Netsuke

The Collection of the Peabody Museum of Salem

Merry Christmas
1991
Love
Dick and Carolyn

LISA A. EDWARDS AND MARGIE M. KREBS

Peabody Museum of Salem
Salem, Massachusetts 1980

Foreword and Acknowledgments

The particular circumstance that initiated the chain of events that resulted in this catalogue and helped shape the character of the special exhibit marking its publication is significant from the vantage point of the museum devotee and enthusiast, whether professional or avocational. The circumstance to which I refer is a visit that Lisa Edwards made to the Peabody Museum in 1969, when, as a youthful museum visitor, she was so intrigued by a small group of netsuke on exhibit that she was prompted to ask at the museum gift shop for more information than the labels provided. The shop manager jokingly suggested that Lisa come back and write a catalogue of the collection—a suggestion which Lisa accepted as reasonable and resulted in the publication of this work. The catalogue is an example not only of personal success but of how museums can successfully stimulate interest and provoke thought.

At the time of Lisa's initial work on the collection back in 1972 there were inadequate resources to publish and insufficient staff to raise the funds and see the work through press. Lisa was an undergraduate at that time and wished to continue her formal education. Currently, she is writing her dissertation for a Ph.D. in English and American Literature at the University of Iowa.

In 1978 Margie (Mitch) Krebs, a volunteer at the Museum since 1971, undertook as a special project the publication of this work and organization of the exhibition. Through her efforts petitions for grants made to the National Endowment for the Arts for the catalogue and the exhibition were successful. Now all that was needed was 800-odd photographs, inclusion of additions to the collection, a little reorganization, and expansion of portions of the text to accommodate new information. Under Mitch's guidance all this was accomplished; however, not without some trying moments arising from the sheer logistics of dealing with such a large collection. Mitch and Markham Sexton, the staff photographer, nevertheless managed to photograph each of the netsuke and sagemono with fidelity to the original.

Guidance and direction in the design of the catalogue were received from book designer David Ford, and

Elizabeth Pollock of the Museum staff.

Frederick Johnson, Frank Duley and John Grimes have been primarily responsible for the design, construction, and installation of the exhibition. Throughout the course of the work Ava Steenstrup, Chieko Conrad, Kathy Flynn, Geraldine Ayers, Lucy Batchelder, Mitch Cole, Bob Dane, and many others have contributed to various aspects of the project. We are thankful to all of these people and to the National Endowment for the Arts for enabling us to bring to fruition this work by Lisa Edwards intended for all who have been inspired to investigate the world of netsuke.

Peter Fetchko Acting Director, Peabody Museum of Salem

Table of Contents

Introduction

Netsuke were a practical invention that filled a specific need over a period of three hundred years, and gradually developed into a unique form of miniature Japanese sculpture. Rarely used today, they are appreciated for their sculptural qualities as well as the insights they give into Japanese life and customs.

The traditional Japanese costume, the kimono, lacked pockets, so Netsuke, pronounced Ne/Tsu/ke (e as in met), were devised as a means to hang pouches, boxes, and other hanging objects called sagemono on a cord from the sash (obi) of the kimono. This enabled the wearer to carry a variety of personal belongings, for sagemono included purses (kinchaku), tobacco pouches and boxes (tabako-ire), medicine or seal cases (inro), writing kits (yatate), even clocks, books, small lanterns, and flint pouches.

The ends of the cord suspending the sagemono were threaded through two openings (himotoshi) in a netsuke

Himotoshi

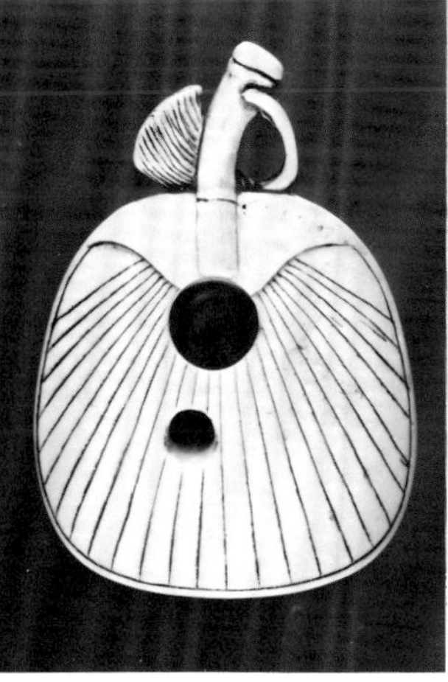

Netsuke

Ojime

Inro

and tied together; then the cord and netsuke were slipped up under the obi and the netsuke hung over the upper edge, acting as a toggle or stop to prevent the sagemono from falling. This entire set was worn at the waist, slightly to the rear, functioning as a portable hip pocket. Often a sliding bead (ojime) was strung on the cord between the sagemono and the netsuke, in order to tighten or loosen the opening of the sagemono. Women were able to tuck small objects in the folds of their very wide, tight obi, but sagemono and netsuke ensembles were worn daily by Japanese men over a three hundred year period, until the adoption of western clothing late in the 19th century made them unnecessary.

Written records of the 16th c. indicate that sagemono such as flint pouches, purses and inro were used in the last half of the century, and it is assumed that netsuke fashioned from roots, seashells, gourds, etc., were worn with them. The word Netsuke itself (Ne: Root; Tsuke: to fasten) denotes that early netsuke were made from natural objects and emphasizes their strictly utilitarian function.

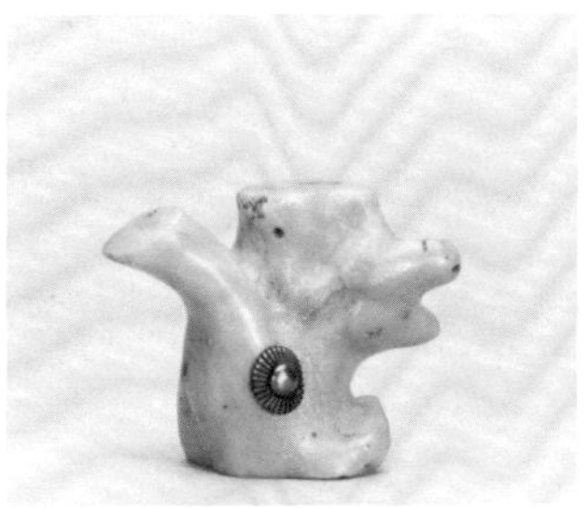

A metal ring fastened through a piece of coral serves as the cord attachment for a polished coral netsuke.

Orange coral, metal ring for cord. 19th-20th c. Katabori. 3.5 cm. E26802

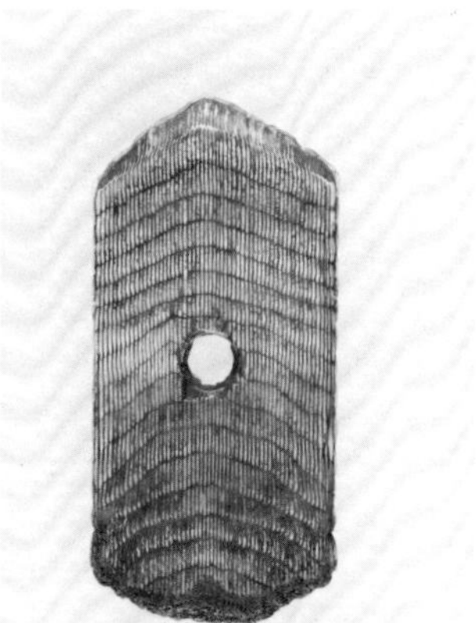

A primitive netsuke made from turtle plastron (breastplate) pierced through with one hole.

Turtle plastron. 17th-18th c. Manju. 6.2 cm. E26918

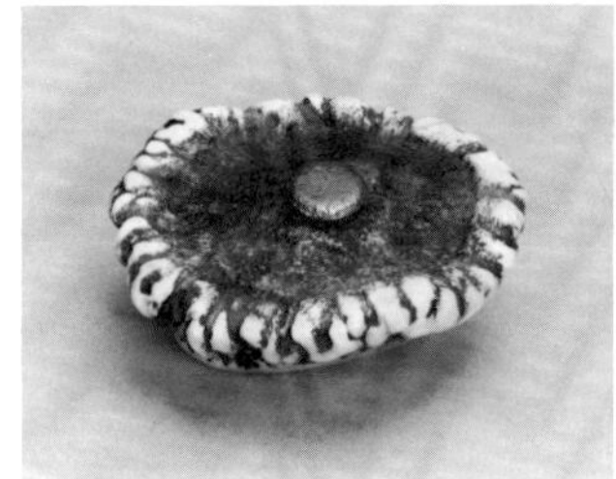

A piece cut from the base of a staghorn has a metal ring attached for the cord.

Staghorn with metal ring. 19th c. Manju. 5.5 cm. E26850

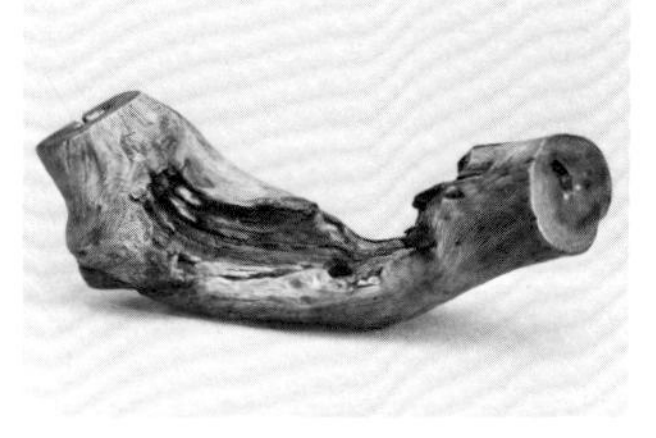

A piece of a root pierced through with one hole makes a distinctive netsuke.

Wood. 17th-18th c. Katabori. 7.5 cm. E63531

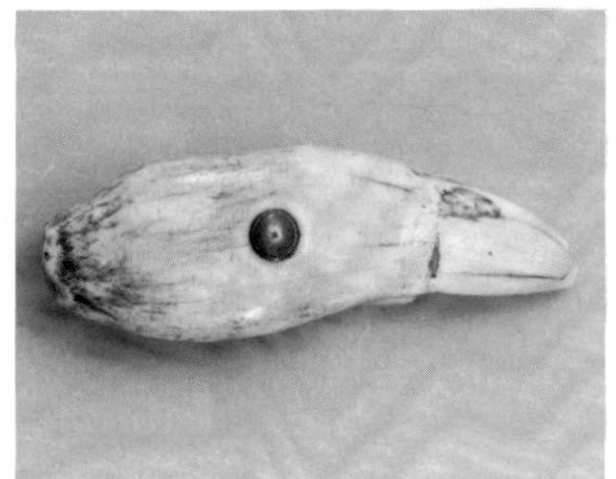

A large animal tooth has been modified to serve as a netsuke by means of a metal ring which has been attached to serve as a cord fastener.

Tooth and metal. 19th c. Katabori. 7.5 cm. E26864

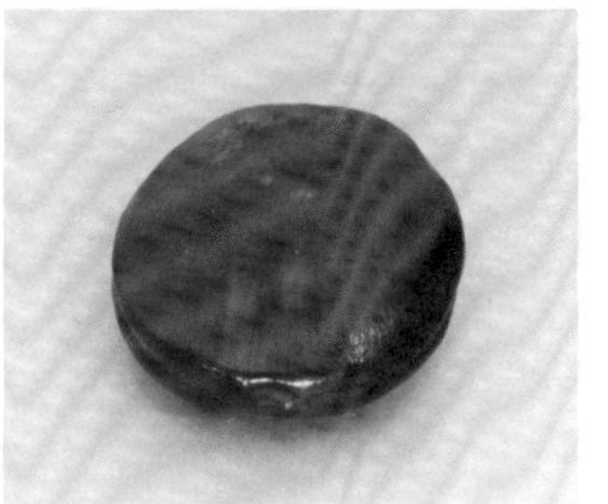

A round brown bean has himotoshi drilled in it.

Bean. early 19th c. Manju. 5.0 cm. E26573

Netsuke could have remained simple toggles and adequately served their purpose but two historic events fostered their further development: the unification of Japan in 1603 under a powerful central government, the Tokugawa Shogunate, that ruled for two and a half centuries; and the introduction of tobacco by the Portuguese in 1543 which would later broaden the popular demand for netsuke enormously.

The restrictive policies of successive Tokugawa Shoguns in the 17th century affected the use and development of netsuke. The extraordinary edict of 1636 excluding foreigners, except for a few Dutch and Chinese who were allowed limited trade on an island in Nagasaki Bay, isolated Japan from foreign ideas and influence for 230 years, and created a concurrent period of peace in which art, especially miniature art, flourished and developed distinctive national characteristics.

In 1617 the shogunate reorganized the social system in order to define class distinctions. Daimyo (land owners) and samurai (military) were ranked at the top, then farmers, artisans and merchants in that order. Sumptuary laws controlling clothing (its cost, type of fabric), food, housing, social functions, etc., and establishing codes of conduct and privileges for each class in the hierarchy were intended to discourage extravagance; they indirectly encouraged the use of netsuke by forbidding jewelry and unnecessary forms of personal adornment. The two swords that samurai were permitted to wear were evidently considered a necessary form, for an edict in 1635 specifically directed to the samurai stated, "*With the exception of military weapons* (italics mine), there must be no indulgence of personal luxury, or fondness for unnecessary utensils or household gear."[1] Swords and military skills were in less demand during the lengthy era of peace and samurai turned to artistic pursuits, indulging in exquisitely ornamented swords and sword fittings to maintain an impressive appearance of power, wealth and refinement. An earlier edict had stipulated that only stamped signatures were valid, necessitating the use of inro by samurai and aristocrats to hold the seal and ink pad for signing documents. Inro and their accompanying netsuke became correspondingly elegant as lacquer techniques incorporating powdered gold developed in the 17th century, creating fashionable and necessary items which were quickly adopted by the upper class.

Meanwhile, a growing merchant class prospered from increased commercial activity in Edo (Tokyo), seat of the new government, and from managing the financial affairs of daimyo and samurai who were required to maintain residences and retinues in that city, but who disdained the concomitant monetary transactions as beneath their rank. Prohibited by the sumptuary laws from dressing, eating, or entertaining as lavishly as their new wealth permitted, merchants began to wear increasingly opulent purses with netsuke that rivaled the ostentatious displays of the samurai and aristocrats.

By 1650 netsuke had evolved from natural forms into a flattened button shape (manju); further changes emanated from a period of intense interest in Chinese literature and art. Imported Chinese articles, carved figures, ornaments and particularly, seal or stamp handles, were converted into netsuke by providing holes for a cord. Chinese toggles were also used as netsuke. The artisans of the period, including architectural sculptors, Buddha image-makers, lacquerers, potters, metal workers, mask and doll makers, etc., created netsuke on the side, and adopted Chinese subject matter from shishi (lions) to sennin (Taoist hermits) for their diminutive sculptures, whose theme and design were often dependent on the aesthetics and assets of a patron.

Early in the 18th century, an edict that finally repealed a century old law prohibiting the cultivation and selling of tobacco had tremendous impact on the development of netsuke; smoking became a national habit, creating an unprecedented need and demand for tobacco pouches and netsuke among men of every social rank, except the samurai, who were forbidden to smoke in public. Matching sets of pouch, ojime and netsuke became universally fashionable; those who could afford them had many ensembles, each appropriate for a specific occasion, but the fashion served every man who smoked, regardless of his wealth.

Craftsmen continued to make netsuke to the buyer's order, but the demand was so great they freely applied their skills and wonderful imaginations to a wide variety of subjects, confident of a market for their work. Gradually, as techniques and individual styles developed, a separate class of artisans formed, the netsuke-shi, artists who carved netsuke for a living, no longer subsidized by wealthy patrons. Netsuke-shi often signed their works, and master carvers opened schools for teaching carving techniques, but despite the freedom to select techniques, subject matter and from a wide variety of materials for carving, the netsuke-shi, like the craftsmen, were restricted by the function of netsuke, which dictated certain limitations. They had to design compact netsuke with no protruding pieces or sharp edges to snag the kimono and with unobtrusive openings for the cord to pass through, openings perfectly placed to balance and show off the proper side of the netsuke. Awareness of these functional requirements, a high degree of originality and fine workmanship were essential to create netsuke that were equally useful objects and sculptured works of art.

The popularity of netsuke reached its zenith early in the 19th c., netsuke being in such common use that a preponderance of all netsuke were produced between 1820-1853. Netsuke-shi of the period painstakingly refined their carving to technical perfection, concentrating on precise details and remarkable fidelity to their subjects. Nevertheless, by the last quarter of the century, the demand for netsuke had diminished. Commander Perry's ships entered Japanese ports in 1853, and he negotiated a treaty that allowed American ships to trade with Japan. Similar concessions were soon made to European traders, ending Japan's long period of isolation. Once trade with the West was established, the adoption of western clothing and the cigarette followed, eliminating the need for netsuke by the end of the century.

Netsuke-shi and other skilled artisans continued to produce netsuke after the Tokugawa shogunate fell and the Mikado was restored to power in the 1868 Meiji Restoration, because early travellers to Japan discovered and began collecting the unique sculptures. At first, numerous old netsuke were available, but increased demand stimulated another period of activity, netsuke made for export to the West. The endeavor was not economically feasible, however, and artisans turned to techniques of mass production and designing for western tastes, resulting in a decline of traditional quality that ultimately disaffected the foreign collectors.

Largely ignored by Japanese art historians because they are works of a utilitarian nature, and because they were made and worn by all classes of people, netsuke have only recently begun to achieve recognition as works of art in Japan. Western collectors and enthusiasts have long admired the artistic qualities of netsuke; in recent years their interest has been revived by exhibits, auctions of large collections, lectures, and in particular, by the many excellent books about netsuke written and published in the West.

Twenty-eight netsuke in the extensive collection of Japanese material gathered by E.S. Morse for the museum during his residence in Japan between 1877 and 1882 became the nucleus of the museum's collection, which has grown to 790 specimens through the generosity of numerous donors in the intervening years. In 1947, Dr. Ernest G. Stillman's generous gift of 628 netsuke provided a comprehensive basis for the collection, not only because of its size (79% of the collection), but because of its diversity in terms of materials and techniques and its representation of a broad range of subjects and artists. Dr. Stillman, a collector of Japanese art and literature, edited one of the first studies of netsuke in English, in 1924, a translation of Albert Brockhaus's *Netsukes,* first published in German in 1905. Many of the photographs in Stillman's edition are of netsuke now in the museum's collection. His preface noted the translation was done "to make this work available to the American collectors who own one or many Netsukes."

This catalogue has been written and organized to increase appreciation of netsuke by both collectors and non-collectors. Explanations of their use and information about their stories and subject matter afford insights into the culture and history of Japan. Individual netsuke in the catalogue are arranged according to subject matter with the following information about each:

Museum number: An identifying number for use within the museum.

Dimension: The greatest dimension of the netsuke is given.

Type: Types of netsuke are determined by their shape and form. In this catalogue each netsuke has been designated as one of the following four types:

Manju The netsuke in this group are shaped like flat buttons, or manju, the Japanese word for round rice cakes. Some are smooth and undecorated; the majority are carved, etched, embossed, inlaid or painted. Ryusa netsuke are a form of manju carved in an openwork design. The cord of a manju made in one piece is attached to a metal ring on the surface. If the manju is divided in half, the cord passes through a hole in one half and a small eyelet in the other.

Kagamibuta This type is in the form of a shallow bowl (made of ivory, wood, metal, etc.) covered with a metal lid, the design almost always being on the lid and rarely on the bowl. The cord passes through a hole in the bowl and an eyelet on the inside of the lid.

Katabori This is the most common type of netsuke, a figure in the round. The cord holes in katabori netsuke are placed so that the front of the netsuke faces forward as it hangs. Often the himotoshi are part of the figure, i.e., natural apertures formed by bent arms, legs, etc.

Sashi Much longer than katabori netsuke, part of a sashi netsuke is tucked into the obi in order to provide better balance and support for the sagemono. The himotoshi in sashi netsuke are at one end rather than in the middle. Some sashi netsuke have curved bottoms which hook onto the bottom of the obi.

Material: An effort has been made to identify the material employed in each piece. When specific woods, ivories, etc. are known, the names are given; otherwise, only the general material (wood, ivory, coral, etc.) is listed.

Signature: Netsuke in the catalogue are unsigned unless the artist's name is listed. Each signature has been identified as accurately as possible, but no determinations as to genuineness have been set forth. Information about the artists comes basically from three sources: *The Netsuke Handbook, Netsuke,* and *Collectors' Netsuke* (see Bibliography). If an artist's name is given, but listed as unrecorded, it means that no mention is made of him in any of the sources listed above.

Circa: Criteria for judging the age of unsigned netsuke included subject matter, wear, himotoshi size and shape, netsuke type, material, inlay work, etc.; if signed by a known artist, the date is that given by one or more of the above sources.

1. J. Carey Hall, "Japanese Feudal Laws III; Tokugawa Legislation Part I," *Transactions of the Asiatic Society of Japan,* vol. 38, 1910-1912, p. 311.

Deities and Demons

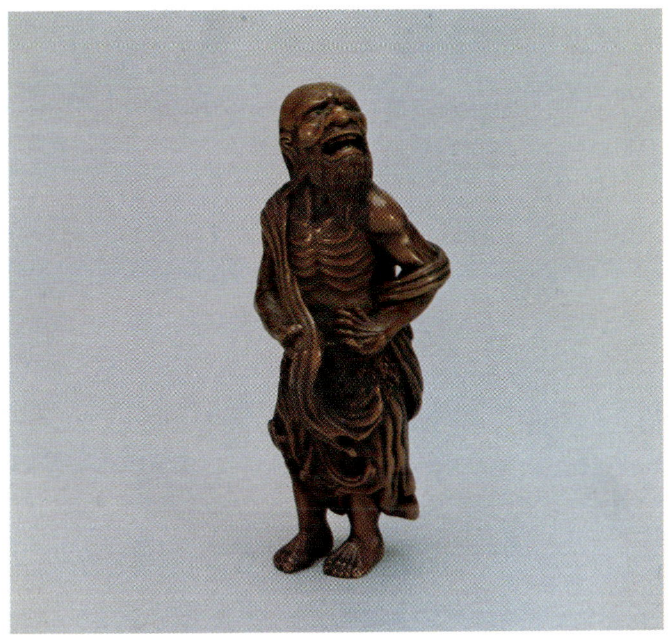

Shintoism, Buddhism, Confucianism and Taoism were the major sources of religious beliefs and philosophies in Japan: four distinct and separate developments that interacted and accommodated one another for centuries, forming an interrelated historical, mythological and spiritual legacy for the nation.

Shinto, the Way of the Gods, is the name given to the original and indigenous religious beliefs of Japan, which evolved from the nature worship of primitive agricultural people. Their gods, or *kami,* were the sacred spirits responsible for the mysterious forces at work in nature: light, dark, wind, thunder, seasons, etc. A mythical account of the cosmological origins of the people and their gods is incorporated in historical records of the early 8th c. that describe the creation of the world, the births of myriad kami and in particular, the birth and origin of Japan and its first ruler, Amaterasu, the Sun Goddess, whose descendants became the rulers of Japan. By means of this myth, the ancient chronicles established and justified the unity of religion and government in Japan, and the divine nature of the Emperor.

In the early ages, gods inherent in natural phenomena, sun, moon, water, etc., were dominant because of the dependence on the elements for successful crops, but ultimately any person, animal, plant, object or skill that evoked a sense of awe, authority or wonder was designated a god: spirits of one's own ancestors, spirits of Imperial ancestors, spirits of national heroes, guardian spirits of clans or villages, occupations and crafts, for example. Shinto gods are worshipped by making offerings of food or material goods, and by driving out evils of mind or body with ritual purification, in order to gain the protection of the particular object, person or venture the god represents. The rite takes place in a shrine that provides the dwelling place for a specific god and is intended to promote harmony and happiness and to ward off misfortune as the petitioner becomes the instrument of the god. These religious traditions of Shinto have made ancient customs a part of daily life in Japan.

Confucianism was introduced to Japan about the 6th c., during a period of intense cultural exchange with China, where its political and ethical philosophies were widespread. It was not established as a religion in Japan, but its philosophy made significant contributions to the development of social order and religious traditions and provided the political organization of the Chinese Empire as a model for governmental changes in Japan.

Confucianism contributed moral concepts of integrity, loyalty, benevolence and justice to government; officials possessing these virtues would set a standard of ethical conduct. The virtues of filial piety and reverence for ancestors, expressed in subordination to authority within the family, were absorbed and expanded into existing Shinto beliefs.

During the Tokugawa period, the shoguns turned to Neo-Confucianism in order to justify the social and political system they had established: Confucian emphasis on a hierarchical family and social order as a part of the cosmic order of heaven to earth, ruler to ruled, laid the foundation for the shoguns' division of society into four classes.

Ethical social and political solutions were the focus of Confucianism. The philosophy of Taoism, which arrived in Japan during the same period, focused on achieving harmony with the Tao, the eternal Way, by withdrawal from civilization and communion with nature. This mystical philosophy deteriorated into a popular belief, Religious Taoism, which employed magic, charms, divination, incantations and other practices that infiltrated Japanese life, legends and religions.

Buddhism reached Japan in the middle of the sixth century by way of Korea, one thousand years after its founding in India by Gautama Buddha. Introduced during a period of enthusiastic cultural exchange with China, its early history is notable for its contributions to temple architecture, Buddha-image sculpture, art, and learning. Its basis was the Mahayana doctrine of India, which taught that by practicing certain virtues, everyone could attain salvation and enlightenment.

Buddhism's early acceptance and influence were apparent: the Buddha was worshipped as a kami and Buddhist priests were performing funeral rites by the 7th c. Ultimately, the co-existence of Shinto and Buddhism became so great that Shinto kami were designated as manifestations of Buddhist divinities.

By the Middle Ages, Buddhism was primarily a religion of the court, upper classes and intellectuals. Closely associated with the ruling powers, its influence was confined to government affairs and monasteries, and rarely filtered down to the people. Then new forms of Buddhism were developed by Japanese Buddhist philosophers during the Kamakura period (1185-1333), creating sects that gained great popularity among the entire nation. One of these was the Pure Land (Paradise) Sect, in which salvation could be attained simply by repeating, "I put my faith in Amida Butsu (Buddha)." Another, Zen Buddhism, stressed the individual's experience of enlightenment that could be brought about by self-discipline and meditation. These innovative Japanese sects, made up of millions of followers, were the last major Buddhist sects in Japan for 600 years, through the Tokugawa period.

New sects failed to develop because Buddhism became the official state religion during the Tokugawa era and the various sects were controlled and financed by the government. This policy effectively ended the introduction of new ideas, reforms and religious activities that would have made Buddhism flourish.

Many people turned to folk religions that incorporated aspects of the major beliefs, using magic formulas, festivals, pilgrimages, charms, etc., to petition sacred spirits for protection. Most Japanese continued to participate simultaneously in the traditions of Shinto, Buddhism, Taoism and Confucianism, which had no basic philosophical differences and which shared common themes of filial piety, ancestor worship, love of nature and a close relationship with the government.

Seven Gods of Good Fortune

A group of seven gods, borrowed from all the religions of Japan, but mostly from Buddhism, became popular in the folk religion of the early 17th century. The individual gods are endowed with physical traits that make for easy identification; further, each has a characteristic object or animal that symbolizes his or her particular area of wealth or plenty. All share an irresistibly good-humored approach to their felicitous task of dispersing wealth and happiness. The Good-Luck Gods are frequently depicted in a lighthearted, even irreverent manner by netsuke artists.

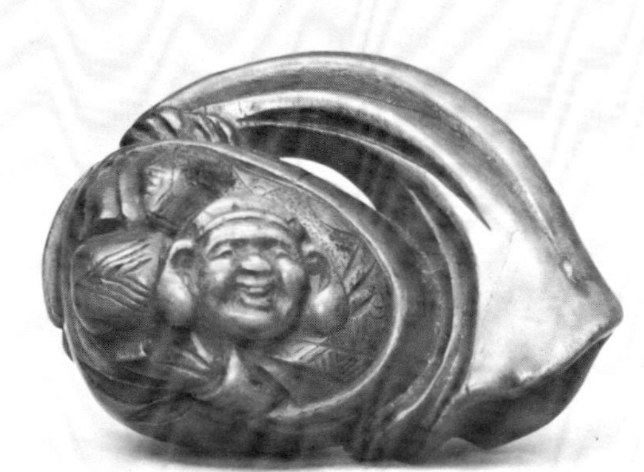

A jolly Daikoku, hammer in hand, looks out from inside his bag.

Boxwood. 18th c. Katabori. 6.7 cm. E26889

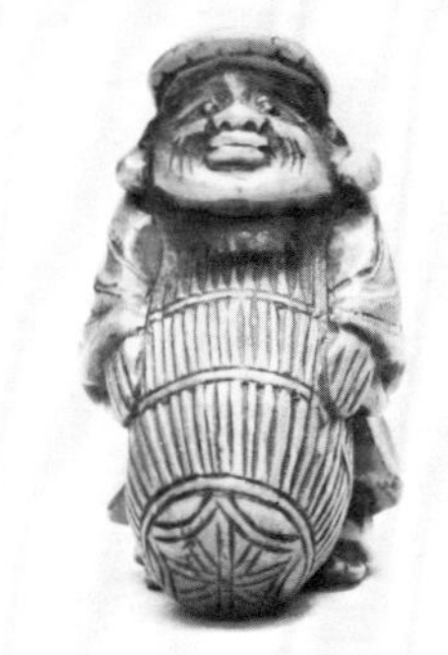

A red-robed Daikoku attempts to lift his rice bale.

Wood with red lacquer. 18th-19th c. Katabori. 4.3 cm. E27064

Daikoku Of Buddhist origin, Daikoku, god of wealth and the land, carries a mallet, a sack, and bulging rice bale, and wears a flat head covering. A rat usually accompanies Daikoku, perhaps symbolizing a harvest with plenty for all.

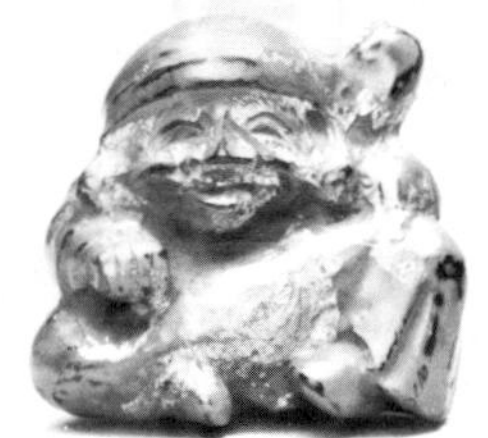

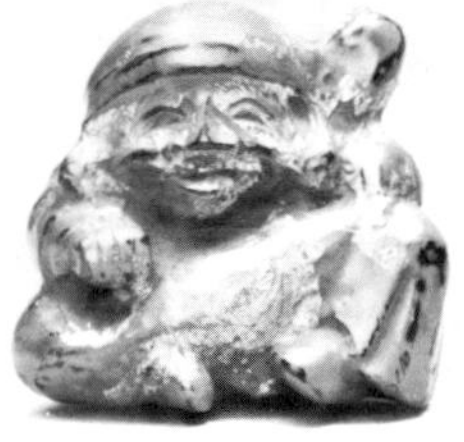

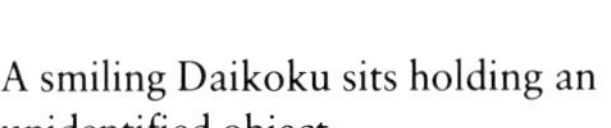

A smiling Daikoku sits holding an unidentified object.

Wood lacquered red and gold. 19th-20th c. Katabori. 2.9 cm. E9415

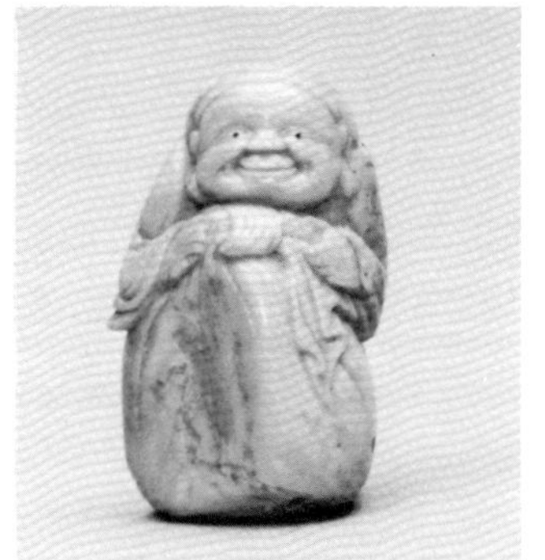

Daikoku kneels with one foot propped on his bag which he holds in front of him.

Pink coral. late 18th-19th c. Katabori. 3.7 cm. E27142

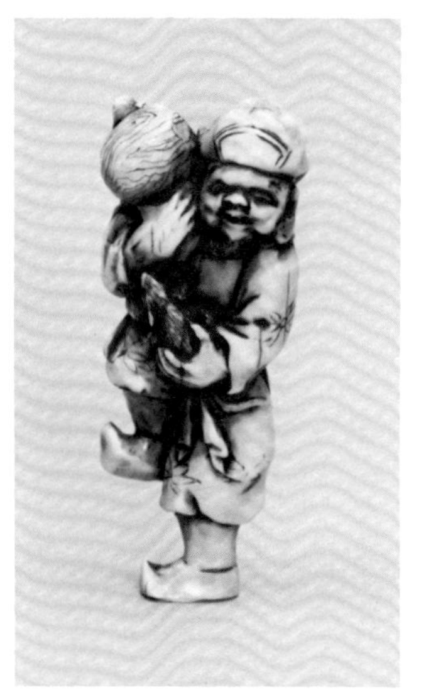

A laughing Daikoku dances while holding his mallet in one hand and a rat friend in the other.

Ivory. 19th c. Katabori. 5.6 cm. E27032

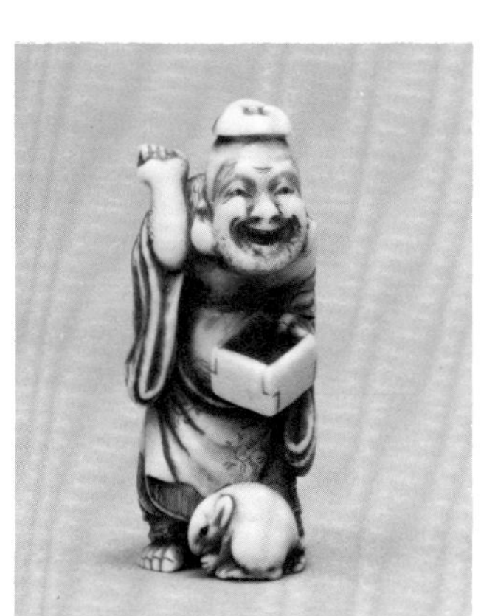

Daikoku, wearing a mask of Okame, Goddess of Mirth, on top of his head, throws peas while a rat eats them. The pea-throwing is part of Setsubun Oni, an annual ceremony to expel oni from homes.

Ivory. 19th-20th c. Katabori. 4.5 cm. E27154

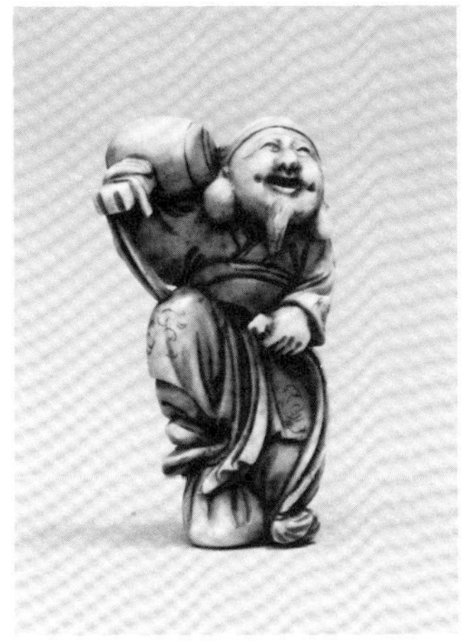

A cheerful Daikoku stands with his right foot on his bag and his mallet slung over his shoulder.

Ivory. 19th-20th c. Katabori. 4.1 cm. E33344

Ebisu Ebisu, "the laughing god," was adapted from Shintoism to become the patron of fishermen as well as a god of food and honest dealing. A sea bream usually accompanies him.

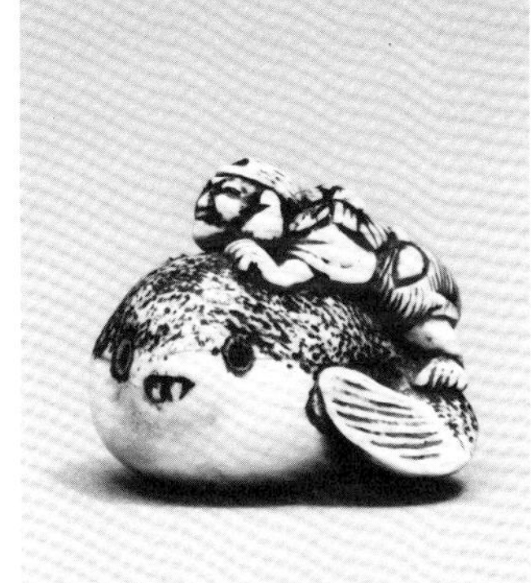

A smiling Ebisu climbs on the back of his companion, the sea bream.

Ivory, ebony eyes. late 18th-19th c. Katabori. 3.7 cm. E26634

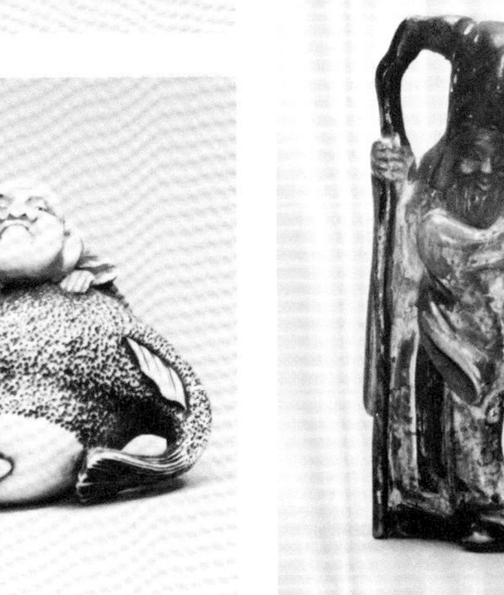

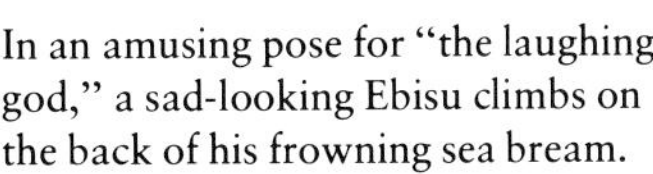

In an amusing pose for "the laughing god," a sad-looking Ebisu climbs on the back of his frowning sea bream.

Ivory, ebony eyes. Sho, unrecorded artist. 18th-19th c. Katabori. 4.0 cm. E26681

Fukurokuju and Jurojin Both of Taoist origin, these two gods look so similar that distinction frequently becomes difficult. Both gods possess an extremely high forehead which perhaps suggests their enormous mental capacities. They have several symbols in common including a crane, a bushy tailed tortoise, a deer, a staff, a scroll and a sacred gem. Fukurokuju, whose name means Wealth, Prosperity, Longevity, is usually depicted in more lighthearted, less distinguished situations than Jurojin, and is known for his love of children. Jurojin is a god of longevity and wisdom, and he dresses in scholars' robes, usually carrying a scroll and fan.

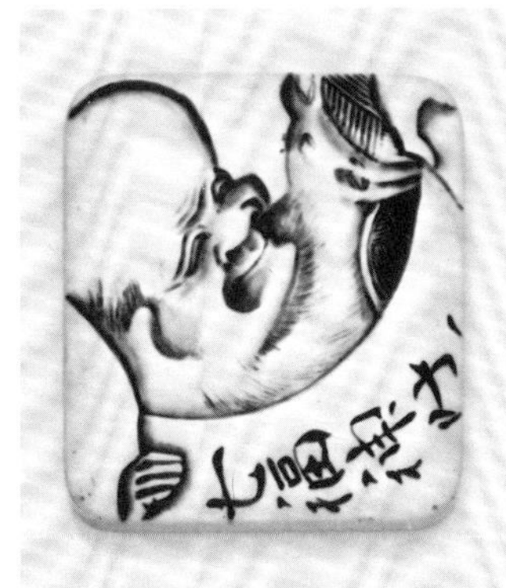

This piece pictures a smiling Jurojin unrolling a scroll which reads "seven gods."

Ivory. Shohosai. 19th-20th c. Manju. 4.5 cm. E26559

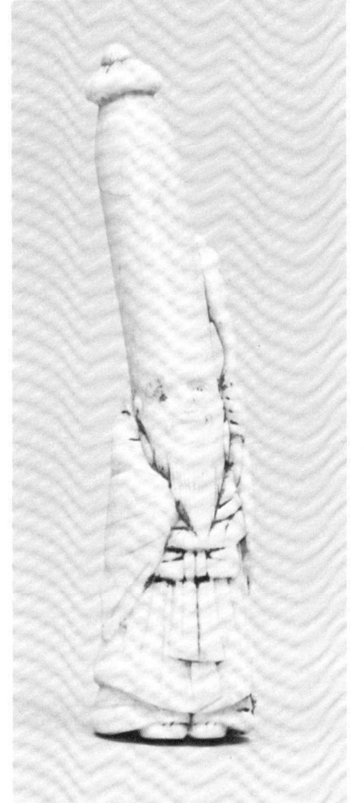

Fukurokuju, with an extremely exaggerated forehead, stands holding a staff.

Bone, the marrow cavity has been plugged. 18th c. Katabori. 9.1 cm. E26939

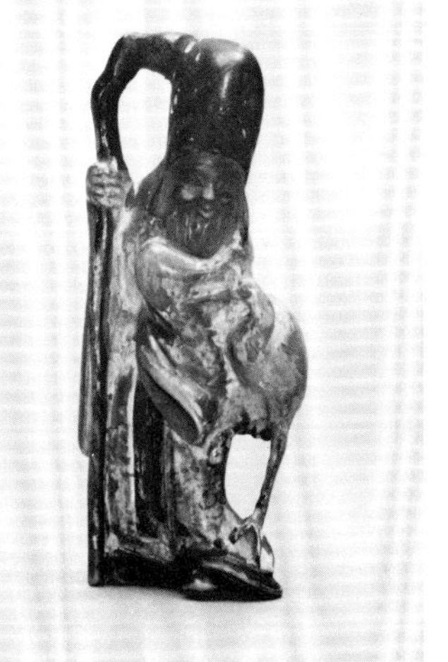

A smiling Jurojin stands with a staff and a crane by his side.

Wood painted blue, red, and white. late 18th-19th c. Katabori. 5.3 cm. E26987

A jolly Fukurokuju stands patiently while a child (visible only on the back of the netsuke) sits on his shoulders playing a string game on the god's high forehead.

Boxwood. Tsuji. 18th c. Katabori. 6.3 cm. E26989

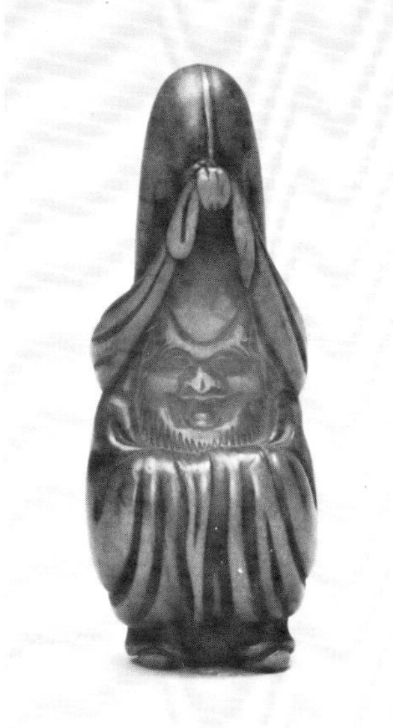

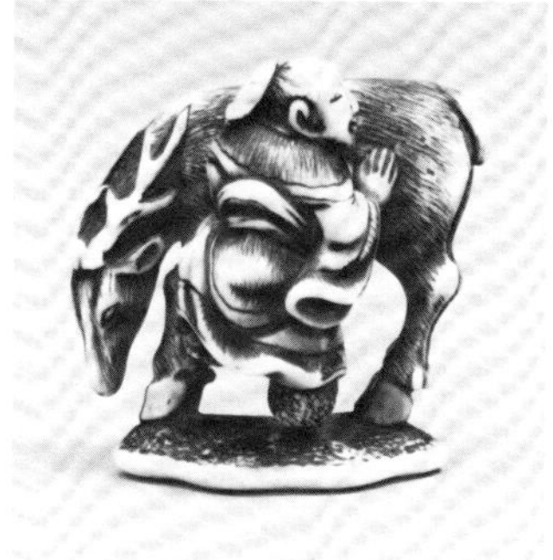

Jurojin/Fukurokuju stands next to his companion the deer. Apparently about to mount, he has one foot raised and both hands on the deer's back.

Ivory. Sadatsugu. 1800-1869. Katabori. 3.4 cm. E27099

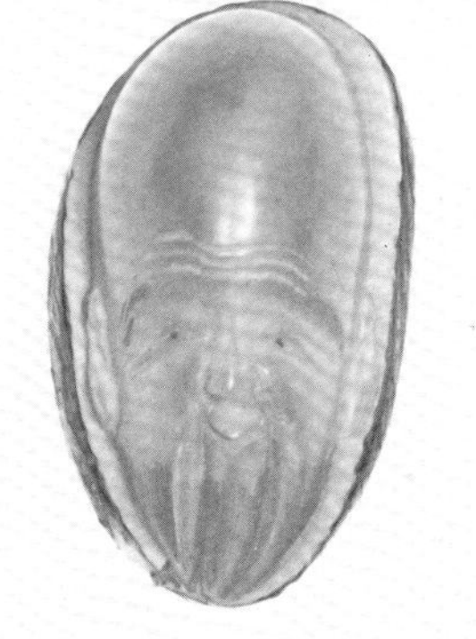

The face of Fukurokuju appears on one side, the back of the nut shell on the other.

Vegetable ivory. Masaharu. 1801-1829. Katabori. 4.4 cm. E38682

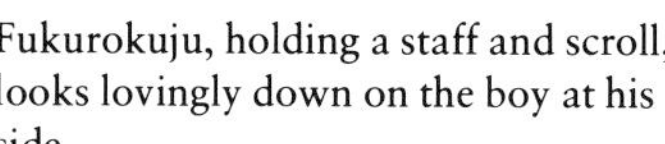

Fukurokuju, holding a staff and scroll, looks lovingly down on the boy at his side.

Ivory. late 18th-19th c. Katabori. 4.2 cm. E27015

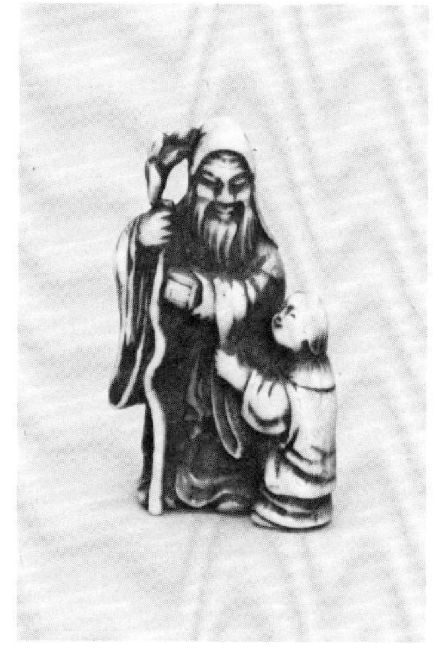

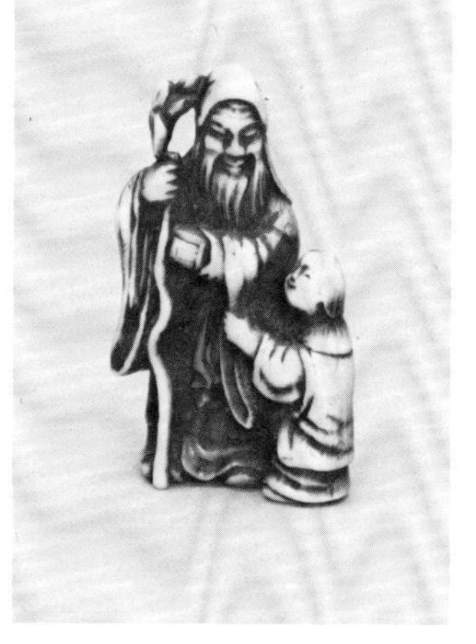

Hotei The original Hotei was a Chinese Buddhist priest of the Liang dynasty (503-557), but the Hotei depicted in netsuke is the god of happiness and the most popular of the Seven Gods of Good Fortune. He can be recognized by his jolly expression, huge belly and his sack of "Precious Things" (which often contains either children or himself); children are his frequent companions.

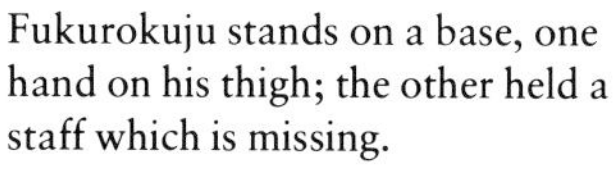

Fukurokuju stands on a base, one hand on his thigh; the other held a staff which is missing.

Ivory. 18th c. Katabori. 5.5 cm. E27053

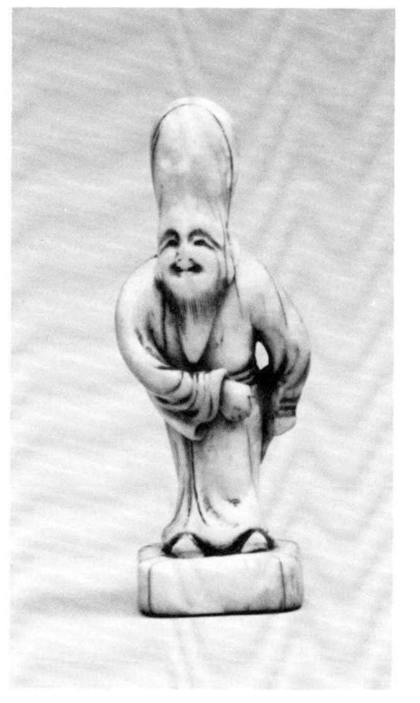

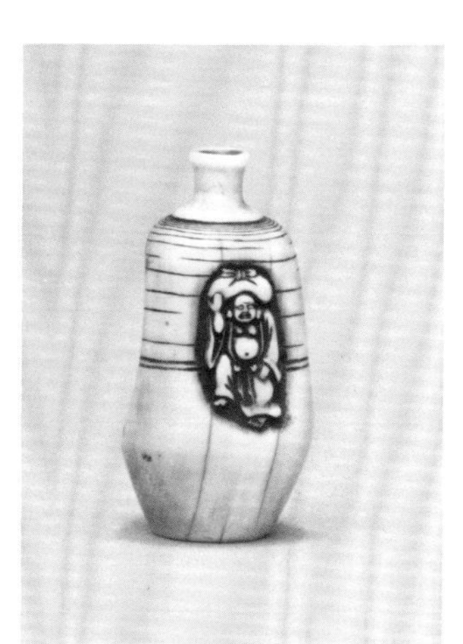

Carved in relief on the side of a sake bottle, Hotei joyfully dances with his sack on his head.

Ivory. Mitsuhiro. 1810-1875. Katabori. 4.0 cm. E26868

Fat Hotei sits atop a three-legged altar.

Wood painted red, blue, green and white. Shuzan (Nagamachi). late 18th c. Katabori. 5.0 cm. E26869

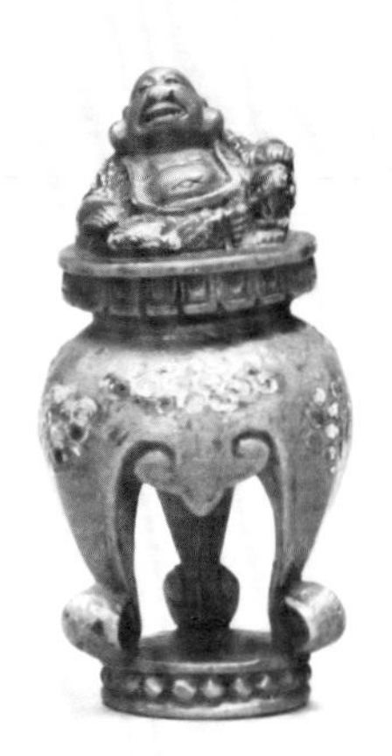

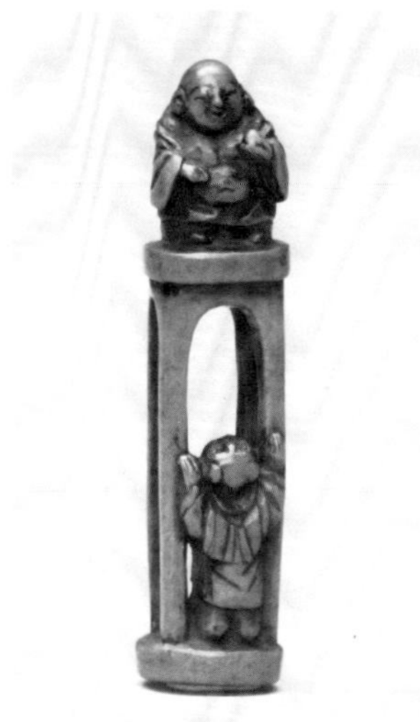

Perched on a high four-legged stand, Hotei holds a ball while far below a young boy reaches up towards him.

Wood. 19th c. Katabori. 5.8 cm. E27012

Hotei dances on his sack.

Ivory. 19th-20th c. Katabori. 4.0 cm. E26974

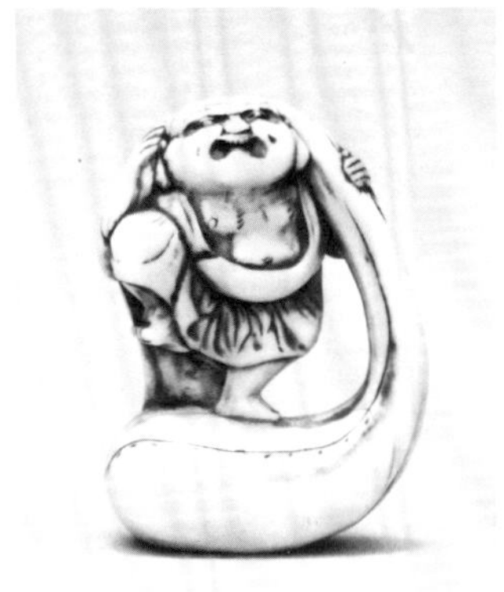

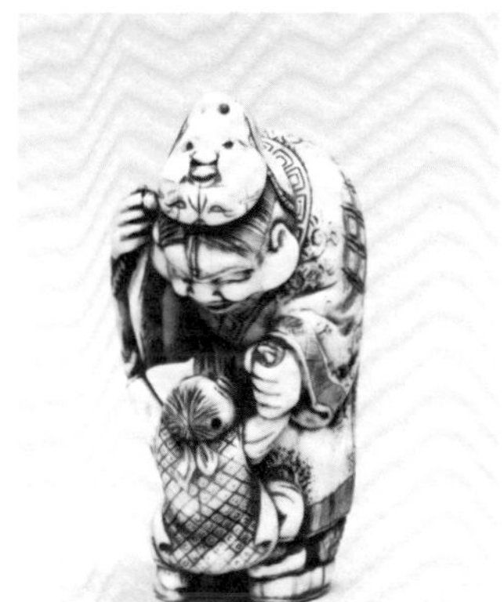

Wearing an Okame mask on top of his head, a laughing Hotei bends over and holds the hands of a boy who is attempting to climb onto Hotei's feet.

Ivory. Sako. before 1800. Katabori. 4.5 cm. E27014

A jolly Hotei sits on his bag and gets pulled and pushed by three happy young boys.

Boxwood. late 18th-19th c. Katabori. 4.3 cm. E26979

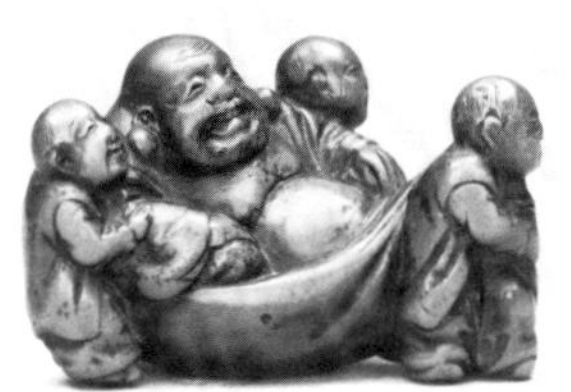

A boy, tucked into Hotei's robe, plays with Hotei.

Ivory. late 18th-19th c. Katabori. 4.7 cm. E27052

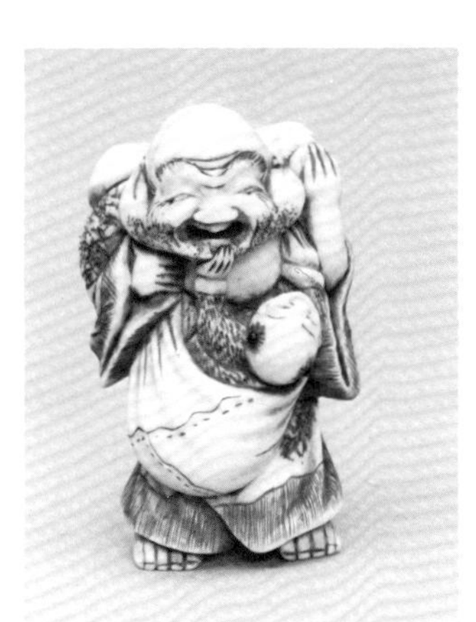

A karako (Chinese boy), hanging in the sack on Hotei's belly, reaches for a prize that the god playfully holds too high.

Ivory, ebony inlays. 19th c. Katabori. 4.5 cm. E27003

Hotei, a sake cup in one hand and the other on a boy's shoulder, watches two boys play Go. A third boy watches from behind Hotei.

Wood, ivory inlays. Norishige. 1772-1788 or 1830-1843. Katabori. 3.0 cm. E27063

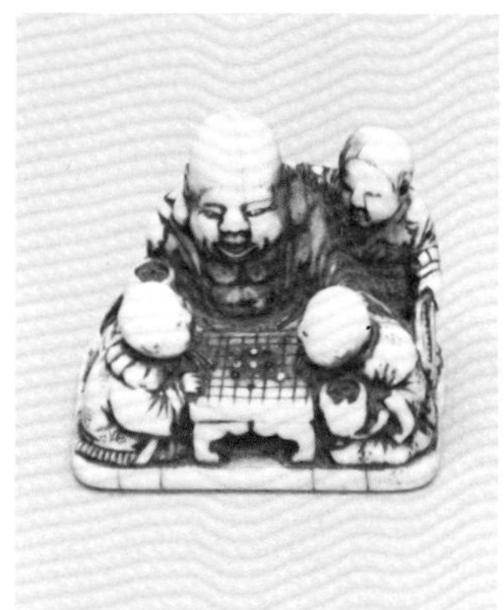

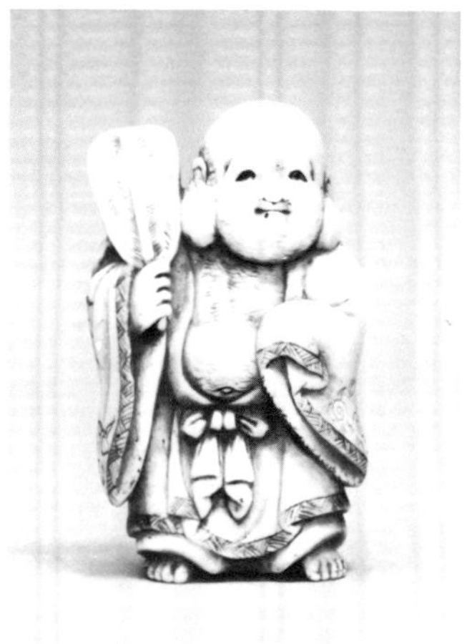

Hotei stands and holds a fan in his right hand.

Ivory. Tomochika I. 1800-1873. Katabori. 4.3 cm. E27122

Hotei, atop his sack, prepares to play a flute.

Wood lacquered black and gold. 18th-19th c. Katabori. 4.2 cm. E27079

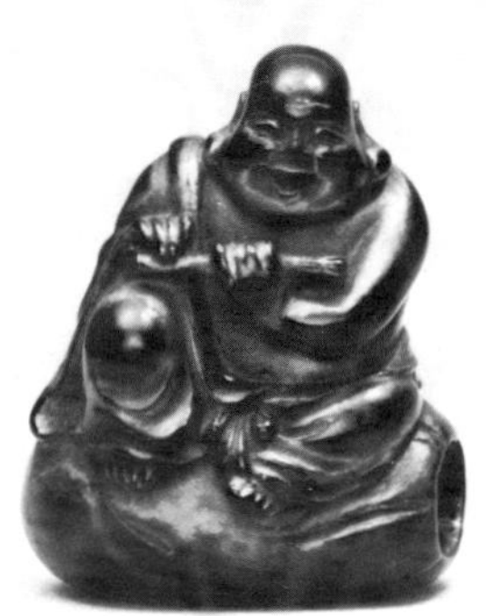

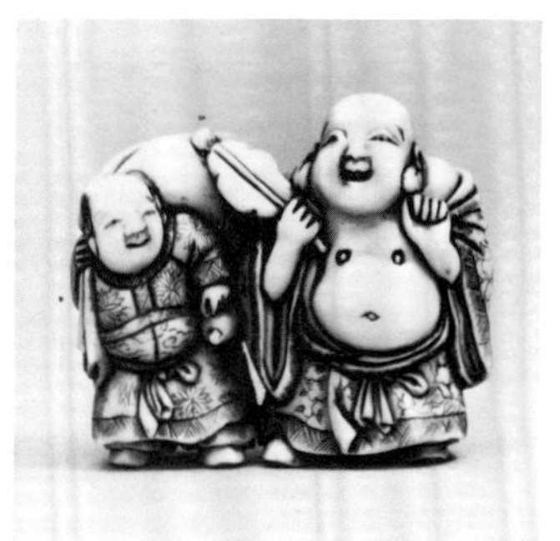

Hotei, holding a fan in his right hand, stands with a companion who carries Hotei's sack. They wear robes decorated with floral designs.

Ivory. Masamitsu. 1852-1902. Katabori. 4.5 cm. E27137

Hotei holds a Hotei mask up to his face. Two karako, one of whom holds a horn, stand beside him.

Ivory. 18th c. Katabori. 4.3 cm. E27116

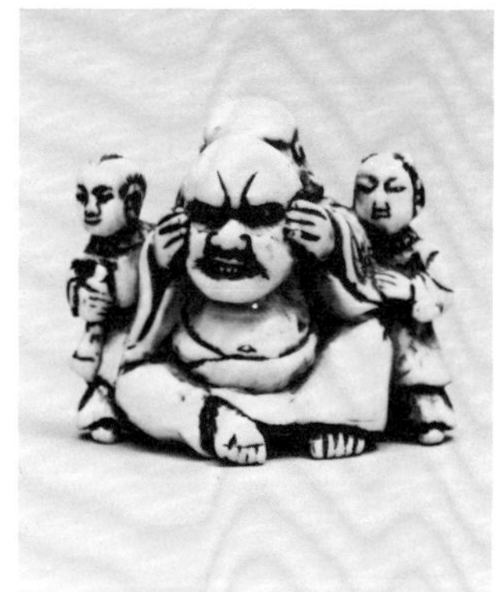

Hotei holds his sack while a karako plays on Hotei's shoulder.

Bone, wood inlays. late 18th-19th c. Katabori. 6.3 cm. E29150

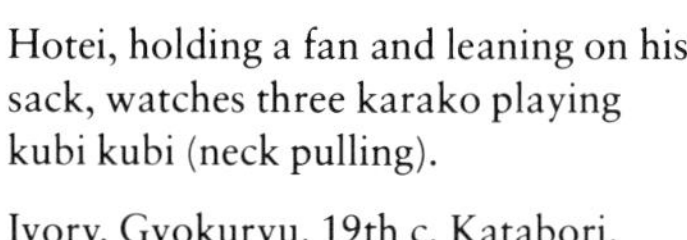

Hotei, holding a fan and leaning on his sack, watches three karako playing kubi kubi (neck pulling).

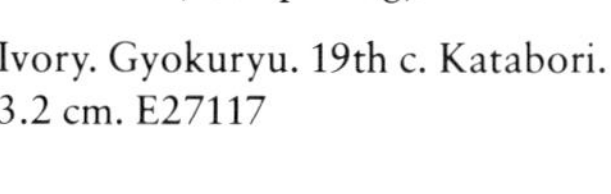

Ivory. Gyokuryu. 19th c. Katabori. 3.2 cm. E27117

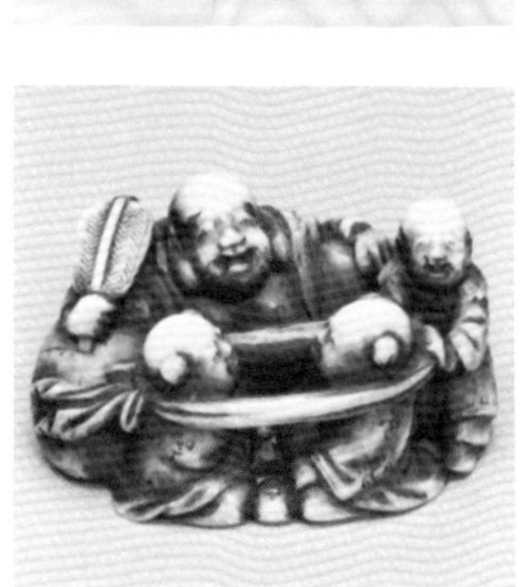

A happy karako bounces on Hotei's stomach while Hotei stands.

Ivory. late 19th-20th c. Katabori. 4.4 cm. E32879

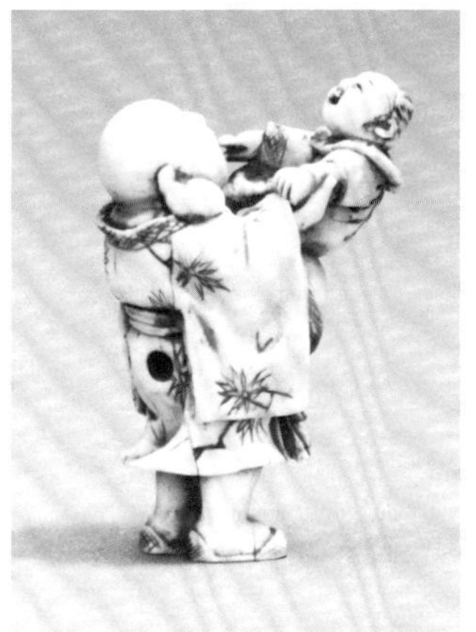

Benten Originating in the Buddhist religion, Benten is a goddess of wealth, learning, speech, divinity and love. Her companions are the dragon and the white serpent. Of the Seven Gods of Good Fortune, Benten is the only female.

A grinning Hotei holds a fan and leans against his sack.

White porcelain. Ipachi, in Owari. 19th c. Katabori. 3.0 cm. E53702

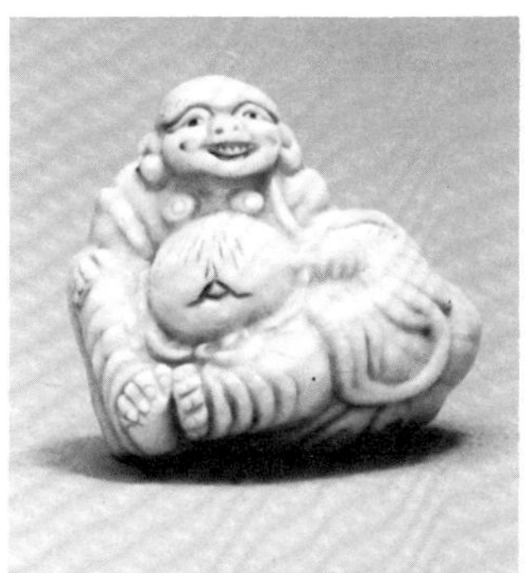

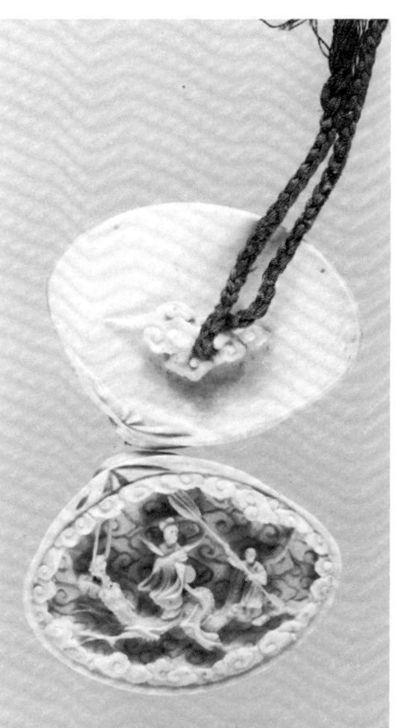

A clam shell opens into two halves to reveal a fragile carving inside. Amidst clouds, the goddess Benten rides on the back of her dragon while a servant fans her from a nearby cloud.

Ivory. 18th-19th c. Katabori. 5.3 cm. E26638

A grinning Hotei holds a fan and leans against his sack.

Blue porcelain (Kairaku-en ware). 19th c. Katabori. 4.3 cm. E60823

Shinto

The Shinto pantheon of "Eight-hundred Myriads of Gods," is described in the *Kojiki* (Records of Ancient Matters) and the *Nihongi* (Chronicles of Japan), historic accounts written in the 8th c. about the mythical beginnings of Japan and Shinto. Many of the gods and goddesses were personified, Amaterasu, the Sun Goddess being the supreme deity; others who formed the divine hierarchy included deities of the moon, wind, tides, storms, etc.

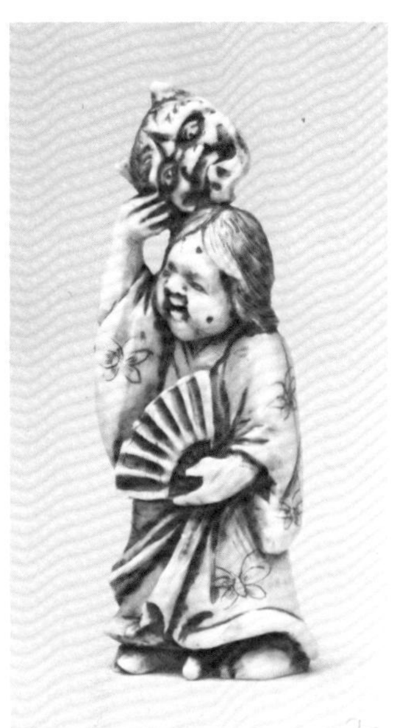

Okame holds an open fan in one hand and a demon mask over her head in the other.

Ivory. 18th-19th c. Katabori.
6.7 cm. E27027

Okame (Uzume) The most famous story about Okame tells how the Sun Goddess Amaterasu, angered by her brother, hid in a cave, thus plunging the earth into darkness. At the urging of other gods, Okame performed a merry (some say lewd) dance in front of Amaterasu's cave which brought such laughter and noise from her audience of gods that Amaterasu looked out and in so doing brought sunshine back to the world. Okame's pudgy cheeks, dotted forehead and jolly smile are unforgettable; her fun-loving personality made her a favorite among netsuke-shi.

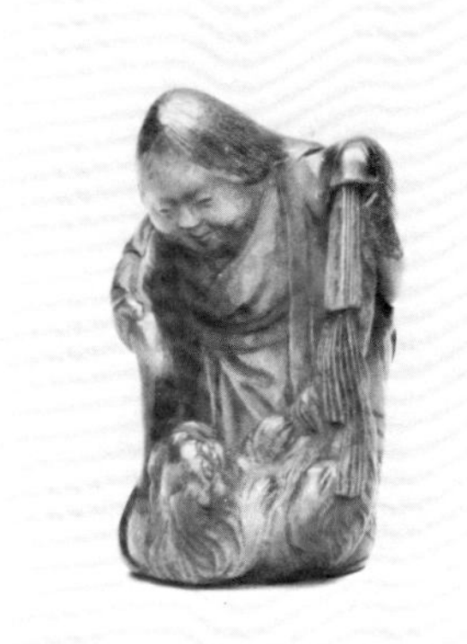

Okame, holding a closed fan in her left hand, plays with a Pekingese dog who lies on his back at her feet.

Boxwood, ebony lined himotoshi.
18th-19th c. Katabori.
4.2 cm. E26992

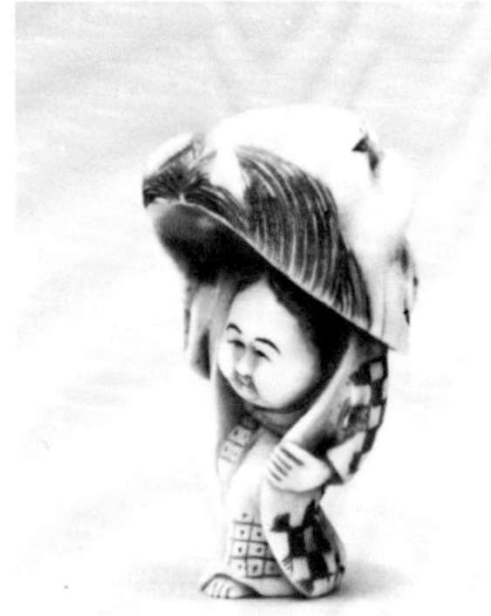

Okame carries a huge demon mask on her back.

Ivory. 19th-20th c. Katabori.
4.0 cm. E27008

Raiden Raiden, god of thunder, looks demonic with his horns and clawed feet, but netsuke-shi usually treat him humorously. He is most often portrayed with his thunder drum decorated with the mitsu tomoe, a three-comma-shaped figure which may be the primitive form of the sign for thunder.

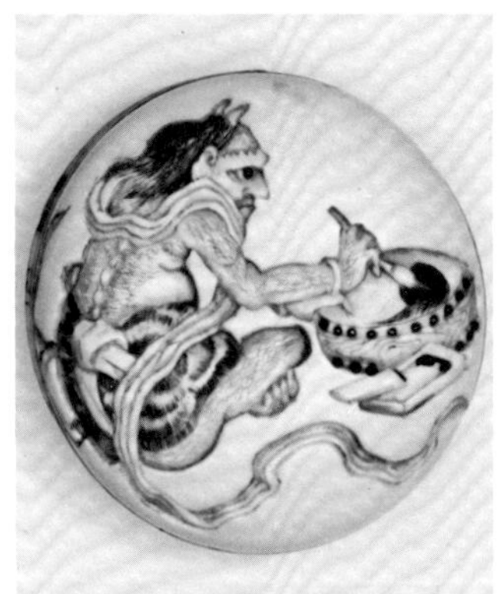

On one half Raiden paints the mitsu tomoe on his drum. An ink box lies next to the drum which is decorated with metal beads. On the other half a teapot, cup and heater stand next to a sack with the words "thunder crunch" (a sweet, puffed rice snack) written on it.

Ivory and metal. 19th c. Manju.
4.8 cm. E23115

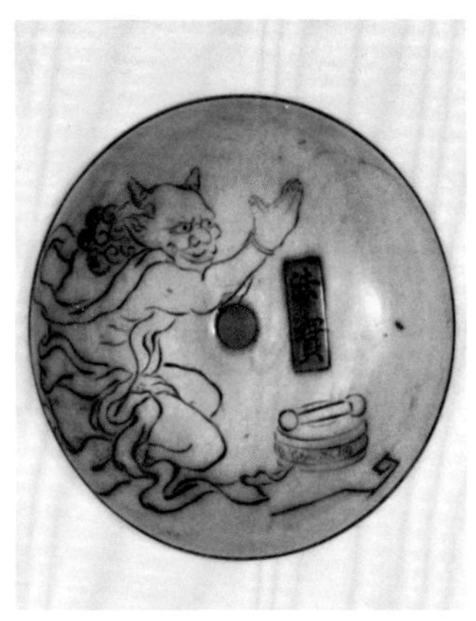

Raiden prays in front of his drum. The signature is on an inlaid red plaque.

Ivory. late 19th c. Hojitsu. Manju.
4.1 cm. E23116

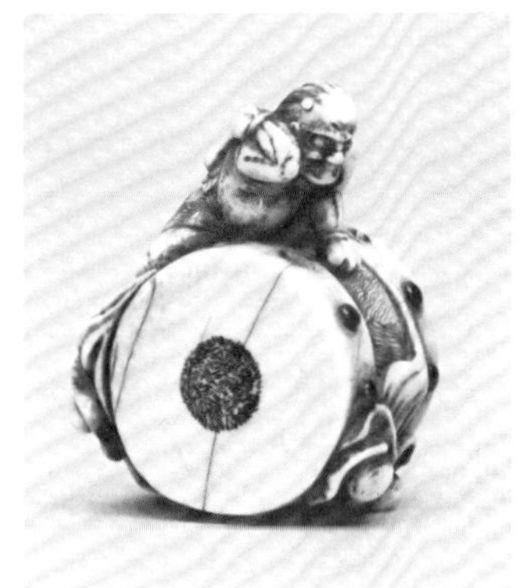

Raiden sits atop his huge drum and beats it with a stick. Black beads are inlaid on the drum for decoration.

Ivory, black inlays. 19th c. Katabori. 4.2 cm. E26874

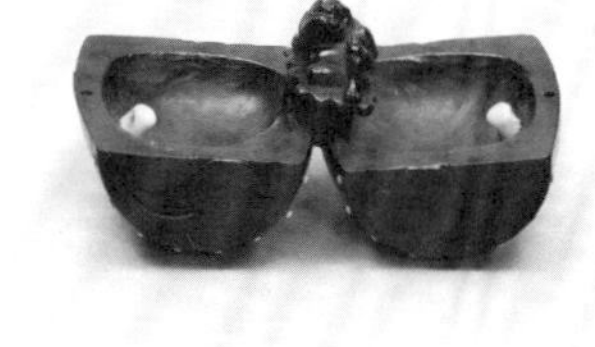

A wooden cylindrical drum, decorated on its rim with ivory beads, opens to reveal Raiden reclining on a stand inside.

Wood and ivory. 19th c. Katabori. 4.0 cm. E26919

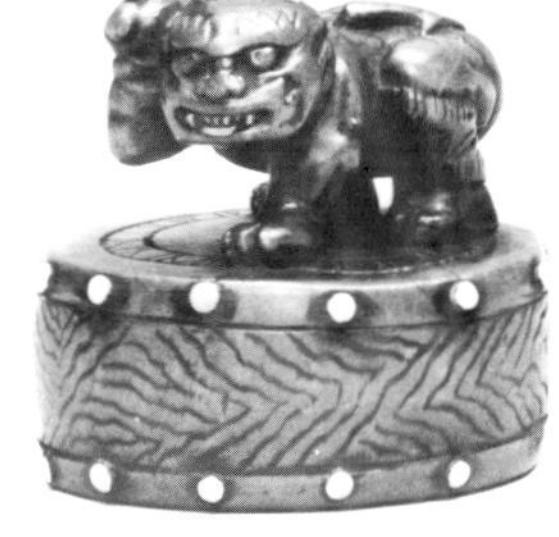

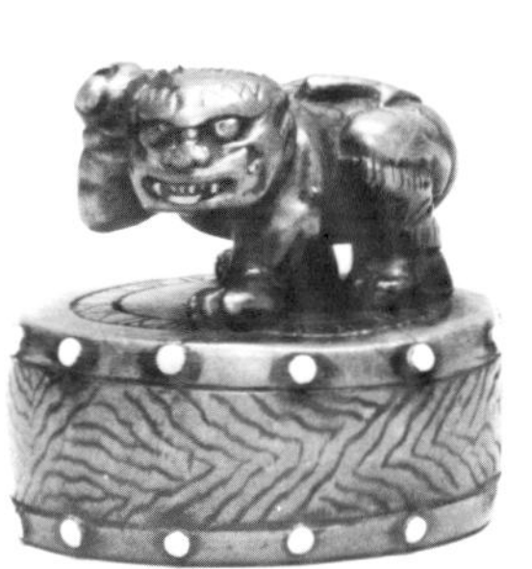

Raiden, with ivory horns and teeth, squats on top of his drum and prepares to make thunder by beating it with a stick. Ivory beads were used to decorate the rim of the drum.

Wood and ivory. late 18th c. Katabori. 3.5 cm. E26929

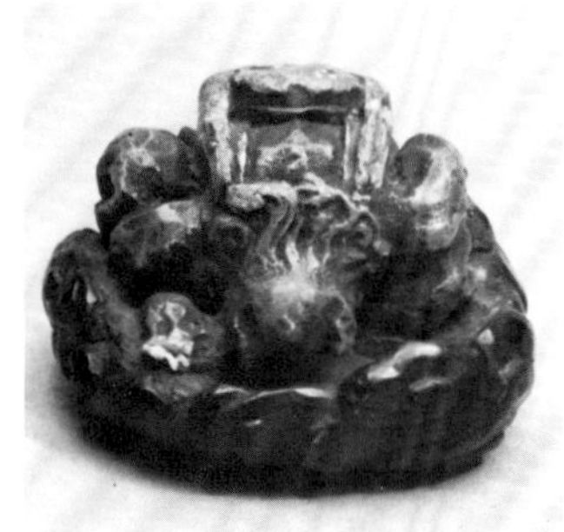

In this clever piece a red and white porcelain Raiden peers down through a hole in the brown wood cloud on which he sits. On the underside Raiden's face can be seen through the hole which doubles as a himotoshi.

Wood and porcelain. Teiji. late 19th-20th c. Katabori. 3.6 cm. E34088

Ryujin Ryujin, god of the sea, controls the waters with a tide-ruling gem. The palace from which he rules is often depicted inside a clam shell.

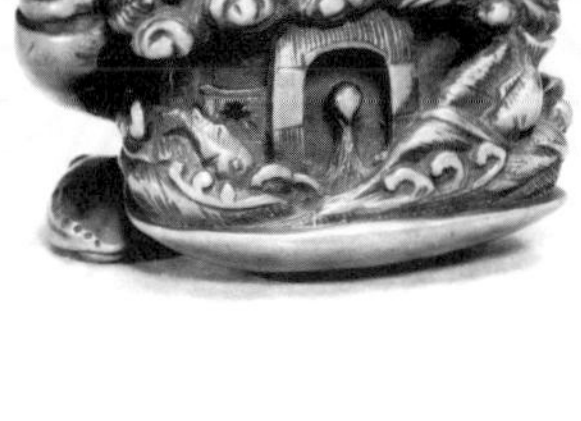

Beside two small shells a partially open clam shell reveals waves, fish and a shrine housing the gem of Ryujin.

Wood. 18th-19th c. Katabori. 5.3 cm. E26748

Ryujin dances while holding high in his left hand a lantern inside of which sits his jewel.

Boxwood, coral jewel. 18th-19th c. Katabori. 7.7 cm. E27024

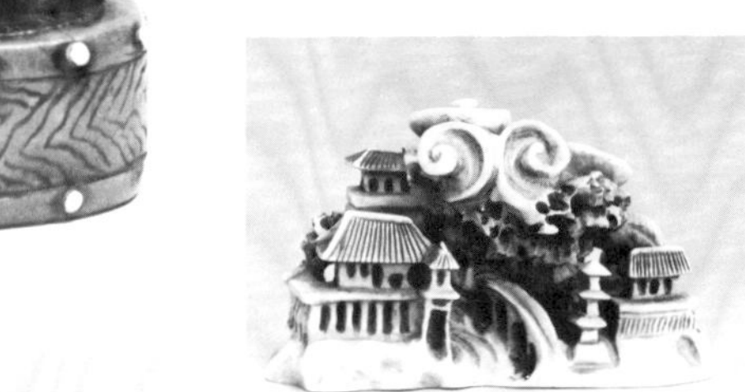

Ryujin's underwater palace

Ivory. Gozan. 19th c. Katabori. 3.5 cm. E61565

Religious procession

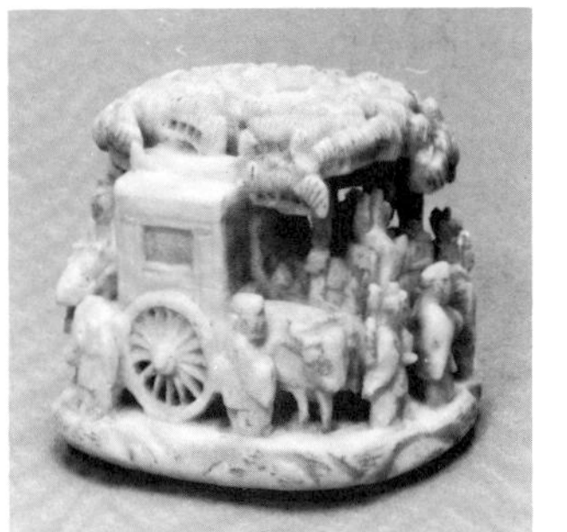

A lively processional scene includes Shinto priests.

Ivory. Kagetoshi. 1800-1869. Katabori. 3.7 cm. E27118

Buddhism

Two main sects of Buddhism, the Hinayana (lesser vehicle) and the Mahayana (greater vehicle)were introduced to Japan, but the Mahayana division had the greatest impact. The Mahayana sect deified Buddha and created a pantheon of Bodhisattvas (Bosatsu, or saints) and other divinities.

Bosatsu A bosatsu is the ideal person of the Mahayana branch of Buddhism. Inferior only to Buddha himself, the bosatsu devotes his life to saving others and refuses to enter Nirvana until every soul on earth reaches enlightenment.

Two bosatsu stand beside an elephant which carries an urn on its back.

Ivory. 19th c. Katabori.
4.0 cm. E27120

Buddha Buddha inspired many legends, but the respect he demands makes him a rare netsuke subject. A large hand holding something usually represents the hand of Buddha. One popular story tells of the time that Buddha, Lao-tzu, founder of Taoism, and Confucius all tasted wine from the same cauldron. One found it sweet, one bitter, one sour; thus demonstrating that though their doctrines seem different, they all flow from the same source.

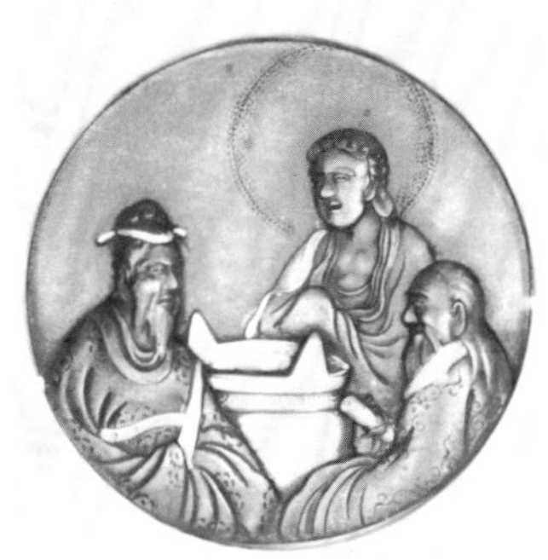

The stark white ivory bowl has no decoration. On the lid is a depiction of Buddha, Lao-tzu and Confucius around the cauldron. Their garments are trimmed in bright gold; the cauldron is silver on the outside and gold on the inside.

Ivory bowl, bronze lid with silver and gold decoration. 19th c. Kagamibuta.
4.6 cm. E5827

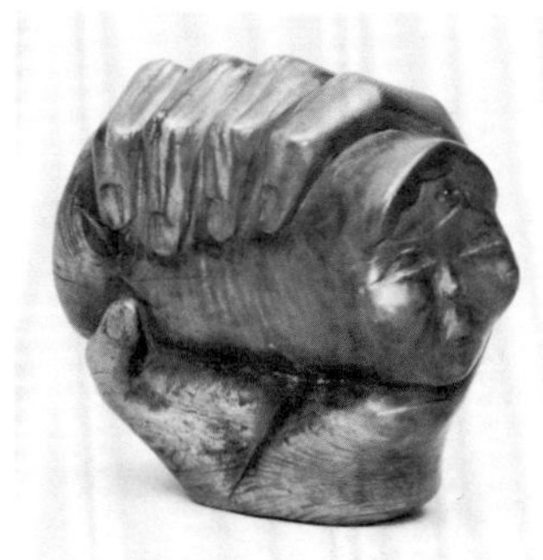
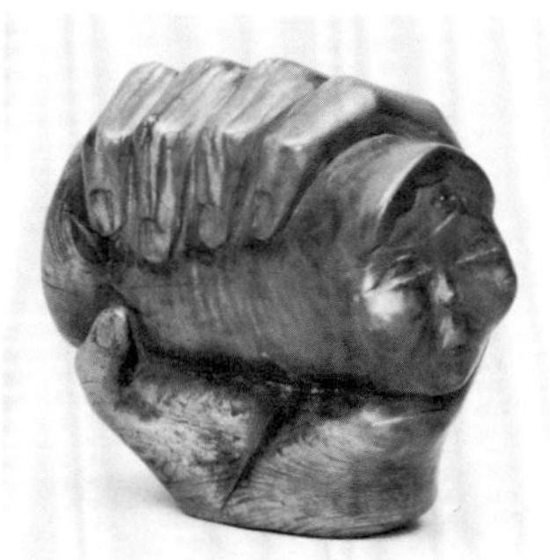

A hand holds a rod with a mushroom carved on one end and the face of Okame at the other. Since the mushroom is a suggestive symbol and Okame is known for her raucous and mischievous behavior, perhaps this piece symbolizes the problems caused by human frailties which fall into the hand of Buddha.

Wood. 19th-20th c. Katabori.
6.2 cm. E26886

Daruma Daruma founded the Zen sect of Buddhism. Though highly respected, netsuke carvers frequently depict him in comical forms. His legendary nine year meditation, in which he sat without moving, gave rise to his most frequent representation, a roly-poly figure without limbs. During those nine years, his legs supposedly withered away from lack of use. The roly-poly figure makes one of the most popular toys in Japan. A symbol of patience and perseverance, it rights itself when knocked over. Netsuke carvers, however, may be questioning Daruma's ability to meditate continuously when they portray him yawning and stretching.

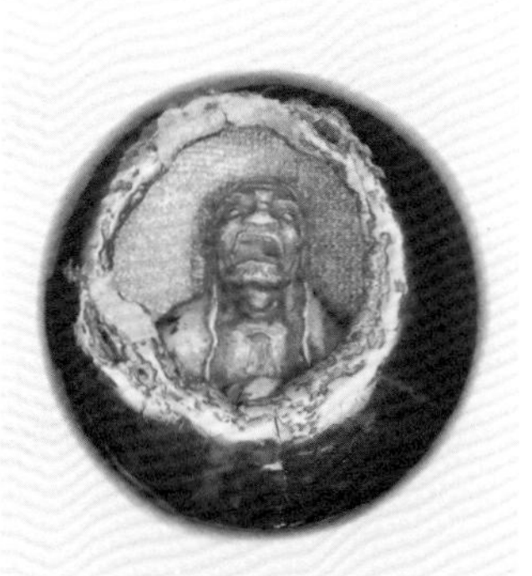

On the back side a red lacquer table and silver urn are pictured on a brown background. A cut-away section of the brown lacquered front reveals a wailing (yawning?) Daruma inside.

Wood with brown, red, and silver lacquer. late 18th-19th c. Manju.
4.3 cm. E26545

A comical looking, roly-poly Daruma has been carved on a peach pit.

Peach pit. 19th c. Katabori. 4.3 cm. E26810

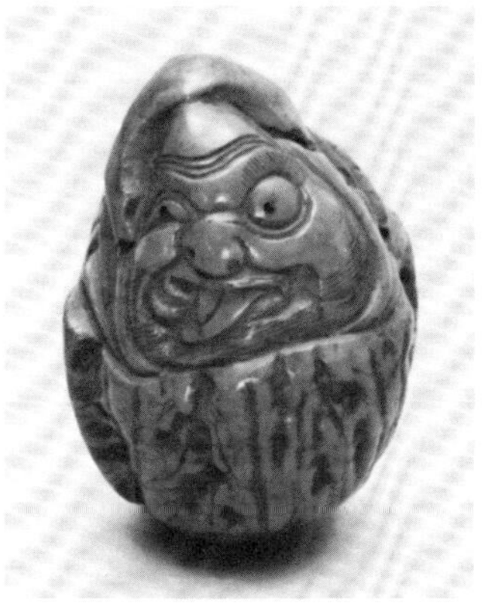

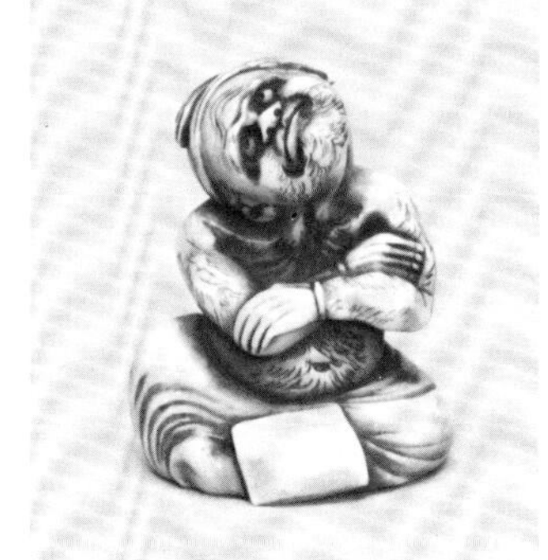

A meditating Daruma sits on a temple whisk (visible from the bottom only).

Ivory. 19th-20th c. Katabori. 3.7 cm. E27111

A frowning Daruma's legs have completely atrophied.

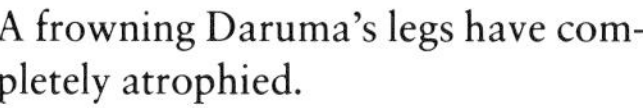

Ceramic, gold paint. 19th c. Katabori. 3.6 cm. E26983

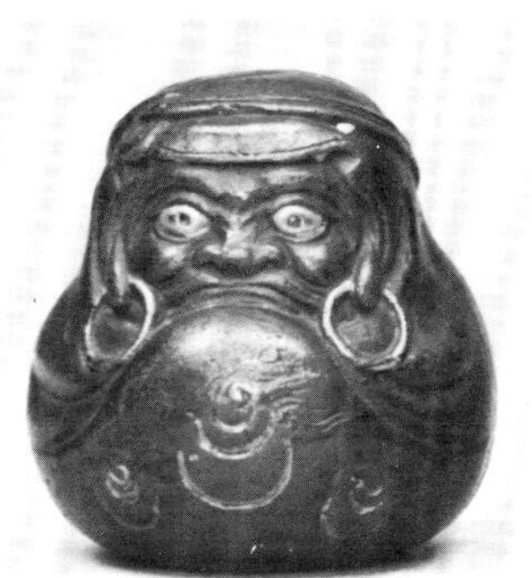

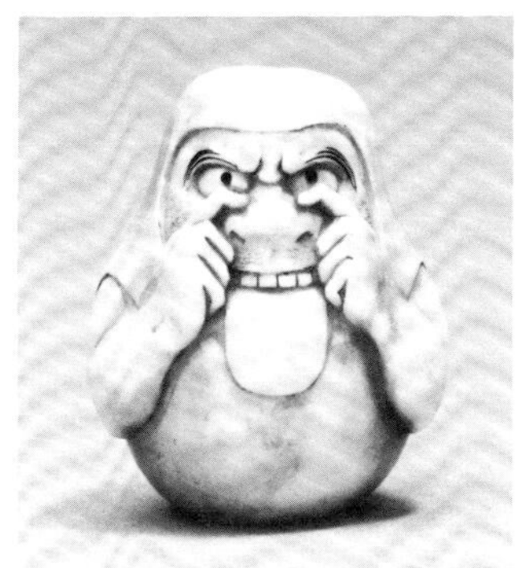

A comical, roly-poly Daruma

Ivory. Doshosai. 1830-1867. Katabori. 3.8 cm. E27124

Daruma yawns and stretches out his arms and legs.

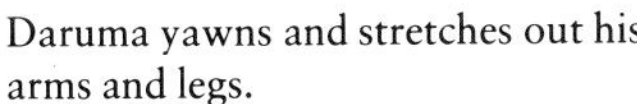

Ivory. 19th-20th c. Katabori. 6.0 cm. E27133

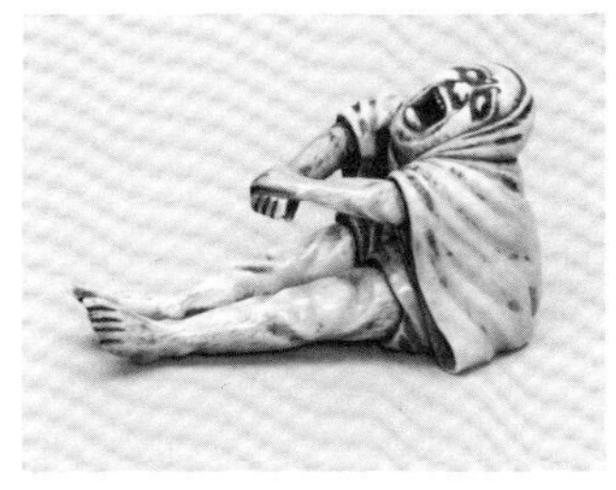

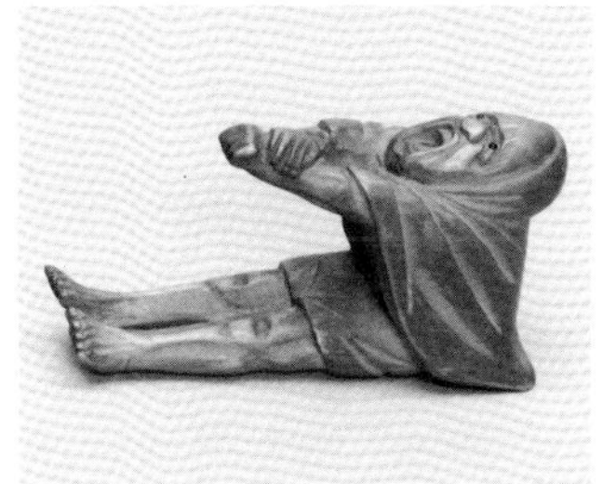

Daruma yawns and stretches out his arms and legs.

Wood painted red, inlaid eyes. 19th-20th c. Katabori. 5.7 cm. E27061

Daruma yawns and stretches his arms after his nine year meditation. The himotoshi, located on the bottom of this piece, make it an awkward netsuke by forcing Daruma to hang either upside down or with his arms sticking out to catch on garments.

Wood painted red. 19th-20th c. Katabori. 5.2 cm. E27068

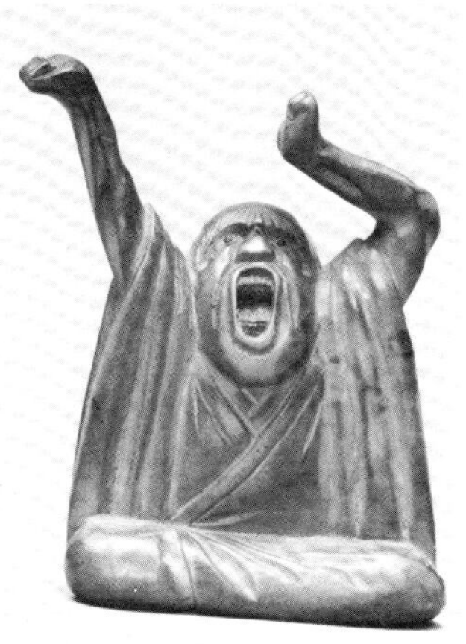

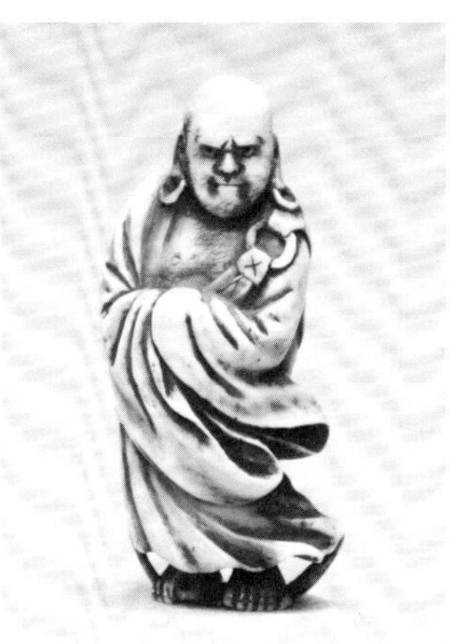

Daruma is depicted here as Bodhidharma, the historical founder of Zen Buddhism. The stern look and stance are common to representations of this Indian Buddhist.

Ivory. Tomochika I. 1800-1873. Katabori. 4.8 cm. E52710

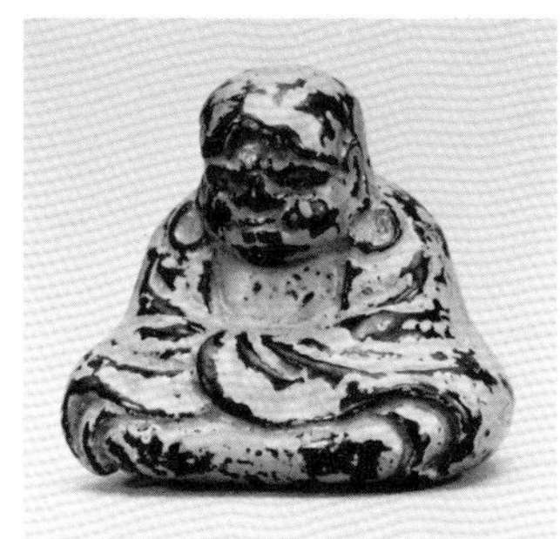

Daruma in meditation

Lacquered wood. Katabori.
3.4 cm. E63530

Emma Emma rules hell and sits in judgment on all sinners. He loves women, but must resist them for they weaken his strict judgments and sentencing of sinners. He usually wears a crown which says "king," and a vicious expression.

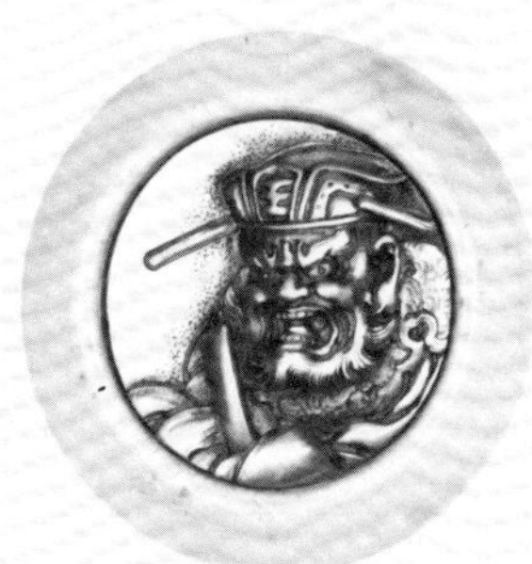

An undecorated bowl is topped by a gold lid depicting the vicious face of Emma.

Ivory bowl with gold metal lid. mid-19th c. Kagamibuta.
3.7 cm. E26539

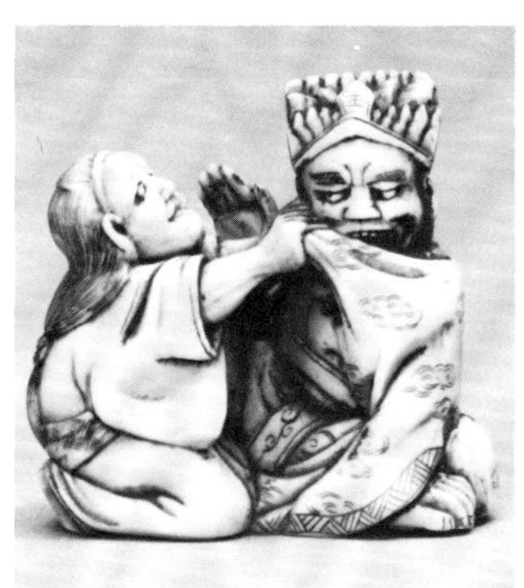

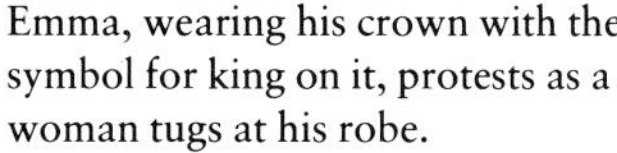

Emma, wearing his crown with the symbol for king on it, protests as a woman tugs at his robe.

Ivory. 19th-20th c. Katabori.
3.8 cm. E27159

Rakan (**Arhats**) The term applied to these Buddhist holy men means "deserving of worship." Rakan are disciples of Buddha and can be identified by their shaven heads, long eyebrows and earlobes, earrings, and their cloaks which leave one shoulder uncovered. Many are said to possess supernatural powers, such as Rakan Panthaka who can conjure up his companion the dragon. The term rakan applies to over a thousand persons, but only about sixteen of them are commonly depicted in netsuke.

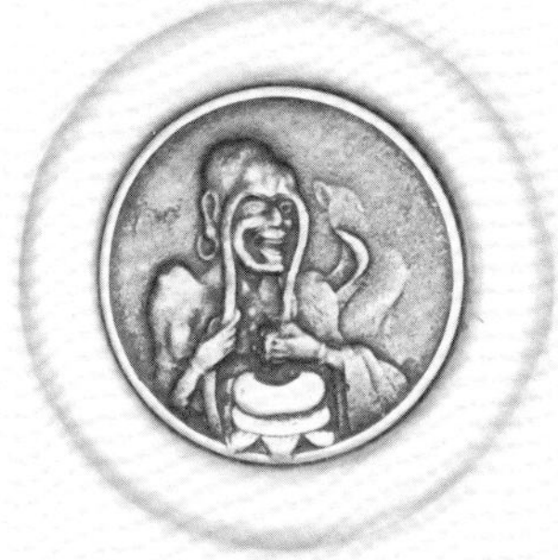

The lid covering an undecorated bowl depicts a rakan with long eyebrows standing over a cauldron.

Gold lacquer bowl, bronze lid. mid-19th c. Kagamibuta.
5.5 cm. E26534

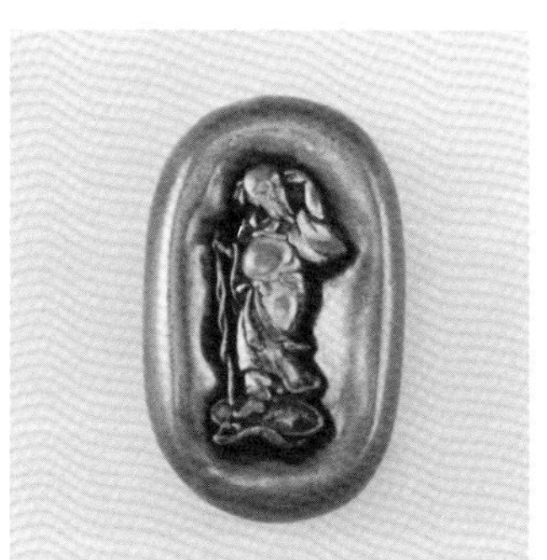

A rakan (in gold colored metal) is set into a gold lacquered piece of wood.

Lacquered wood and metal. 18th-19th c. Manju. 3.5 cm. E26536

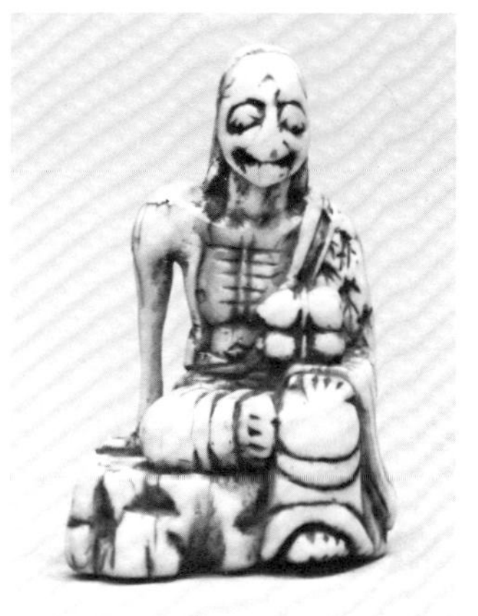

An emaciated rakan sits in fasting meditation on a rock. Two water gourds hang over his shoulder.

Ivory. 18th c. Katabori.
4.8 cm. E27103

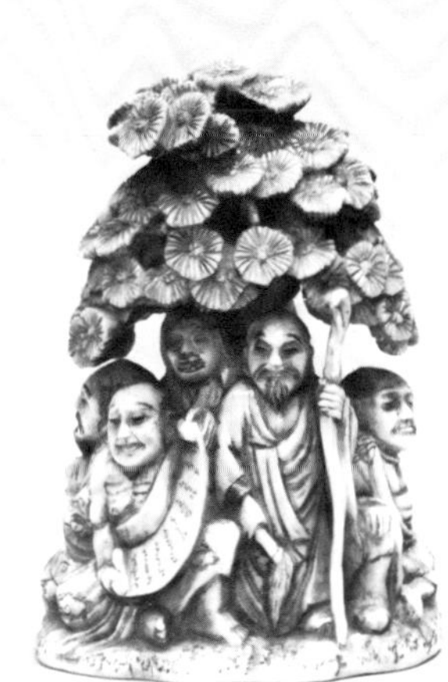

The rakan and other holy persons gathered here under a blossoming tree may illustrate Prince Shotoku's idea that the three religious and ethical systems of Japan can be compared to the root (Shinto), stem and branches (Confucianism), and flowers and fruits (Buddhism) of a tree.

Ivory. Shomei, unrecorded artist. late 19th-20th c. Katabori.
5.4 cm. E27164

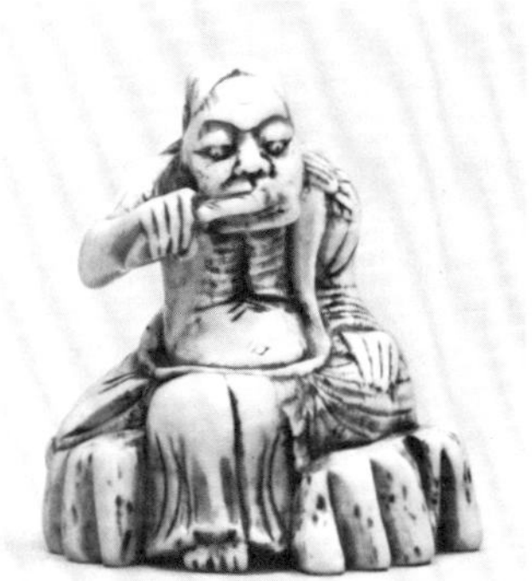

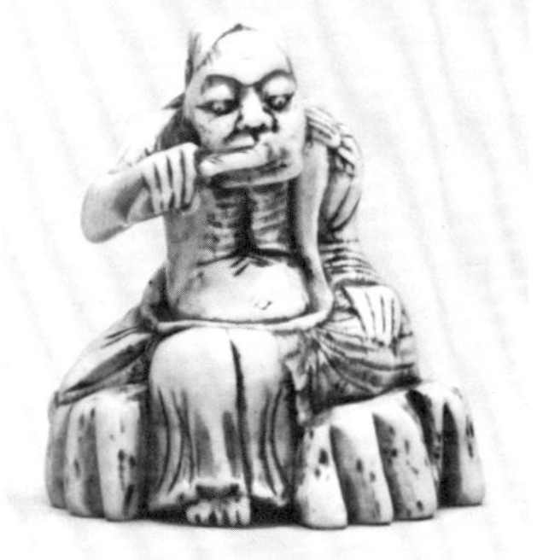

A rakan sits on a rock and washes his mouth, a compulsory act performed before praying.

Ivory. 18th c. Katabori.
4.0 cm. E27147

Rakan Panthaka

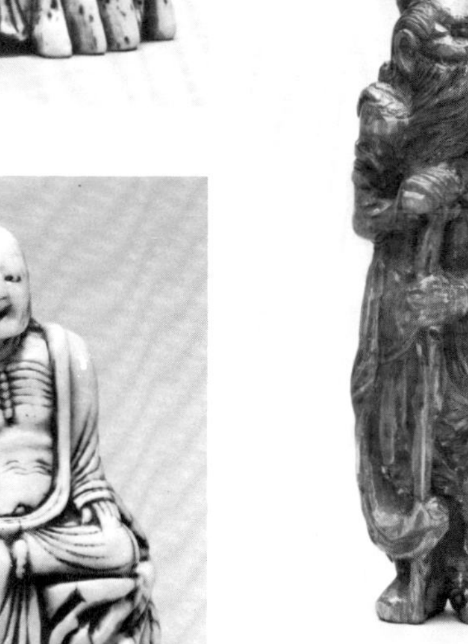

Panthaka's dragon peers over the top of Panthaka's head.

Painted cypress. early 18th c. Katabori.
10.5 cm. E26956

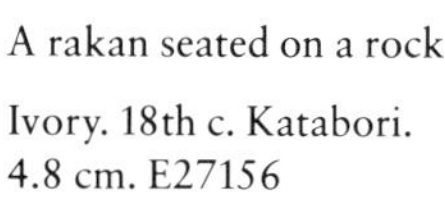

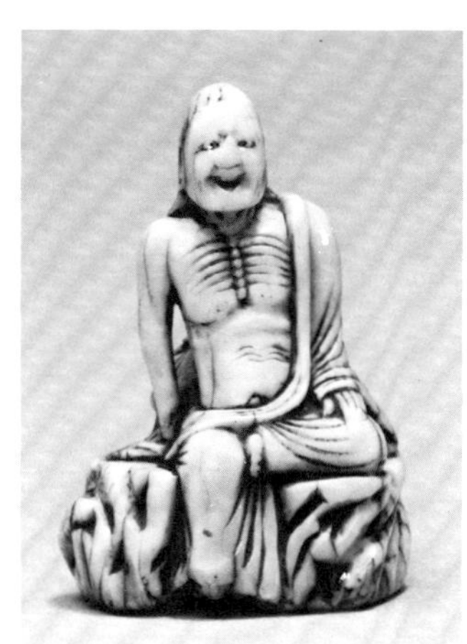

A rakan seated on a rock

Ivory. 18th c. Katabori.
4.8 cm. E27156

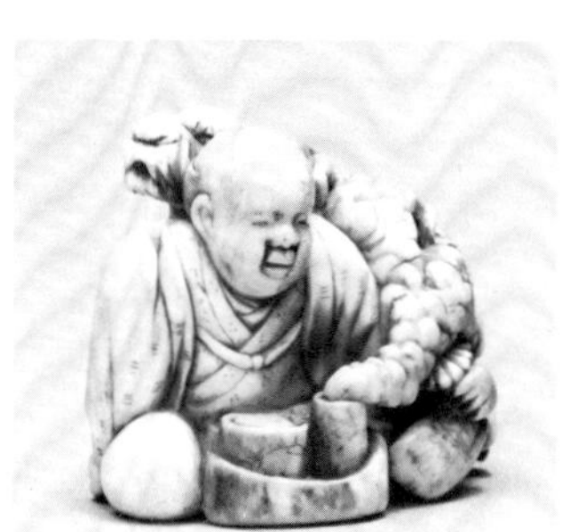

Panthaka's dragon issues forth from a bowl and slithers onto Panthaka's back.

Ivory, brass signature plaque. Hojitsu. mid-19th c. Katabori.
3.7 cm. E27102

Tennin Tennin are female inhabitants of the Buddhist heaven. Clothed in flowing scarves and robes of feathers, they fly through the air carrying a musical instrument or a lotus flower.

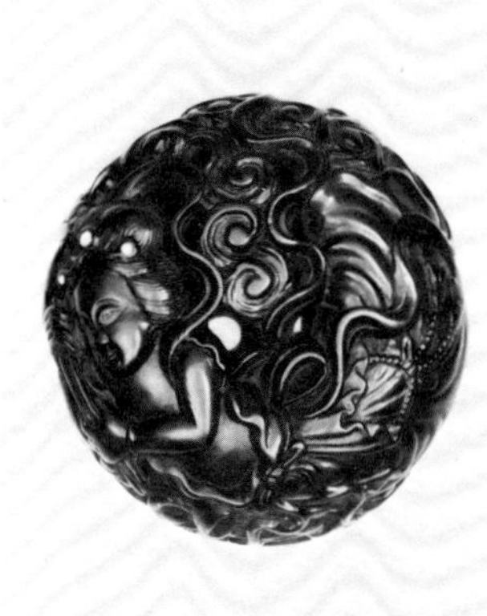

This piece depicts a tennin flying through clouds carrying a flower. On the other side, musical instruments (a drum, a flute, a sho) float in the clouds.

Boxwood with ivory inlays. Isshinsai. before 1800. Manju-ryusa. 4.2 cm. E26572

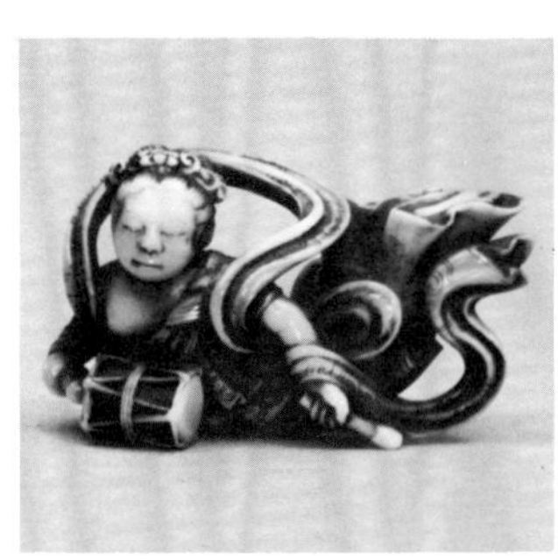

A tennin flies through the air playing a hand drum.

Ivory. 19th c. Katabori. 4.3 cm. E27002

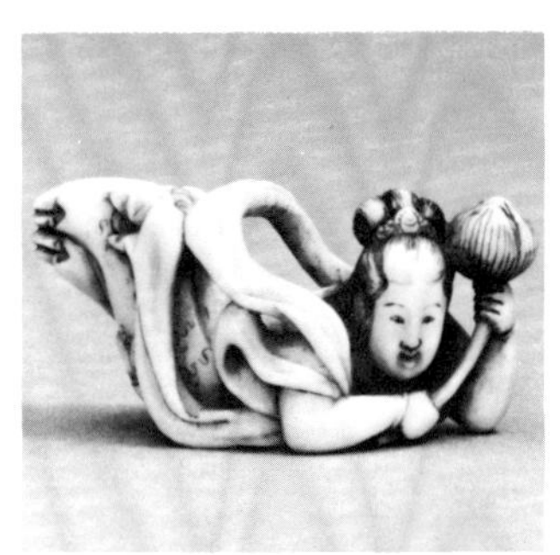

A tennin flies through the air holding a lotus flower.

Ivory. Tomochika I. 1800-1873. Katabori. 4.5 cm. E27131

Wago Jin These two karako (Chinese boys) represent Harmony and Concord. One carries a lotus, the other a scepter and gems.

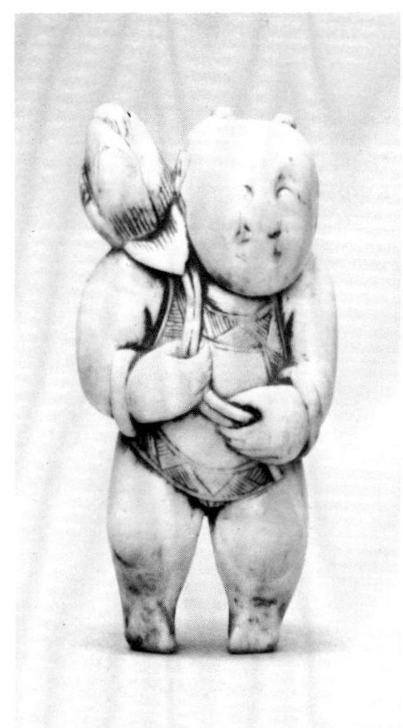

The karako of Harmony holds a lotus flower.

Ivory. 18th c. Katabori. 5.7 cm. E27036

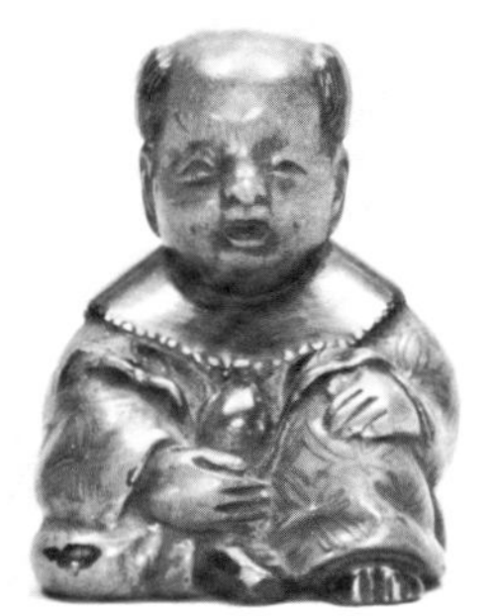

The karako of Concord holds an amber jewel. Inlaid in the black collar of his red and gray robe are tiny pieces of pearl.

Lacquered wood, amber and pearl inlays. 19th c. Katabori. 4.0 cm. E27066

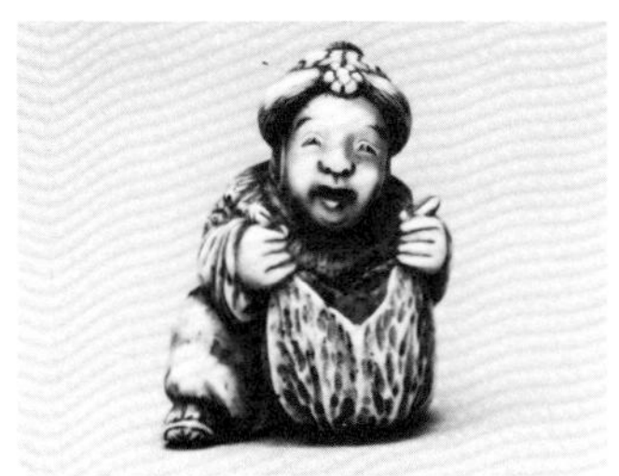

This karako of Harmony's lotus flower has a coral jewel inside.

Ivory, coral inlay. Tomochika I. 1800-1873. Katabori. 3.0 cm. E27121

Taoism

A mystical alliance with the Tao, or eternal Way, can be attained by retreating from civilization, living simply and communing with nature. Mountain mystics from Chinese Taoism became sennin in Japan, and were believed to inhabit Japanese mountains.

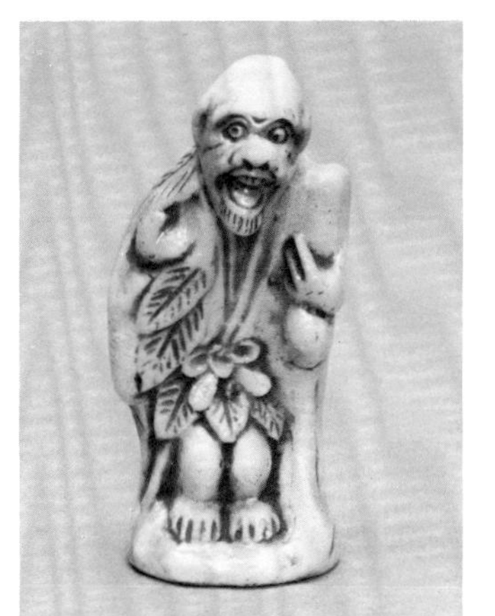

A sennin stands with his arm around a tree trunk.

Porcelain. late 18th-19th c. Katabori. 5.5 cm. E10063

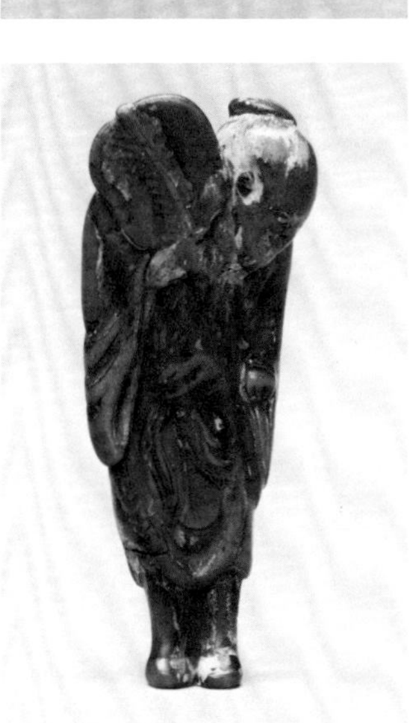

A leaf-collared sennin holds a fan.

Painted cypress. Shuzan. late 18th c. Katabori. 6.4 cm. E26936

Sennin H. L. Joly (see Bibliography) states that sennin are actually of Buddhist origin though they clearly follow Taoist teachings. Among the most common of netsuke subjects, sennin are the Taoist Immortals who have achieved immortality by meditation and asceticism. Many sennin possess magical powers, living in the mountains amidst magical animals. Sennin can be easily identified in netsuke by their leaf aprons and collars, and their long hair. The identity of individual sennin can often be determined by the attributes associated with them.

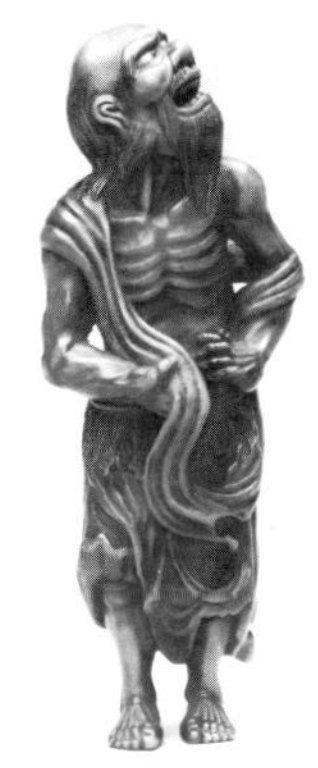

A bearded sennin wears a shawl, skirt and leaf apron.

Boxwood, inlaid eyes. Rokuko. 19th c. Katabori. 9.2 cm. E26951

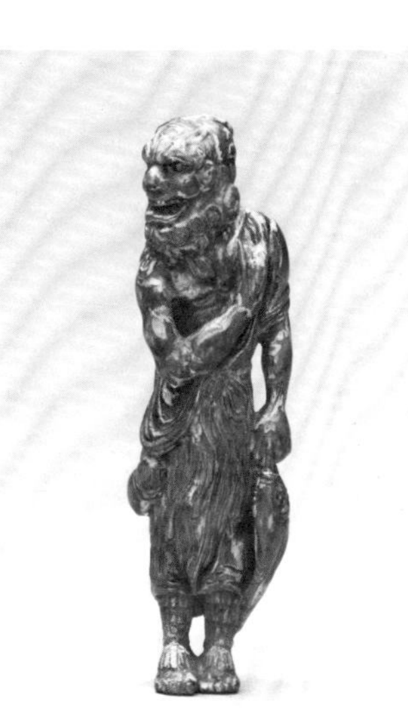

A bearded sennin stands with a large fish slung over his shoulder and two smaller fish in his left hand.

Cypress painted blue and red. 18th c. Katabori. 11.0 cm. E26955

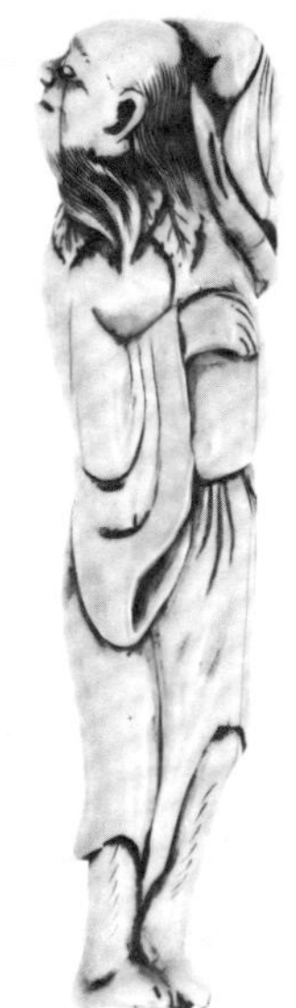

A piece whose form is clearly dictated by the shape of the ivory from which it was carved, this bearded, leaf-collared sennin stands with his left arm over his head and his right hand on his stomach.

Ivory. 18th c. Katabori. 12.7 cm. E26961

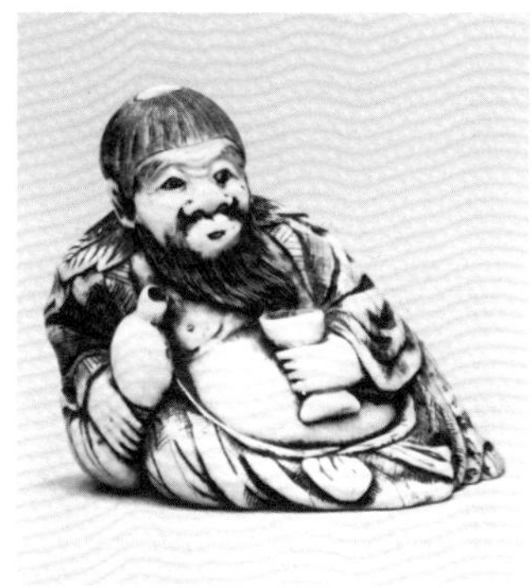

A fat, bearded, reclining sennin pours sake from a gourd bottle into his cup.

Ivory. Masamori. early 19th c. Katabori. 4.0 cm. E27105

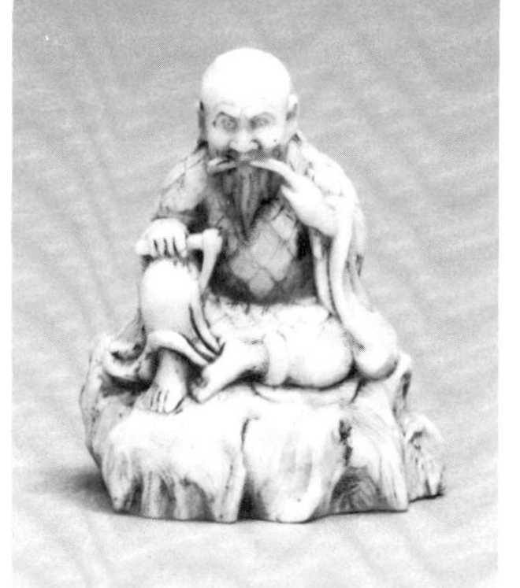

A horned sennin chews a string which he apparently has been working on with the tool he holds in his right hand.

Ivory. 19th c. Katabori. 4.2 cm. E27110

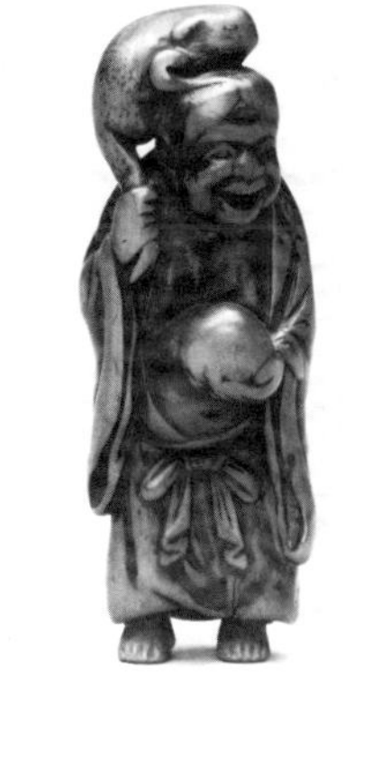

This sennin carries the symbols of three famous sennin. He holds Gama Sennin's frog, Tobosaku's peach, and wears Chokwaro's gourd at his belt.

Wood. late 18th c. Katabori. 9.4 cm. E29141

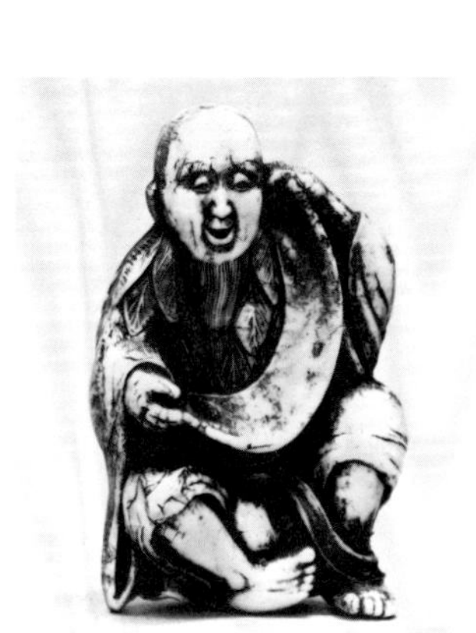

A seated sennin (perhaps Bushishi) holds a scroll.

Cast from a mold. 1940-1958. Katabori. 5.4 cm. E36984

Sennin playing Go Two sages lived unbeknownst to anyone inside of two huge oranges which hung from a tree. One day the owner of the tree cut open the oranges, the sages walked out and sat down together to play Go. Later, one of the sages conjured up a dragon which took them to heaven on a cloud.

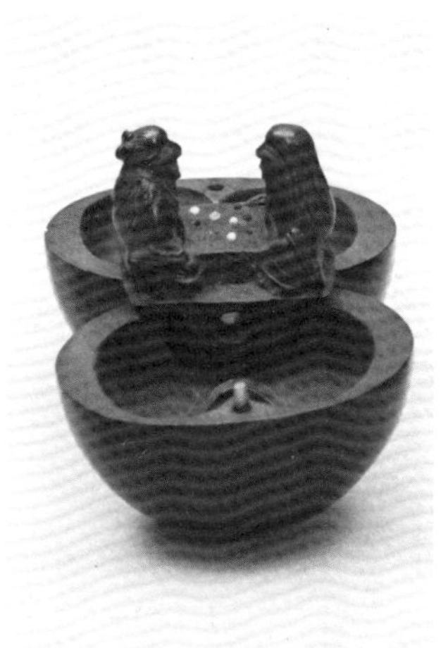

A hinged orange opens to reveal two sennin playing a game of Go.

Wood, ivory and ebony inlays. 19th c. Katabori. 3.5 cm. E26547

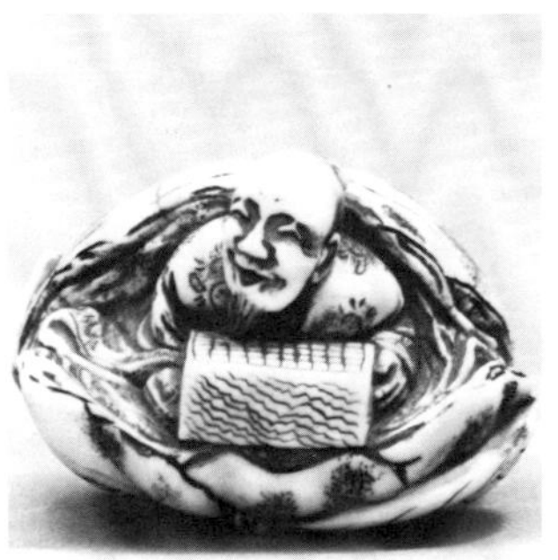

In a somewhat different representation of the story, one of the sages emerges from the fruit, Go board in hand.

Ivory. Hidemasa. early 19th c. Katabori. 3.3 cm. E27088

Sennin Chokwaro Sennin Chokwaro can summon forth his horse from a gourd by spitting on it. This provides him with swift transportation at a moment's notice.

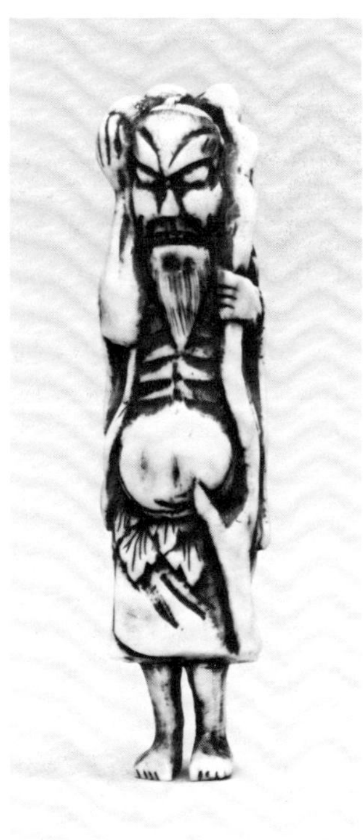

A mean looking Chokwaro, wearing a leaf apron and collar, holds up his staff and gourd.

Ivory. late 18th c. Katabori. 7.8 cm. E3964

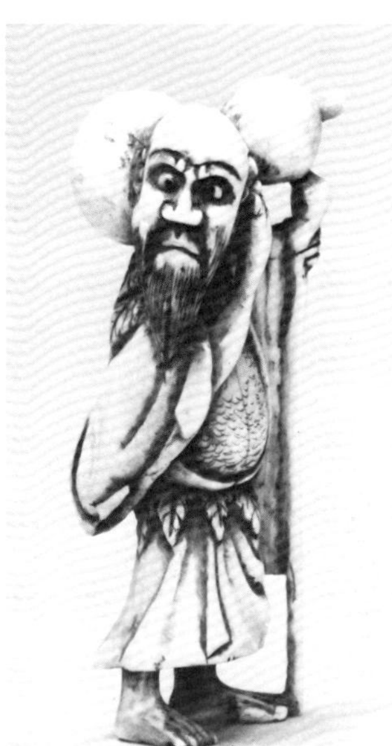

Chokwaro stands with a staff and his gourd on his shoulders.

Ivory with ebony eyes. late 18th-19th c. Katabori. 7.0 cm. E27034

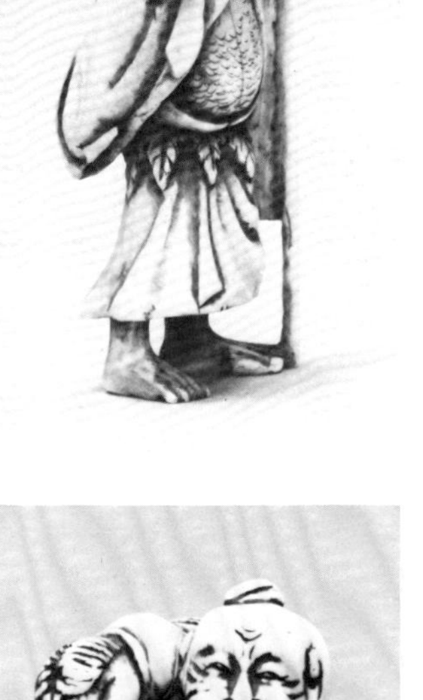

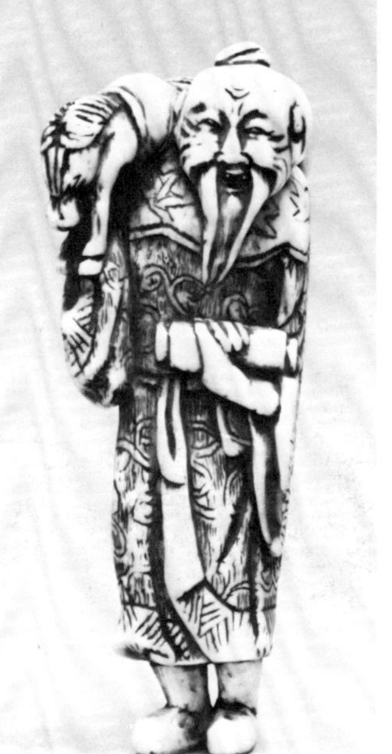

A bearded Chokwaro, wearing robes and holding a scroll, holds his gourd on his shoulder as his horse emerges from it.

Ivory. 18th c. Katabori. 7.7 cm. E26942

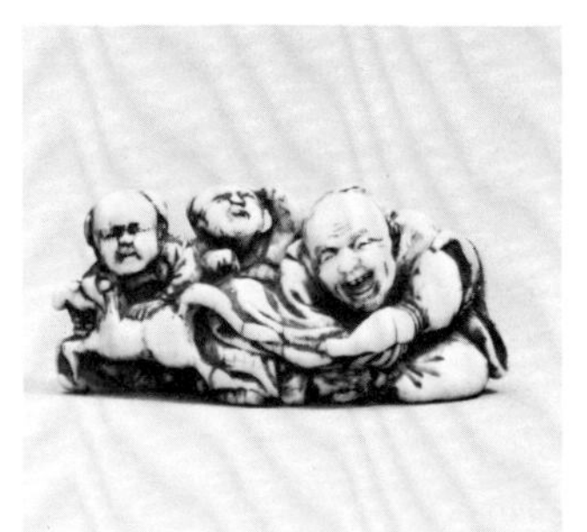

Chokwaro amuses two boys by releasing his horse from the gourd.

Ivory. Yamada. 19th c. Katabori. 4.8 cm. E27109

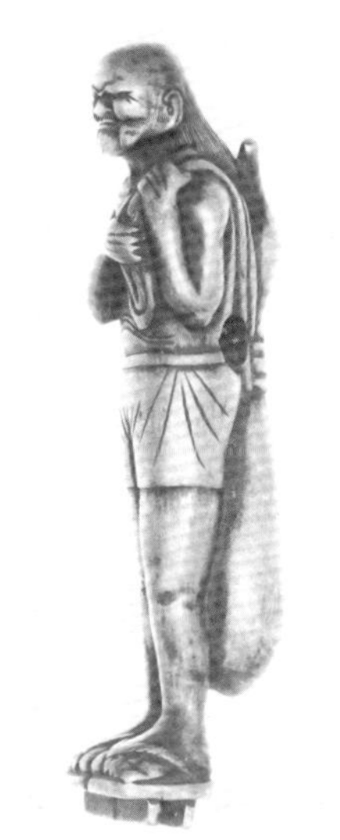

Chokwaro, wearing sandals, stands with his large gourd slung over his shoulder.

Boxwood. 18th c. Katabori.
11.7 cm. E29144

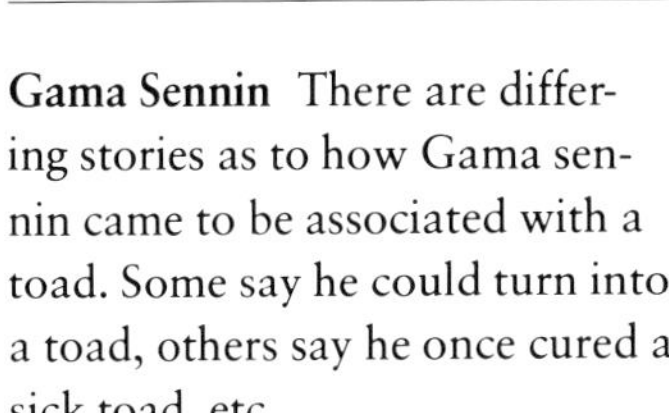

Gama Sennin There are differing stories as to how Gama sennin came to be associated with a toad. Some say he could turn into a toad, others say he once cured a sick toad, etc.

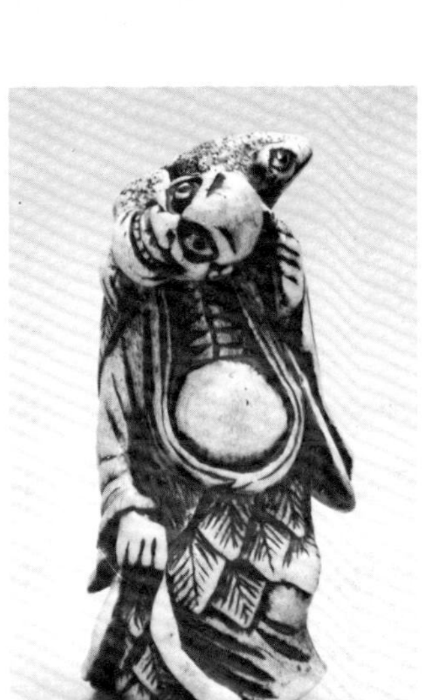

A frog plays on Gama sennin's shoulders.

Bone, ebony eyes. late 18th-19th c. Katabori. 6.0 cm. E26934

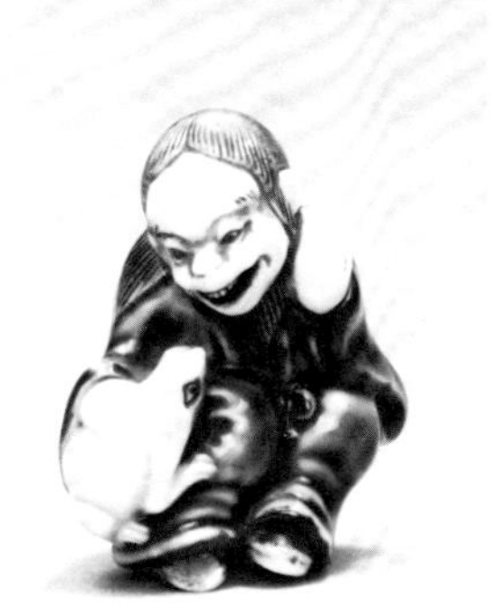

A cheerful looking Gama sennin squats to pet his frog.

Porcelain—blue, white, brown, gray. late 18th-19th c. Katabori.
4.0 cm. E26990

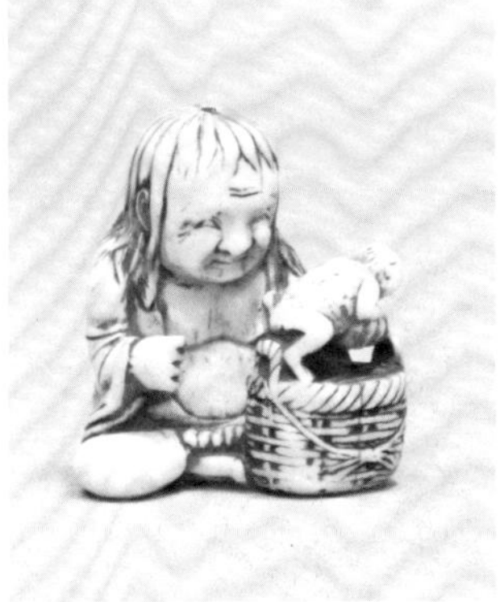

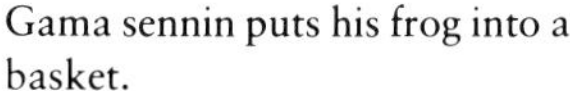

Gama sennin puts his frog into a basket.

Ivory, red stain. 19th c. Katabori.
3.3 cm. E27149

Koreijin Sennin A tiger accompanies this sennin.

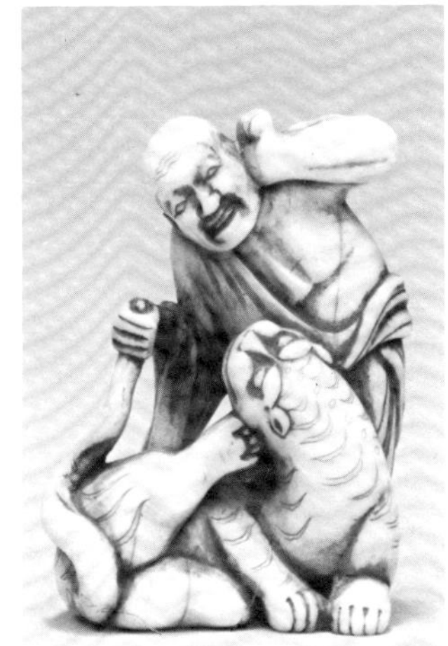

Koreijin sennin stretches and holds the tail of his tiger in one hand as the beast reclines at his feet. The tiger scratches his chin with one of his rear paws.

Ivory. 18th c. Katabori.
5.0 cm. E27119

Kyoyu and Sofu An emperor offered the rule of his land to Kyoyu, a Chinese sage. Kyoyu refused and washed his ears in a nearby stream to rid himself of the defilement caused by this worldly temptation. His companion, Sofu, the sennin, also washed himself clean, and then, discovering that his ox drank from the contaminated waters, led him away in order to prevent the beast's defilement.

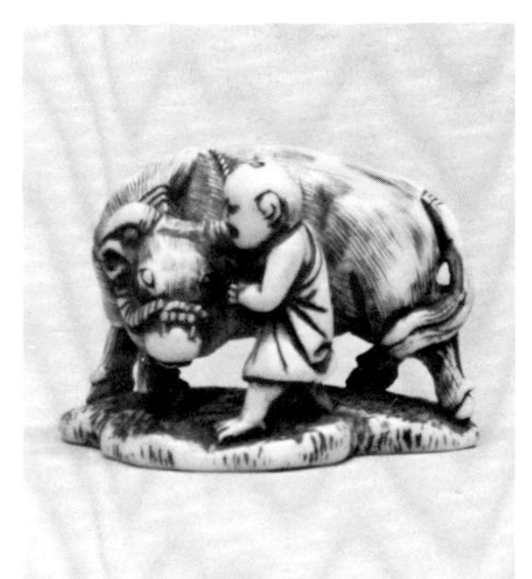

Sofu leads his ox away from the contaminated water.

Ivory. 19th c. Katabori.
4.5 cm. E26714

Seiobo Seiobo, the Chinese queen of the fairies, usually carries a peach (symbol of longevity) which she grows in her orchard. Legend has it that anyone who eats a peach from this orchard will live 3000 years.

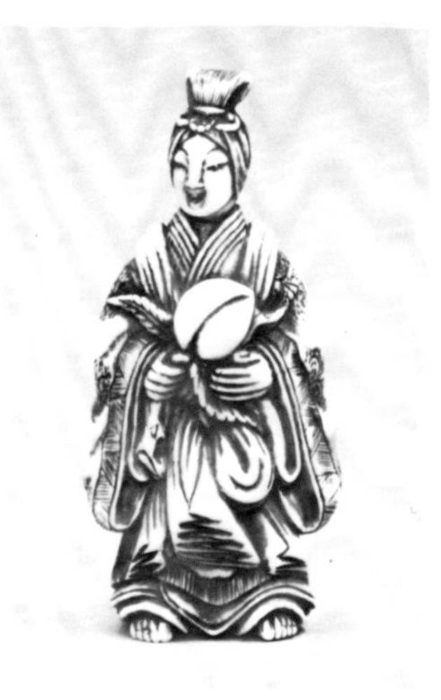

Seiobo, dressed in elegant robes, holds a peach from her orchard.

Ivory. late 18th-19th c. Katabori. 5.7 cm. E27051

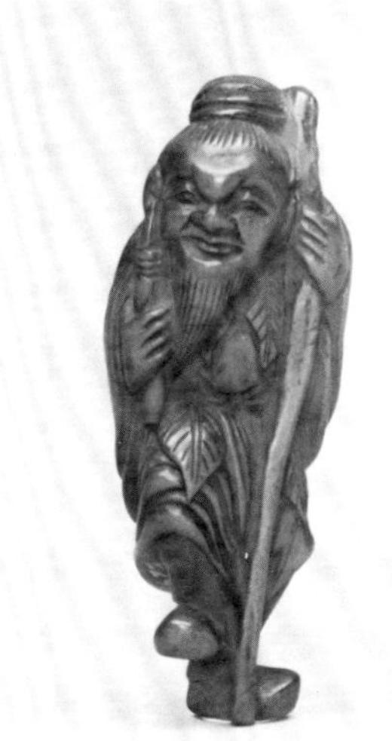

A smiling Tekkai has a staff in one hand and a writing brush in the other.

Wood. late 18th-19th c. Katabori. 6.7 cm. E29143

Sennin Tekkai In order to travel to heaven to speak with Lao-tzu, Tekkai's spirit could leave his body. On one of these journeys, however, Tekkai lost his body by staying away too long; thereafter he hobbled about (with the help of a staff) in the body of a beggar.

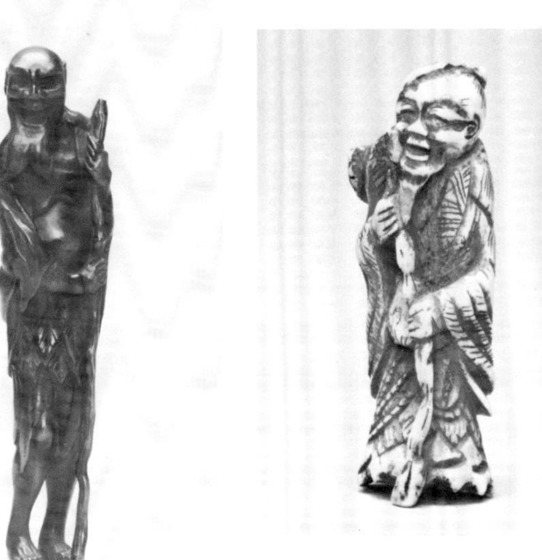

A bearded Tekkai stands holding his staff and laughing.

Wood, ebony eyes. early 18th c. Katabori. 12.2 cm. E26962

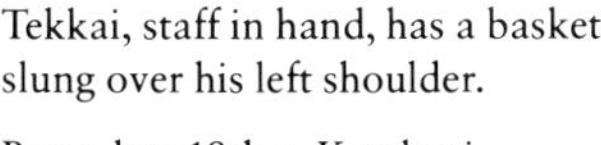

Tekkai, staff in hand, has a basket slung over his left shoulder.

Bone. late 18th c. Katabori. 8.6 cm. E29149

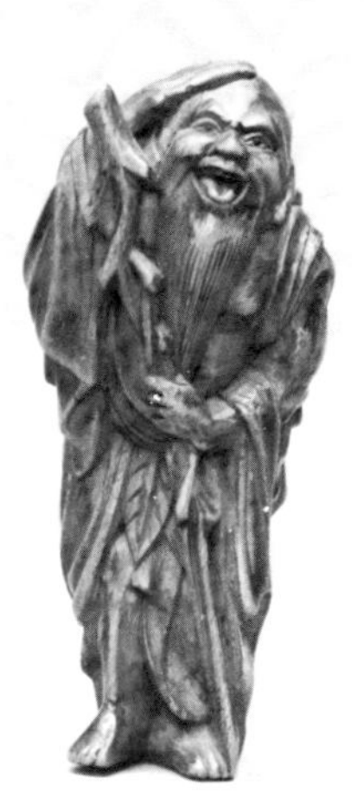

A bearded Tekkai has one hand on top of his head and his staff in the other.

Wood. 19th c. Katabori. 5.5 cm. E27023

Tobosaku Sennin As a youth, Tobosaku ate three peaches from the orchard of Seiobo and thus acquired godly wisdom and a life-span of 9000 years.

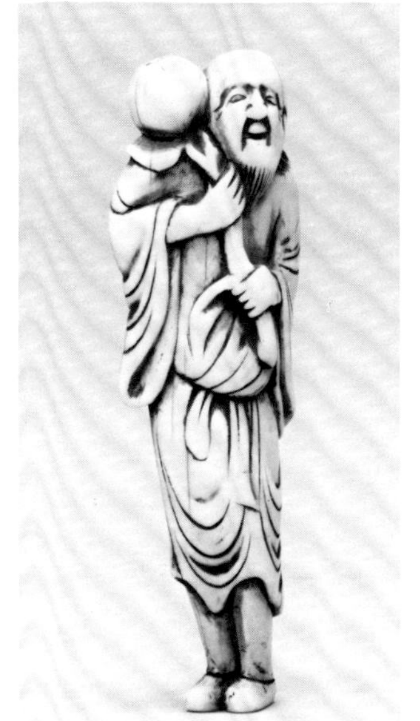

Tobosaku stands with a peach and branch in his hands.

Ivory. early 19th c. Katabori. 8.2 cm. E24907

Tobosaku scratches his ear as he stands next to a large peach. Inside the peach, another carving of Tobosaku depicts him studying a scroll.

Ivory. late 18th c. Katabori. 6.0 cm. E27041

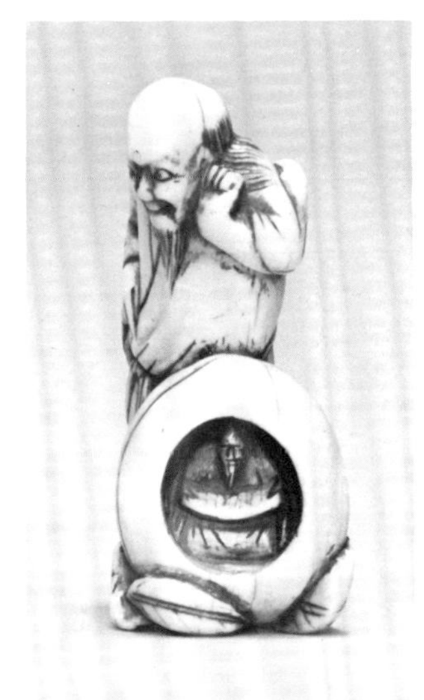

In this amusing piece three legendary figures, each holding a symbol of longevity, sit back-to-back in a saucer. Tobosaku holds a peach: Fukurokuju has his fan and stork; and Urashima Taro holds his box and bushy-tailed turtle.

Ivory. Masamine. early 19th c. Katabori. 2.7 cm. E27130

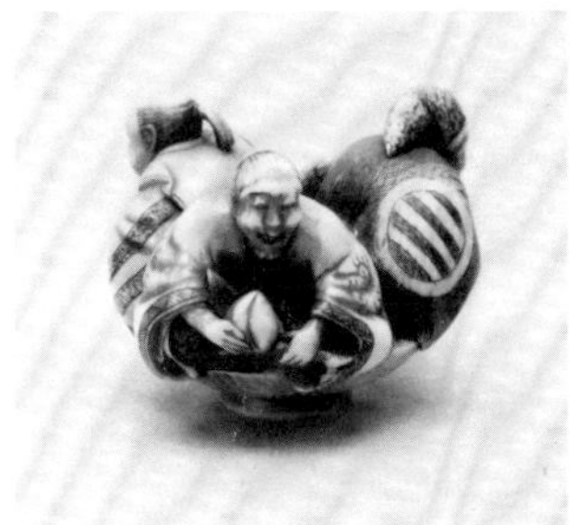

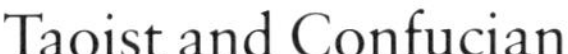

Taoist and Confucian

Kanzan and Jittoku These two friends are almost always portrayed together. Kanzan, a thinker, philosopher and poet usually carries a scroll. Jittoku, a simple kitchen worker, holds a broom. Kanzan symbolizes meditation while Jittoku symbolizes material, bodily concerns. Since the two spoke a sort of gibberish to each other which no one else understood, they were thought to be madmen or halfwits. Frequently depicted in art, they usually appear as comical, boyish figures. There is poetry extant that is attributed to Kanzan.

On one side Kanzan holds a scroll while Jittoku sweeps the grounds around the temple. On the other side a general comes to the temple to pray.

Walnut or peach pit. 18th-19th c. Manju. 3.3 cm. E26853

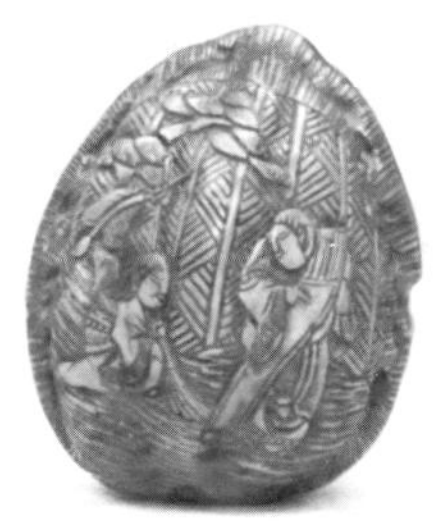

Demons

The folk religions and legends of Japan are populated not only by countless good deities, but by demons as well. Their half human, half animal forms made interesting subjects for netsuke carvers. In addition to their aesthetic value, netsuke of deities and demons served as charms to ward off evil and invite good spirits into the lives of those who wore them.

Bakemono Bakemono is a generic term for ghosts and goblins. As with other frightening or austere figures in Japanese religions and legends, the netsuke-shi tend to treat bakemono with humor.

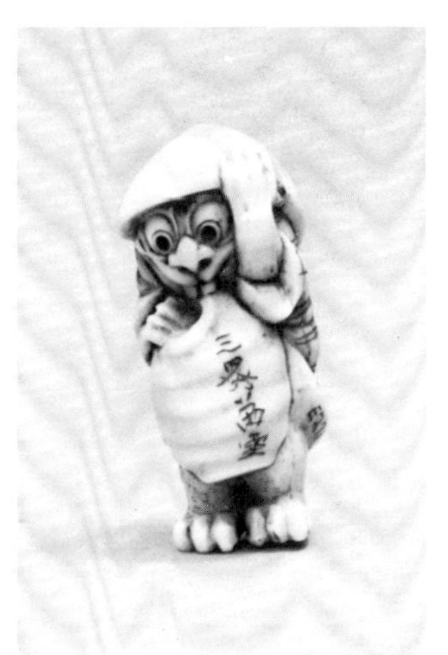

An animal-like bakemono, wearing a farmer's jacket and hat, holds a jug with writing on it which says that he is the spirit of past, present and future.

Ivory. Chi or Zoroku. 19th-20th c. Katabori. 4.0 cm. E27143

Oni Oni are mischievous and sometimes evil demons. Physically, they resemble Raiden the thunder god, with their horns, fangs, clawlike toes and three-fingered hands. They serve as assistants to Emma, king of Hell, and they take on a variety of disguises in order to engage in mischievous activities. Oni are terrified of dried peas (perhaps because peas are emblematic of strength and health), and on Setsubun oni (the first day of Spring) peas are ceremoniously thrown about in an effort to exorcise oni. Oni are often depicted hiding in and under such shelters as boxes and priests' helmets trying to avoid the peas. Common netsuke subjects, oni are most often depicted in humorous ways.

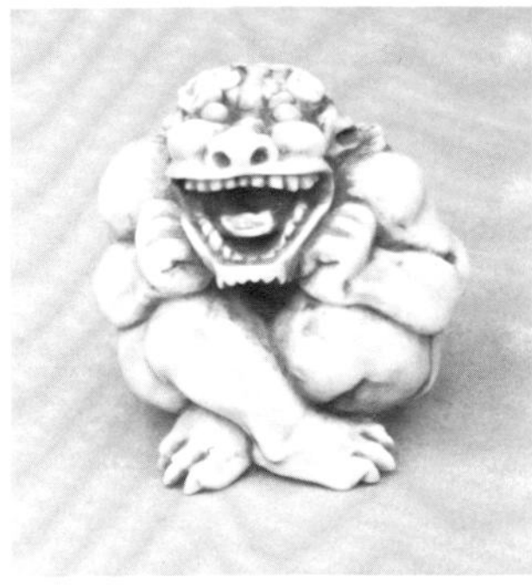

A laughing oni fiendishly displays his fangs.

Ivory, pearl eyes. Koichi. late 19th-20th c. Katabori. 3.2 cm. E26675

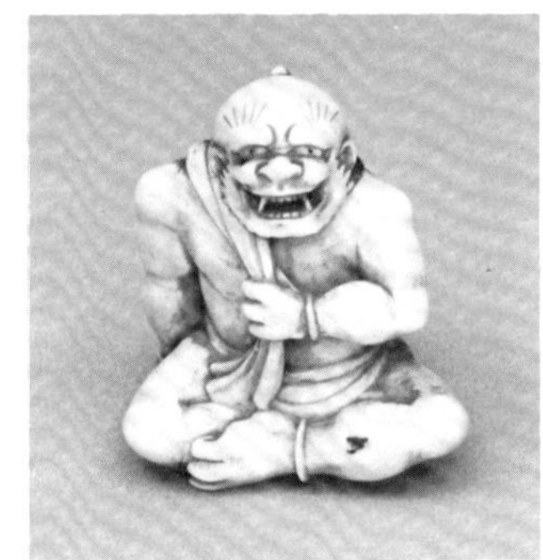

An oni sits cross-legged with a sack slung over his shoulder.

Ivory. 19th-20th c. Katabori. 3.3 cm. E26999

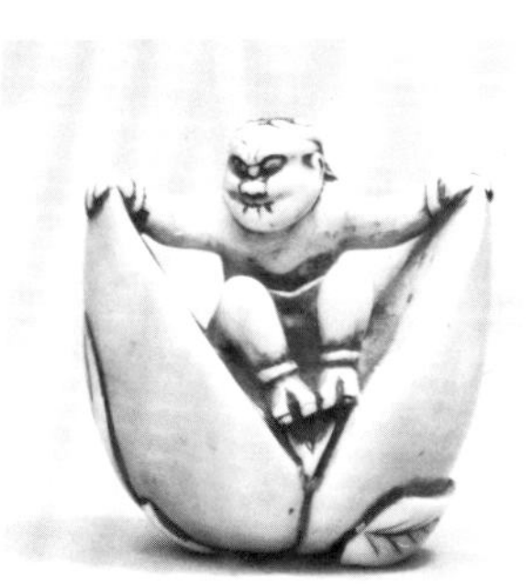

This oni sitting inside a split-open peach probably refers to the visit of Momotaro "Little Peachling" to the Island of the Devils.

Ivory. late 18th-19th c. Katabori. 3.3 cm. E26795

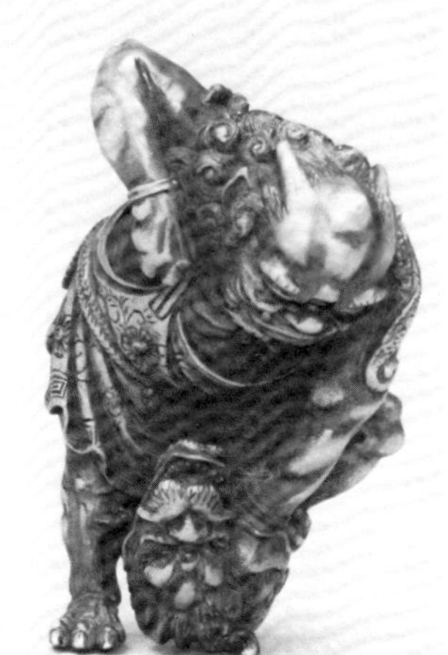

This piece depicts an oni fighting a dragon. The dragon's body is curled around the oni's back.

Wood. late 18th c. Katabori. 6.0 cm. E27013

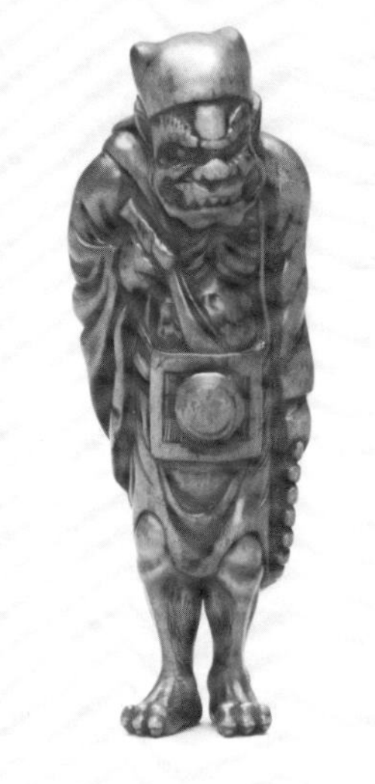

An oni disguises himself as a priest. The wear on this piece suggests that the cord was strung through the oni's mouth, rather than through the himotoshi.

Boxwood. 18th c. Katabori. 11.5 cm. E26960

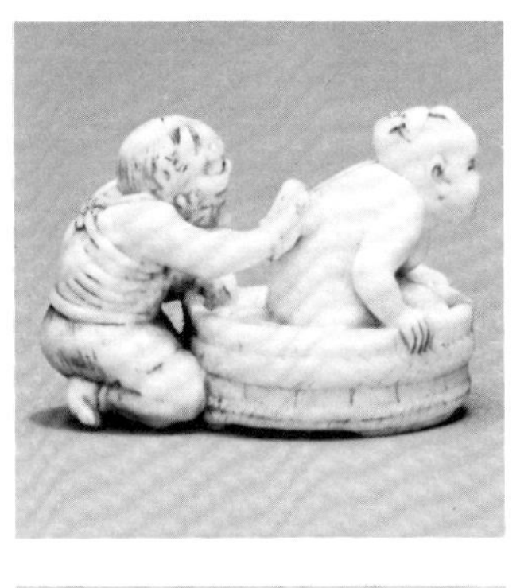

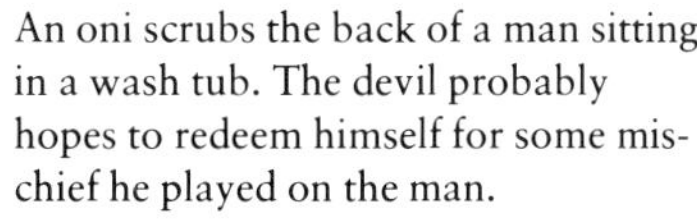

An oni scrubs the back of a man sitting in a wash tub. The devil probably hopes to redeem himself for some mischief he played on the man.

Ivory, inlaid eyes. Ranko. early 19th c. Katabori. 3.8 cm. E27086

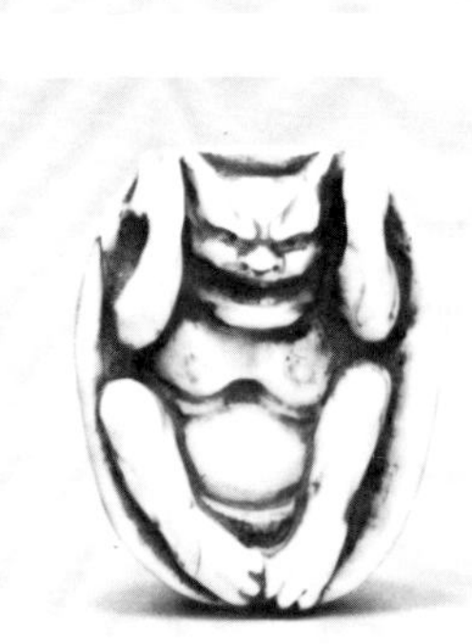

An oni hides under a priest's helmet in order to avoid the peas being thrown at him. On the reverse side the peas can be seen on the helmet.

Ivory. 19th c. Katabori. 3.3 cm. E26996

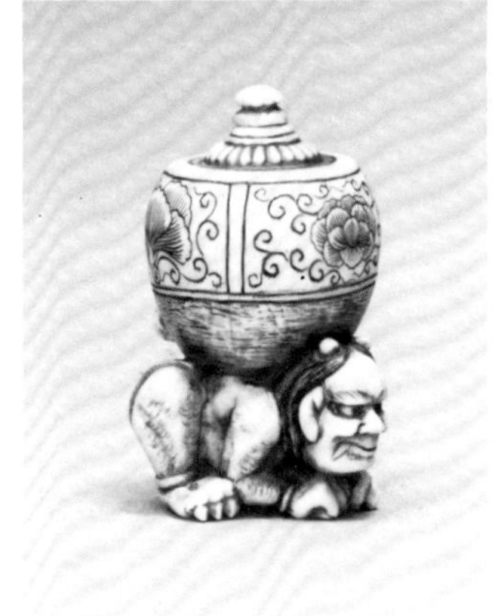

This crouching oni has an urn on his back. The oni wears a tiger skin loin cloth, common attire for oni. The plug in the urn is removable and the urn is hollow.

Ivory. 19th c. Katabori. 4.0 cm. E27127

An oni disguised as a priest

Cast from a mold. mid 20th c. Katabori. 5.3 cm. E36988

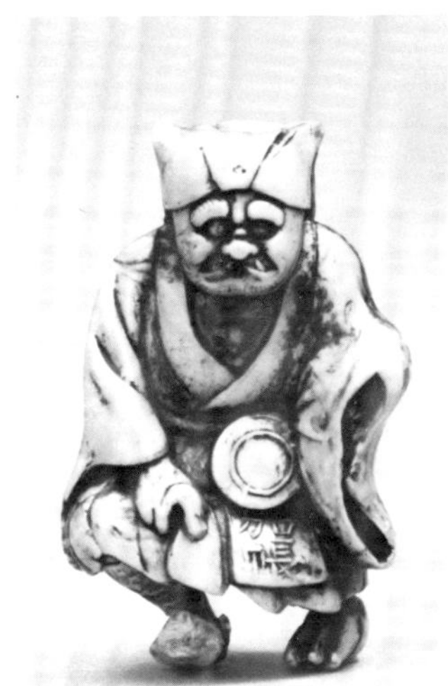

Tengu Possessed of supernatural powers, these inhabitants of mountains and forests take two different forms. The Karasu (crow) tengu with its birdlike beak and wings is often depicted hatching from an egg. The Konoha tengu has a more human form, though it has wings and an extremely long nose. Some tengu supposedly help humans, while others cause them difficulties.

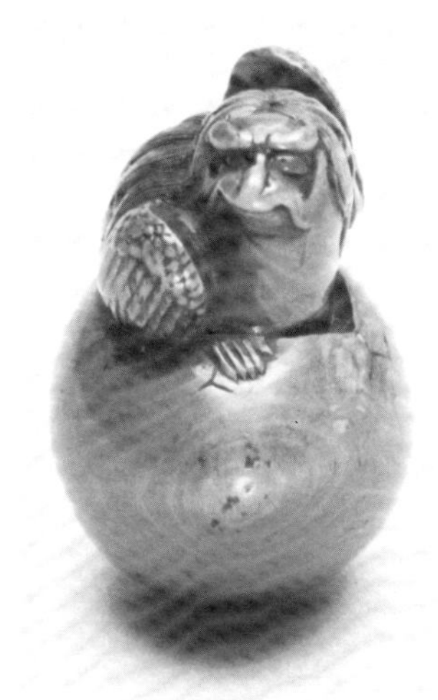

A karasu (crow) tengu hatches from an egg.

Wood, inlaid eyes. 18th c. Katabori. 4.8 cm. E26770

Folk Tales

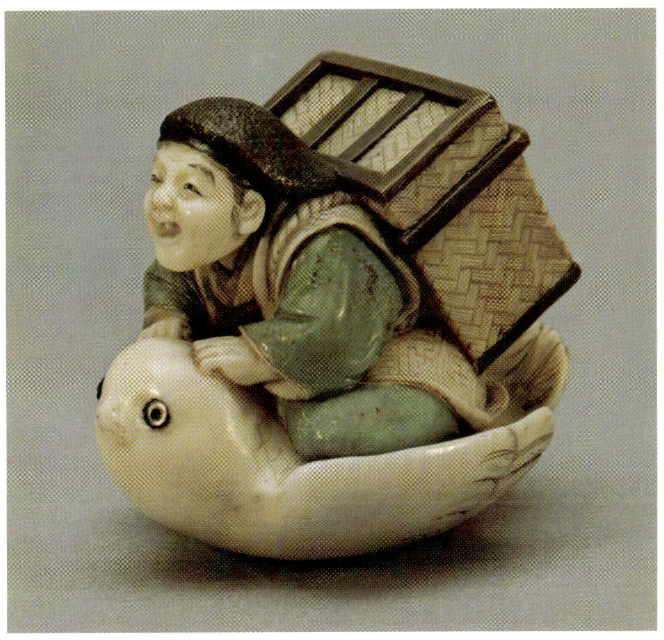

Folk tales, i.e. fairy tales and legends, have been generated in profusion in Japan. Some have been recorded in written texts but most have been passed from one generation to the next by word of mouth; all have provided a stimulus to Japanese artists, particularly the carvers of netsuke.

The proliferation of legends, ancient tales based on historic events, and fairy tales, based on fabricated events, began early in Japan's history. The *Kojiki* and the *Nihongi* set the pattern for mixing fact with fancy in the 8th c. by documenting mythical tales of the origin and traditions of the Japanese. The tradition of Shinto, an ancient faith by that time, was to deify awe-invoking spirits, *kami,* believed to be the source of phenomena in nature. In ensuing ages, when inspiring historic events occurred, this tradition deified remarkable heroes and warriors, even ancestors, as kami, or gods. Legends grew describing the events and heroic or virtuous acts, and although based on fact, they were invariably embellished and often associated with a local clan or community. Later, Chinese legends were adapted by the Japanese and Buddhism contributed a whole new set of deities and religious heroes whose miraculous deeds became the basis of popular legends.

Legends were remembered, retold and retained partly because Shinto shrines were built for the spirits of extraordinary heroes, preserving their names and stories; religious festivals honoring the memory of illustrious men or deities also maintained the legends. Lastly, legends and fairy tales were a principal source for the Japanese drama, and are reenacted in the performances of the Noh and Kabuki theatres.

Legends

Ancient folk tales based on historic events and personalities were common subject matter for netsuke carvers of the 18th c.

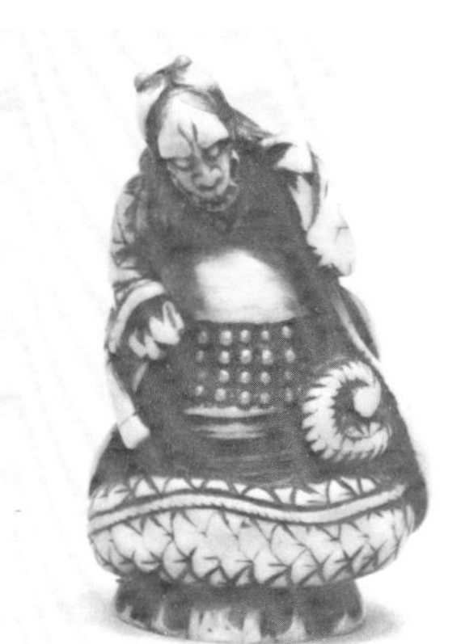

Kiyohime, with green coral demon's face and horns, has wrapped herself around the bell, hammer in hand. The bell is inlaid with small brass dots for decoration.

Ivory, with green coral and brass inlays. 19th c. Katabori. 4.5 cm. E26997

Anchin and the Bell The priest Anchin accidentally invoked the love of the sorceress Kiyohime and had to spurn her overtures by hiding in a huge bell. Furious, Kiyohime felled the bell, trapping Anchin inside, then changed herself into a serpent dragon and coiled herself around the bell. The heat of her anger was sufficient to melt the bell, burning Anchin to ashes.

Ashinaga and Tenaga The legendary Longlegs and Longarms of Japan, Ashinaga has legs twenty feet long, and Tenaga's arms are even longer. Usually portrayed fishing, they live on the seafood Tenaga catches with his long arms while perched on the back of the long-legged Ashinaga, who can wade into deep water. They are almost always together, for they demonstrate cooperation and the benefits of working together.

Kiyohime is wrapped around the bell, peering into a small hole in it. When the bell hanger of this netsuke is turned, Anchin's face can be seen turning from red to white to blue as he burns.

Wood, ivory lined himotoshi and ivory face inside bell. Minko. 1735-1816. Katabori. 4.0 cm. E26973

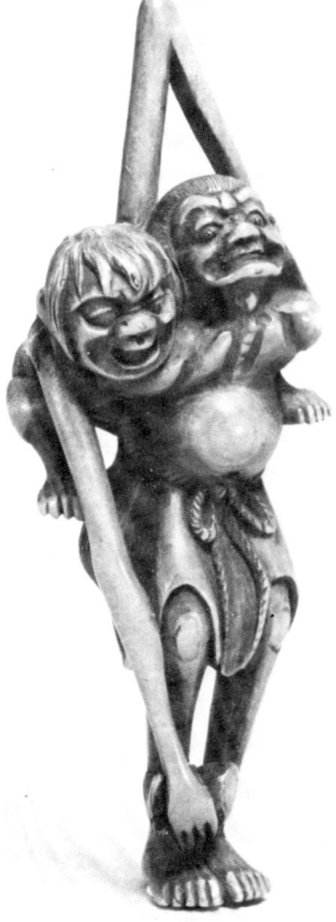

Ashinaga and Tenaga are fishing. Tenaga grabs a fish while hoisted onto Ashinaga's back.

Boxwood, inlaid eyes. Tomokazu. late 18th-early 19th c. Katabori. 9.0 cm. E26938

Ashinaga, legs bent, knees in the air, sits on a drum. He bends over a book while two little men sit on his feet and presumably help him read.

Ivory. 19th c. Katabori.
3.7 cm. E27087

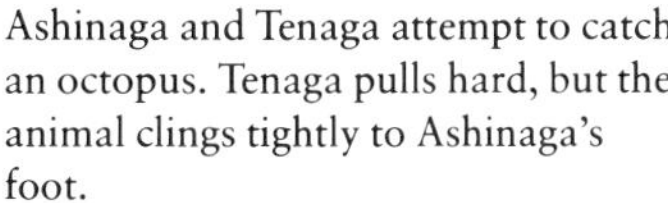

Ashinaga and Tenaga attempt to catch an octopus. Tenaga pulls hard, but the animal clings tightly to Ashinaga's foot.

Wood. Masanobu. 1838-1900.
Katabori. 16.3 cm. E26964

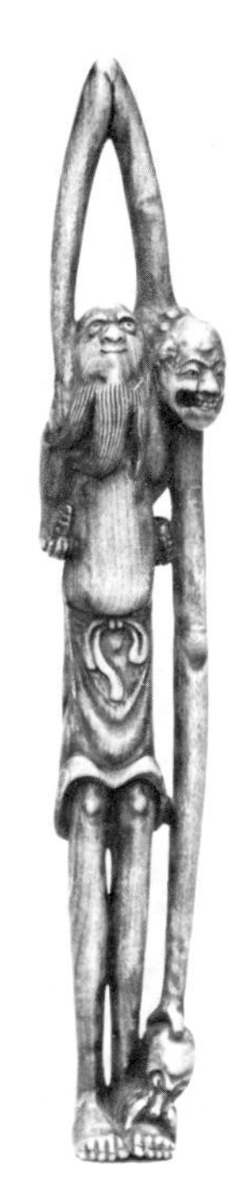

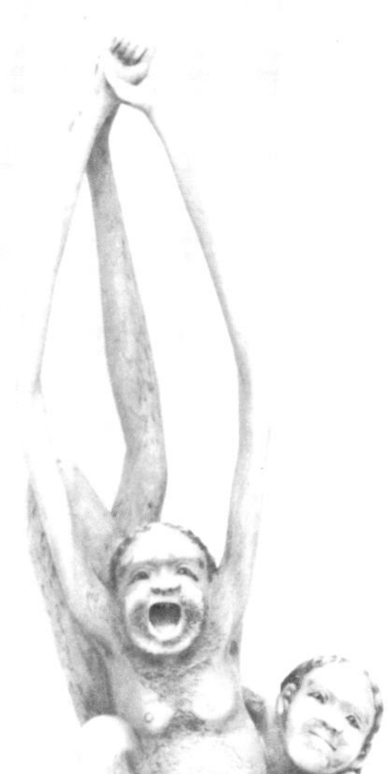

The comical Ashinaga and Tenaga relax. Tenaga sits and stretches his long arms into the air while Ashinaga stretches one of his long legs far into the air.

Ivory. Tomomasa. early 19th c.
Katabori. 7.5 cm. E27101

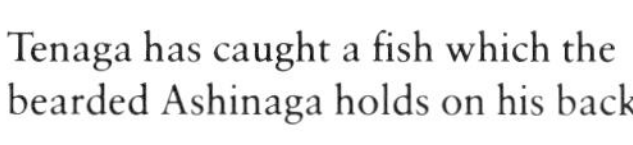

Tenaga has caught a fish which the bearded Ashinaga holds on his back.

Ivory. late 18th c. Katabori.
9.3 cm. E27026

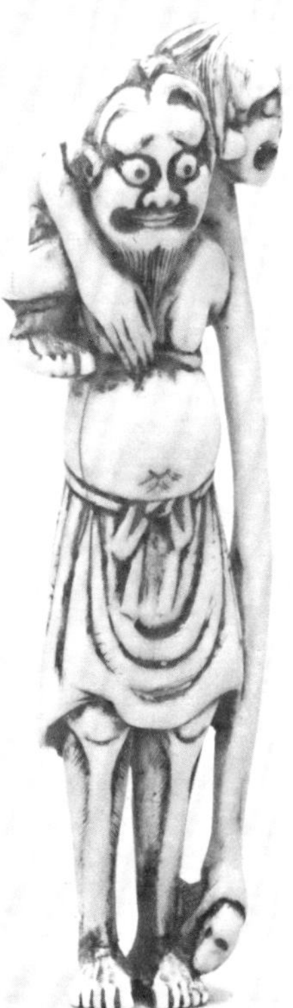

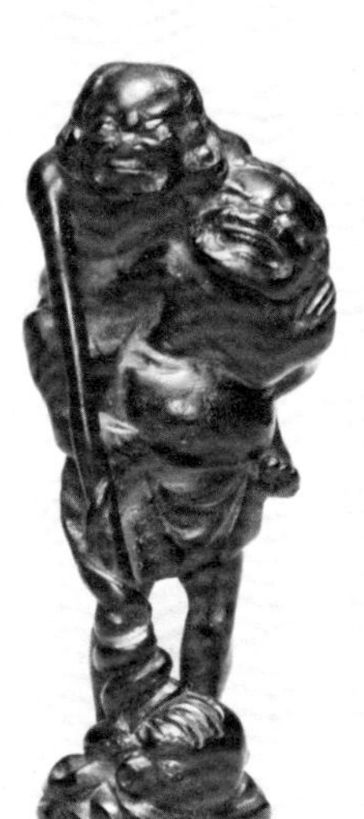

Ashinaga and Tenaga have gone fishing and caught an octopus.

Ebony, glass inlaid eyes. 19th c.
Katabori. 6.0 cm. E53703

Benkei Benkei is a hero of the 12th c. whose feats of supernatural strength (he was as strong as a hundred men) and courage were in keeping with his extraordinary height of eight feet. A hellion as a child, Benkei joined the yamabushi, (itinerant Buddhist priests) at age 17, but priesthood failed to curb his irrepressible spirit of adventure. He became a lawless warrior, determined to prove his prowess by collecting 1,000 swords from soldiers he waylaid and challenged. He had successfully acquired 999 when the youth Yoshitsune, another hero, defeated him in an encounter on the Gojo Bridge in Kyoto. A chastened Benkei became Yoshitsune's loyal, resourceful retainer for the rest of his life, providing countless legends of their exploits together.

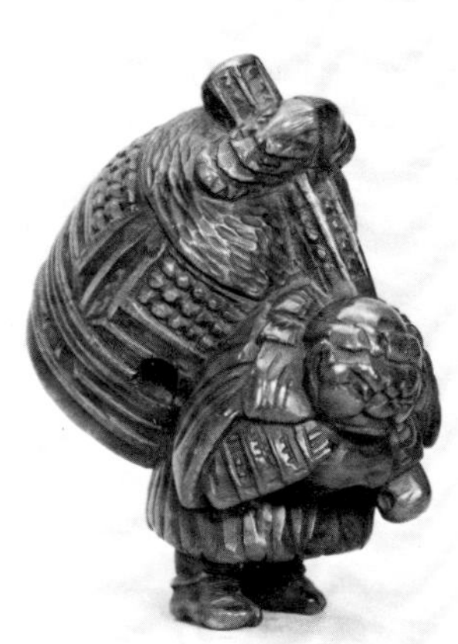

Benkei's most remarkable feat was carrying the huge bell from a monastery in Miidera to the top of Mt. Hiei. The bell, however, refused to ring, muttering only "I want to return to Miidera." Enraged, Benkei moved it to the mountain's edge, and kicked it back to the monastery.

Boxwood. Sanko. 1772-1788. Katabori. 5.0 cm. E29152

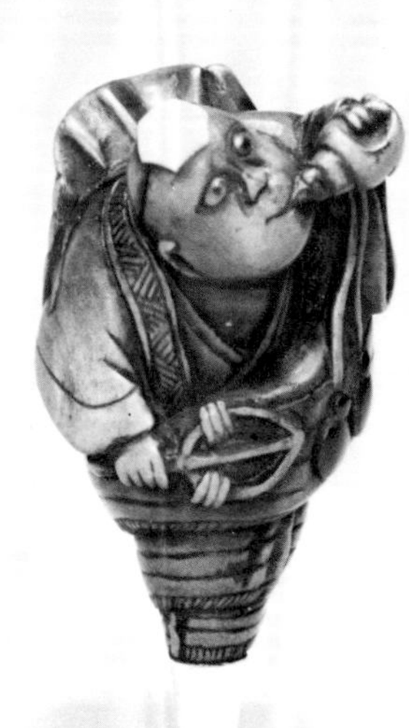

Benkei, with amber eyes, wears the hexagonal cap and hair style of the yamabushi. He reclines in a giant conch shell, one of the attributes of that Buddhist sect, blowing a smaller shell.

Boxwood with ivory, ebony and amber inlays. mid-18th c. Katabori. 6.0 cm. E26967

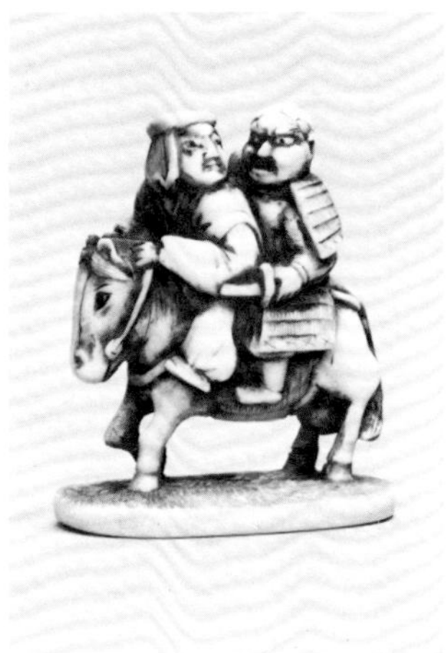

Benkei and Yoshitsune ride together on horseback, Yoshitsune holding the reins. Benkei, mounted behind Yoshitsune, is wearing armor.

Ivory. Norishige. 1830-1843 or 1772-1788 (opinions vary). Katabori. 4.0 cm. E27083

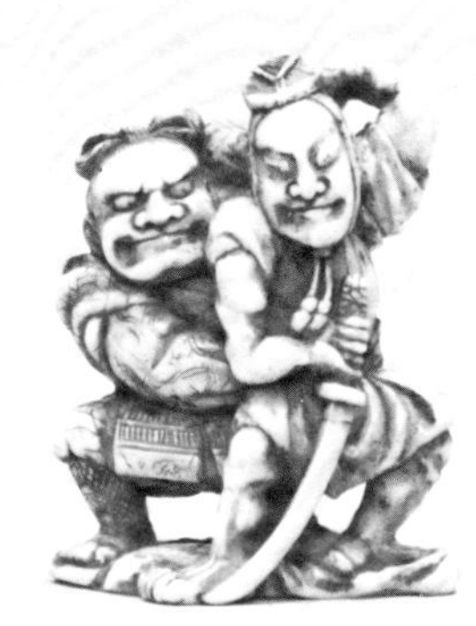

Benkei's swordsmanship was not equal to that of Yoshitsune, who, as a child, had received lessons in fencing and martial arts from the King of Tengu. Here, Benkei grabs Yoshitsune from behind, demanding his sword.

Ivory. Soun. 1913-1940. Katabori. 4.2 cm. E27132

Choryo and the Sandal A famous tale about Choryo, the celebrated Chinese general, explains how he received his great wisdom. One day an old man stopped Choryo on a bridge and demanded that he retrieve a sandal which the old man had just dropped. Choryo, out of respect for the old man's age, did so and had to threaten a dragon to recover the shoe. As a reward, the old man said he would teach Choryo, calling for a meeting several days later. Choryo complied, but had to prove his perseverance by returning to the meeting place several times, although each time he received nothing. Finally, the old man gave Choryo a scroll which, through careful study, enabled Choryo to become a great statesman and the wisest man in China.

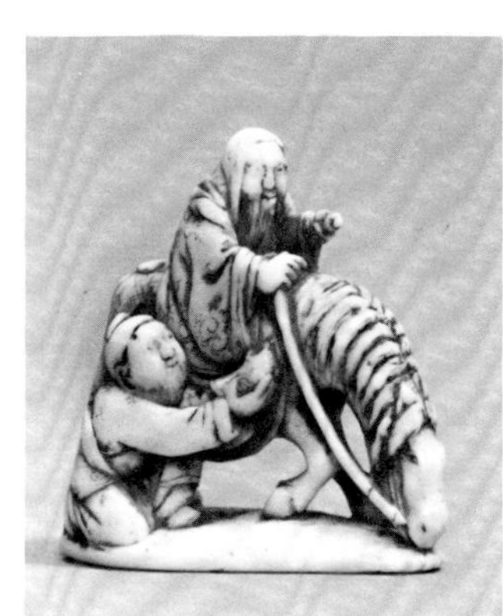

Choryo, kneeling at the old man's feet, returns the sandal. The old man sits on his horse holding a scroll, while the horse eats the grass at his feet.

Ivory. Yuraku. early 19th c. Katabori. 4.0 cm. E27157

Fukusuke Fukusuke, a large-headed dwarf, gained tremendous popularity as a legendary comic, entertainer and story-teller.

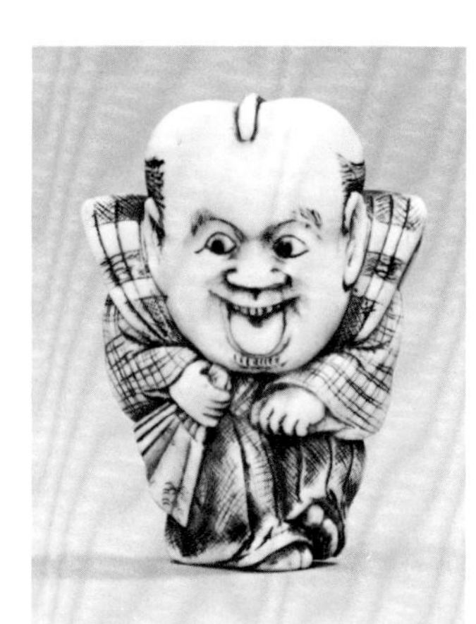

The large-headed dwarf holds a fan and sticks out his tongue.

Ivory, ebony eyes. Yoshitomo. 1800-1835. Katabori. 5.2 cm. E27047

A smiling Fukusuke carries a mask of Okame slung over his shoulder.

Resin. early 20th c. Katabori. 5.4 cm. E27058

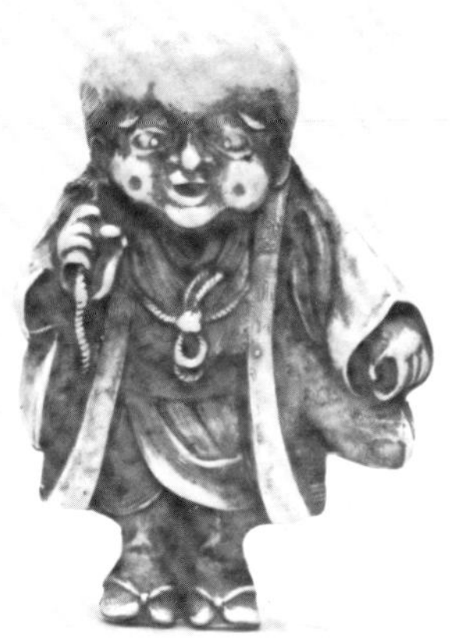

Hankwai Hankwai served as minister to the Emperor Ryuho. Hearing of a plot against the emperor's life, Hankwai, by removing a door, forced his way into the hall where the conspirators feasted. Then, joining in the feast, Hankwai managed to give the emperor a chance to escape.

Hankwai, forcing his way into the hall, holds the door under his arm.

Boxwood, pearl and ivory inlays. Shuzan (Ranrinsai). early 19th c. Katabori. 5.0 cm. E26972

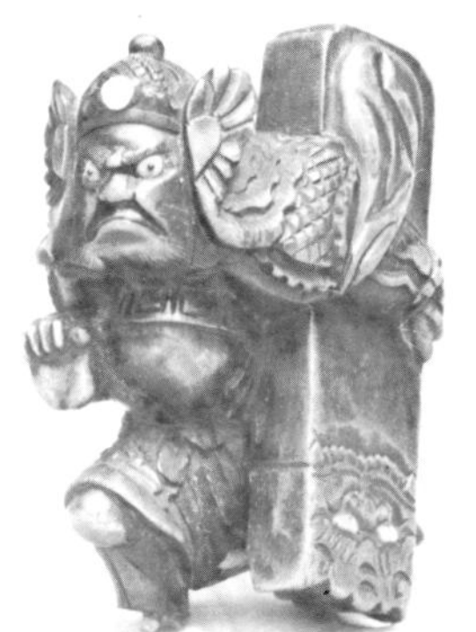

Jo and Uba This old couple symbolizes long life, happiness, and conjugal fidelity. They personify two ancient pine trees (symbols of longevity), which grew on the spot where Jo and Uba spent their lives sweeping pine needles with a broom and rake. Many stories evolved about these two, and they became common subjects in the theatre.

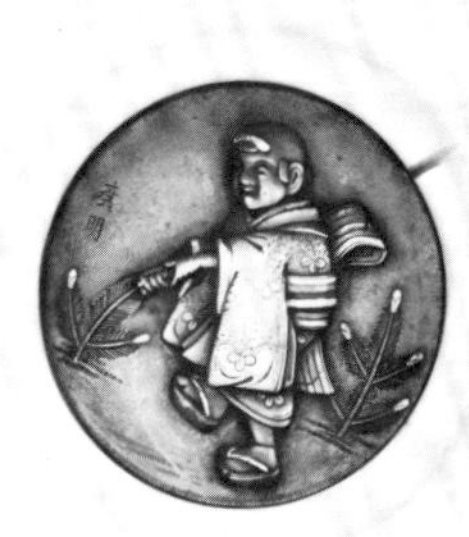

On the lid, Uba gaily pulls at a small evergreen bush. The bowl lacks decoration.

Ivory bowl, bronze lid. Hiroaki. 19th c. Kagamibuta. 4.6 cm. E5826

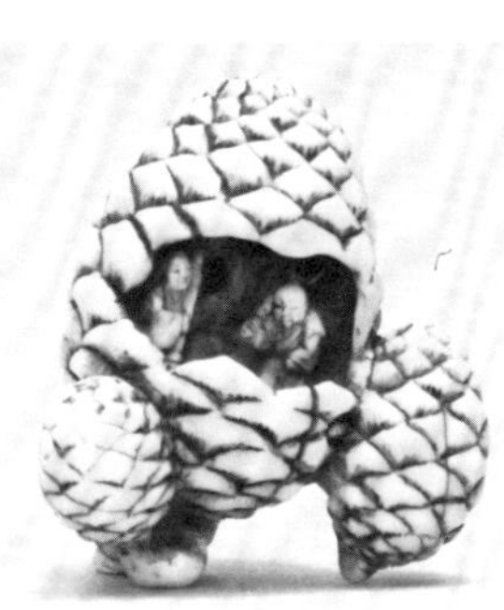

Two small pine cones rest on either side of a larger pine cone. A section of the larger pine cone has been cut away to reveal Jo and Uba standing inside with a broom and rake. Jo and Uba were carved separately from a different type of ivory and fastened inside the piece.

Ivory. Kaigyokusai. 1863-1892. Katabori. 4.0 cm. E26816

Kanshin Kanshin was a great Chinese general of the Han dynasty. In his youth, a young ruffian challenged him to a street fight; rather than engage in such a crude act as a street brawl, Kanshin submitted, and crawled between the legs of his challenger.

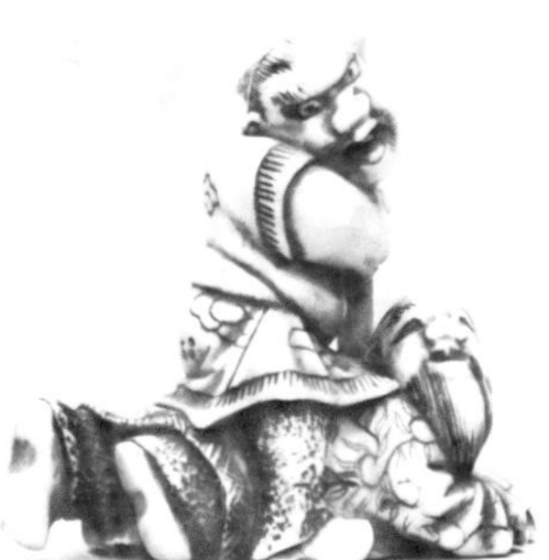

Kanshin crawls between the legs of his challenger.

Ivory. late 18th-19th c. Katabori. 4.4 cm. E27158

Kidomaro A legendary bandit, Kidomaro planned to attack his brother while the latter played the flute, but became so entranced with the beautiful melody, he was unable to complete the dastardly assault.

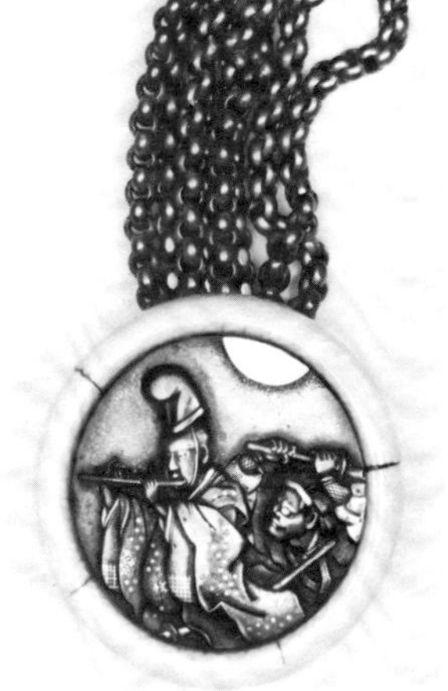

The metal cover shows Kidomaro preparing to attack his flute-playing brother.

Ivory. early 19th c. Kagamibuta. 4.8 cm. E24908

Kintaro A legendary boy who became lost in the mountains as a child, Kintaro grew very strong wrestling and fighting with the forest animals. His companions are invariably animals, and he carries an ax for a weapon.

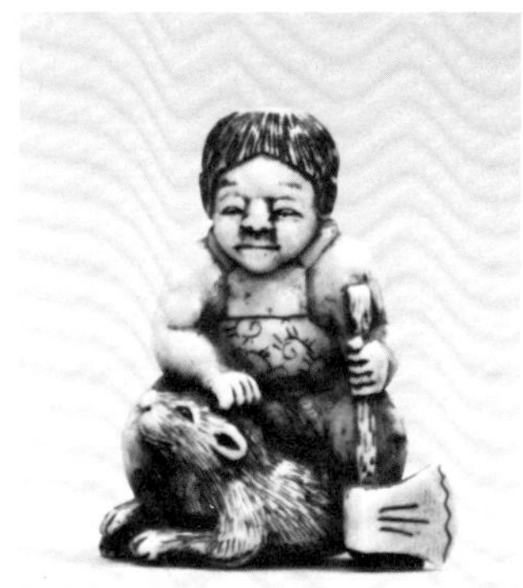

Holding his ax in his left hand, Kintaro straddles an animal.

Ivory. Norishige. 1772-1788 or 1830-1843. Katabori. 4.0 cm. E27144

Kwanyu A Chinese general of the Han Dynasty, Kwanyu can be identified by his black beard and Chinese halberd. Kwanyu is one of the Three Warrior Heroes of Han China and is known for his loyalty. H. L. Joly (see Bibliography) notes that Kwanyu was canonized as an immortal in 1128, deified as a God of War in 1594, and made a chief object of national worship in 1878. He is often depicted with a retainer.

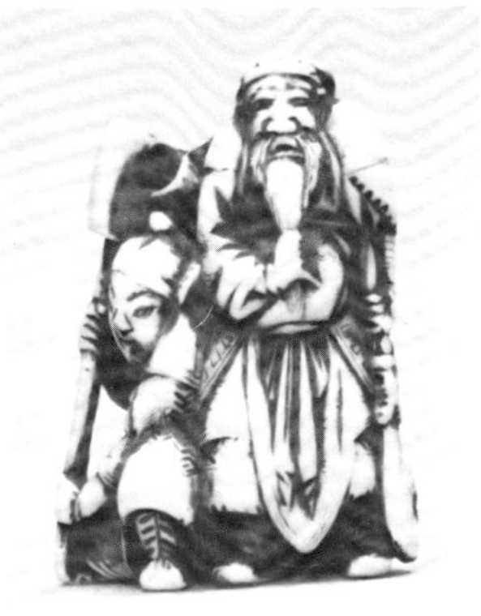

Kwanyu, grasping his beard and halberd, stands next to his kneeling retainer.

Ivory. Horyusai, unrecorded artist. early 19th c. Katabori. 4.4 cm. E27108

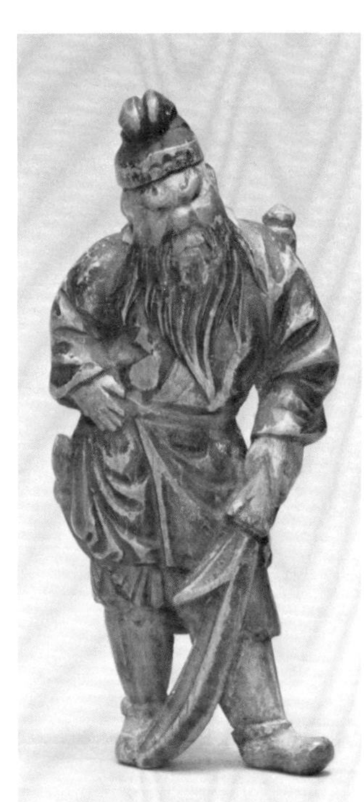

The black-bearded Kwanyu, attired in blue robe, green skirt, red boots and black hat, holds his halberd.

Painted cypress wood. late 18th-19th c. Katabori. 7.8 cm. E27025

Moso One of the twenty-four paragons of filial piety, Moso showed total devotion to his mother. She became deathly ill and would eat nothing available, but craved some soup made from bamboo shoots. Moso went to the bamboo grove, but being midwinter, the earth was frozen solid. Despairing, he began weeping profusely and to his surprise, his warm tears thawed the ground and caused tiny bamboo shoots to sprout. He took them home, and cured his mother with bamboo sprout soup.

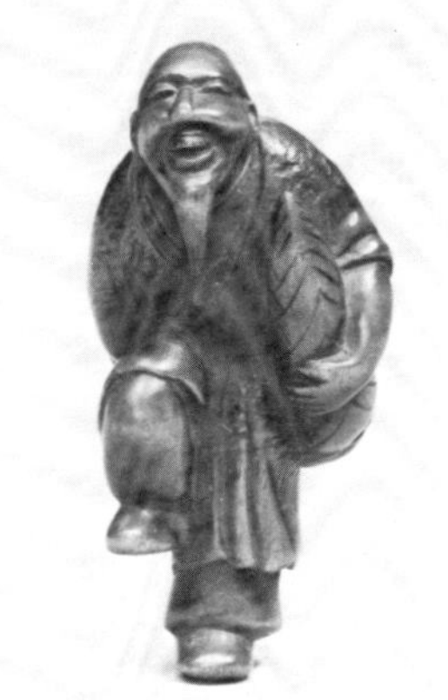

Moso runs back home with a bamboo shoot under one arm, his shovel in the other.

Boxwood. 19th c. Katabori. 4.8 cm. E26988

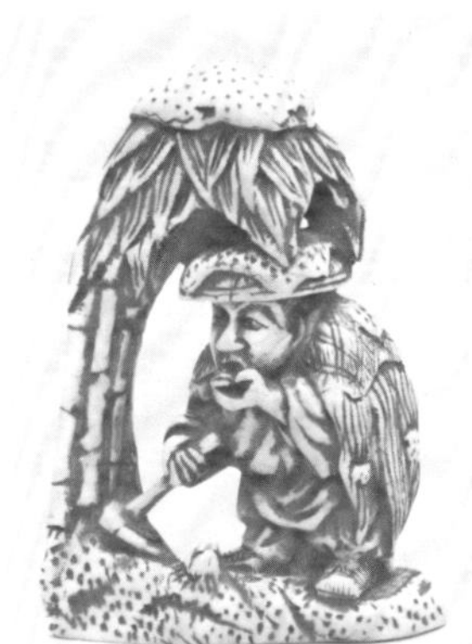

Moso stands in a bamboo grove. With one hand he digs with his spade and a tiny bamboo shoot grows at his feet. With the other hand he holds a piece of bamboo shoot to his mouth.

Ivory. 19th c. Katabori. 5.8 cm. E26995

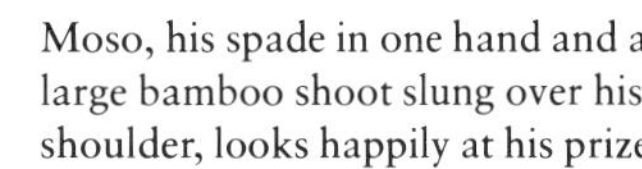

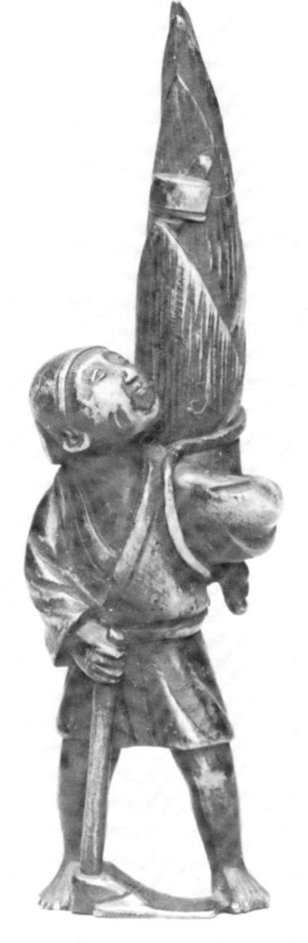

Moso, his spade in one hand and a large bamboo shoot slung over his shoulder, looks happily at his prize.

Wood. Toshihito, unrecorded artist. 19th c. Katabori. 10.1 cm. E29140

Narihira A poet of the 9th c., Narihira became one of the Rokkasen, the Six Famous Poets. A man of legendary handsomeness, as well as poetic ability, he was exiled from the Court over an affair with the Empress. During his ensuing travels he composed a renowned poem describing the snow on Mt. Fuji.

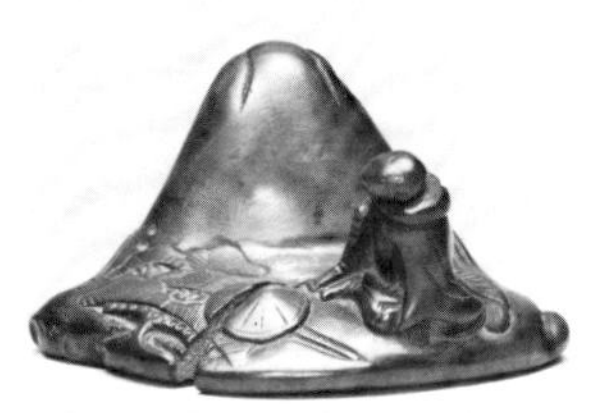

Narihira rests in front of Mt. Fuji. Trees are engraved on the ground between Narihira and the mountain and their roots can be seen on the bottom of the netsuke.

Wood. 19th c. Katabori. 5.5 cm. E27001

Ono-no-Komachi A legendary beauty and poetess of the 9th c., Ono-no-Komachi was one of the Rokkasen, the Six Famous Poets. Deprived of her true love by court intrigue, she went into seclusion, refused all suitors and devoted her life to writing poetry. Her story is used to exemplify the dangers of vanity and pride, for after rejecting all her suitors as unworthy of her, she aged into an ugly hag, unwed and unwanted.

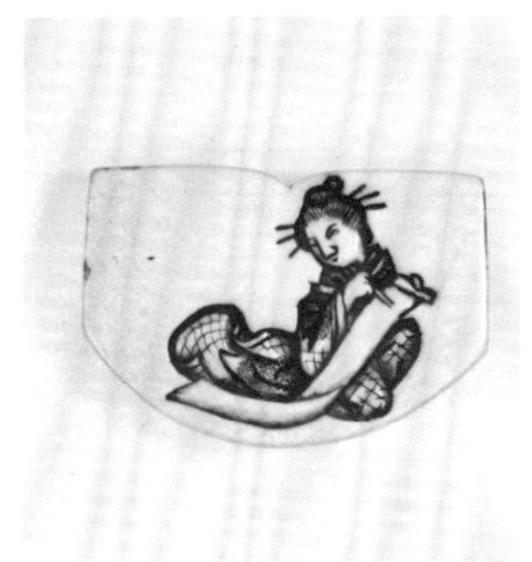

On one side the poetess Ono-no-Komachi kneels and writes on a scroll. A writing brush is engraved on the other side.

Ivory. 19th-20th c. Manju. 4.0 cm. E26561

Ranryo Ranryo was a legendary Chinese prince who could count on victory if he wore this grotesque mask in battle.

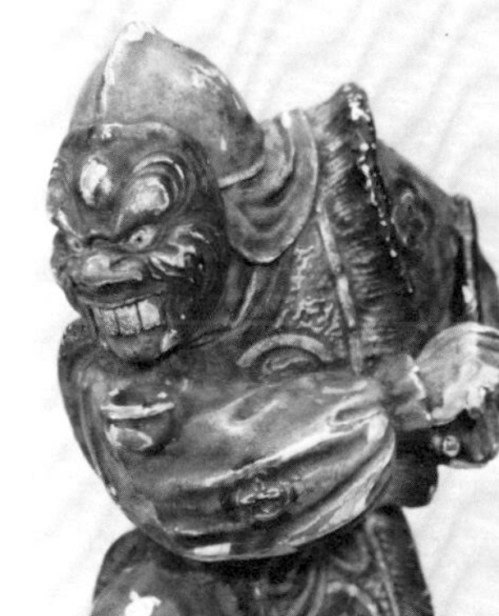

Because Ranryo became the hero of a Noh play, this netsuke could be a depiction either of Ranryo himself or of an actor playing that role.

Painted cypress wood. after 1750. Katabori. 8.3 cm. E26947

Shoki The demon queller Shoki is a mythical Chinese hero who became a favorite of the Japanese. As a student, Shoki failed his examinations, so committed suicide. His spirit appeared in a dream of the Emperor, who belatedly honored him with a splendid funeral. Shoki's spirit was so grateful he promised to protect the Emperor and his people from demons for evermore. The most prevalent demons in Japan are oni, and netsuke artists invariably portray Shoki as an old, bearded man futilely pursuing oni who have outwitted him.

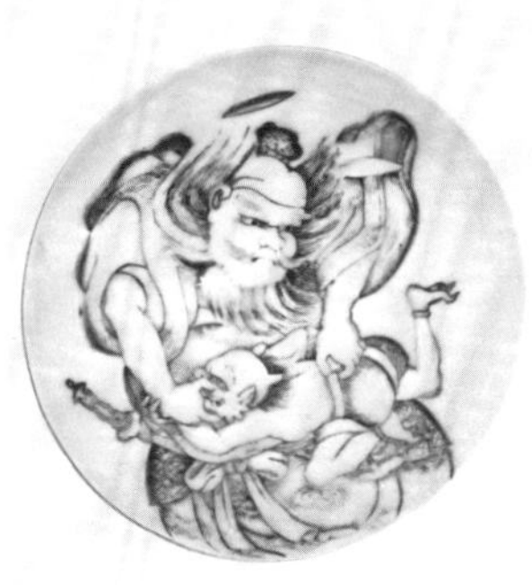

On one half, a triumphant Shoki holds a captured oni over his knee. On the other half, a flute and sack represent Shoki's first good deed; he recovered these items which had been stolen by an oni and returned them to the Emperor Genso.

Ivory. Kosai Suzuki. late 19th-20th c. Manju. 4.5 cm. E23113

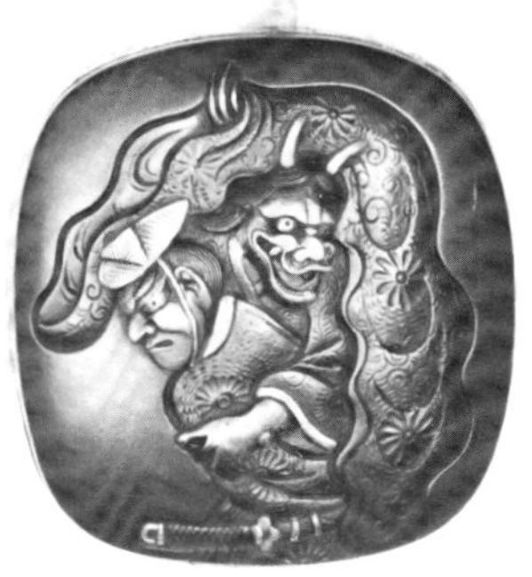

On the front a gold-horned oni is depicted climbing onto Shoki's back in an attempt to put Shoki into a large sack which the oni carries. On the reverse there is a river.

Metal alloys, gold. Haruaki. 1785-1859. Manju. 3.2 cm. E23995

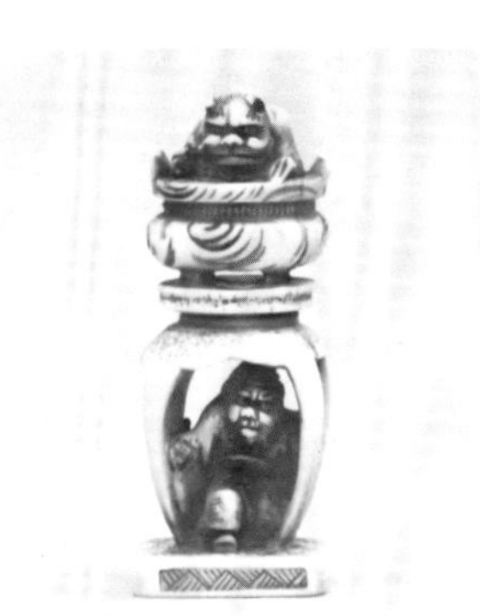

A comical Shoki pursues an oni. Shoki hides in waiting under an altar while the mischievous oni hides on top of the same altar.

Ivory. 19th-20th c. Katabori. 4.0 cm. E26875

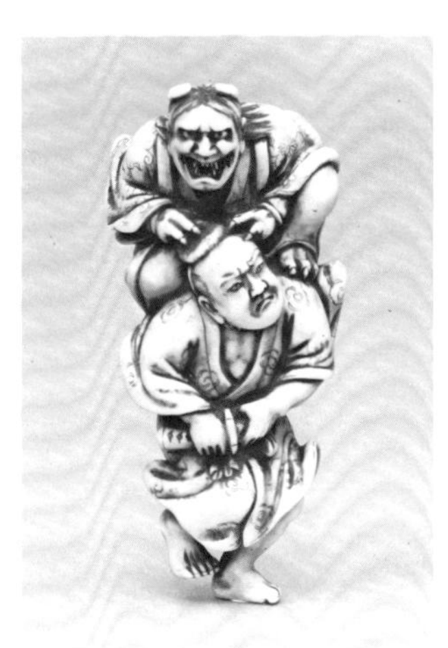

An angry Shoki draws his sword while an oni sits on his shoulders, digging his claws into Shoki's head.

Ivory. Ikkosai. 1804-1876. Katabori. 7.5 cm. E27044

Shoki, standing on one foot, reaches up and grabs the arm of an oni who hides on Shoki's helmet.

Boxwood, with horns of ivory on oni. late 18th c. Katabori. 7.6 cm. E29142

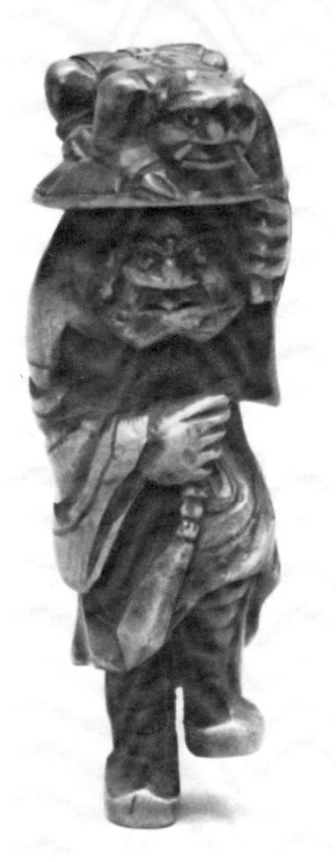

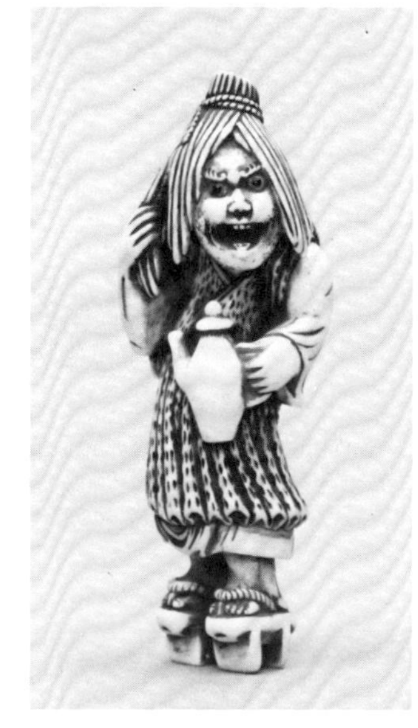

Tadamori and the Oil Thief Taira no Tadamori bravely ventured forth in search of a fire-breathing monster which reportedly lurked on the grounds of a temple. Spying something moving in the dark, he attacked the creature, which turned out to be a temple servant in the act of stealing oil.

The fierce looking servant holds the pitcher of oil he stole.

Ivory, ebony eyes. late 18th-19th c. Katabori. 6.8 cm. E27030

A triumphant oni leans against a sack. The conquered Shoki's head peers from the top of the sack.

Boxwood with ivory lined himotoshi, ivory horns and ebony eyes. late 18th-19th c. Katabori. 4.1 cm. E29151

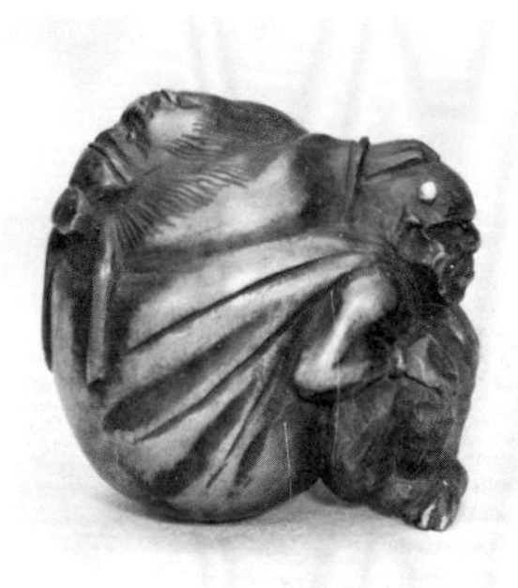

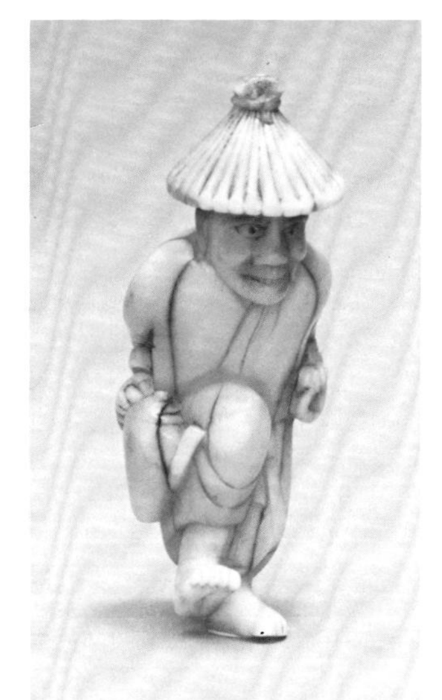

The temple servant, clutching his pitcher of oil, sneaks away from the temple.

Ivory. late 18th-19th c. Katabori. 5.8 cm. E27049

"Smart Boy" M. E. Tollner (see Bibliography) recounts a tale of "smart boy," a child who fell into a huge water jar, but "used his head" to escape.

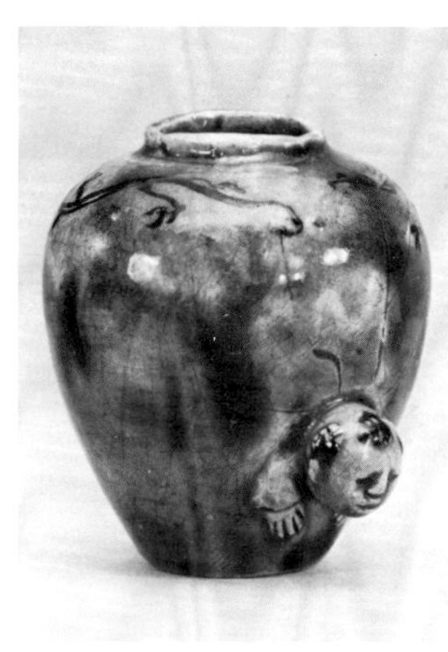

"Smart Boy" forces his way out of the jar by "using his head."

Ceramic, brown, blue glaze. Kenya. 1850. Katabori. 3.8 cm. E60821

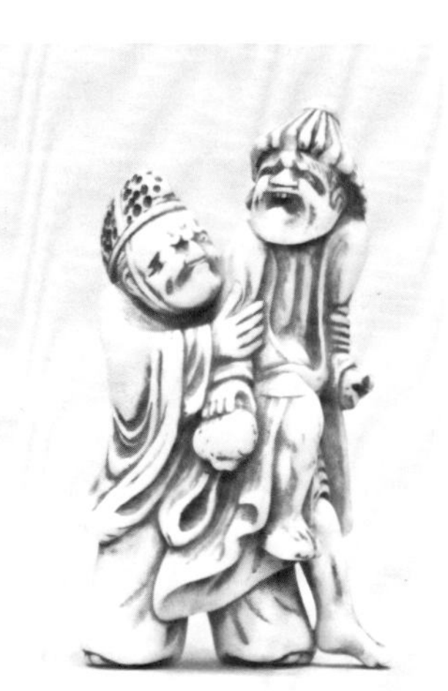

Tadamori grabs the oil thief, lifting him off the ground.

Ivory. late 18th-19th c. Katabori. 5.2 cm. E27067

Yamato and the Serpent Yamato Take, a legendary prince, involved himself in countless adventures. Once he fought a serpent that plagued the province of Omi. Yamato successfully killed the serpent, but not before the snake stung and nearly killed him.

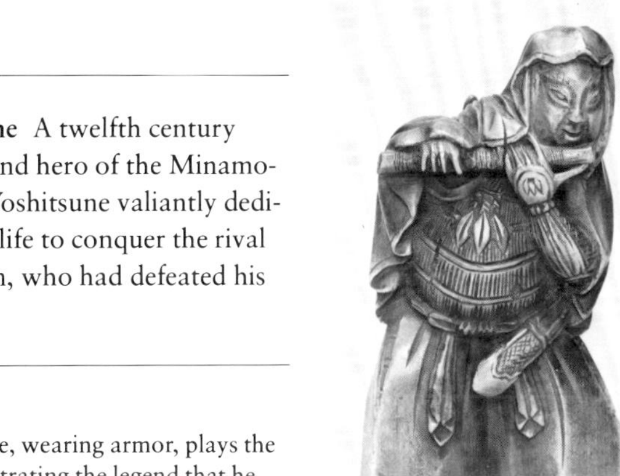

Yamato confronts the serpent. The aperture for the cord is through the snake's coiled body.

Ivory, ebony eyes. 19th c. Katabori. 5.6 cm. E26752

Yoshitsune A twelfth century warrior and hero of the Minamoto clan, Yoshitsune valiantly dedicated his life to conquer the rival Taira clan, who had defeated his father.

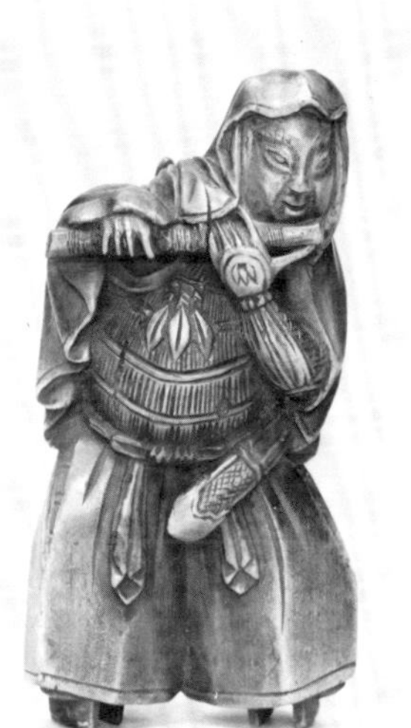

Yoshitsune, wearing armor, plays the flute, illustrating the legend that he once seduced a young girl by answering her music with music from his flute.

Wood. late 18th c. Katabori. 9.0 cm. E26959

Fairy Tales

A favorite theme in Japanese fairy tales, and one often portrayed by netsuke-shi, was the unpredictable and eccentric behavior of familiar animals.

The Crackling Mountain A farmer caught a wily badger stealing his pet hare's food and tied him to a tree while he went hunting. As soon as he was gone, the evil badger tricked the farmer's wife into freeing him; then he killed her, made soup out of her, and assumed her form. Welcoming the unsuspecting farmer on his return, the badger served the soup to the farmer for supper, told him that he had eaten his wife, and ran away to a nearby mountain. The farmer's loyal pet hare set out after the badger, determined to avenge his master, and soon found him on the mountain. Observing that he had a load of sticks tied to his back, the hare surreptitiously set them on fire. When the badger asked what the strange noises on his back were, the hare replied that it was just the mountain they were on, the "Crackle-Crackle Mountain," and he managed to burn the badger badly. Then for good measure, he poured pepper on the burns to cause even more pain. Finally, the hare persuaded the badger to sail with him to the moon, but he let the foolish badger make his boat out of clay, which dissolved in the water, causing the badger to drown.

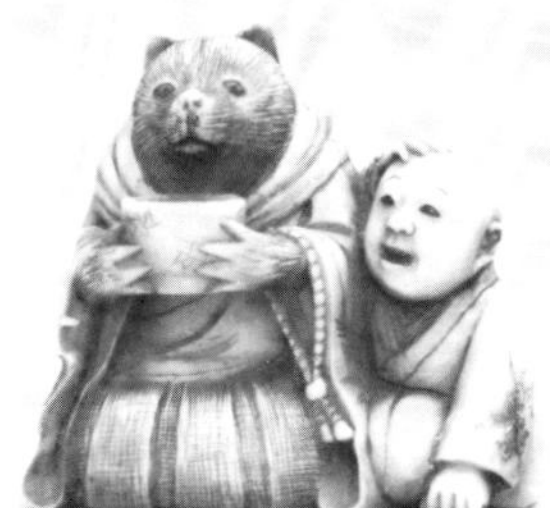

The badger, in the guise of the farmer's wife, offers the farmer the broth made from his dead wife.

Ivory. 19th-20th c. Katabori. 3.5 cm. E24906

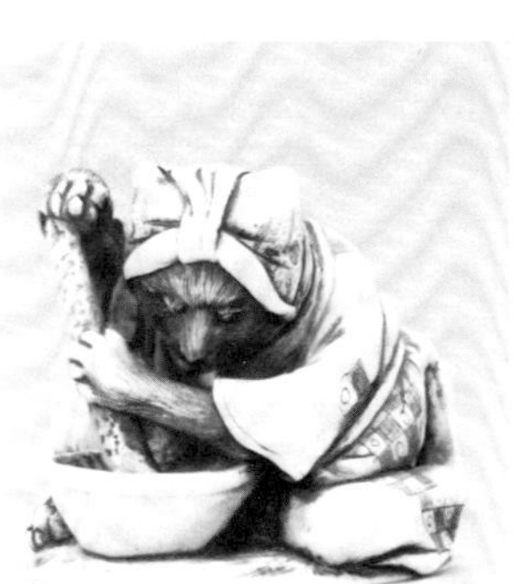

The badger, dressed as the farmer's wife, makes a broth from the wife's body. A temple whisk and beads are engraved on the bottom of this piece.

Ivory. Gyokusai. 1800-1868. Katabori. 3.5 cm. E26740

Hana-Saka-Jiji, the Man Who Made Dead Trees Grow One day Hana-Saka-Jiji's dog sniffed a spot on the ground which revealed a buried treasure of coins to his master. Envious neighbors, hoping for similar treasure, stole the dog, but when the spot he disclosed to them only yielded garbage, they killed him. That night, the dog's spirit instructed Hana-Saka-Jiji to make a mortar from the tree where the dog lay buried. The old man discovered that the rice he ground in the magic mortar turned to gold, whereupon the greedy neighbors stole the mortar. It turned their rice into horse dung however, so they burned it. The dog's spirit returned to tell his owner to sprinkle the mortar's ashes on dead trees and they would sprout. Hana-Saka-Jiji became famous for his miraculous power to make dead trees grow and blossom. His greedy neighbors, trying to work the same magic with stolen ashes, were severely punished by the angry people whose trees they damaged.

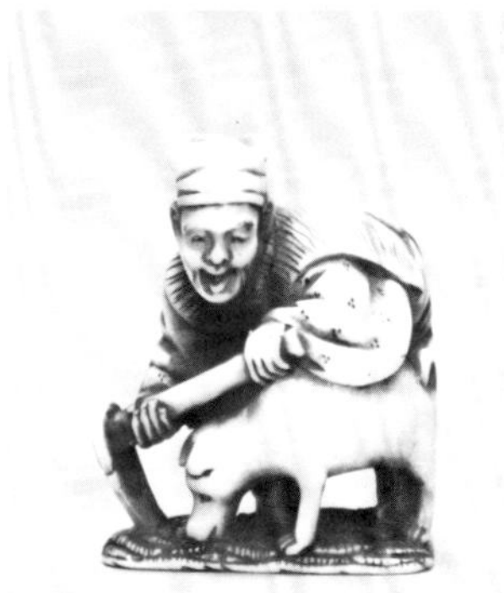

Hana-Saka-Jiji's dog indicates where his master should dig for treasure. Coins are carved on the bottom of the netsuke. This piece is similar to E25279, and bears the same signature, but the two pieces were not carved by the same artist. The carving schools of the late 18th and 19th centuries developed characteristics of technique and design and many pupils openly copied their master's work. A master might sign his name to a pupil's work, or the pupil might sign his own work with his master's name out of respect.

Ivory. Tomochika I. 1800-1873. Katabori. 3.6 cm. E27115

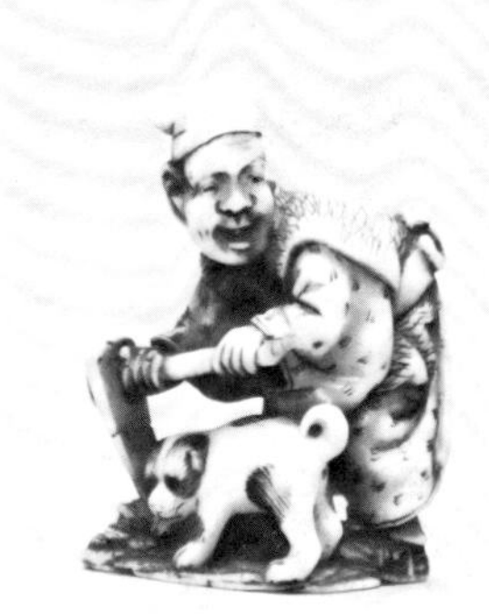

Hana-Saka-Jiji digs the spot his dog points out. On the underside of the piece, one can see the coins that the man will soon dig up.

Ivory, inlaid eyes. Tomochika I. 1800-1873. Katabori. 3.8 cm. E25279

The Magic Kettle A priest's teakettle unexpectedly turned into a badger then back into a teakettle, so he quickly sold it to an unsuspecting tinker. The tinker soon discovered the magic antics of his kettle and traveled throughout Japan entertaining crowds with his remarkable performing badger. He amassed such a fortune that he returned the kettle to the temple along with a sizable donation. As for the kettle, it remained in the temple and was worshipped as a precious treasure.

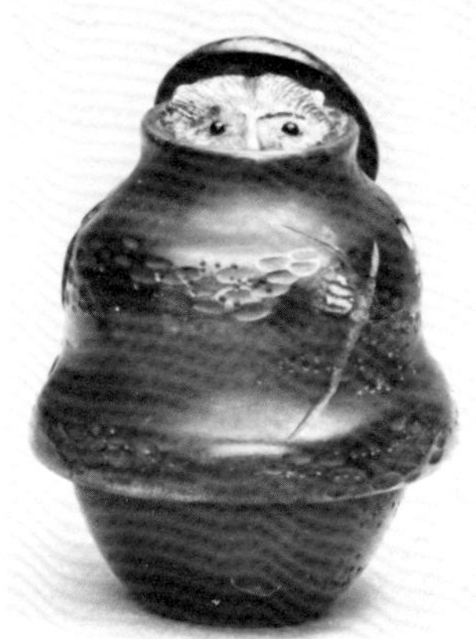

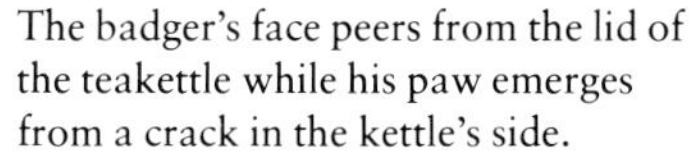

The badger's face peers from the lid of the teakettle while his paw emerges from a crack in the kettle's side.

Wood kettle, ivory badger, ebony eyes. 19th c. Katabori. 4.3 cm. E26915

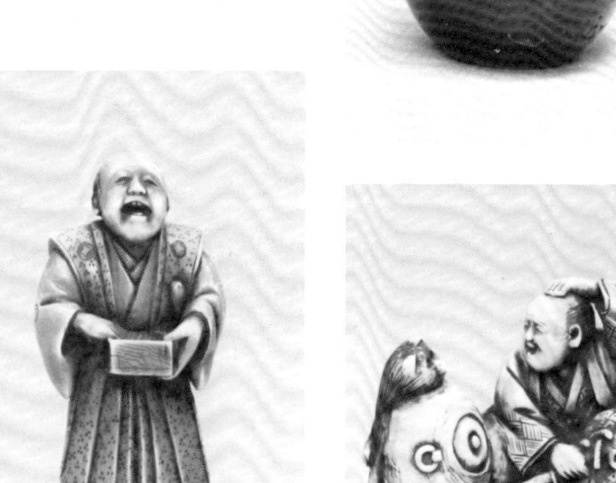

The old man throws the ashes which make withered trees grow.

Ivory. Mitsuhiro. 1810-1875. Katabori. 4.8 cm. E27057

The tinker scratches his head in wonder as he watches his new teapot turn into a badger.

Ivory. Tomomasa. 1800-1869. Katabori. 4.5 cm. E27112

The Tongue-Cut Sparrow The pet sparrow of a kindly man hid in the woods after his wicked neighbor slit its tongue. The man searched for the sparrow and when he found him, the sparrow offered him a choice of gifts for his kindness: a heavy or a light basket. Modestly, he chose the light basket, and found it full of treasure. The evil neighbor immediately demanded a choice of baskets too, and greedily chose the heavy one, which contained not treasure, but goblins who killed her.

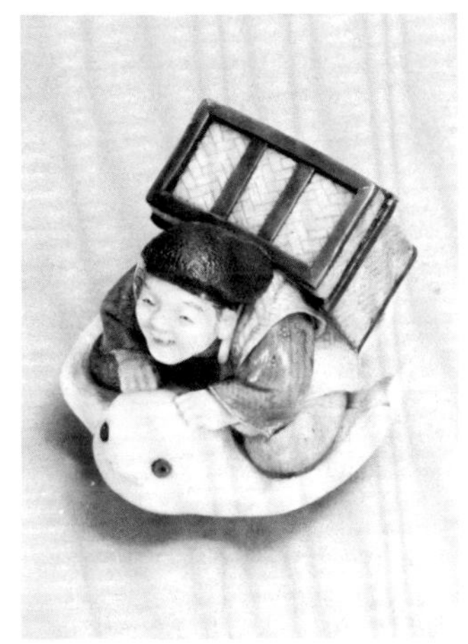

The kindly man, with the sparrow's gift basket on his back, rides on the back of his sparrow friend.

Ivory with horn, coral and pearl inlays, and green stain. Minun. 19th-20th c. Katabori. 3.8 cm. E27076

Urashima Taro One day Urashima, a simple fisherman, caught a tortoise which he threw back into the sea, for he was reluctant to cut short its long life. The tortoise gratefully offered to carry Urashima to the Palace of the Dragon King Ryujin, an underwater paradise. On their arrival, the tortoise revealed herself to be the Dragon King's beautiful daughter, and she and Urashima were married. Eventually, Urashima became very homesick for his relatives on land, and asked his wife to take him back for a visit. Changing to her tortoise form, she agreed to carry Urashima back to the shore and gave him a box which would enable him to return to her, provided he didn't open it. To his amazement, Urashima discovered that hundreds of years had gone by and that his family had perished. In his panic, Urashima opened the box, releasing a vapor that enveloped him and within seconds he aged four hundred years and died.

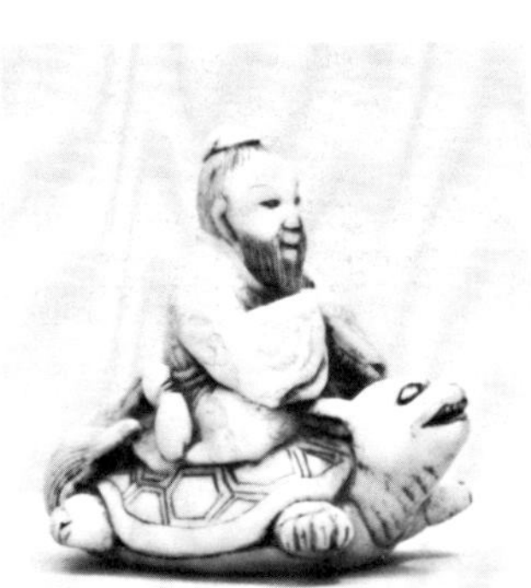

Urashima rides on the back of his tortoise wife.

Ivory. Minsei. early 19th c. Katabori. 3.6 cm. E27106

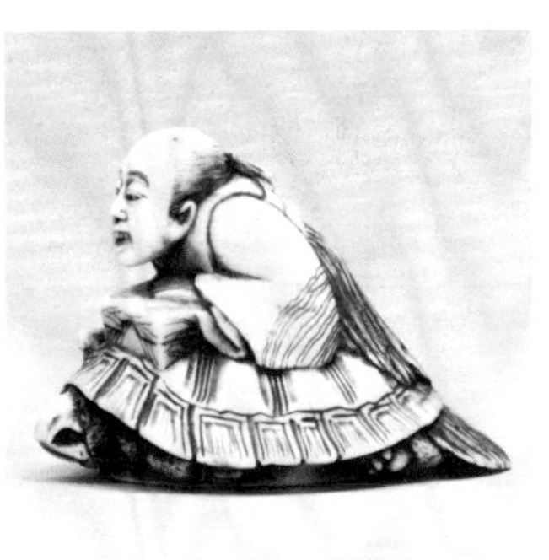

Urashima rides his tortoise wife on his return to land to visit his family, carrying the box she gave him.

Ivory, ebony eyes in turtle. 19th-20th c. Katabori. 5.0 cm. E27126

People

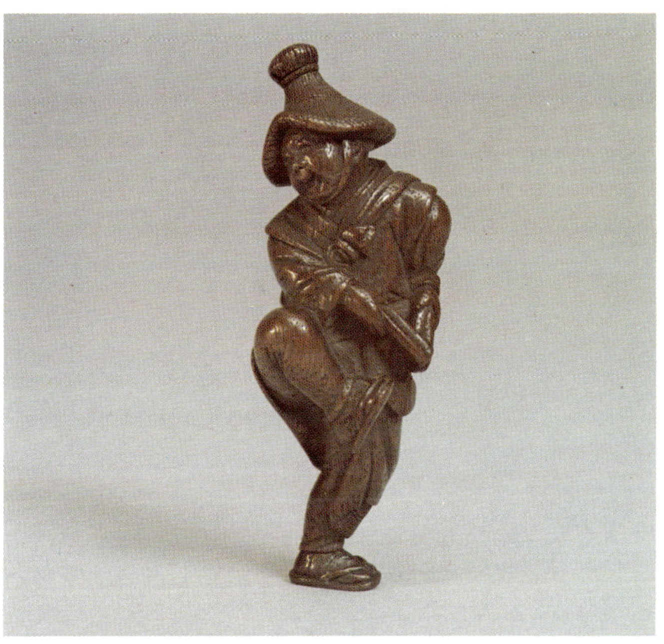

Though imagination may be the main ingredient in any netsuke design, netsuke-shi frequently sought inspiration for subjects in the real world. Every social class and nearly every occupation, as well as countless typical and extraordinary activities of the Japanese have been examined and depicted by netsuke artists. As a consequence of the carvers' keen observations and their tendency to make social commentary, a great deal can be learned about Japanese culture and history by studying their presentation of Japanese and foreigners. Netsuke not only portray the habits, dress, activities, tools, toys, traditions, etc. of the people, but the art of the netsuke-shi and the popularity of netsuke reveal much about the interests, the sense of humor, the appreciation of craftsmanship and art of the Japanese people as a whole.

Foreigners

Japan had so little contact with foreigners from the mid-17th to the mid-19th centuries that those who were seen were considered oddities.

"Southern Barbarians" (Europeans) From 1539 Japan engaged in limited trade with "Southern Barbarians" (Europeans) who were restricted to trade at Nagasaki. In 1639 Japan began its virtually total two-hundred-year isolation, and a handful of Dutch traders on an island at Nagasaki was the only contact with Europe. The interest in the strangers' clothing, large features, long curly hair and mysterious tools is apparent in netsuke. Since most carvers never saw a European, they based their work on rumor and imagination, creating, perhaps deliberately, caricatures of the foreign traders.

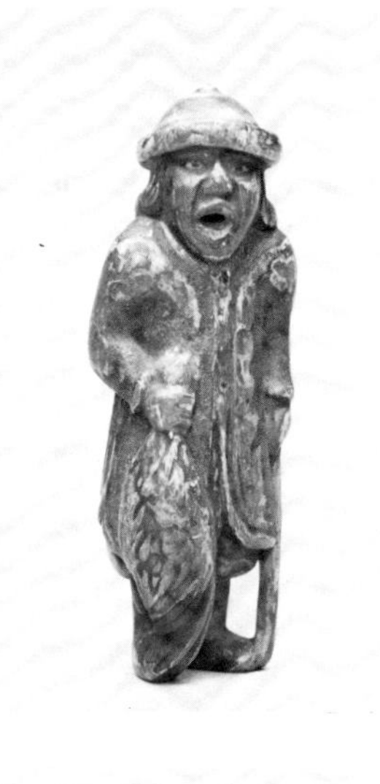

A Dutchman, wearing green coat and wide brimmed hat, stands with a rooster in one hand and a stick in the other.

Cypress wood, painted. 1750 or after. Katabori. 7.8 cm. E26937

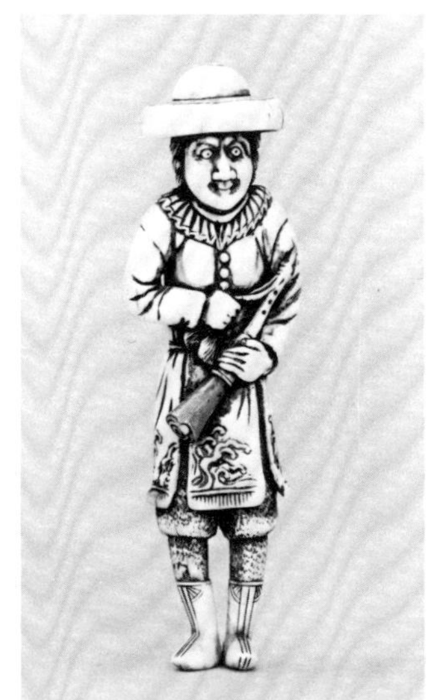

A Dutchman, with curly hair and wide brimmed hat, holds a brass horn.

Ivory, brass inlay. mid-late 18th c. Katabori. 10.3 cm. E26950

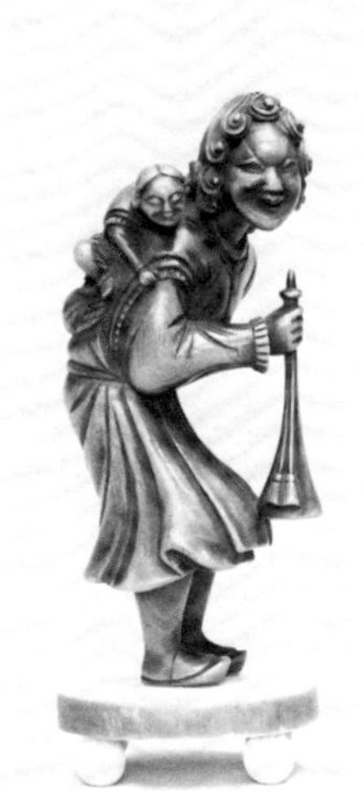

A curly-haired, foreign musician holds a horn in one hand and a child on his back. Their clothing is decorated with metal buttons. The oval ivory base is not part of the original piece and was probably added for display purposes.

Wood, metal inlays. early 19th c. Katabori. 8.0 cm. E26943

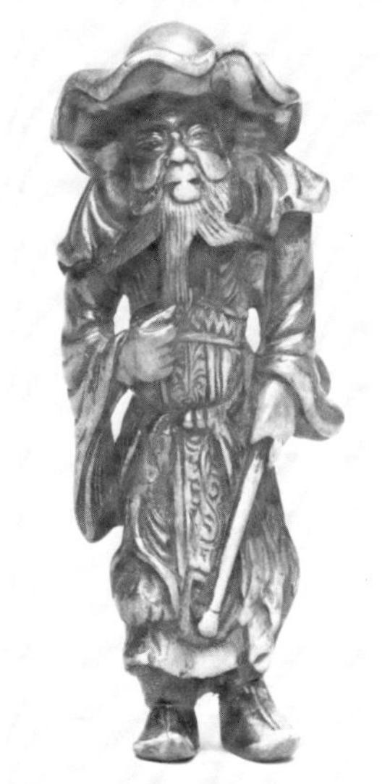

An archer

Boxwood. 18th c. Katabori. 10.0 cm. E26958

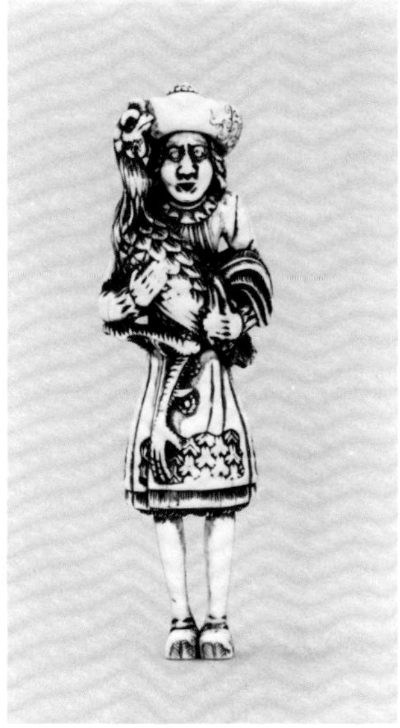

A Dutchman, with long hair and wide brimmed hat, holds a rooster.

Ivory. 18th c. Katabori. 11.0 cm. E26949

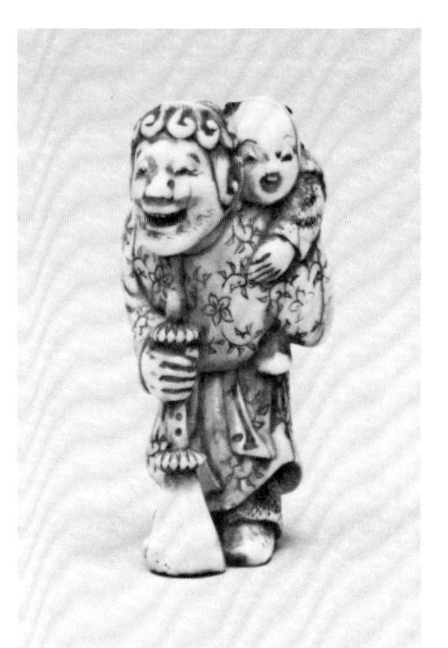

A foreign musician holds a horn in one hand while supporting a child on his back with the other.

Ivory. 19th c. Katabori. 4.6 cm. E26993

South Sea Islanders The black islanders of the South Pacific, commonly depicted in grass skirts holding a coral branch or small drum, were often made to look rather fierce.

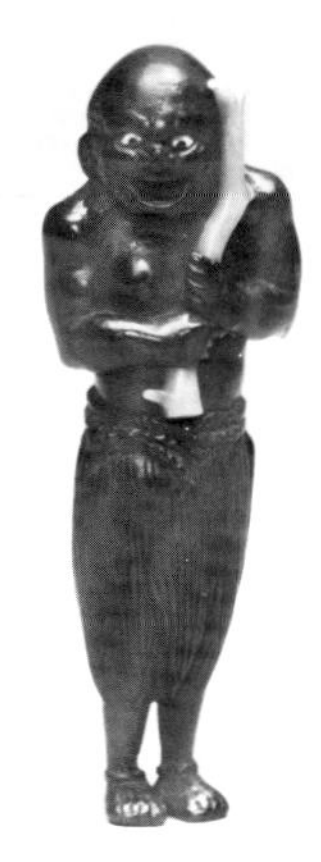

A fierce-looking south sea islander holds a coral branch.

Boxwood, coral branch, ivory eyes. 1750 or after. Katabori. 8.7 cm. E26941

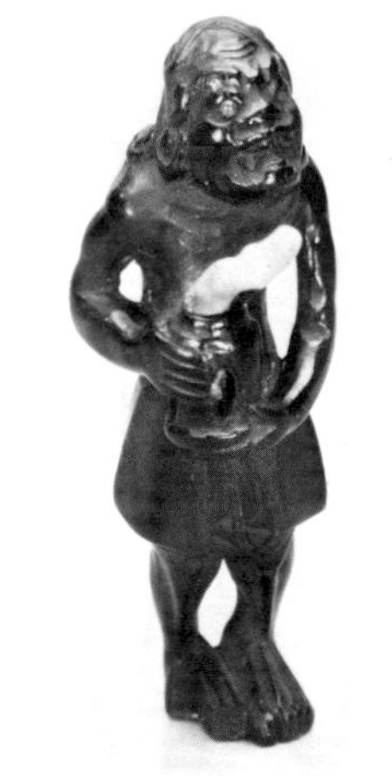

A south sea islander holds a firepot with a flame made of pink coral rising from it.

Ebony wood, pink coral inlay, glass inlaid eyes. 19th c. Katabori. 5.5 cm. E26998

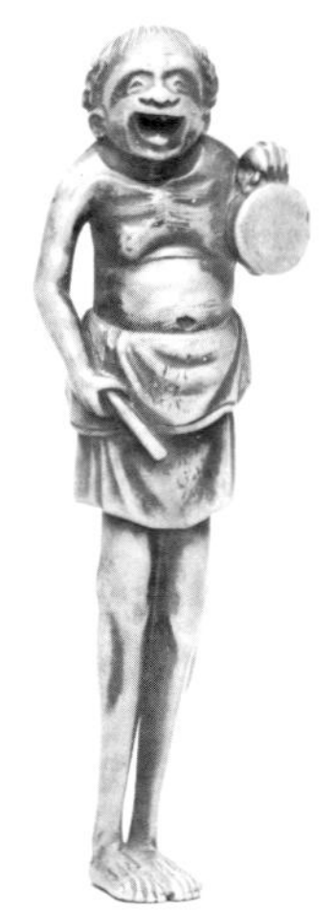

A long-legged islander holds a drum and drum stick.

Wood. 19th c. Katabori. 10.0 cm. E26957

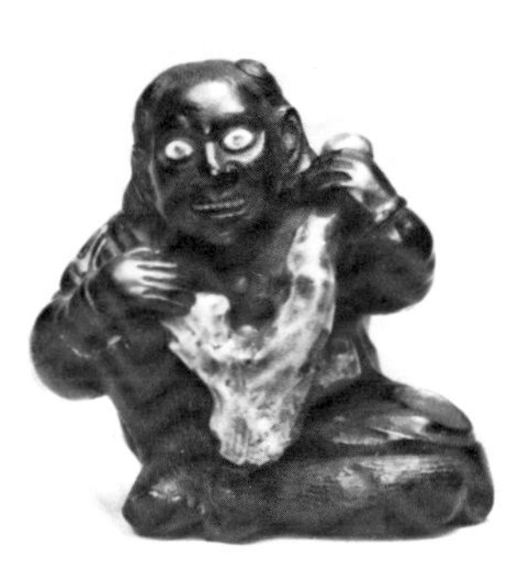

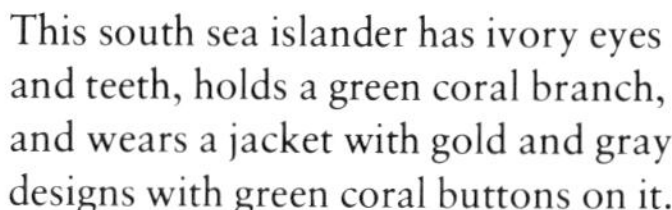

This south sea islander has ivory eyes and teeth, holds a green coral branch, and wears a jacket with gold and gray designs with green coral buttons on it.

Ebony wood, lacquered gold and gray, green coral and ivory inlays. Ryukei. probably late 18th-19th c. Katabori. 3.5 cm. E27009

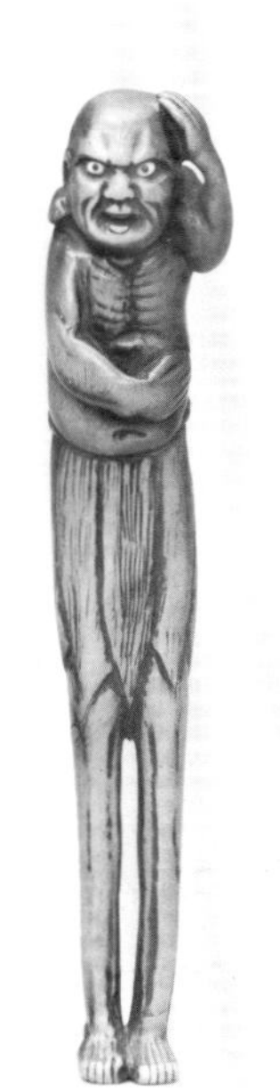

This long-legged, fierce-looking south sea islander has one hand on his stomach and the other on his head.

Wood, ivory eyes. 18th c. Sashi. 12.5 cm. E26963

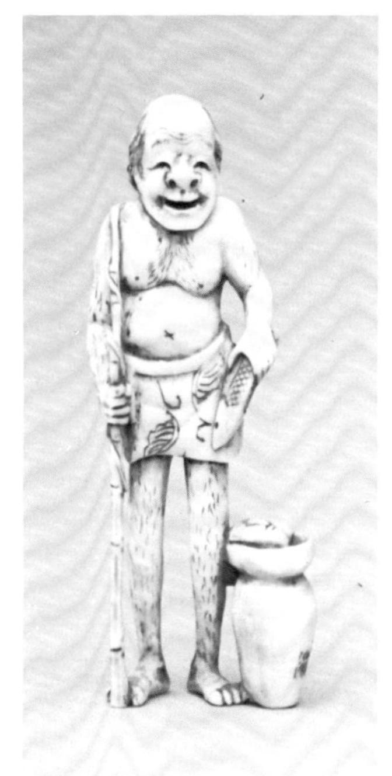

This frail carving of an islander fisherman may not have been carved for use as a netsuke; the wear on the piece suggests that it was used as one.

Ivory. 19th c. Katabori. 6.5 cm. E27045

Japanese

When Westerners began to take an interest in netsuke, particularly in the late 19th and early 20th centuries, netsuke-shi, perhaps believing that everyday life in Japan would be as strange and intriguing to Westerners as Japanese deities, demons and fairy tales, turned to the real world around them for netsuke subjects.

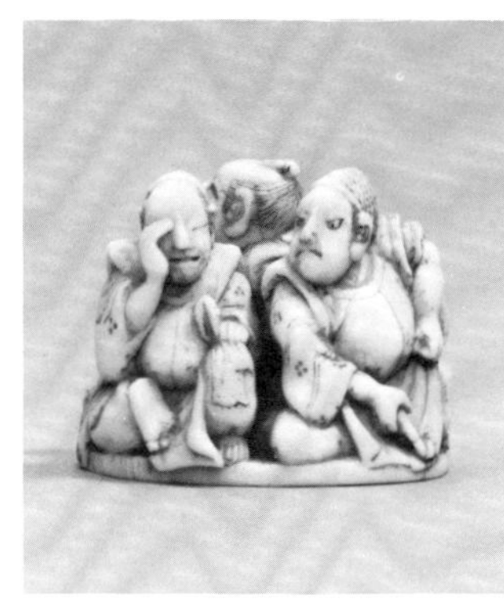

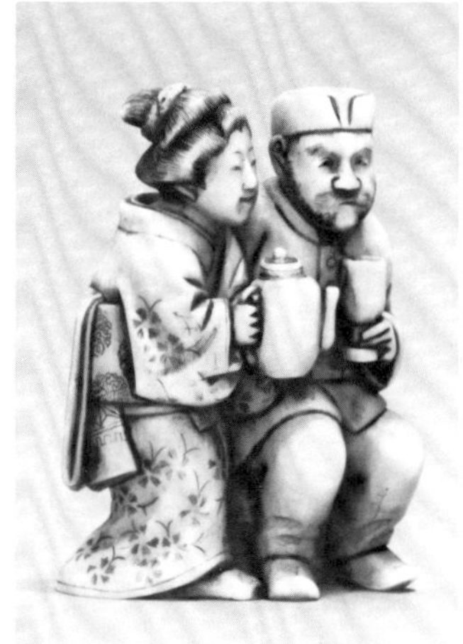

A Japanese woman, dressed in an elaborate kimono, pours tea for a gentleman in foreign attire.

Ivory. Tomochika III. late 19th c. Katabori. 5.0 cm. E27085

Diverse Activities Activities of ordinary people may help create a picture of Japan during the period in which the pieces were carved, but given the netsuke carvers' propensity for humor and whimsy, netsuke cannot be relied upon for a literal portrait of Japanese life.

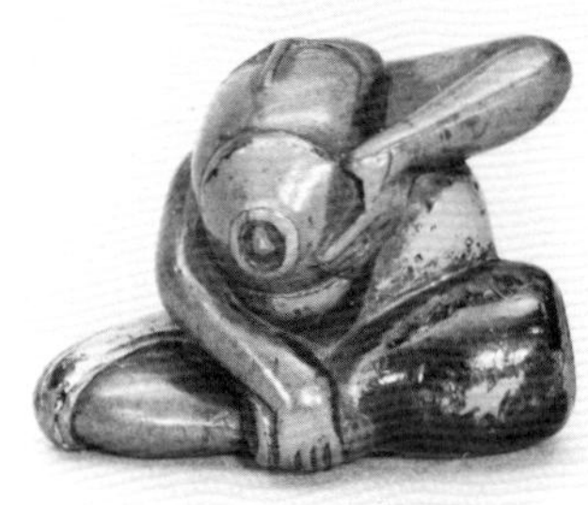

A man in red jacket and black pants holds a big black hat.

Lacquered wood. 19th-20th c. Katabori. 3.8 cm. E27072

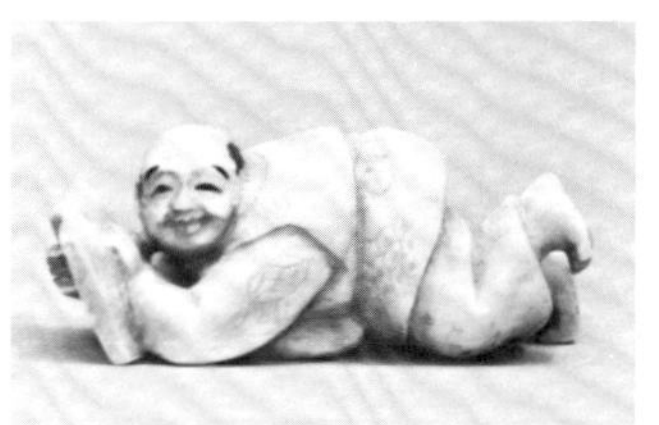

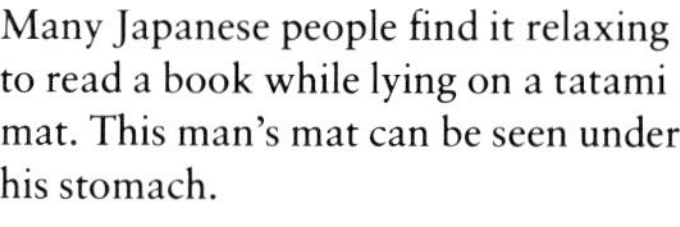

Many Japanese people find it relaxing to read a book while lying on a tatami mat. This man's mat can be seen under his stomach.

Ivory. Gyokushi. mid 20th c. Katabori. 4.5 cm. E36985

In this group of three men having tea one holds the cup and teapot (not visible in photo), one holds a cloth in one hand and rubs his right eye with the other hand, the third empties his pipe into an ashtray netsuke.

Ivory. Ryukosai. early 19th c. Katabori. 3.3 cm. E25276

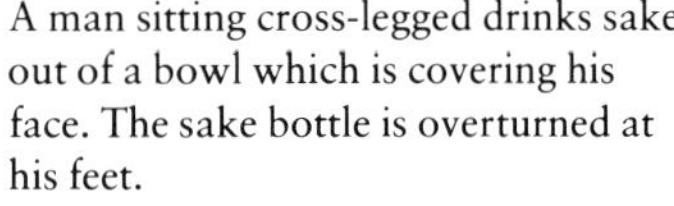

A man sitting cross-legged drinks sake out of a bowl which is covering his face. The sake bottle is overturned at his feet.

Wood and lacquer. 19th c. Katabori. 2.5 cm. E26981

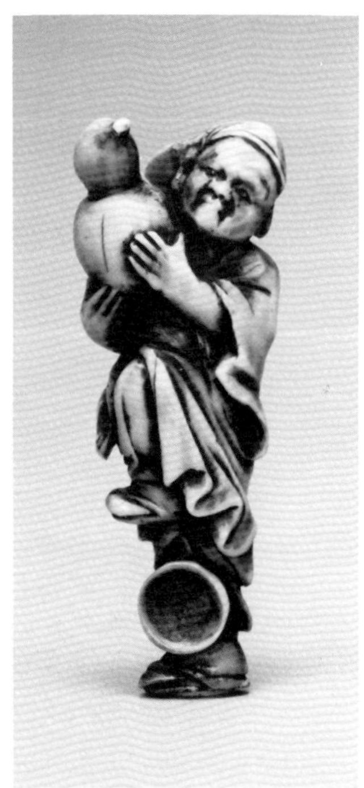

A bowl is leaning against the leg of a man who is holding up a gourd bottle.

Ivory. 19th c. Katabori. 6.5 cm. E27056

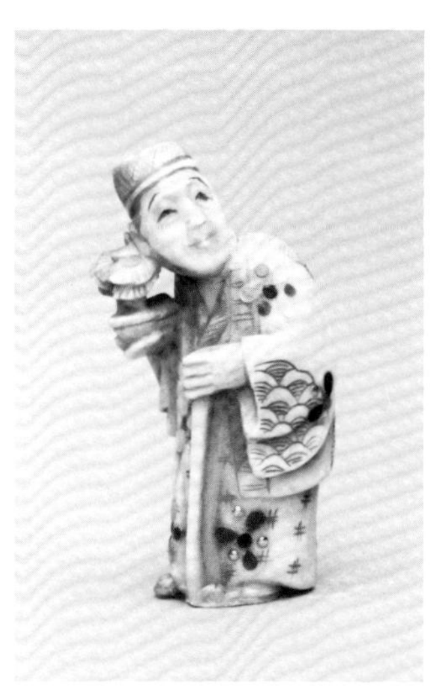

A man holds a cane and a bonsai tree.

Ivory, inlays of nacre, silver metal, green, red and black stone. mid 20th c. Katabori. 4.6 cm. E36993

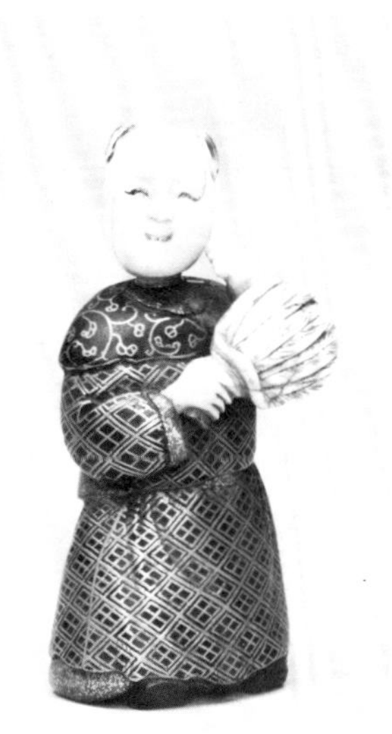

The head, hands and fan of this Chinese man are ivory; his body and robe are wood decorated with gold paint and red lacquer.

Lacquered wood and ivory. 19th-20th c. Katabori. 5.2 cm. E24902

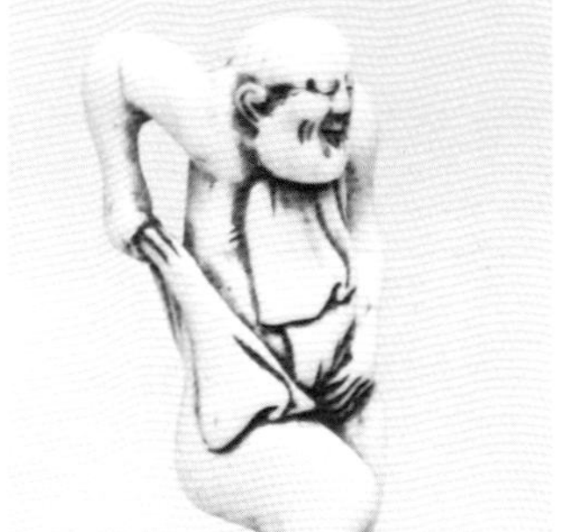

A laughing man attempts to put on his girdle.

Ivory. 19th c. Katabori. 5.0 cm. E27016

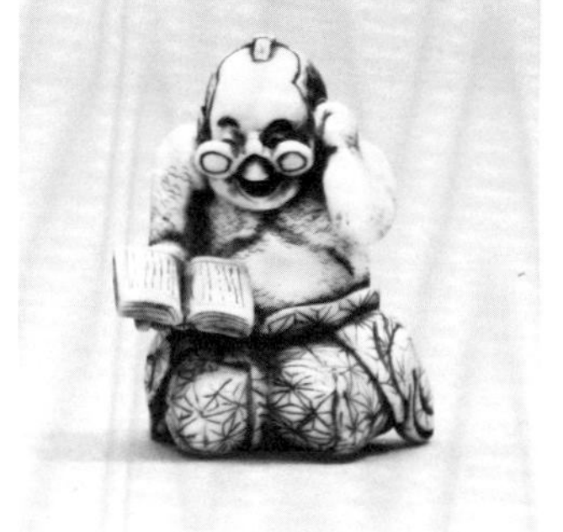

A man with glasses is reading a book. His book and right hand are a separate, removable piece.

Ivory. 19th-20th c. Katabori. 3.5 cm. E27055

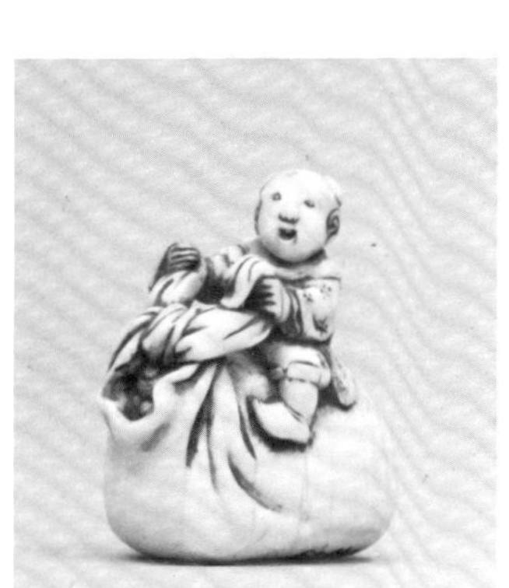

A karako plays on top of Hotei's bag.

Ivory. Gyokkosai (Gyokko). 1830-1867. Katabori. 3.3 cm. E24905

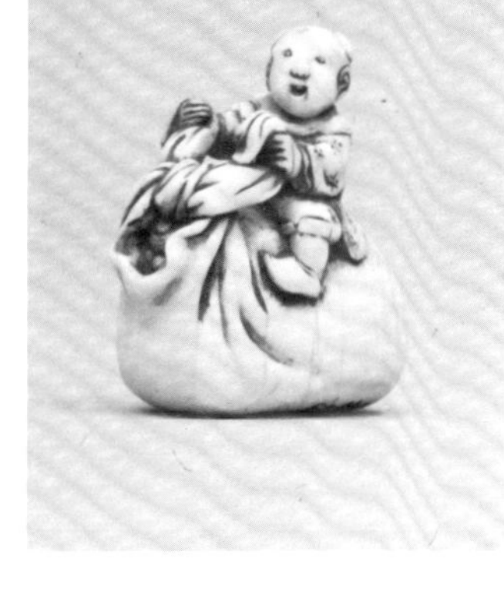

A woman with black hair and a red kimono is softening and pressing cloth by beating it with a pestle on a millstone.

Lacquered wood. 19th c. Katabori. 4.0 cm. E27062

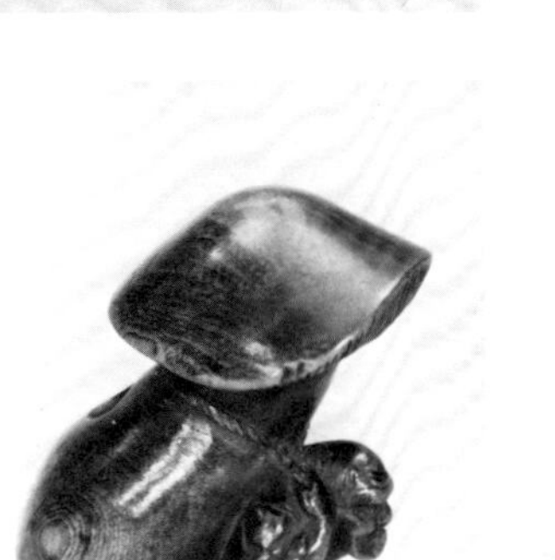

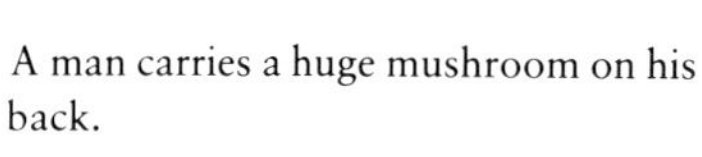

A man carries a huge mushroom on his back.

Wood. late 18th-19th c. Katabori. 5.0 cm. E26848

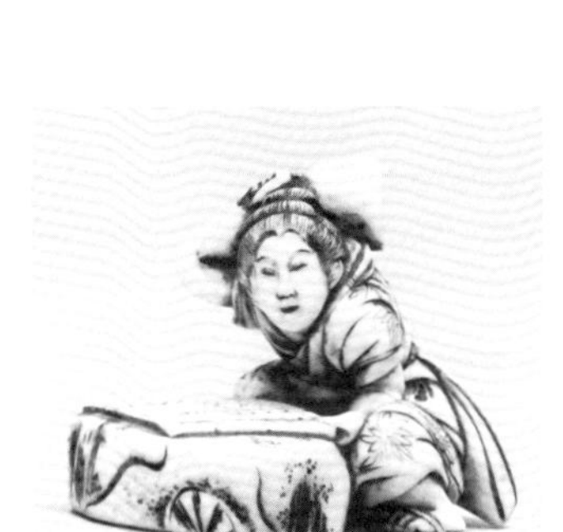

A woman holding a mallet prepares to beat cloth.

Ivory. Gyokuzan. late 19th c. Katabori. 4.5 cm. E27162

A man carries a bundle of scrolls on his back. Wooden inlays represent the poles that pass through such scrolls.

Ivory, ebony inlays. 19th-20th c. Katabori. 4.5 cm. E27070

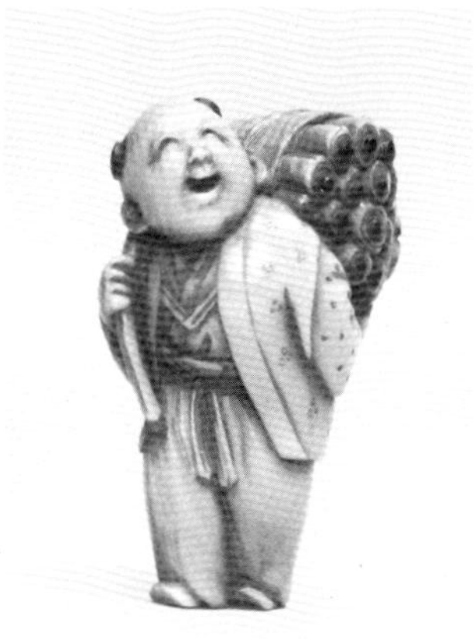

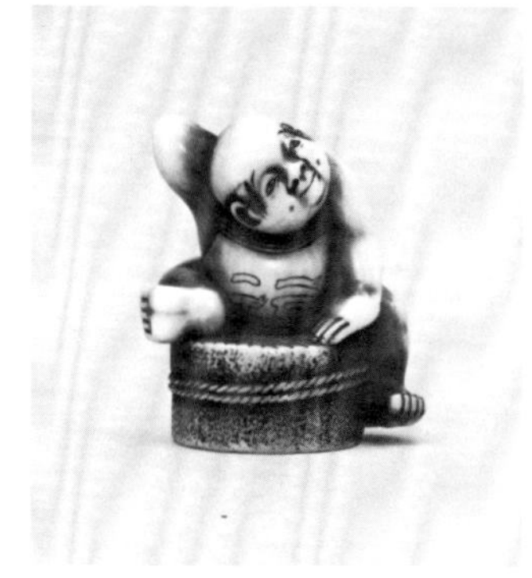

This man sitting on a millstone seems to be adjusting a chest protector.

Ivory. Hidemasa. 19th c. Katabori. 3.2 cm. E27091

In this common and amusing netsuke design, a man uses a nose tickler (the ivory stick in his right hand) to make himself sneeze.

Wood and ivory. Hokei. early 19th c. Katabori. 3.6 cm. E27077

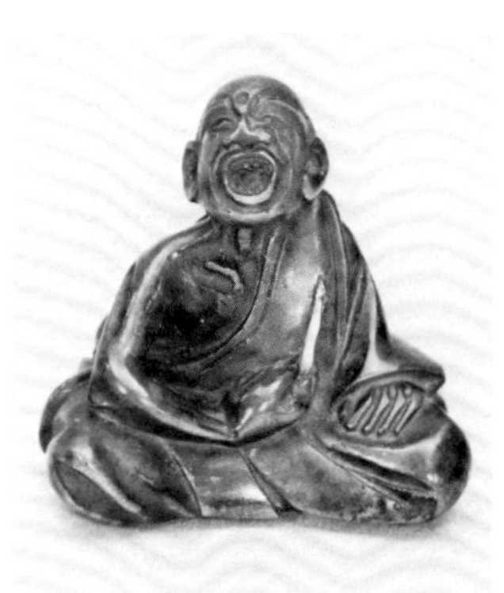

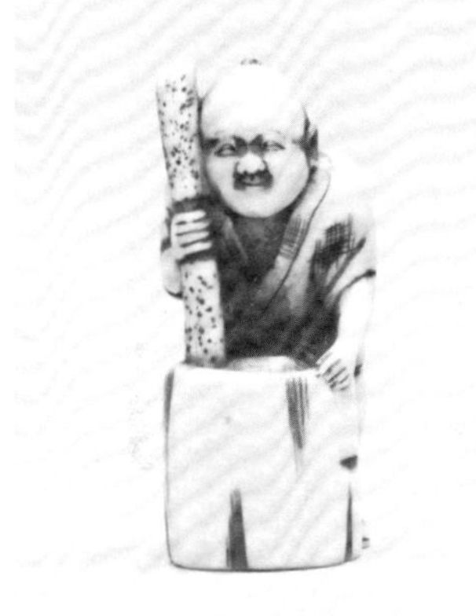

A man works with a large mortar and pestle.

Ivory. late 19th-20th c. Katabori. 4.4 cm. E27123

A man holding a mask of Okame behind his back and pulling on his eyelid is playing Akambe, a children's game which centers around the derisive gesture called Bekkanko. The gesture, pulling down the eyelid and sometimes sticking out the tongue, means "see my eye."

Ivory. Masatoshi. late 19th-20th c. Katabori. 4.2 cm. E27082

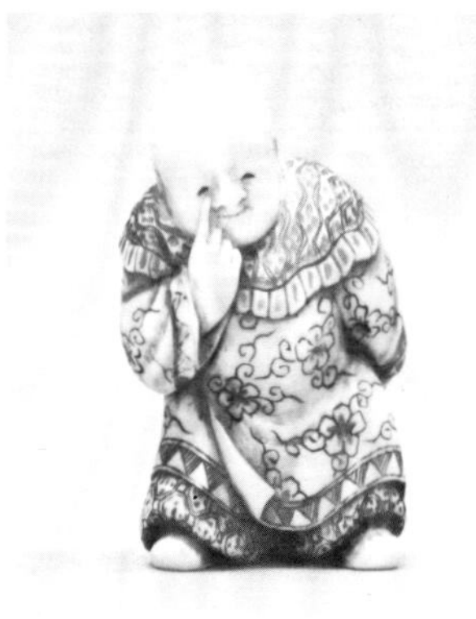

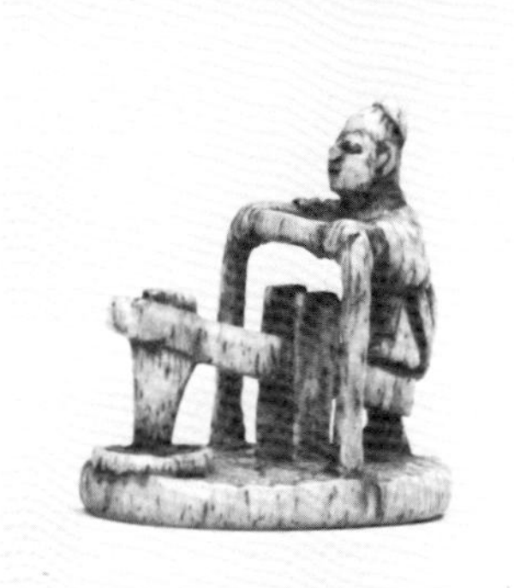

A man polishes rice in a mortar with a foot operated pestle in order to convert brown rice into white rice.

Bone. Juzan. 19th c. Katabori. 3.4 cm. E27138

This boy playing Akambe is holding a mask of Okame behind his back. Carved with fine details, the boy's tongue is of pink coral, his pants are decorated with bushy-tailed turtles, and he wears a pouch and netsuke at his waist.

Boxwood, coral, pearl inlay. signature plaque Kotekisai. 19th c. Katabori. 3.4 cm. E52712

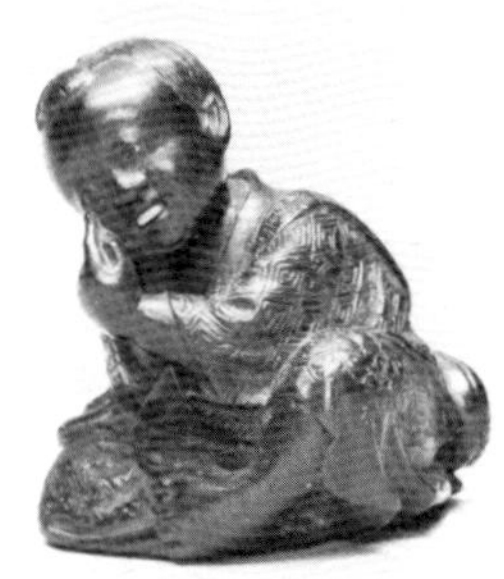

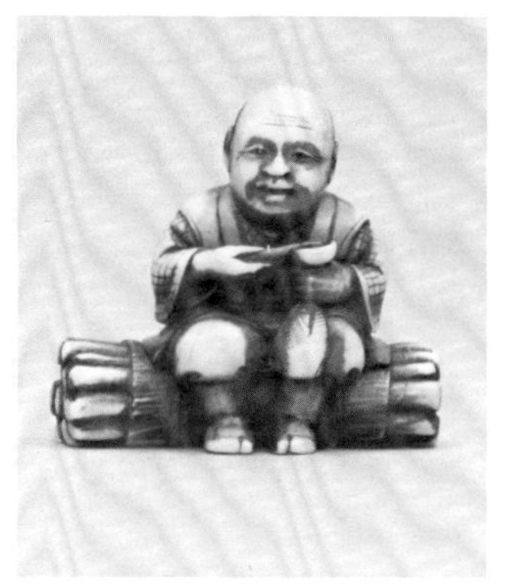

A man, sitting on a bundle of sticks, empties his pipe into an ash tray netsuke attached to a tobacco pouch.

Ivory. Masakazu. 1868-1911. Katabori. 3.2 cm. E27151

This man is making a henro (pilgrimage).

Ivory. Tamakazu or Gyokuichi. 20th c. Katabori. 5.5 cm. E36983

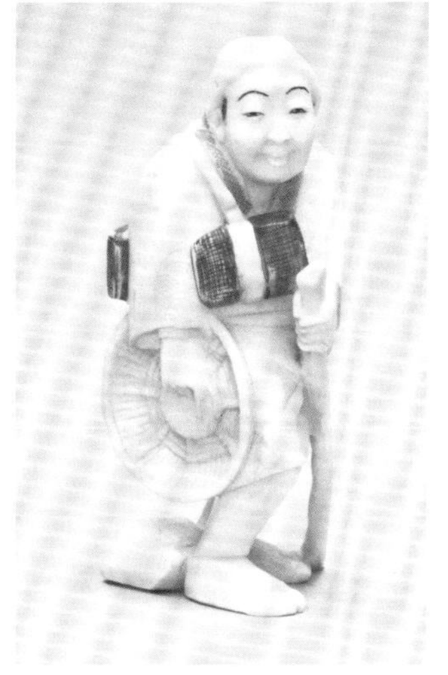

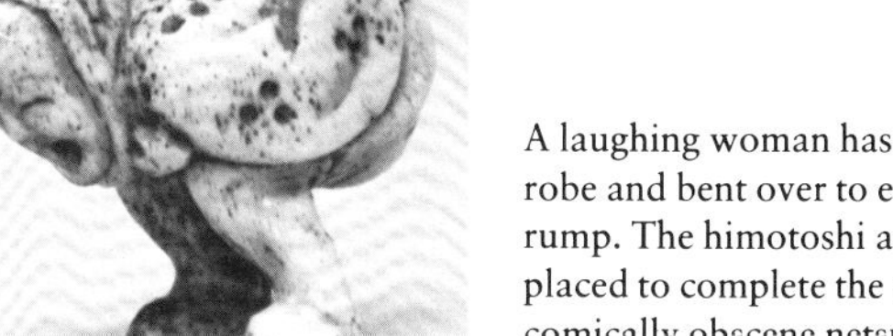

A laughing woman has lifted her robe and bent over to expose her bare rump. The himotoshi are strategically placed to complete the effect of this comically obscene netsuke.

Bone. late 19th-20th c. Katabori. 4.0 cm. E53704

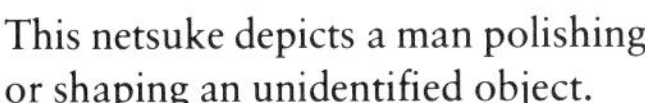

This netsuke depicts a man polishing or shaping an unidentified object.

Ivory. Bizan, unrecorded artist. 20th c. Katabori. 3.5 cm. E36986

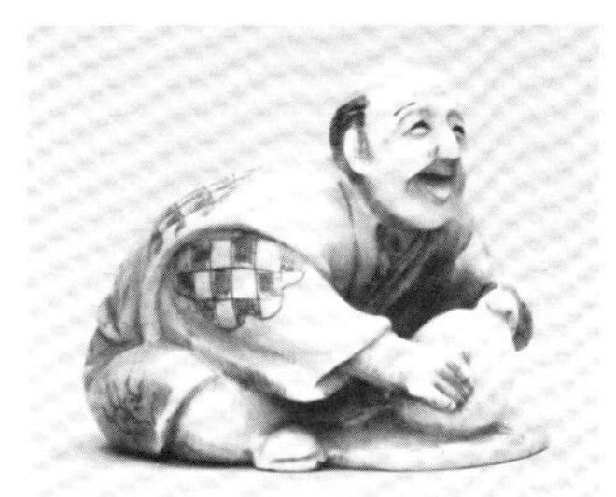

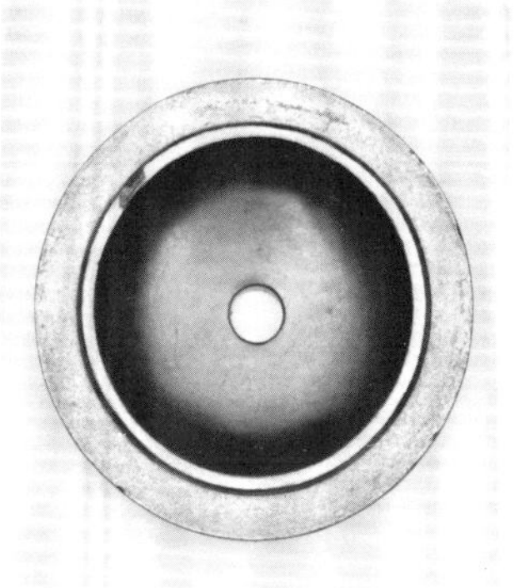

On the top lid of this "hidden delight" netsuke a man sleeps atop a pile of rumpled cloth. Inside the lid a man and a woman are making love.

Lacquered wood and metal. late 19th-20th c. Manju. 4.0 cm. E53706

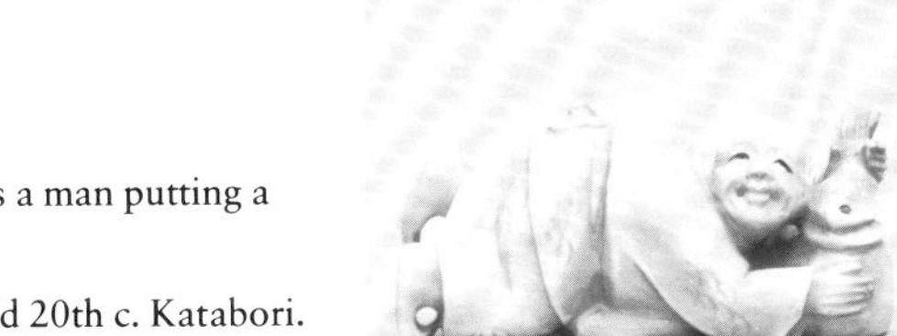

This netsuke depicts a man putting a fish into a jar.

Ivory. Gyokuho. mid 20th c. Katabori. 4.7 cm. E36990

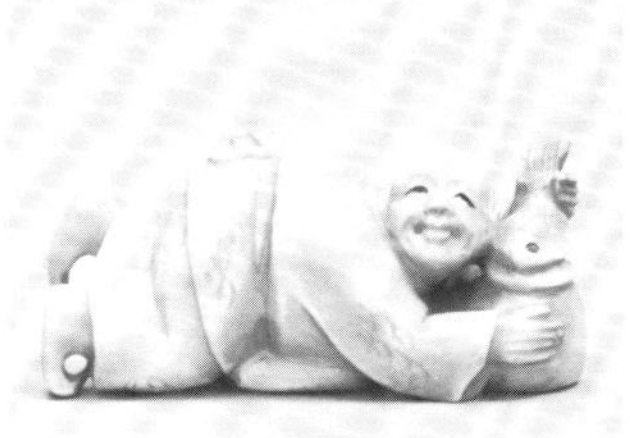

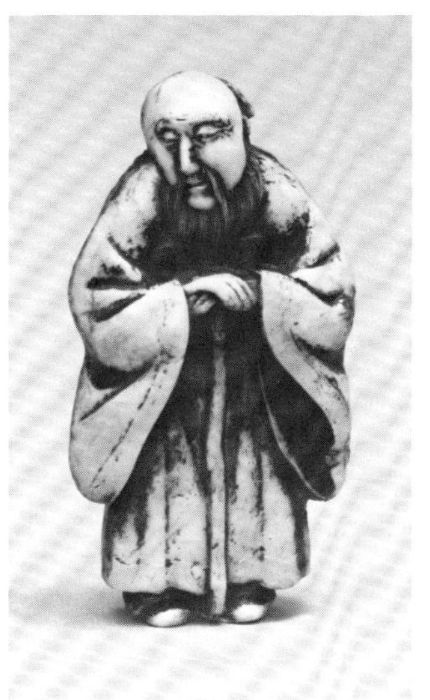

An old bearded man leans on his cane.

Cast from a mold. 1940-1958. Katabori. 5.9 cm. E36992

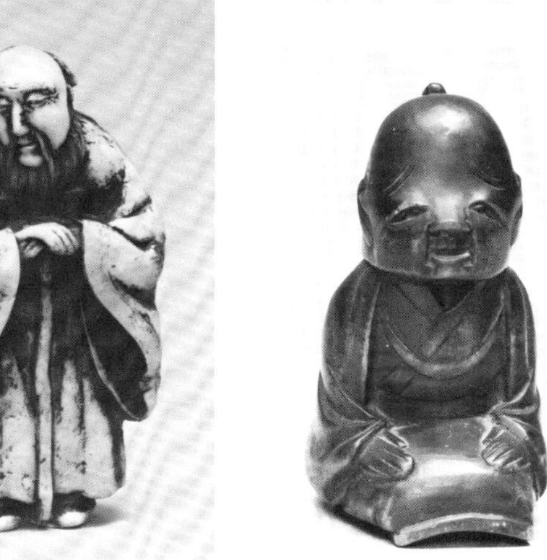

A kneeling man

Wood. 19th c. Katabori. 4.7 cm. E4445

This landscape scene depicts people working in the mountains. On one side a man carries a bundle over a bridge while two people wait for him. On the other side a man with a bundle walks toward a hut.

Boxwood. Issan. 19th c. Katabori. 4.2 cm. E26870

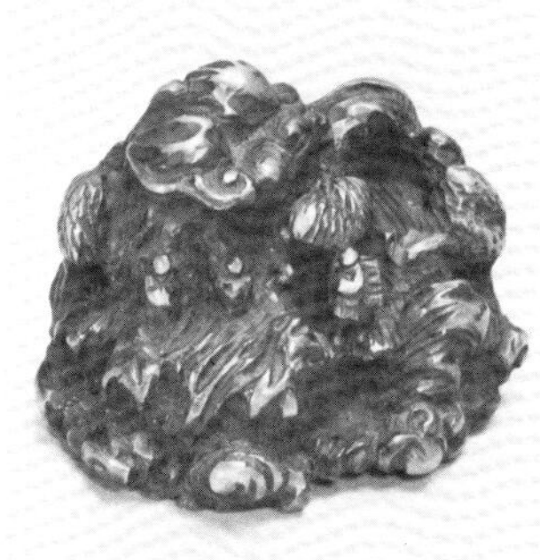

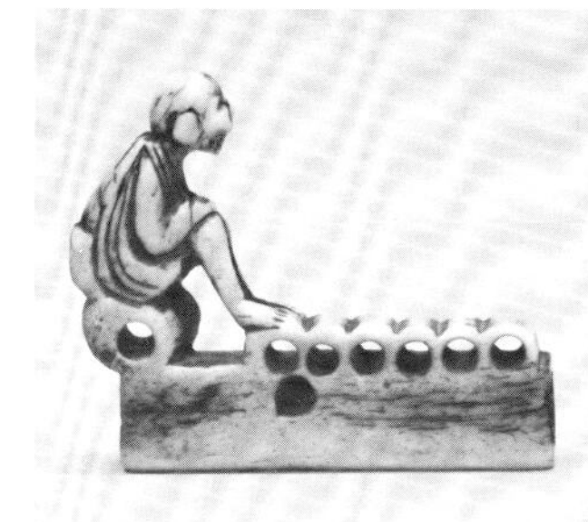

A man sits at the end of a row of hollow tubes.

Bone. early 19th c. Katabori. 6.0 cm. E27073

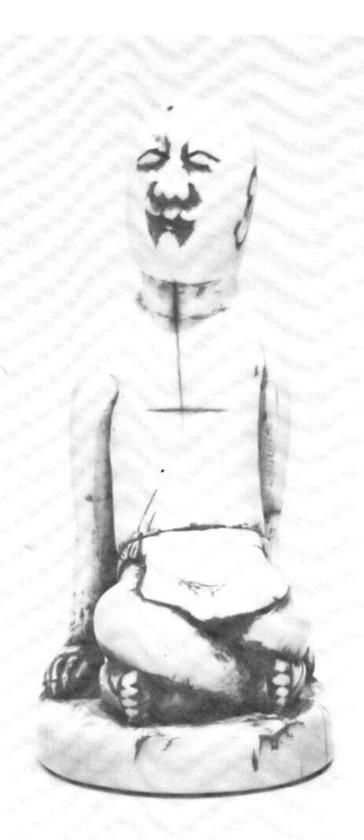

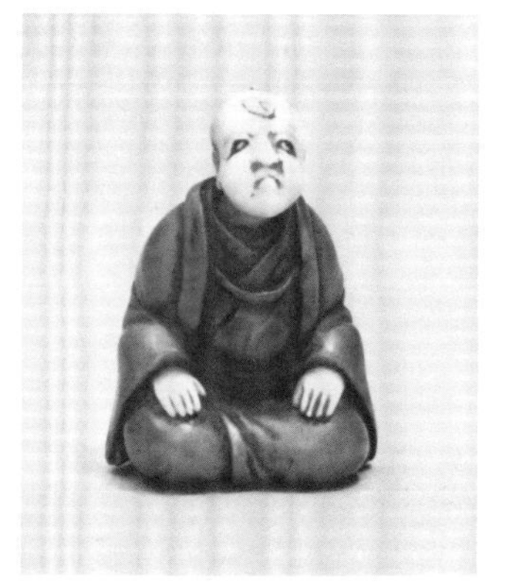

The head and hands of this frowning man are ivory, the rest of the carving is wood.

Wood and ivory. 19th-20th c. Katabori. 3.4 cm. E27074

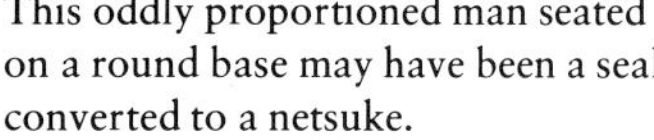

This oddly proportioned man seated on a round base may have been a seal converted to a netsuke.

Ivory. 18th c. Katabori. 7.0 cm. E26933

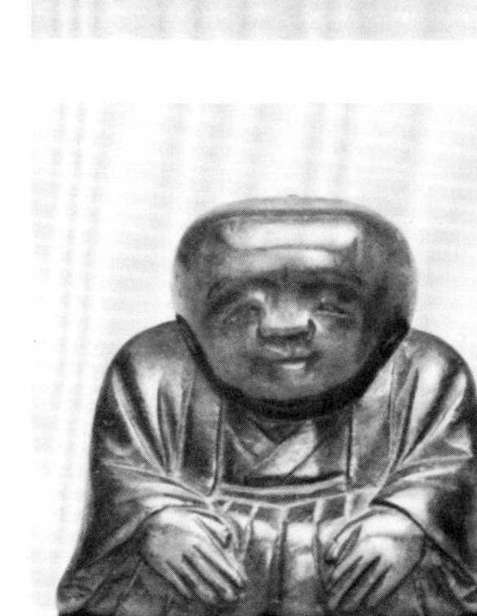

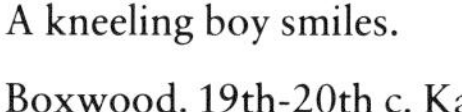

A kneeling boy smiles.

Boxwood. 19th-20th c. Katabori. 3.4 cm. E34087

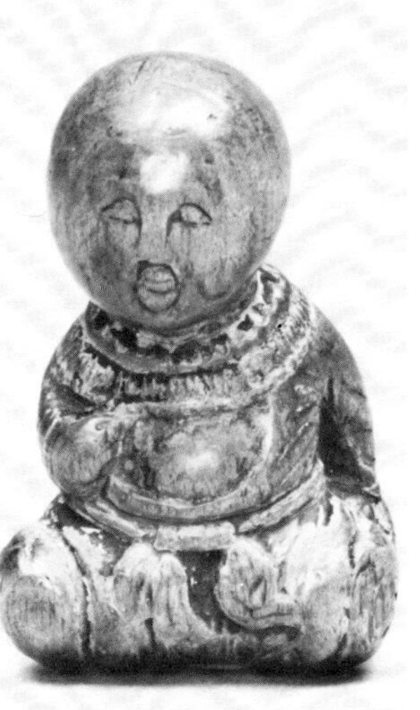

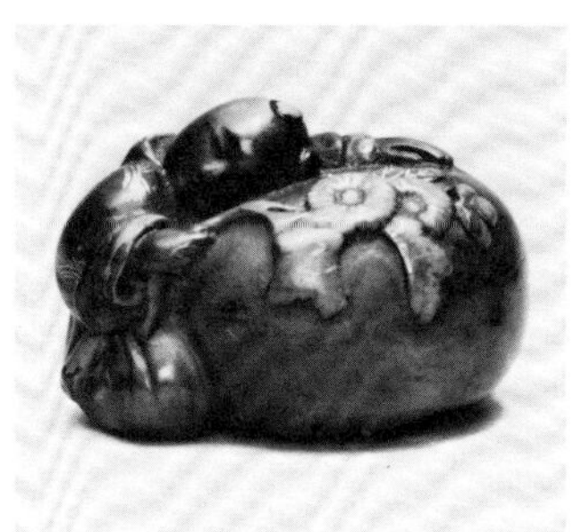

A sleeping karako (Chinese boy), his head resting on a sack, holds the stems of two chrysanthemums (symbol of purity) which lie atop the sack. The boy's robe and flowers are trimmed in red and gold lacquer.

Wood and lacquer. late 18th-19th c. Katabori. 4.1 cm. E26970

This seated bald boy wears a pouch and netsuke at his belt (not visible in photo).

Soft painted wood. early 19th c. Katabori. 5.2 cm. E27010

A woman washes her hair.

Boxwood. 19th c. Katabori.
4.5 cm. E26978

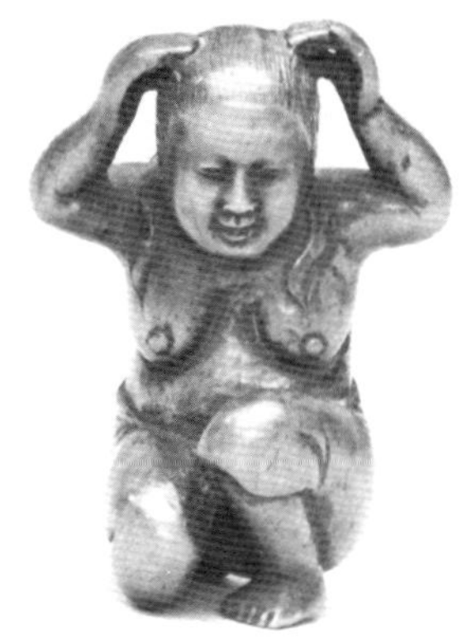

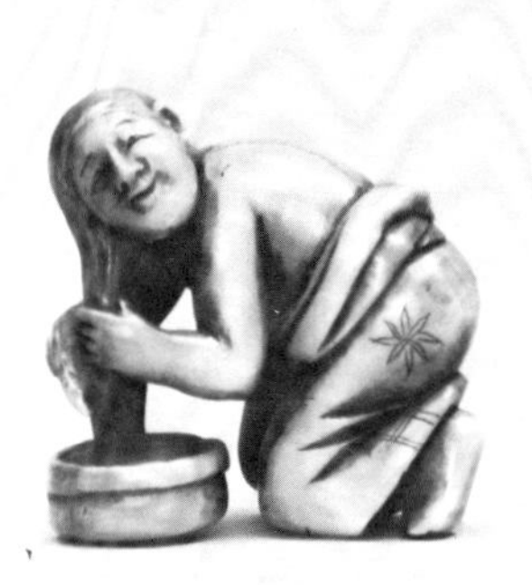

A woman combs her hair as she washes it.

Ivory. Tomochika, III. mid-19th c.
Katabori. 3.5 cm. E27152

A boy clings to a woman preparing to wash her hair.

Ivory. Ryoji. early 19th c. Katabori.
3.7 cm. E27069

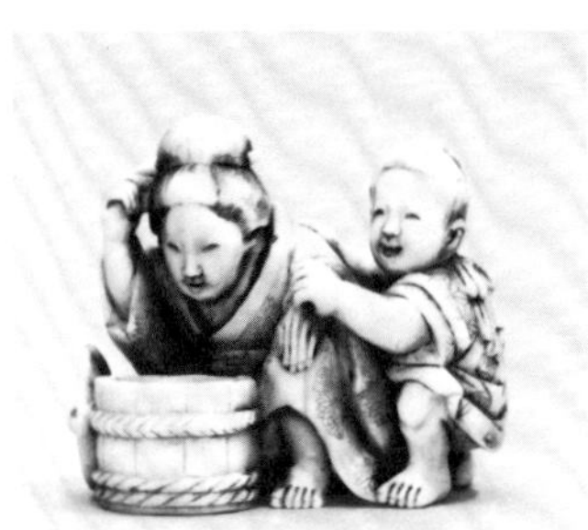

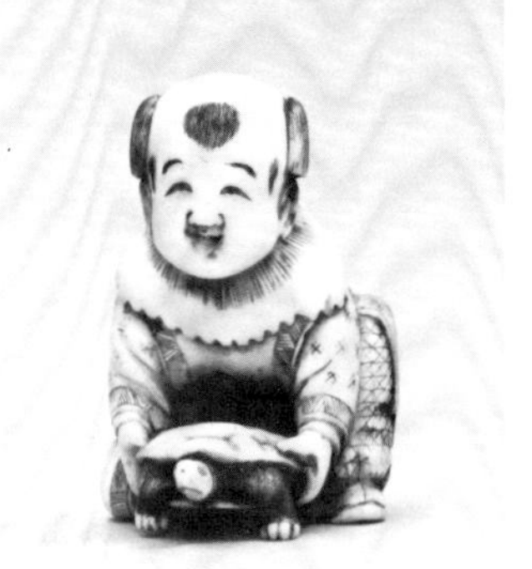

A smiling karako grabs a turtle by its shell.

Ivory. Shungetsu. 19th c. Katabori.
4.4 cm. E24904

This woman is washing a sign of the letter signifying life. The piece perhaps illustrates the expression, "enjoying life when the husband is away." An English equivalent would be "when the cat is away the mice will play."

Ivory. Tomomasa. early 19th c.
Katabori. 4.4 cm. E27097

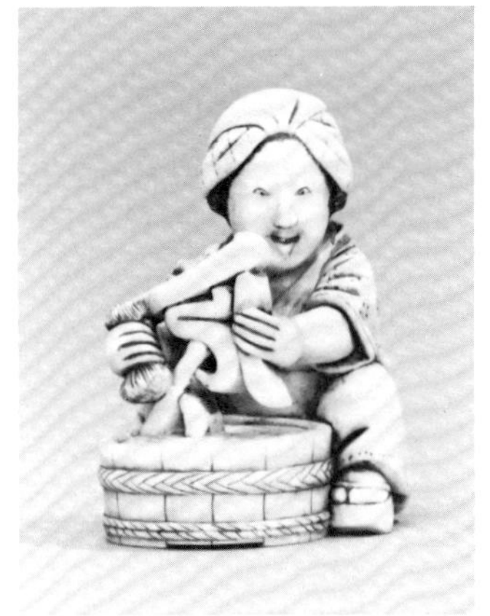

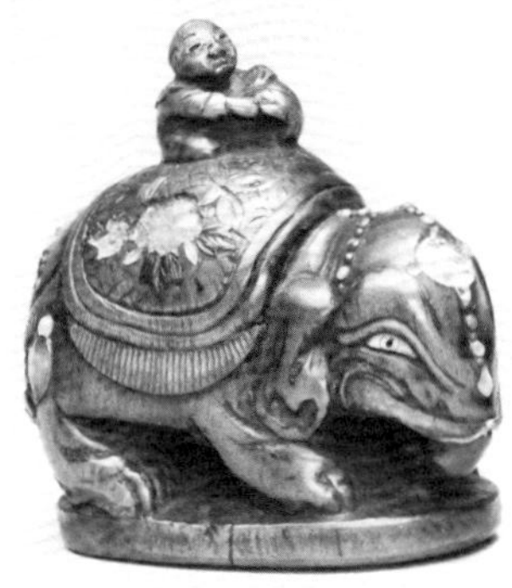

A small karako (Chinese boy) plays a drum while sitting on the back of an elaborately decorated elephant. The elephant's eyes and tusks are nacre, his decorations include green and red coral and nacre.

Boxwood, coral, nacre. 18th c.
Katabori. 5.0 cm. E26747

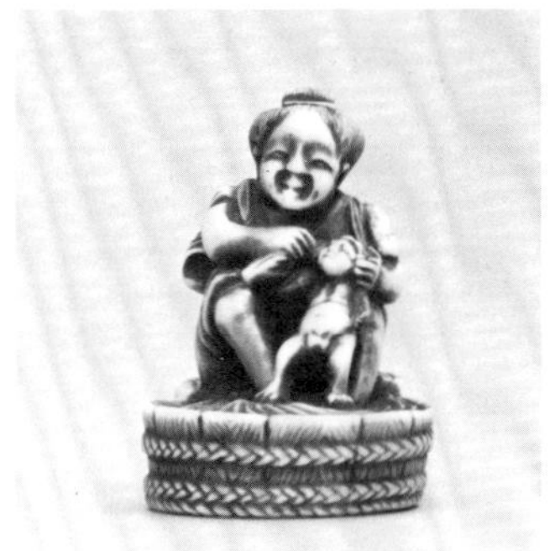

A woman, sitting on a box with her feet in a tub of water, washes her child who stands reluctantly in the water.

Ivory. 19th-20th c. Katabori.
3.7 cm. E27141

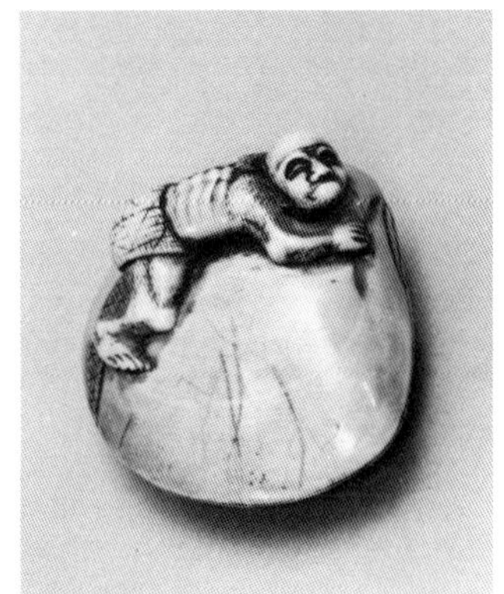

This man comically struggles to free his loin cloth which is caught in the giant clam on which he climbs.

Ivory. 19th c. Katabori. 4.3 cm.
E26755

A hawk is perched on his trainer's fist.

Painted wood. Shuzan, Nagamachi. late 18th c. Katabori. 5.1 cm. E27060

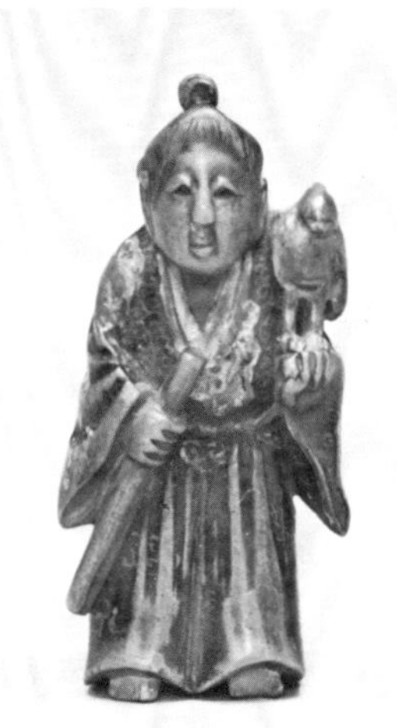

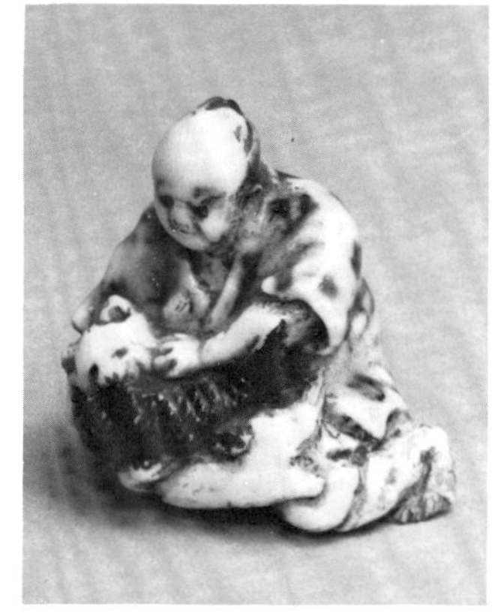

A seated man holds a white dog who holds a black fish in its mouth.

Porcelain. 19th c. Katabori. 3.6 cm. E27128

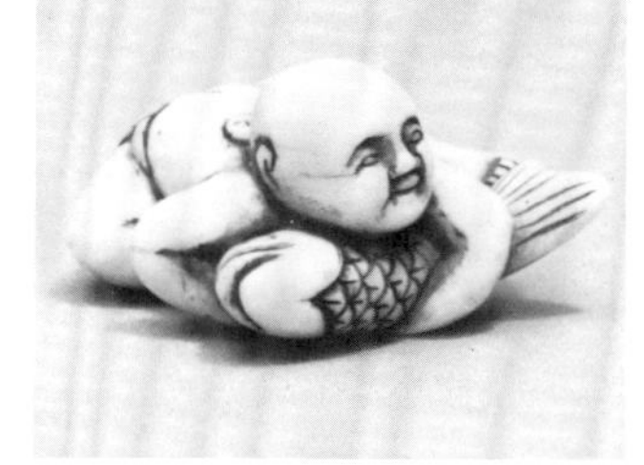

A man grabs hold of a carp.

Ivory. early 19th c. Katabori. 3.3 cm. E27135

This scholar holds a boy in his lap. Their heads and hands are made of ivory, their bodies of wood. The man's robe is decorated with green coral and white ivory flowers.

Wood, ivory, coral. Kokoku. late 19th-20th c. Katabori. 3.1 cm. E27065

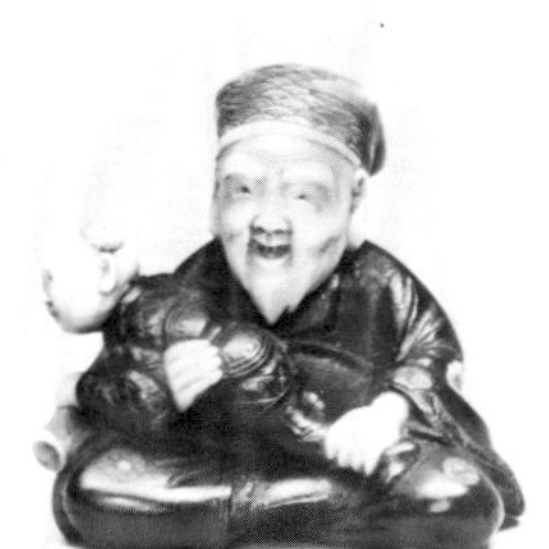

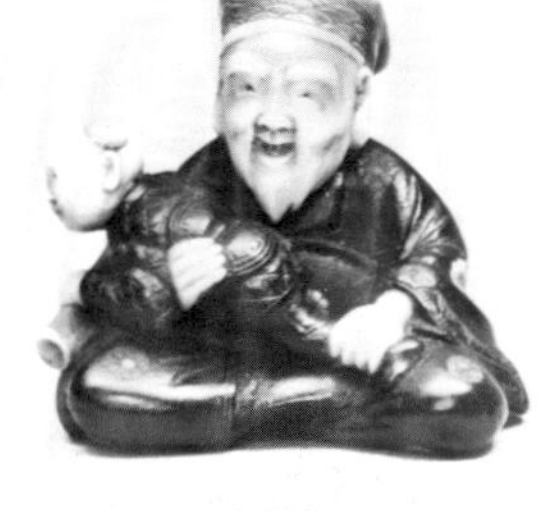

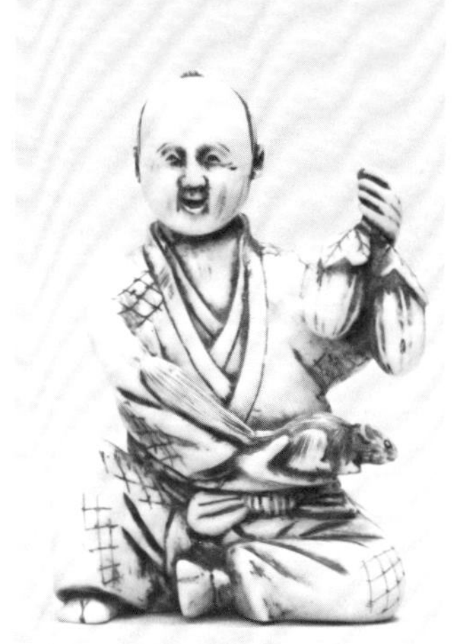

A man holds a bushy-tailed squirrel in one hand and two fruits in the other.

Ivory. 19th-20th c. Katabori. 5.3 cm. E27136

A squatting man holds a boy on his back.

Porcelain. 19th c. Katabori. 3.3 cm. E27096

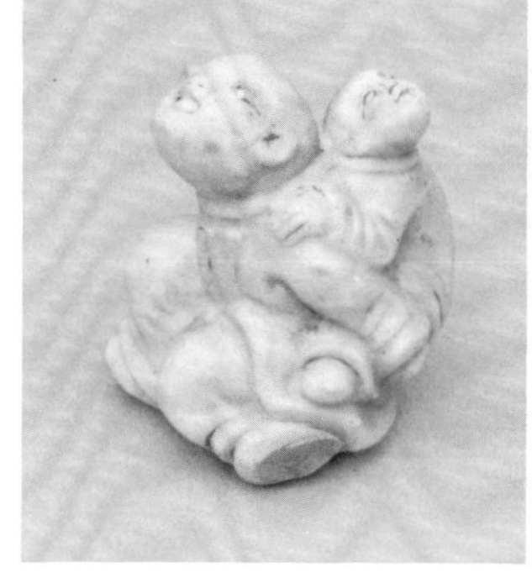

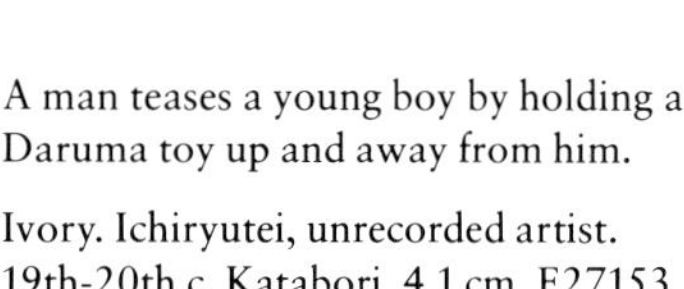

A man teases a young boy by holding a Daruma toy up and away from him.

Ivory. Ichiryutei, unrecorded artist. 19th-20th c. Katabori. 4.1 cm. E27153

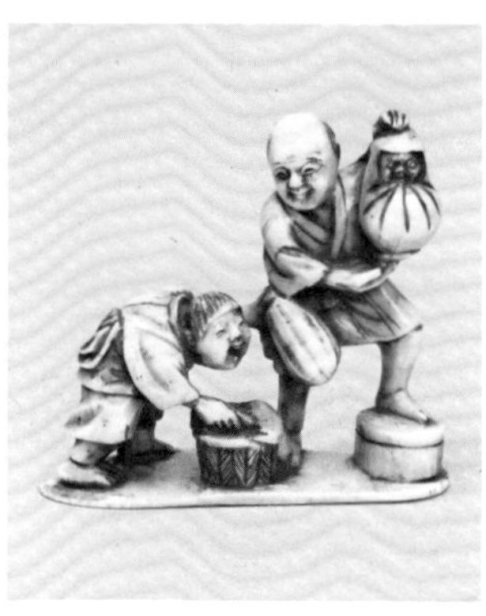

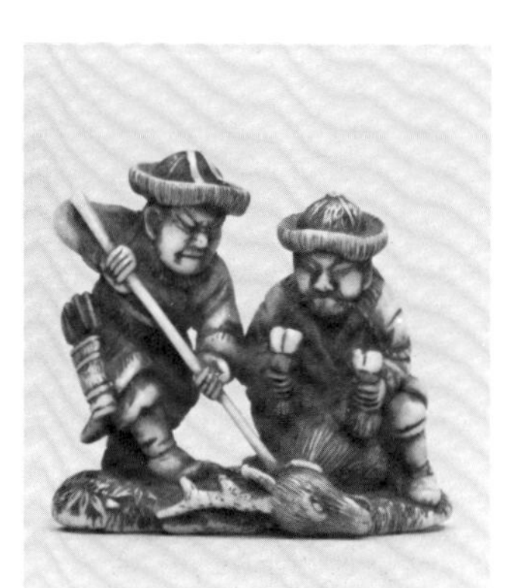

Two hunters subdue a deer. One man sits on the deer's stomach and holds its front legs while the other man stabs a spear into the deer's neck.

Ivory. early 19th c. Katabori. 3.5 cm. E27139

A child with an unrolled scroll sits at the feet of a sage.

Ivory. 19th-20th c. Katabori. 4.2 cm. E27146

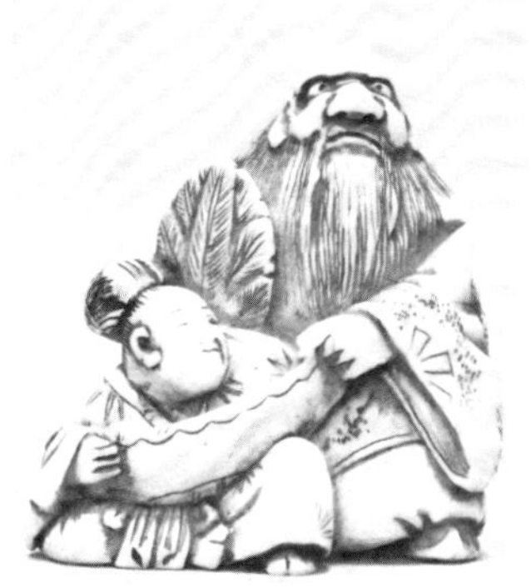

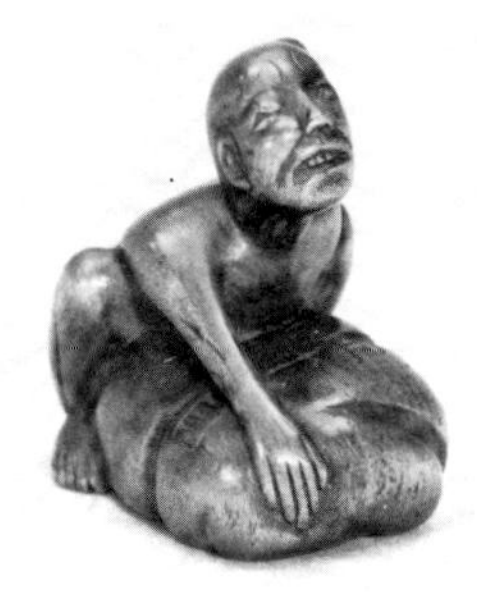

This blind man with a wen (lump on his head) strains to lift a stone with the inscription "50 eyes." The artist may be playing on both the man's blindness and the more common strength stone inscription "50 kan" (a weight measurement). (cf. plate 115 in the Bushell collection catalogue, see Bibliography)

Boxwood. 19th c. Katabori. 3.5 cm. E26976

A man holds a demon mask in front of his face while a karako looks up at the mask and pulls on its cords.

Ivory, stone inlays. Hidemasa. 1800-1834. Katabori. 5.0 cm. E27155

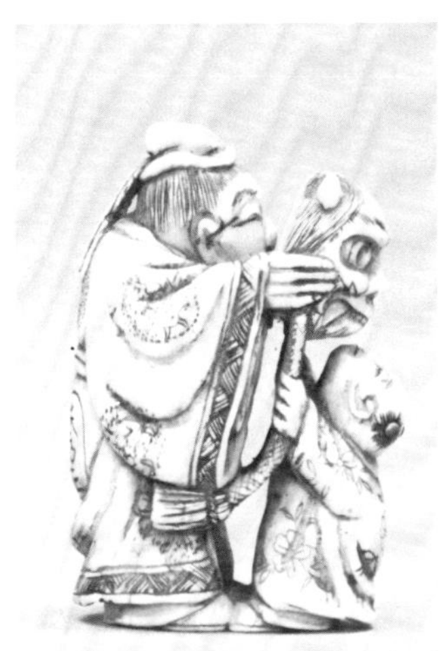

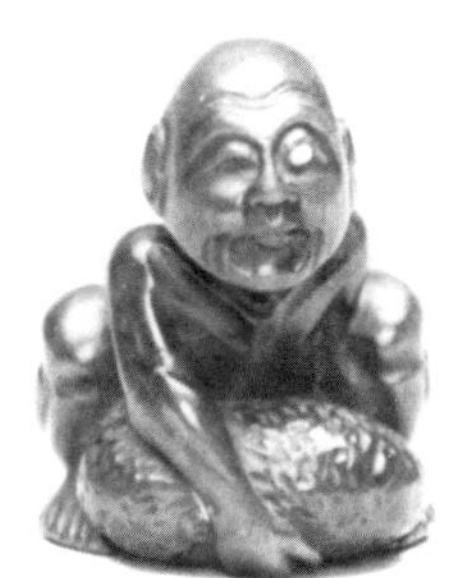

A man with a wen and one ivory eye, stoops and strains to lift the strength stone.

Boxwood, ivory inlays. Gyokkei. 1781-1800. Katabori. 3.4 cm. E27080

Occupations

Carpenters

A boy lifts a rock which he apparently intends to bring down upon the back of a turtle.

Ivory, inlaid buttons. Shigemasa. 1820-1850. Katabori. 3.2 cm. E27160

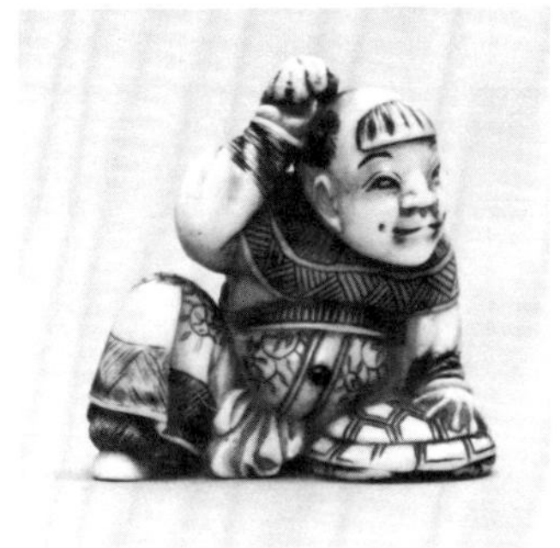

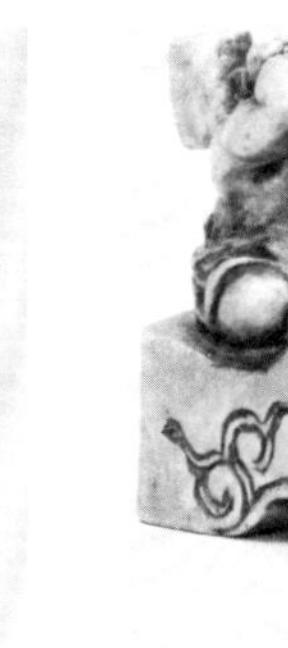

A carpenter sitting on top of a gigantic inkline holder, chisels a mortise for the ink, pad and line.

Wood. 19th-20th c. Katabori. 4.0 cm. E26980

A boy, perhaps a student, kneels beside a small desk or table.

Ebony. 19th c. Katabori. 2.8 cm. E53730

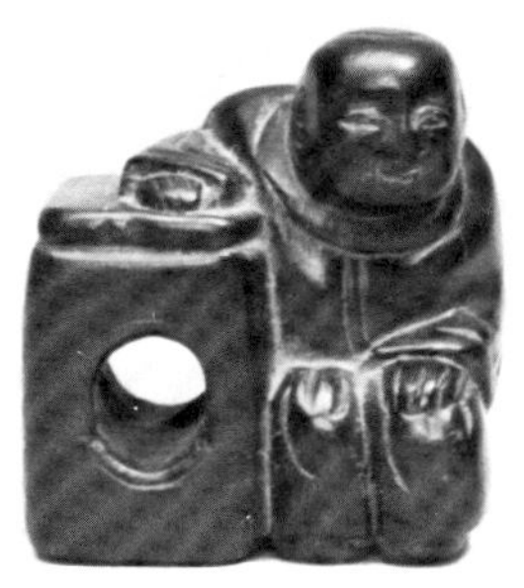

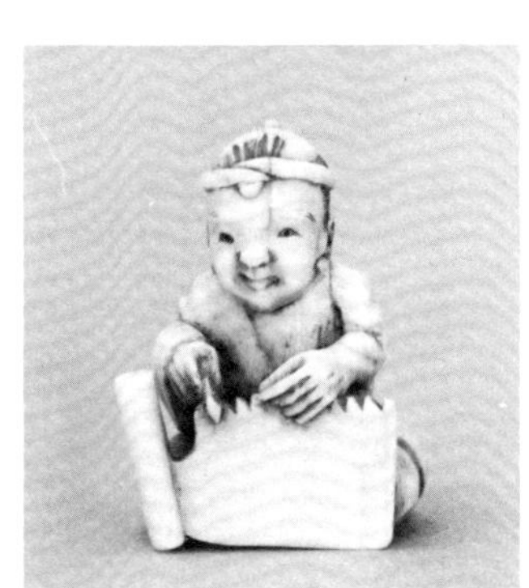

A carpenter sharpens a saw with a file.

Ivory. 19th-20th c. Katabori. 3.3 cm. E27100

A carpenter saws an inclined board.

Ivory. Masaaki. late 19th c. Katabori. 4.0 cm. E27125

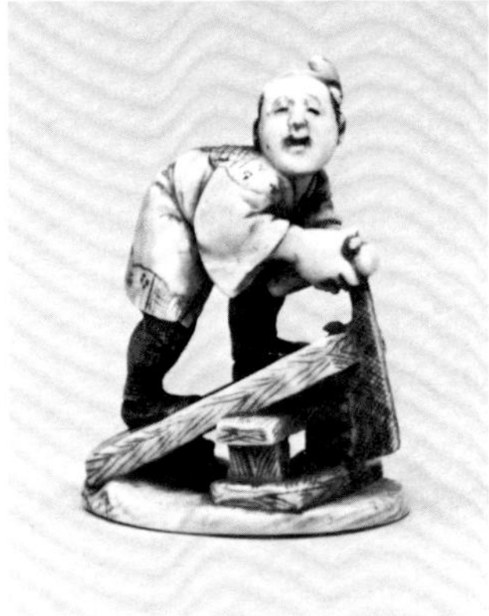

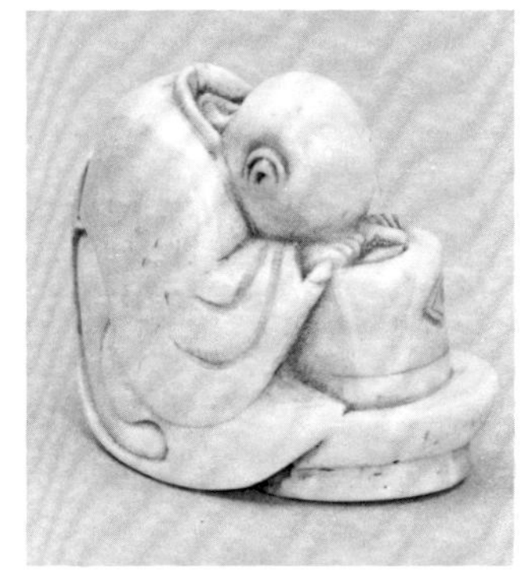

Chajin

H. L. Joly notes that netsuke carvers made fun of Chajin (tea experts) by depicting them asleep at their tea mills. The Peabody Museum has two such figures in its collection.

Ivory. 18th c. Katabori. 3.4 cm. E27094

A carpenter with a dragon head tattoo on his back is planing a board.

Ivory. 19th c. Katabori. 4.7 cm. E27140

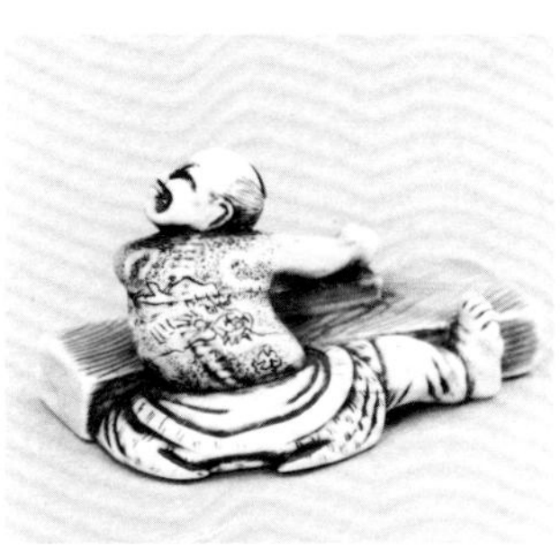

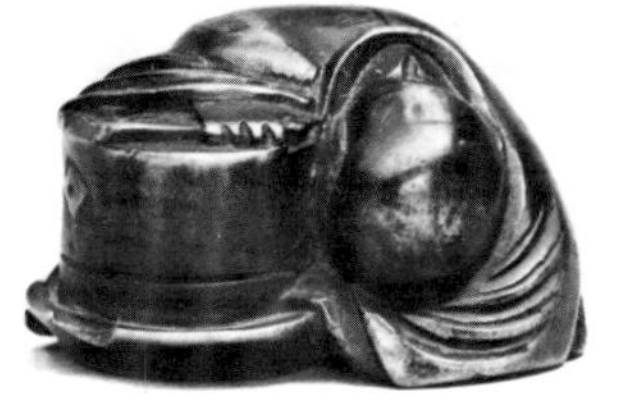

Wood. 19th c. Katabori. 3.7 cm. E34090

Carvers

A carver sculpts a figure of Kwannon, a Buddhist deity of mercy.

Ivory. Tama, unrecorded artist. 20th c. Katabori. 4.5 cm. E36981

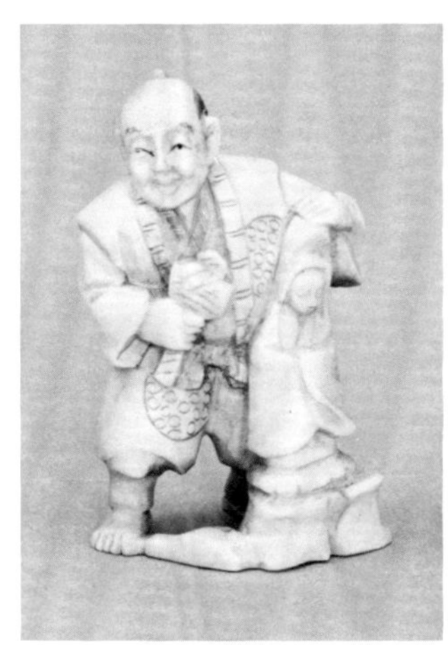

Farmers

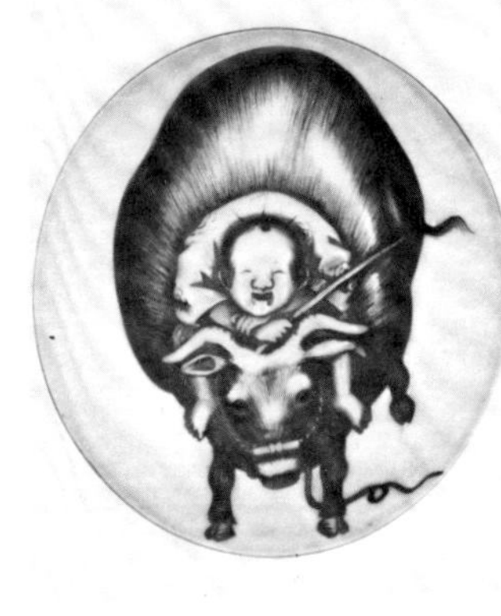

On the photographed side of this piece a farmer sits atop a water buffalo. The design on the other side is of a basket of wheat and a sickle.

Ivory. 19th-20th c. Manju. 4.3 cm. E23114

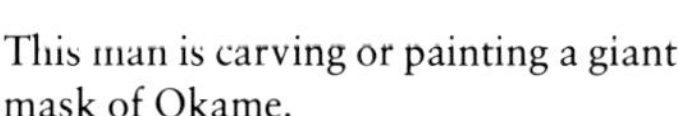

This man is carving or painting a giant mask of Okame.

Ivory. Isshi (Shibayama). late 19th-20th c. Katabori. 5.6 cm. E36987

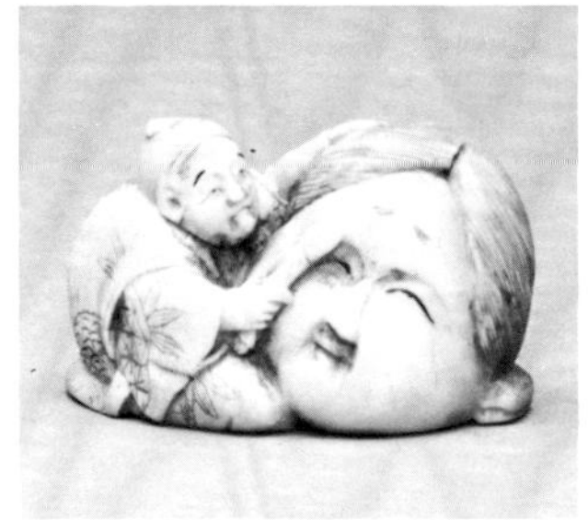

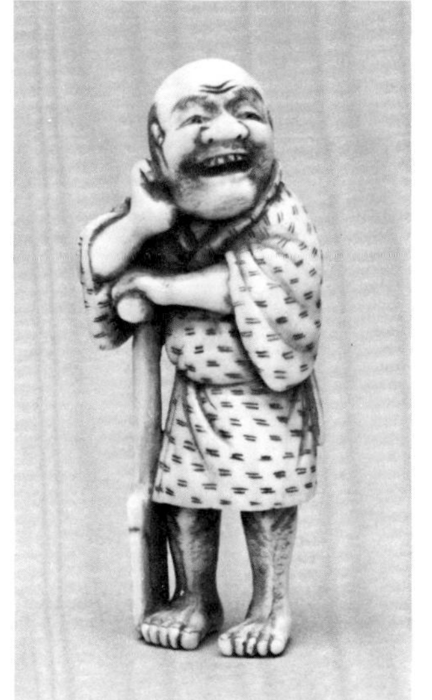

A farmer, resting on his spade, wears a netsuke and a tobacco pouch with the inscription "Be aware of fire." (Pouch and netsuke not visible in photo.)

Ivory. late 19th-20th c. Katabori. 5.6 cm. E27017

A farmer, carrying his harvest, wears a robe decorated with sparrows, a symbol of his industriousness.

Ivory. Minkoku II. early 19th c. Katabori. 4.6 cm. E27059

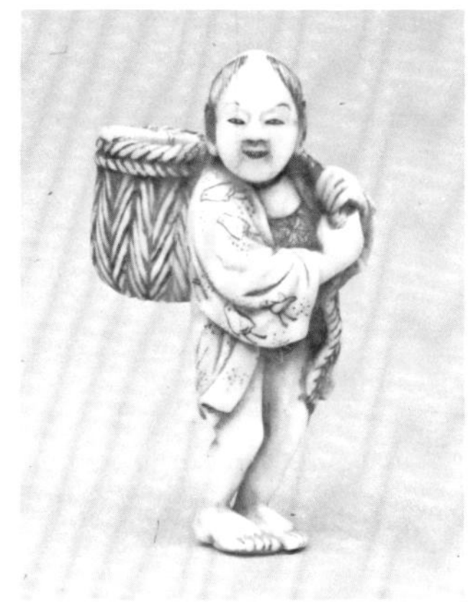

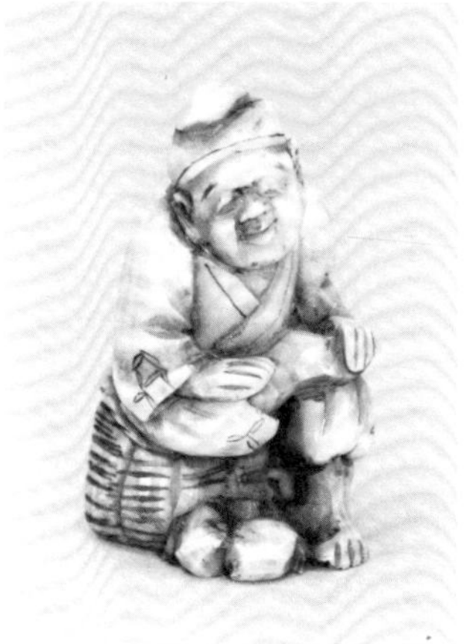

A fisherman sits on his fish basket.

Ivory. 20th c. Katabori. 4.5 cm. E27042

Fishermen

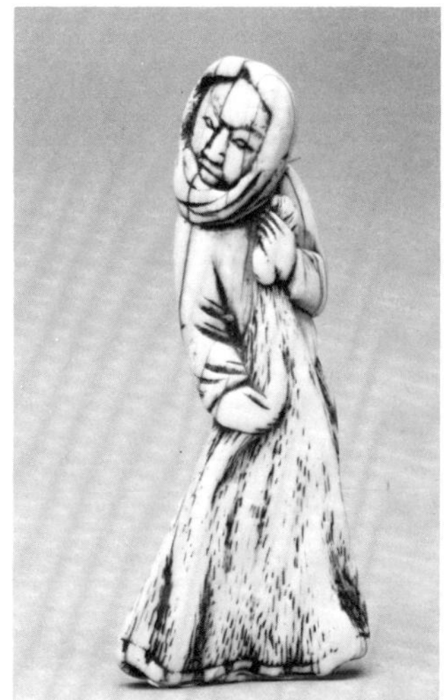

A fisherman hauls in his net.

Ivory. 18th c. Katabori. 8.7 cm. E26953

Health Occupations The Japanese believed in both curative and preventive medicine. Doctors and druggists worked to cure sickness; amma (blind masseurs) were specially trained to give massages, a widely used method for gaining a feeling of well-being.

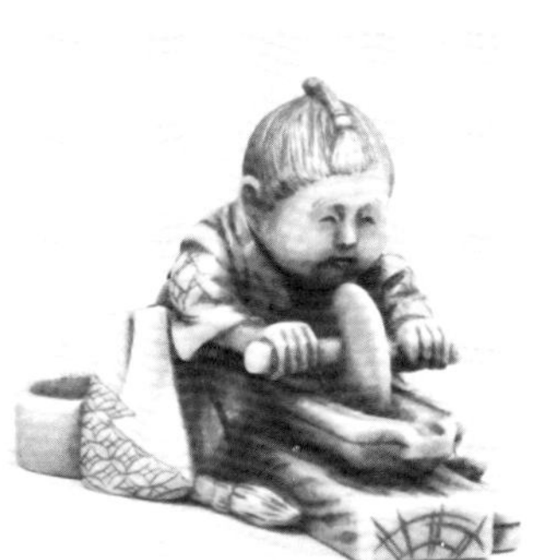

Surrounded by various sacks, spoons, brushes and bowls of his trade, a druggist grinds medicine with a wheel and mortar.

Ivory. Masayuki. mid 19th-20th c. Katabori. 4.5 cm. E27092

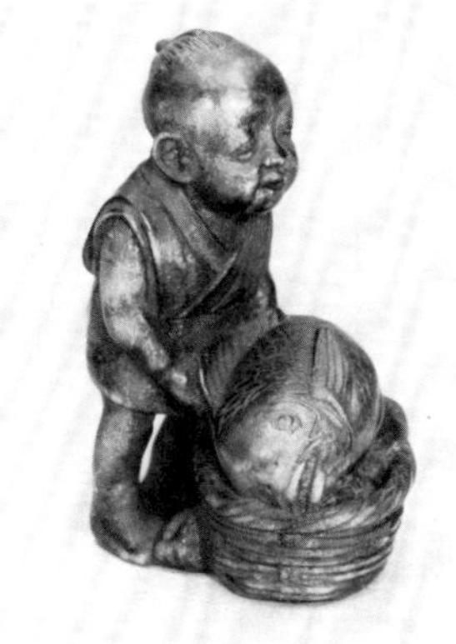

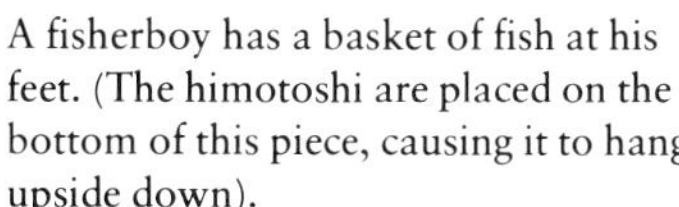

A fisherboy has a basket of fish at his feet. (The himotoshi are placed on the bottom of this piece, causing it to hang upside down).

Boxwood. Temmin, unrecorded artist. 19th-20th c. Katabori. 4.1 cm. E27005

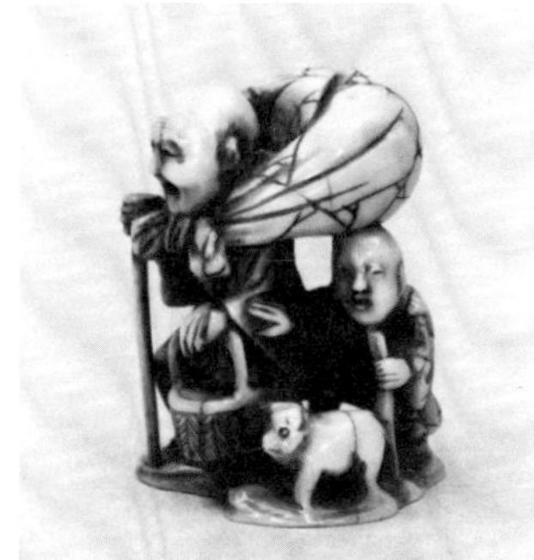

Two blind amma (a man and a boy) make their way down a road with the help of canes and a dog. Amma generally move around until they find work as masseurs.

Ivory. Ikkan, unrecorded artist. late 19th-20th c. Katabori. 3.5 cm. E27161

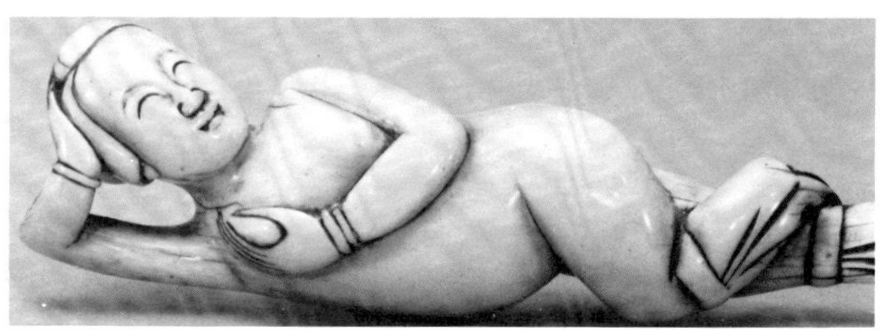

Chinese doctors used small female models which enabled a modest patient to point out the area that ailed her without revealing her body to the doctor. Many of these models were later employed as netsuke, and this one was probably made in China.

Ivory. 18th c. Katabori. 14.2 cm. E26965

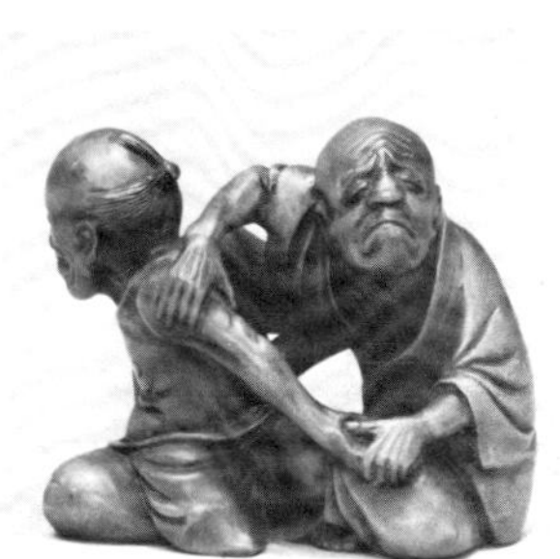

An amma gives a massage. The amma wears a netsuke and inro at his waist (not visible in photo), and in fact this carving may have been an okimono (carving made for display) used as a netsuke.

Wood. illegible signature. 19th c. Katabori. 5.0 cm. E33343

Mirror polishers Some Japanese mirrors are metal and must be kept highly polished. Mirrors have a significant place in Shinto shrines and are the subject of numerous proverbs. F. H. Davis in *Myths and Legends of Japan* (see Bibliography) writes that in Shinto the mirror "typifies the human heart, which, when perfectly placid and clear, reflects the very image of the deity." An old Japanese proverb says, "when the mirror is dim the soul is unclean."

The Peabody Museum collection includes three mirror polishers, all in the same pose.

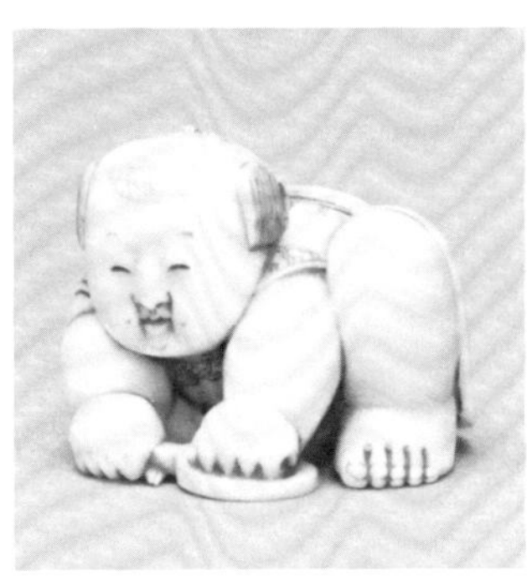

Ivory. Gyokuzan. late 19th-20th c. Katabori. 2.5 cm. E27104

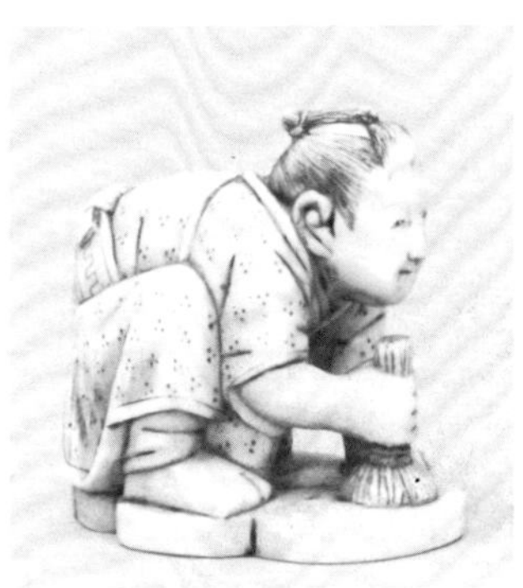

Ivory. Tomoharu. early 19th c. Katabori. 3.3 cm. E27107

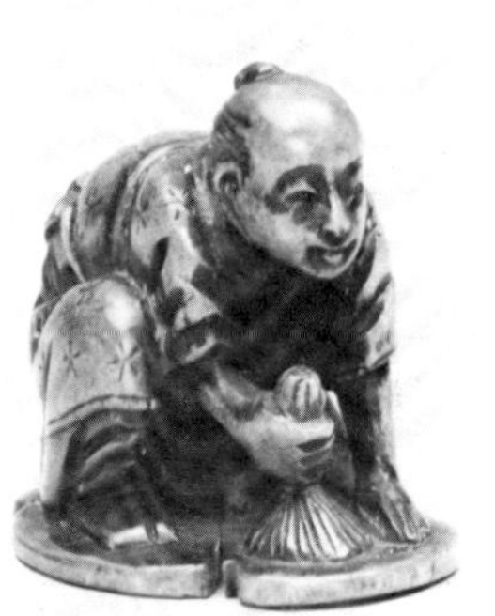

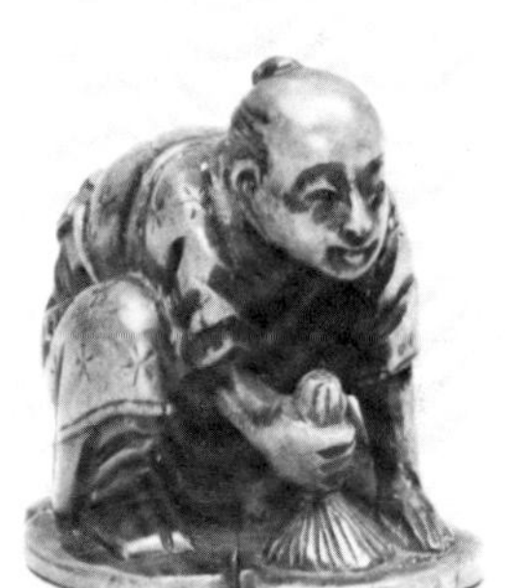

Wood. 19th-20th c. Katabori. 3.5 cm. E27129

Monks and Priests

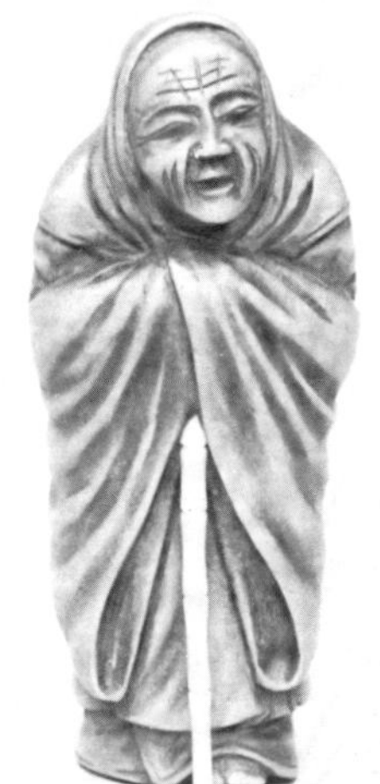

A blind monk with a white ivory cane

Wood and ivory. late 19th-20th c. Katabori. 5.7 cm. E27031

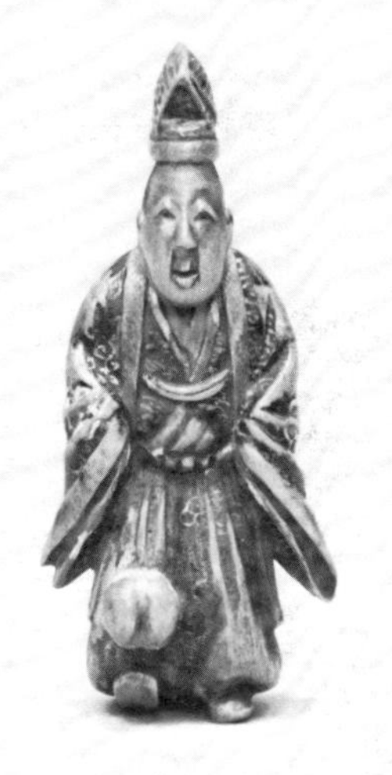

This priest wears a blue and red robe and green pants.

Painted wood. Shuzan, Nagamachi. late 18th c. Katabori. 5.5 cm. E27075

Noblemen

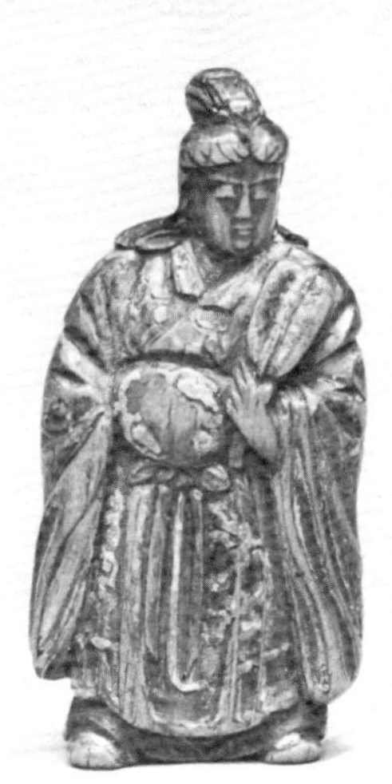

A nobleman in flowing robes of green and red holds a fan.

Painted wood. late 18th-19th c. Katabori. 5.4 cm. E27020

Rat catchers Modern devices did not exist for getting rid of these pests.

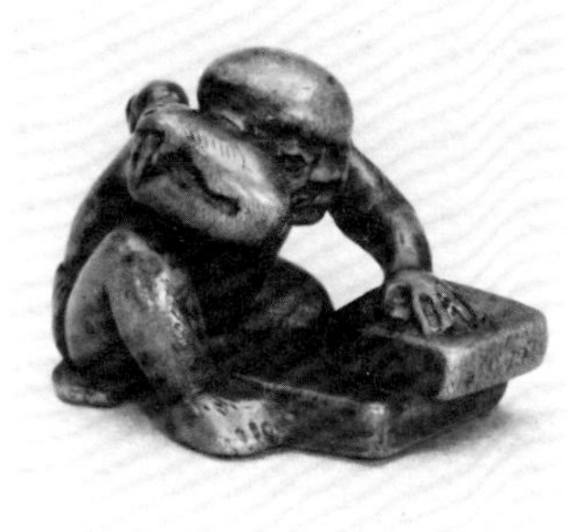

A rat catcher reaches over his shoulder in an attempt to grab the tail of the rat that is running down his back.

Boxwood. Naoshige. 19th c. Katabori. 4.0 cm. E26969

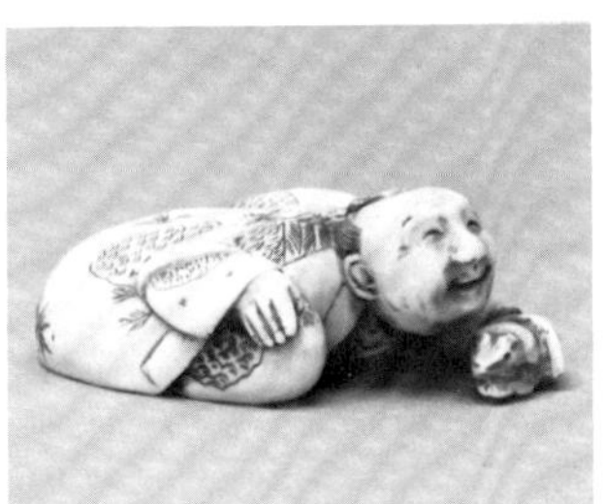

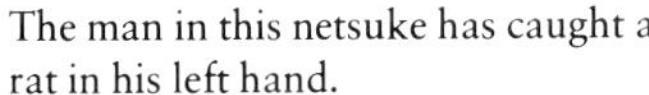

The man in this netsuke has caught a rat in his left hand.

Ivory. illegible signature. 20th c. Katabori. 5.0 cm. E36991

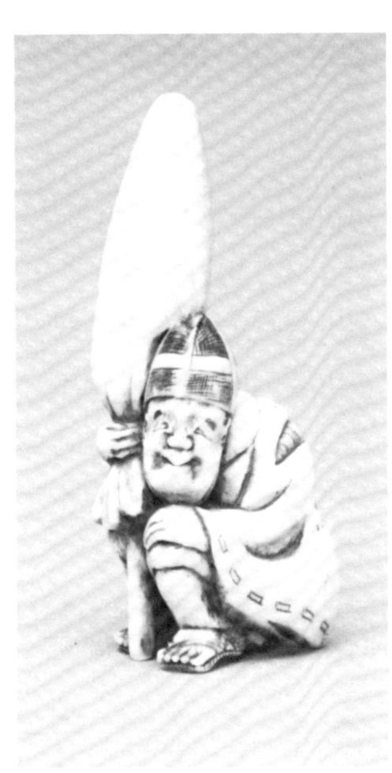

Servants

A servant holds his master's umbrella, a symbol of wealth and distinction.

Ivory. Ikko. early 19th c. Katabori. 6.0 cm. E27134

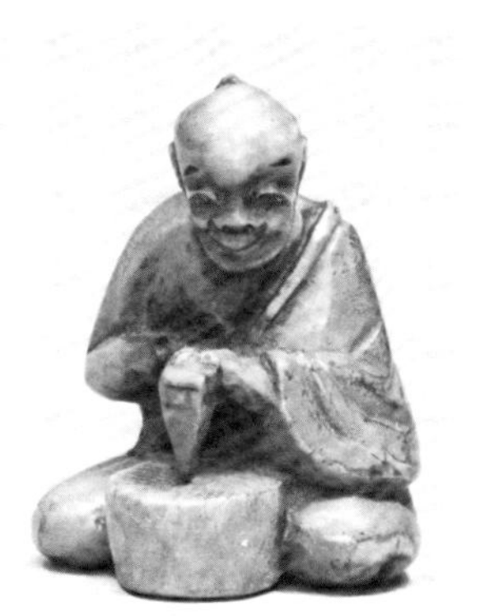

Stone Cutters

A stone cutter works with the tools of his trade.

Wood and red lacquer. 19th c. Katabori. 4.1 cm. E4171

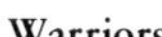

Warriors

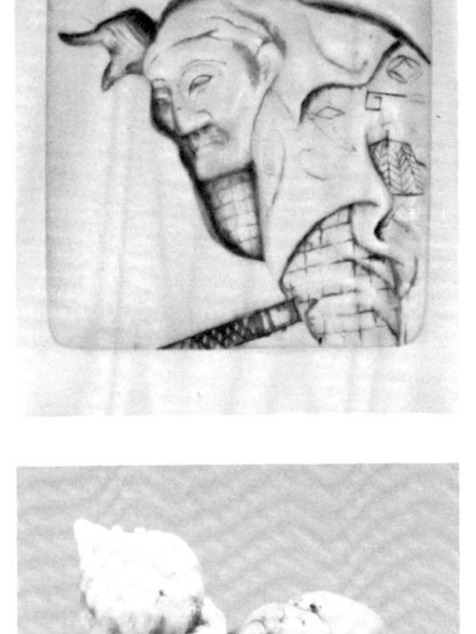

The warrior pictured here may be headed toward battle. On the reverse side is a stalk of bamboo (symbol of virtue, fidelity and constancy) and three bales of wheat.

Ivory. Koraku. early 19th c. Manju. 4.5 cm. E26558

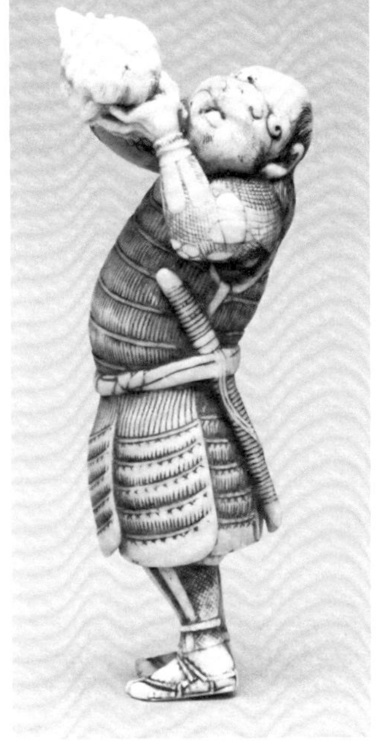

A warrior in a coat of armor blows a Buccinum, a Buddhist sacred shell, in a signal of victory.

Ivory. 19th c. Katabori. 7.2 cm. E27033

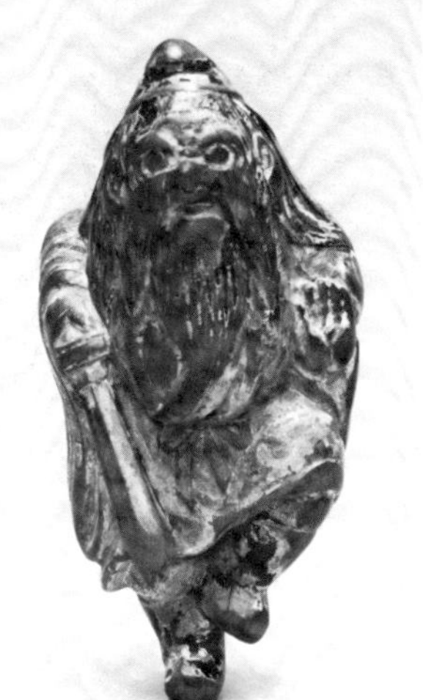

A bearded warrior stands on one foot with his sword drawn.

Cypress painted green and black. late 18th c. Katabori. 7.8 cm. E26944

Wrestlers

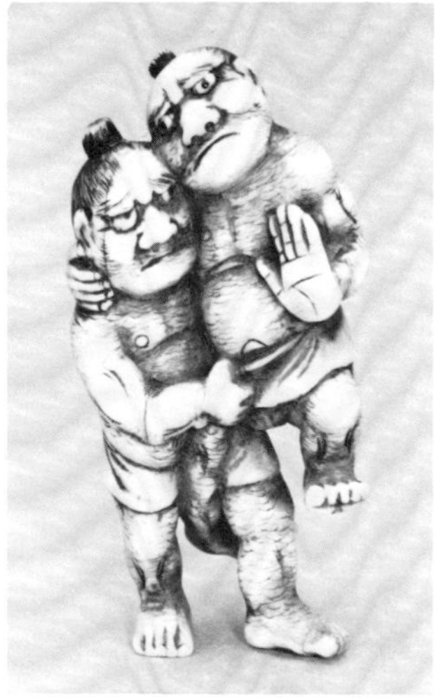

One wrestler lifts another into the air by grabbing hold of his loincloth.

Ivory. Masatsugu (Kaigyokusai). 1823-1833. Katabori. 5.5 cm. E21273

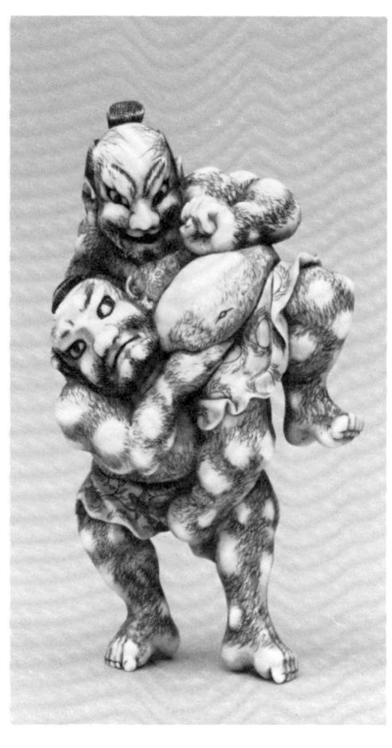

The wrestler being lifted by his loincloth is about to be overcome by the "kawazu throw." His mouth is closed, the other wrestler's is open possibly illustrating the principle of dualism in nature: female and male (Yin and Yang or In and Yo), up and down, open and shut, etc.

Ivory. Mitsukuni Anrakusai. 1869-20th c. Katabori. 7.5 cm. E27011

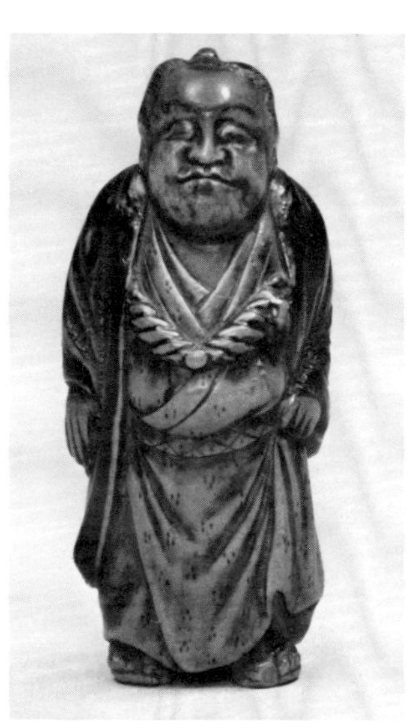

A sumo wrestler with black hair and black robe.

Wood and lacquer. 19th c. Katabori. 6.3 cm. E27028

Entertainment: Yose and Street Performers Jugglers, acrobats, comics, musicians, dancers and other performers made up the variety shows of Yose theater; they also provided street entertainment on festival (and other) days.

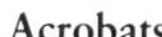

Acrobats

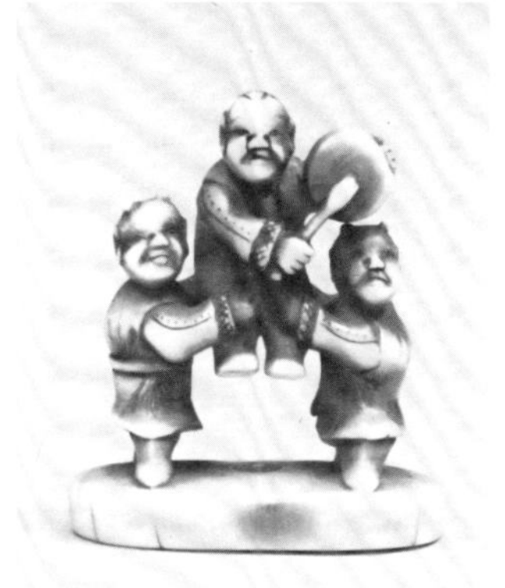

Three Acrobats

Ivory. late 19th-20th c. Katabori. 3.8 cm. E27004

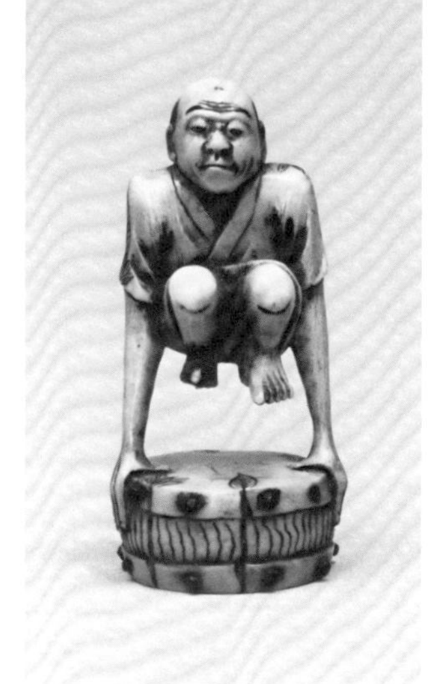

An acrobat performs a stunt on a drum decorated with wood beads.

Ivory, wood inlays. Masatsugu. mid 19th c. Katabori. 5.0 cm. E27098

Comedians

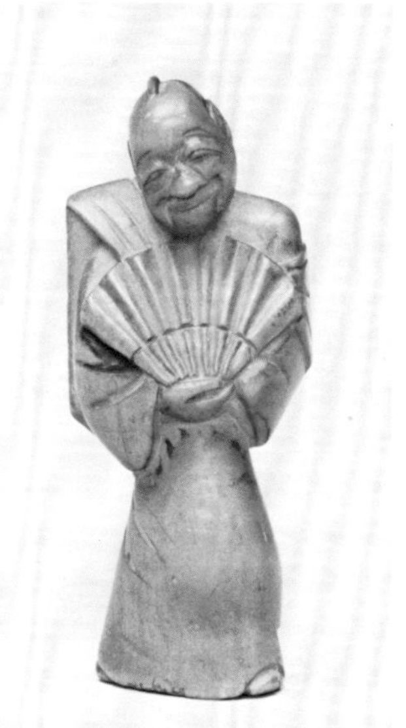

A taikomochi is a professional male comedian who entertains prior to a geisha performance.

Wood. 19th c. Katabori. 5.8 cm. E4484

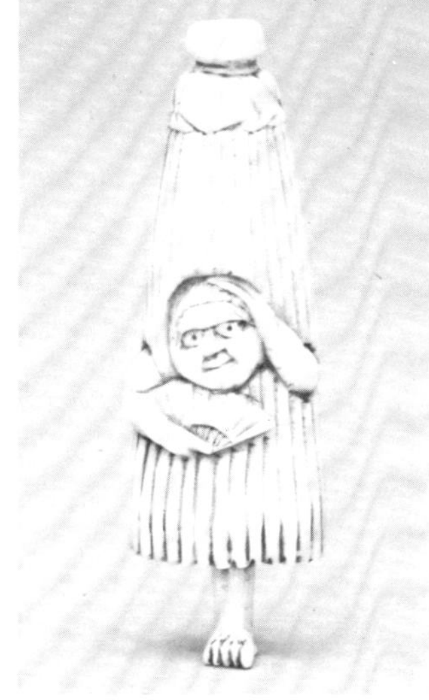
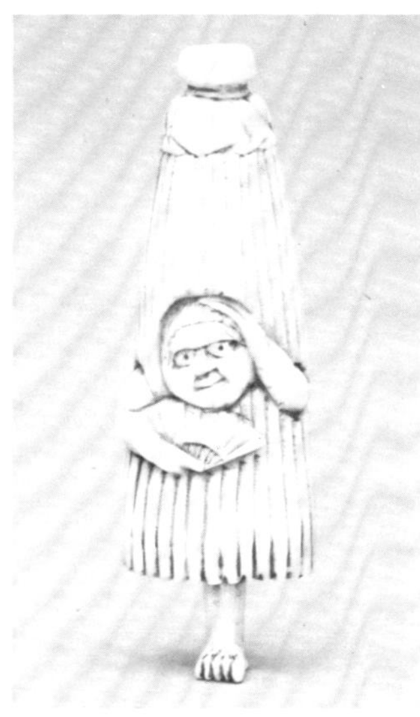

Folded into a symbol of wealth and distinction (umbrella) while unfolding a sign of proper dress (fan), this man's expression seems appropriate to his predicament. The design may have been taken from the netsuke carver's imagination, rather than a real performance.

Ivory. 19th-20th c. Katabori. 6.2 cm. E26930

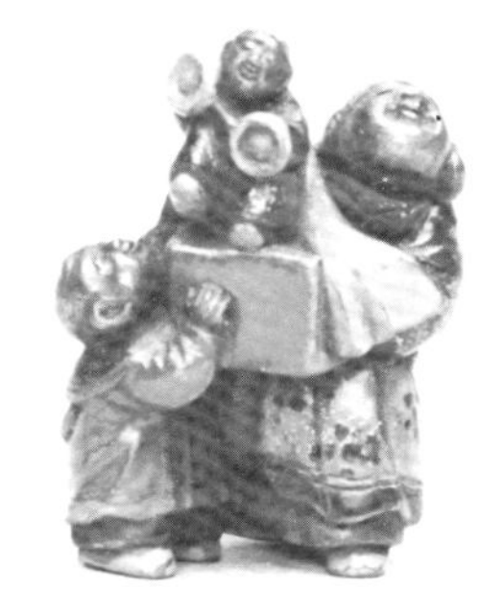

On a stage strapped to his waist, a puppeteer amuses a boy by making a puppet dance. This piece is lacquered in red, green and yellow.

Wood and lacquer. 19th-20th c. Katabori. 4.5 cm. E26985

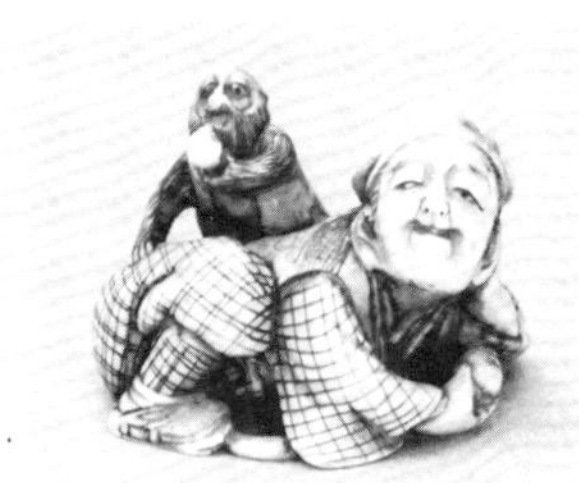

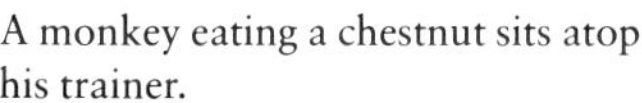

A monkey eating a chestnut sits atop his trainer.

Ivory. late 19th-20th c. Katabori. 3.0 cm. E27000

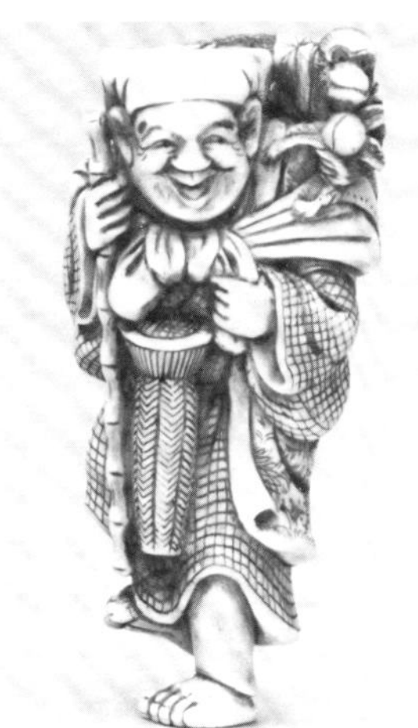

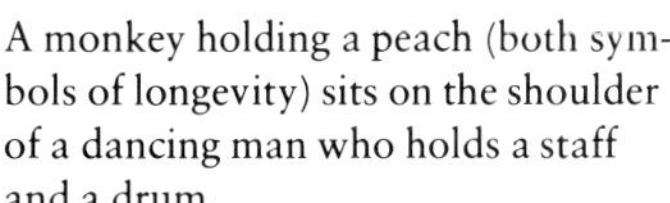

A monkey holding a peach (both symbols of longevity) sits on the shoulder of a dancing man who holds a staff and a drum.

Ivory. Yoshitomo. 1800-1830. Katabori. 6.4 cm. E27050

Dancers and Musicians

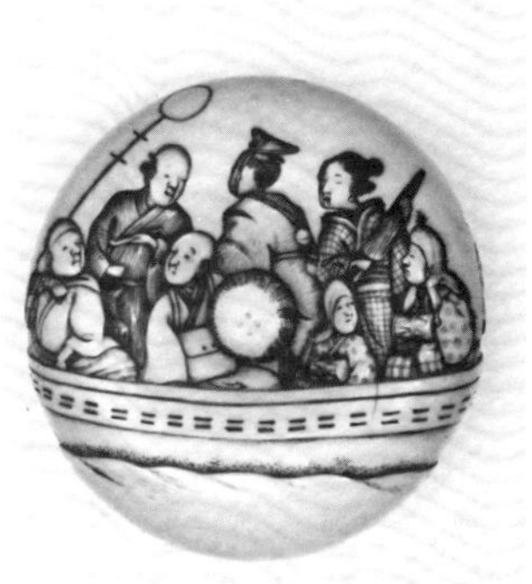

Seven people, including a chonin (tradesman) couple, a Shinto priest, a Buddhist monk and three entertainers (one leader, two young acrobats), travel to Kyoto on a ferryboat. The boatman (who can be seen from the side only) wears a robe with the word "Miyako" (now the city of Kyoto) on it. On the back of this piece is a Shinto shrine, perhaps the destination of the travelers.

Ivory. Moritoshi (Kosai). 1854-1911. Manju. 5.4 cm. E23058

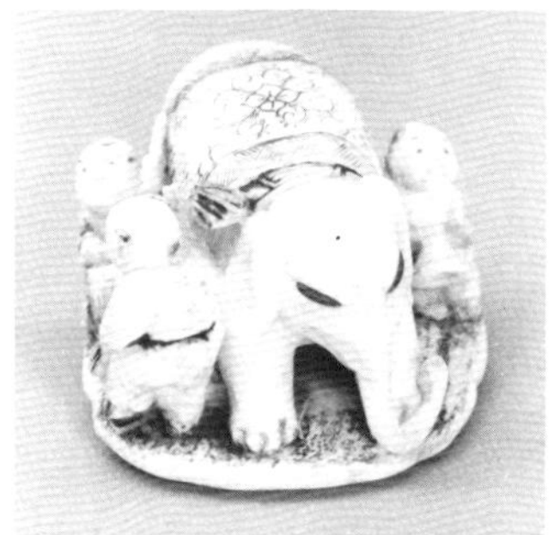

Perhaps in a festival performance, a dancer and two musicians stand beside an elephant (symbol of wisdom).

Ivory, inlays. Nagai Rantei Seiyo, unrecorded artist. 19th-20th c. Katabori. 4.5 cm. E26707

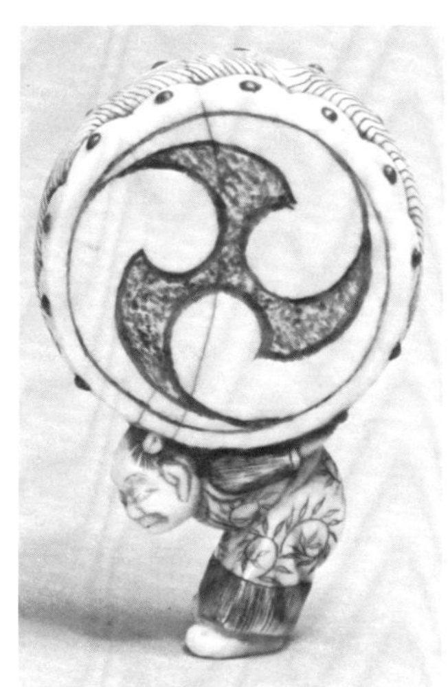

This man carrying a large drum may represent the day of grievance (fifth day of the eighth month) which H. L. Joly describes as a tradition originating in China in which people could beat on a giant drum (decorated with the three-comma mitsu tomoe design) and present petitions to government officials.

Ivory, inlays. 19th-20th c. Katabori. 4.3 cm. E26871

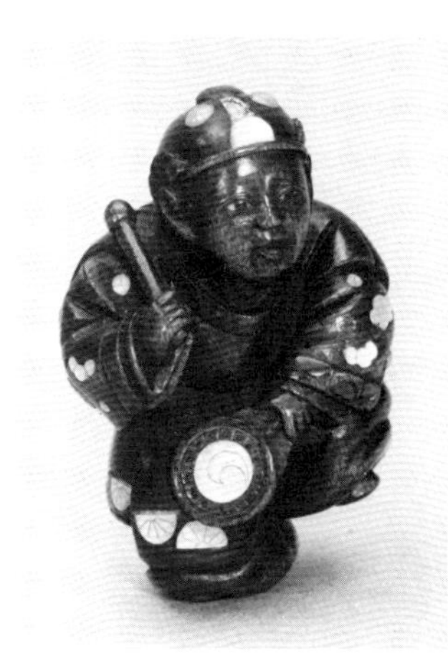

Inlay work highlights this carving of a dancing musician.

Wood with coral, pewter, mother-of-pearl inlays. Hirotada. mid-19th c. Katabori. 4.5 cm. E26977

A drummer

Wood and lacquer. early 19th c. Katabori. 5.3 cm. E26994

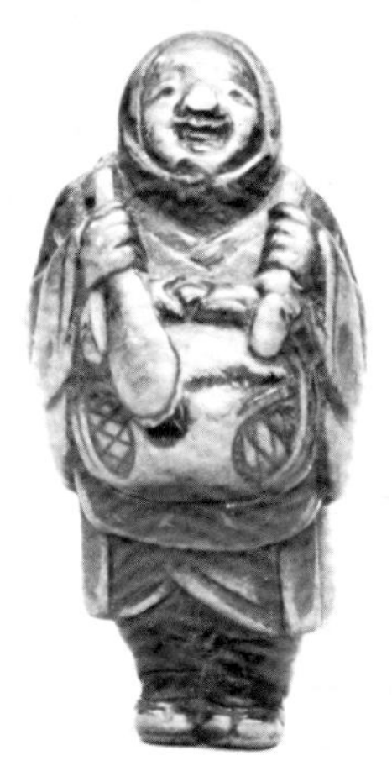

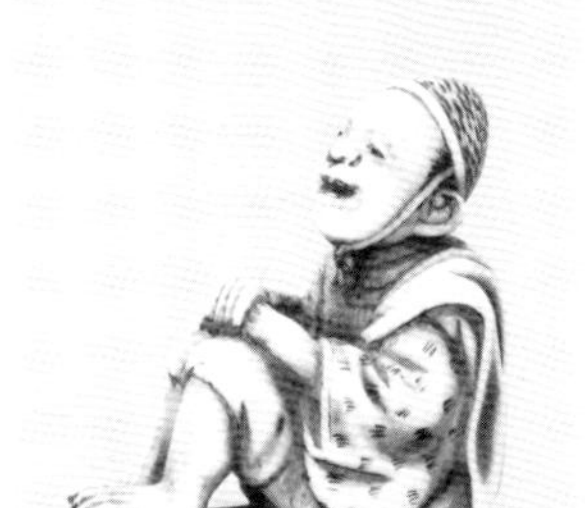

A seated festival dancer

Ivory. Tomochika III. late 19th c. Katabori. 3.6 cm. E27095

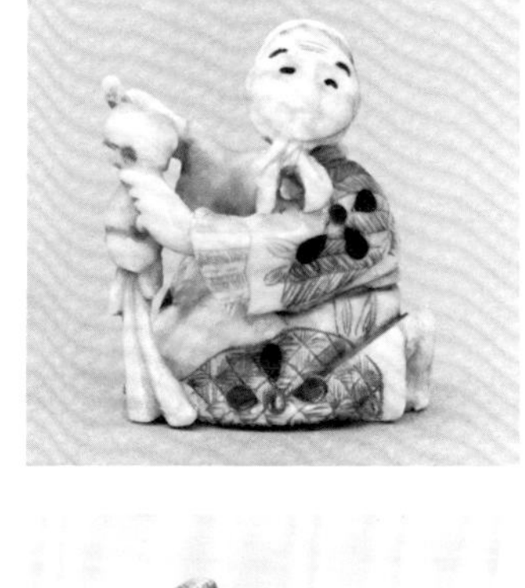

This netsuke depicts a kneeling man playing two gongs.

Ivory with colored inlays. mid 20th c. Katabori. 3.5 cm. E36989

A horn player

Brass. 19th c. Katabori. 5.5 cm. E27019

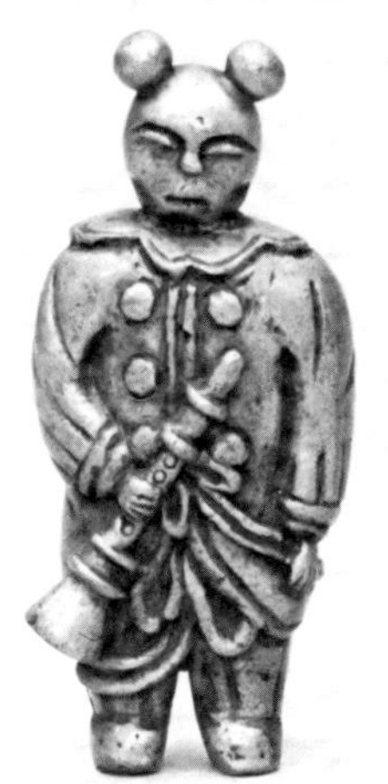

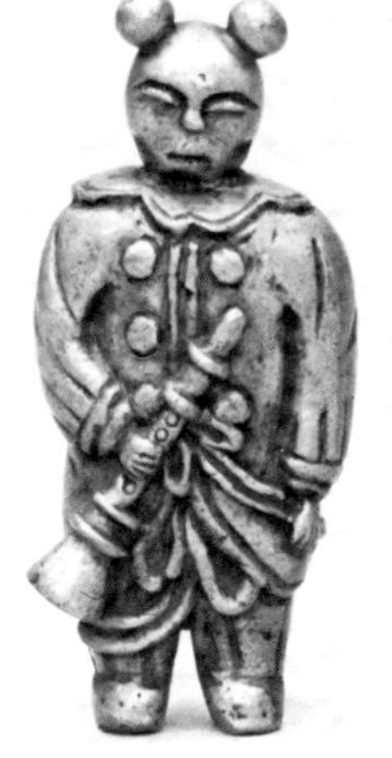

Folk Dancers

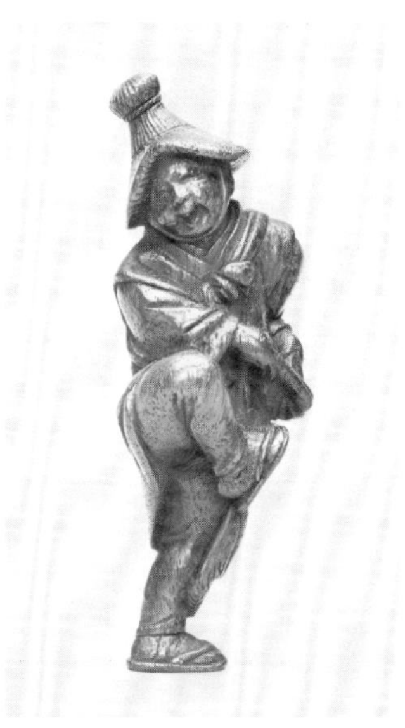

A farmer dances and plays wood blocks. He is probably dancing the traditional peasant dance for Bon, the annual festival of the dead.

Wood. early 19th c. Katabori. 9.3 cm. E26946

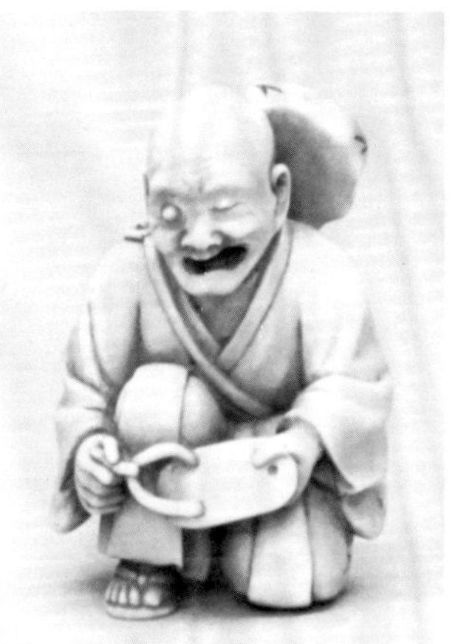

A blind musician kneels on one knee to examine his broken sandal. His instrument (probably a biwa), protected by a sack, is strapped to his back.

Ivory. 19th c. Katabori. 4.3 cm. E27093

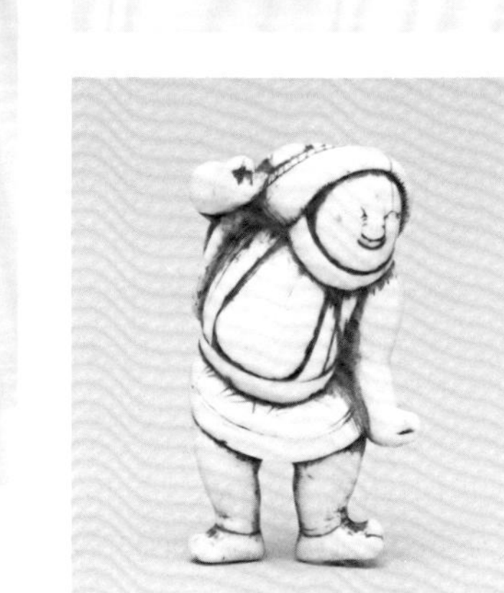

A peasant dancer

Ivory. 19th c. Katabori. 5.5 cm. E27048

Lion Dancers The lion dance takes place both in the Noh theatre and as a street dance during the New Year festival. The main dancer wears a lion mask with a cloth attached to cover his body. Some of the lion dancers are part of the Manzai performances.

This sleeping dancer's mask is leaning against his back.

Ivory. Masatoshi. late 19th c. Katabori. 3.0 cm. E4486

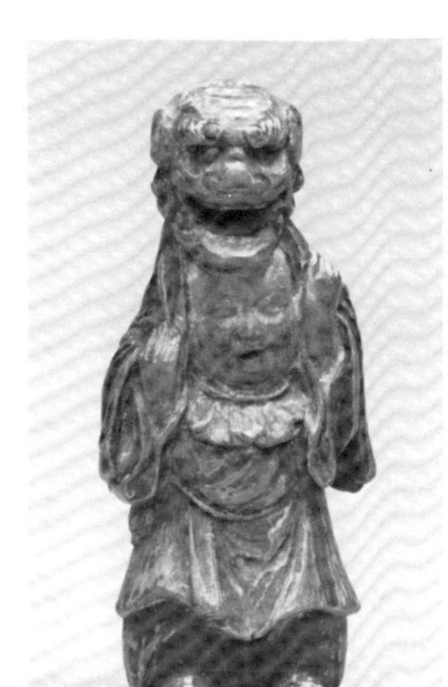

A dancer holds a lion mask over his head.

Painted cypress. 19th c. Katabori. 7.6 cm. E26952

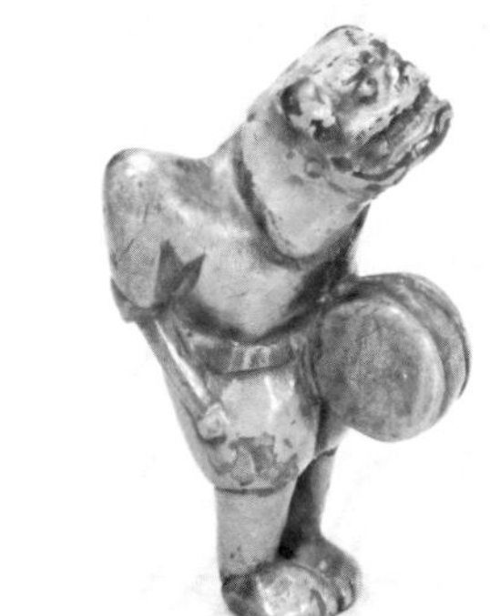

An actor wearing the lion mask beats on a drum which hangs from his waist. His pants and mask are red.

Wood and lacquer. 19th c. Katabori. 5.0 cm. E26968

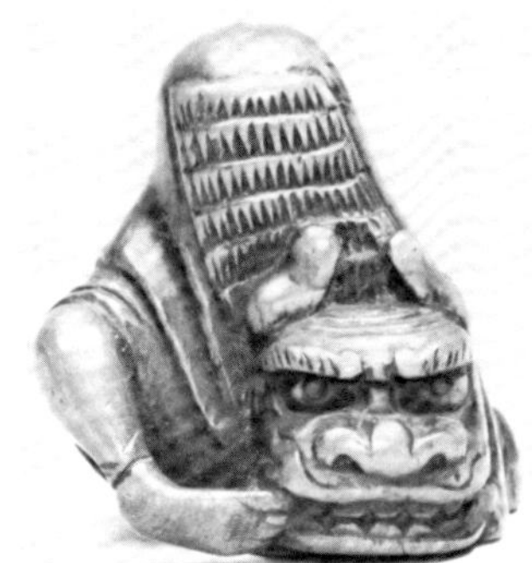

A lion dancer manipulates his mask so that it bites his foot.

Boxwood. 19th c. Katabori. 4.2 cm. E27007

Manzai Performers Manzai is a dance performed by wandering dancers or mummers at the New Year. "Manzai" is a salute meaning "10,000 years," or "long life". Masks of the lion (Shishimai), Hyottoko and Okame are popular in Manzai performances.

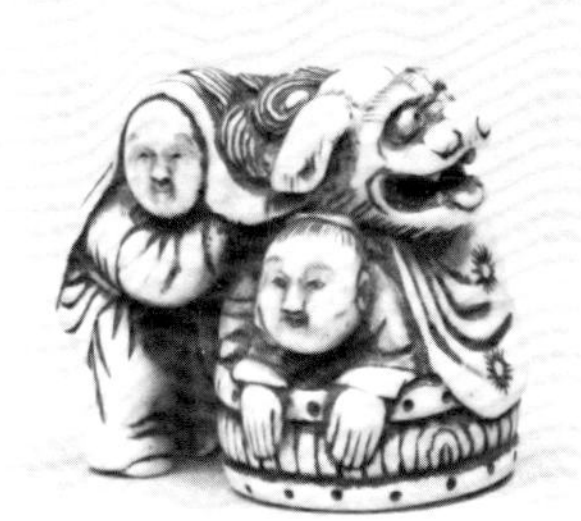

A lion mask is draped over these two Manzai entertainers.

Ivory. 19th c. Katabori. 3.2 cm. E26777

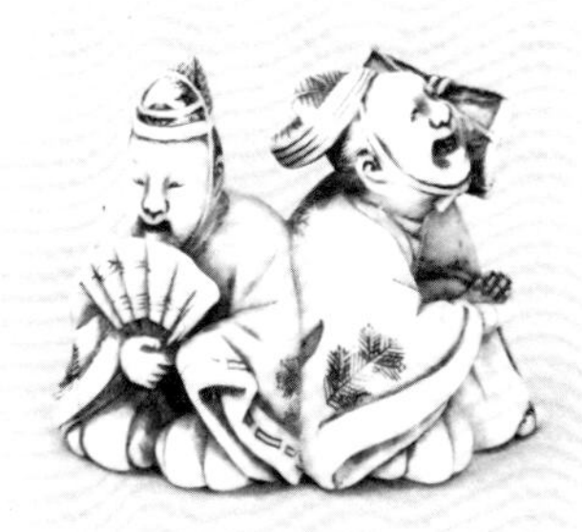

Two Manzai performers wear robes decorated with evergreens, a symbol of longevity.

Ivory. Tomochika I. 1800-1873. Katabori. 3.0 cm. E27084

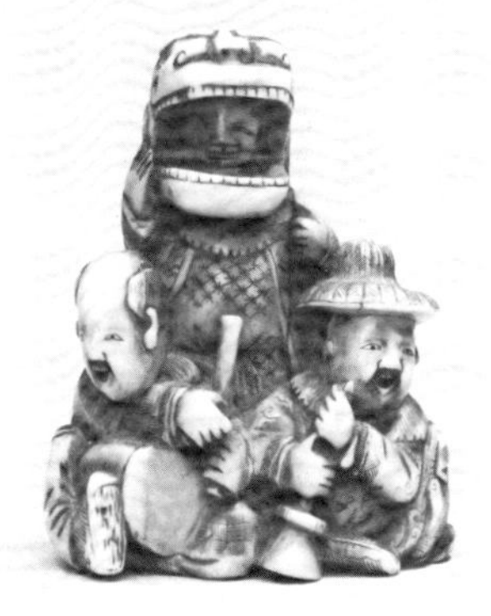

While standing between two other Manzai performers, a lion dancer peers out from the mouth of his lion mask.

Ivory. Harushige. late 19th-20th c. Katabori. 5.5 cm. E27113

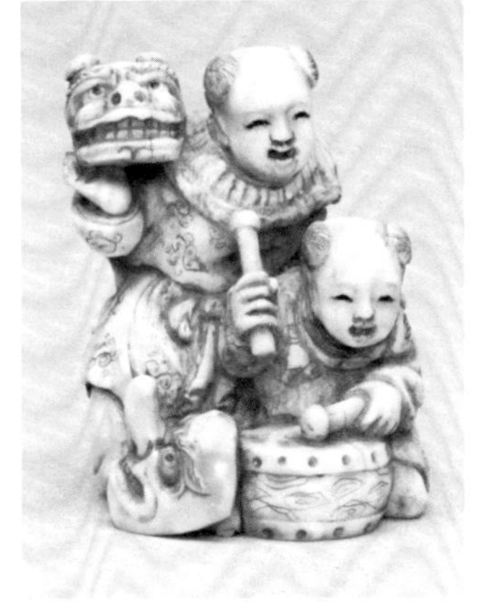

Standing behind a drummer and a mask of the long-nosed god Saruta Hiko No Mikoto, a Manzai dancer holds up his lion mask.

Ivory. Hoichi, unrecorded artist. 19th c. Katabori. 4.3 cm. E27114

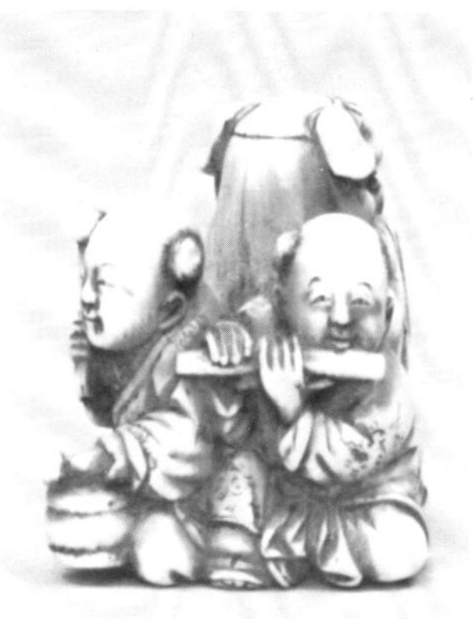

A masked lion dancer stands with his back to two other Manzai performers.

Ivory. 19th-20th c. Katabori. 3.8 cm. E27145

Story Teller

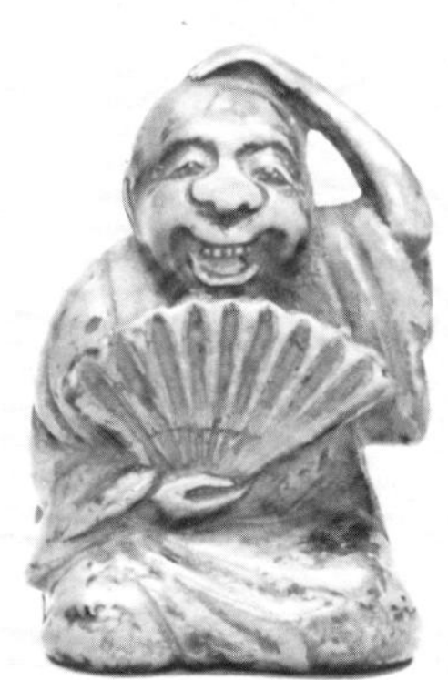
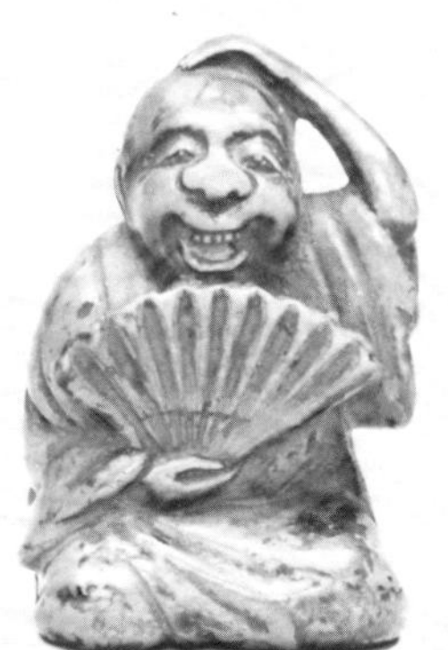

A poor person could supplement his income by going to wealthy households and reciting folk tales and legends. At the end of his stories, he would spread out his fan in hopes of receiving money.

Lacquered wood. 19th c. Katabori. 4.3 cm. E27078

Entertainment: Actors The Noh and Kabuki drama make up the two main branches of traditional theatre in Japan. Noh plays are an ancient formal and aristocratic drama, consisting of a combination of recited poetry and formal dance performed by masked male performers. Arthur Waley (see Bibliography) points out that the origin of the word "Noh" is a Chinese character meaning "to be able". It implies, then, an exhibition of talent. Kyogen (wild words) are comic interludes staged during breaks in the day long Noh performances. Kabuki (from Kabuku, "to deviate") is the popular theater of Japan and is filled with elaborate scenery and stunts as well as poetry and dance. As in the Noh theatre, Kabuki plays were performed exclusively by men, and both Noh and Kabuki dramas are based on legends and historical events.

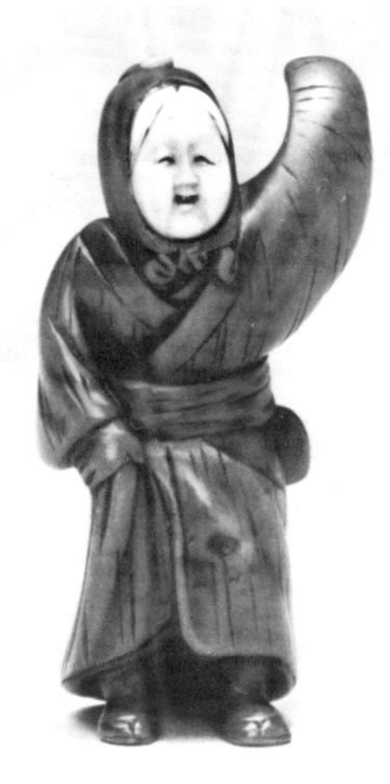

This dancer wearing an Okame mask is also wearing a pouch with a pearl ojime and ivory manju netsuke (not visible in photo).

Boxwood with ivory, coral and pearl inlays. late 18th-19th c. Katabori. 5.8 cm. E26935

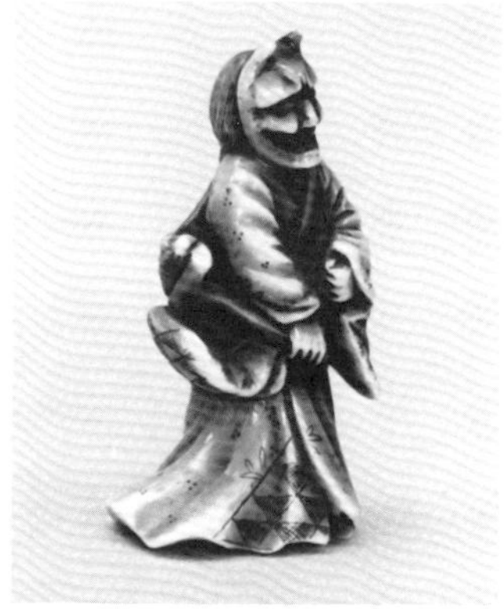

An actor in a demon mask

Ivory. late 19th-20th c. Katabori. 4.3 cm. E27018

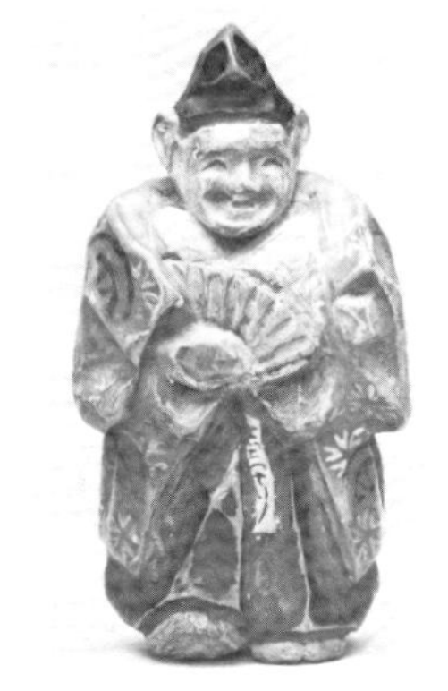

This masked Noh actor wears a black cap, blue pants and red robe with blue and white decorations. In *Collectors' Netsuke* R. Bushell (see Bibliography) discusses this type of painted wood carving. Carved in the style of Toen, it is known as a Nara ningyo (souvenir doll from the city of Nara). The style of carving, called ittobori (one-knife), can be recognized by its angular lines.

Painted wood. illegible signature. late 19th c. Katabori. 5.9 cm. E27021

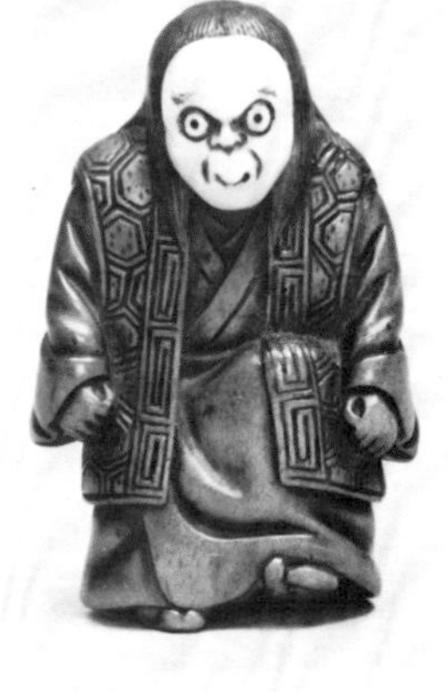

An actor wears a monkey mask.

Wood and ivory. Hojitsu. 1800-1872. Katabori. 4.6 cm. E27022

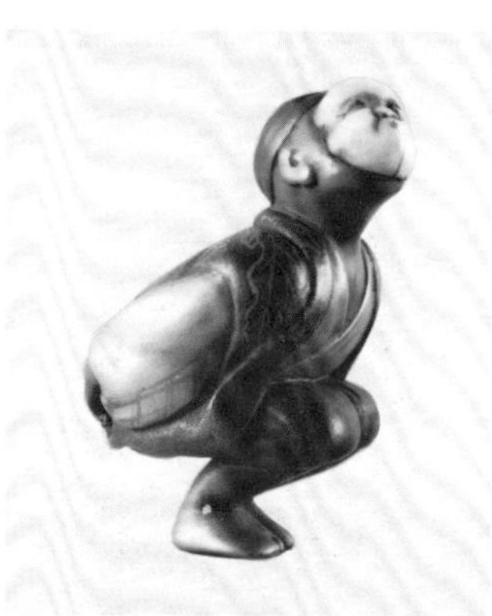

This actor wearing an ivory Hyottoko mask squats in an awkward position, but the piece balances perfectly when set down on a flat surface. The actor wears a gold shirt, black and gold vest decorated with a gold turnip, black pants, gold boots and a green hat.

Lacquered wood and ivory. 19th c. Katabori. 4.0 cm. E27039

This carving painted red, blue, green and white depicts a masked Noh actor holding a leaf fan.

Painted cypress wood. Ikko III. early 19th c. Katabori. 5.5 cm. E27040

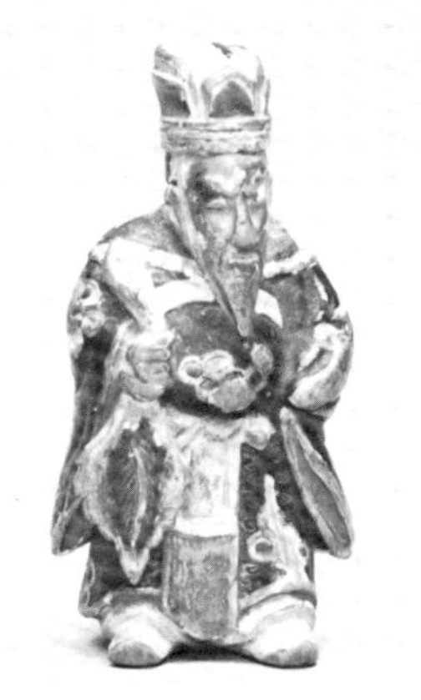

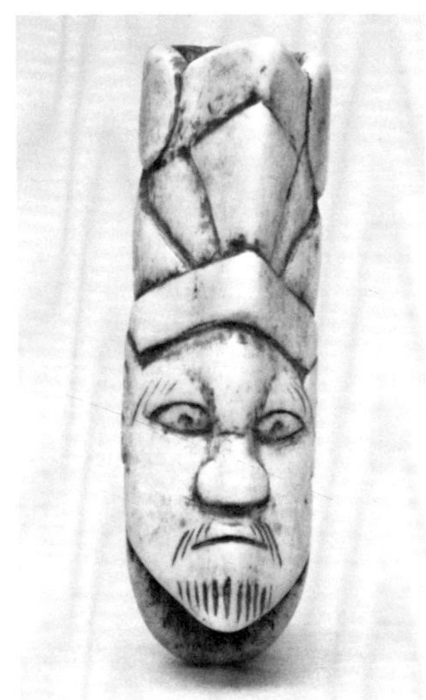

The head and helmet of a fierce warrior are simply carved on a hollow piece of bone.

Bone. late 18th c. Katabori. 5.9 cm. E26940

In this Nara ningyo piece the colorfully painted Noh actor wears the red mask and wig of the drunken Shojo character.

Painted wood. mid-19th c. Katabori. 5.0 cm. E27046

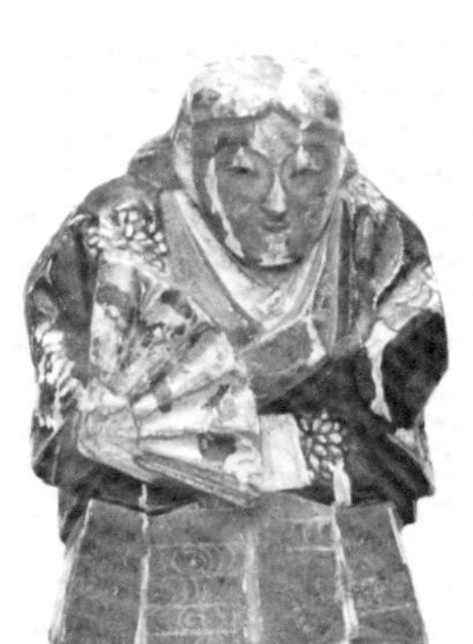

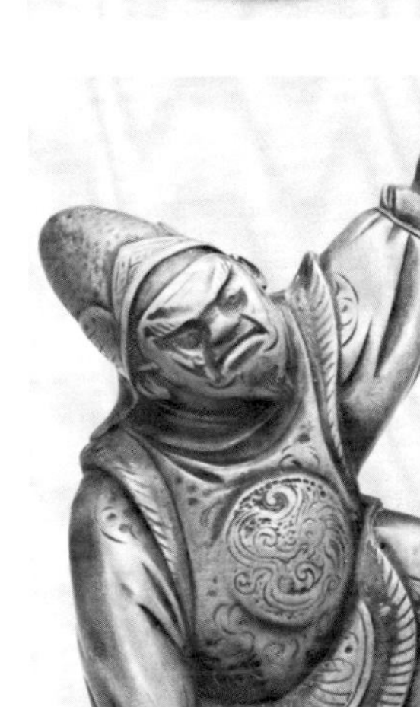

An actor playing an angry warrior.

Painted wood. early 19th c. Katabori. 9.8 cm. E26948

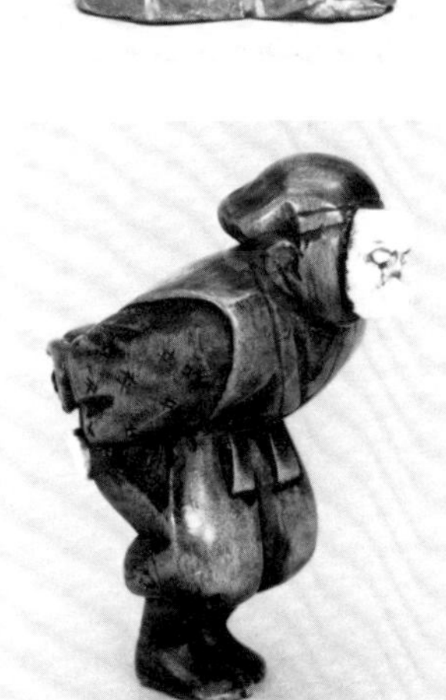

An actor wears a Hyottoko mask.

Wood and ivory. mid 18th-19th c. Katabori. 5.1 cm. E27071

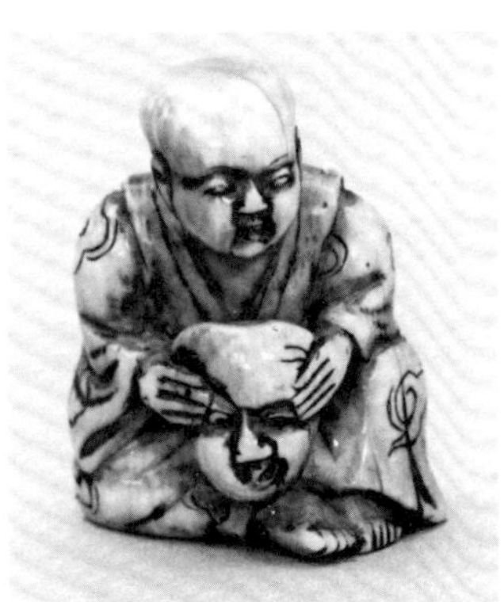

This actor holds a Hyottoko mask.

Ivory. 19th c. Katabori. 4.0 cm. E27150

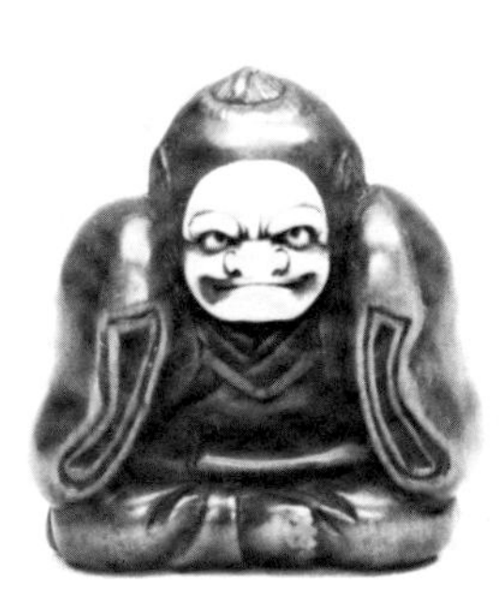

An actor wears a Beshimi mask.

Wood and ivory. Houn. 1800-1834. Katabori. 3.3 cm. E26984

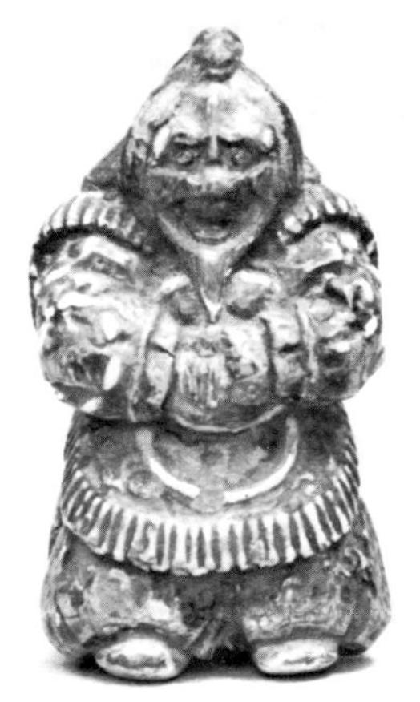

An actor-dancer wears an elaborate costume decorated in blue, green and white.

Painted wood. 19th c. Katabori. 5.1 cm. E27029

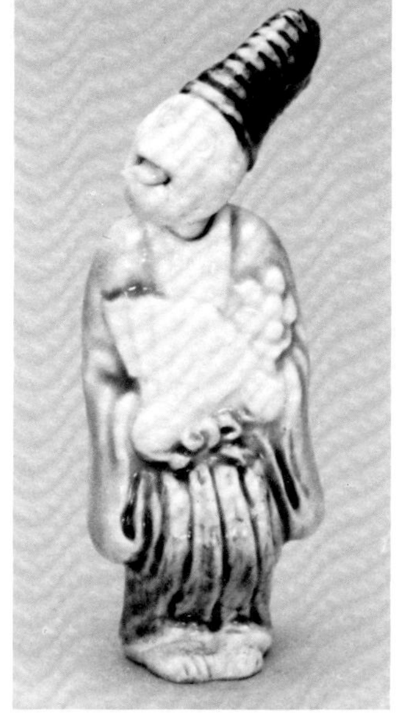

This monkey-faced Sambaso dancer has a movable head which slides up and down from the neck, and a tongue which goes in and out. He wears a dark brown hat, light blue jacket and light brown pants.

Porcelain. 19th c. Katabori. 7.2 cm. E4668

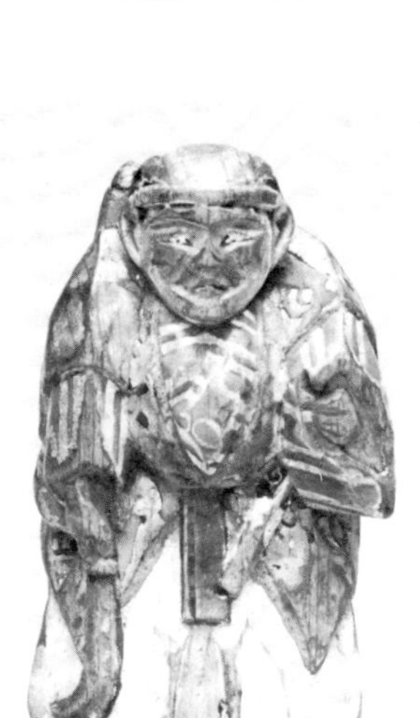

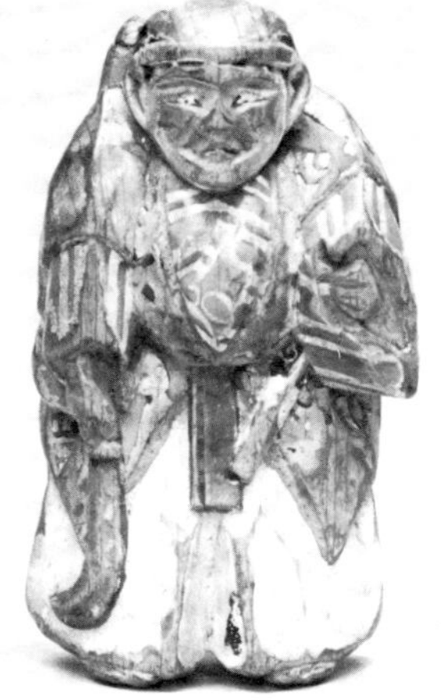

This Nara ningyo type carving depicts an elaborately dressed entertainer in red and white striped shirt, a green robe and white pants.

Painted wood. early 19th c. Katabori. 5.5 cm. E27035

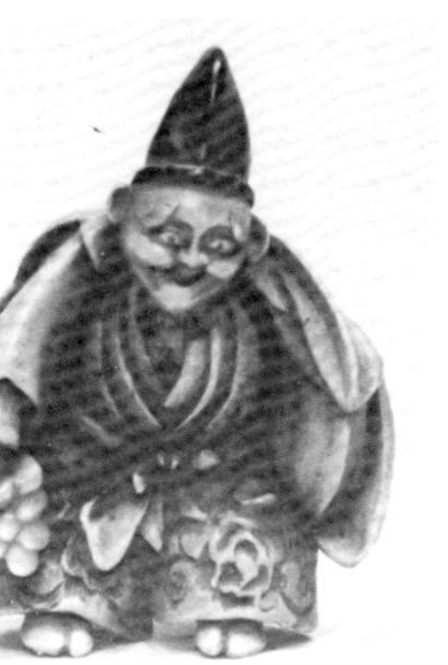

The natural wood carving of a Sambaso dancer has a variety of other materials both inlaid and attached, including a nacre rattle, a dark wood cap with ivory inlaid circles, ivory feet and an ivory inlaid beak on the crane design of the dancer's jacket. The inlaid ivory signature plaque reads Shibayama, the name of the foremost inlay artist, whose name became a generic term for this style of inlay work.

Wood, ivory, nacre. Shibayama. early 19th c. Katabori. 4.5 cm. E27089

Sambaso Dancers The Sambaso dance precedes a drama to appease the gods so that any errors in the performance will be forgiven. The Sambaso is supposed to have originated in the 9th century as a religious dance intended to thwart an earthquake. The dancers wear high hats and carry fans and rattles.

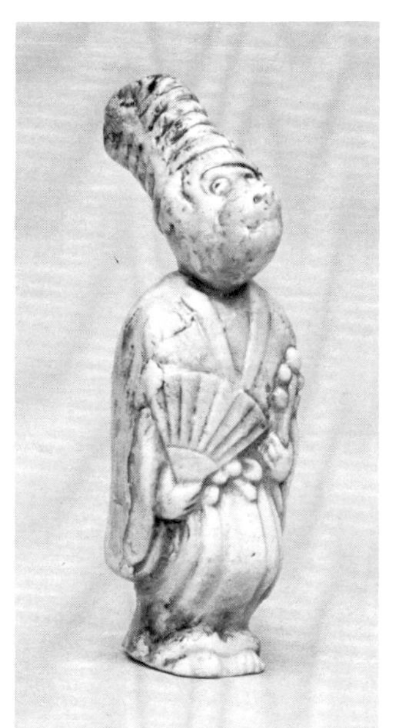

A cream colored Sambaso dancer has a monkey's face.

Porcelain. late 18th-19th c. Katabori. 5.7 cm. E4667

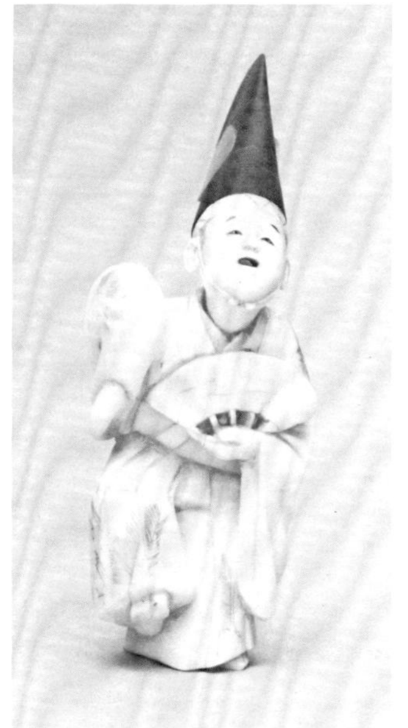

The red tongue of an ivory Sambaso dancer moves in and out of his mouth. The hat is of wood with red circle inlays.

Ivory, wood. Nobuyasu (Shinan), unrecorded artist. late 19th-20th c. Katabori. 7.6 cm. E32880

Masks

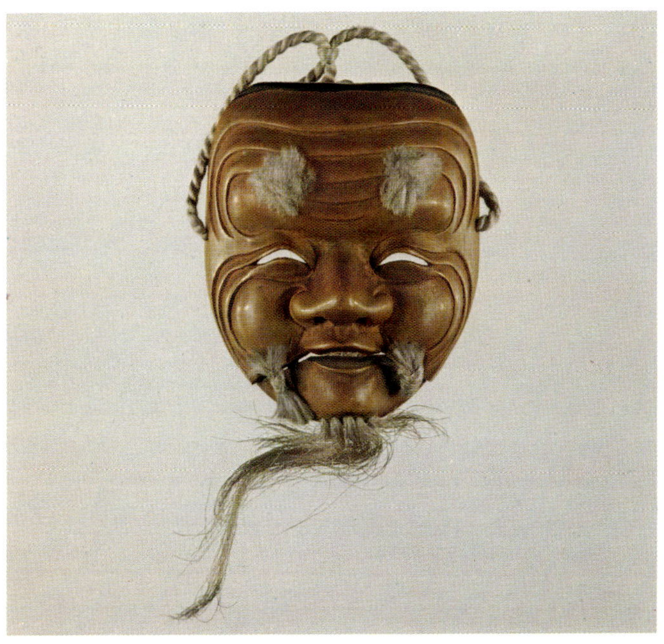

Masks have been worn in Japanese dance-dramas for over a thousand years beginning with Gigaku religious dances and Bugaku dances performed at court in the 7th and 8th centuries. Noh drama developed in the 14th and 15th centuries and adapted and refined early mask forms to accommodate its restrained, elegant style of acting.

In the Tokugawa period (1603-1868) master carvers standardized and formalized Noh masks. Named masks represented an idealized person, his character, age, rank and form, and these masks can be generally categorized as Gods, Men, Women, Ghosts and Demons. The two main actors in Noh drama depend on expressive movements and shadows falling on their masks to convey emotions, which are primarily tragic. Noh drama's heavy overtones are lightened by brief, humorous plays called Kyogen, which are interspersed between Noh acts for comic relief and performed by actors who often wear ludicrous masks.

Netsuke masks are usually replicas of those worn in the Noh and Kyogen drama; masks are rarely worn in

Kabuki performances, as Kabuki actors rely on make-up for characterizations. An extraordinary number of mask netsuke were produced, many of which merely represent comic faces or portraits, partly because many apprentice netsuke carvers learned to carve by making masks. In addition, master mask carvers may have made duplicates of their work in netsuke, or skilled carvers may have created facsimiles of outstanding masks.

Animal Masks Kyogen actors did not always wear masks, but masks were a necessity for portraying animals in the comic pieces of the Noh theatre.

Lion Masks Shishi-guchi is the name for lion masks worn in Noh drama, which are identical to those worn in shishimai, lion dances. Shishimai were introduced in the Gigaku dance-drama and are part of the New Year's festivals as well as the Noh theatre. In Noh however, the lion mask is worn by one actor, who stands upright; usually the lion dance is performed by two people.

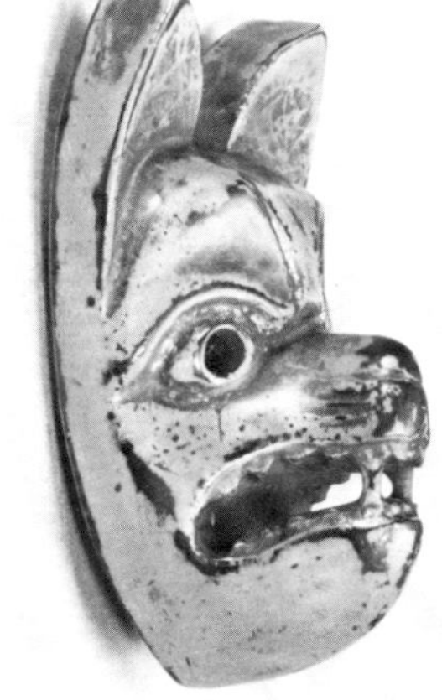

A red lacquered kitsune (fox) has black and gold trim, hollow eyes and an open mouth.

Lacquered wood. late 18th c. Katabori. 5.3 cm. E26591

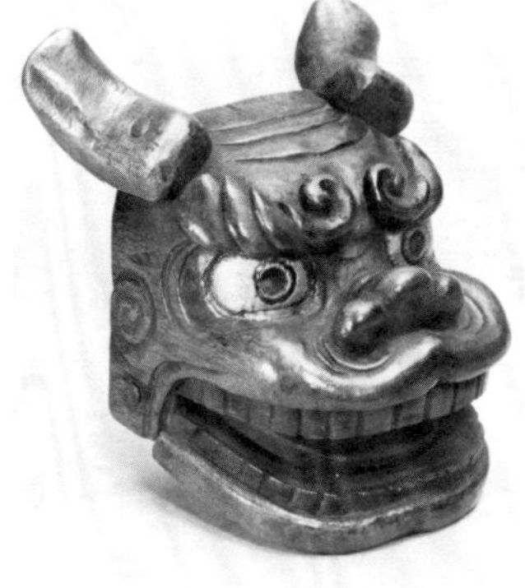

The jaw and ears of this large lion mask are movable, its eyes are gold. A metal ring served as cord fastener.

Wood and metal. 19th c. Katabori. 5.0 cm. E26585

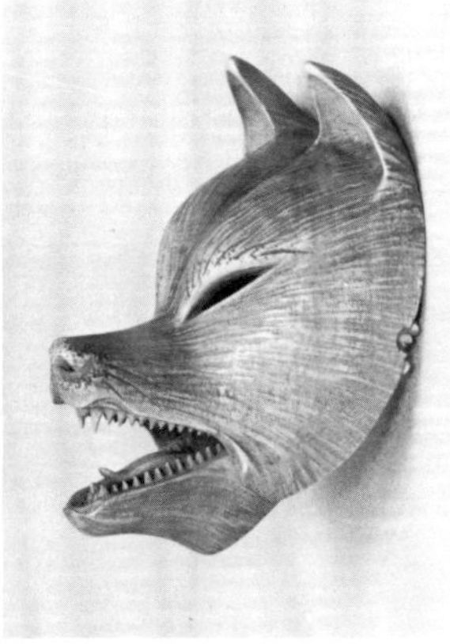

The mouth of this articulated kitsune mask opens to reveal a full set of tiny, sharp teeth and a curled red tongue.

Wood. 19th c. Katabori. 4.8 cm. E26592

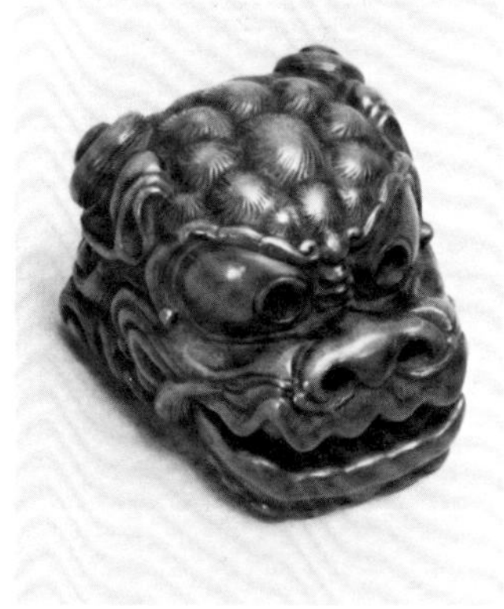

A highly-carved lion mask has an articulated jaw.

Boxwood. Minko. late 18th-19th c. Katabori. 4.0 cm. E26586

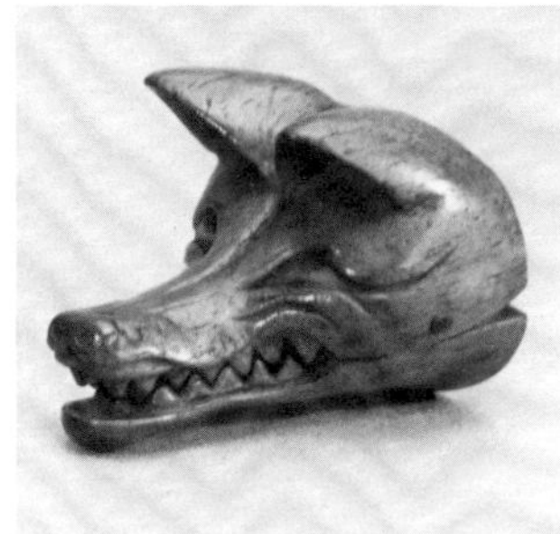

A kitsune mask with a movable jaw displays a sly grin and full set of teeth.

Wood. 19th c. Katabori. 3.3 cm. E26593

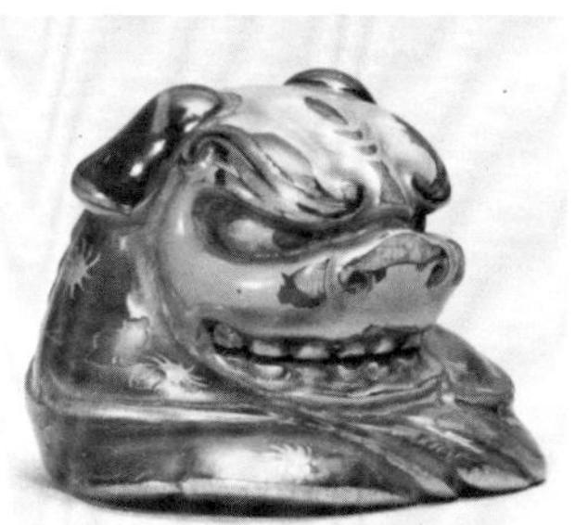

A lion rests on the cloth attached to it. Its head is red with black ears; gold designs decorate the black cloth.

Wood and lacquer. 19th c. Katabori. 3.5 cm. E26932

Beshimi Mask Beshimi means clenched mouth, or to set one's mouth firmly. The Beshimi character in the Noh theater was sometimes demonic, an aged tengu, or took the part of Emma, the King of Hell.

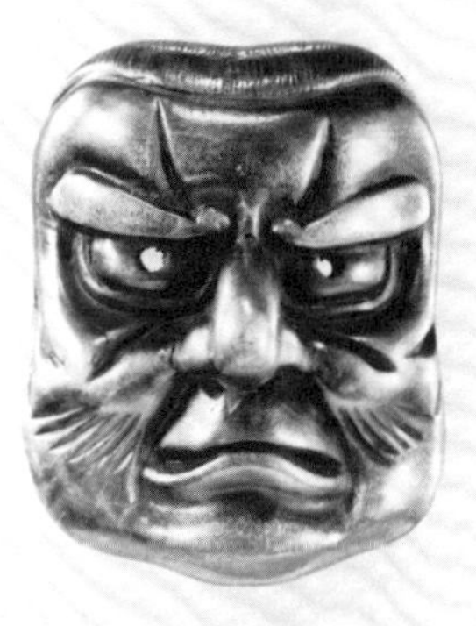

A Beshimi mask expresses fierce determination.

Boxwood, ivory signature plaque. Ikko. early 19th c. Katabori. 4.5 cm. E26599

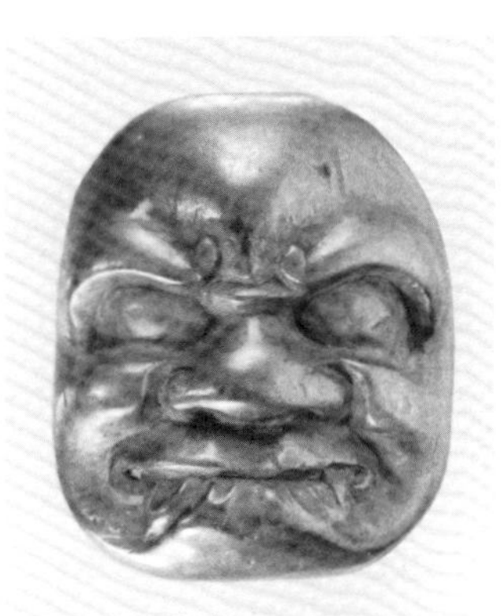

A grim Beshimi mask, mouth firmly set

Wood. 18th c. Katabori. 4.4 cm. E29145

Hannya Masks The Noh character Hannya is the embodiment of a jealous female's rage and vituperation. Masks of the demon Hannya snarl with hate and outrage.

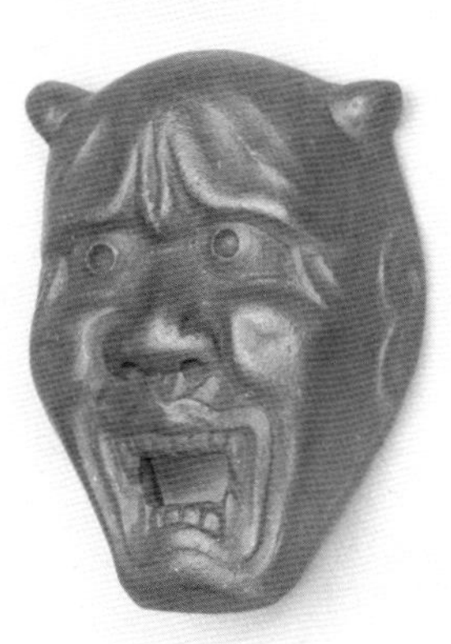

A Hannya mask howls with fury.

Ceramic. 19th c. Katabori. 4.7 cm. E26601

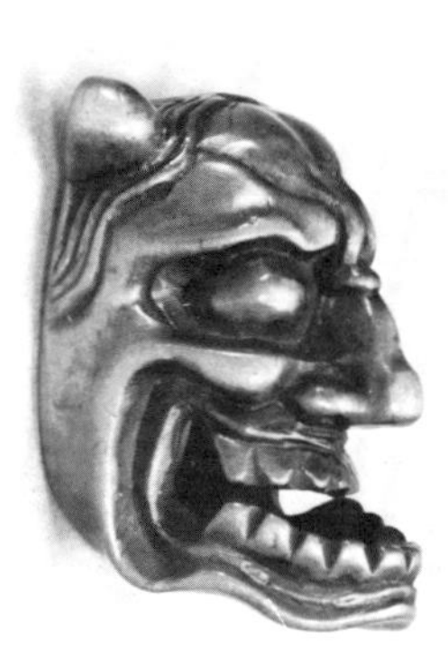

Hannya mask with incipient horns, long lower jaw

Wood. 19th c. Katabori. 3.8 cm. E26600

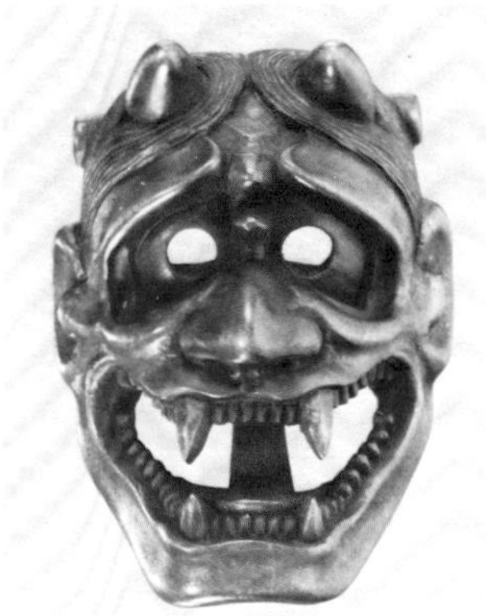

A hollow-eyed Hannya mask has prominent fangs.

Wood. Chikusai. Katabori. 4.2 cm. E26614

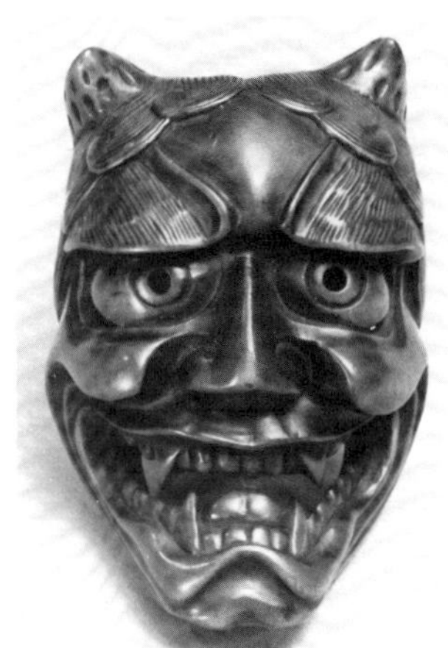

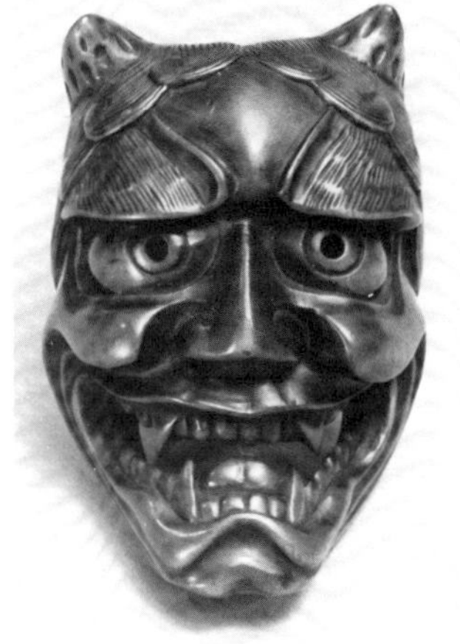

The characteristic open mouth on this Hannya mask exposes a full set of teeth and fangs.

Wood. early 19th c. Katabori. 6.5 cm. E26625

Hyottoko Mask Hyottoko is a comical character in Kyogen who has a twisted, puckered mouth and often one squinting and one bulging eye.

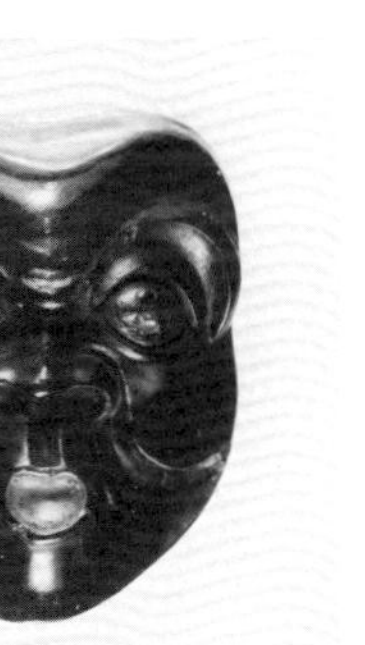

A black Hyottoko mask with red mouth

Lacquered wood. late 18th-19th c. Katabori. 4.3 cm. E3453

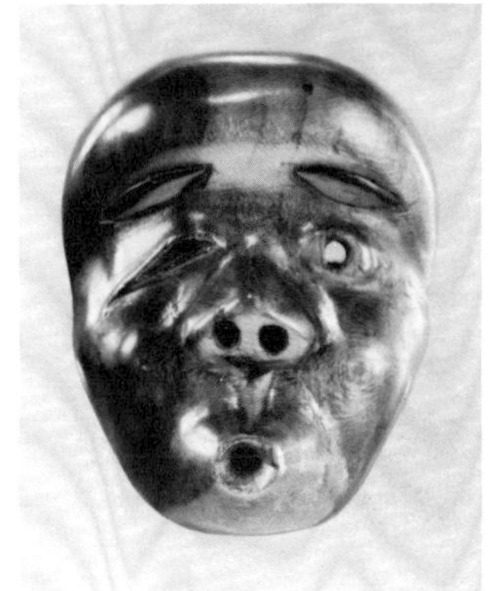

A light brown wood Hyottoko mask with dark wood inlaid eyebrows.

Wood. late 18th-19th c. Katabori. 5.2 cm. E26606

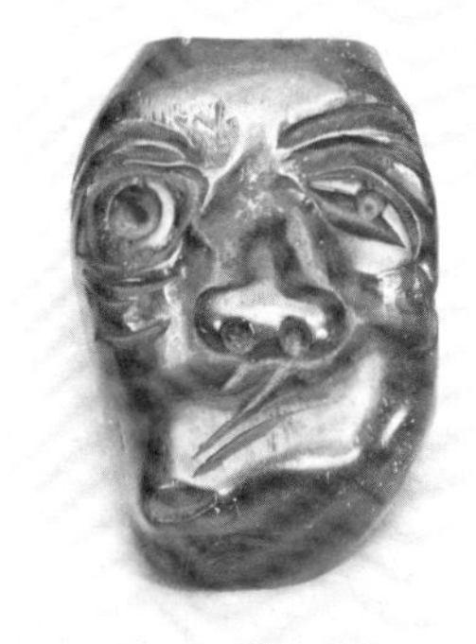

The mouth of this Hyottoko mask twists absurdly low to the extreme right.

Wood. late 18th-19th c. Katabori. 4.7 cm. E26609

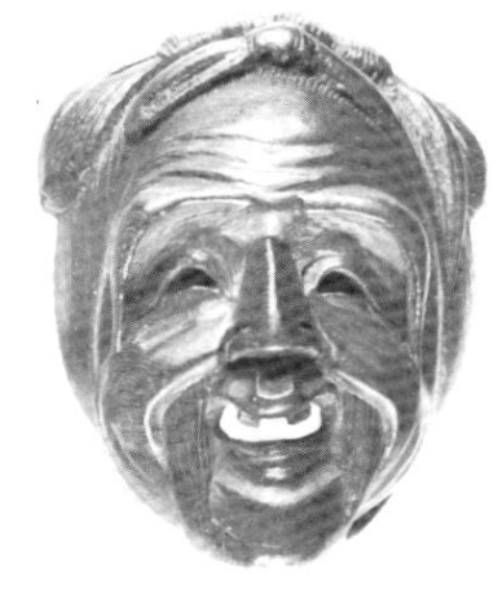

A smiling, wrinkled Jo mask

Boxwood. Deme, family name. before 1800. Katabori. 3.5 cm. E26618

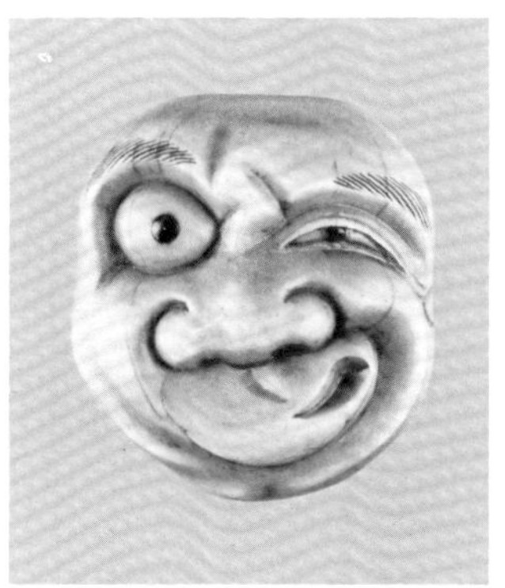

A Hyottoko mask with mouth twisted to the left

Ivory, inlaid eyes. 19th c. Katabori. 3.5 cm. E26617

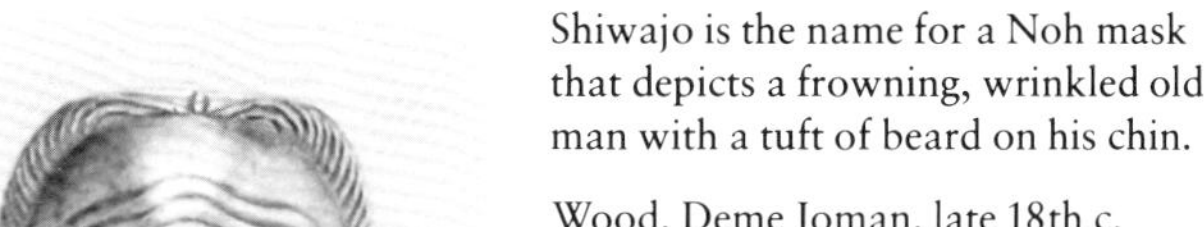

Shiwajo is the name for a Noh mask that depicts a frowning, wrinkled old man with a tuft of beard on his chin.

Wood. Deme Joman. late 18th c. Katabori. 4.0 cm. E26620

Kappa Mask A mask of the amphibious demon who snatches unsuspecting swimmers (especially children who go out too far in the water) and people on land, as well.

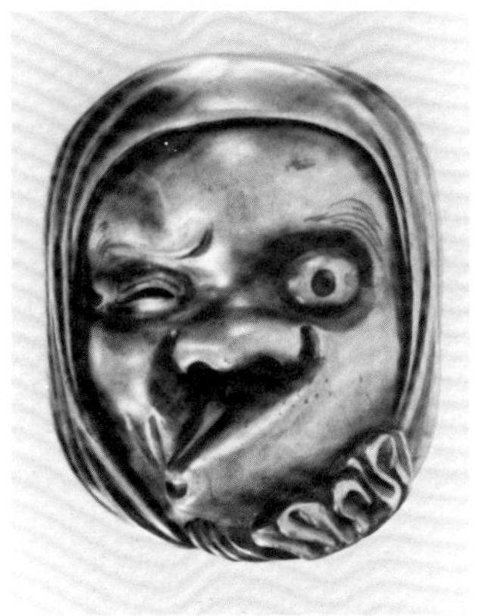

A Hyottoko mask's mouth twists to the right and the entire face is framed in cloth for added comic effect.

Wood. late 18th-19th c. Katabori. 4.5 cm. E26624

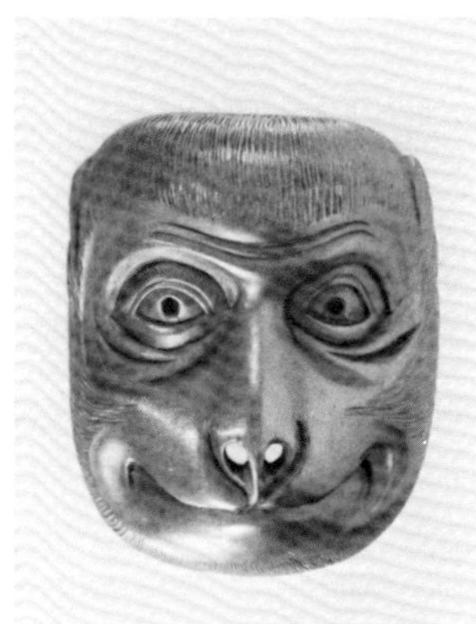

A kappa mask appears to have just swallowed someone.

Wood. 19th c. Katabori. 5.0 cm. E26607

Jo Masks Jo means old man and is the generic term for masks of old men in Noh drama. Jo masks are often used to portray woodcutters or peasants in the first act of a play, then different masks are used in the second act to portray the deities or anguished souls they really are.

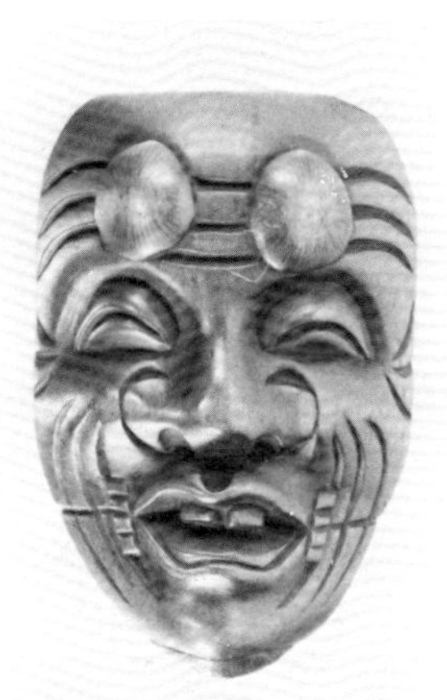

Chichi-Ni-Jo masks represent an old, smiling patriarch, similar to Okina, with an articulated jaw but fewer wrinkles and no beard.

Wood. Deme, inscription "Knife cut." early 19th c. Katabori. 5.7 cm. E24900

Mask Groups

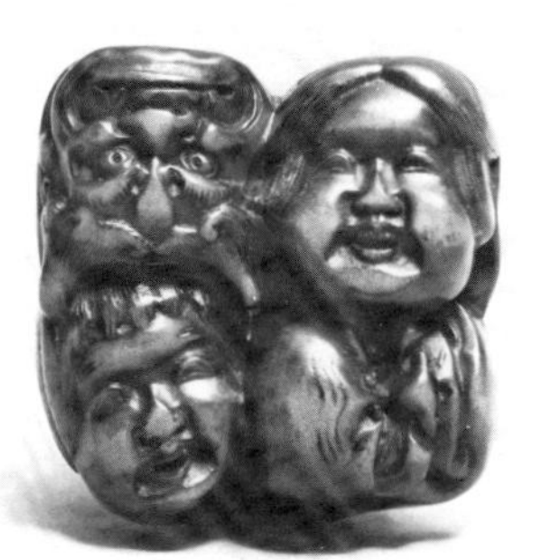

Masks of Shojo, a young woman, Beshimi and Okame rest back to back with masks of Hyottoko, Okina and a demon.

Wood. Gyokuzan. 19th c. Katabori. 4.0 cm. E26588

A group of masks is displayed on each side of this netsuke: on the himotoshi side, masks include Okame, Karasu tengu, Kitsune and a demon; on the other side are Okame, Hyottoko, Hannya, a comic mask, demon and Okina.

Resin. 19th c. Katabori.
4.5 cm. E26589

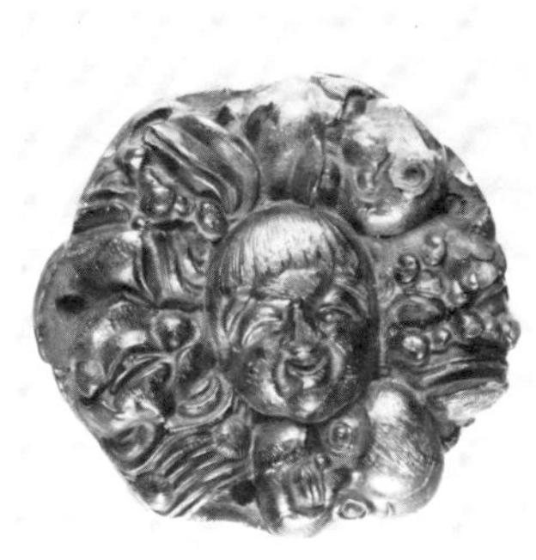

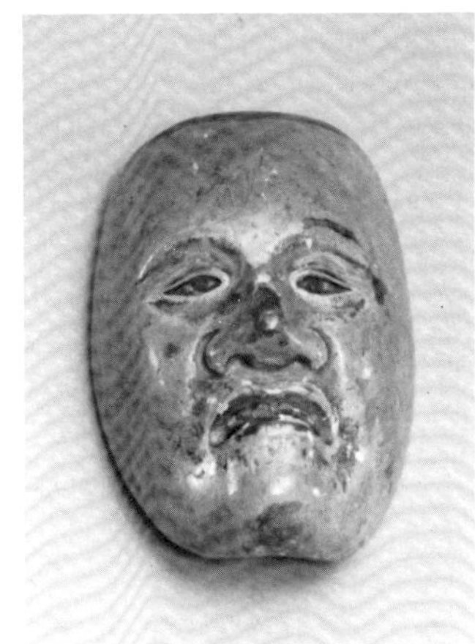

A sorrowful red-faced man

Wood, painted Deme Uman, inscription "tenka-ichi," meaning "best under heaven" a title bestowed to master craftsmen by the shogun. late 18th c. Katabori. 5.0 cm. E26603

A highly polished light brown peach pit provides the shape for Hotei's round bag. Masks of Okame and Hyottoko, comic characters, peer out of the bag.

Peach pit. Tomochika III. late 19th c.
Katabori. 3.2 cm. E26897

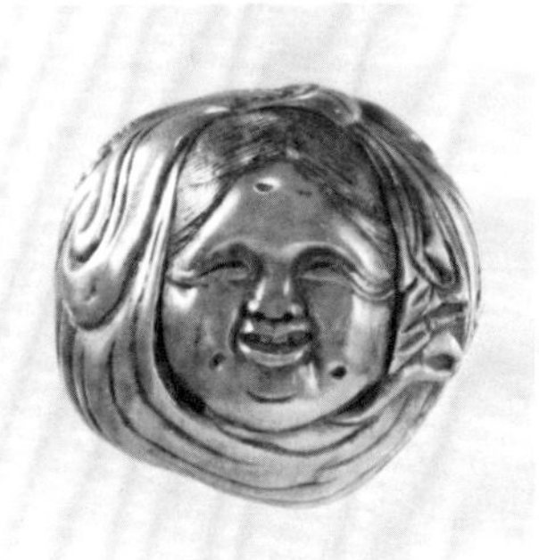

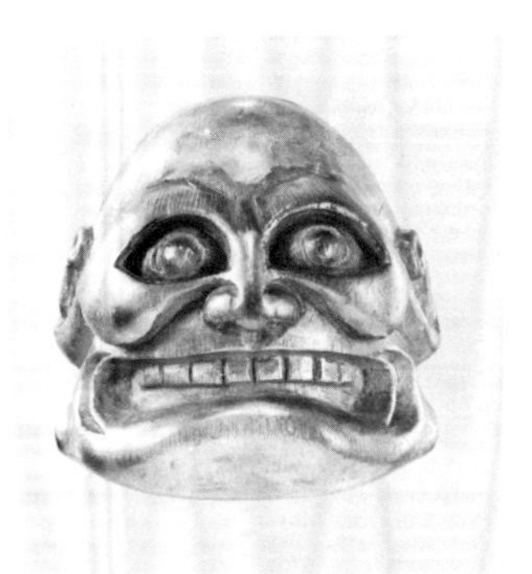

A grim-faced mask with clenched teeth

Wood. 18th c. Katabori.
4.5 cm. E26610

Non-theatrical Masks The following masks are not replicas of theatrical masks but imaginative faces invented by carvers, or possibly portraits of people.

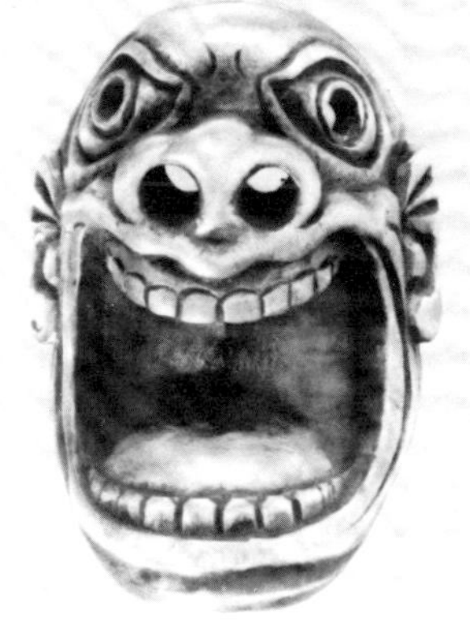

A mask with hollowed-out nostrils and a cavernous mouth

Wood. Morimitsu. early 19th c.
Katabori. 4.8 cm. E26587

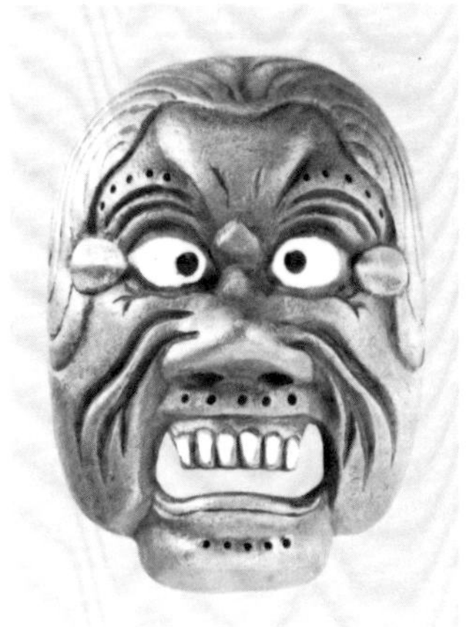

A comical cross-eyed brown ceramic mask with white eyes and teeth

Ceramic. Sekisen, unrecorded artist.
19th c. Katabori. 4.5 cm. E26615

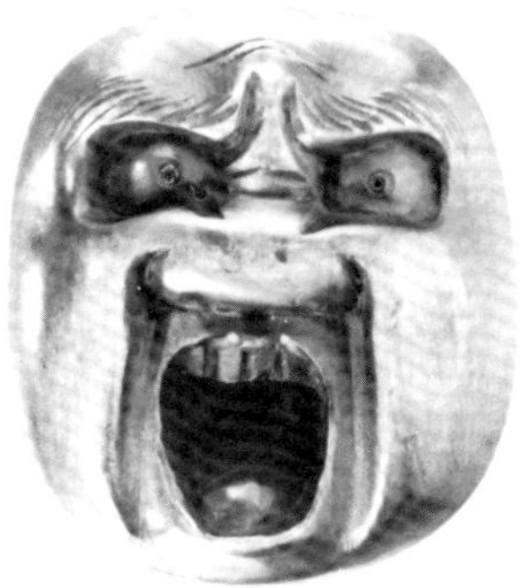

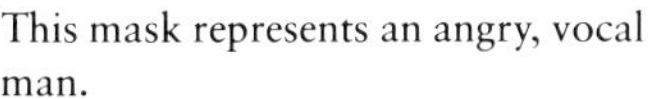

This mask represents an angry, vocal man.

Wood, bead eyes. 19th c. Katabori.
4.5 cm. E26605

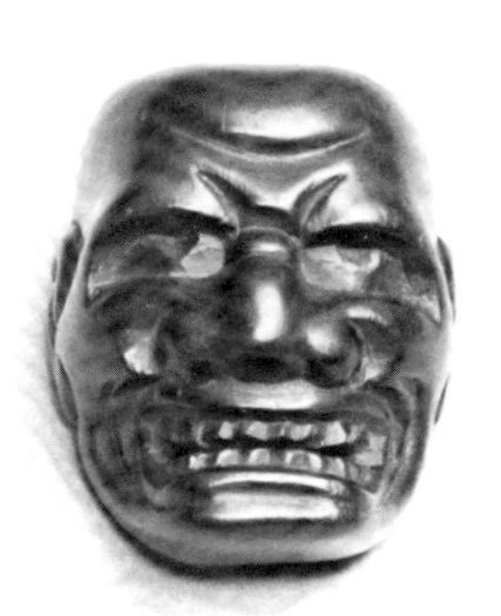

A sinister mask with bared teeth

Wood. Deme Josei. late 18th c.
Katabori. 3.3 cm. E26619

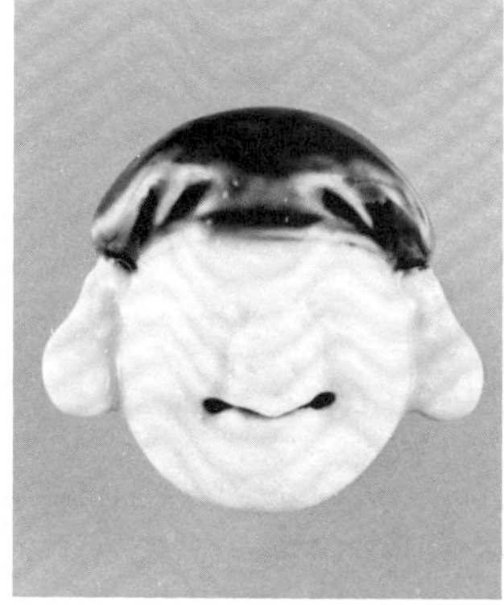

A mask of a white-faced Daikoku, god of plenty, wearing a blue cap.

Porcelain. late 18th-19th c. Katabori. 4.0 cm. E26621

A gray faced Okame mask with red lips and black hair, eyes and eyebrows

Porcelain (unpolished). 19th c. Katabori. 4.0 cm. E26598

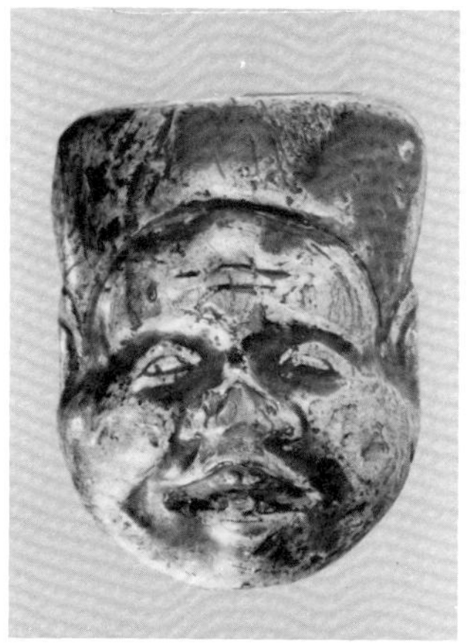

A smiling mask

Wood. 18th c. Katabori. 5.5 cm. E26626

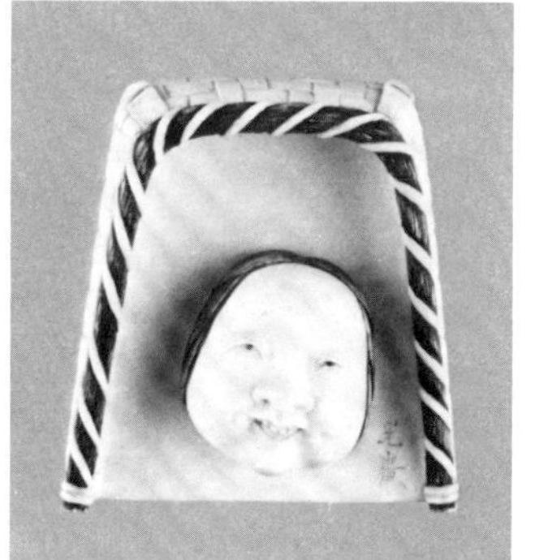

An Okame mask in a straw rice scoop

Ivory. Mitsuhiro. late 19th-20th c. Katabori. 3.6 cm. E26887

Okame Masks Noh masks of Okame express the same joyous, effervescent quality as do all representations of the goddess of mirth.

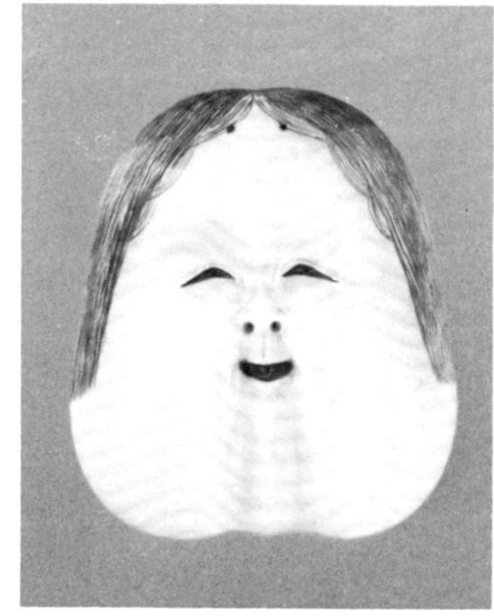

A smiling Okame mask has finely carved hair.

Ivory. Hidemasa. 1800-1830. Katabori. 3.5 cm. E26596

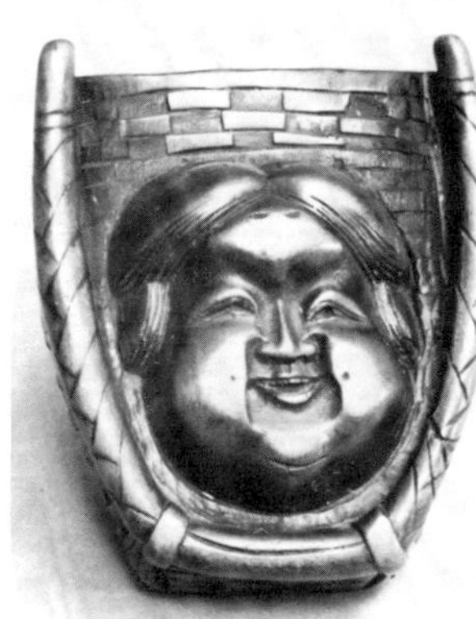

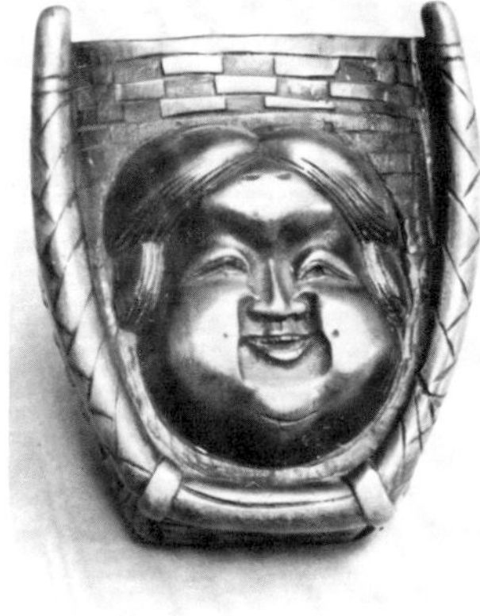

A mask of Okame rests in a winnowing basket.

Boxwood. Gyokuzan. 18th-19th c. Katabori. 4.3 cm. E26931

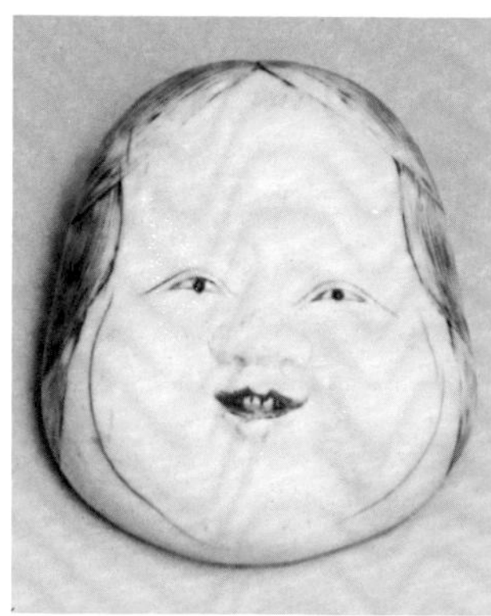

An Okame mask's cheeks bulge, its lips are painted red.

Ivory. Masamitsu. 1836-1909. Katabori. 4.5 cm. E26597

Okina Masks A mask used in Noh drama, Okina represents a happy old man. An Okina mask always has a movable jaw attached by a cord and tufts of hair on eyebrows and chin.

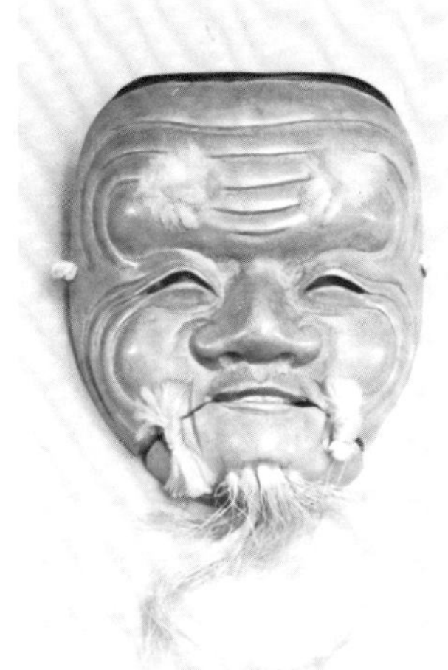

An Okina mask exudes happiness.

Wood, silk cord. early 19th c. Katabori. 5.2 cm. E26608

Oni Mask The fiendish demons, Oni, had roles in Noh plays.

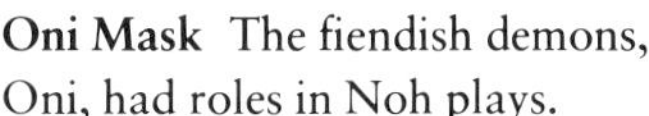

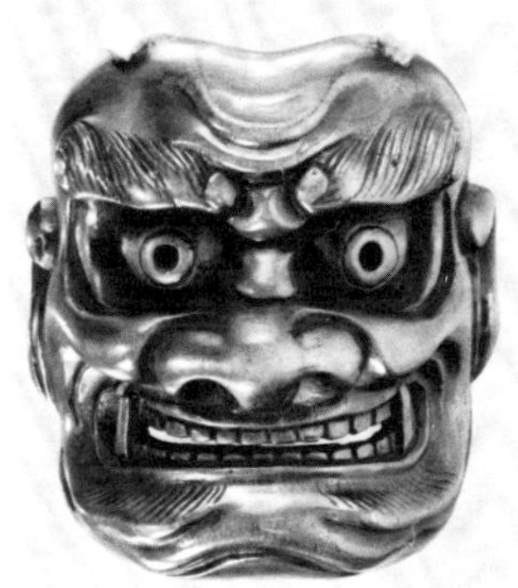

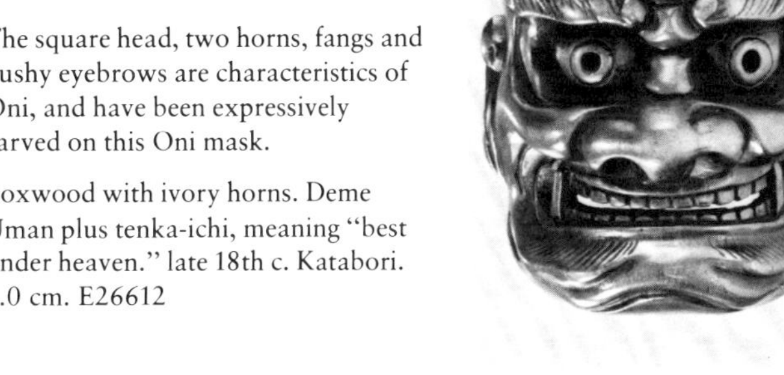

The square head, two horns, fangs and bushy eyebrows are characteristics of Oni, and have been expressively carved on this Oni mask.

Boxwood with ivory horns. Deme Uman plus tenka-ichi, meaning "best under heaven." late 18th c. Katabori. 4.0 cm. E26612

Otobide Mask The name given to the mask used to portray fierce gods, including Raiden, god of thunder. In keeping with its use for ferocious deities and supernatural beings in the Noh theatre, it has glittering, bulging "eyes that fly out."

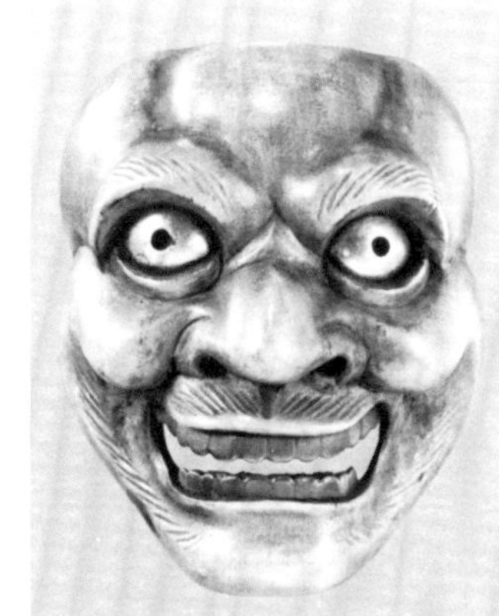

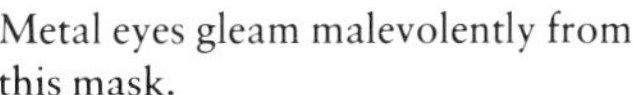

Metal eyes gleam malevolently from this mask.

Wood and metal. 19th c. Katabori. 4.5 cm. E26604

Shojo Mask Red-haired Shojo are mythical beings who are habitual drinkers. Believed to be water sprites in the form of young men, they are the characters of a Noh play.

A mask of Shojo smiles foolishly.

Ceramic, glaze. Deme Yoshinari. late 19th-20th c. Katabori. 4.4 cm. E26616

Tengu Masks Tengu, belligerent forest demons, took the form of either Konoha Tengu, who had human faces with grossly exaggerated noses, or Karasu Tengu, who had a bird-like beak. Tengu appear in Kyogen plays.

A Karasu Tengu's beak dominates the mask.

Ivory. Naomasa, unrecorded artist. 19th c. Katabori. 4.0 cm. E26594

This mask portrays a Konoha Tengu disguised as a member of the yamabushi, Buddhist warrior monks who roamed the forests and mountains wearing distinctive small caps.

Ivory. 19th c. Katabori. 4.5 cm. E26595

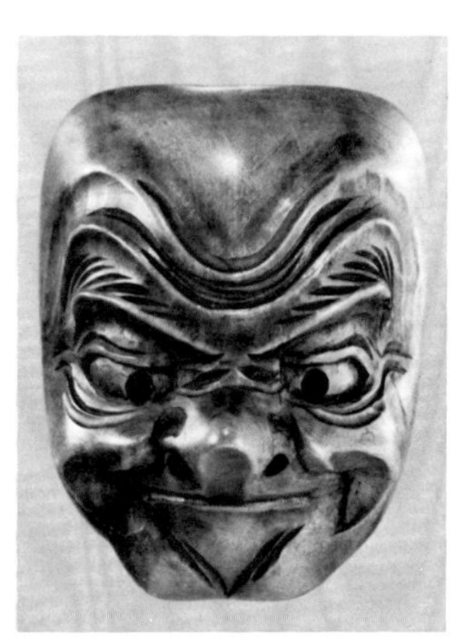

A Konoha Tengu mask

Wood. late 18th-19th c. Katabori. 4.0 cm. E26602

A Konoha Tengu mask

Wood. late 18th-19th c. Katabori.
4.8 cm. E26611

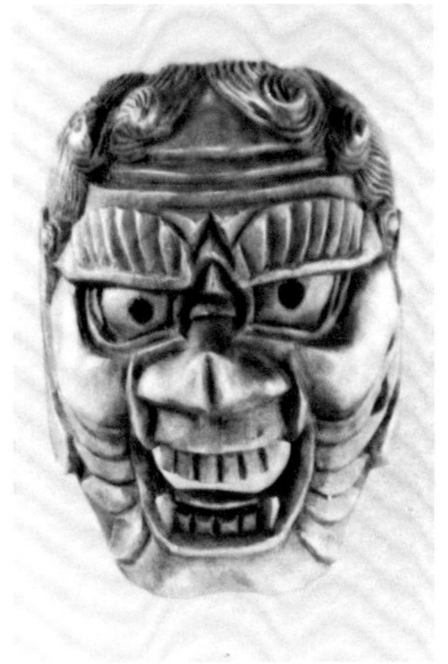

The yamabushi cap on this mask indicates that Konoha Tengu is disguised as a yamabushi.

Porcelain. 19th c. Katabori.
4.0 cm. E26622

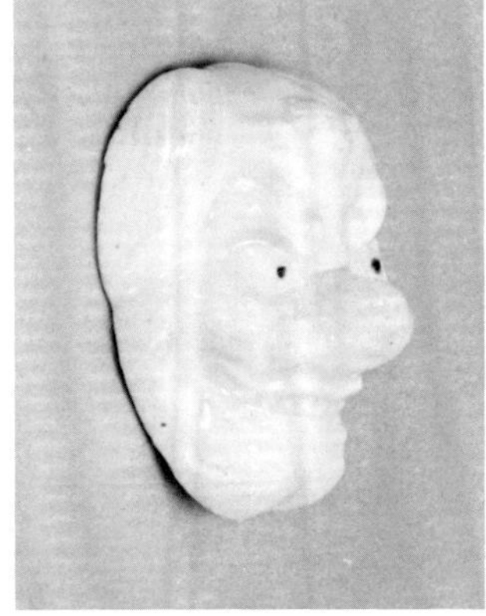

Yase-Otoko Mask In the Noh drama, a mask of a thin-faced man is worn to represent a departed soul.

The eyes of a cadaverous man dominate his ghostly face.

Ivory. 19th-20th c. Katabori.
4.0 cm. E47099

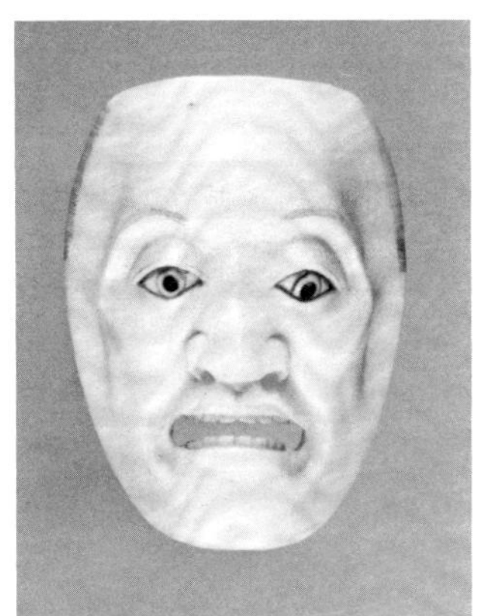

Animals

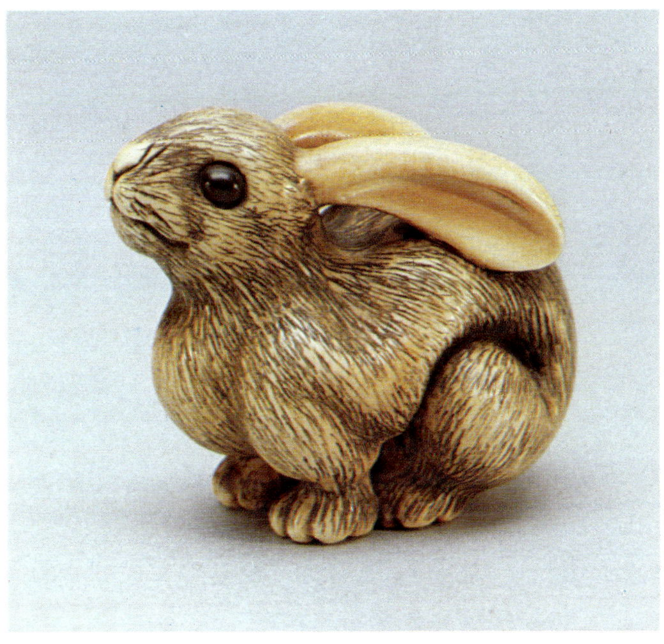

While Japanese and Westerners may find netsuke of animals charming, in Japan animals are more than just amusing or interesting creatures. The folk religions of Japan as well as its formal religions of Shinto and Buddhism have imbued animals with special significance. Shinto's concept of kami deifies some animals. In addition, images of animals guard entrances to Shinto shrines, and images of animals who attend certain kami can be found inside shrines. Buddhism taught that Buddha took on the forms of many different animals in order to teach their admirable traits to humankind and individual human beings might be reincarnated as another animal or as a plant during the journey of the human soul toward nirvana. Such beliefs naturally inspired great reverence for all living things.

Other beliefs regarding animals were disseminated through superstitions, folktales, traditions and folk religions to which nearly every Japanese person is exposed from childhood, including the belief that animals can take possession of human beings.

A good many animals have also become part of everyday

expressions or have come to symbolize certain ideas because of a play on words. The three wise monkeys ("hear no evil, see no evil, speak no evil"), for example, express a Buddhist idea, but actually come from a play on the words for monkey (saru) and for evil (zaru). The bat became a symbol of happiness because in Japanese the characters for "bat" and "happiness" are pronounced the same way.

All of this is not to say that every netsuke-shi who carved an animal netsuke necessarily knew the origins of the symbolic significance of that animal, or even had the symbolism or religious connections or folktales in mind. Like people the world over, the Japanese are amused and awed by the animal kingdom, and animal subjects certainly give netsuke-shi an opportunity to display their talents.

Furthermore, the choice of animal subjects in netsuke was as influenced by popular taste as by other considerations. In the 18th century netsuke artists were concerned more with religious, legendary and mythical creatures, and their choice of animals reflects that interest. Zodiac, mythical animals and shishi, for example, were common 18th century netsuke subjects. In the 19th and 20th centuries, first because of influences from other arts and later because of Japan's increasing westernization and the Westerners' interest in netsuke, carvers of animal subjects became more interested in carving realistic looking animals than in choosing a subject because it illustrated a folktale or had religious or symbolic overtones.

Whatever the individual carver's motive for choosing a particular subject and design for an animal netsuke, it is important to remember that Japanese culture is inseparably tied to the animal world in complex, long-standing and deep-seated ways.

Mythical and Supernatural Animals

The folklore of Japan contains many tales of mythical animals and of animals believed to possess supernatural powers.

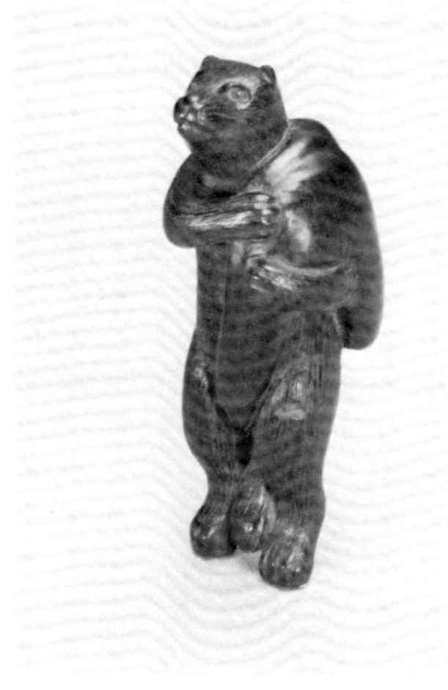

A badger on his hind legs carries a sack over his shoulder.

Boxwood. 19th-20th c. Katabori.
5.6 cm. E4490

Badger Among its powers the badger can take on human form and usually does so in order to bring trouble to innocent people. In its animal shape the badger can make its belly swell and produces a drumlike sound by beating it.

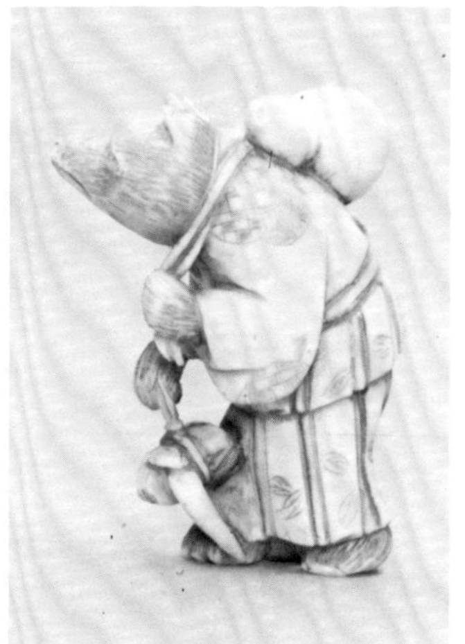

A badger, dressed as a man, carries a dead octopus in one hand and a wine gourd slung over his shoulder.

Ivory. 19th-20th c. Katabori.
4.5 cm. E26649

A badger beats his swollen belly.

Ivory, inlaid eyes. Shunkosai (Chogetsu). 1826-1892. Katabori. 3.5 cm. E26700

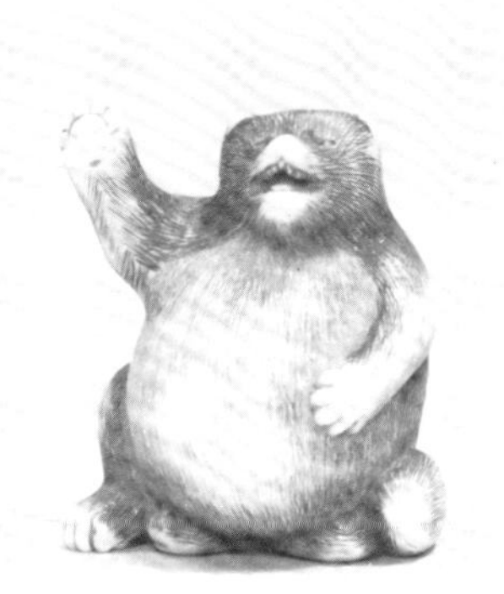

Baku This strange creature has a trunk like an elephant, a body like a shishi (lion) or a horse, and clawed feet. Known as an eater of bad dreams, the baku is a friend to humans despite its often fierce-looking expression.

This netsuke of a baku was done in the lacquering technique known as Negoro, a splotched red-on-black layering technique developed by the priests of Negoro Temple.

Lacquered wood. 18th c. Katabori. 5.7 cm. E26667

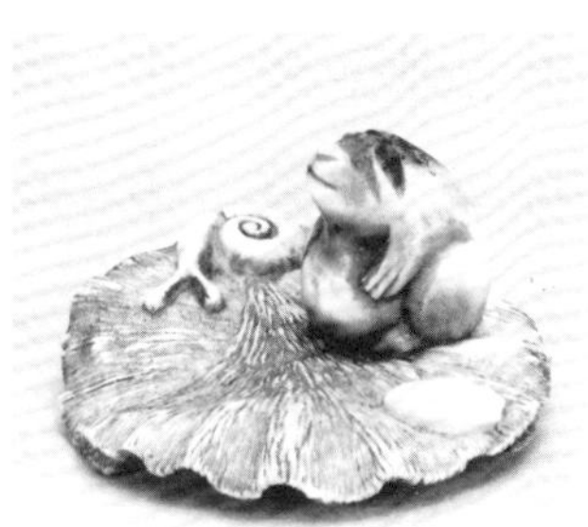

This badger beating its swollen stomach is carved from a different piece of bone than the lotus leaf, snail and shell.

Bone. 19th-20th c. Katabori. 4.1 cm. E26775

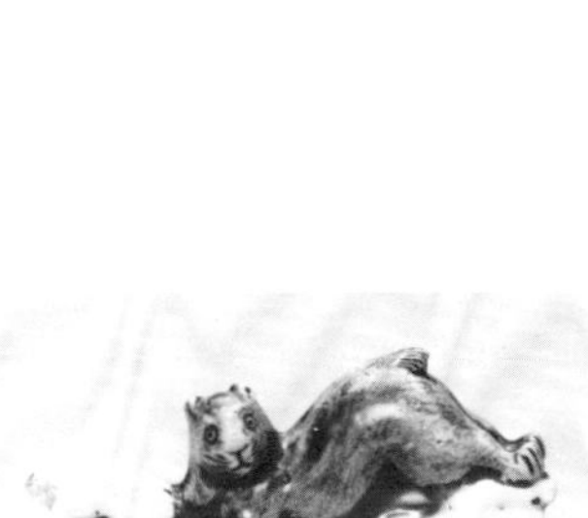

Cat Long-tailed cats, as opposed to the Japanese stub-tail cats, are considered evil. These cats take on disguises to surprise their victims and are said to avenge murders of other cats by killing the murderers.

The Japanese cat finds favor with sailors who believe a cat on board ship will keep away the evil spirits that lurk in the water. The whitecaps on waves symbolize the grasping hands of the deep over which the cat has control.

Porcelain: gray, blue and white. 18th-19th c. Katabori. 3.6 cm. E26686

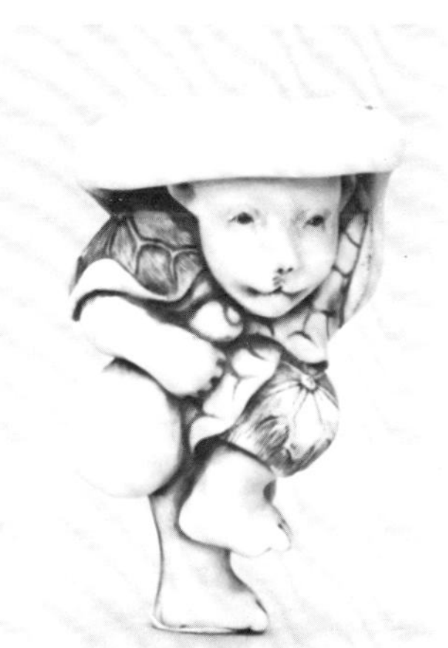

A happy-go-lucky badger, wrapped in a leaf and holding a sake gourd, playfully dances and pulls his bushy tail up over his head like a hat.

Ivory. Hidemasa. early 19th c. Katabori. 4.8 cm. E27037

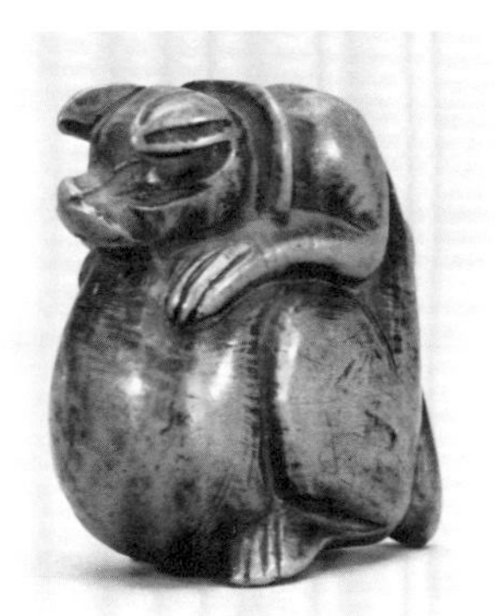

A badger in dog-like form swells his belly.

Wood. 19th-20th c. Katabori. 4.3 cm. E34086

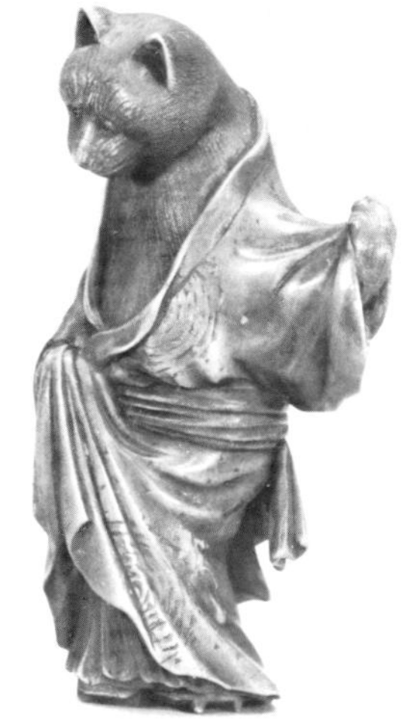

A cat disguised as a woman

Wood. 19th-20th c. Katabori. 6.0 cm. E26756

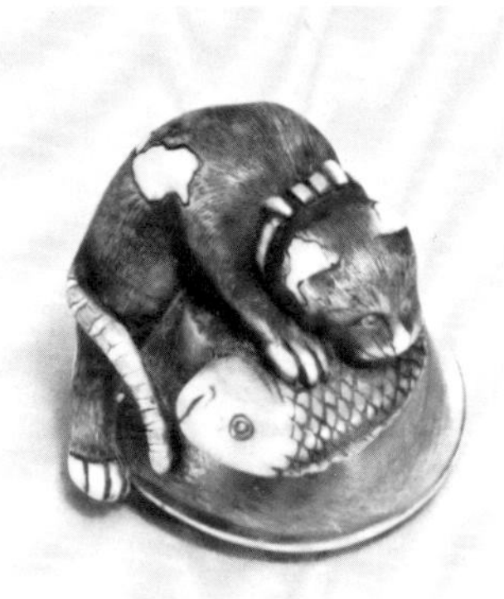

A cat hungrily devours a fish on top of an overturned bowl.

Ivory, glass eyes. 19th-20th c. Katabori. 3.3 cm. E26759

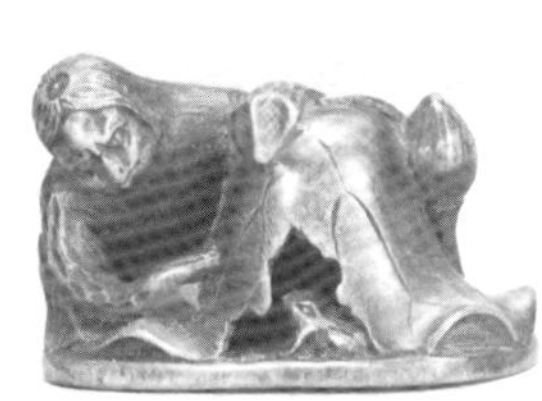

A kappa tries to catch a frog who hides under a lotus leaf.

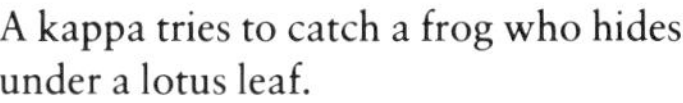

Boxwood. Masatoshi. 18th c. Katabori. 3.1 cm. E52709

Kappa Kappa inhabit deep ponds and other bodies of water and are said to be responsible for the drownings of swimmers who venture out too far. Supposedly, the kappa pulls them under and then feasts upon them. Odd-looking creatures, kappa have the shell of a tortoise, the legs of a frog and the head of a monkey (though some have beaks). The top of a kappa's head is shaped like a shallow bowl, and when on land (where they also seize prey) a kappa must keep this bowl filled with water or else lose all its strength and die. This "Achilles heel" provides a means of conquering the kappa for, always polite, a kappa will bow to anyone who bows to it, and in so doing of course, will spill the precious water it carries on its head.
As usual with evil creatures, netsuke-shi treat kappa with humor.

Kirin (unicorn) The emblem of kindness and virtue, the kirin is a vegetarian and is so gentle a creature that it will not even walk on grass lest it crush the living beings that take shelter there. The kirin somehow lost the magical powers it once possessed, but its presence is believed to be a sign of the coming of an important person.

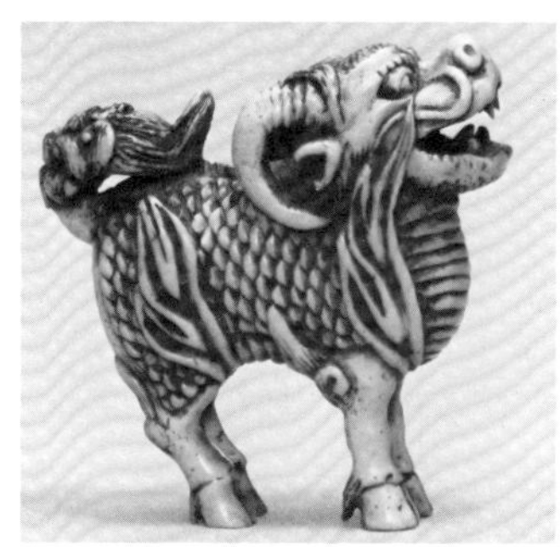

A two-horned kirin depicted in fine detail

Ivory. 19th c. Katabori. 4.8 cm. E26744

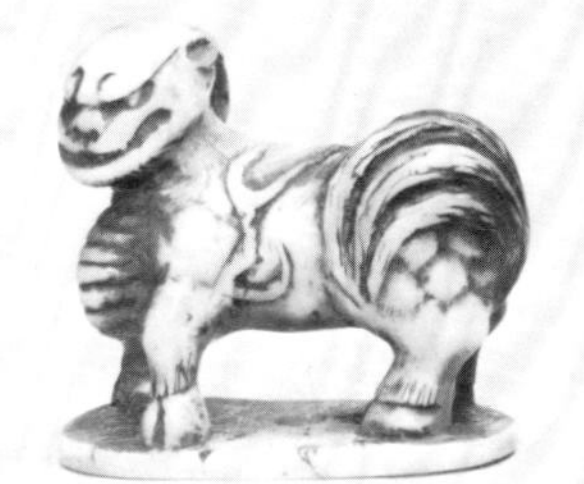

An unusually fierce-looking one-horned kirin

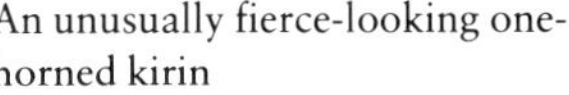

Ivory. 19th c. Katabori. 3.0 cm. E26768

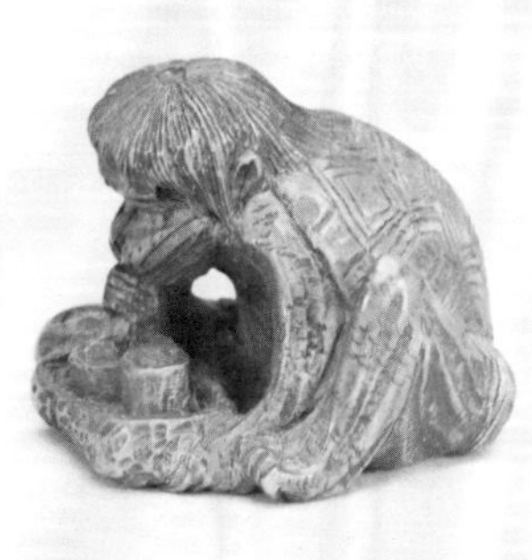

A kappa plays with a pipe and several bowls.

Wood, ivory lined himotoshi. late 18th-19th c. Katabori. 4.0 cm. E26766

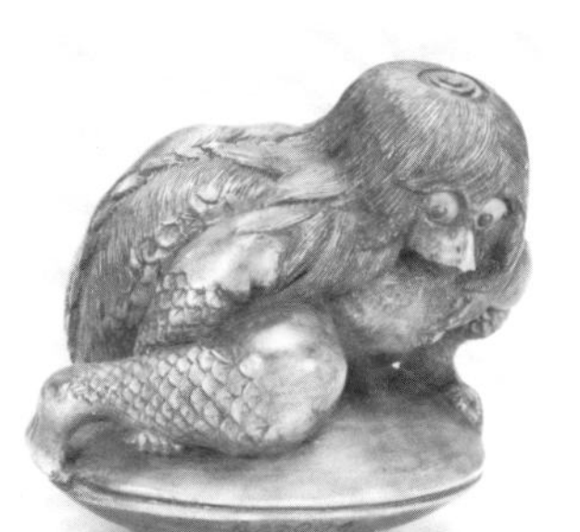

A kappa struggles to extricate his foot from the tight grip of a clam. The over-amorous kappa is commonly depicted in predicaments from which escape is difficult, serving as a warning to all who would love too freely.

Boxwood, inlaid eyes. Hideharu. mid 19th-20th c. Katabori. 4.7 cm. E27006

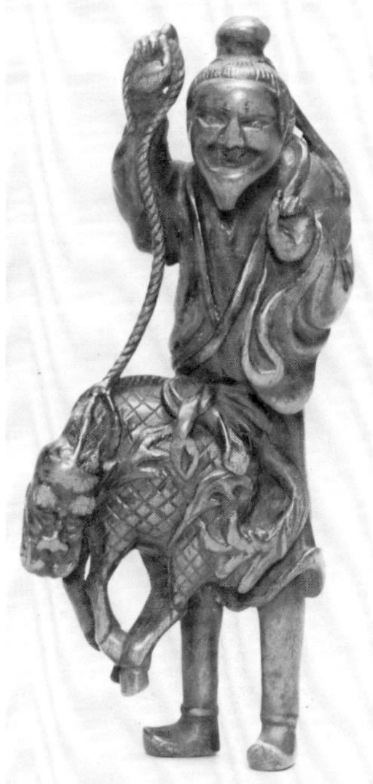

A sage holds a kirin on a leash. Judging from the wear on this piece, the himotoshi were not used.

Boxwood. 18th c. Katabori. 9.5 cm. E26945

Kitsune (fox) Tradition holds the fox as both a good and an evil creature. When disguised as a woman or as a priest, the fox brings harm to people. No doubt the fox's slyness and nighttime activities have given rise to the legends of evil foxes. However, the fox is also the messenger for the Shinto rice god, Inari, and statues of Inari foxes guard Shinto shrines that have been erected to the rice god.

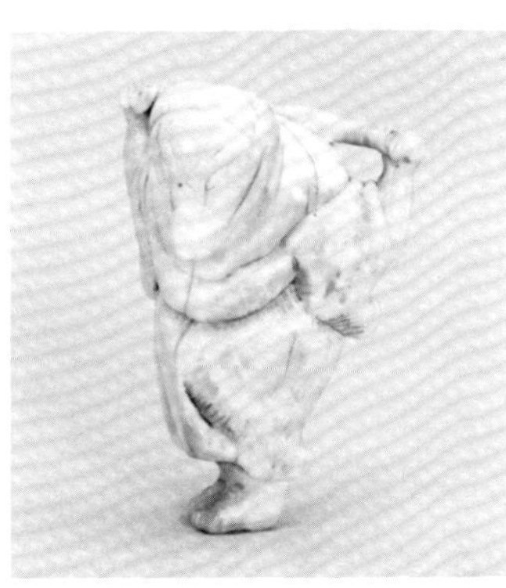

A kitsune in human clothing appears to be dancing.

Ivory. 19th-20th c. Katabori. 4.2 cm. E26660

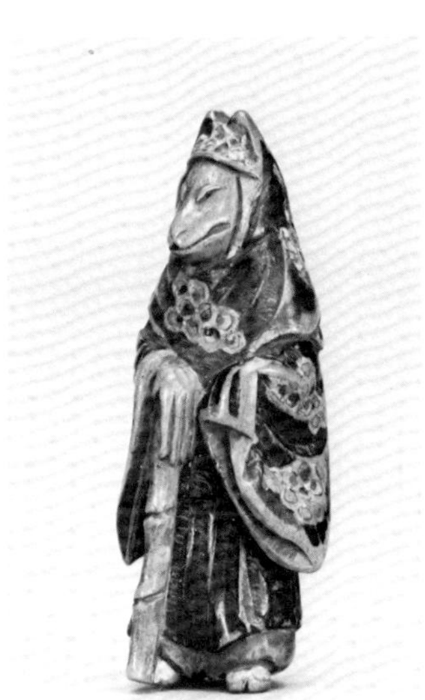

A kitsune dressed as a priest

Wood painted blue, green and red. Shuzan (Nagamachi). late 18th c. Katabori. 5.7 cm. E26697

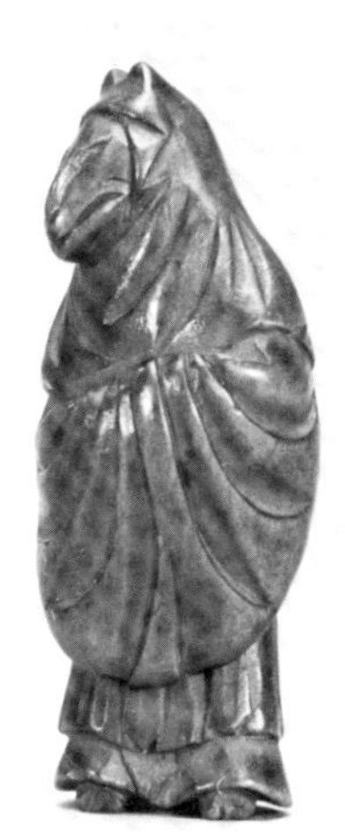

A kitsune disguised as a priest

Wood. 19th-20th c. Katabori. 5.3 cm. E26760

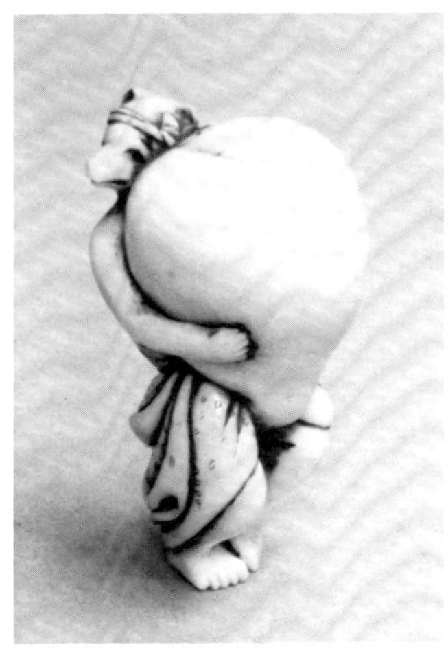

A kitsune holding his over-developed sexual organ

Ivory. Sadatomo. late 19th-20th c. Katabori. 4.5 cm. E53705

Mermaid The mermaid, though mythical, has a basis in fact in the sea cow, a mammal who suckles her young. Mermaids supposedly learn the secrets of the ocean by listening to shells. According to legend, eternal youth comes to anyone who eats mermaid flesh, and thus the mermaid has become a symbol of eternal youth.

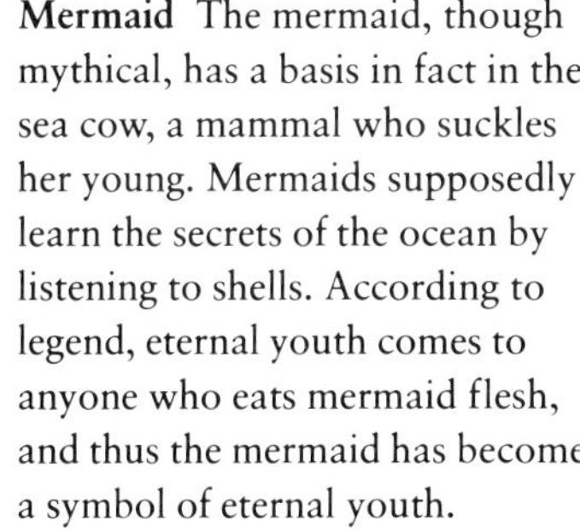

A mermaid nursing her child

Cypress wood. 19th c. Katabori. 5.1 cm. E26741

Namazu (earthquake fish) According to legend, when this giant ocean-dwelling fish wriggles, the earth quakes, but it can be quieted by rubbing its back with a magic gourd.

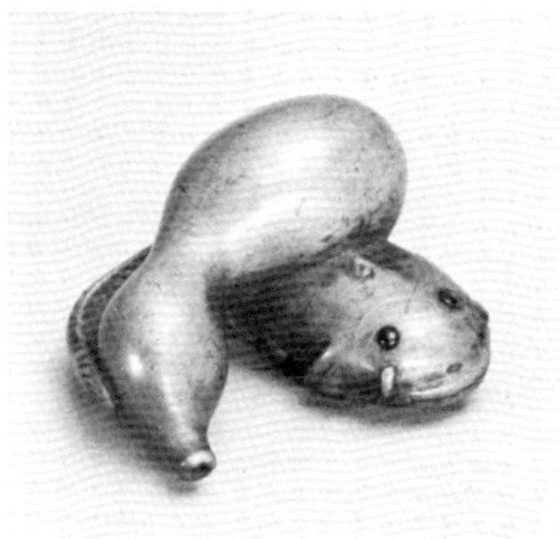

An earthquake fish and gourd

Wood, inlaid eyes. Tomochika. early 19th c. Katabori. 4.0 cm. E26839

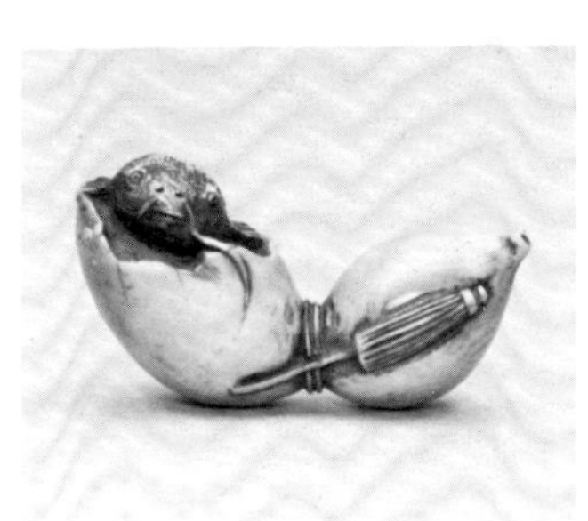

An earthquake fish emerges from a gourd on which a closed umbrella and a rope are carved.

Ivory. Tomochika. early 19th c. Katabori. 3.9 cm. E33345

Shachihoko Because of their watery associations, the mythical shachihoko (dragonfish or dolphins) are mounted on the top two tile pieces of castle roofs in order to put out fires.

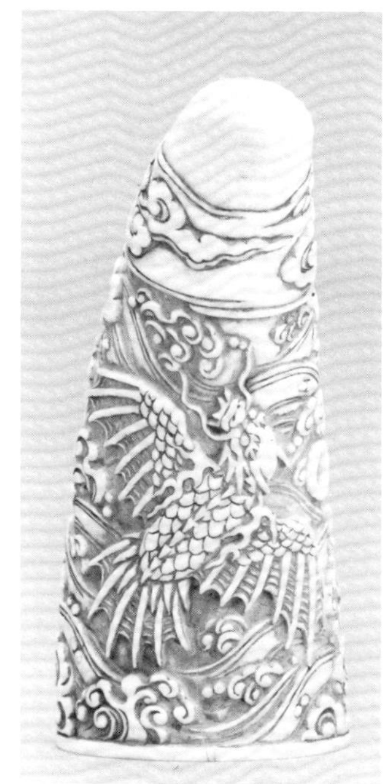

Shachihoko are carved on both sides of a whale's tooth.

Whale's tooth. 19th c. Katabori. 7.5 cm. E26877

Legendary and Symbolic Animals

Many real animals play key roles in legends or symbolize various beliefs and attributes.

Bat The Chinese word for bat is pronounced the same as the word for happiness, so in the Orient the bat carries none of the evil connotations it has in the West. Instead, bats symbolize only good wishes, "the five happinesses": longevity, riches, peacefulness, love of virtue, and a happy death.

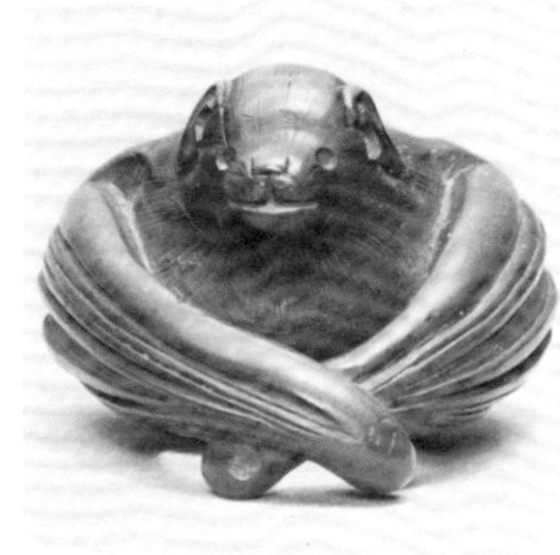

A bat with crossed wings

Boxwood. 19th-20th c. Katabori. 4.0 cm. E24901

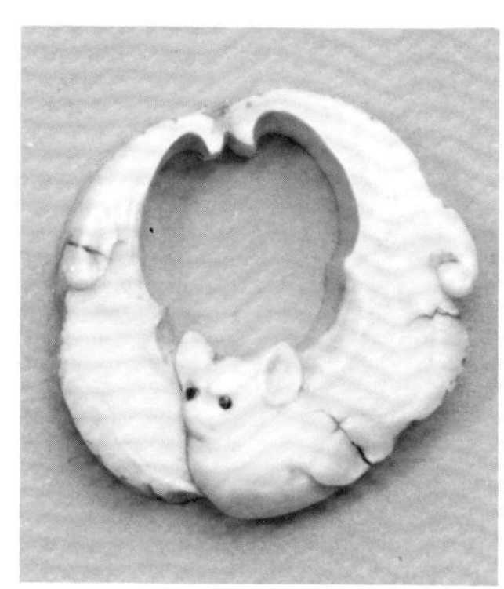

This carving of a bat with its wings over its head has an undetailed (unfinished?) back, atypical of netsuke.

Ivory, inlaid eyes. 19th-20th c. Katabori. 3.6 cm. E26656

Carp Because carp swim upstream and even up waterfalls in order to spawn, they have become a symbol of strength and perseverance. According to a Chinese legend, if a fish manages to reach a certain sacred place on a river, it will be sent to heaven on a cloud, be changed into a dragon and live happily ever after. Only the carp have the perseverance and strength to succeed at this, and consequently they have become an important symbol for young boys and especially for young samurai. The giant paper carps which fly on poles during the Boys' Festival remind young boys of the carp's traits. M. Allen (see Bibliography) tells of an ancient samurai custom of eating a live carp. The carp remains quiet during the vivisection "giving its silent lesson to man that the most bitter and painful death must be endured for the preservation of self-respect." The Japanese word for carp (koi) also means love, so the carp is a symbol of love as well.

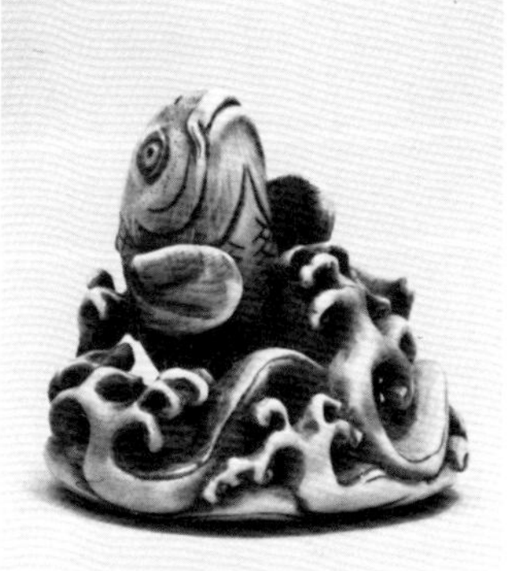

A carp struggles against strong waters to reach its destination.

Ivory. Gyokuzan. 1867-1923. Katabori. 4.0 cm. E26666

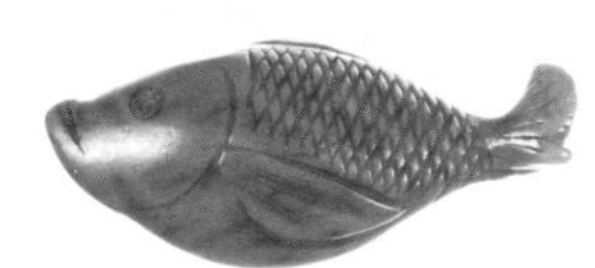

A carp

Boxwood. 19th-20th c. Katabori. 7.5 cm. E26715

Cicada Prized for their music, cicadas symbolize humaneness. In *Real and Imaginary Beings,* M. Neill and B. Okada (see Bibliography) point out that because cicadas go through a chrysalis stage they also symbolize longevity and afterlife, thus cicada netsuke were worn during the Festival of the Dead.

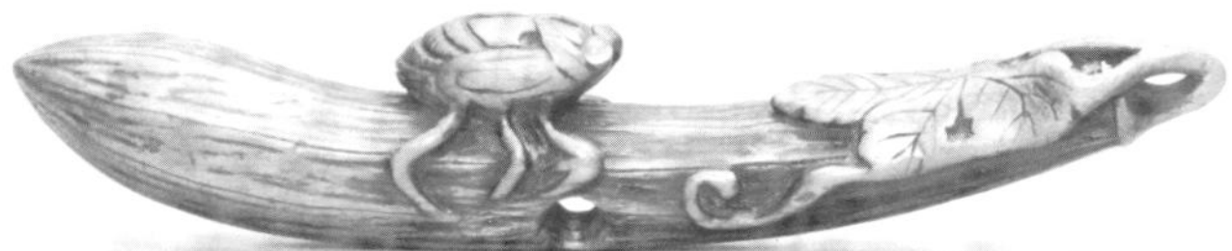

A cicada crawling on a long squash.

Boxwood, inlaid eyes. late 18th-19th c. Katabori. 10.7 cm. E26852

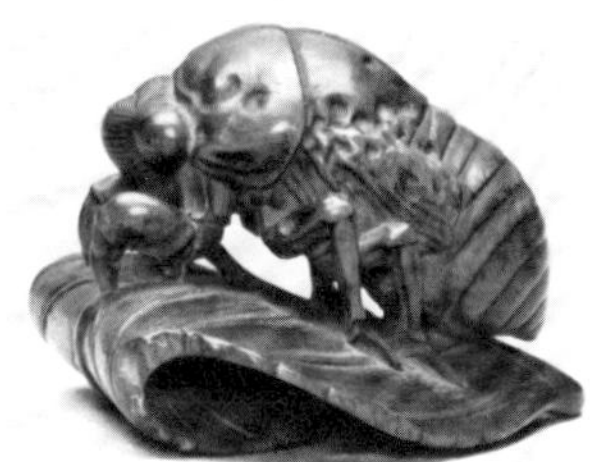

A cicada attaches itself to a leaf in preparation for its annual change of shell.

Wood. Masanao, Shawa. mid-19th c. Katabori. 3.8 cm. E24897

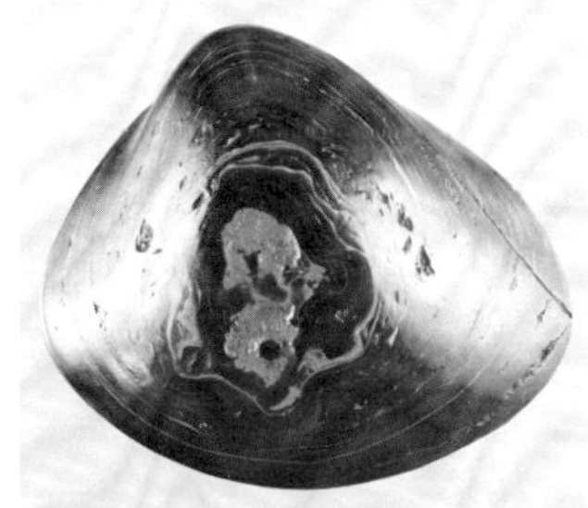

A closed clam is painted with many coats of lacquer which form a swirling pattern of green, black and red.

Clamshell and lacquer, ivory lined himotoshi. 19th c. Katabori. 5.5 cm. E26662

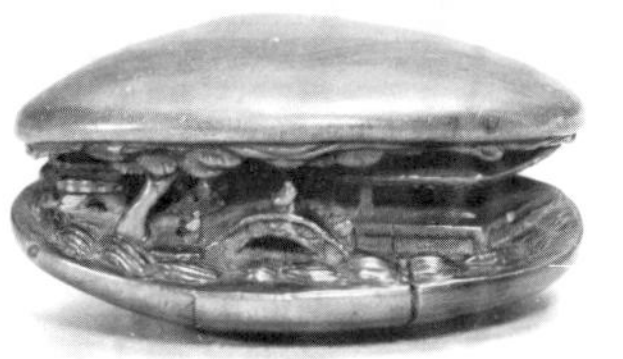

A partially opened clamshell reveals a scene inside (not visible in photo), probably of Horai, in which people bearing gifts are crossing a bridge from a temple to a small altar.

Boxwood. 19th-20th c. Katabori. 5.2 cm. E26698

Clam The underwater palace of Ryujin and the underwater island of Horai (isle of eternal life) are both believed to appear in the breath of a clam. Netsuke depict such landscapes inside clam shells.

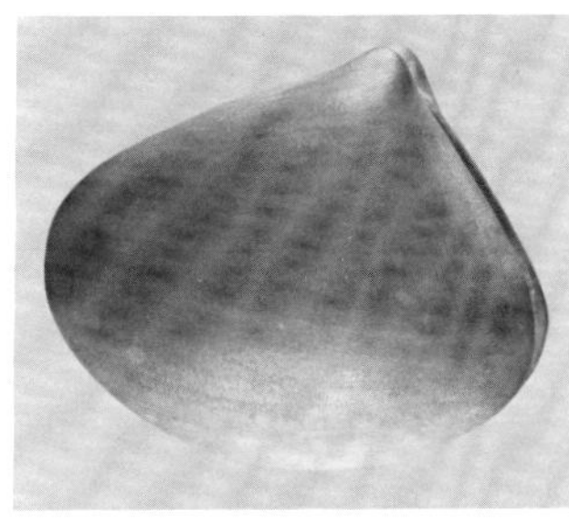

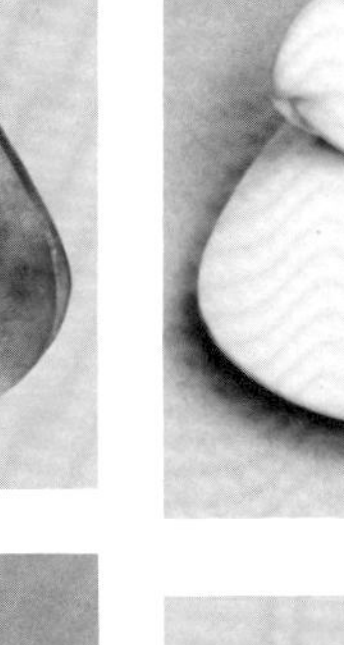

The narrow opening in this smooth, undecorated clamshell reveals people at a shrine, probably on the island of Horai.

Wood. 19th c. Katabori. 3.9 cm. E15467

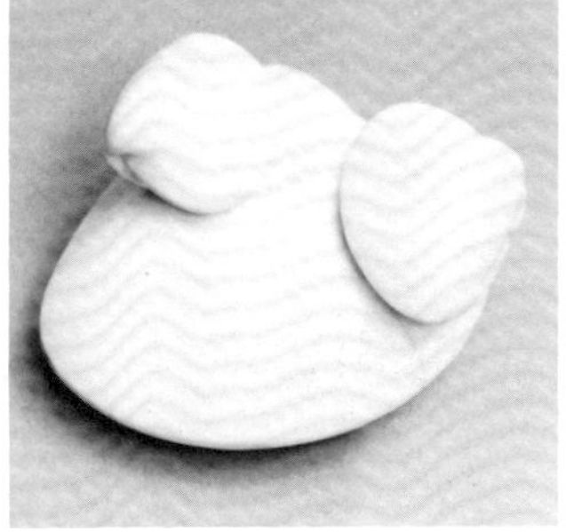

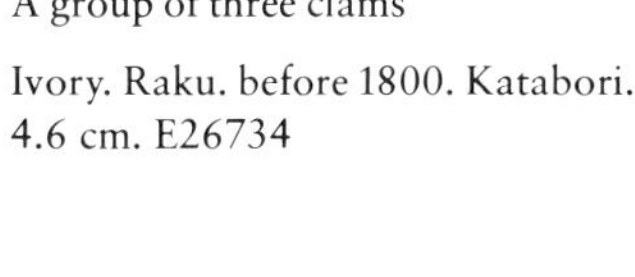

A group of three clams

Ivory. Raku. before 1800. Katabori. 4.6 cm. E26734

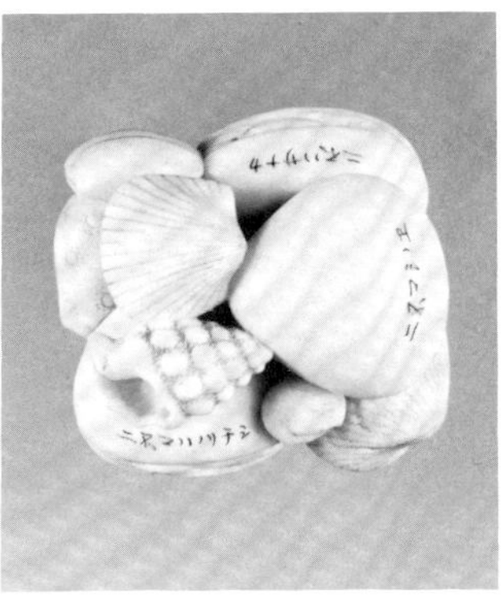

This group of shells includes three partially open clamshells each with a different view of Mt. Fuji inside. Written on the tops of the clamshells are the names of the places from which the mountain is being viewed: Kanasawa Fuji, Enoshima Fuji, Shichiriga-hama Fuji. The fact that all three locations are along a shoreline accounts for the appearance of the other shells in the carving.

Ivory. Gyokuho. 1868-1900. Katabori. 3.5 cm. E25278

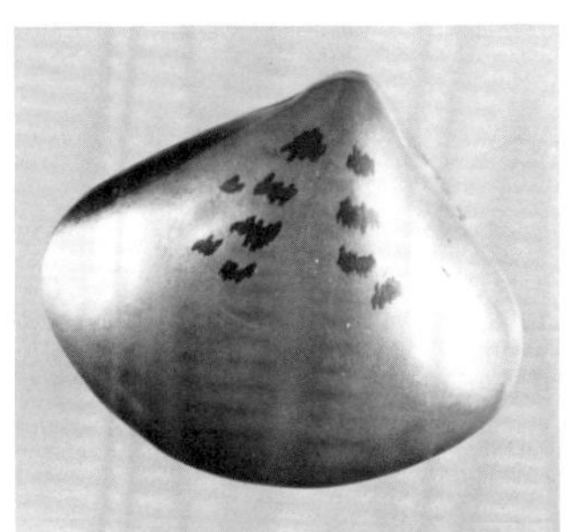

A partially opened clamshell (lacquered gold and black) reveals a scene (not visible in photo) probably of Horai, with people, trees, river, a bridge and a building.

Wood. 19th-20th c. Katabori. 4.0 cm. E26754

Crab A creature of cleverness and foresight, a crab outsmarts a monkey in the tale about the two animals. Another legend reports that Heike-gani crabs are reincarnations of dead Heike warriors, and therefore the Heike crab serves as protection from misfortune. (see Bibliography, M. Neill and B. Okada, *Real and Imaginary Beings;* M. and E. Jahss, *Inro*)

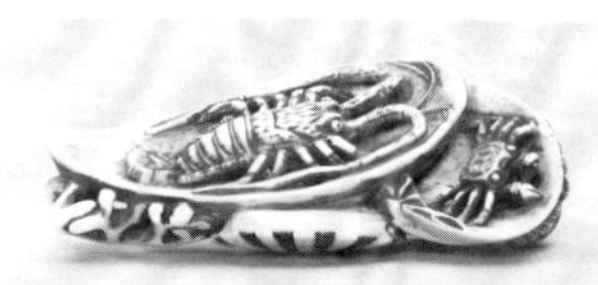

A crab and a lobster (symbol of longevity because of its bent back) rest inside two shells which are piled atop several other shells and a coral branch (symbol of rarity and perfection).

Ivory. 19th c. Katabori. 7.5 cm. E26664

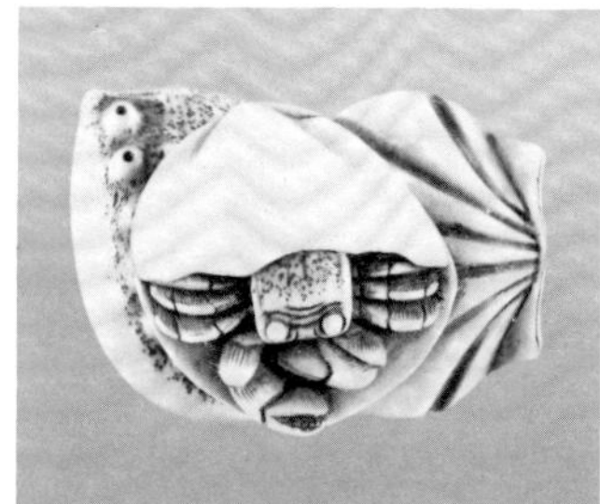

A crab peers out of a clam shell which sits on top of two other shells.

Ivory. 19th c. Katabori. 4.0 cm. E26705

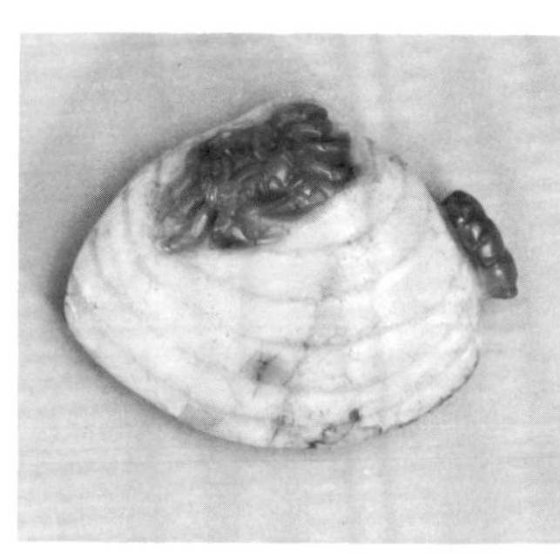

The artist has taken full advantage of his material in this carving of a red shell and red crab on a white clam. The red shell and crab appear to be attached to the white clam shell when in fact they are all carved from one piece.

Agate. 19th c. Katabori. 4.3 cm. E26733

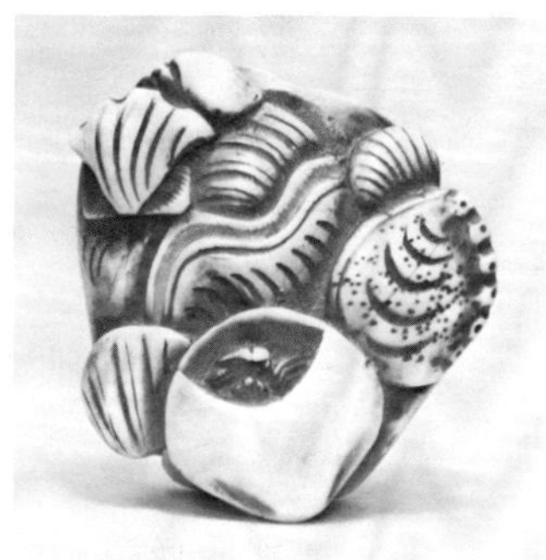

A crab peeks out of a broken clam shell which is piled on other shells.

Bone. 19th c. Katabori. 4.5 cm. E26764

Deer "The animal bringing good fortune" symbolizes long life and good luck. A deer is thought to be the incarnation of Buddha, and it is also a companion to the gods Jurojin and Fukurokuju. A pair of deer symbolizes a happy married life.

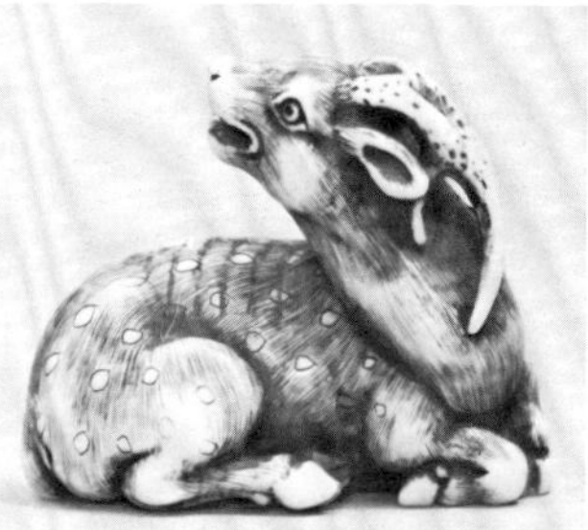

Okatomo and Tomotada were famous for their animal carvings, but they also had many students who, by way of complimenting their masters and bringing honor to themselves, were allowed to sign their master's name to their own work.

Ivory, inlaid eyes. Okatomo. before 1781. Katabori. 4.5 cm. E26636

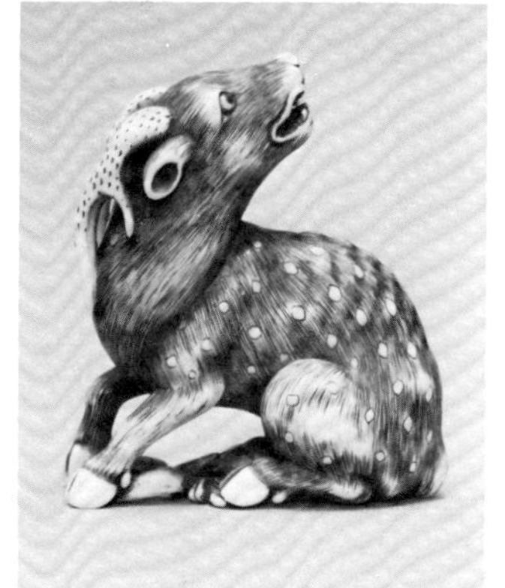

A deer sitting on some grape leaves

Ivory, inlaid eyes. Tomotada. 1781-1800. Katabori. 4.8 cm. E26637

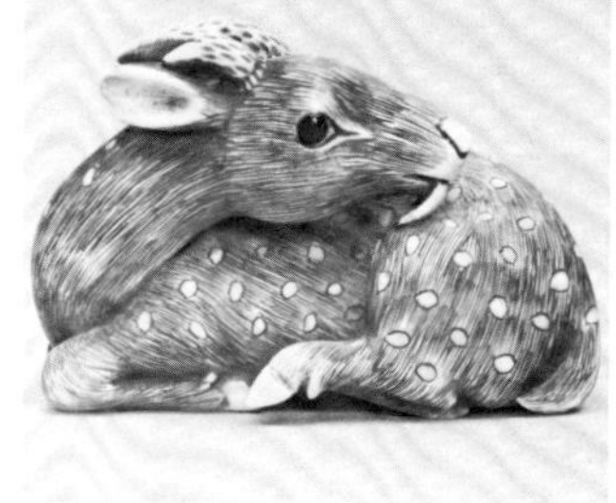

A deer cleaning itself

Ivory, inlaid eyes. late 18th c. Katabori. 4.8 cm. E26728

Dragonfly The dragonfly is the emblem of Japan because the first emperor likened the shape of the islands to a dragonfly licking its tail and named the country Dragonfly Islands. The dragonfly's ability to fight has made it a symbol of victory and courage as well.

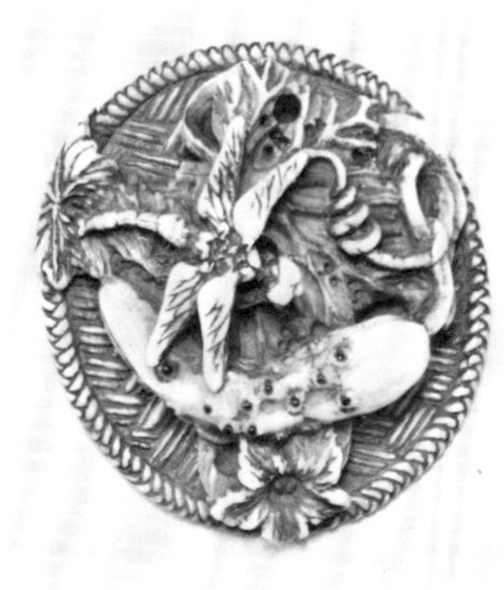

A cucumber (with wooden inlays), vine and dragonfly on a round straw mat

Ivory, wood inlays. Issen. early 19th c. Katabori. 4.2 cm. E26762

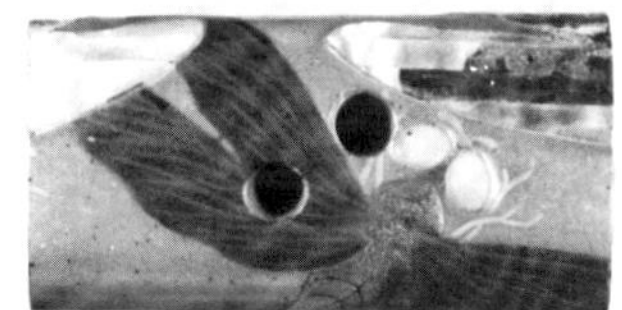

Dragonflies in red and gray lacquer with nacre inlays on a gold lacquered background.

Lacquered wood and nacre. 19th-20th c. Manju. 3.6 cm. E26906

Elephant The elephant, though not indigenous to Japan, is important because it accompanies the Buddhist deity Fugen Bosatsu, and is also a symbol of wisdom.

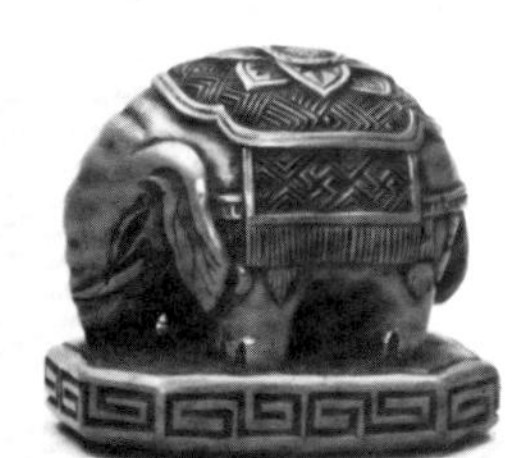

An elephant wearing a blanket decorated with a chrysanthemum

Wood with cinnabar lacquer. 19th-20th c. Katabori. 2.9 cm. E26774

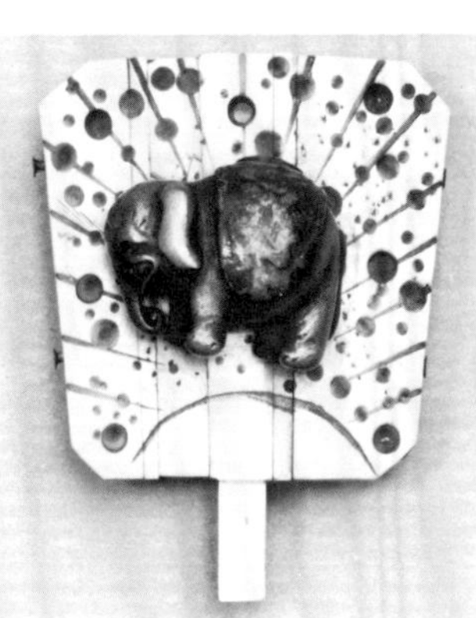

A brass elephant is fastened to a fan made of strips of ivory pegged together.

Ivory and brass. illegible signature. 19th-20th c. Katabori. 4.7 cm. E26899

Frog A symbol of rain, luck and persistence, frogs also represent many stories and proverbs. Basho's proverb, "A frog in a well knows not the great sea" describes a man of limited experience and narrow views, and a netsuke of such a frog serves as a constant reminder to its owner. A frog on a lotus represents the story of the emperor Go Toka who, annoyed by the croaking of certain frogs, ordered them silent. They remain silent to this day.

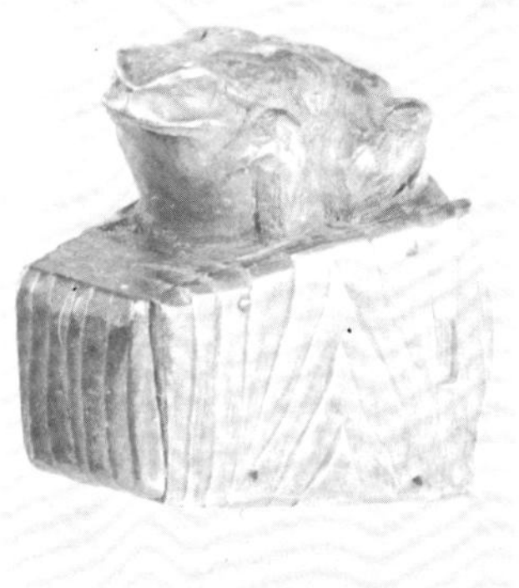

A frog sits on the side of an overturned bucket.

Wood. Masanao. late 19th-20th c. Katabori. 3.3 cm. E4489

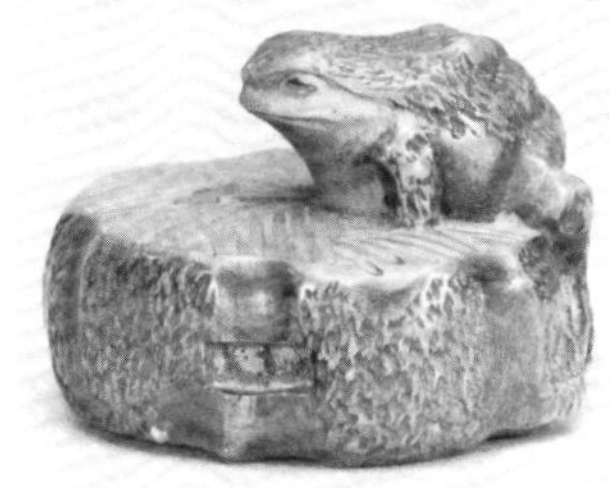

A frog on a grinding block

Wood. Masanao. late 19th-20th c. Katabori. 3.0 cm. E4491

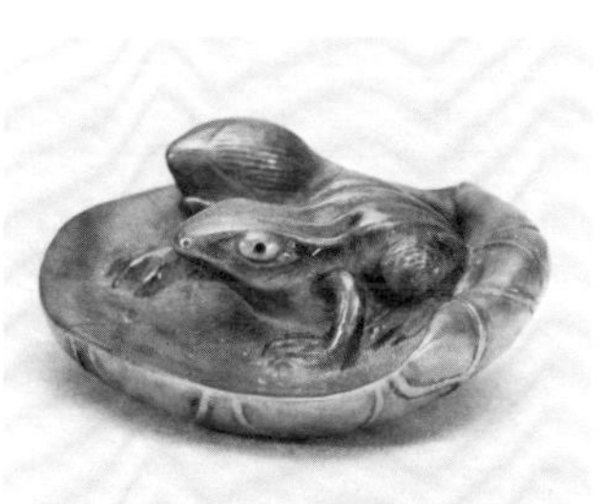

A frog sits on a lotus leaf next to a lotus flower.

Wood. Tomonobu. 1781-1800. Katabori. 4.5 cm. E25281

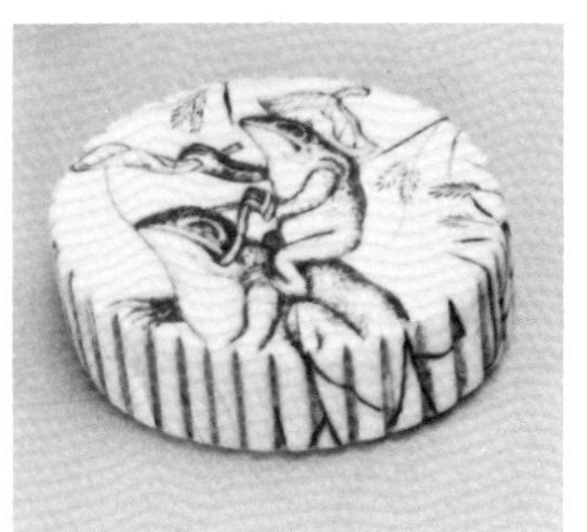

On one side, a frog, in leaf helmet and carrying a leaf whip, holds the reins of another frog upon whom it sits. On the other side is a river and reeds. The engraved areas on this netsuke are stained brown and black.

Ivory. Kochosai. 1830-1843. Manju. 4.0 cm. E26560

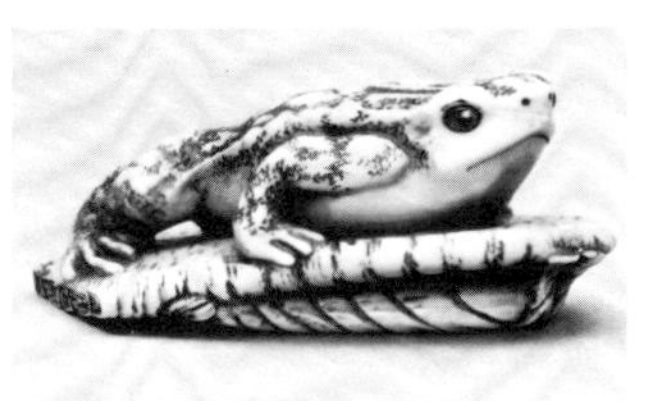

A frog sits on an upside down straw sandal.

Ivory, amber eyes. Sukeyuki. 19th c. Katabori. 6.0 cm. E26753

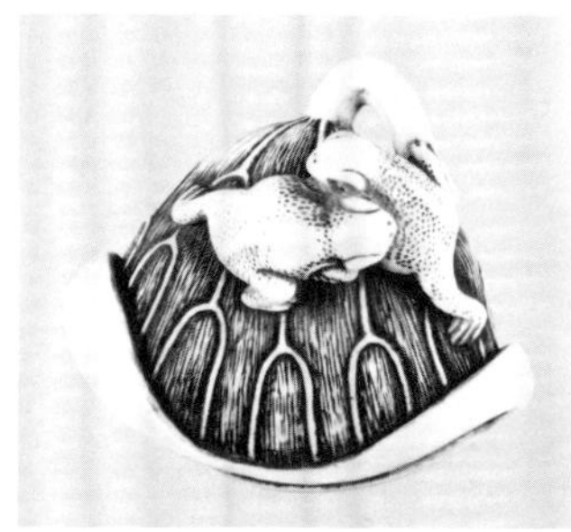

Two frogs wrestle atop a lotus leaf.

Ivory. 19th-20th c. Katabori. 5.1 cm. E26761

Hawk Hawks and falcons, associated with the aristocracy because they used them as hunting birds, also symbolize generosity and heroism. Several stories give the hawk these attributes such as the tale which tells of the hawk who warmed its frozen feet on the body of a small bird and then let the bird go.

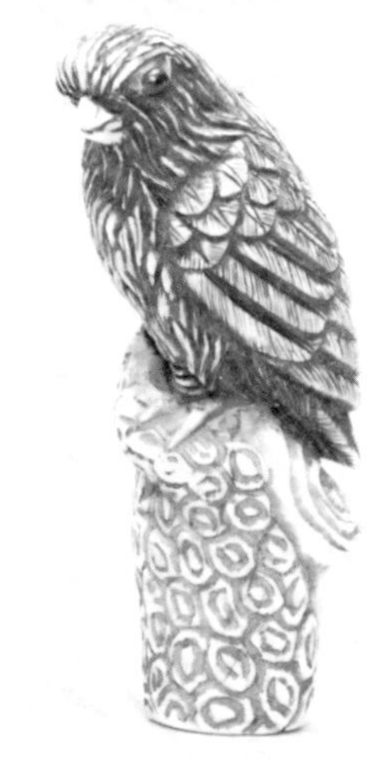

A hawk on a perch

Ivory, inlaid eyes. 19th c. Katabori. 5.7 cm. E26716

A frog emerges from inside a lotus leaf.

Ivory, ebony eyes. 19th-20th c. Katabori. 5.0 cm. E26778

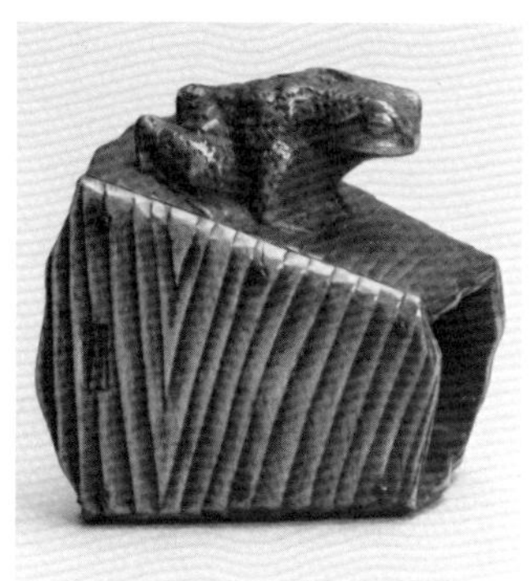

The bucket upon which the frog sits looks as though it was made from four separate pieces of wood, but in fact the carving is all one piece.

Boxwood, ebony inlays. Masanao. after 1900. Katabori. 3.2 cm. E26895

Heron The white heron is a symbol of longevity, and the species is a common one in Japan.

A heronlike bird is perched on a thatched roof on which a squash plant is growing. It is a common practice to grow vegetable vines on roofs in Japan.

Ivory. 19th c. Katabori. 3.6 cm. E26735

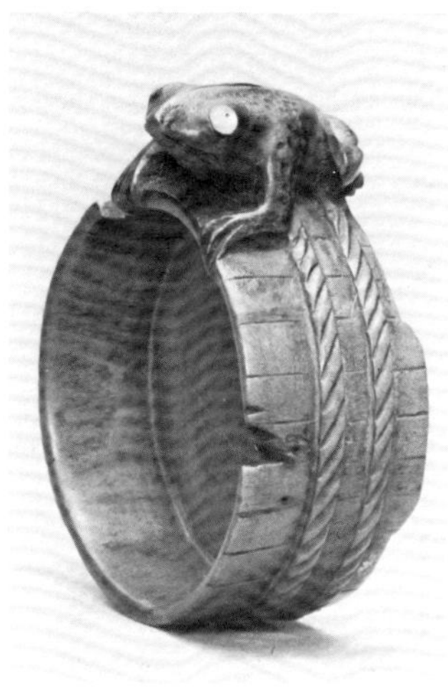

A frog hangs on the side of a wooden grinding base.

Wood with nacre eyes and signature plaque. Chikukoku. 19th-20th c. Katabori. 5.0 cm. E26903

Shiosake (Salmon) A common food source, salmon is often depicted in its dried form in netsuke.

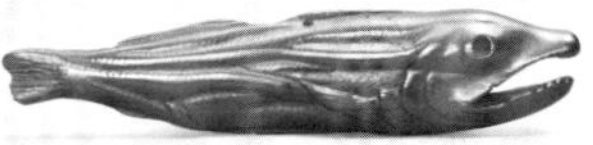

A dried salmon

Wood. early 19th c. Katabori. 7.0 cm. E26678

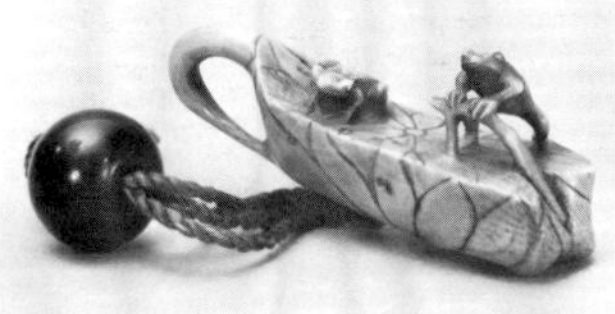

Two frogs ride in a leaf boat. A lacquered wood ojime is attached.

Ivory. Yugyokusai. early 19th c. Katabori. 6.0 cm. E34091

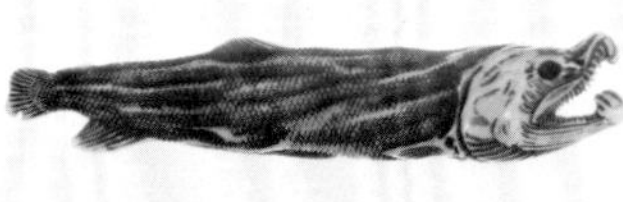

A dried salmon

Ivory. 19th c. Katabori. 10.5 cm. E26709

A fish and shell on a sea cucumber

Ivory. Mitsuhiro. late 19th-20th c. Katabori. 5.3 cm. E26829

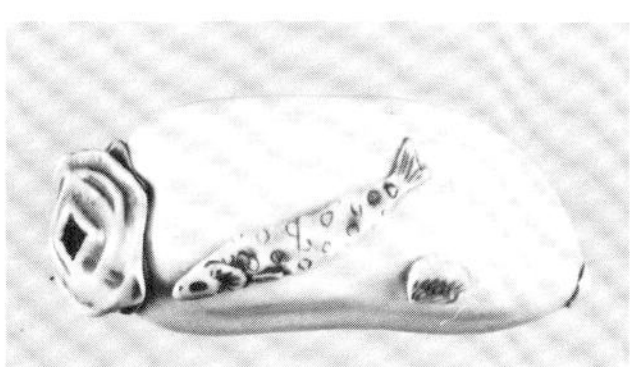

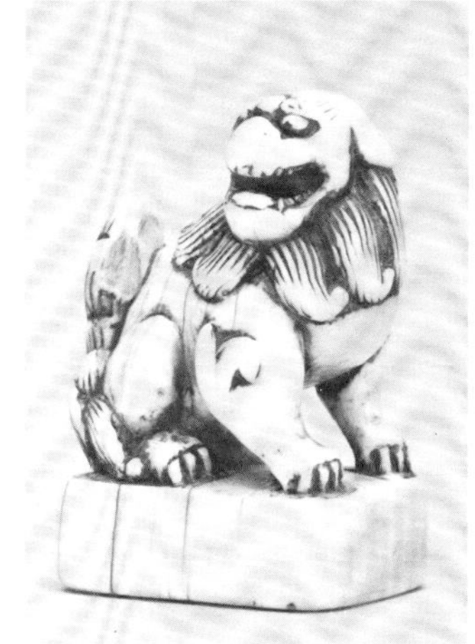

A shishi seated on a thick rectangular base was a very common design for Chinese seals, and many such carvings, as may be the case with this piece, were converted to netsuke.

Ivory. 18th c. Katabori. 4.3 cm. E26631

Lion (Shishi) The lion is not native to Japan, and its unrealistic appearance in netsuke is based on Buddhist artwork from India and China. The shishi, though its form tends to vary somewhat, generally appears to be half lion, half dog, with a curly mane and bushy tail. Statues of shishi can be found in pairs guarding the entrances of important buildings including Buddhist and Shinto shrines. Shishi also guard the tama, jewel of omnipotence, and when depicted with this jewel in its mouth or between its paws, the shishi symbolizes divine protection. Female shishi are often depicted with their young, a symbol both of family and of endurance and strength, for a female shishi is said to expose her young to grave danger in order to ensure that her lineage is courageous and strong.

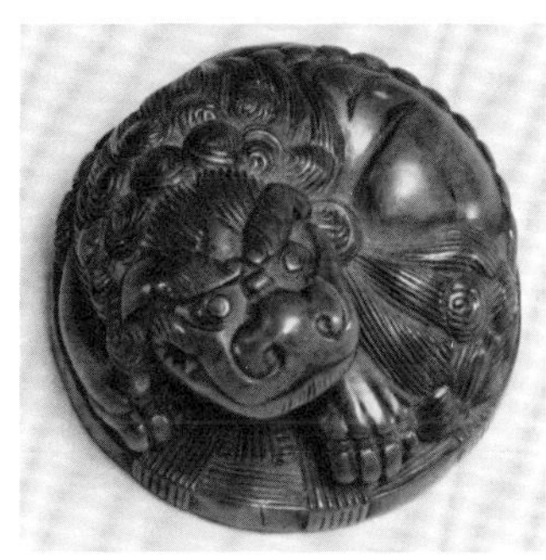

A shishi curled up on a round straw mat

Wood. late 18th c. Katabori. 3.3 cm. E4492

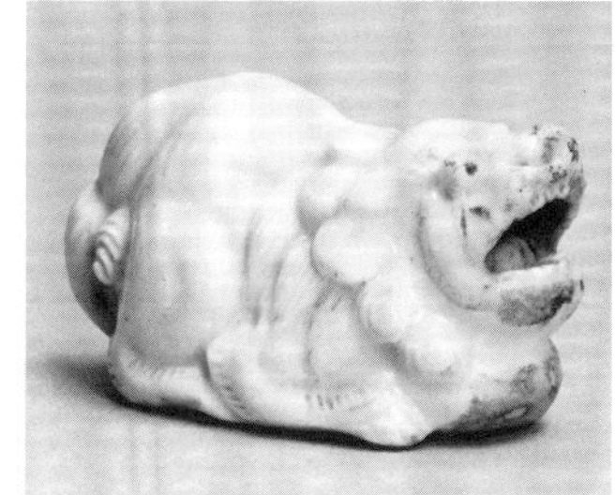

A white shishi guards the sacred jewel which rolls loosely in its mouth.

Porcelain. 19th c. Katabori. 5.0 cm. E26641

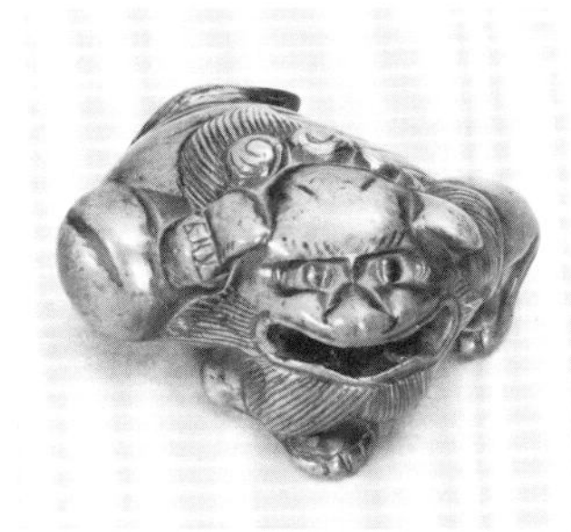

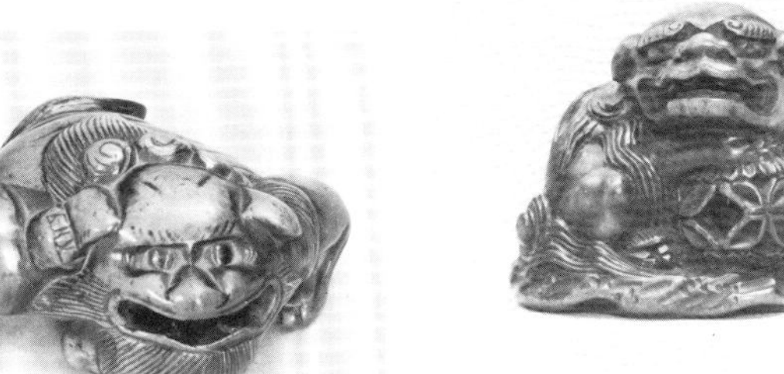

A fierce-looking shishi guards the sacred jewel which rolls loosely in its mouth.

Wood. 18th-19th c. Katabori. 5.1 cm. E19157

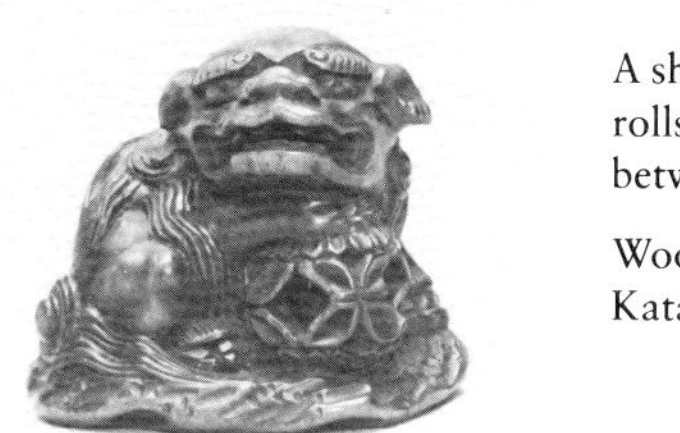

A shishi guards the sacred jewel which rolls loosely inside a container held between its paws.

Wood. Minkoku II. early 19th c. Katabori. 3.7 cm. E26688

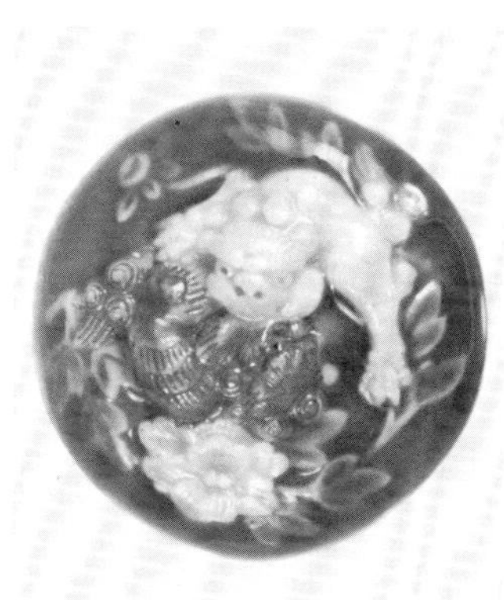

A brown shishi, a white shishi and a white chrysanthemum on a bright blue background

Porcelain. 19th c. Manju. 4.5 cm. E26546

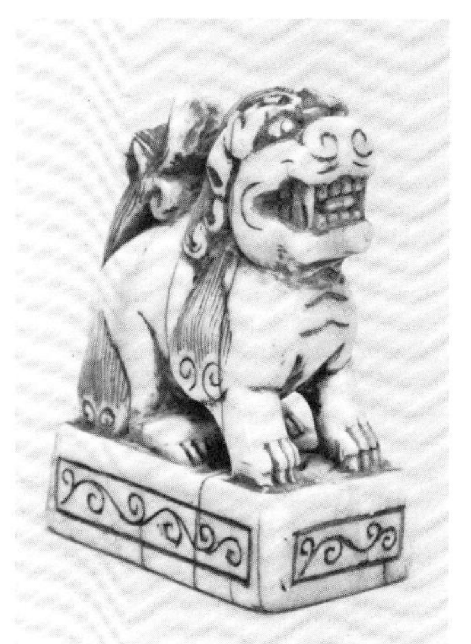

One of the pair of shishi that guard temple entrances, this one has an open mouth because it utters the first sanskrit vowel *aum*, its partner would have a closed mouth, uttering the last vowel *um*. Together they symbolize the Buddhist concepts of the Beginning and End. Like E26631, this carving may have been carved as a Chinese seal and then converted to a netsuke.

Ivory. 18th c. Katabori. 4.7 cm. E26689

A reclining parent shishi with baby shishi on its back

Ivory. 18th-19th c. Katabori. 5.4 cm. E26693

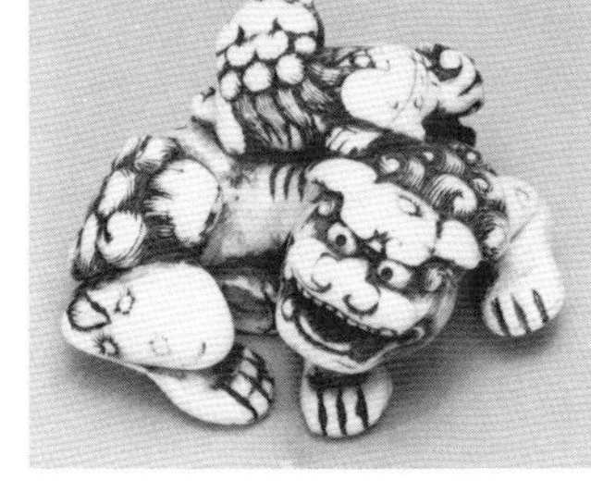

A white shishi reclines on a large blue stone, perhaps representing the sacred jewel.

Porcelain. 19th c. Katabori. 4.2 cm. E26711

A shishi rests on a stone or sack while holding a sacred jewel (made of wood) loosely in its mouth.

Ivory and wood. 18th-19th c. Katabori. 4.0 cm. E26757

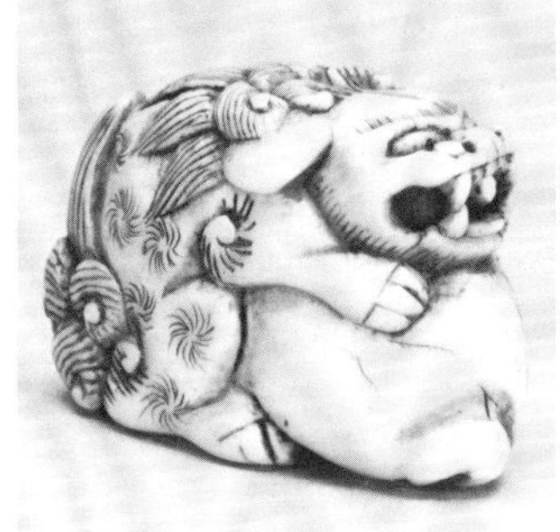

This shishi sits on a Ko, (thunderbolt) an implement used for exorcism by Japanese Buddhist priests and a symbol of supernatural power and the power of prayer.

Ivory. 19th c. Katabori. 3.8 cm. E26878

Another shishi on a base inspired by or carved as a Chinese seal

Ivory. 18th-19th c. Katabori. 3.8 cm. E29147

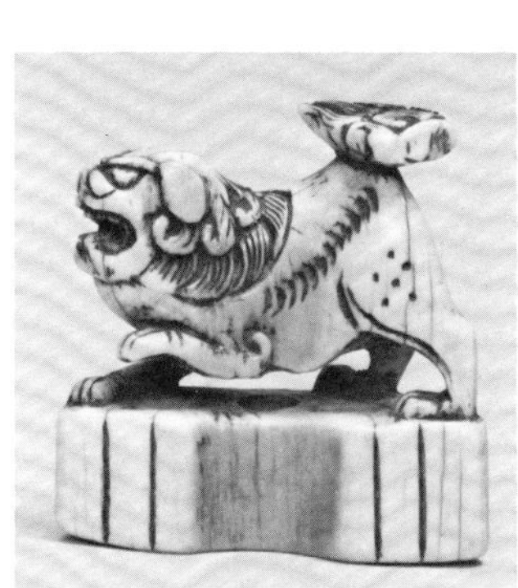

Mandarin Ducks Always depicted in male and female pairs, these ducks symbolize wedded bliss, and depictions of them are common wedding gifts. It is said that a duck will pine away if its mate dies rather than take a new mate. Buddha supposedly was reincarnated for a time as a mandarin duck in order to teach their attributes to humans.

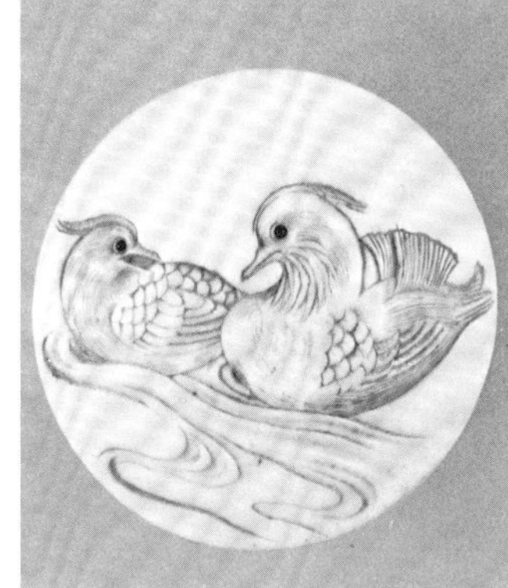

On one side of this manju netsuke are two mandarin ducks swimming; the other side is undecorated.

Ivory, inlaid eyes. Kojyu, unrecorded artist. 19th-20th c. Manju. 3.8 cm. E26550

Nightingale Most often depicted with plum blossoms, the bird and blossoms announce the coming of spring.

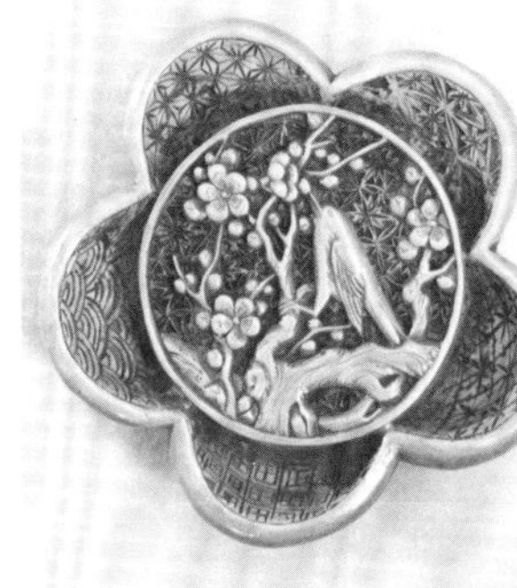

This piece, shaped like a plum blossom, has diaper patterns on its outer petals and a nightingale on blossoming plum tree branches on the inner circle.

Cinnabar lacquered wood. 18th-19th c. Katabori. 4.5 cm. E26832

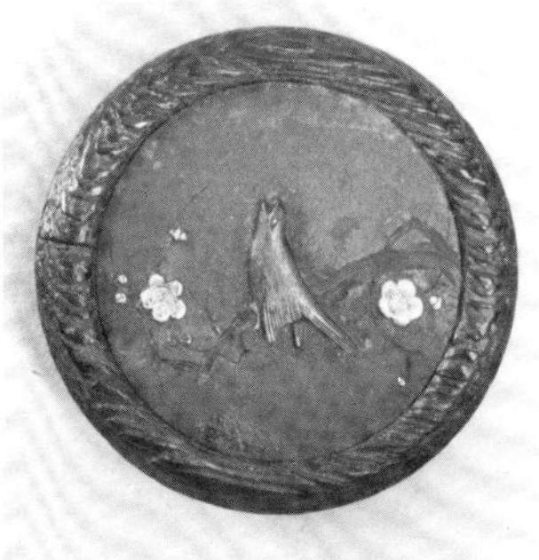

On the lid a nightingale sings from a plum tree branch displaying gold colored flowers. The bowl is plain wood.

Wood and metal. 19th c. Kagamibuta. 4.2 cm. E52486

Octopus In addition to providing a common food source in Japan, the octopus plays two contradictory roles. Named Umi Bozu, the priest of the sea, its bald head is reminiscent of the shaven heads of priests, but the firm grip of the octopus makes it a comical symbol of amorousness.

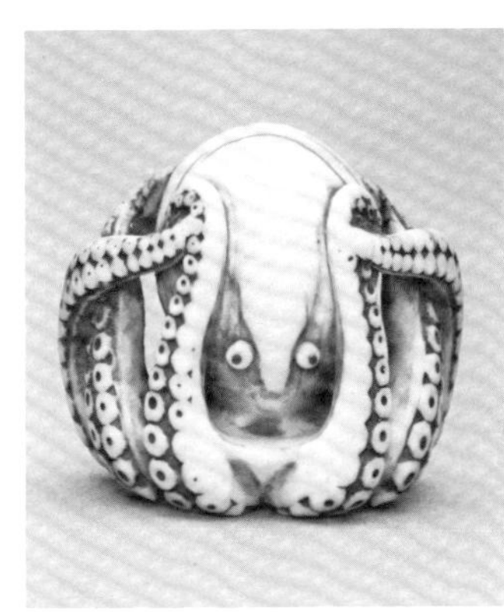

An octopus sits with all eight arms on its head.

Ivory, inlaid eyes. Tomotada. 1800-1869. Katabori. 4.0 cm. E26647

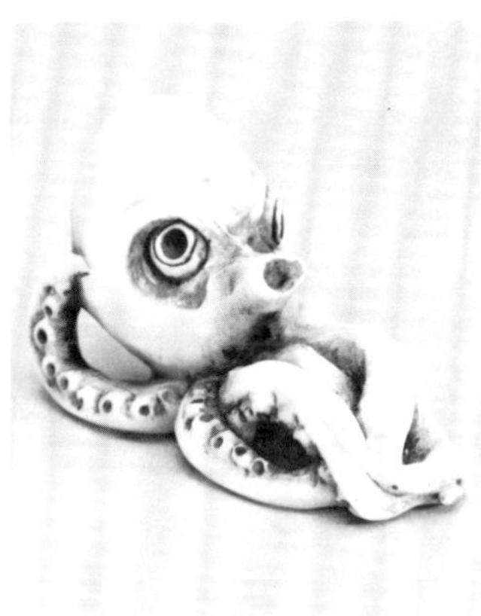

A comical looking octopus reclines with its head resting on two of its arms.

Ivory. 19th-20th c. Katabori. 4.3 cm. E26648

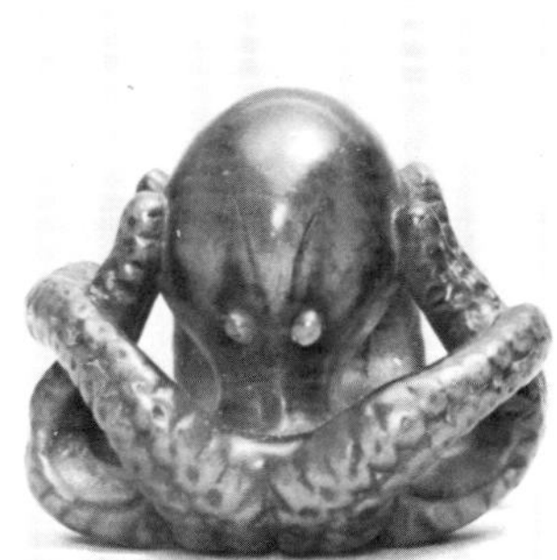

An octopus with all eight arms on its head

Wood, inlaid eyes. 19th c. Katabori. 4.0 cm. E26690

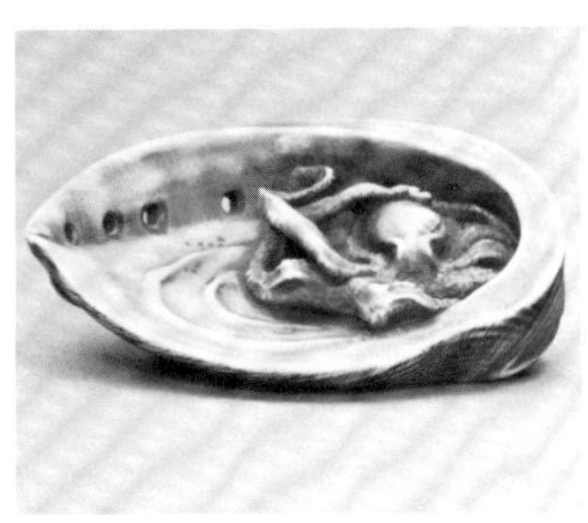

An octopus lounges on a shell. A long narrow leaf on the other side of the shell forms a natural aperture for the cord.

Ivory, inlaid eyes. Josetsu. after 1853. Katabori. 5.3 cm. E26701

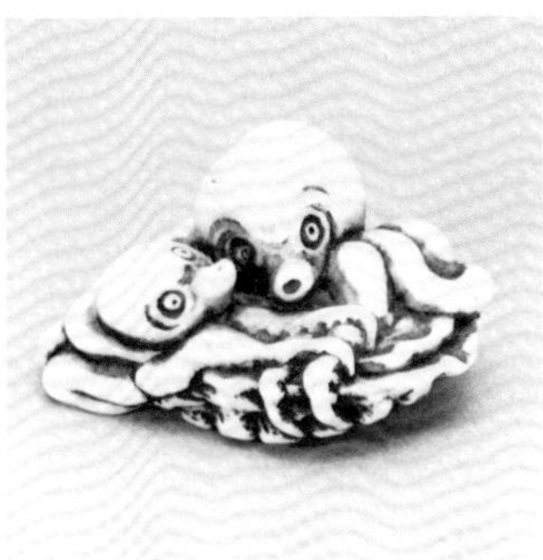

Perhaps to suggest the result of too much amorousness, the artist of this piece carved an octopus and its baby.

Ivory. 19th-20th c. Katabori. 3.5 cm. E26758

Quail According to M. and E. Jahss (see Bibliography), quail on millet represent autumn. Since quail were once kept as fighting birds they can also represent the martial spirit; because of their ragged appearance they can signify poverty.

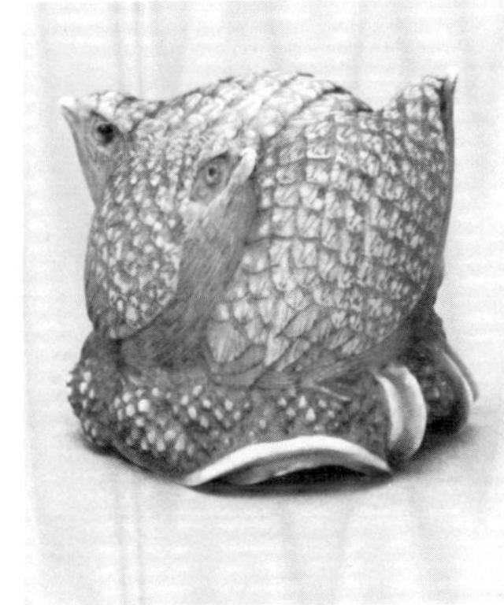

Quail on millet was a famous design by the master Okatomo, and as Bushell points out in *Collectors' Netsuke* (see Bibliography), as such it was frequently reproduced (signature and all) by inferior artists.

Ivory, inlaid eyes. Okatomo. late 19th-20th c. Katabori. 3.5 cm. E26677

Snail The snail symbolizes the impermanence of earthly power and belongs to the triad of mutual deterrence: the frog can eat the snail, the snake can eat the frog, the snail's slime can poison the snake.

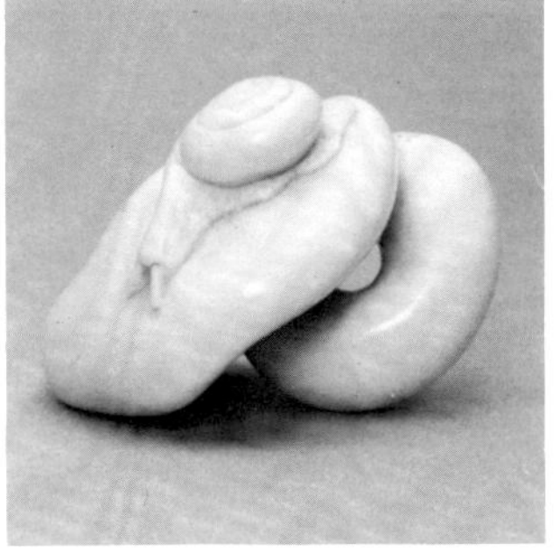

A snail crawls on the cap of a mushroom whose stem curves gracefully under its cap to form a natural aperture.

Ivory. late 19th-20th c. Katabori. 2.6 cm. E25280

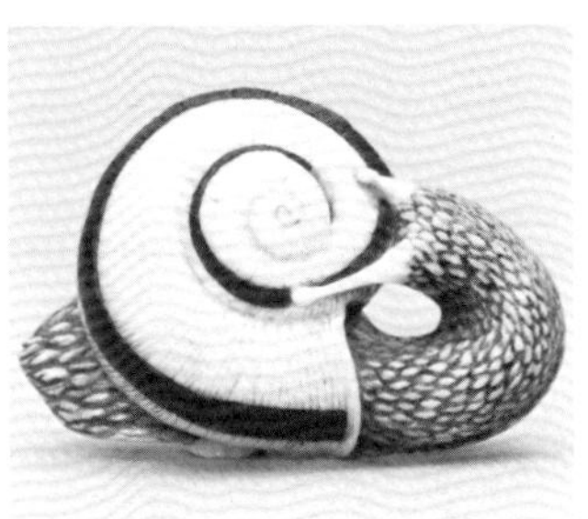

The stripes in the snail shell are made of horn inlays.

Ivory, horn. 19th c. Katabori. 4.0 cm. E26633

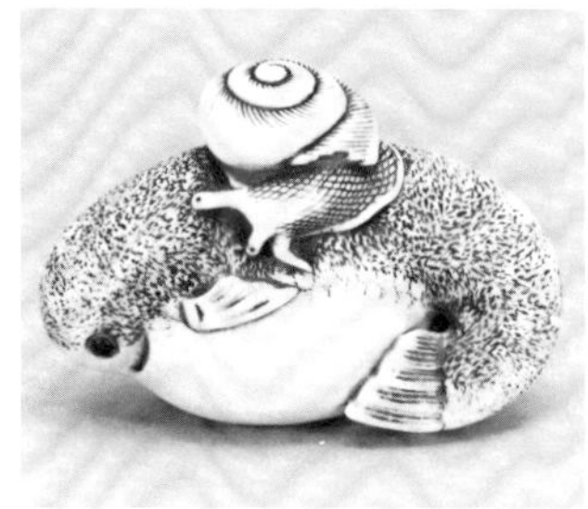

A snail atop a sea bream

Ivory, ebony eyes. late 19th-20th c. Katabori. 4.8 cm. E26682

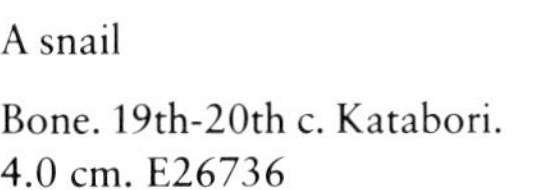

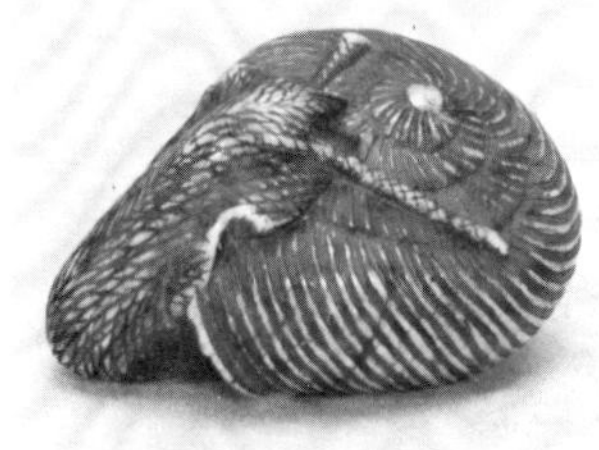

A snail

Bone. 19th-20th c. Katabori. 4.0 cm. E26736

A snail on the underside of a mushroom

Ivory. Tomotada. early 19th c. Katabori. 4.7 cm. E26806

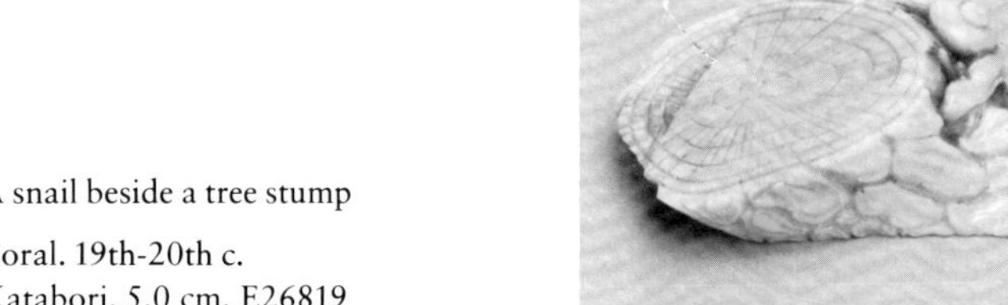

A snail beside a tree stump

Coral. 19th-20th c. Katabori. 5.0 cm. E26819

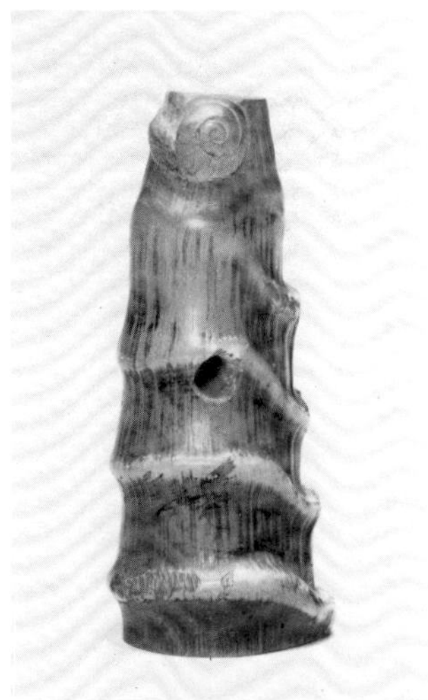

A snail on a piece of bamboo

Horn. 19th-20th c. Katabori. 6.5 cm. E26888

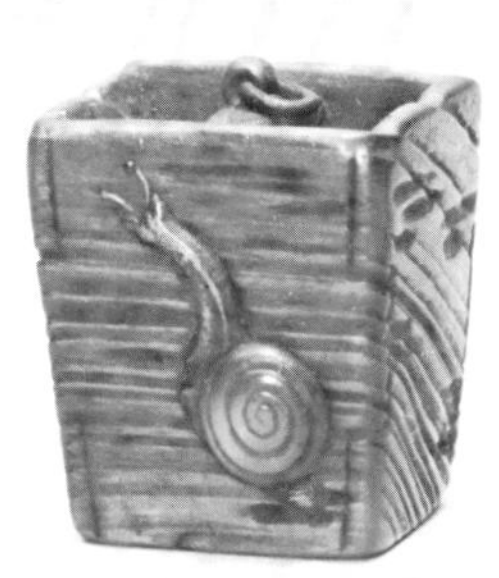

A snail (neck, head and tail of bone, shell of horn) crawls on the side of a wooden bucket.

Wood, bone, horn. 19th-20th c. Katabori. 2.7 cm. E26909

Squirrel Because it carefully prepares for winter, the squirrel is known for its foresight.

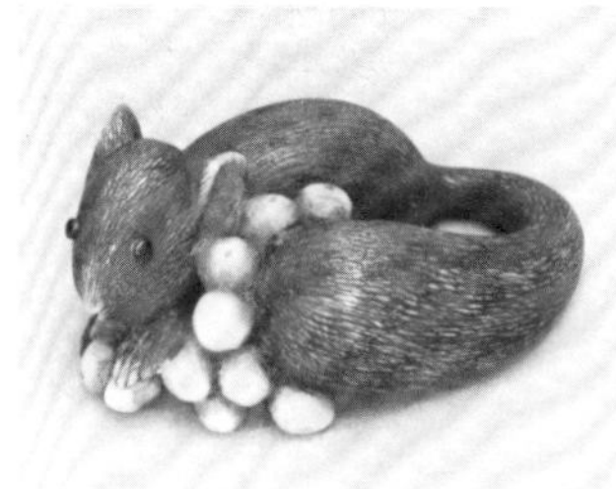

A squirrel on a pile of nuts

Ivory, ebony eyes. 19th-20th c. Katabori. 3.9 cm. E26769

Sparrow Besides its roles in fairy tales, the sparrow symbolizes many attributes including friendship, industry, grace and charm. The inflated sparrow (fukura suzume) is a popular children's toy which is often recreated in netsuke, embellished with designs and symbols. Neill and Okada (see Bibliography) suggest that the flight of the sparrow is also a reminder of the Buddhist ideal of the individual freed from worldly concerns.

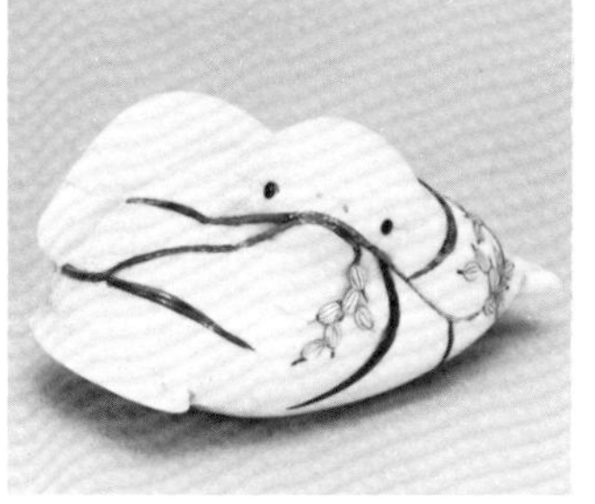

A fukura suzume holds green leaves (coral inlay) and white flowers (pearl inlay) in its mouth, perhaps as a harbinger of spring. The artist's name and the generic term for inlay work (Shibayama) appear on an inlaid pearl plaque.

Ivory, coral, pearl. Senzo. 18th-19th c. Katabori. 4.6 cm. E26643

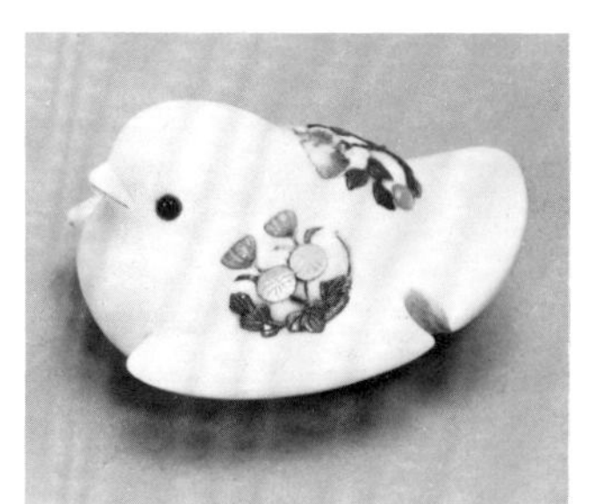

The back of this fukura suzume is decorated with pearl, and green and pink coral inlaid floral designs. It is signed Shibayama, the generic term for inlay work.

Ivory, coral, pearl. Shibayama. 19th c. Katabori. 5.2 cm. E26669

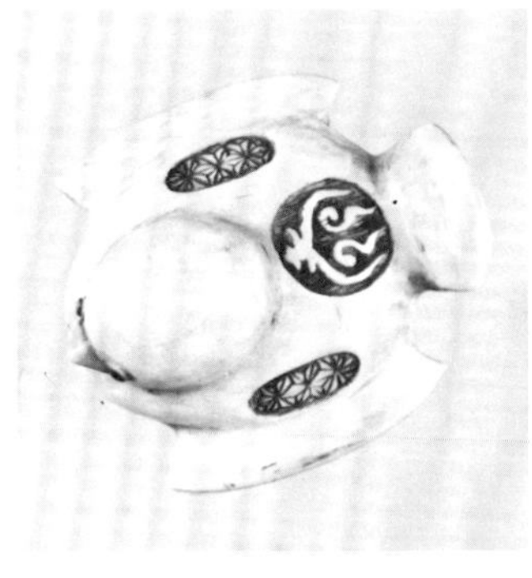

A fukura suzume with designs engraved on its back

Ivory, ebony eyes. 19th-20th c. Katabori. 3.8 cm. E26670

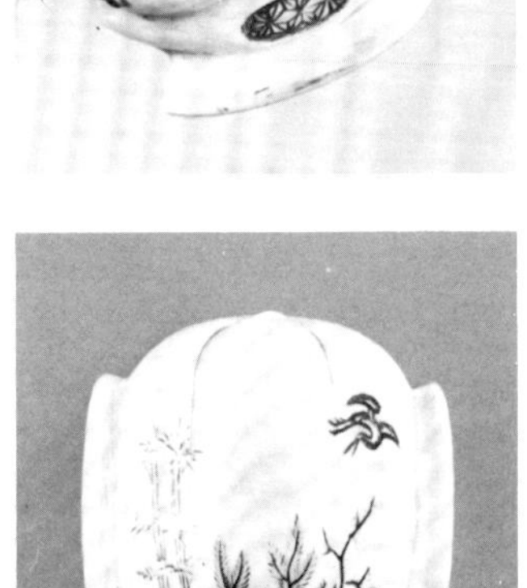

Engraved on the back of fukura suzume are several symbolic plants and animals often depicted together: a bushy-tailed turtle, a crane, and some pine and bamboo branches which all together symbolize extreme longevity and joyfulness.

Ivory. Shounsai. 1800-1869. Katabori. 3.4 cm. E26727

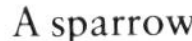

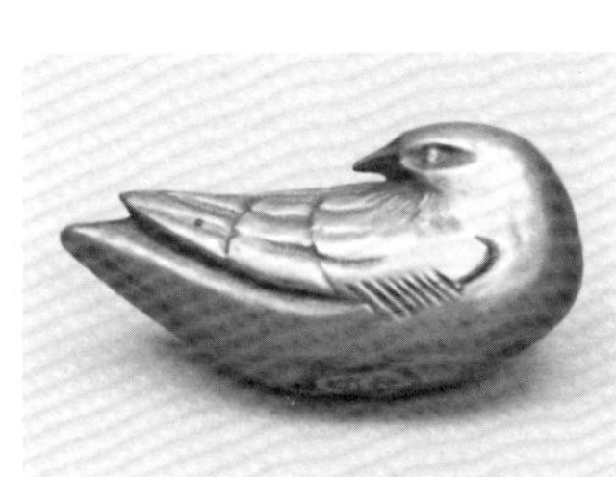

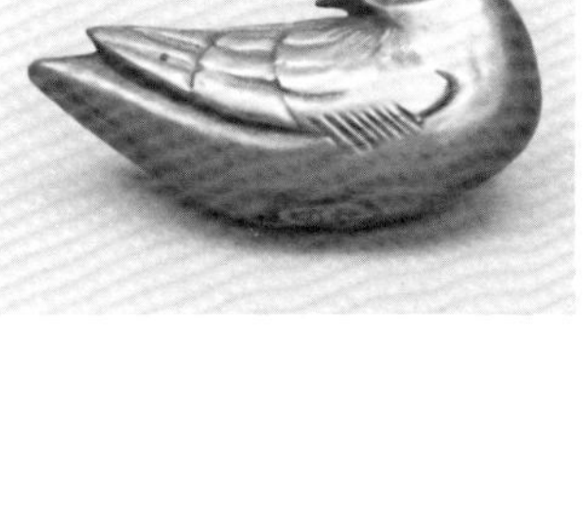

A sparrow

Wood with gold lacquer. 19th-20th c. Katabori. 5.4 cm. E26750

Tortoise The tortoise symbolizes longevity: the plain-tailed tortoise is said to live at least a thousand years and the bushy-tailed tortoise supposedly acquires its tail when it reaches the age of ten thousand. (Scientists explain that a plant parasite actually attaches itself to the turtle's shell and forms a veil which resembles a bushy tail.) According to legend tortoises descend from dragons and serve as messengers for the queen of the world under the sea. A stack of tortoises symbolizes numerous descendants; empty tortoise shells can be used for divining omens and messages from the gods.

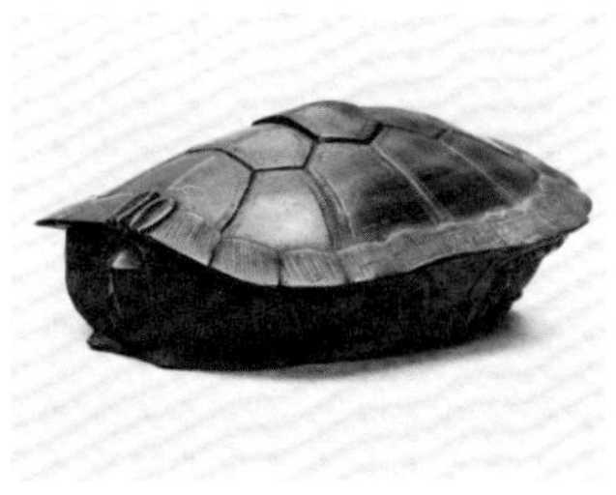

A tortoise withdrawn into its shell

Wood. Sekishu. 18th-19th c. Katabori. 5.0 cm. E7968

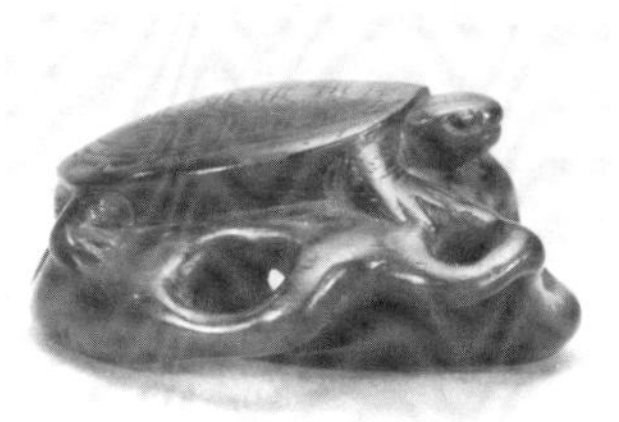

A turtle on an open cut wood base

Wood. 19th-20th c. Katabori. 4.8 cm. E26640

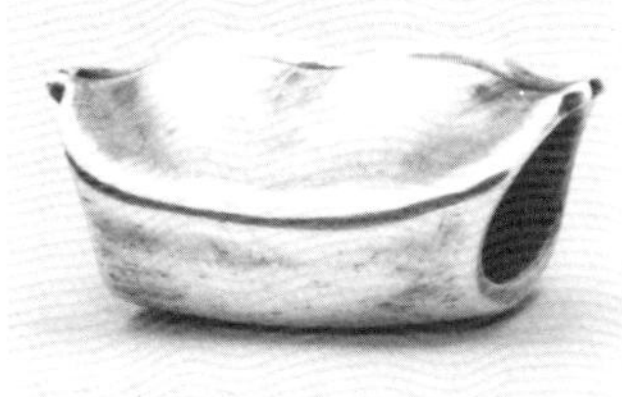

An uninhabited tortoise shell

Bone. 19th c. Katabori. 3.5 cm. E26644

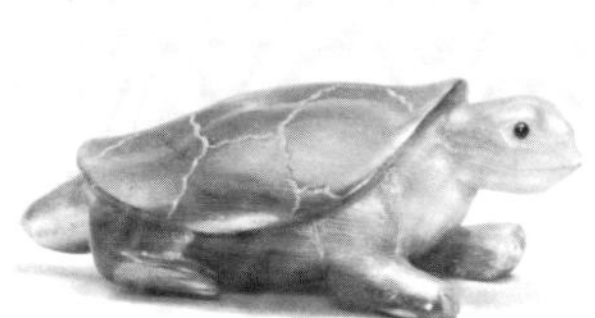

A turtle

Horn, inlaid eyes. 19th-20th c. Katabori. 5.0 cm. E26654

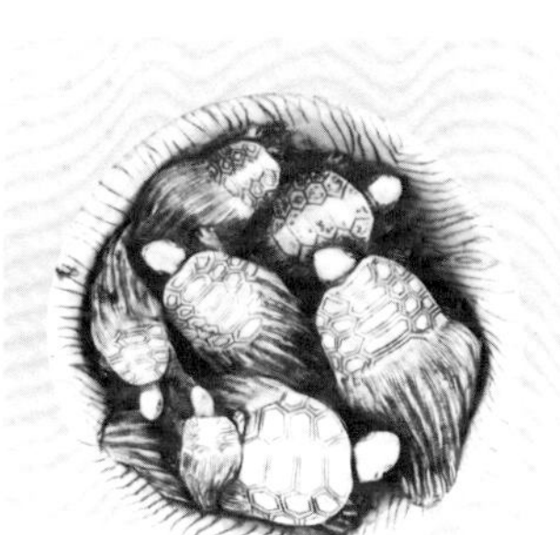

Seven bushy-tailed tortoises in a bowl

Ivory, inlaid eyes. Donkosai, unrecorded artist. 19th c. Katabori. 5.5 cm. E26732

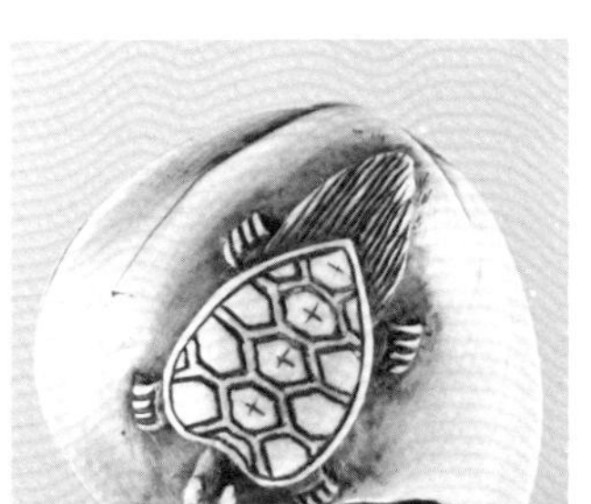

A bushy-tailed tortoise stands on the outside of a clamshell; a crab peeks out from within.

Ivory. 19th c. Katabori. 3.8 cm. E26749

A tortoise on a leaf

Ivory, ebony eyes. 19th-20th c. Katabori. 6.0 cm. E26776

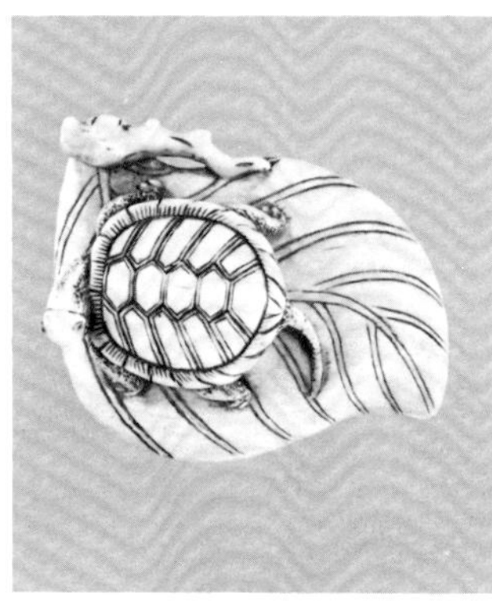

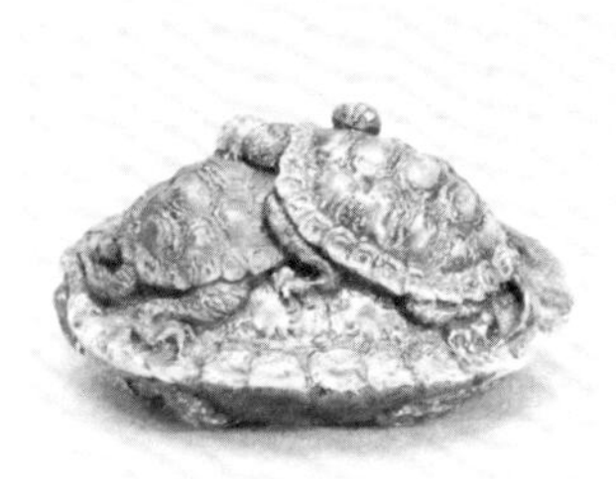

Two small turtles atop a larger one

Brown porcelain. Teiji. late 19th c. Katabori. 4.0 cm. E53700

A tortoise, lotus leaf, loquats on a branch and a beetle are grouped on a flat round base.

Ivory, metal eyes. late 19th-20th c. Katabori. 4.0 cm. E26820

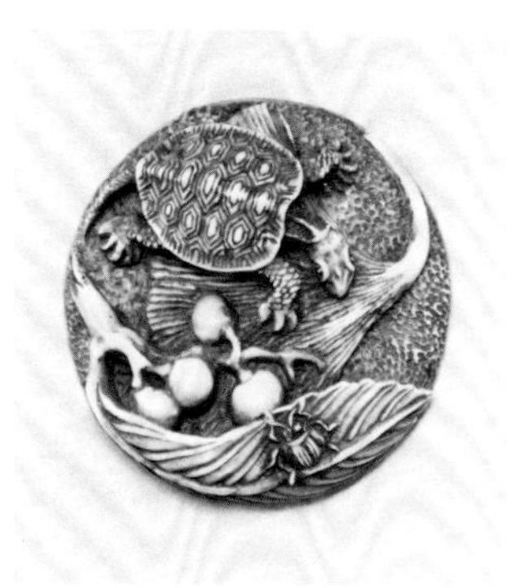

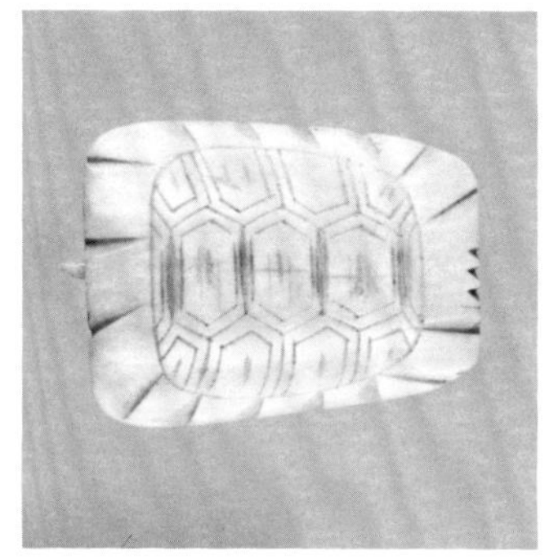

An empty tortoise shell

Bone. 19th c. Katabori. 5.5 cm. E64727

A stack of turtles

Wood, ebony eyes and himotoshi. Gekkosai. 19th c. Katabori. 6.6 cm. E37162

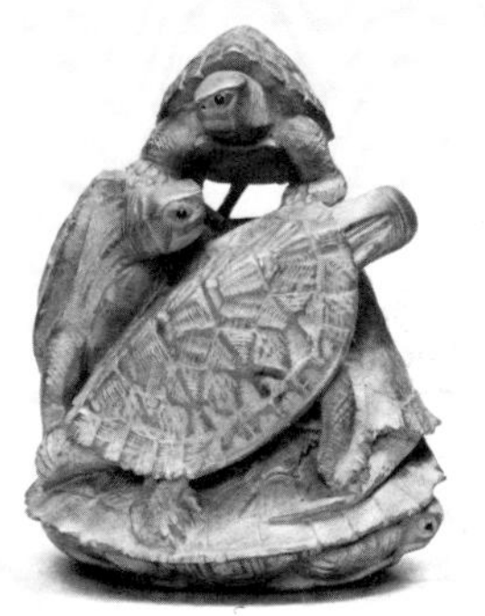

Wasp Wasps appear so frequently in netsuke that they are thought to have been symbolic; but according to Okada and Neill (see Bibliography), their significance has been lost.

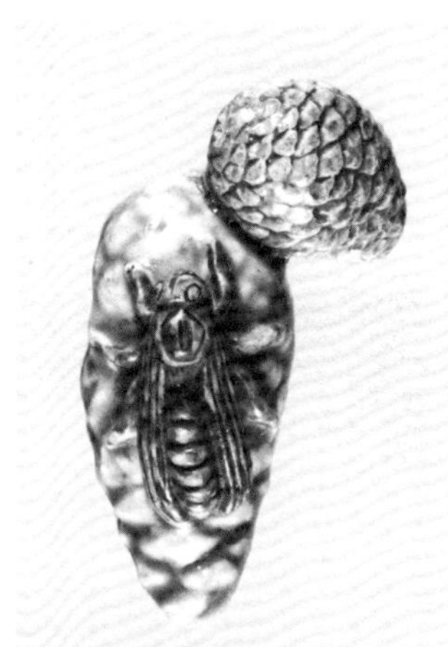

A brown wasp crawls on a blue pine cone which is beside a small green pine cone.

Porcelain. 19th c. Katabori. 4.6 cm. E26796

A stack of turtles

Wood, ebony eyes and himotoshi. Gekko. 19th c. Katabori. 6.1 cm. E37163

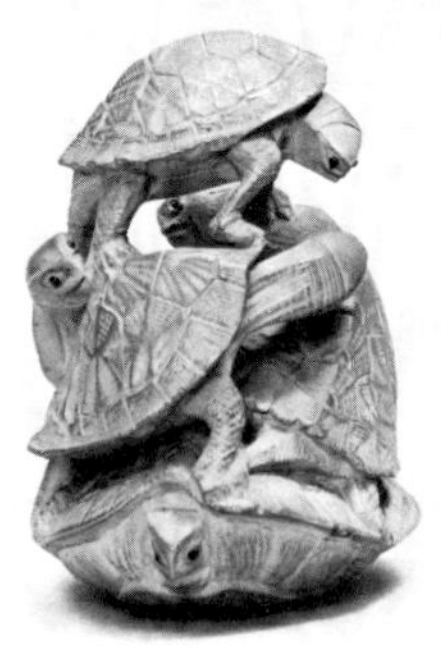

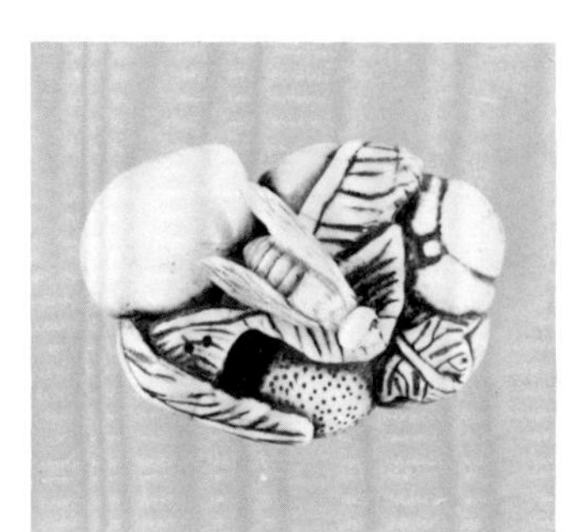

The wasp atop this bunch of fruit was carved from a separate piece of ivory, and may have been added by another artist.

Ivory. 19th-20th c. Katabori. 4.0 cm. E26991

Wild Goose Flying across a full moon, a formation of geese symbolizes autumn. Since geese break their line only in the presence of danger, these birds also symbolize caution.

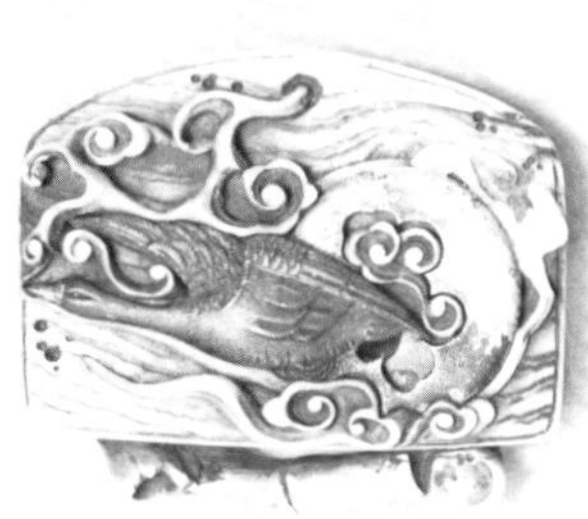

On the front of the manju netsuke, a solitary goose flies in front of a full moon; broken stalks of bamboo appear on the top and back of this piece. Since bamboo is a symbol of flexibility because it can bend under heavy weight without breaking, this netsuke design is unusual.

Ivory, metal. 19th c. Manju. 4.0 cm. E26562

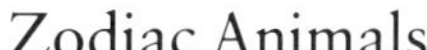

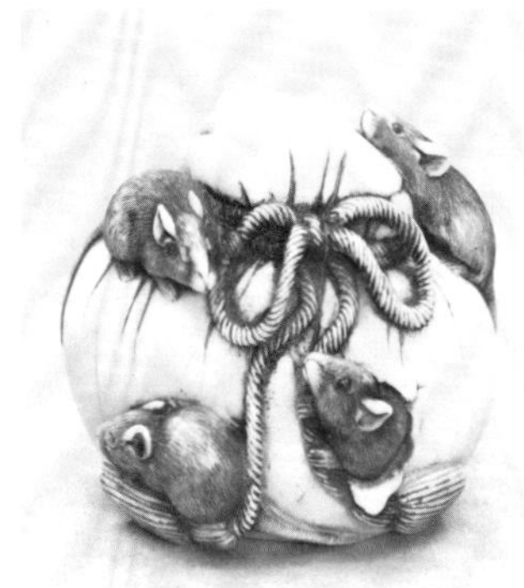

Five rats crawl over and through a bag of grain.

Ivory, inlaid eyes. Tomokazu. 19th c. Katabori. 4.2 cm. E24903

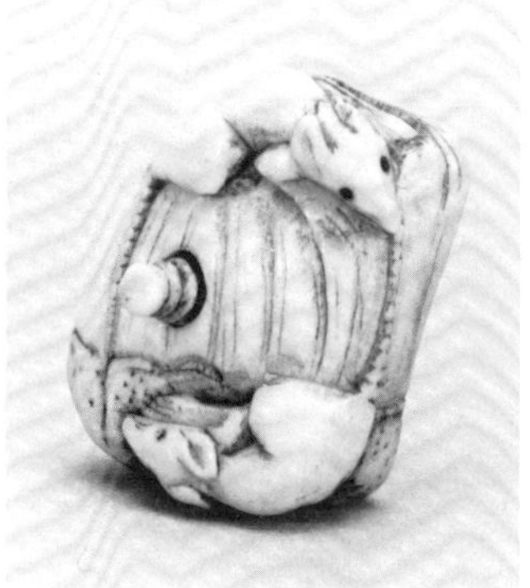

A worm slides in and out of a hole in a chestnut upon which two rats climb.

Bone. early 19th c. Katabori. 3.5 cm. E26658

Zodiac Animals

Each animal of the Japanese zodiac represents a whole year of a twelve year cycle and is assigned to specific hours, days and points of the compass. Many people who believed their destinies were dependent on their date of birth chose a netsuke of the corresponding animal. In addition to their place in the zodiac, the animals play roles in folk tales and traditions.

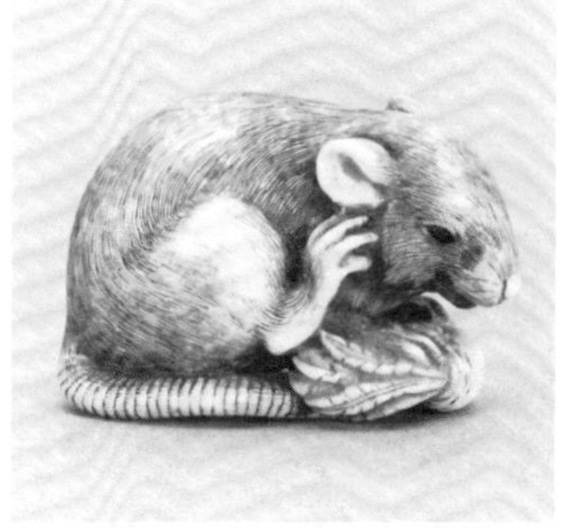

Huddled over a parsnip, a rat scratches his ear with his right hind leg.

Ivory, inlaid eyes. Okatomo. before 1781. Katabori. 4.3 cm. E26680

Rat (first sign) Persons born in the year of the rat are creative and charming. Japan's multitude of rats suggests why it is a symbol of fertility and wealth, an emblem of good luck and the companion of the beloved god of wealth, Daikoku.

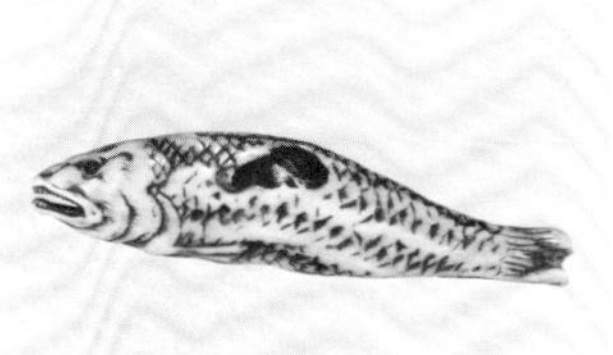

A rat crawls out of a hole in the back of a dead fish.

Ivory. early 19th c. Katabori. 7.7 cm. E26706

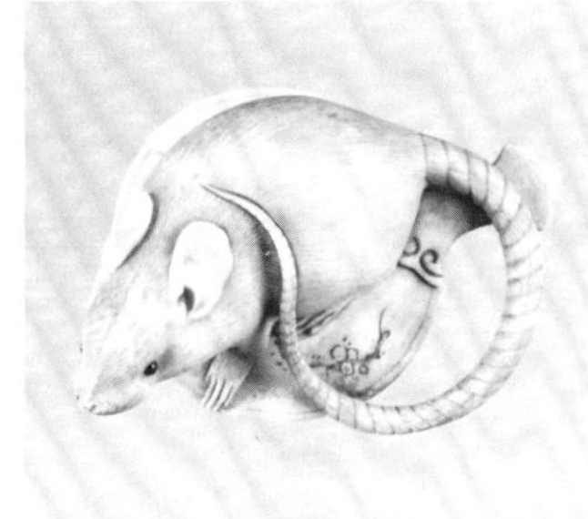

A rat reclines on a fan decorated with cherry blossoms.

Ivory, inlaid eyes. Masatami. 1848-1853. Katabori. 5.2 cm. E21250

Two rats on leaves and mushrooms

Ivory, ebony eyes. 19th c. Katabori. 6.0 cm. E26708

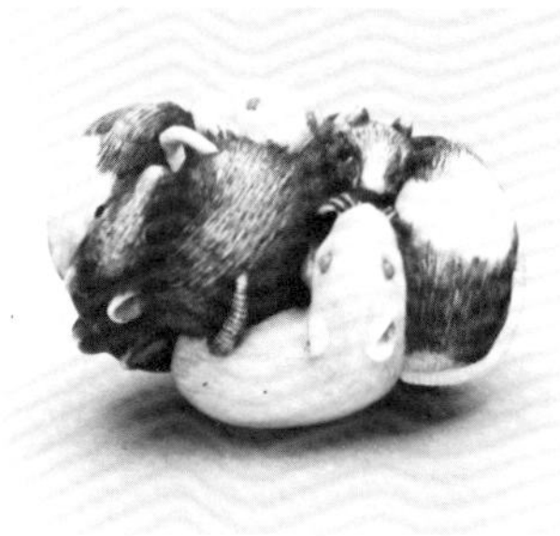

An entanglement of seven black and white rats

Ivory, coral and ebony eyes. Tomochika I. 1800-1873. Katabori. 4.4 cm. E26729

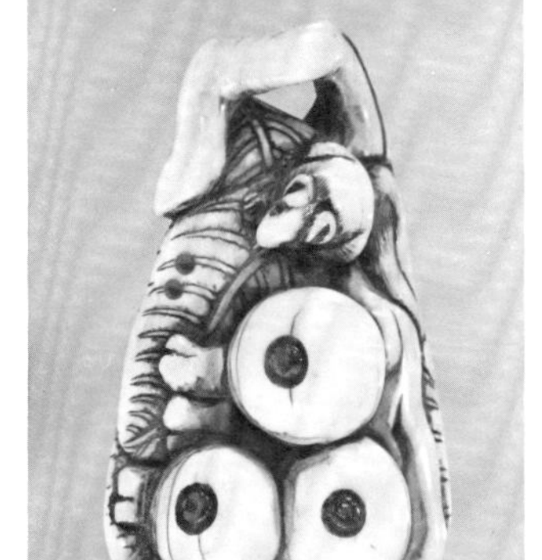

A rat with leaves and fruit

Ivory, wood inlays. 19th c. Katabori. 6.2 cm. E26808

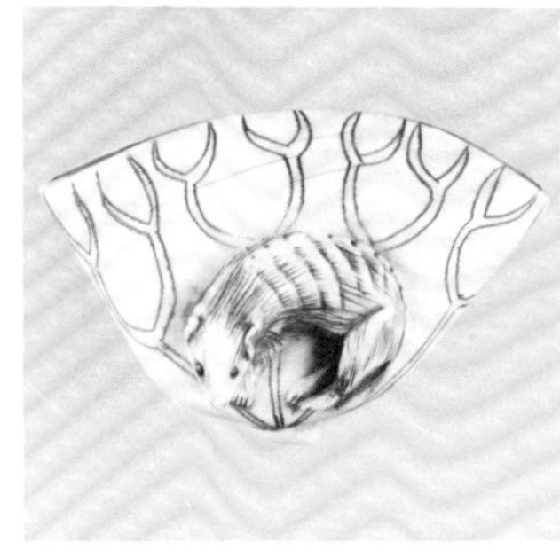

A rat on a curled lotus leaf

Ivory, ebony eyes. 19th-20th c. Katabori. 5.6 cm. E26737

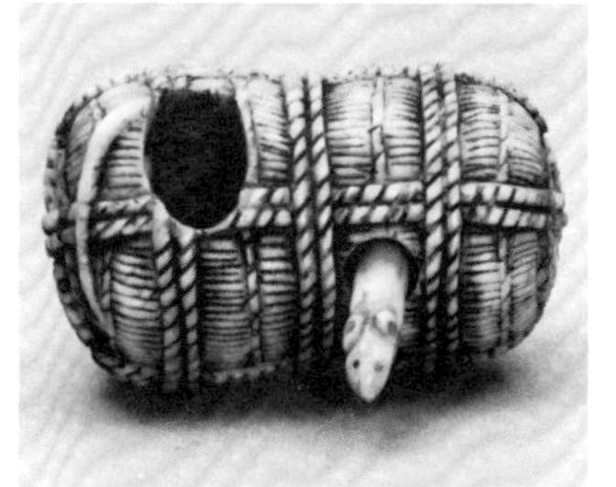

A rat's head slides in and out of a hole in a rice bale. (Another large hole and a tail of a rat carved on the outside of the bale suggest that another movable rat has been lost from the piece).

Bone. 19th c. Katabori. 4.0 cm. E26872

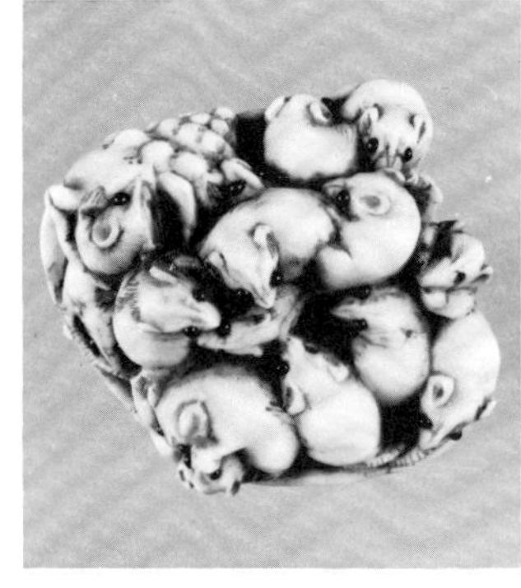

Fifteen rats climb on a pile of shells.

Ivory, inlaid eyes. Masamitsu. late 1800's-1909. Katabori. 4.5 cm. E26763

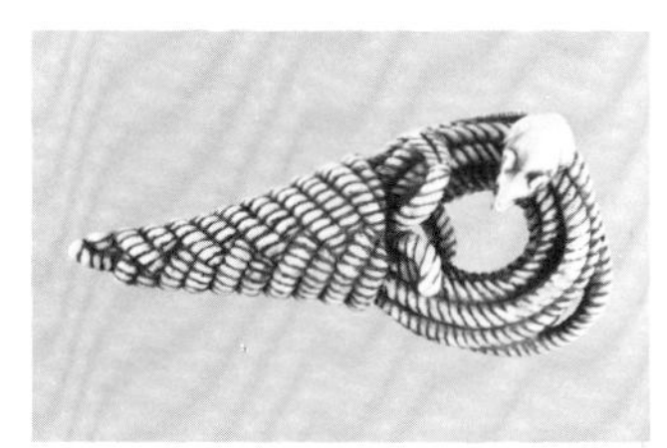

A tiny rat climbs on a coil of rope.

Ivory, inlaid eyes. 19th-20th c. Katabori. 6.5 cm. E26880

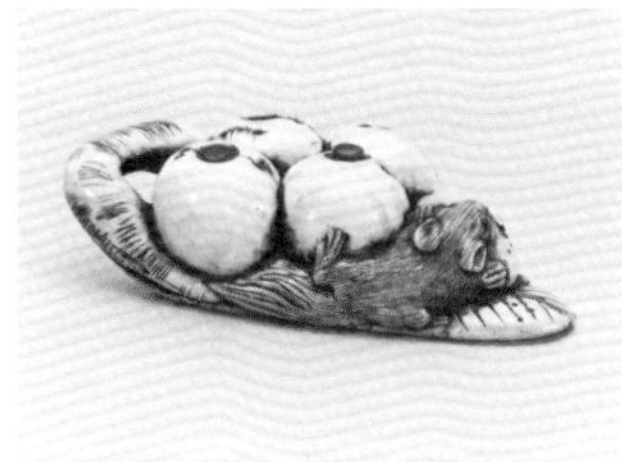

A rat with five fruits

Ivory, wood inlays. Kogyokusai. late 19th-20th c. Katabori. 5.8 cm. E26790

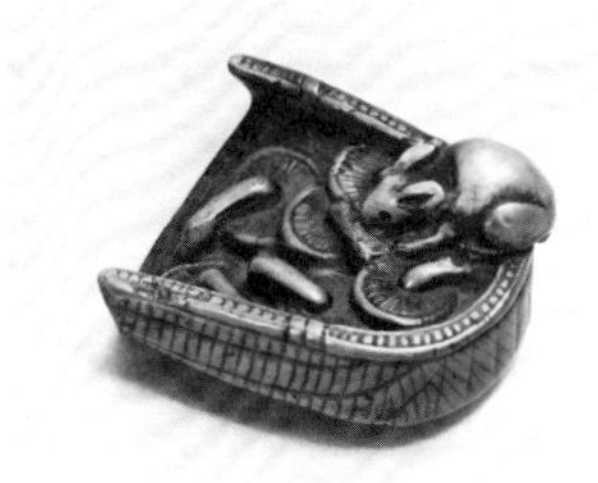

A rat sits on the edge of a rice scoop filled with mushrooms.

Wood. early 19th c. Katabori. 5.0 cm. E26884

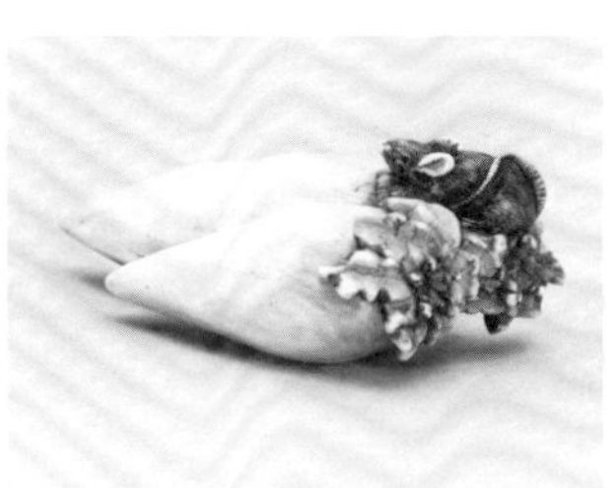

A small rat on two large parsnips

Ivory. late 19th c. Katabori. 7.0 cm. E26803

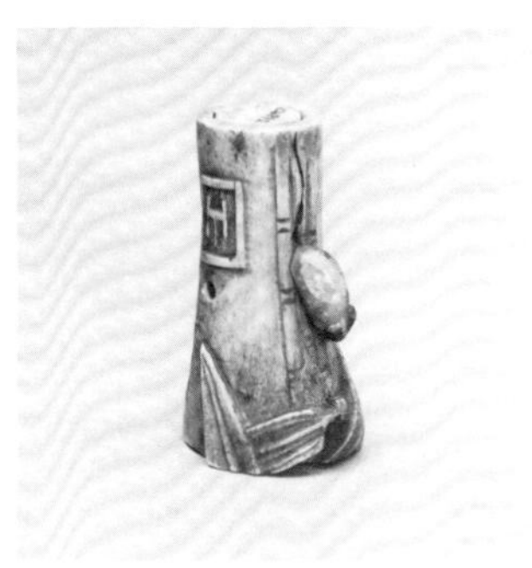

A rat made of quartz runs down a bamboo stalk made of bone.

Bone and quartz. 19th-20th c. Katabori. 5.0 cm. E26892

Ox (second sign) A person born in the year of the ox is patient and inspires confidence. The ox is the emblem of the Zen sect of Buddhism. A standing ox represents agriculture; lying down, it is the symbol of the god of calligraphy.

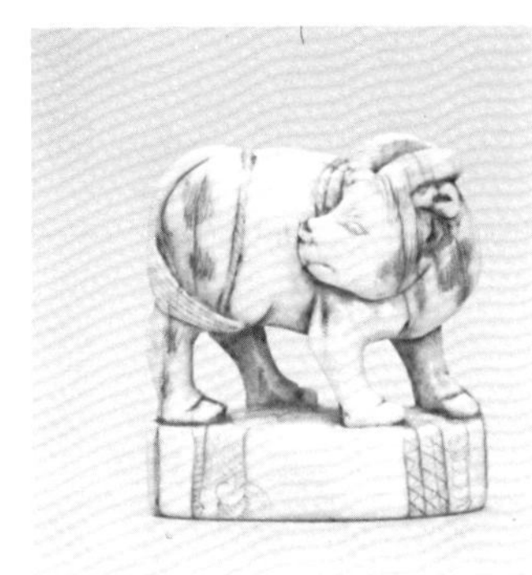

A carving appropriately designed to serve as a seal depicts an ox with a ring in its nose.

Ivory. 19th c. Katabori.
3.5 cm. E26653

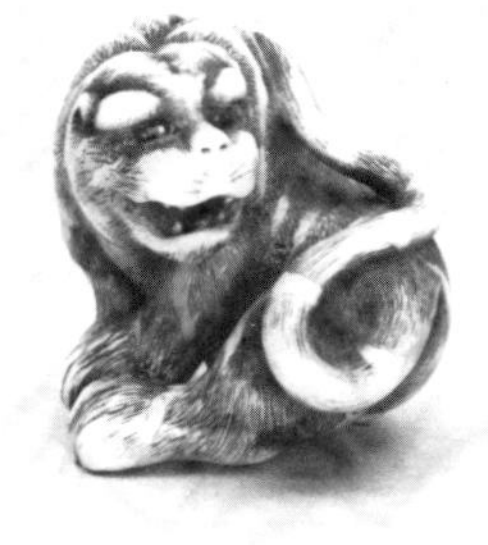

A tiger with gold eyes and red tongue

Ivory. Hakuryu. 19th c. Katabori.
3.2 cm. E26676

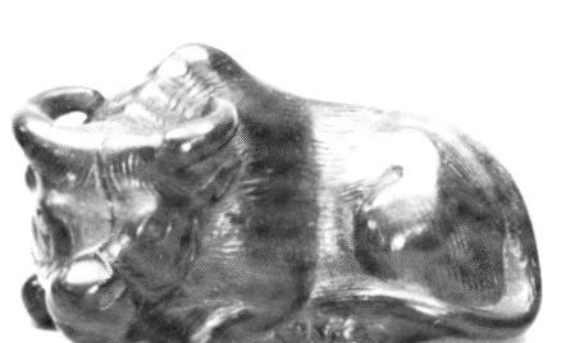

A reclining ox

Wood. 19th-20th c. Katabori.
5.8 cm. E33342

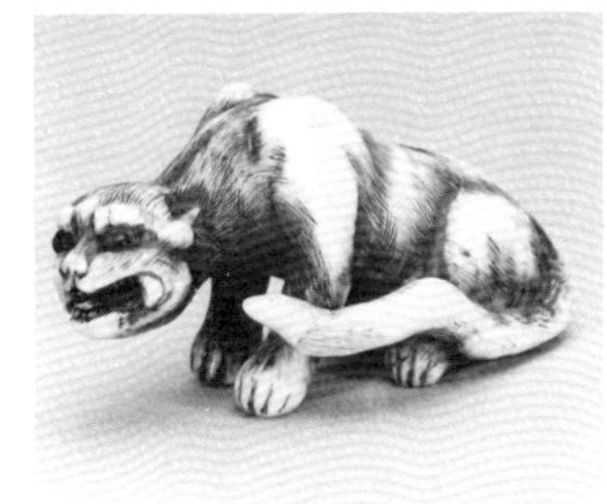

A vicious-looking tiger crouches as if ready to pounce.

Ivory, inlaid eyes. 19th c. Katabori.
5.0 cm. E26692

Tiger (third sign) A person born in the year of the tiger is fortunate, for the tiger is the zodiac sign for luck, as well as courage and strength. As with other animals and people that are foreign to Japan, the tiger's appearance in netsuke is based on verbal descriptions and other artists' conceptions; consequently the tiger appears in caricature only. The tiger in bamboo became a symbol stressed in netsuke: just as the mighty tiger needs the flimsy bamboo for protection, so the strong need the weak.

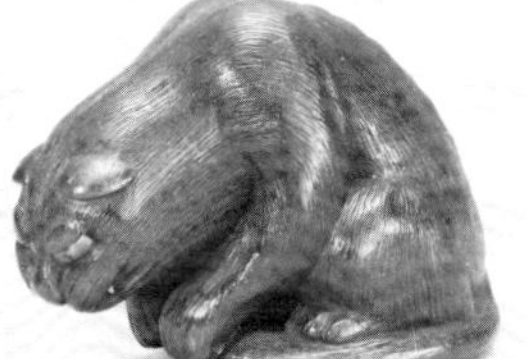

The tail of this crouching tiger loops around under its feet to help form the natural aperture for the cord.

Wood, amber eyes, ivory fangs.
Tomotada. 19th-20th c. Katabori.
4.5 cm. E26694

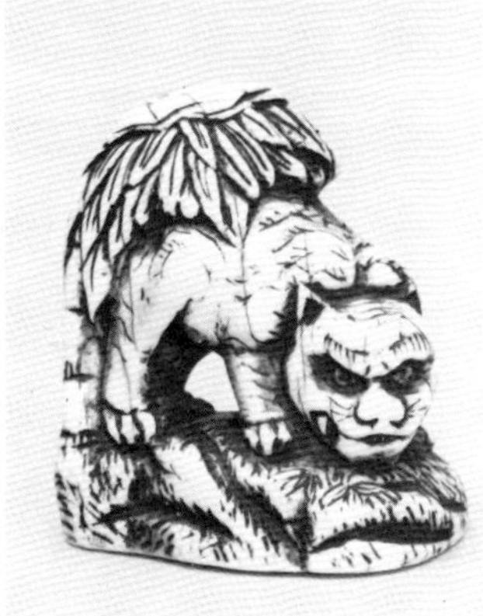

A tiger crouches under a bamboo tree.

Ivory. early 19th c. Katabori.
4.9 cm. E26639

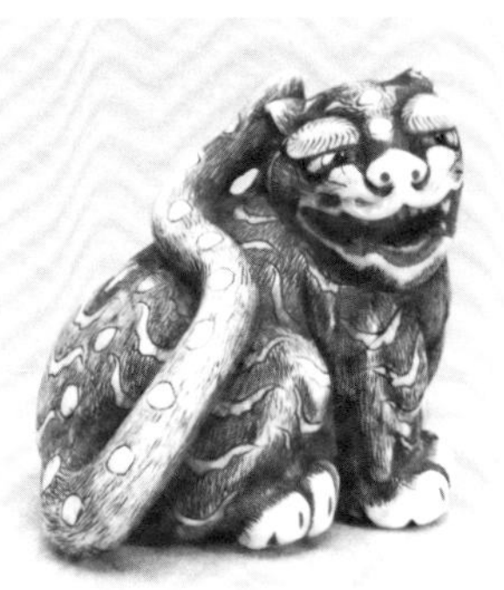

A seated tiger

Ivory, ebony eyes. mid-19th c.
Katabori. 4.3 cm. E26704

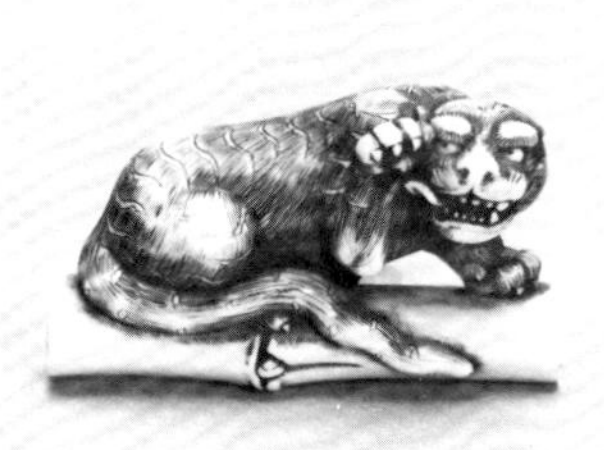

Crouching on a stalk of bamboo, a tiger licks its paw.

Ivory. 19th c. Katabori.
5.2 cm. E26655

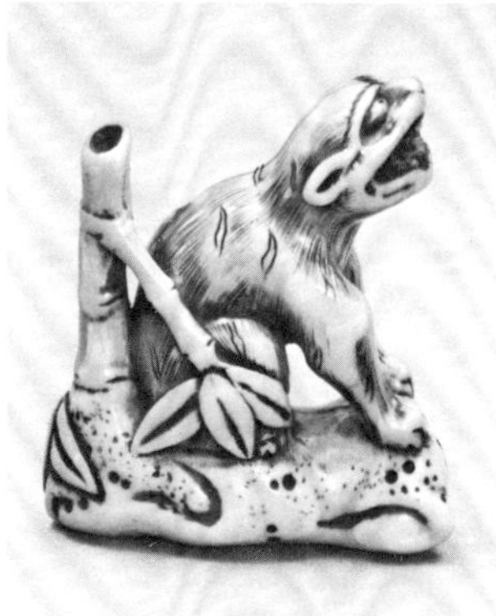

A tiger sits on rocky ground next to a bamboo stalk.

Ivory. Minamoto, unrecorded artist. late 18th-19th c. Katabori. 4.0 cm. E26712

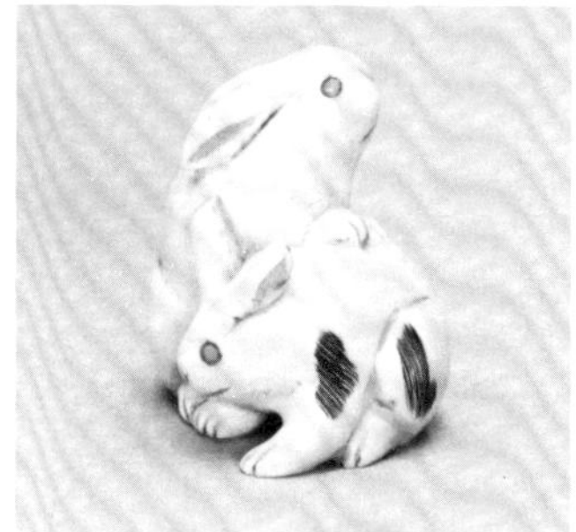

Rabbit group

Ivory, pink coral eyes. late 19th-20th c. Katabori. 3.2 cm. E26719

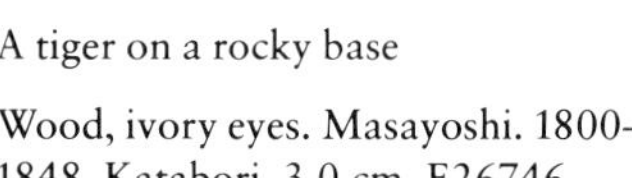

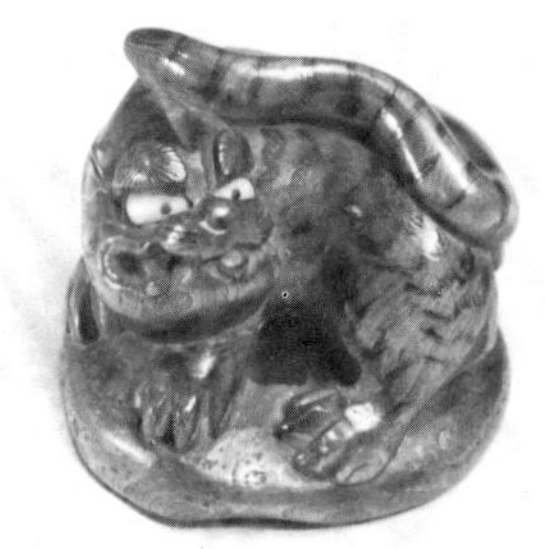

A tiger on a rocky base

Wood, ivory eyes. Masayoshi. 1800-1848. Katabori. 3.0 cm. E26746

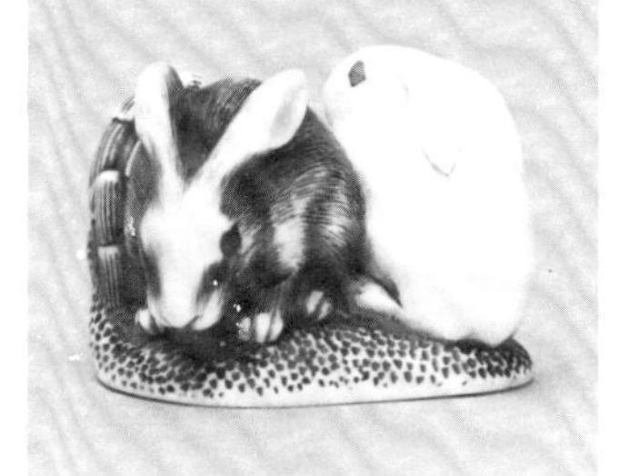

Two rabbits sit near some bamboo shoots.

Ivory, inlaid eyes. 19th-20th c. Katabori. 3.5 cm. E26720

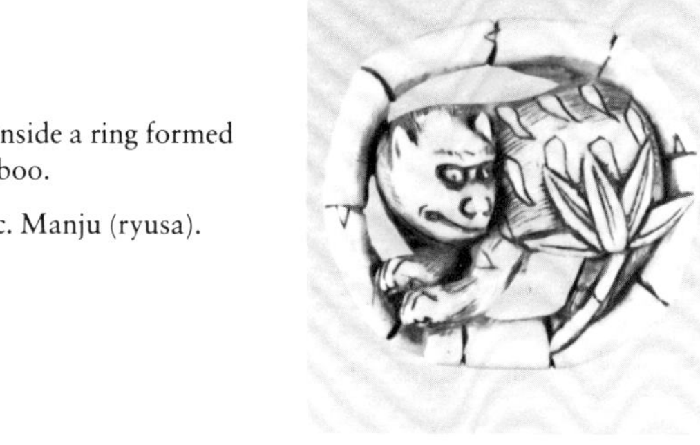

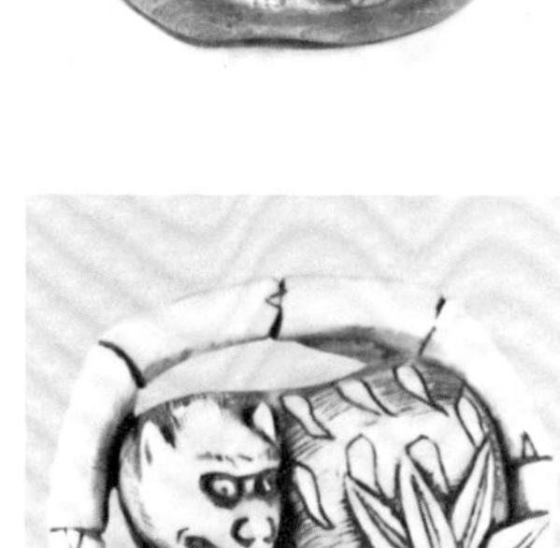

A tiger crouches inside a ring formed by a stalk of bamboo.

Ivory. 19th-20th c. Manju (ryusa). 3.7 cm. E26773

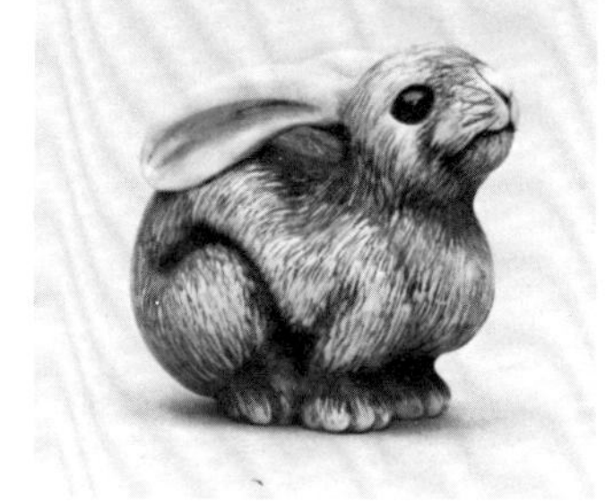

A crouching rabbit depicted with very fine detail

Ivory, inlaid eyes. Toyomasa. late 18th-19th c. Katabori. 4.1 cm. E26721

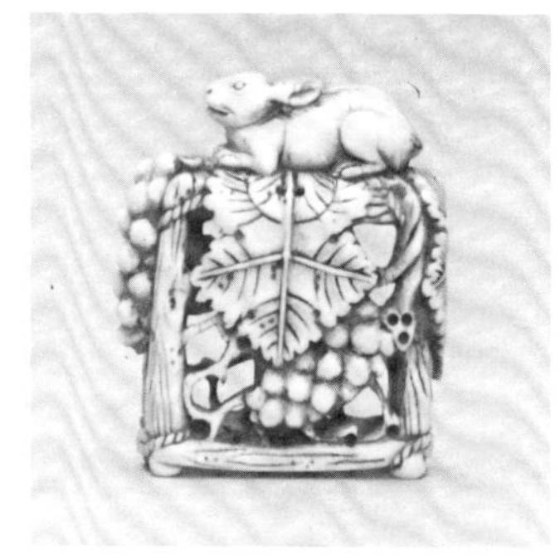

A rabbit lies atop a grape arbor.

Ivory. 19th c. Katabori. 3.7 cm. E26785

Hare (fourth sign) People born in the year of the hare are conservative, talented and ambitious. A symbol of longevity, the hare supposedly turns white at five hundred years of age and lives to be one thousand. The Japanese see a "rabbit in the moon" pounding rice for the rice-cake offerings made in Shinto shrines.

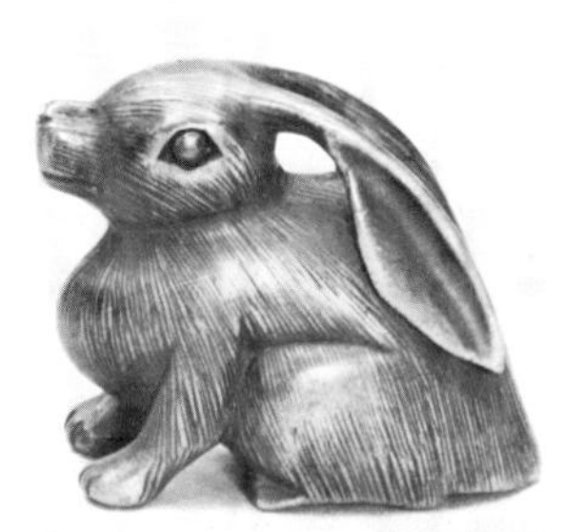

A rabbit

Boxwood. 19th-20th c. Katabori. 4.5 cm. E26674

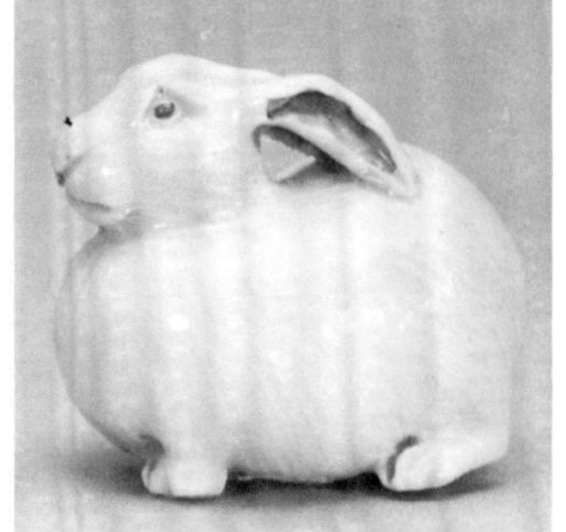

A grayish rabbit with pink ears, eyes and mouth

Porcelain. illegible signature. 19th c. Katabori. 4.0 cm. E53701

Dragon (fifth sign) Those born in the year of the dragon enjoy longevity and success. The dragon is the supreme animal power in the sky, symbol of the emperor, though it also lives at times in the sea. Its watery breath creates clouds that lift it to heaven.

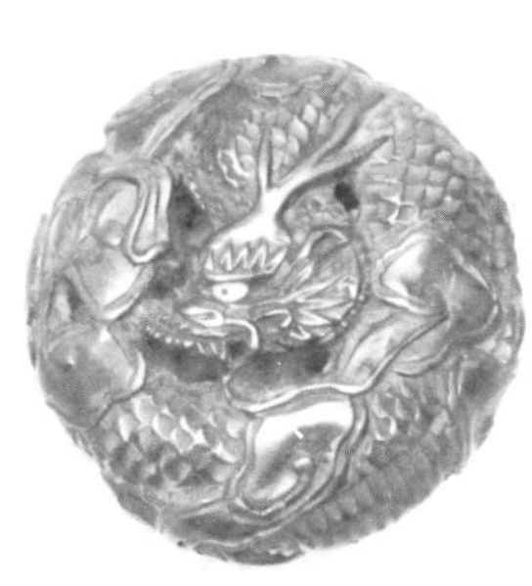

Through the hole in this clam a green dragon can be seen curled up.

Porcelain. illegible signature. late 18th-19th c. Katabori. 4.8 cm. E26699

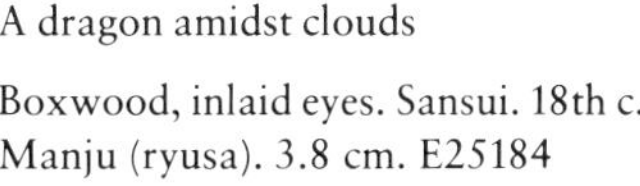

A dragon amidst clouds

Boxwood, inlaid eyes. Sansui. 18th c. Manju (ryusa). 3.8 cm. E25184

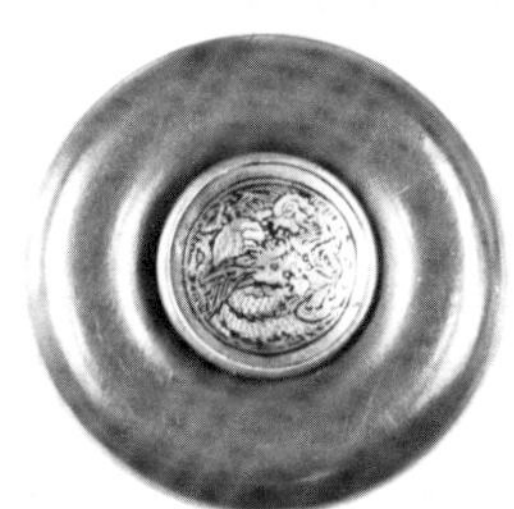

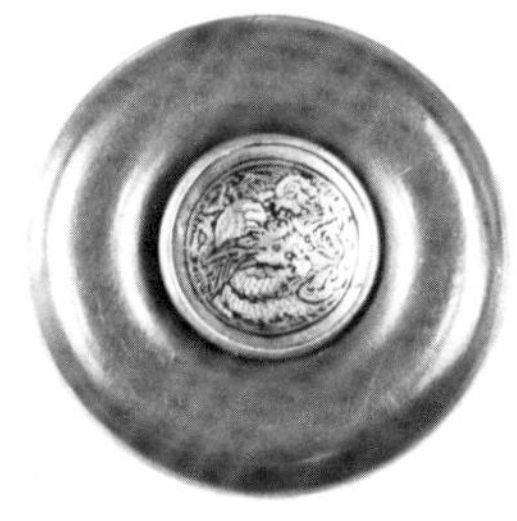

A pink coral dragon entwined in clouds

Wood and coral. mid-18th-19th c. Manju (ryusa). 4.3 cm. E26916

A dragon appears on a gold metal button in the center of a plain gold lacquered bowl.

Lacquered wood and metal. 19th c. Manju. 3.0 cm. E26537

Snake (sixth sign) People born during the year of the snake are meditative and attractive people who attain their goals. A member of the triad of mutual deterrence, the snake is also a symbol of jealousy, retaliation, deceit, and cunning.

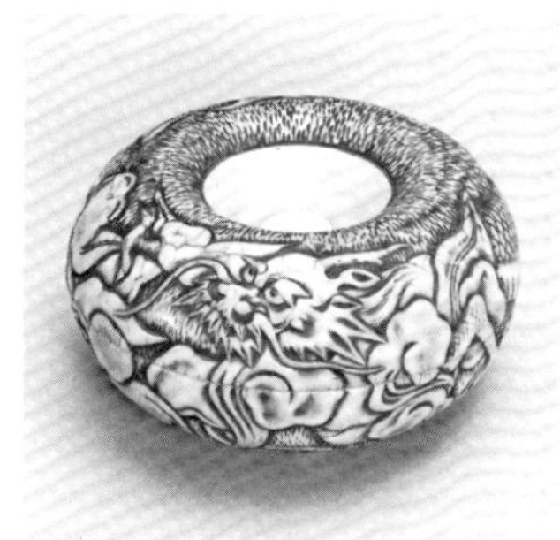

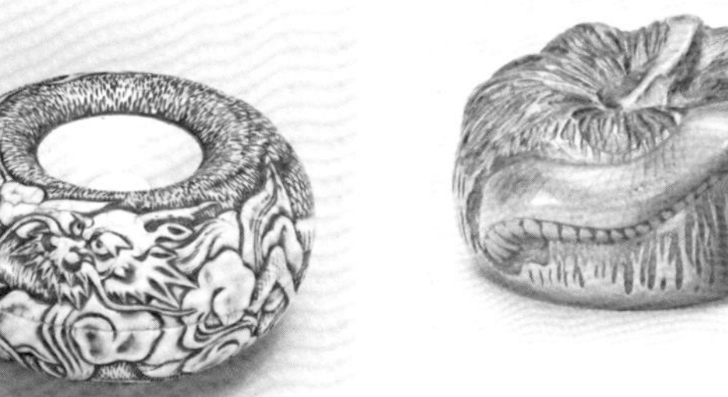

A dragon amidst clouds and rain is engraved around this unusually large manju netsuke. A small metal button (not visible in photo) is engraved with evergreens and bamboo, and writing which reads Temmin, age 63.

Ivory and metal. Temmin. mid-19th c. Manju. 8.0 cm. E26541

A snake crawls through a pumpkin.

Boxwood. Ranju. 19th c. Katabori. 4.5 cm. E4483

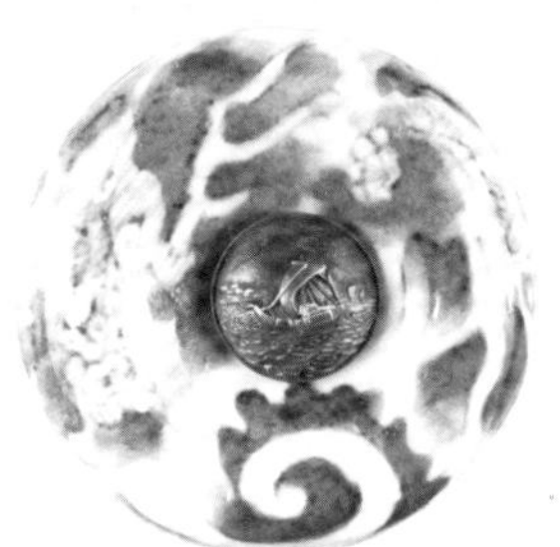

A porcelain manju netsuke is decorated with a blue dragon on a white background. On the small metal button a ship is sailing in front of Mt. Fuji.

Porcelain and metal. 19th c. Manju. 4.3 cm. E26542

A coiled snake swallows a frog.

Ivory, inlaid eyes. 19th c. Katabori. 4.0 cm. E26642

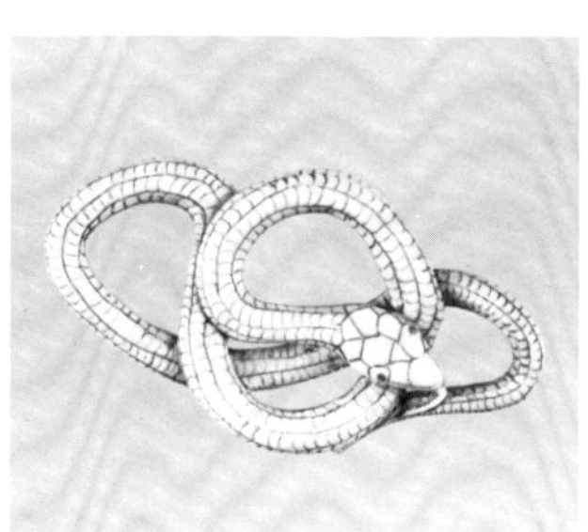

The body of this snake forms several natural apertures.

Ivory, inlaid eyes. late 19th-20th c. Katabori. 6.0 cm. E26672

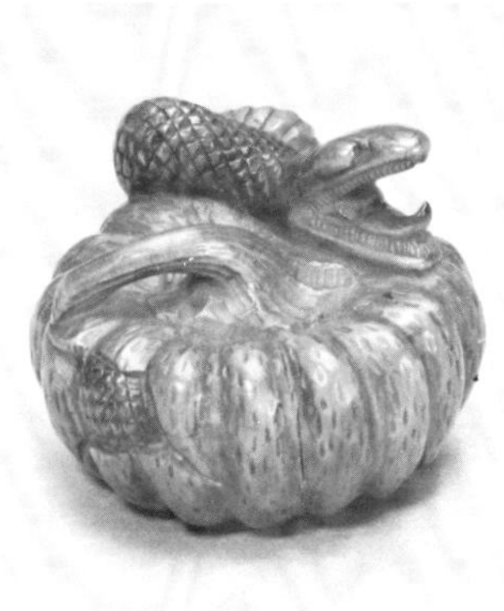

A wicked looking snake crawls through a pumpkin.

Wood. Shigemasa. early 19th c. Katabori. 4.3 cm. E26702

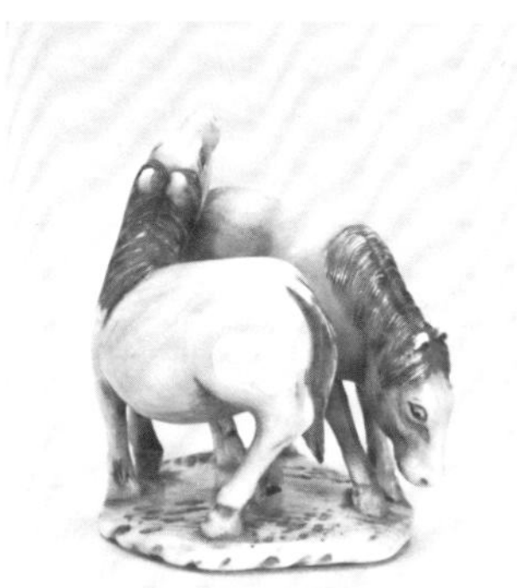

Two horses, one looking up, one looking down

Ivory. Gyokuyosai. 1781-1868. Katabori. 3.1 cm. E26724

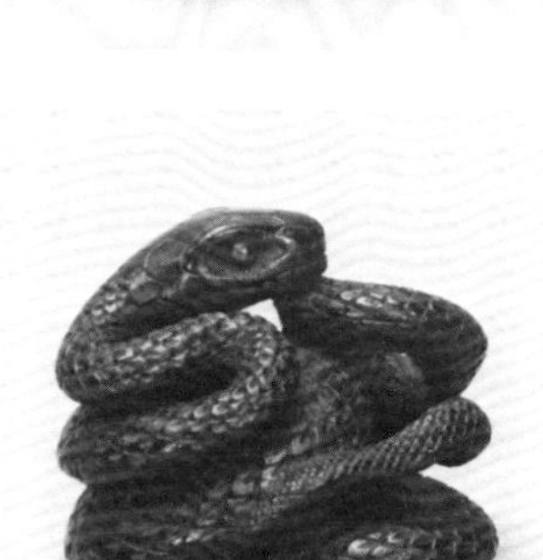

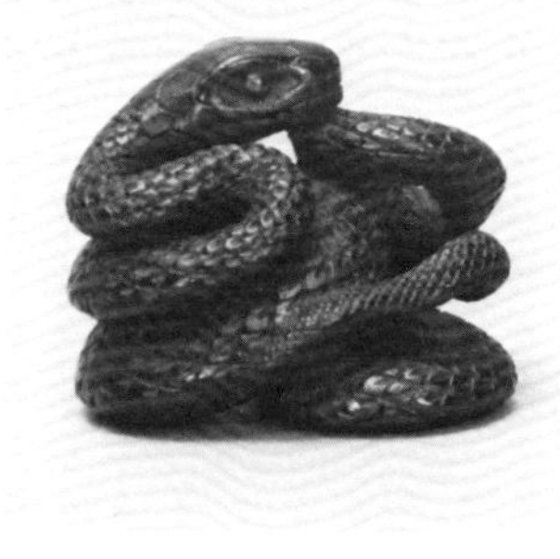

A coiled black snake

Wood. 19th-20th c. Katabori. 3.8 cm. E26731

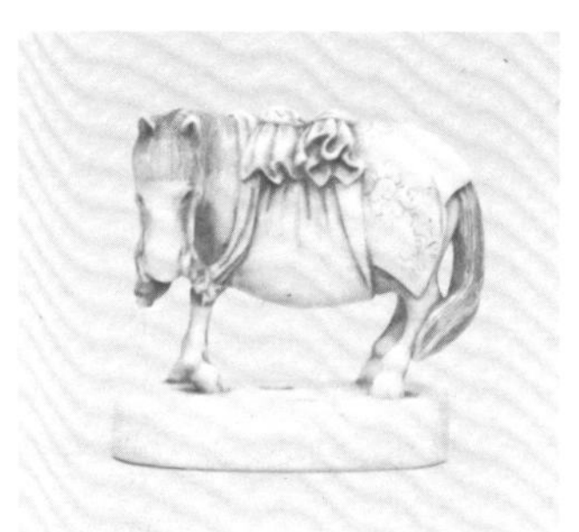

A fully saddled horse on an oval base

Ivory. Gyokuyosai. 1781-1868. Katabori. 3.3 cm. E26725

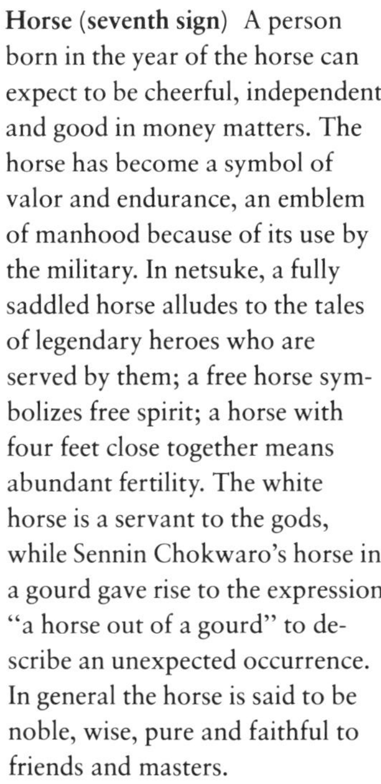

Horse (seventh sign) A person born in the year of the horse can expect to be cheerful, independent and good in money matters. The horse has become a symbol of valor and endurance, an emblem of manhood because of its use by the military. In netsuke, a fully saddled horse alludes to the tales of legendary heroes who are served by them; a free horse symbolizes free spirit; a horse with four feet close together means abundant fertility. The white horse is a servant to the gods, while Sennin Chokwaro's horse in a gourd gave rise to the expression "a horse out of a gourd" to describe an unexpected occurrence. In general the horse is said to be noble, wise, pure and faithful to friends and masters.

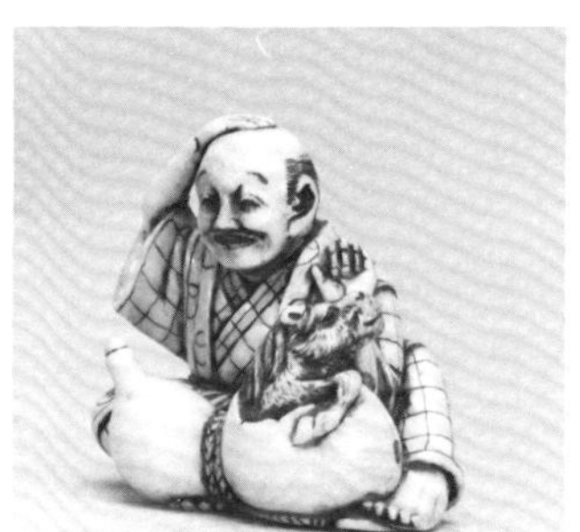

A seated man wearing netsuke, pipe case and tobacco pouch (not visible in photo) shows surprise as a horse emerges from the gourd in front of him.

Ivory. Tomochika I. 1800-1873. Katabori. 2.7 cm. E27038

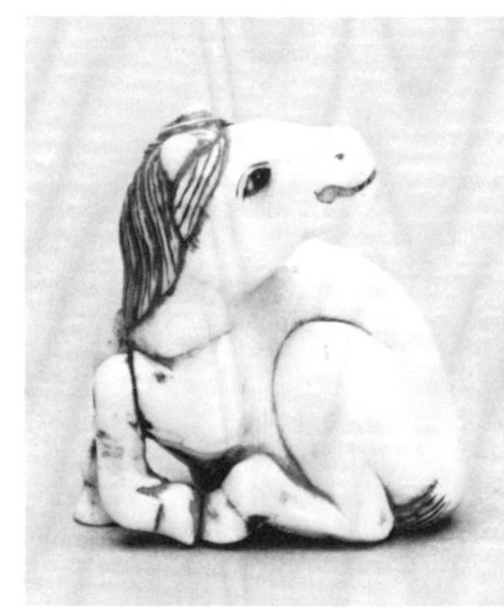

A sacred white horse

Ivory, ebony eyes. Kokusai. 19th c. Katabori. 3.2 cm. E26696

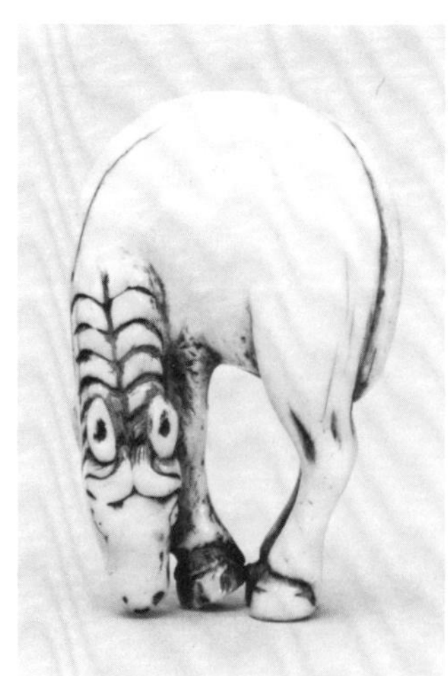

This carving of a horse with legs and head close together will stand upright on a flat surface.

Ivory. early 19th c. Katabori. 5.4 cm. E29139

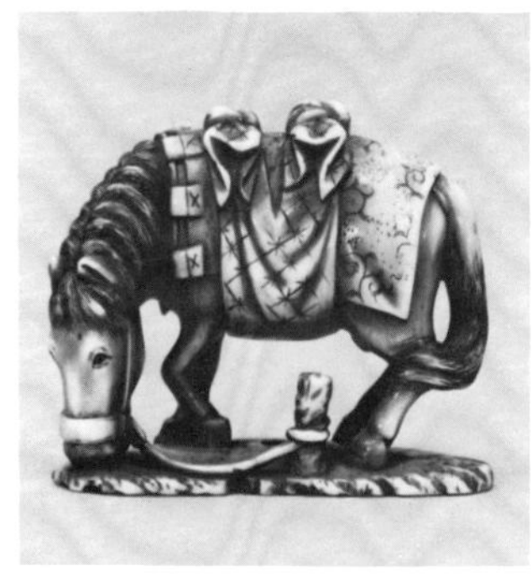

A fully saddled horse, reins tied to a post, grazes on a plot of grass.

Ivory. Hojitsu. mid 19th c. Katabori. 4.5 cm. E26723

Goat (eighth sign) The Peabody Museum collection contains no netsuke of goats.

A mother monkey picks fleas off her baby.

Ivory, inlaid eyes. Okatomo. before 1781. Katabori. 4.0 cm. E26635

Monkey (ninth sign) Clever, good leaders with common sense are born in the year of the monkey. Monkeys are among the most popular of netsuke subjects in part because they are heroes of so many stories, and their human qualities permit netsuke-shi to depict them in amusing situations. Especially when holding a peach, the monkey is a symbol of longevity. From Buddhism comes the three wise monkeys, *sambiki no saru,* servants of Koshin, god of roads, who warn against evil through their familiar pose meaning "hear no evil, see no evil, speak no evil." The expression plays on the Japanese words for monkey *(saru)* and evil *(zaru)*.

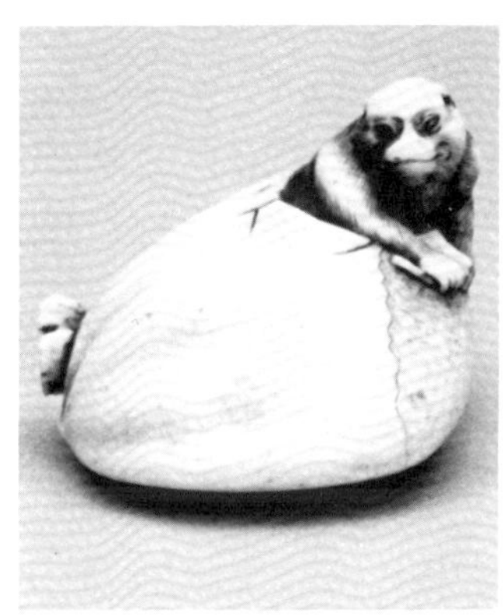

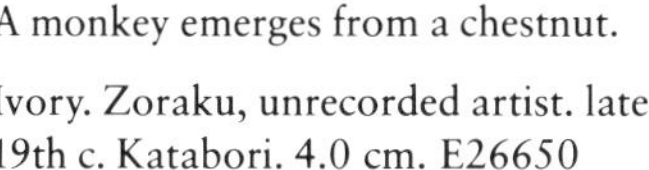

A monkey emerges from a chestnut.

Ivory. Zoraku, unrecorded artist. late 19th c. Katabori. 4.0 cm. E26650

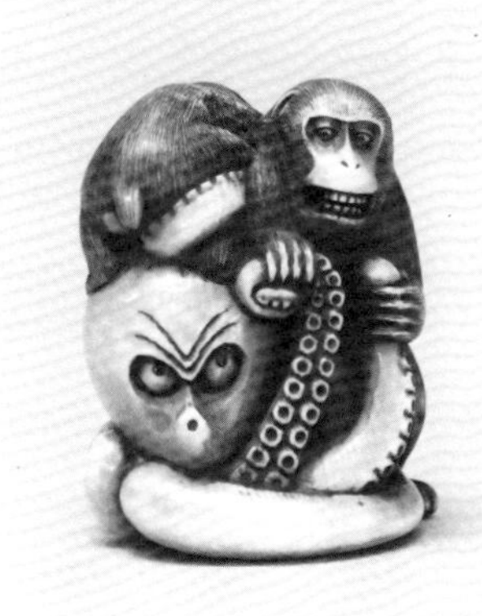

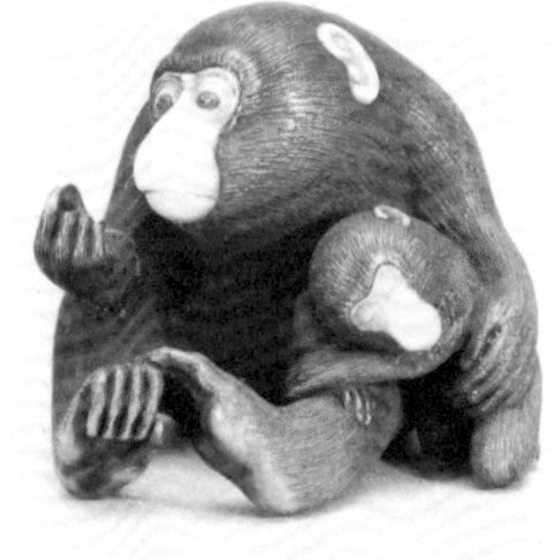

A monkey in a jacket hugs a sack.

Wood, inlaid eyes. 18th-19th c. Katabori. 3.9 cm. E3454

A mother monkey looks at something in her hand (object is missing) while her baby sleeps beside her. The ears and faces of the monkeys are pink coral, the eyes amber.

Wood, coral, amber, ivory signature plaque. Hojitsu. mid 19th c. Katabori. 4.3 cm. E26652

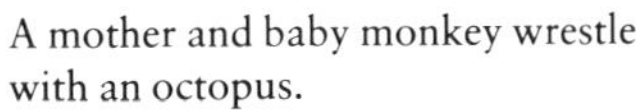

A mother and baby monkey wrestle with an octopus.

Ivory. 19th-20th c. Katabori. 4.0 cm. E26629

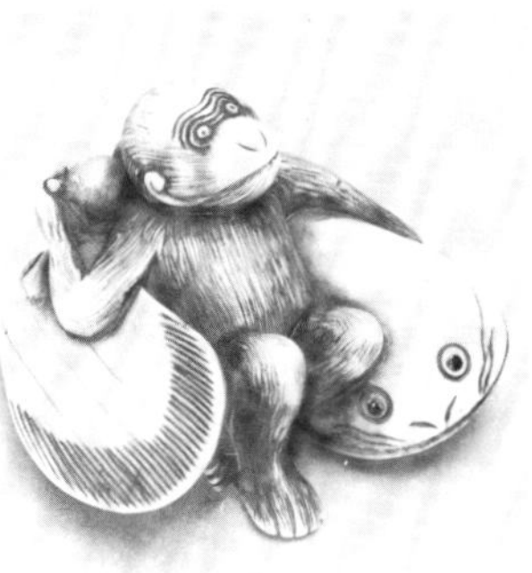

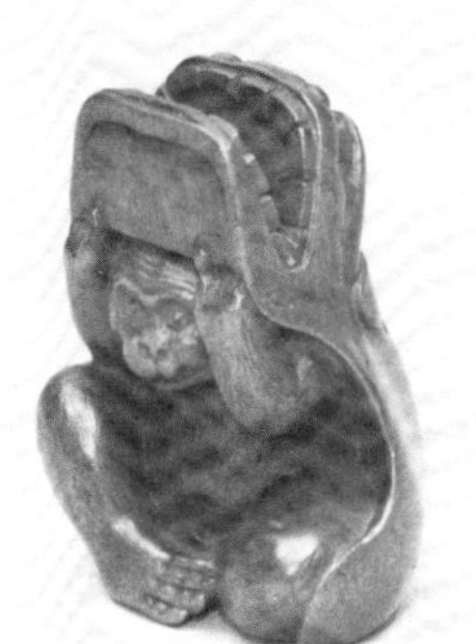

A monkey holds a lion mask over its head.

Wood. 19th-20th c. Katabori. 3.5 cm. E26668

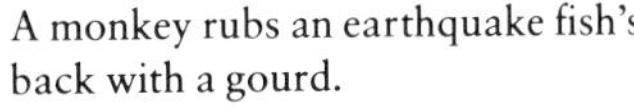

A monkey rubs an earthquake fish's back with a gourd.

Ivory, inlaid eyes. late 18th-19th c. Katabori. 4.5 cm. E26630

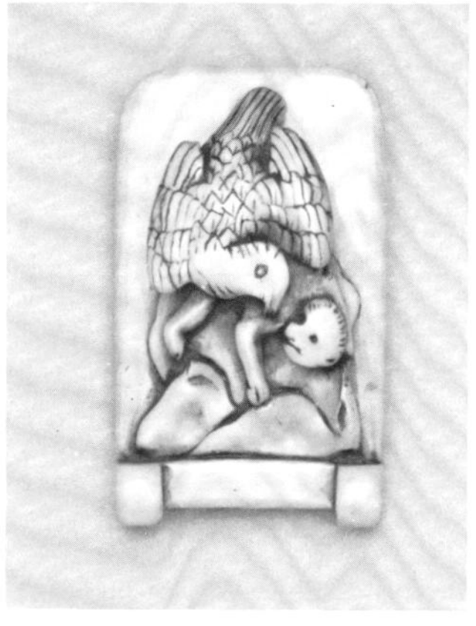

Depicted in three dimensions on a screen, a bird carries a monkey over some mountains.

Ivory. 19th c. Katabori.
4.3 cm. E26683

A monkey can be seen through the hole in this loquat.

Wood. 19th-20th c. Katabori.
4.0 cm. E26570

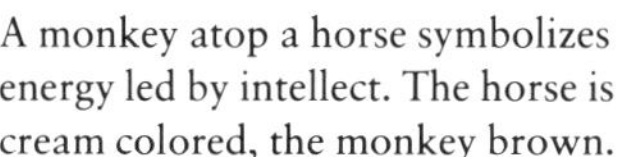

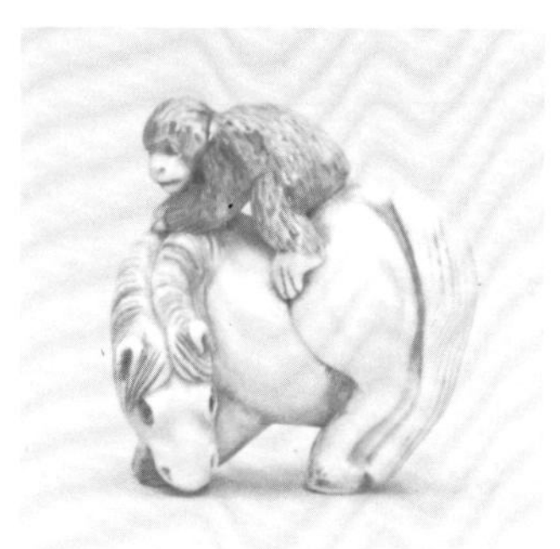

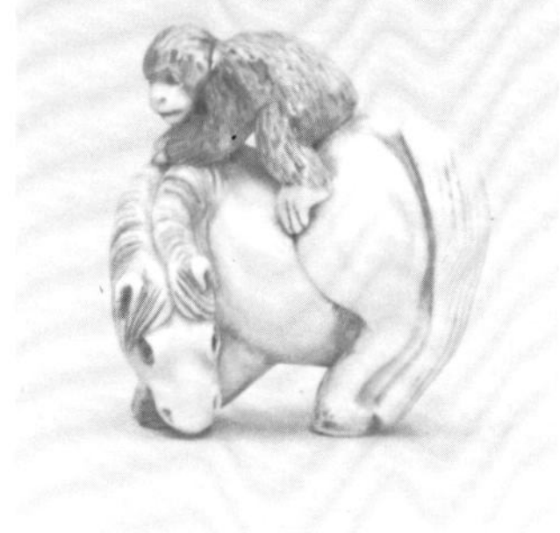

A monkey atop a horse symbolizes energy led by intellect. The horse is cream colored, the monkey brown.

Porcelain. Masakazu. late 19th-20th c. Katabori. 3.6 cm. E26684

A monkey (longevity) sits inside a ring formed by a stalk of bamboo (flexibility).

Ivory. late 19th-20th c. Manju (ryusa).
4.0 cm. E26695

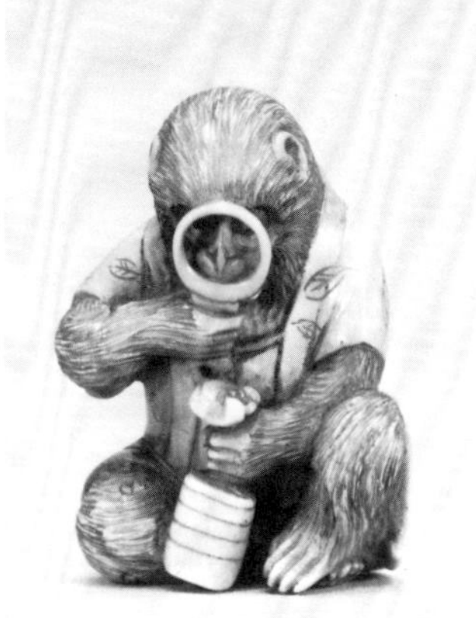

A monkey in a jacket examines an Okame mask netsuke and an inro through a magnifying glass. The artist may be making an amusing comment about "experts."

Ivory. late 19th-20th c. Katabori.
3.8 cm. E26703

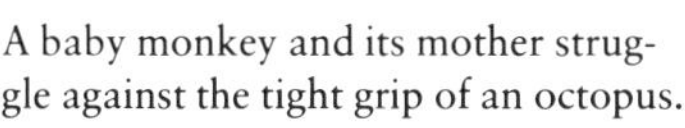

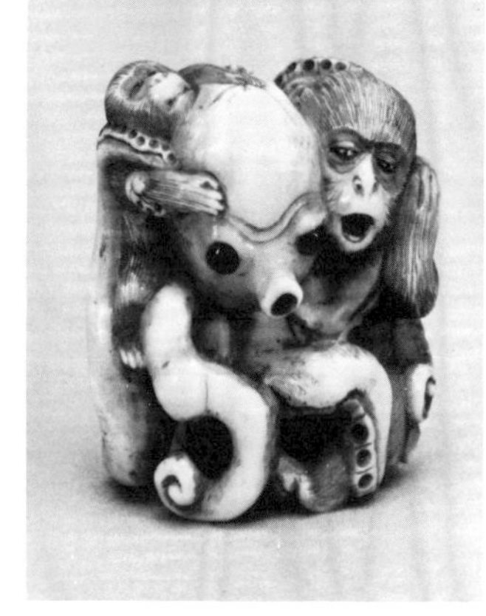

A baby monkey and its mother struggle against the tight grip of an octopus.

Ivory, ebony eyes. Gyokuzan. 1864-1923. Katabori. 3.7 cm. E26687

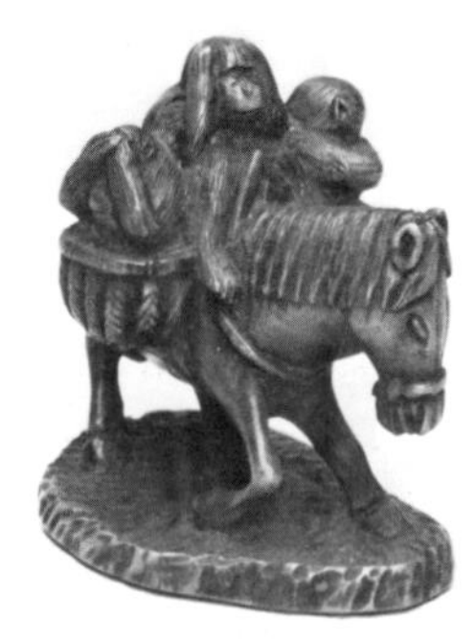

The "hear no evil" monkey sits in the saddle on the back of a horse while the "speak no evil" and "see no evil" monkeys sit in baskets hanging on the sides of the saddle.

Wood. Shuzan. 19th c. Katabori.
4.0 cm. E26691

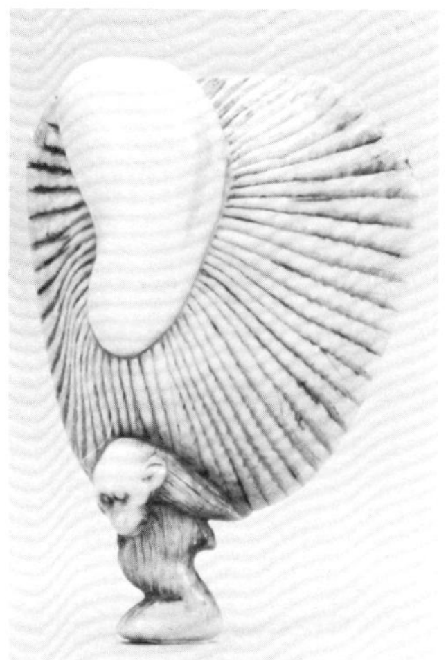

A tiny monkey carries a huge mushroom on its back.

Ivory. 19th c. Katabori.
4.7 cm. E26718

A simply carved monkey with a peach balances perfectly on a flat surface.

Boxwood. early 19th c. Katabori. 5.2 cm. E26765

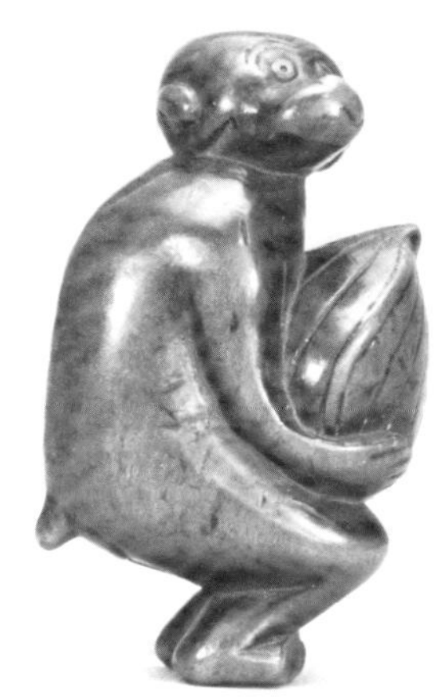

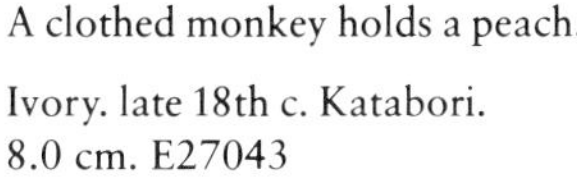

A clothed monkey holds a peach.

Ivory. late 18th c. Katabori. 8.0 cm. E27043

A monkey sits in the crook of a giant gourd.

Ivory, inlaid eyes. Okatomo. before 1781. Katabori. 5.0 cm. E26794

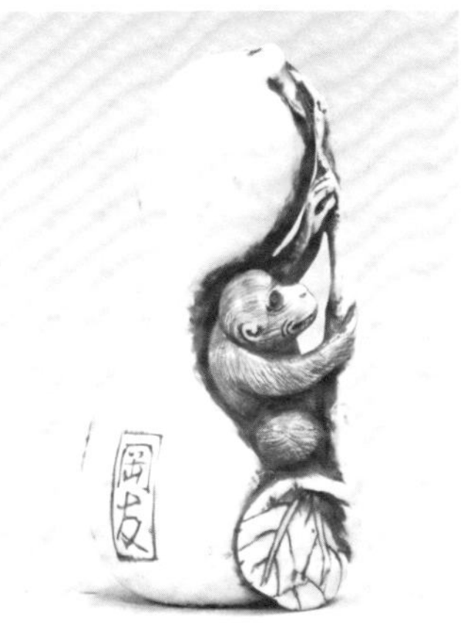

A design similar to E27043; a robed monkey holds a peach.

Boxwood. 19th c. Katabori. 6.3 cm. E34089

A monkey in a jacket rides a horse.

Wood, ivory inlaid eyes and himotoshi. Shunsai. 1800-1834. Katabori. 3.8 cm. E26975

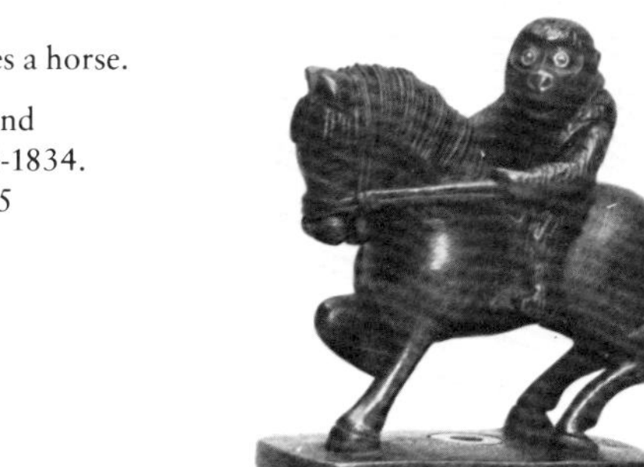

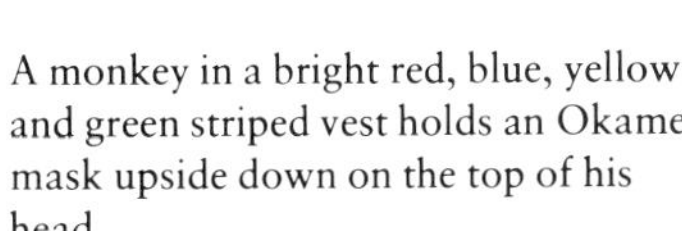

A monkey in a bright red, blue, yellow and green striped vest holds an Okame mask upside down on the top of his head.

Porcelain. Teiji. 19th-20th c. Katabori. 2.8 cm. E26986

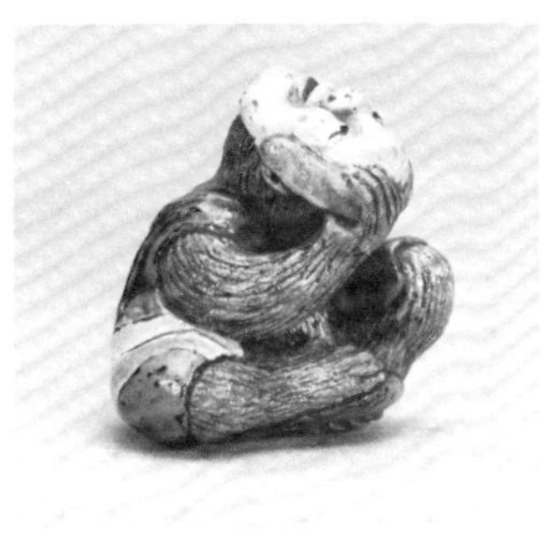

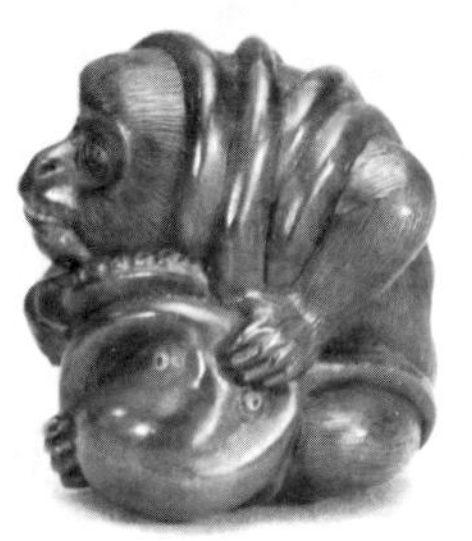

A monkey, wrestling with an octopus, bites one of its tentacles. The monkey's eyes are amber, its teeth, the octopus' eyes and the himotoshi linings are ivory.

Wood, ivory and amber inlays. Ryukei. 1844-1867. Katabori. 3.0 cm. E52711

Cock (tenth sign) Despite enthusiasm and bravery, people born in the year of the cock (rooster) are selfish and the loners of the oriental zodiac. The cock's faithful crowing at dawn is thought to drive away the evil spirits of the night and thus makes the bird both a symbol of faithfulness and a protection against evil. The cock is also known for its courage as a fighter and so symbolizes valor as well. A cock on a drum, however, is a sign of peace, for it is said that peace was kept so long during the reign of the Emperor Kotoku in the 7th c. that the drums of war went unused except as a perch for cocks.

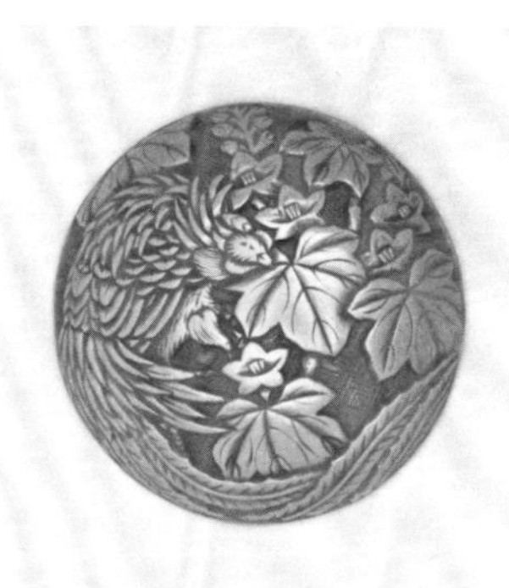

On one half of this manju netsuke a long-tailed fighting cock is depicted amidst flowers; on the other half a man holding a scroll stands in a landscape.

Wood and lacquer. early 19th c. Manju. 4.0 cm. E26552

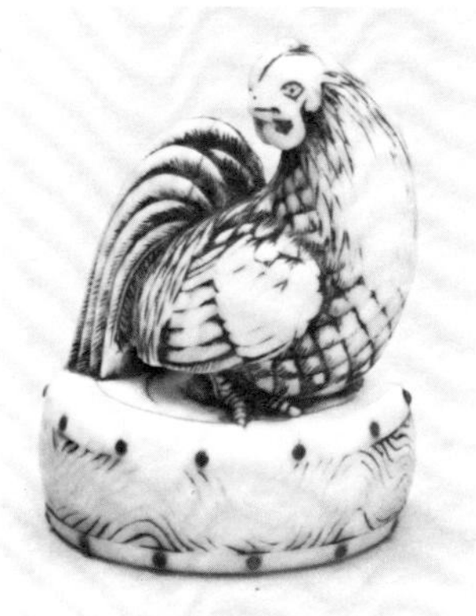

A cock on a drum decorated with wooden beads

Ivory, wood inlays. Tomotada. early 19th c. Katabori. 4.6 cm. E26627

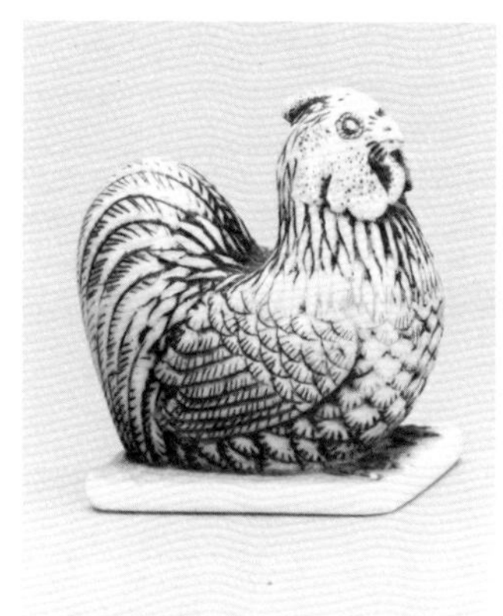

A rooster on a rectangular base

Ivory, metal eyes. 19th c. Katabori. 3.8 cm. E26646

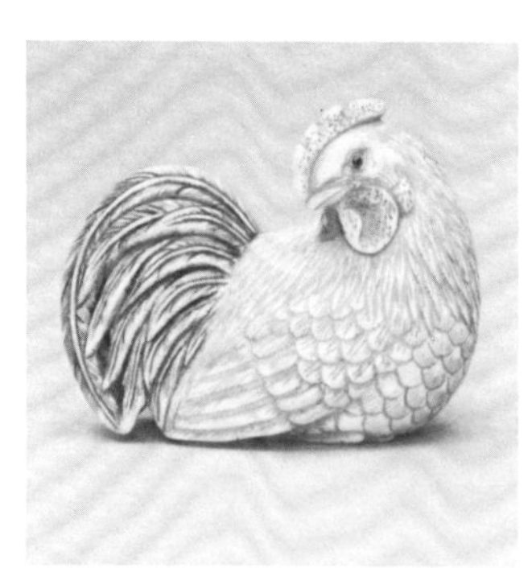

A cock

Ivory, inlaid eyes. Okakoto. 1830-1843. 4.5 cm. E26722

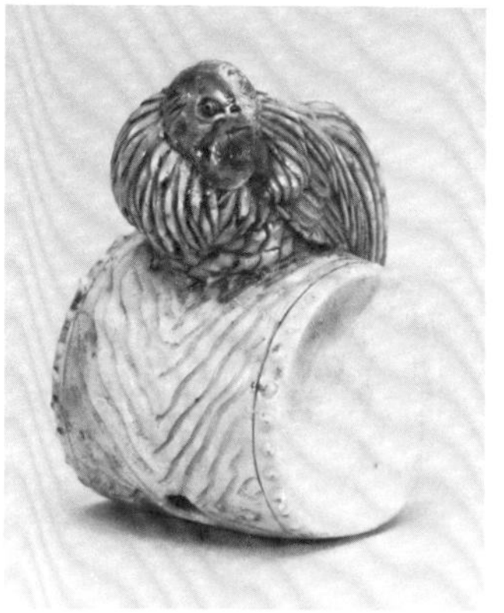

A brown rooster atop a cream-colored drum

Porcelain. 18th c. Katabori. 4.8 cm. E26730

Dog (eleventh sign) Though loyal and sincere, people born in the year of the dog are fault-finders. Dogs are known for the ease with which they give birth, and a netsuke of a dog (especially with puppies) can represent a wish for an easy childbirth. The dog is also a dispeller of evils (the badger, fox and cat lose their supernatural powers in the presence of a dog), and amulets of a dog are said to protect against a variety of evils. An emaciated dog attacking a skull represents a legendary animal that will do no harm if treated kindly. Dogs are also honored as deities in Japanese folklore.

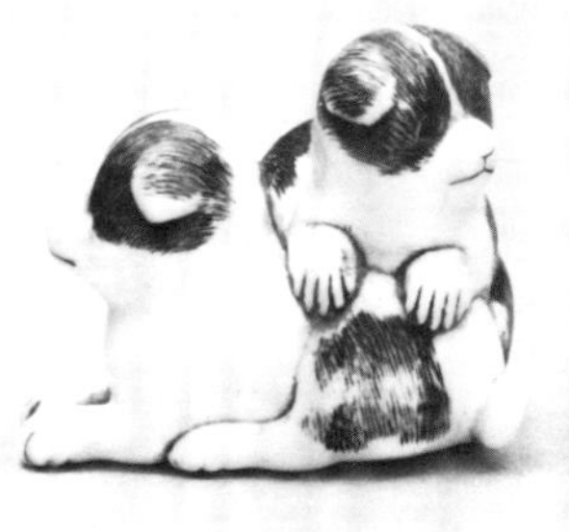

Two black and white puppies

Ivory. late 19th-20th c. Katabori. 3.2 cm. E25277

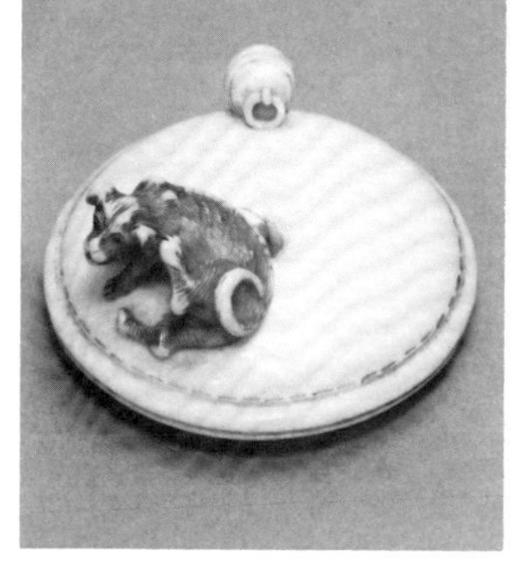

A bell and a dog scratching its ear sit atop a simple manju shaped piece of ivory.

Ivory, inlaid eyes. 19th-20th c. Manju. 3.7 cm. E26548

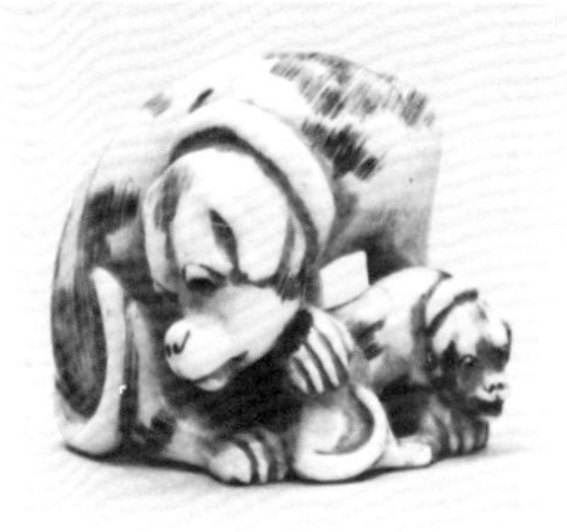

A mother dog with her pup

Ivory, inlaid eyes. 19th c. Katabori. 4.8 cm. E26628

A dog curled up on a mat

Ivory. late 18th-19th c. Katabori.
4.1 cm. E26657

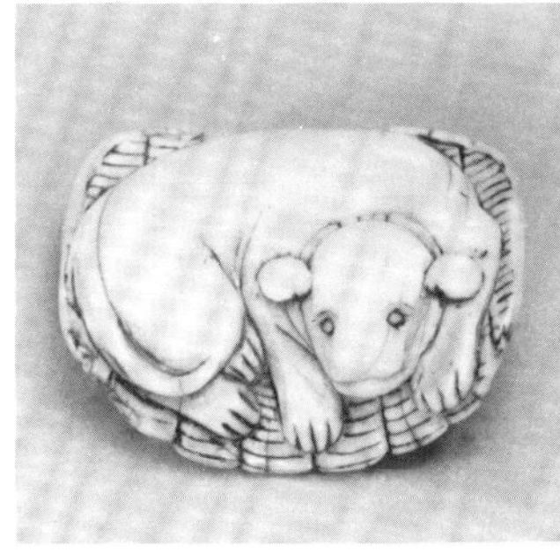

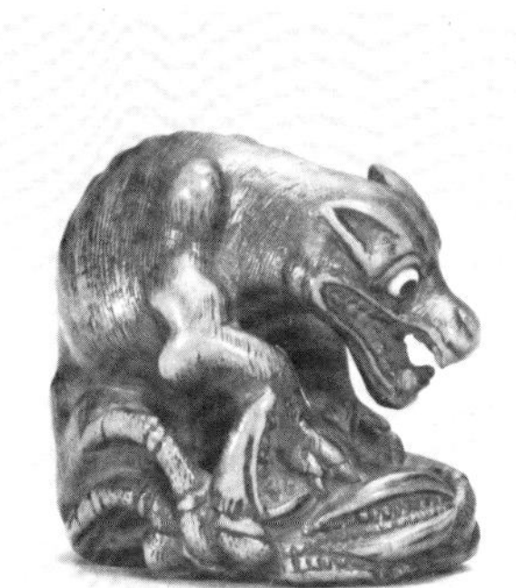

An emaciated dog appears painfully surprised that its foot is being pinched by the crab it is fighting.

Boxwood, ivory eyes. late 18th-19th c.
Katabori. 3.7 cm. E26671

This dog resting its front paws on a bag was carved to conform to the triangular shape of the ivory.

Ivory. late 19th-20th c. Katabori.
4.5 cm. E26659

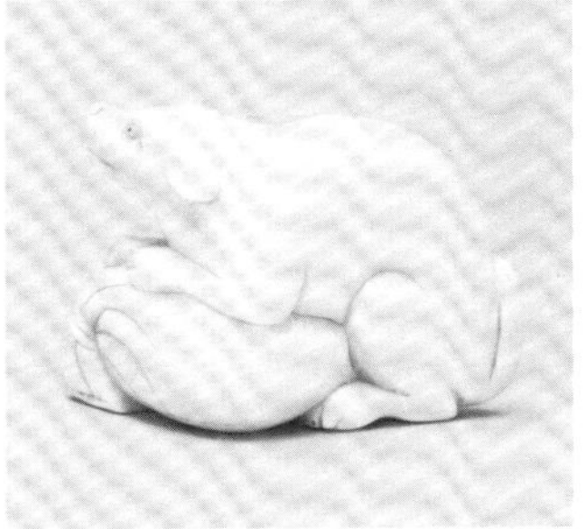

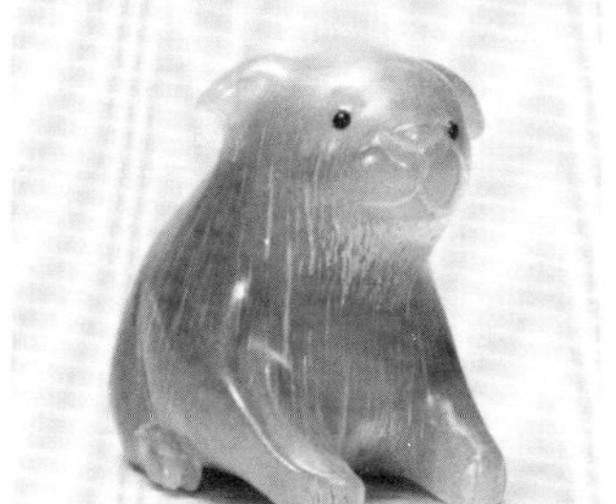

A seated puppy

Horn, inlaid eyes. 19th-20th c.
Katabori. 3.3 cm. E26685

Carved on one side only from a flawed piece of coral, this netsuke depicts a dog lying with one foot on a drum.

Pink coral, inlaid eyes. 19th c.
Katabori. 4.7 cm. E26661

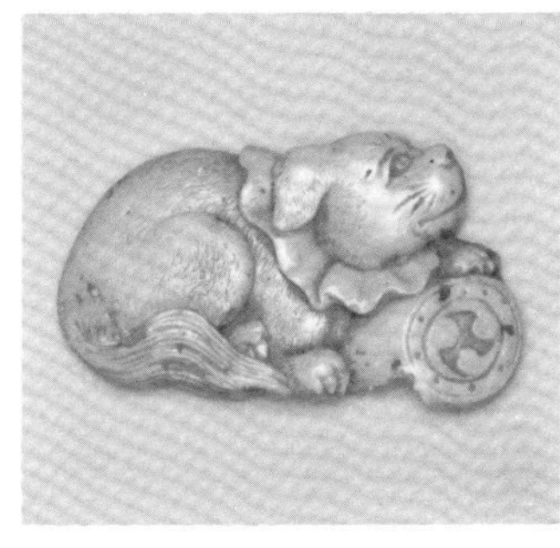

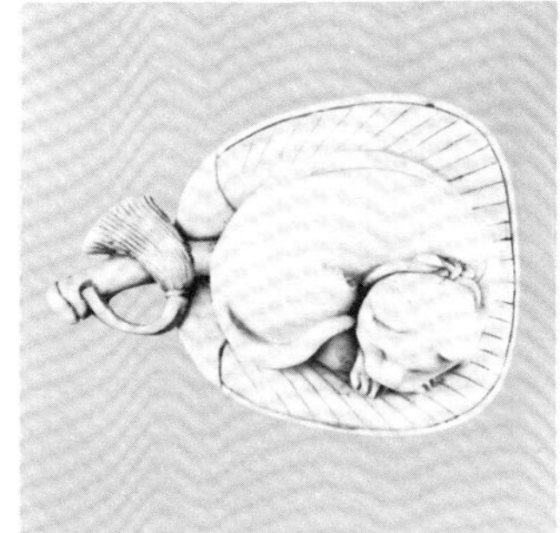

A sleeping dog curled up on a fan

Ivory. 19th c. Katabori.
5.2 cm. E26710

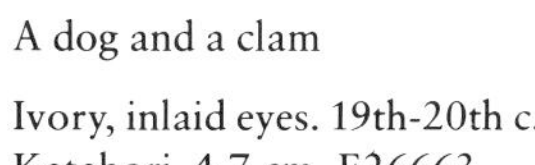

A dog and a clam

Ivory, inlaid eyes. 19th-20th c.
Katabori. 4.7 cm. E26663

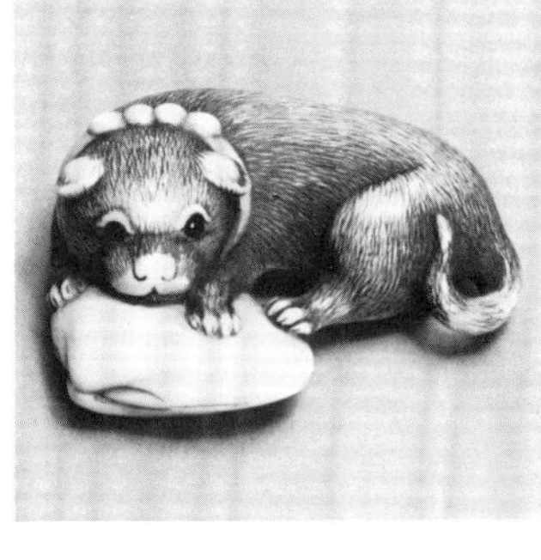

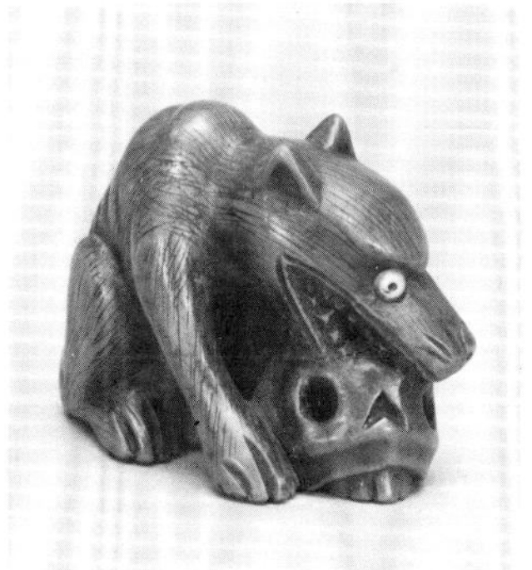

An emaciated dog chews on a skull.

Boxwood, ivory eyes. 19th-20th c.
Katabori. 4.6 cm. E26713

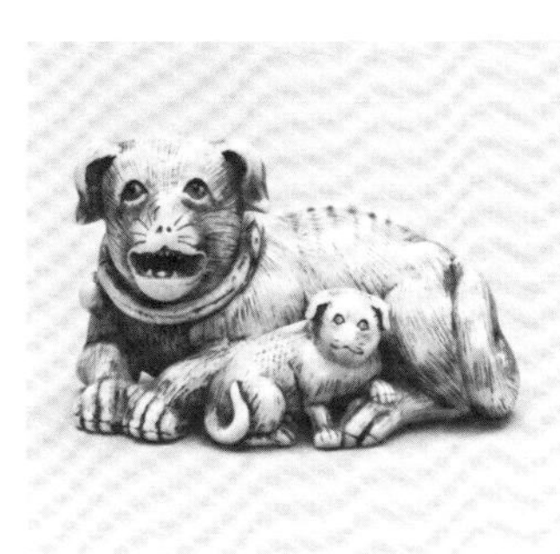

A mother dog with her puppy

Ivory, inlaid eyes. Tomotada. before 1781. Katabori. 5.3 cm. E26665

The three puppies climbing on their mother were carved separately.

Ivory, inlaid eyes. illegible signature. late 19th-20th c. Katabori. 3.7 cm. E26771

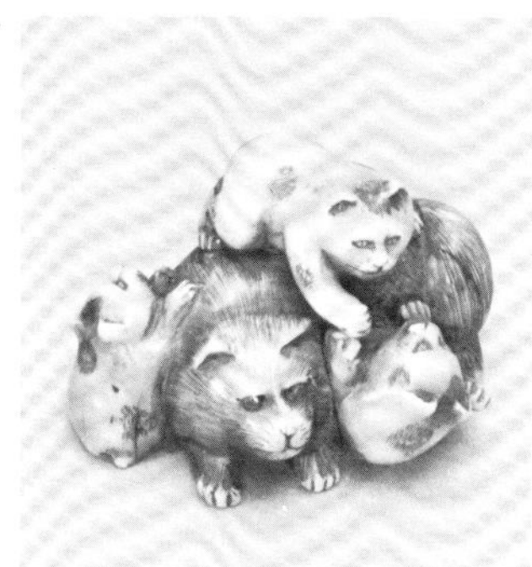

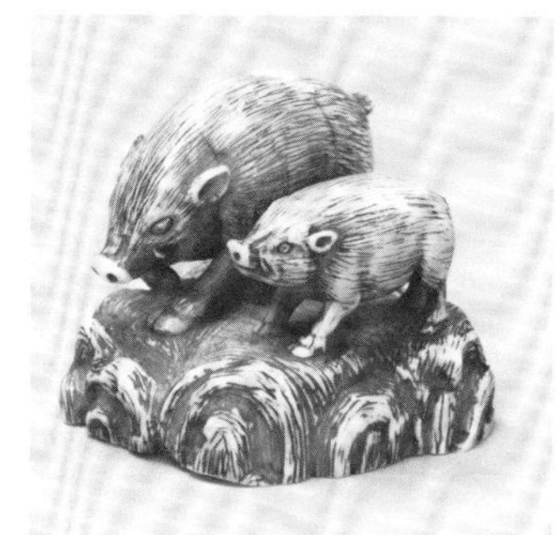

Two boars on a rocky base

Ivory, metal eyes. early 19th c. Katabori. 4.5 cm. E26651

A puppy on a fan

Ivory, inlaid eyes. Gyokuyosai Mitsuhina. 1781-1868. Katabori. 4.1 cm. E26772

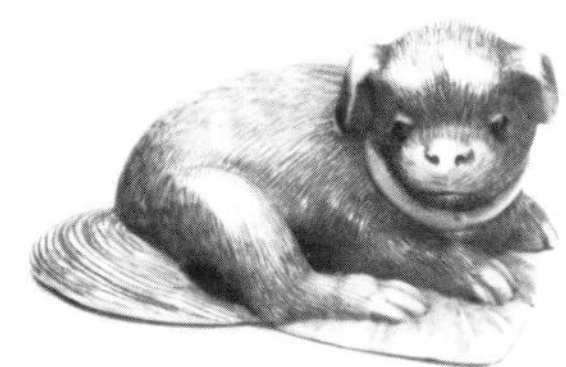

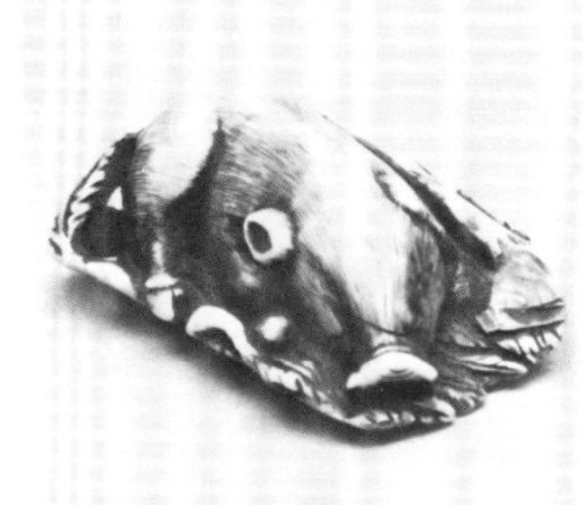

A boar sleeps on some leaves.

Ivory. early 19th c. Katabori. 4.5 cm. E26726

A puppy guards a ball with the character for dragon on it.

Ivory, inlaid eyes. late 18th-19th c. Katabori. 3.8 cm. E26779

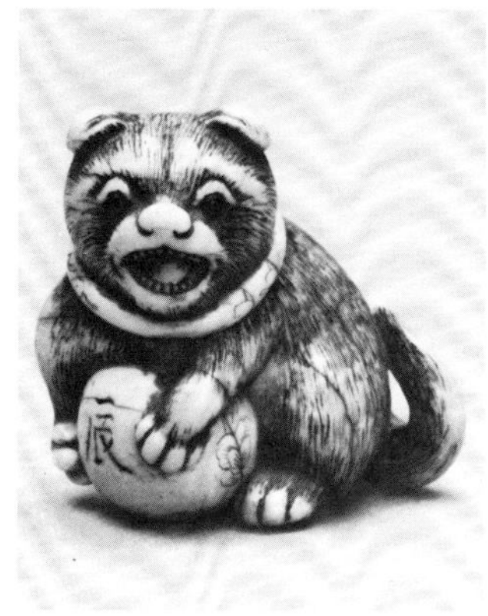

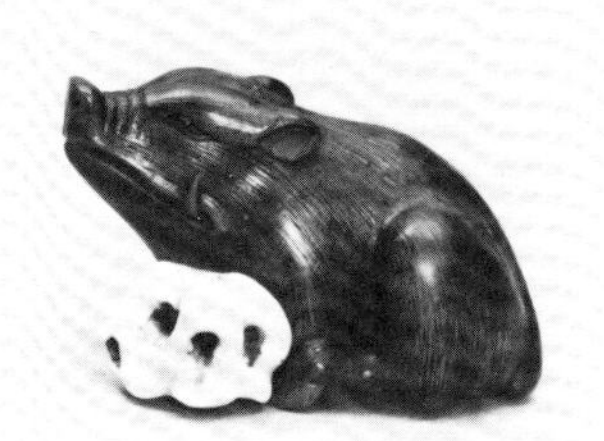

A boar carved from wood sits beside an ivory rock.

Boxwood and ivory. Masakiyo. late 19th-20th c. Katabori. 4.4 cm. E26767

Boar (twelfth sign) The most mannerly, though strong-willed people are born in the year of the boar. They are brave and reckless like the boar who hurls itself at its enemies without looking right or left, a symbol of resolve and determination.

A boar sleeps among some flowers.

Ivory. 19th c. Katabori. 5.0 cm. E26632

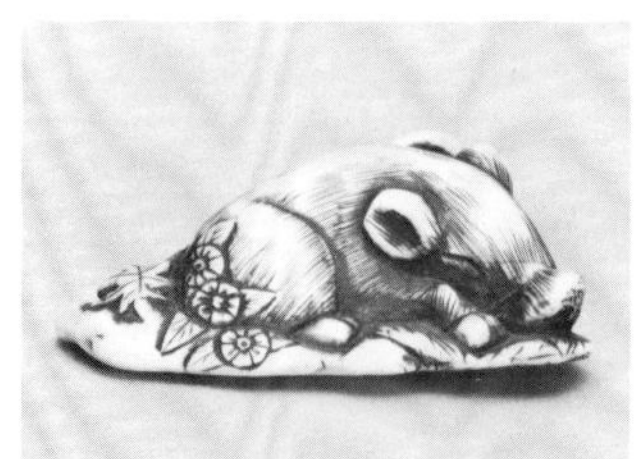

Plants

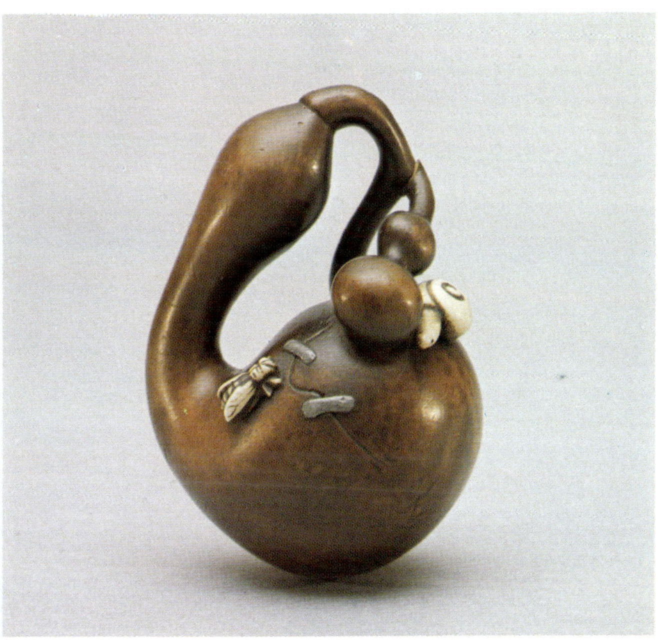

Japan's majestic volcanoes, mountain ranges, hills and lush valleys, surrounded by thousands of miles of beautiful seacoast, have inspired a keen awareness of the beauty of nature among the Japanese, which has been reinforced over the centuries by their religious beliefs and philosophical teachings.

The agricultural people of early Japan ascribed sacred or divine powers to the phenomena they observed in nature, establishing from the beginning the importance of the individual's response to the awe-inspiring processes of nature. As this religion, Shinto, became organized and shrines were erected, the close relationship between man and nature was further developed, for shrines were located in beautiful wooded or scenic areas, evoking a sense of the beauty and grandeur of nature.

Buddhism and Taoism also emphasized the relationship between man and nature in Japan. Taoist ascetics lived as mountain hermits, communing with nature in order to gain a sense of harmony with nature, and union with the Tao, the eternal way; certain sects of Buddhist monks also retreated to the mountains. The Zen sect of Buddhism was effective in stimulating appreciation of natural beauty, since it stressed that an understanding of the universe could be achieved by meditating in the presence of nature.

The innate appreciation of the Japanese for plant life is apparent in the work of the netsuke-shi who carefully observed the plants they portrayed and carved them realistically and artistically, concerned with texture and form. Their faithfulness to nature often included evidences of blight or decay which are as inherent in nature as beauty.

Flowers, Fruits and Vegetables

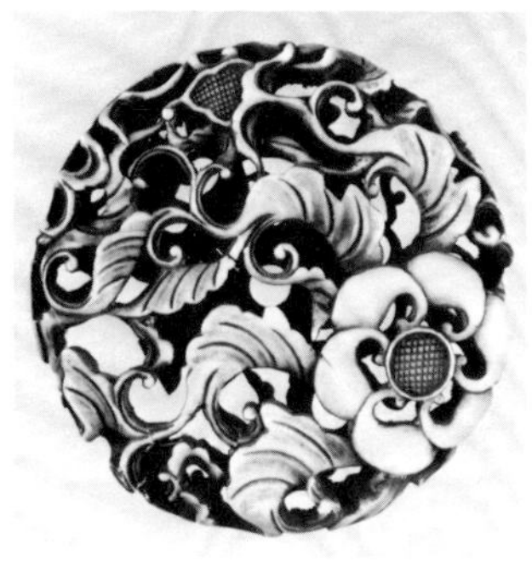

An openwork carving of flowers, leaves, and vines

Ivory. 19th c. Manju (ryusa). 5.5 cm. E26571

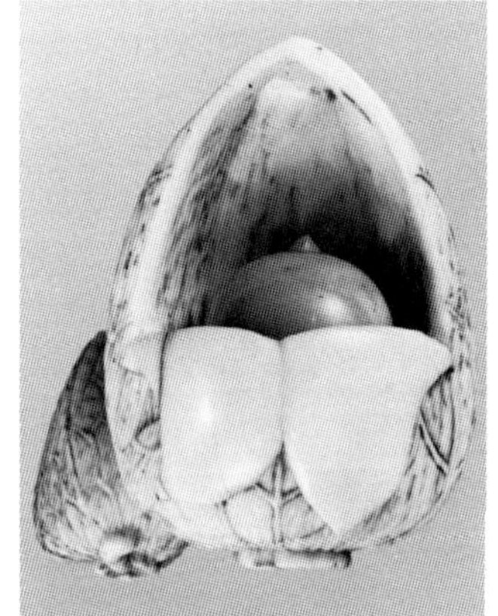

Two Chinese lantern calyces, one with a red coral fruit inside

Ivory, coral inlay. 19th-20th c. Katabori. 4.2 cm. E26833

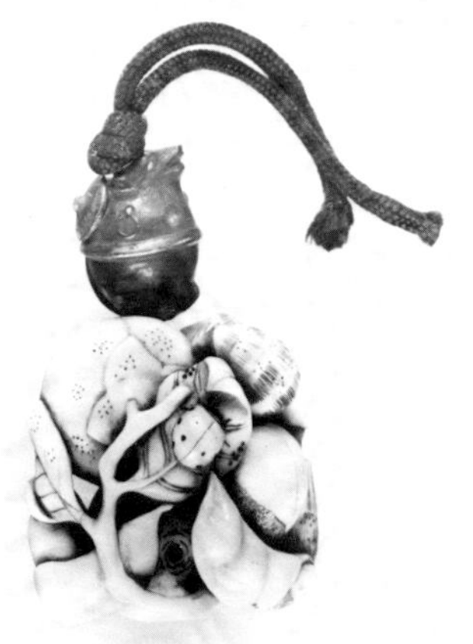

A group of assorted vegetables and fruits includes pea pods, a persimmon, bamboo shoots, chestnuts and leaves and branches. A ladybug crawls on one of the leaves. An ojime attached to the netsuke depicts in metal the adaptable badger from the fairy tale of the magic kettle.

Ivory. Gyokuyosai Mitsuhima. 1781-1868. 3.5 cm. E26831

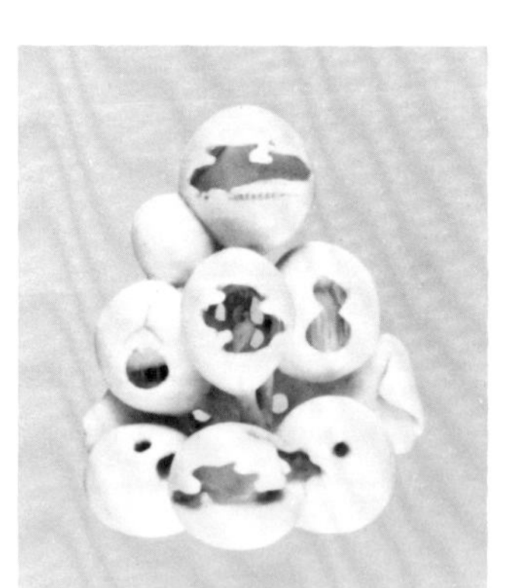

A bunch of grapes on a vine includes five that have scenes carved in them. The scenes are of Mt. Fuji, a temple, a hawk, a waterfall and a rocky landscape.

Ivory. 19th c. Katabori. 3.8 cm. E26845

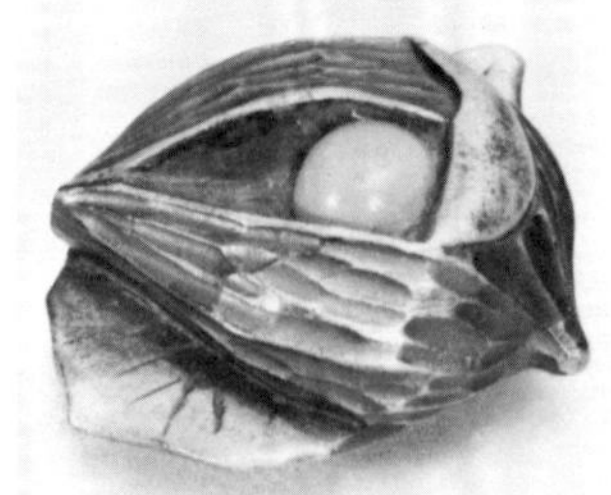

A red coral fruit lies inside the opened calyx of a Chinese lantern plant.

Wood, coral. 19th c. Katabori. 4.0 cm. E26809

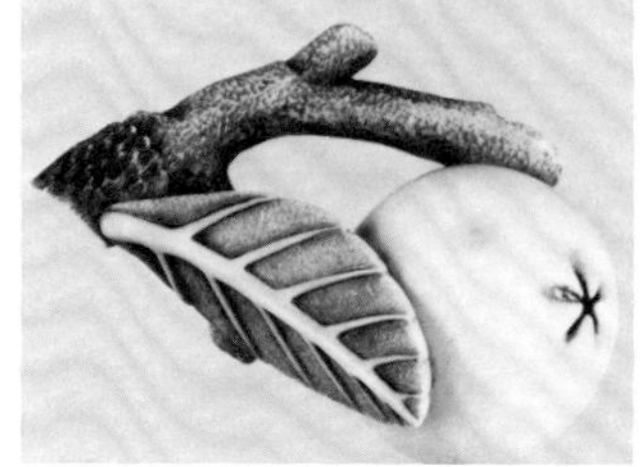

A loquat, branch and leaf

Ivory. Mitsuhiro. 1810-1875. Katabori. 5.0 cm. E26805

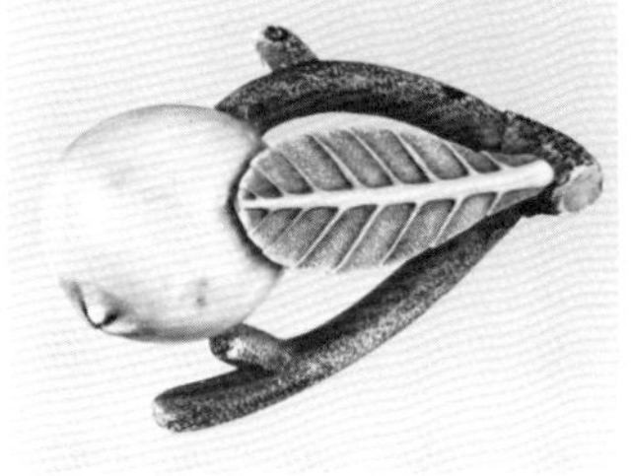

A loquat hangs from its branch.

Ivory. Mitsuhiro. 1810-1875. Katabori. 5.3 cm. E26824

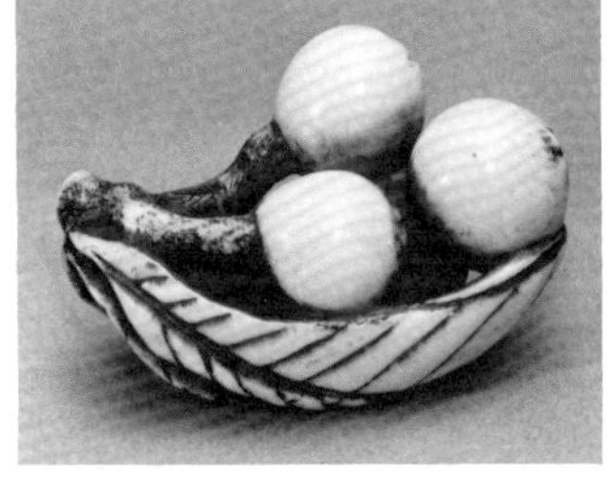

Four loquats and two leaves hang from a branch.

Ivory. Yoshinao. 19th c. Katabori. 4.5 cm. E26843

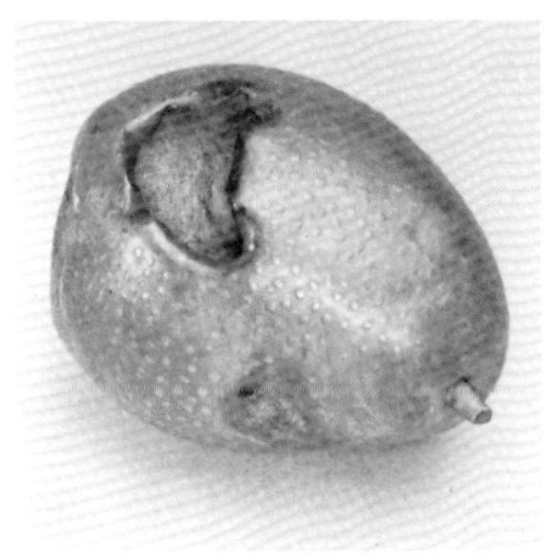

A realistic rotting pear

Wood. 19th c. Katabori. 3.8 cm. E26797

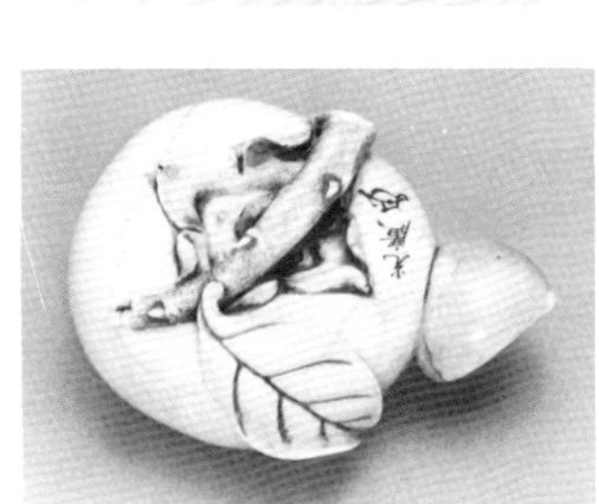

A small brown chestnut is carved alongside a reddish persimmon, its branch and leaf. Persimmons are associated with chestnuts because both ripen in the fall.

Ivory. Mitsuhiro. 1810-1875. Katabori. 5.3 cm. E26793

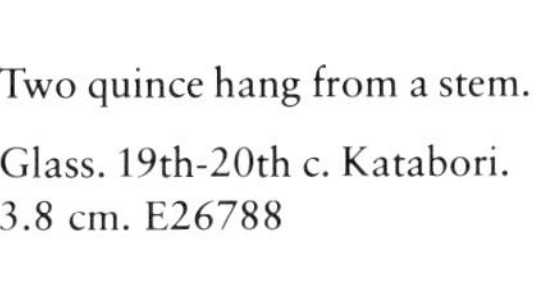

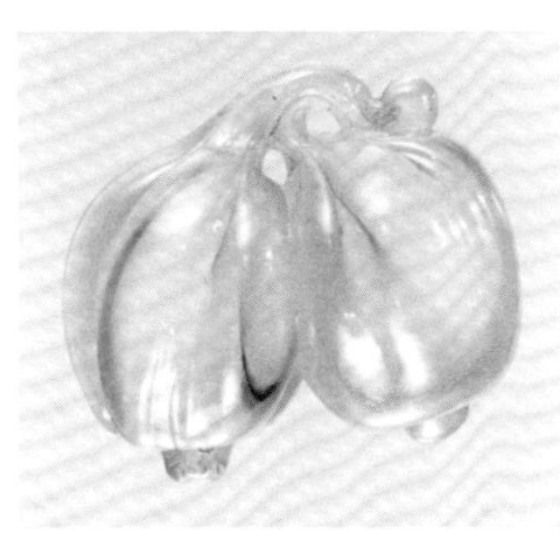

Two quince hang from a stem.

Glass. 19th-20th c. Katabori. 3.8 cm. E26788

A radish and leaves

Bone. 19th c. Katabori. 6.0 cm. E26826

Blue and white squash and leaves

Porcelain. late 18th-19th c. Katabori. 3.8 cm. E26780

A long narrow squash is decorated with red, gray and gold leaves. Its stem forms the cord opening.

Bone. 19th c. Katabori. 5.8 cm. E26791

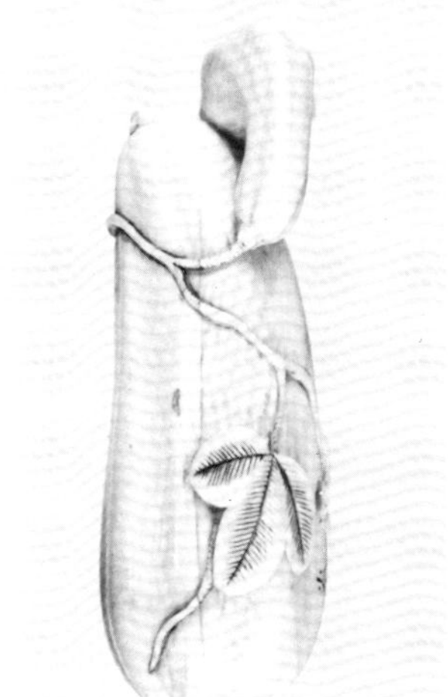

A small squash with vine and leaves rests against a larger squash.

Ivory. Mitsutsugu. Katabori. 5.5 cm. E26812

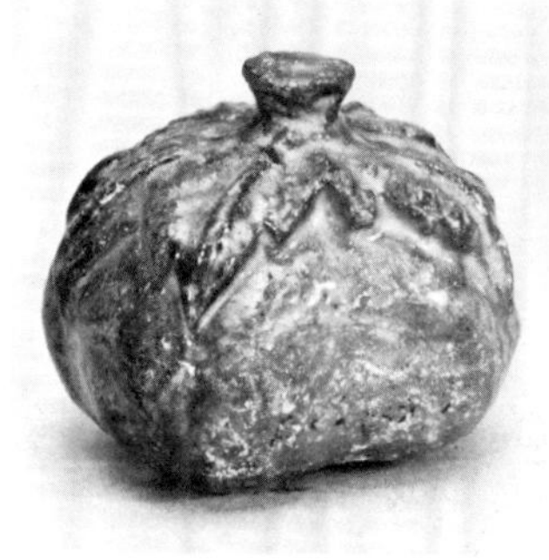

An orange-red squash with olive-green leaves

Ceramic, glazed. Yamata Michu. 19th c. Katabori. 3.0 cm. E60824

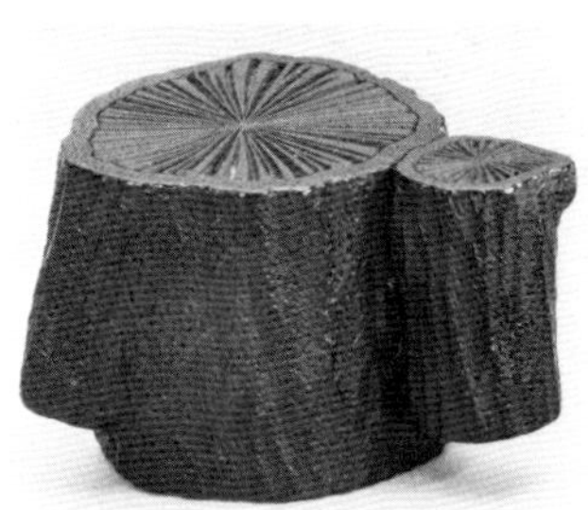

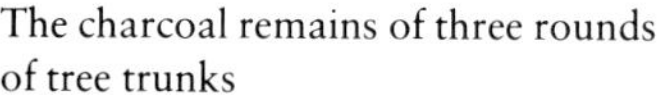

The charcoal remains of three rounds of tree trunks

Ebony. 19th c. Katabori. 3.0 cm. E26807

Nuts and Seed Pods

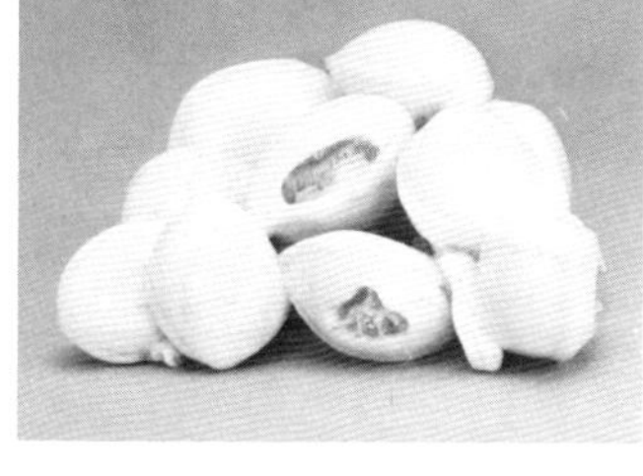

Five of the ginkgo nuts in this cluster have scenes carved inside them. The scenes include a man on horseback, boats on water, and three landscapes with people, buildings, bridges, and water.

Ivory. 19th-20th c. Katabori. 5.5 cm. E26799

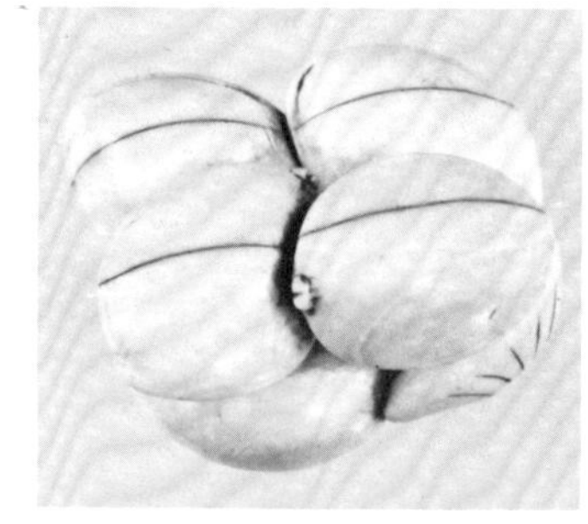

A group of five ginkgo nuts and a leaf

Ivory. Mitsuharu. before 1781. Katabori. 3.5 cm. E26823

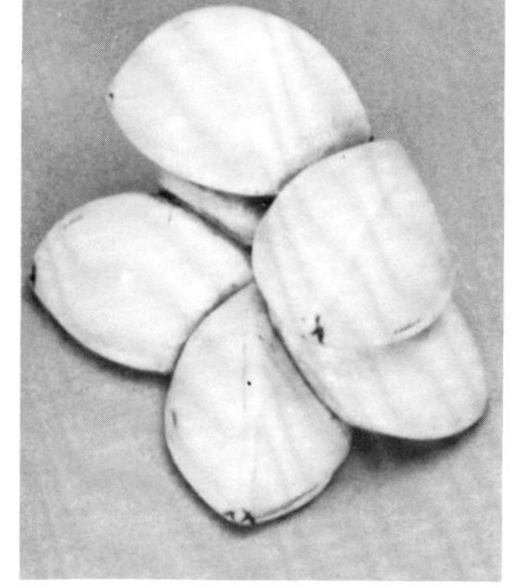

A cluster of ginkgo nuts

Ivory. 19th-20th c. Katabori. 3.5 cm. E26837

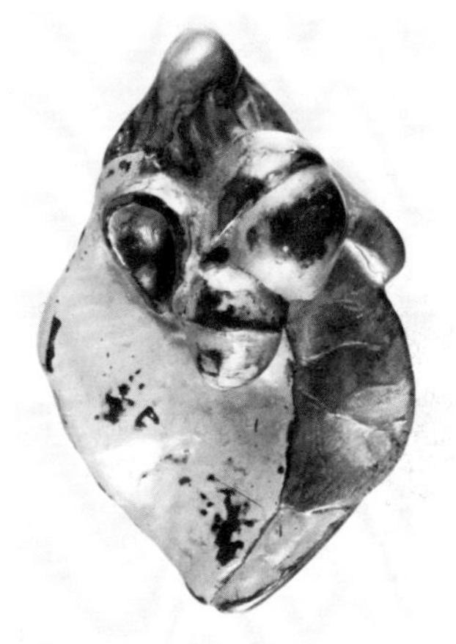

Two acorns, an acorn cap, and brown and red leaves hang from a stem.

Wood, lacquer. early 19th c. Katabori. 6.0 cm. E26830

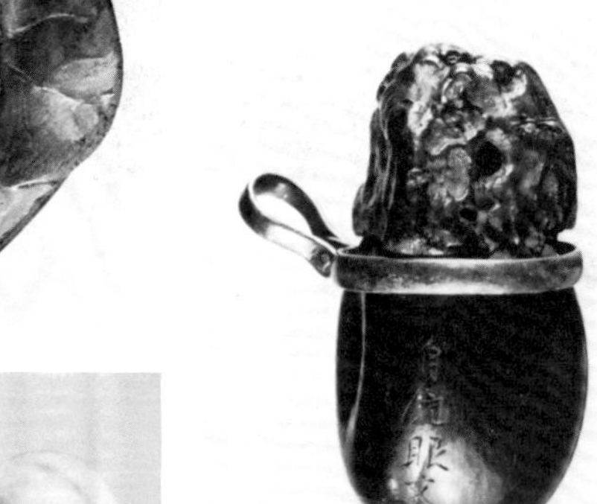

A carved, rotting half of a nut has been fitted into an actual nut. Three metal ants crawl over the rotted half; a metal ring provides the cord aperture.

Nut, wood, metal. Gambun, "white, aged man." early 19th c. Katabori. 3.8 cm. E26818

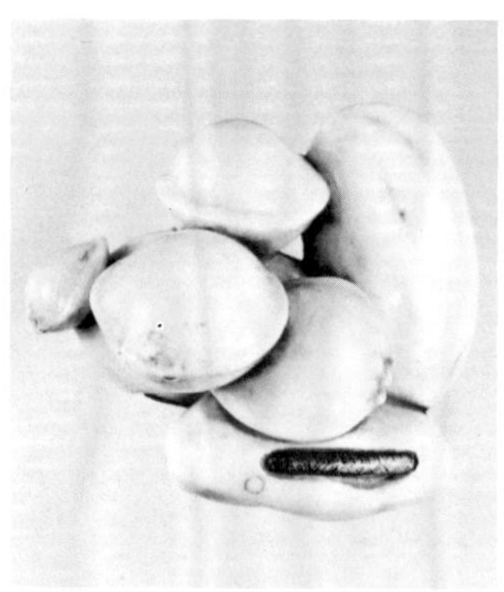

Four ginkgo nuts rest on three stones.

Ivory. 19th c. Katabori. 3.5 cm. E26781

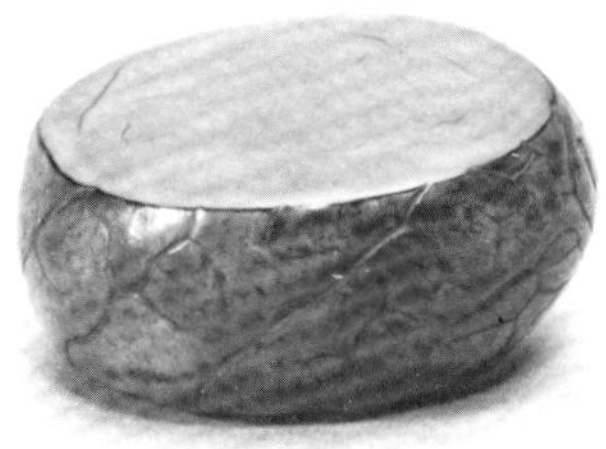

A section of a vegetable ivory nut has been polished and painted red.

Vegetable ivory. late 19th c. Katabori. 3.5 cm. E26827

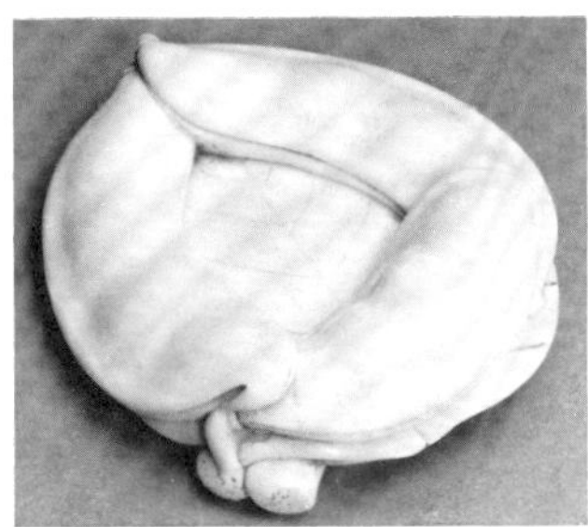

Three pea pods form a triangle on a leaf. On the back, a branch crosses over the leaf to form an aperture for the cord.

Ivory. Garaku. 1772-1780. Katabori. 5.7 cm. E26846

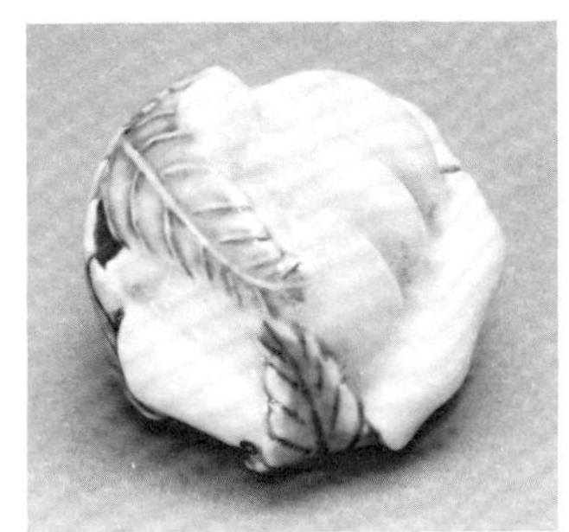

Blue leaves enclose an open seed pod containing three seeds.

Porcelain. 19th c. Katabori. 3.1 cm. E26800

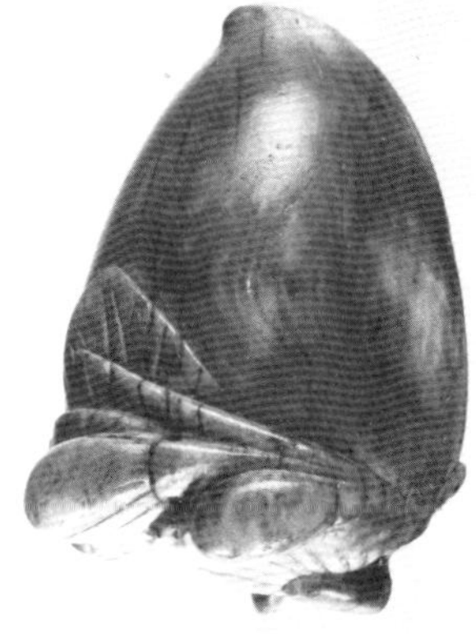

A bamboo shoot

Animal tooth. 19th c. Katabori. 4.4 cm. E26821

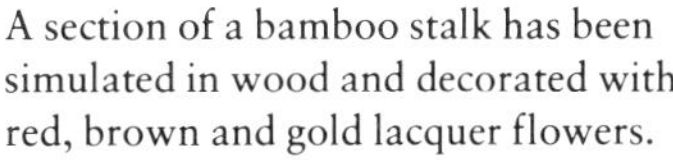

A section of a bamboo stalk has been simulated in wood and decorated with red, brown and gold lacquer flowers.

Wood and lacquer. 19th-20th c. Katabori. 4.5 cm. E26873

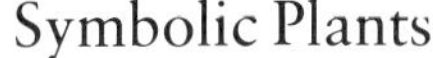

Symbolic Plants

Bamboo Bamboo is indigenous to Japan and is utilized for both food and innumerable objects used in daily life. Its widespread use has led it to become associated with symbols and legends that are portrayed in every art form. An evergreen plant of long life, virtually indestructible, bamboo signifies longevity. Its resilience and ability to withstand snow or wind without breaking symbolize strength from yielding. Associations of bamboo and specific animals suggest loyalty, happiness, safety, etc.

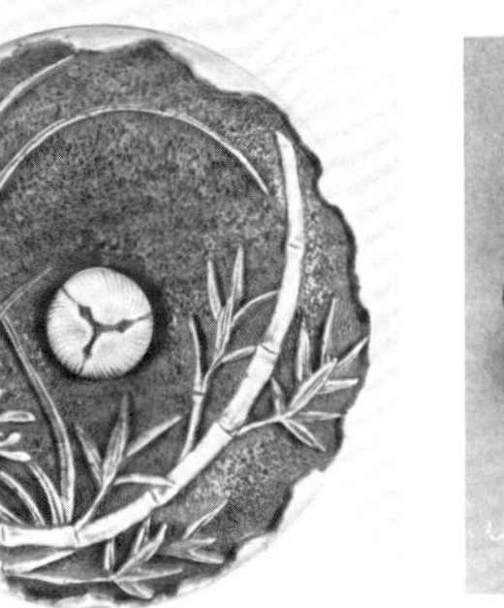

Bamboo stalks are carved on one side of a large manju netsuke; peonies on the other.

Ivory. illegible signature. 19th c. Manju. 7.0 cm. E23057

Chestnut The word chestnut, *Kachigiri,* contains the word *Kachi,* meaning victory; consequently, chestnuts became a symbol of the New Year festival, representing success in the new year.

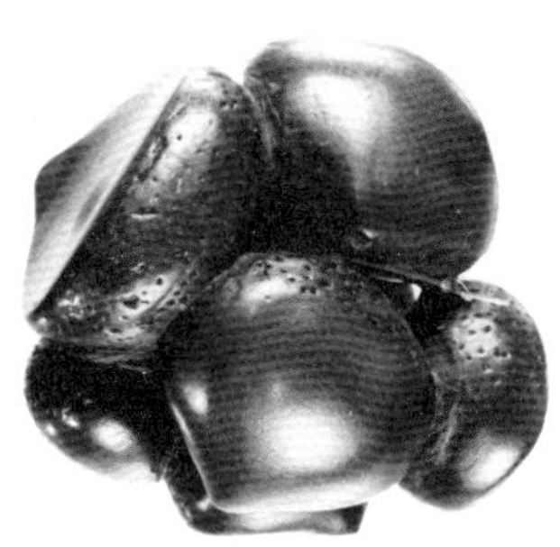

A cluster of chestnuts

Wood. 19th c. Katabori. 4.0 cm. E4482

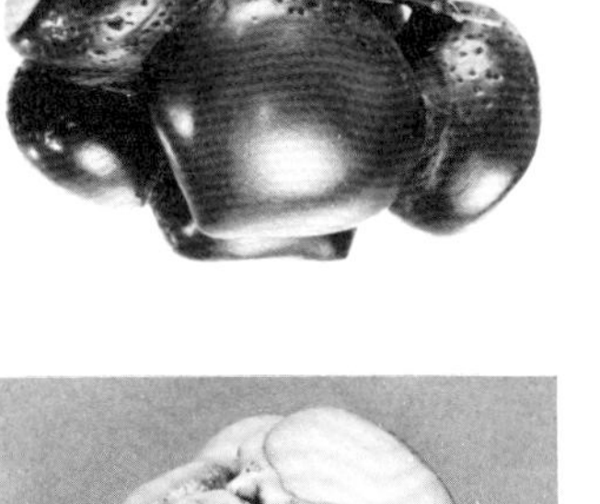

A snail and a branch rest on a cluster of eight chestnuts. Views of Mt. Fuji are carved inside two of the nuts.

Ivory. 19th c. Katabori. 4.0 cm. E26783

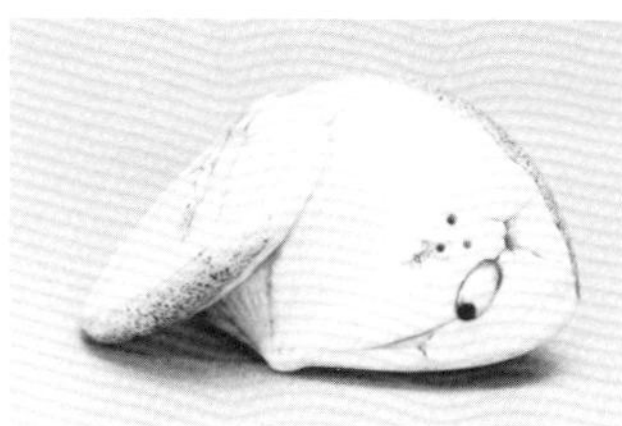

A cross-section slice of a chestnut lies against a chestnut that has several worm holes. A worm crawls from one of them. An ivory signature plaque is plugged into the root hole of the ivory tooth this netsuke is made from.

Ivory. Seishun, unrecorded artist. 19th c. Katabori. 4.0 cm. E26784

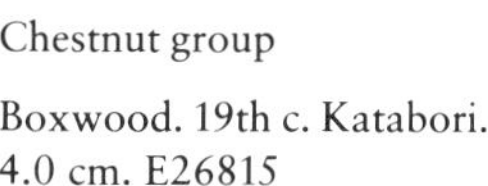

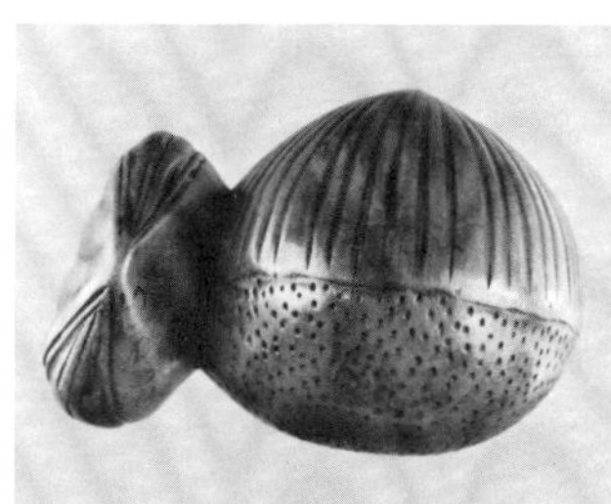

Chestnut group

Boxwood. 19th c. Katabori. 4.0 cm. E26815

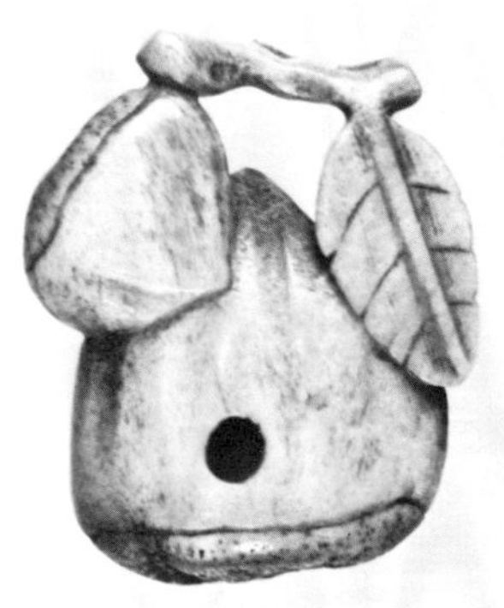

Two chestnuts, a branch and leaf; a worm hole in the larger chestnut

Bone. 19th c. Katabori. 3.8 cm. E26854

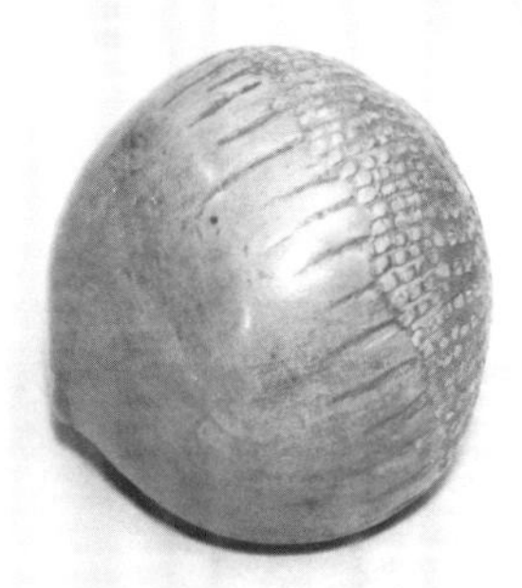

A chestnut has been carved with a flat side for the himotoshi.

Wood. Ichiyu or Kazutomo. 19th-20th c. Katabori. 3.8 cm. E29155

Chrysanthemum One of the most widely used motifs in Japanese art, both realistically and in stylized form, the chrysanthemum symbolizes consistency and long life, for it not only stays in bloom for a long period, it blooms throughout the year. The official crest of the Emperor, its petals suggest the sun's rays, symbolic of the sun goddess who was the progenitor of the Imperial Family.

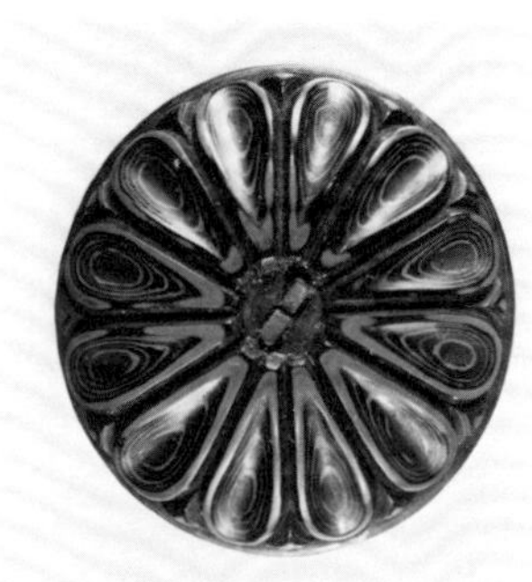

A chrysanthemum carved on one half of this netsuke has petals lacquered in black and red.

Wood, lacquer. 19th c. Manju. 4.0 cm. E26549

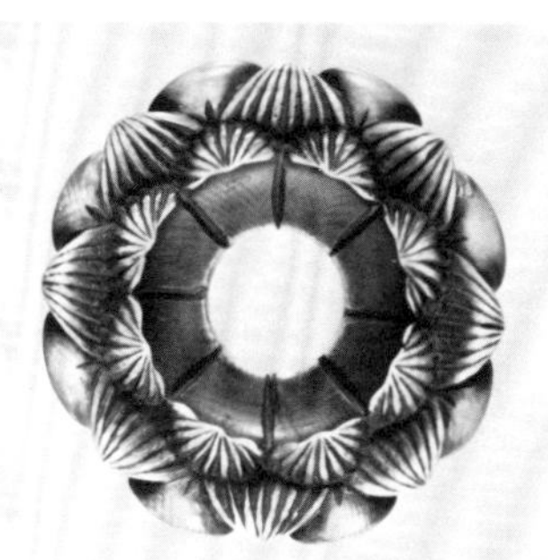

A stylized chrysanthemum

Ivory. late 19th-20th c. Katabori. 4.2 cm. E26554

Eggplant A dream about three eggplants is a lucky sign that the dreamer will have a long life. The egg-shaped fruit and its abundance of seeds are symbols of fertility.

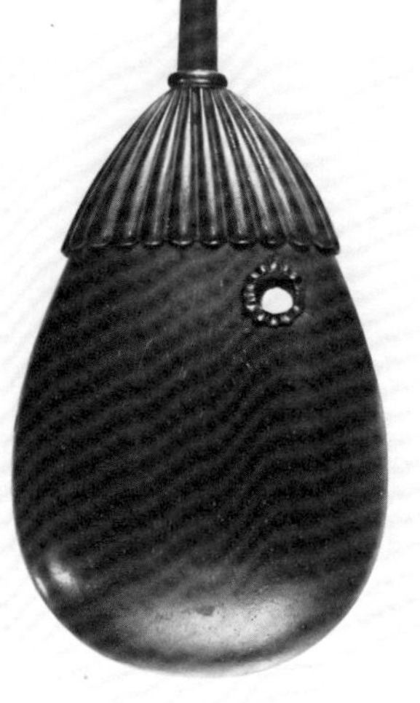

A wooden eggplant has a metal stem and calyx.

Wood, metal. 19th c. Katabori. 7.8 cm. E2279

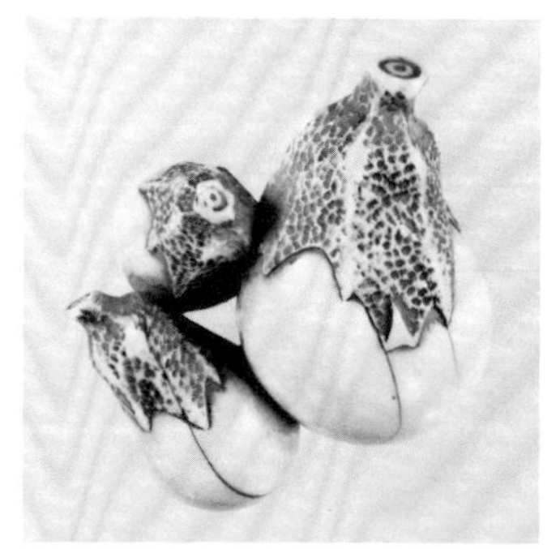

A group of three eggplants predict long life if seen in a dream.

Ivory. Naokazu. Katabori. 4.7 cm. E26847

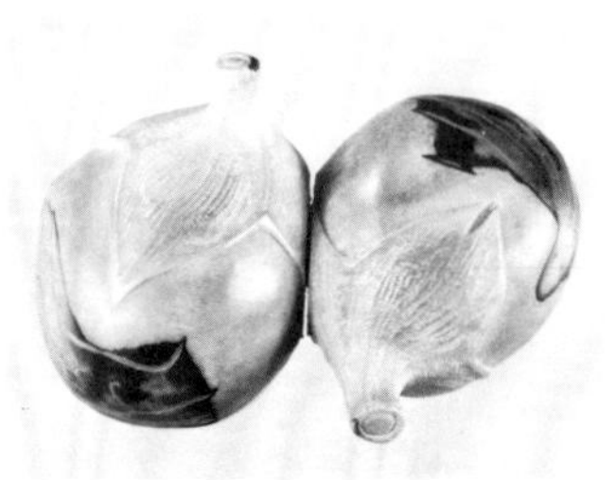

Two eggplants carved in vegetable ivory are pegged together.

Vegetable ivory. Dosho. late 19th-20th c. Katabori. 4.7 cm. E26851

The plant's calyx is outlined on a glass eggplant.

Glass. late 19th-20th c. Katabori.
5.3 cm. E26920

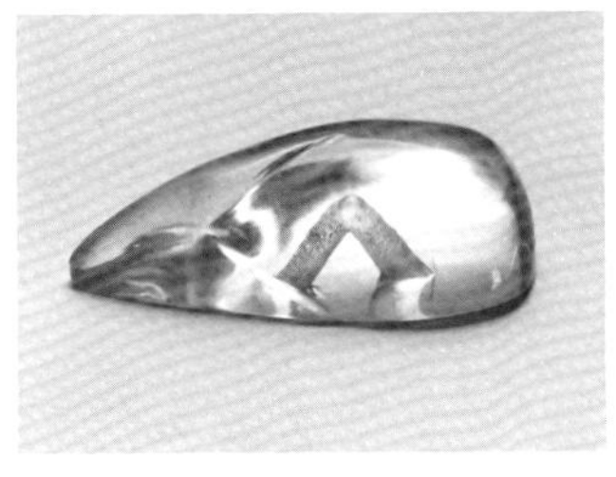

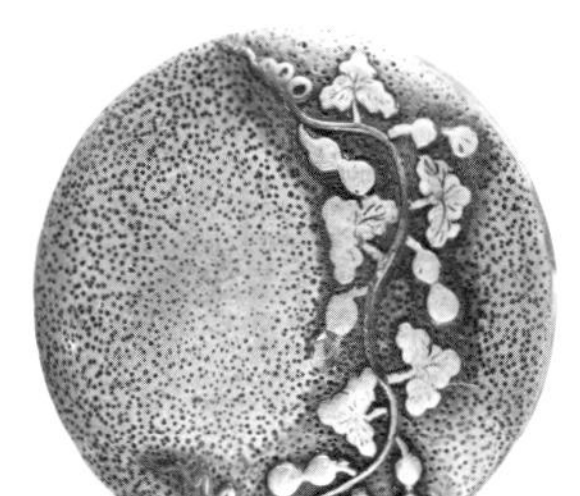

A gourd vine, covered with gourds, trails across one side of a gold metal manju netsuke.

Metal. late 19th c. Manju.
4.7 cm. E29154

Gourd A gourd's profusion of seeds symbolizes fertility and plenty; dried gourds denote longevity and health. The magic powers of gourds are described in legends such as Chokwaro, the earthquake fish, etc. Netsuke carvers admired and copied the shape of the narrow-waisted gourd in a variety of materials.

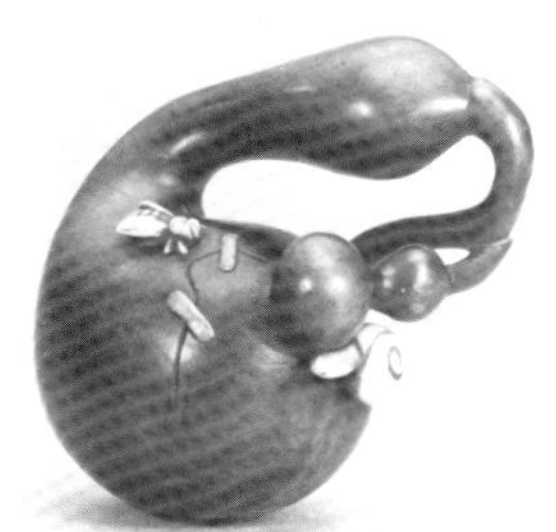

A small gourd, ivory snail and fly rest on a larger gourd. Metal staples apparently keep a crack in the larger gourd from expanding. This is not a repair, the crack was intentionally carved by the artist, whose signature is engraved on an ivory plaque inlaid in the larger gourd.

Wood, metal and ivory inlays. Minko.
19th c. Katabori. 4.8 cm. E26840

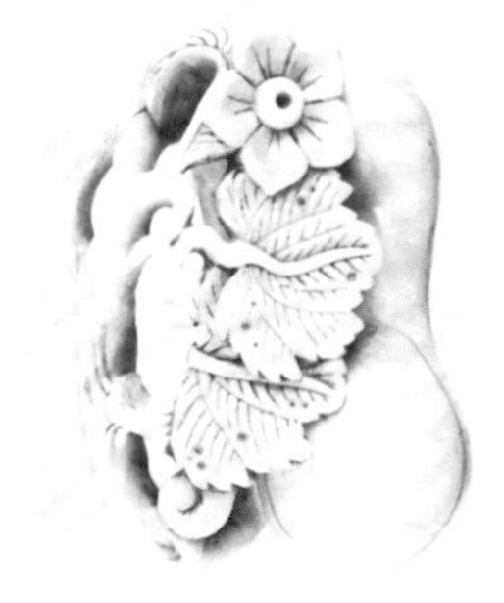

Leaves, a flower and a gourd grow along a gourd vine.

Ivory. 19th-20th c. Katabori.
4.6 cm. E26855

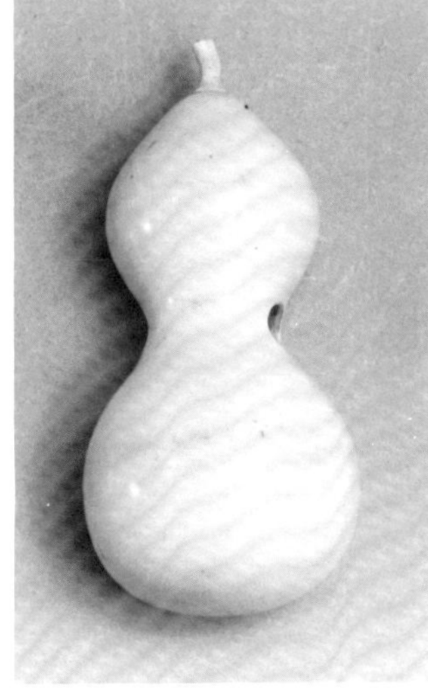

A large, heavy undecorated white ivory gourd has himotoshi running horizontally through its middle.

Ivory. 19th-20th c. Katabori.
7.0 cm. E26858

Lotus The water lily, which emerges pure from a muddy origin, is associated with Buddhism, for Buddha is invariably represented either standing or sitting in a lotus flower. The flower symbolizes wisdom and purity, the arrangement of its petals represents the Buddhist wheel of perpetual existence.

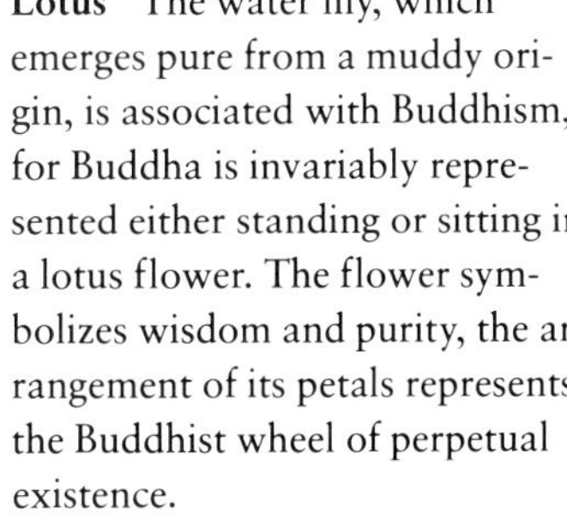

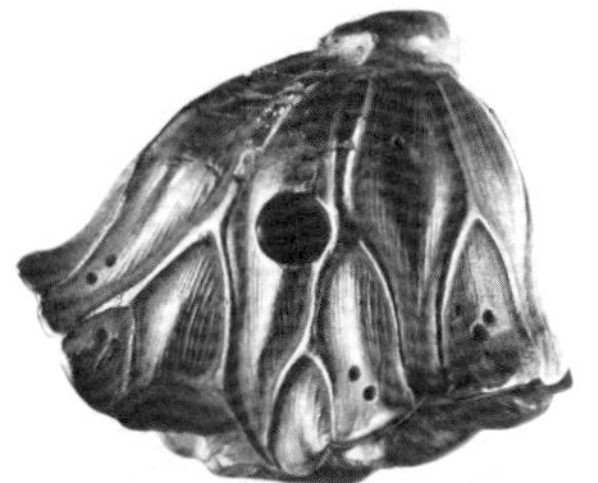

The leaf, curled up flower and stem of a lotus

Wood. 19th c. Katabori.
4.5 cm. E24898

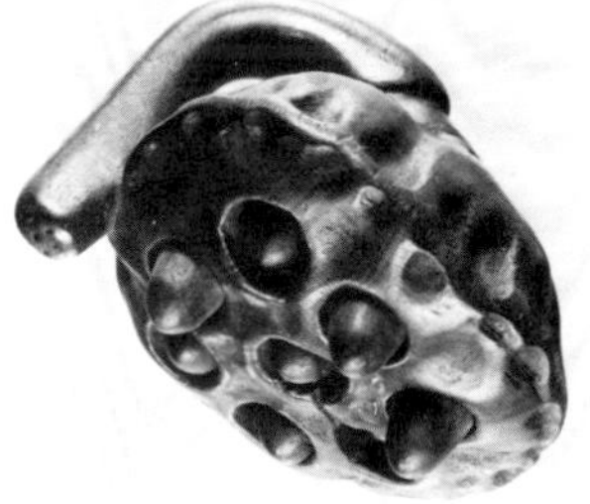

The seeds of this lotus seed pod slide in and out.

Wood. 19th-20th c. Katabori.
4.7 cm. E24959

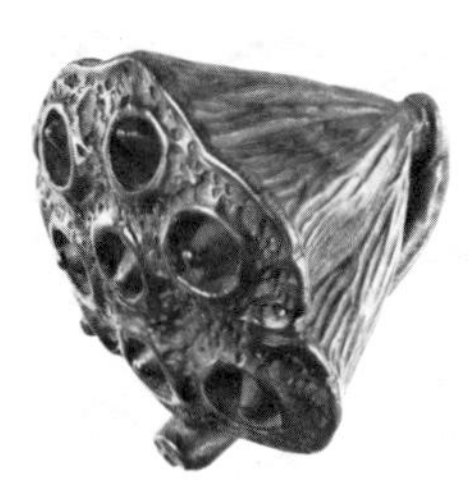

A stem and seed pod of a lotus has seeds that move in and out.

Wood. 19th c. Katabori.
3.2 cm. E26782

A segment of bone has been carved to simulate a curled up lotus leaf and stem.

Bone. 19th c. Katabori.
6.3 cm. E26789

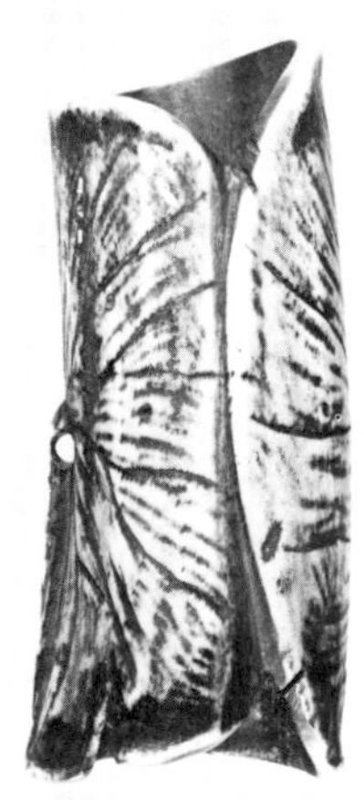

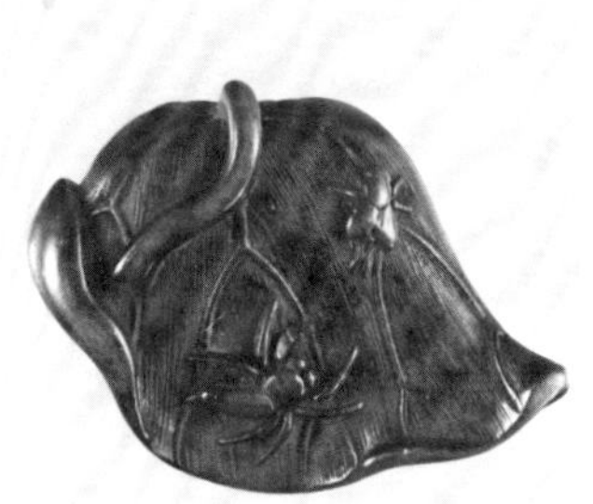

A spider pursues a fly on a curled lotus leaf.

Boxwood. 19th c. Katabori.
4.5 cm. E26849

Mushroom Mushrooms are emblems of longevity, as well as phallic symbols.

A lotus flower and seed pod are carved in a lotus leaf shaped like a bowl. Two ants, one metal and one wooden, crawl inside.

Bone, metal fastener, brass and wood. 19th c. Katabori. 3.8 cm. E26792

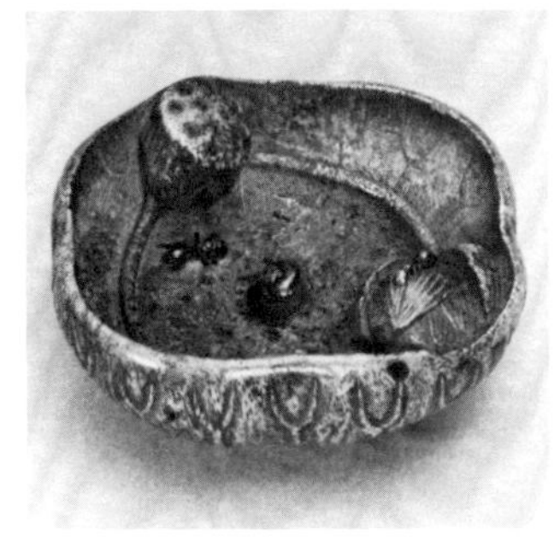

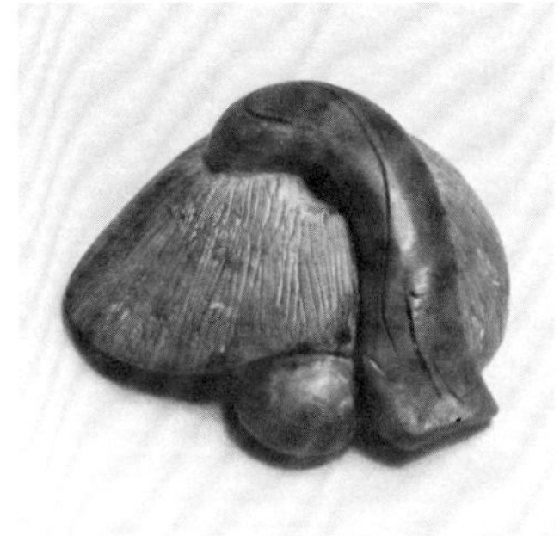

A large mushroom partially covers a smaller mushroom.

Wood. 19th c. Katabori.
4.3 cm. E4485

Two mother-of-pearl flies are inlaid on a lotus seed pod that has movable seeds.

Wood, mother-of-pearl inlay. 19th c. Katabori. 3.3 cm. E26813

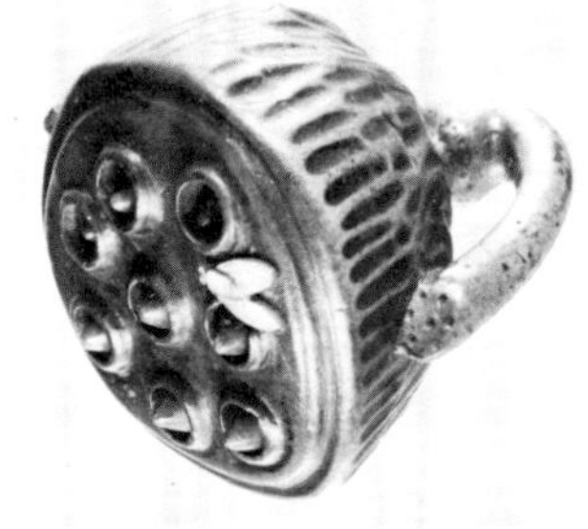

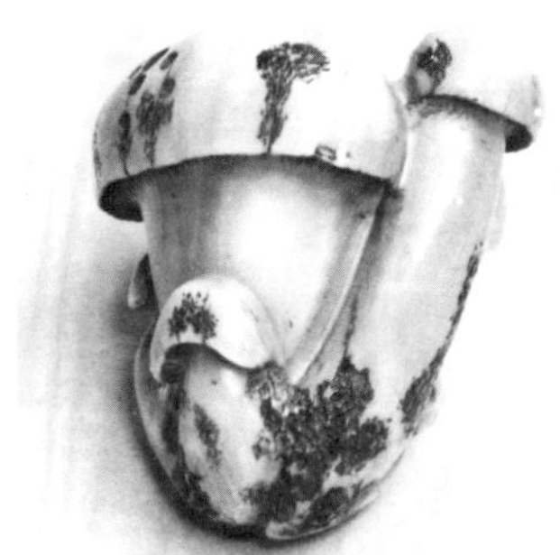

A group of mushrooms are covered with fungus.

Ivory. 19th c. Katabori.
3.5 cm. E26804

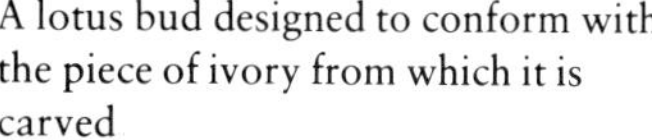

A lotus bud designed to conform with the piece of ivory from which it is carved

Ivory. 19th c. Katabori.
4.5 cm. E26814

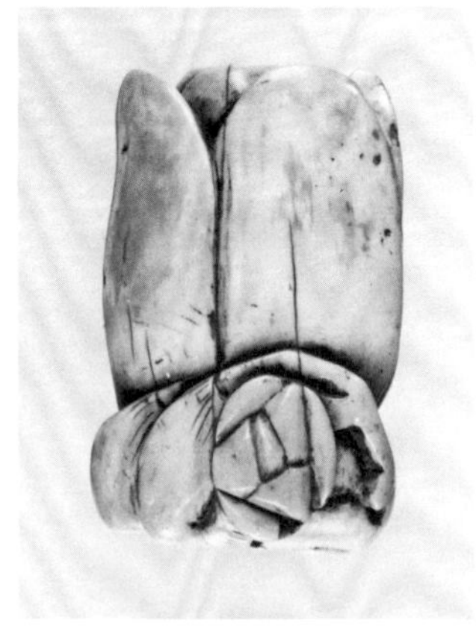

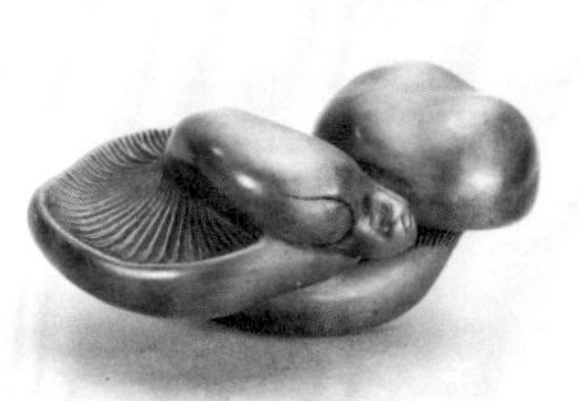

Two mushrooms have been worn smooth from handling.

Wood. 19th c. Katabori.
5.8 cm. E26834

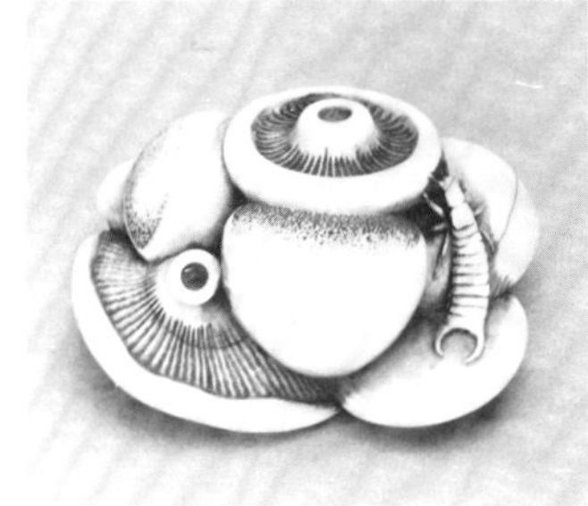

An insect crawls over a group of chestnuts and mushrooms.

Ivory. Gyokuhosai, Ryuchin. 1865-1911. Katabori. 4.8 cm. E26838

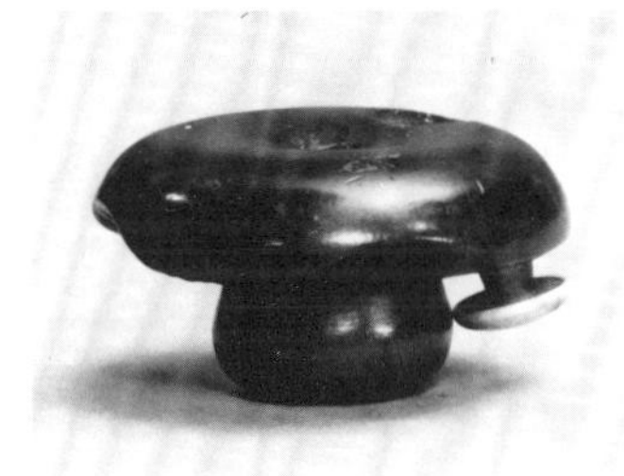

A tiny bone mushroom hangs from a large wood mushroom.

Wood, bone. Isshun. early 19th c. Katabori. 4.0 cm. E26842

Peach Chinese Taoist myths concerning the sennin Seiobo, whose peach tree bore fruit that bestowed eternal life, established peaches as the symbol of longevity.

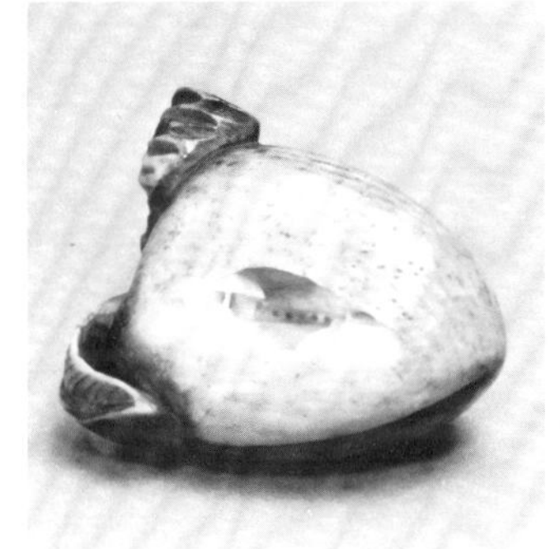

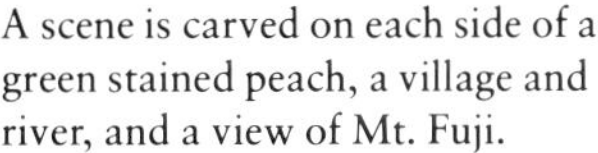

A scene is carved on each side of a green stained peach, a village and river, and a view of Mt. Fuji.

Ivory. 19th c. Katabori. 4.0 cm. E26787

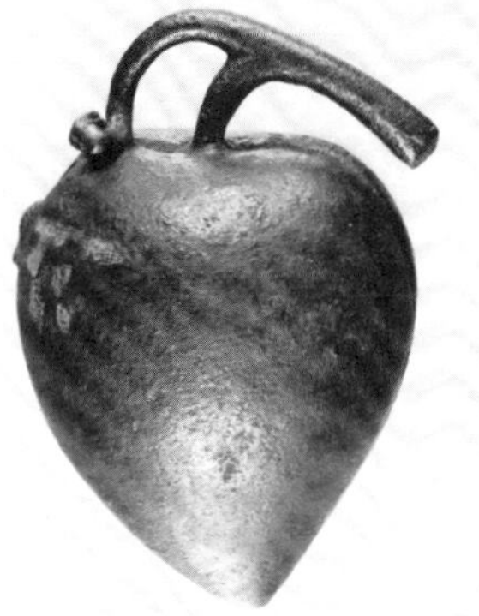

A worm crawls out of a hole in a metal peach. Gold paint decorates the fruit.

Metal, gold paint. illegible signature. 19th c. Katabori. 4.7 cm. E26857

Replicas of Man-Made Objects

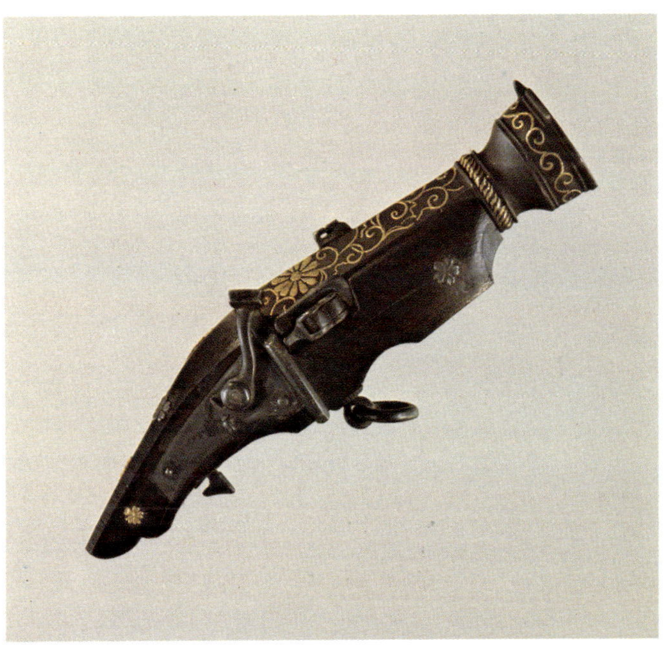

Limited only by the functional requirements of netsuke, netsuke-shi created replicas of virtually everything used in daily life to serve as netsuke. Articles from temple bells to tea jars served as models, leaving a catalog of familiar objects that were used by all classes of Japanese.

Coins

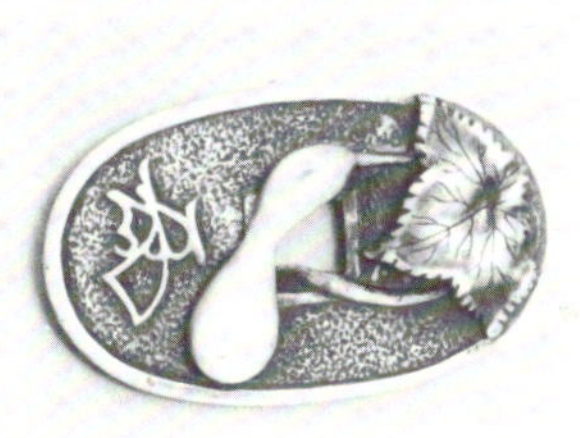

A gourd, vine and leaf lie on one side of a coin. A leaf attached to the vine lies on the other side of the coin.

Ivory. 19th c. Katabori.
4.2 cm. E26856

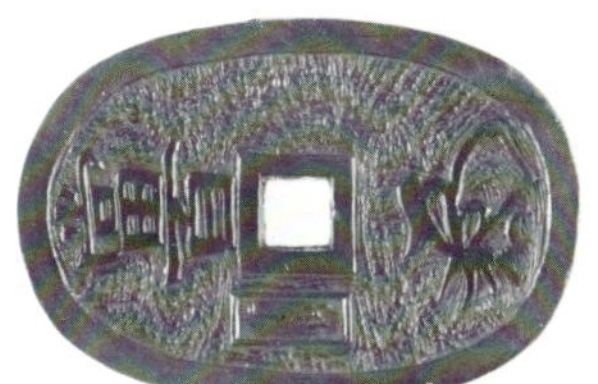

Three oval coins in a stack are tenpotsuho, copper coins made after 1830 until the Meiji Restoration. A decorative signature on the coins is the trademark of Mitsutsugu Goto, who was in charge of coin making under the first Tokugawa shogun.

Wood. Bokuzan. 19th c. Katabori.
4.8 cm. E26901

An amazingly real looking pile of coins tied to a cord is carved from one piece of wood.

Wood, ivory signature plaque. Mitsuhiro. 1810-1875. Katabori.
5.5 cm. E26925

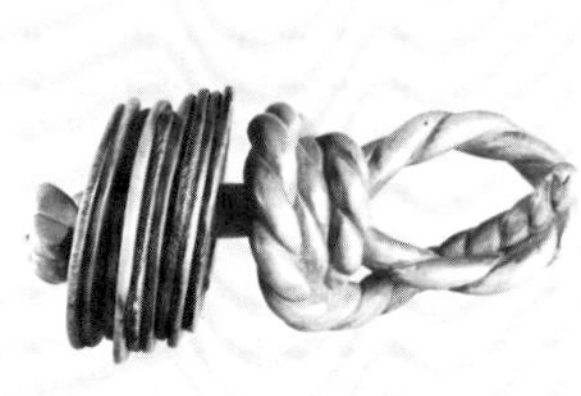

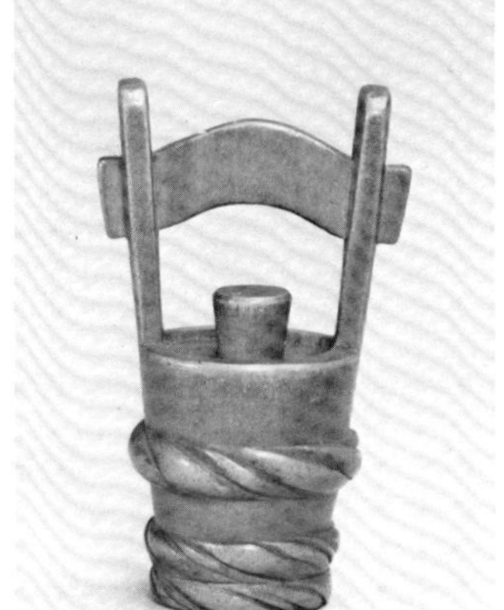

A replica of a bucket

Wood. late 19th-20th c. Katabori.
4.0 cm. E26924

Containers

A wood replica of a charcoal basket contains pieces of charcoal carved in relief.

Wood. 19th c. Katabori.
4.0 cm. E4487

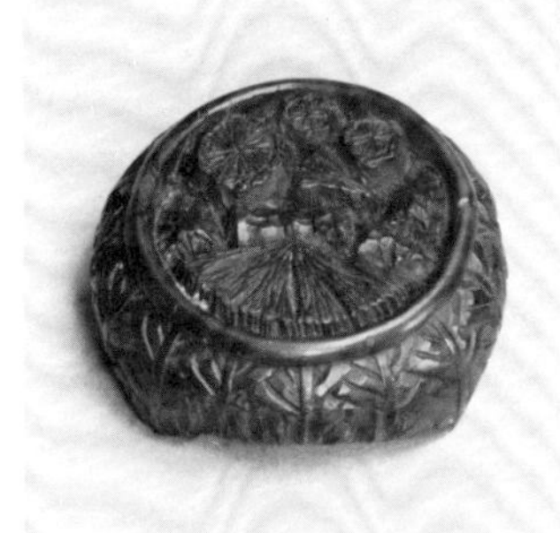

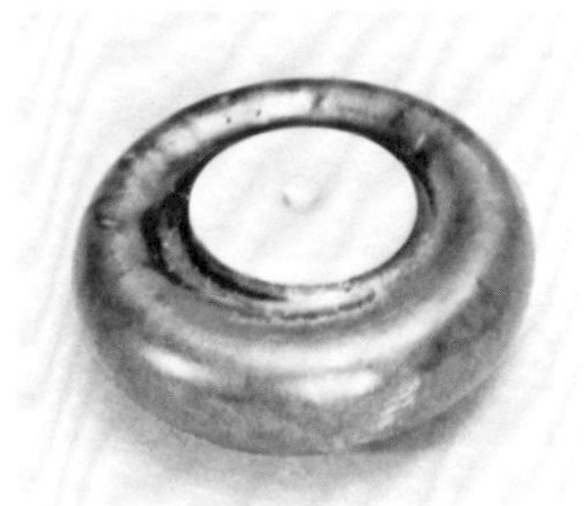

A miniature tea jar is made of Takatori ware; the cord passes through holes in the ivory lid.

Ceramic and ivory. 19th c. Manju.
1.4 cm. E60822

Chrysanthemums decorate this jar that has animal head handles and a pewter lid.

Wood and pewter. 19th c. Katabori.
3.7 cm. E26538

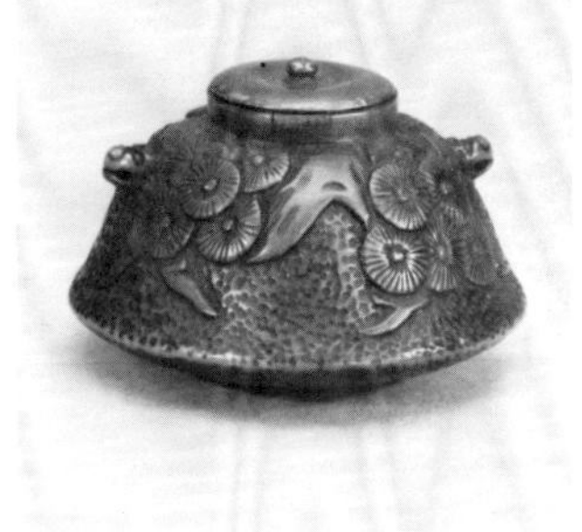

Fan

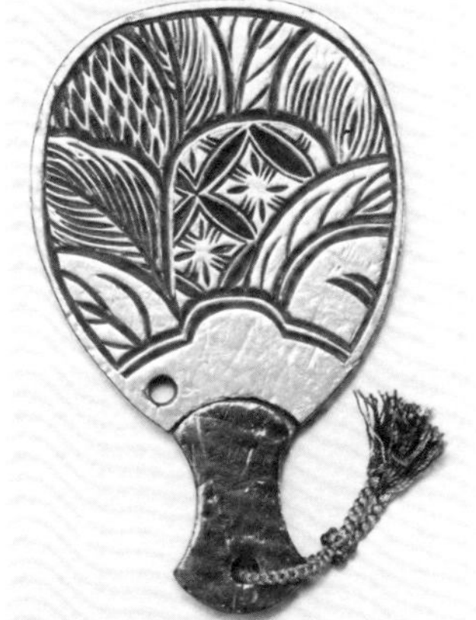

An Uchiwa fan (one which does not fold), with a black handle and red body, is made of two pieces of wood, the handle being the separate piece. Leaves and designs decorate the red fan.

Lacquered wood. 19th c. Katabori.
7.5 cm. E26910

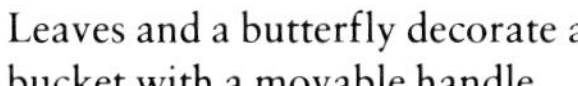

Leaves and a butterfly decorate a bucket with a movable handle.

Bone. 19th c. Katabori.
4.3 cm. E26917

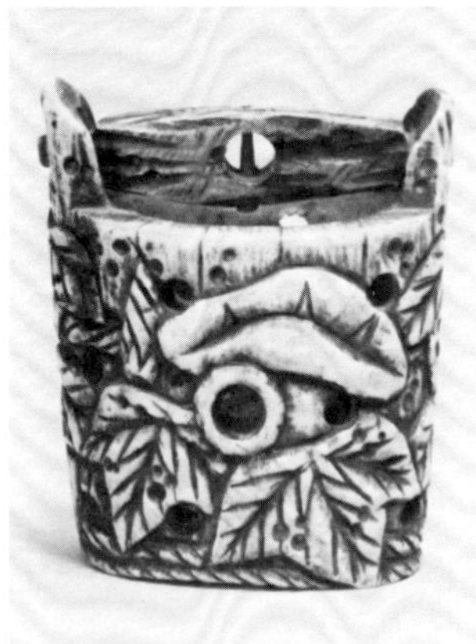

Farm Implements

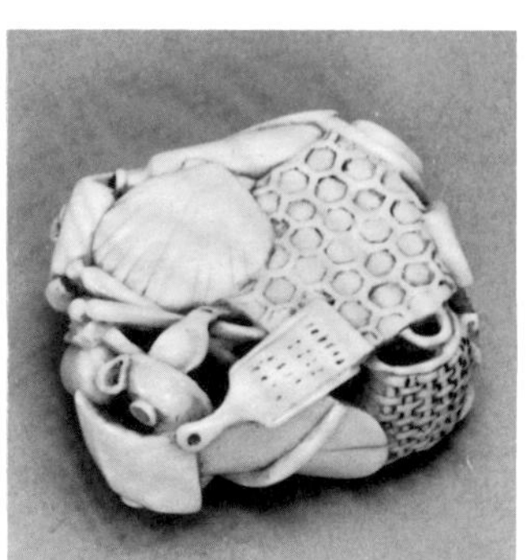

A group of everyday implements from a farming household forms a rectangular shape. Implements include spoons, dishes, bowls, shovel, bees' wax, fan, rice scoop and hoe.

Ivory. late 19th-20th c. Manju (ryusa).
4.0 cm. E26867

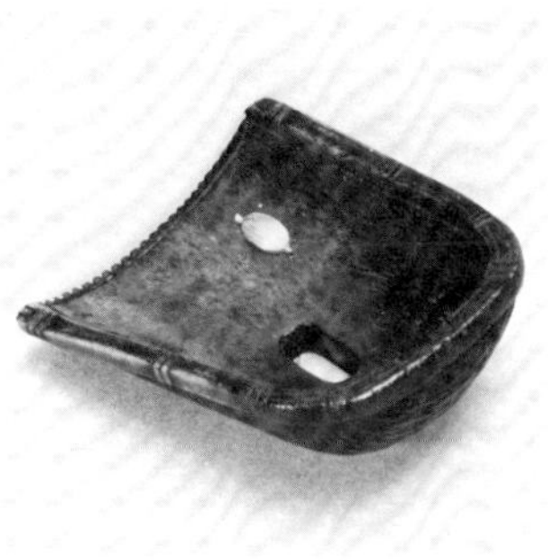

A bone replica of a straw rice scoop displays one gold grain and one black grain in the scoop.

Bone, metal. 19th-20th c. Katabori. 4.0 cm. E26879

House

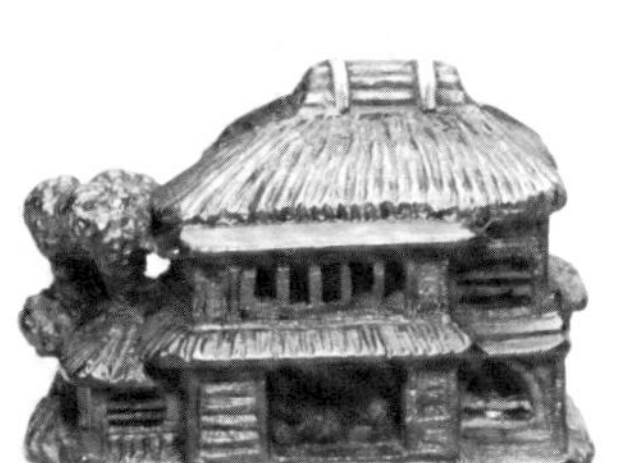

A large tree grows next to a two-story house. The ridge pole on top of the thatched roof is formed of bamboo poles and thatch bound by green coral tiles. One can look into all the windows of the house, and inside the door two men sit facing each other over a low table.

Wood, green coral inlay. 19th c. Katabori. 3.3 cm. E26902

Map

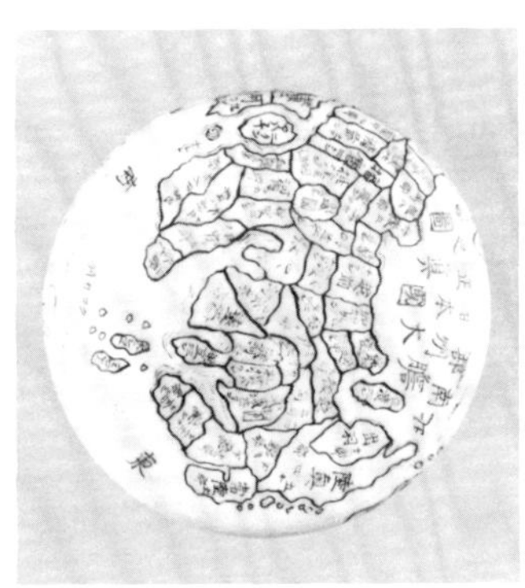

Maps of various prefectures in Japan are accompanied by written labeling and explanation on both halves of this manju netsuke.

Ivory. 19th c. Manju. 3.7 cm. E20861

Matchlock Guns

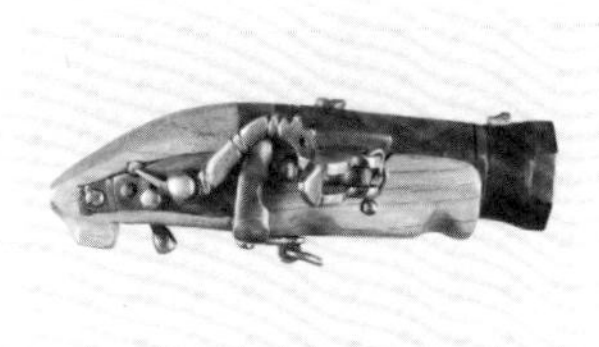

A small matchlock gun has a light wood stock with a brass hammer, lock and short barrel. Matchlock guns were introduced to Japan by the Portuguese.

Wood and metal. 19th c. Katabori. 7.0 cm. E9464

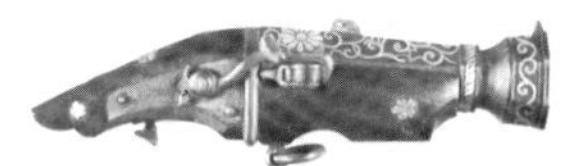

A dark wood stock with iron hammer, lock and barrel, all inlaid with gold and silver floral designs, forms a matchlock gun replica.

Wood, iron, and gold inlay. 19th c. Katabori. 7.0 cm. E26866

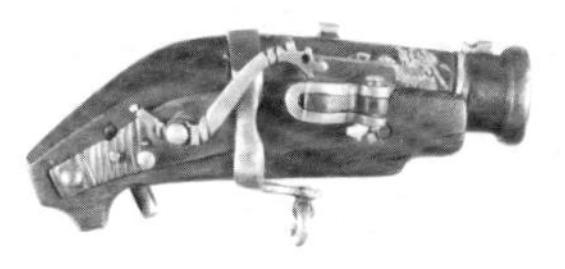

A matchlock gun displays a red wood stock with a brass hammer and lock and an iron barrel decorated with a dragon, painted in gold.

Wood, brass and iron. 19th c. Katabori. 6.7 cm. E26912

Musical Instruments: Entertainment

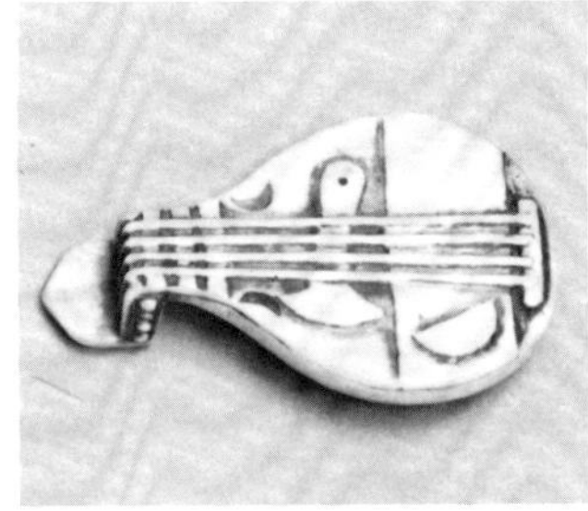

Biwa To play the biwa, a stringed instrument resembling the mandolin, one strikes the strings or the body of the instrument with a large plectrum.

A biwa with the plectrum tucked under the strings for storage

Ivory. 19th c. Katabori. 4.0 cm. E26865

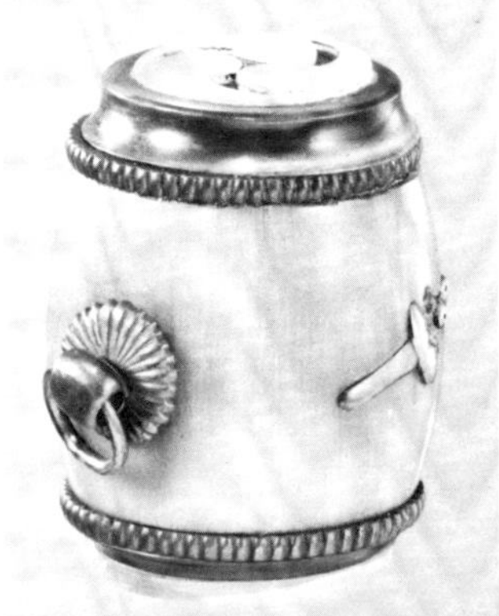

Drums Japanese entertainers make use of three basic types of drums: a plain cylindrical drum, a tsuzumi or dumbbell-shaped drum, and a drum suspended by braces or cords from the body.

A cylindrical horn drum with a metal ring himotoshi has mother-of-pearl inlay tomoe designs on either end, a green coral and brass rattle, and coral drumsticks inlaid on the side.

Horn with mother-of-pearl, coral and metal inlay. 19th c. Katabori. 4.0 cm. E26893

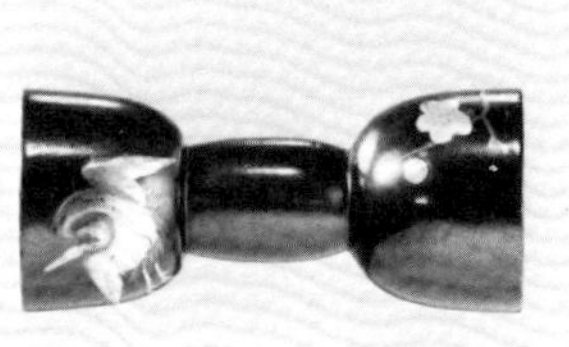

A gold lacquered cherry blossom and a gold lacquered crane decorate the black base of an actor's tsuzumi, a hand drum that had covers stretched across each end held taut by lacing from one end cover to the other.

Lacquered wood. Sho-o. 19th c. Katabori. 4.8 cm. E26894

Musical Instruments: Religious

Bells A Buddhist tsuri-gane (suspended bell) produces a mellow sound. These bells have no clappers; instead, a large wooden beam, hung perpendicular to the bell, is pushed against the outside of the bell. These huge bells, often weighing several tons, are the type that Anchin was trapped under and that Benkei stole from the Miidera monastery.

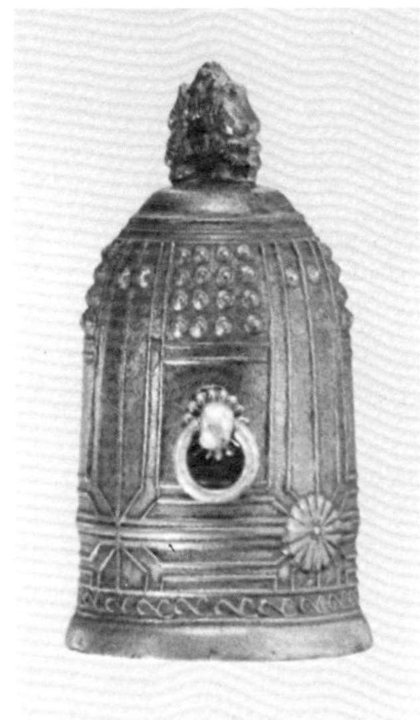

A brass ring provides a cord fastener on the side of a geometrically decorated bronze bell. This bell could also be used as an ashtray.

Bronze and brass. 19th c. Katabori. 5.5 cm. E26881

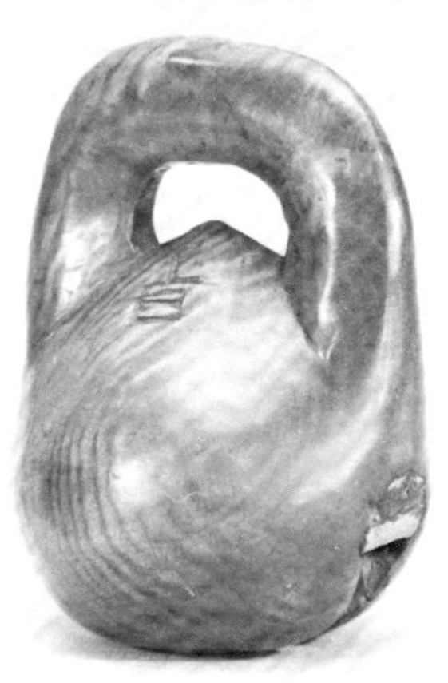

This large, undecorated wooden gong makes a pleasant sound when tapped with a wooden stick.

Wood. 19th-20th c. Katabori. 5.3 cm. E26882

Gongs Small Buddhist temple gongs, called mokugyo (wooden fish), originally resembled a fish with its head and tail meeting; later it was carved with two confronting fish or dragons at the top, keeping the body rounded and hollow for a mellow sound. Chanting a Buddhist sutra, a priest strikes the gong with a padded stick for emphasis.

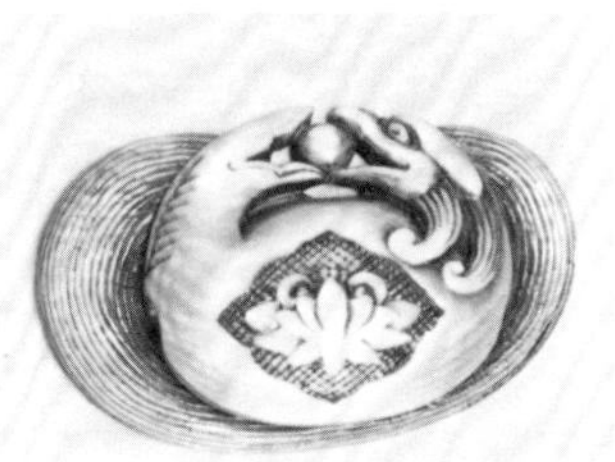

A dragon holds a sacred jewel between its mouth and tail at the top of a mokugyo decorated with a chrysanthemum. The gong rests on top of a temple whisk.

Ivory. late 19th-20th c. Katabori. 4.0 cm. E26885

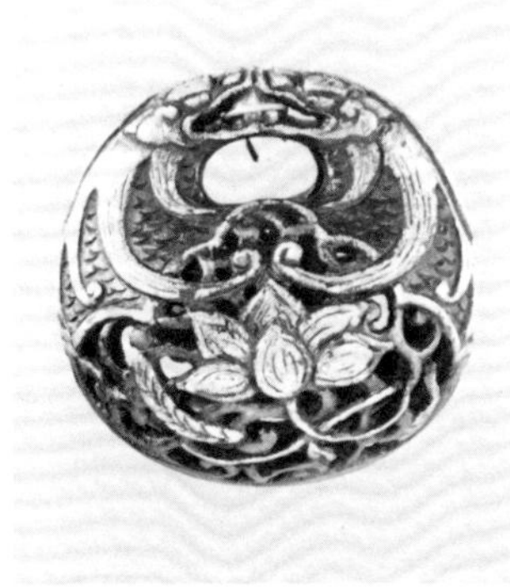

A temple gong is topped by two dragon heads holding a sacred jewel between them. One half of the netsuke is in metal with gold trim and displays a lotus flower. The other half is in bone and displays a chrysanthemum; both halves are carved in an openwork design.

Metal and bone. 19th c. Katabori. 3.5 cm. E26553

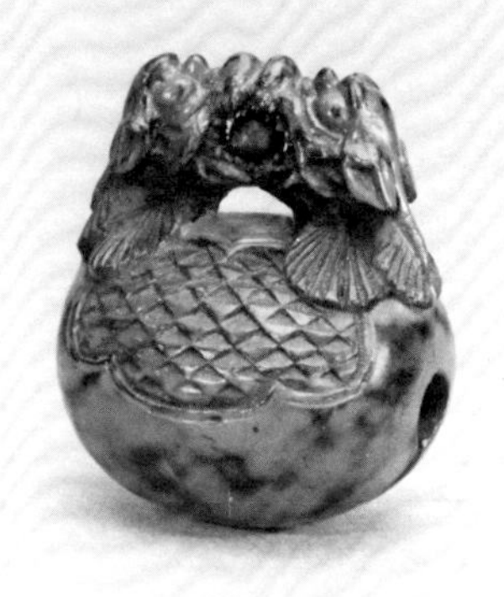

A temple gong is topped by two dragon heads holding a sacred jewel loosely in their mouths.

Wood, black and red lacquer. 19th c. Katabori. 3.5 cm. E26896

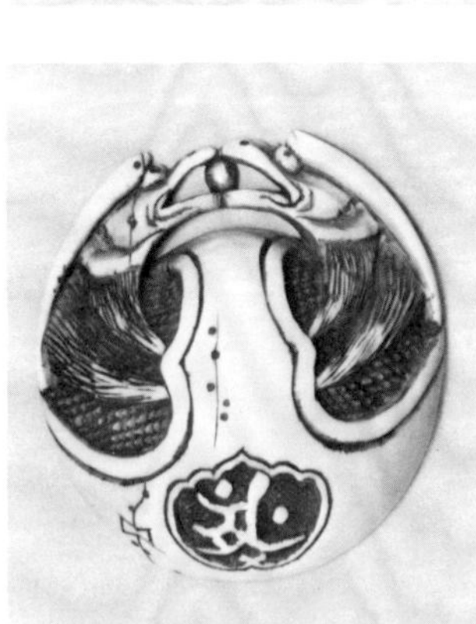

This piece displays half of a mokugyo, with two dragon heads meeting at the top with a sacred jewel held in their mouths. On the back of this piece (inside the gong) are a lotus flower and leaf, Buddhist symbols of purity.

Ivory. 19th-20th c. Katabori. 4.0 cm. E26863

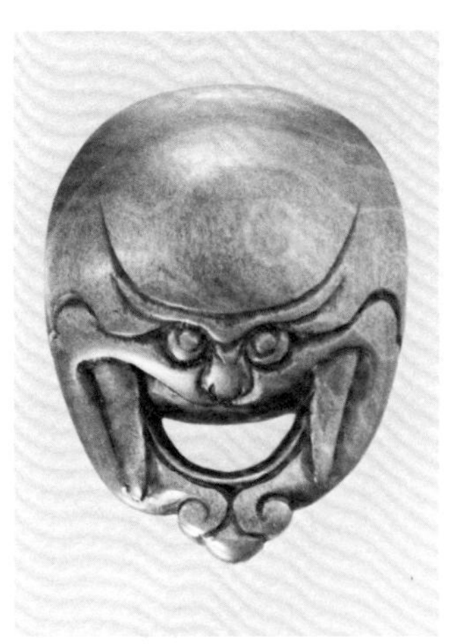

A light wood mokugyo, with a crab carved on one side, makes a beautiful sound when tapped.

Wood. Hojitsu. late 19th-20th c. Katabori. 4.2 cm. E26905

A wood mokugyo makes a pleasant sound when tapped. Two identical dragon heads meet at the top and hold a sacred jewel in their mouths.

Wood. 19th c. Katabori.
3.8 cm. E26921

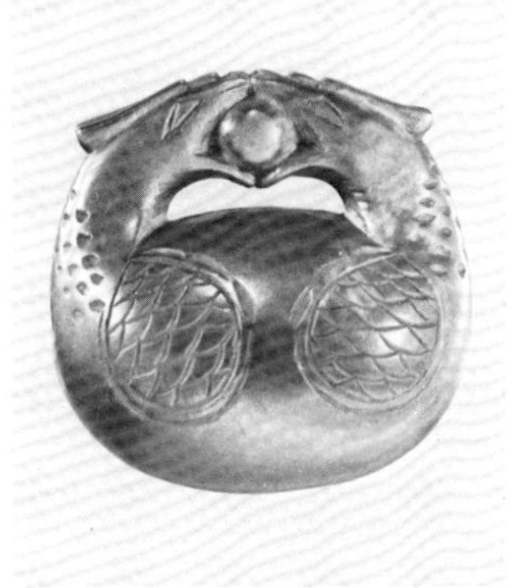

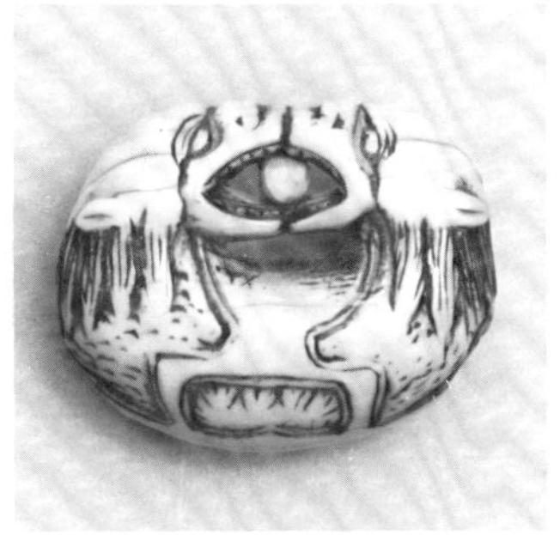

A mokugyo displays two identical animal heads meeting at the top, holding a sacred jewel in their mouths.

Ivory. 19th-20th c. Katabori.
3.6 cm. E26928

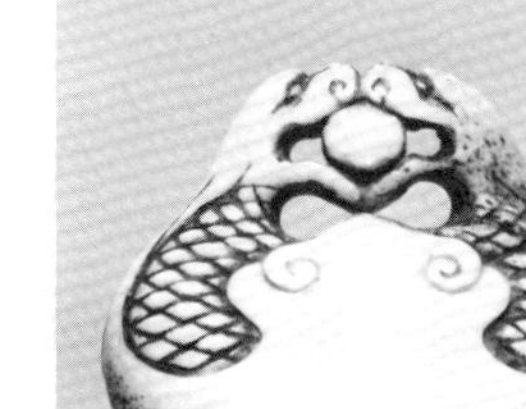

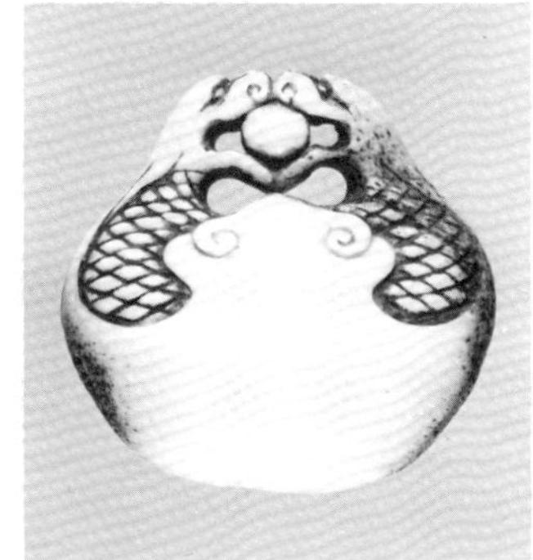

Two identical dragon heads meet at the top of this mokugyo. They hold a sacred jewel in their mouths.

Bone. 19th c. Katabori.
4.2 cm. E36982

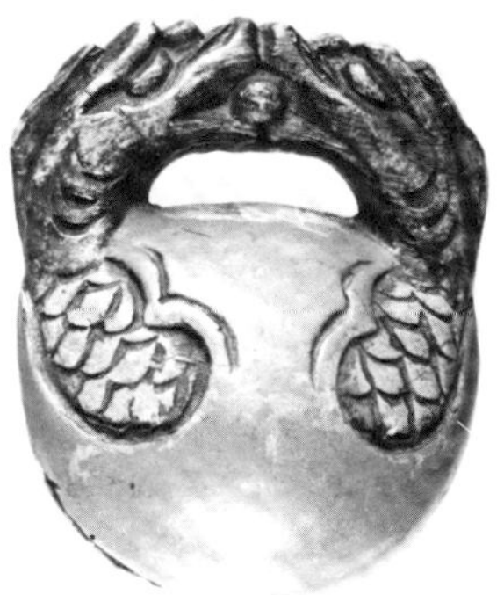

Two lacquered dragons confront each other holding a sacred jewel in their mouths at the top of a red lacquered mokugyo.

Lacquered wood. 19th c. Katabori.
4.0 cm. E63538

Teakettle

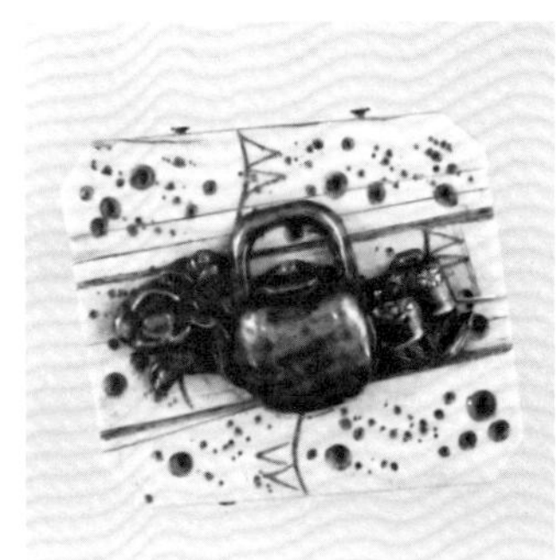

A brass piece in the shape of a teakettle, two tea cups, and a chrysanthemum are attached to a plaque made from strips of ivory nailed together. The brass is decorated with red paint.

Brass and ivory. late 19th c. Manju.
4.1 cm. E26574

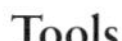

Tools

Two tools of a sandal maker, a mallet for softening and a cutter, lie on top of a sandal.

Ebony. Toshimasa. 19th-20th c.
Katabori. 4.4 cm. E29146

Functional Netsuke

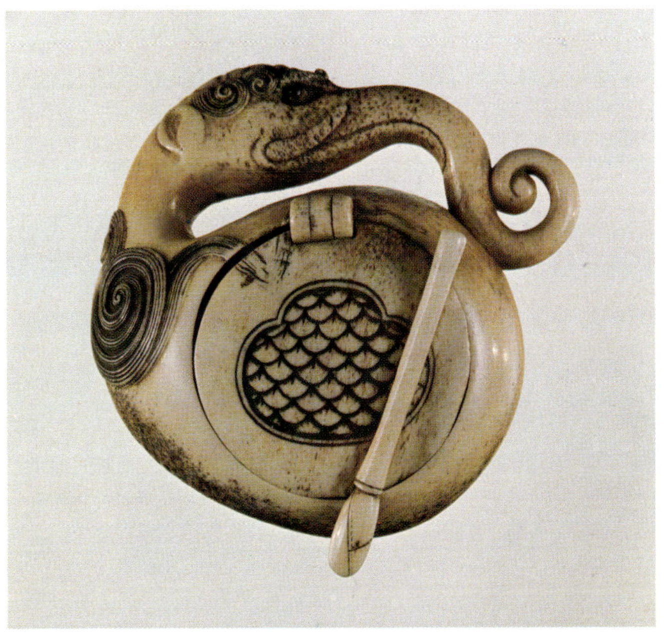

Many netsuke were designed to combine a secondary function with their primary one as a toggle. The use of Chinese seals as netsuke at an early period may be the earliest example of dual-purpose netsuke. Widespread use of tobacco pouches, beginning in the 18th c., spurred the production of ashtray netsuke and flint and steel lighter-netsuke, and the trend for functional netsuke continued to expand.

The technical accuracy of many dual-purpose netsuke indicates they were produced by craft specialists, such as metalworkers, rather than by netsuke-shi. The practicality and convenience of wearing functional netsuke is apparent, for some of the devices modified into netsuke included the abacus, brush rests, firefly cages, chopstick cases, divining rods, tea whisks, etc. Other examples are the following netsuke from the museum's collection.

Ashtrays Ashtray netsuke were popularly used with tobacco pouches, and were often made of cast metal or cloisonne. A typical smoke consisted of three puffs on the pipe; this accounts for the small size of the ashtrays.

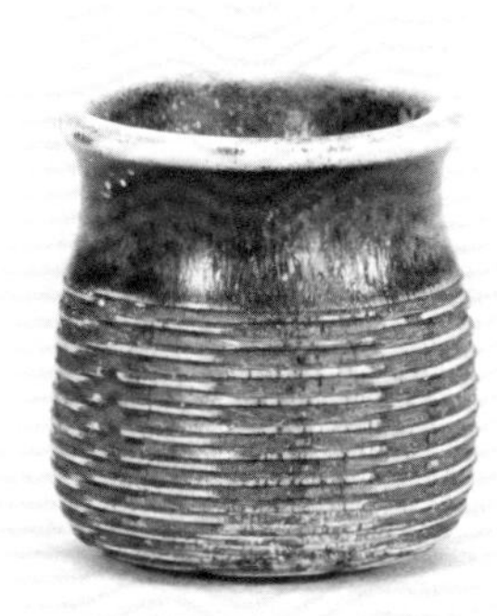

An ashtray carved from bone simulates a decorated ceramic pot.

Bone. 19th c. Katabori. 3.7 cm. E4488

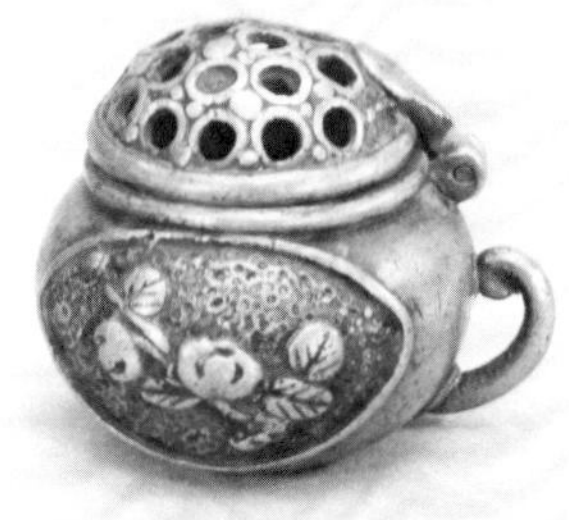

A kettle-shaped container with a hinged lid served as an ashtray. Bamboo stalks and lotus flowers decorate the sides of the bowl.

Copper alloy. late 18th c. Katabori. 3.8 cm. E14797

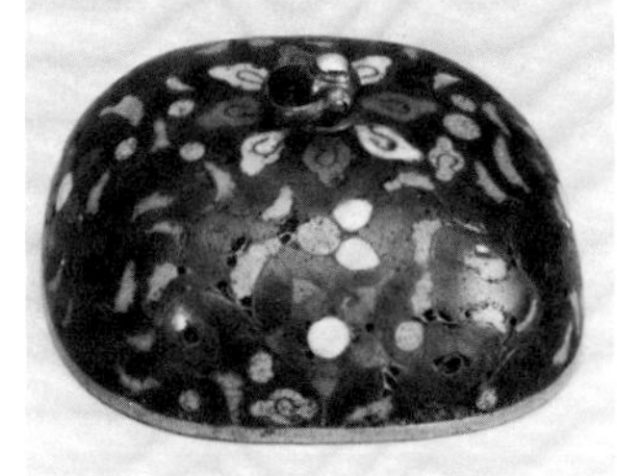

A square metal bowl with rounded corners has a floral pattern in red, gold, blue, white, and black cloisonne on its back, and served as an ashtray.

Metal and cloisonne. 19th c. Manju. 3.8 cm. E26578

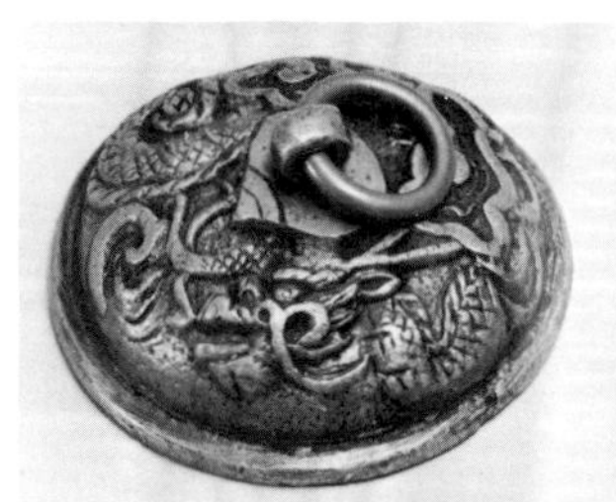

An ashtray is decorated on the outside with a dragon.

Copper alloy. 19th c. Manju. 5.0 cm. E26579

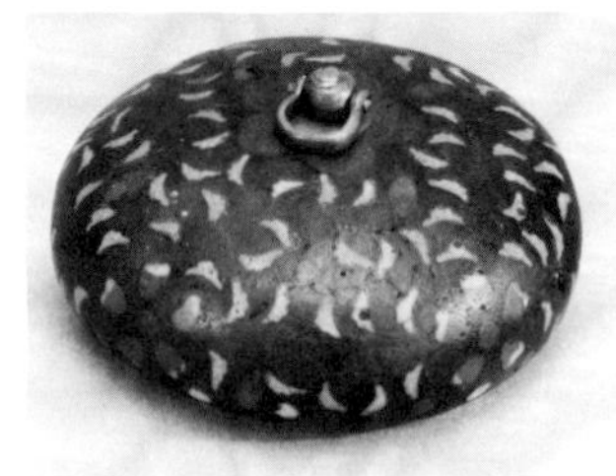

The white porcelain bowl has a blue landscape design inside; the back is blue, red, white, gold and green cloisonne.

Porcelain, cloisonne, metal cord fastener. 19th c. Manju. 4.8 cm. E26580

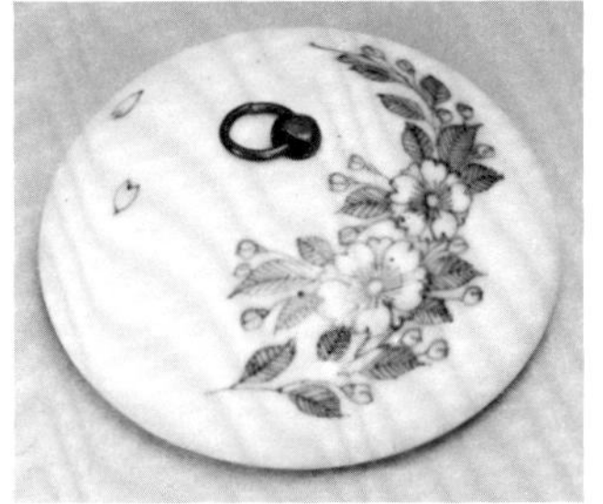

A white porcelain bowl, decorated with blue flowers on the outside and blue ducks and plants on the inside, served as an ashtray.

Blue and white porcelain, metal cord fastener. 19th c. Manju. 5.0 cm. E26581

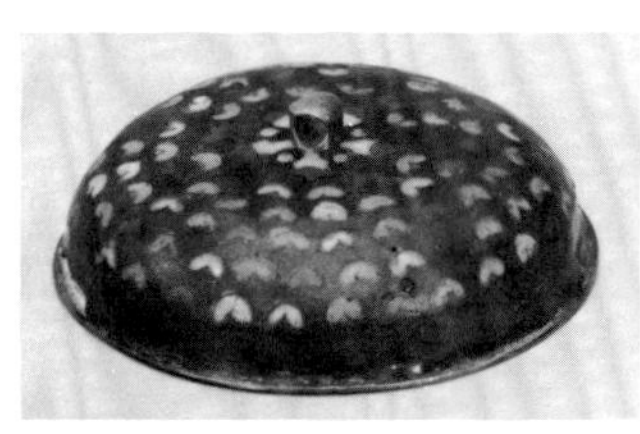

A metal bowl with metal cord fastener served as an ashtray. The inside is plain blue cloisonne, the outside is decorated with red, brown, yellow, and white flower-like designs on a blue background.

Metal and cloisonne. 19th c. Manju. 5.1 cm. E26582

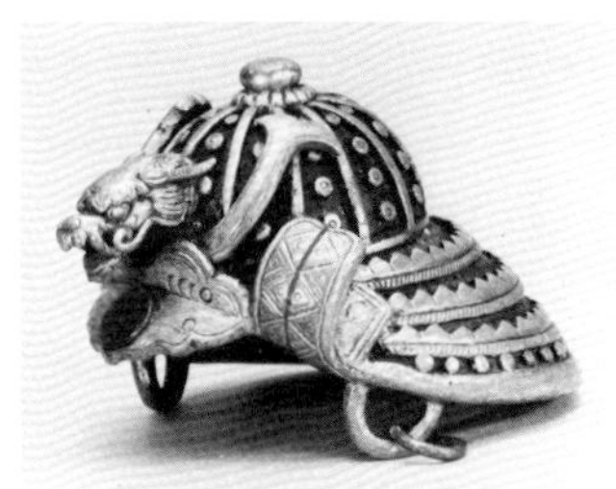

A highly decorated helmet has a dragon's head projecting over the visor.

Copper alloy. 18th c. Katabori. 6.0 cm. E26876

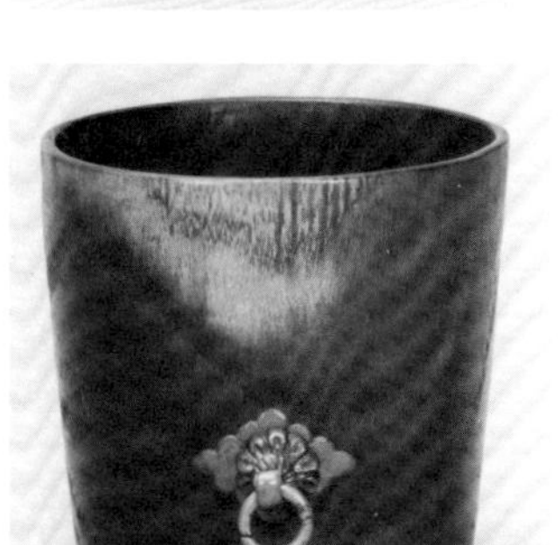

A large wood bucket may have served as an ashtray. A ring on the side of the bucket provides the cord fastener.

Wood and copper alloy. late 19th c. Katabori. 5.2 cm. E26891

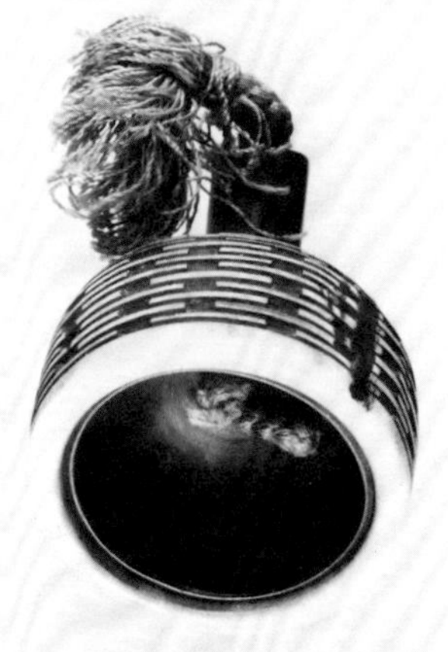

A bone bowl, carved to resemble a straw basket, is lined with dark wood to serve as an ashtray.

Bone, wood, glass. 19th c. Katabori. 3.0 cm. E26907

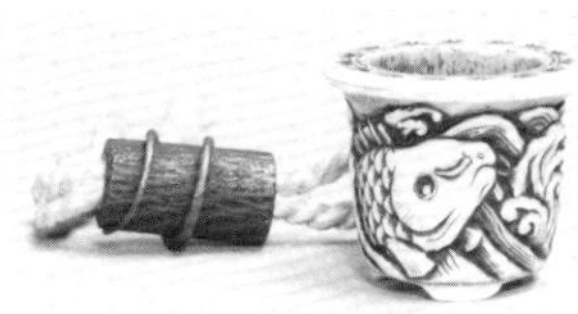

A carp, swimming in waves, decorates the outside of a bone urn which served as an ashtray. A snake is wrapped around a metal ojime log.

Bone, metal. 19th c. Katabori. 3.1 cm. E26908

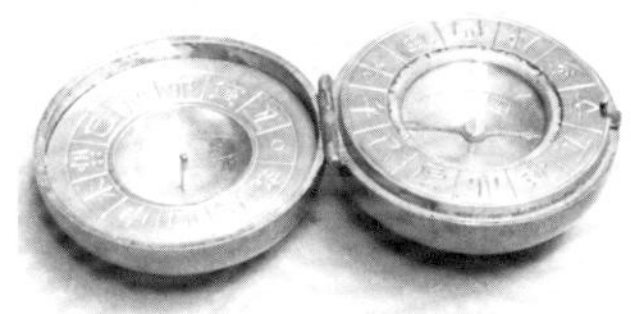

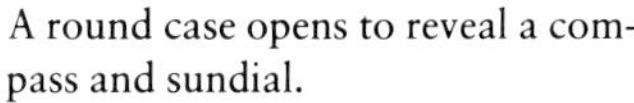

A round case opens to reveal a compass and sundial.

Copper alloy, metal, glass. 19th-20th c. Manju. 3.2 cm. E26564

Compasses, Sundials, and Mag nifiers These netsuke were useful for telling time as well as direction, for one half contained a sundial marked off with the animals of the zodiac for hours; the other side contained a compass. A magnifier was sometimes included for convenience.

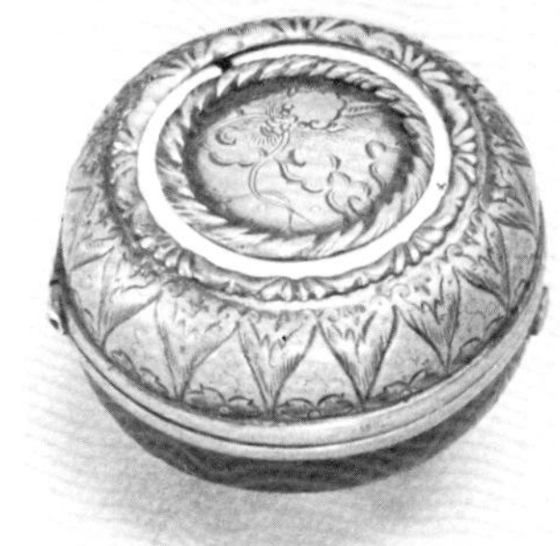

A case decorated with ivory inlay contains a compass and sundial.

Copper alloy, silver, glass, and ivory inlay. 19th c. Manju. 4.2 cm. E26565

Within an engraved copper case are a compass and sundial.

Copper alloy, glass. 19th c. Katabori. 3.5 cm. E4502

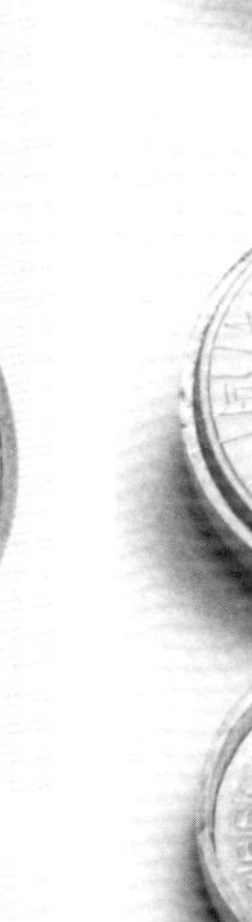

A round case opens to reveal a compass and a dial that indicates high and low tides and phases of the moon for each day of the month.

Copper alloy, metal, glass. 19th-20th c. Manju. 3.2 cm. E26566

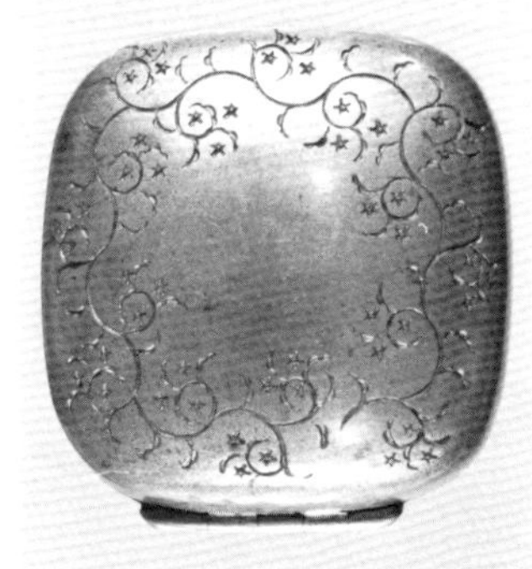

A square case opens to reveal a compass inside one half and a sundial inside the other.

Copper alloy, metal, glass. 19th-20th c. Manju. 3.4 cm. E15619

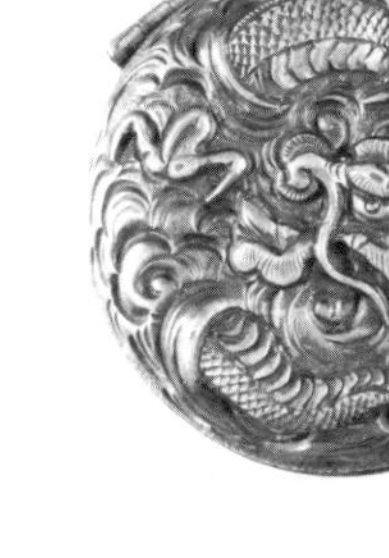

A silver case, decorated with a dragon and waves, opens to a compass and sundial.

Copper alloy, silver, glass. 19th c. Manju. 4.8 cm. E26567

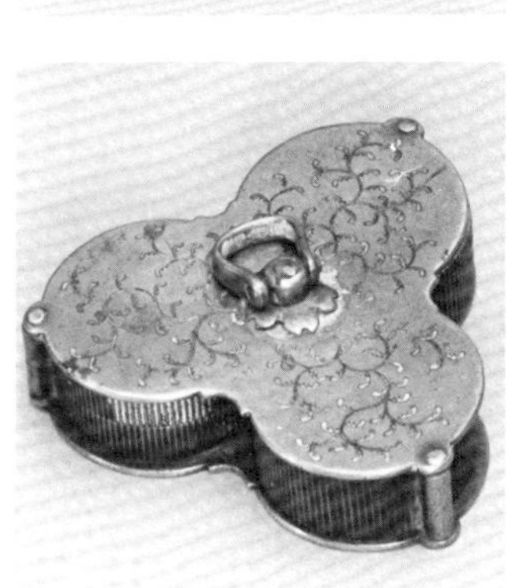

A magnifying lens, a sundial, and a compass unfold from a three-leaf case.

Copper alloy, metal, glass. 19th-20th c. Manju. 4.0 cm. E15620

Containers Properly designed, many netsuke served as small storage boxes or containers to supplement the inro and pouches that they held on the sash.

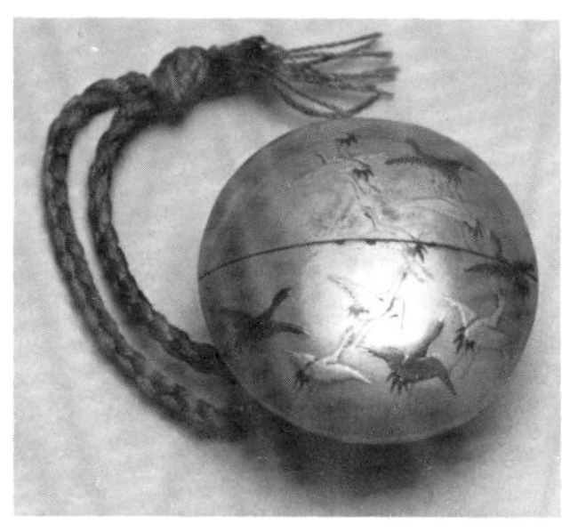

This netsuke opens to reveal a compartment inside similar to that of an inro, and probably accompanied an inro of similar design. On the outside of the piece, gray and gold cranes with black tails and red legs, symbols of longevity, fly on a gold background.

Lacquered wood. 19th c. Manju. 4.0 cm. E26544

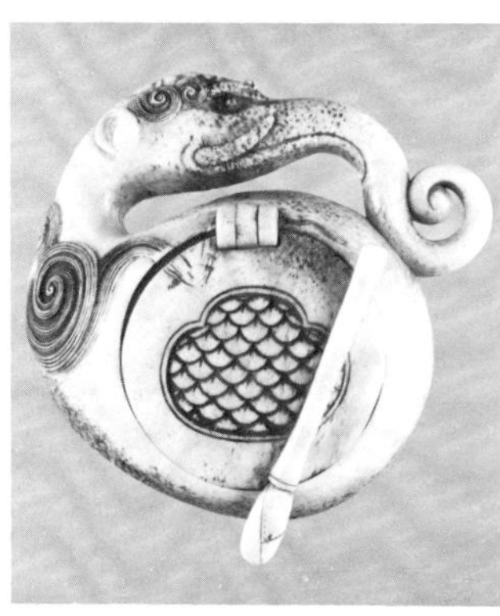

This large piece, in the shape of a mokugyo, could have been used either as an inro or a netsuke. The animal head on top of the gong belongs to a baku, a mythical creature believed to eat bad dreams. The stick with which one would beat the gong provides a handle to a round lid on the belly of the gong. When lifted, the lid reveals a fairly large storage compartment.

Bone, ebony eye. 18th-19th c. Katabori. 7.0 cm. E26861

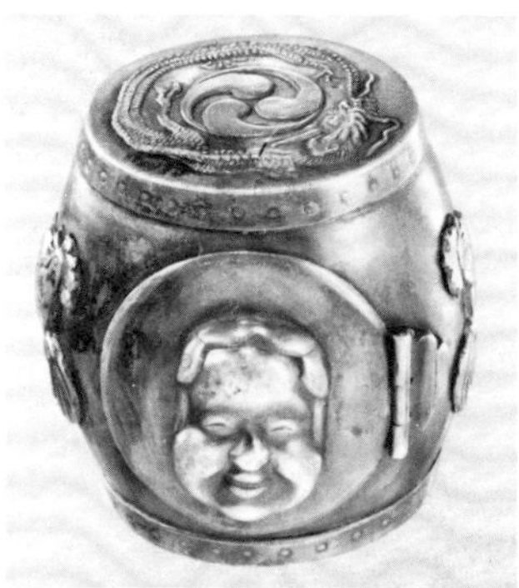

A dragon and a tomoe decorate both ends of a drum, two red roosters decorate the surface. The face of Okame smiles from a small door on the side of the drum which opens to reveal a compartment.

Copper alloy. 18th-19th c. Katabori. 3.7 cm. E26862

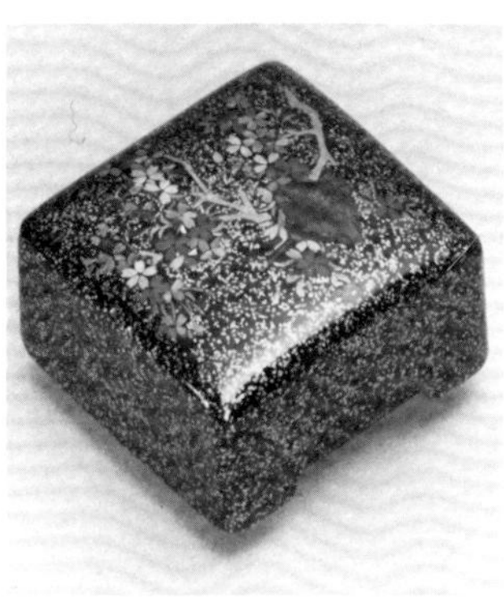

A small square box provides a tiny storage space. An inlay of mother-of-pearl flowers growing on gold branches decorates the lid of the box. The rest of the box is decorated with black lacquer spattered with gold.

Lacquered wood, mother-of-pearl, gold. 19th c. Manju. 2.8 cm. E26890

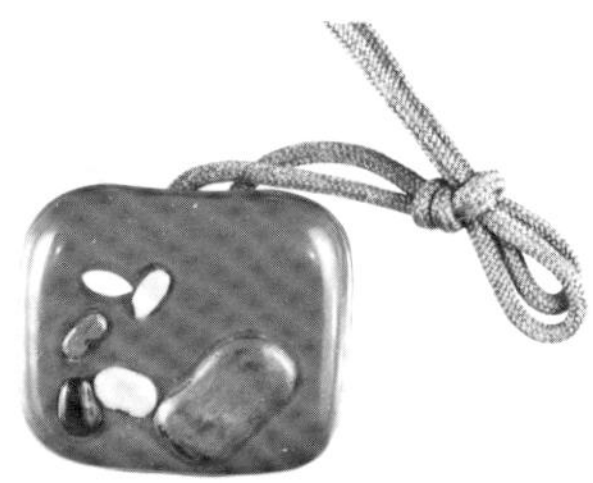

Red, white, yellow, black, and brown stones decorate the top of a small red lacquer box which is lined with painted paper.

Lacquered wood, paper, stone. 19th c. Manju. 4.0 cm. E26898

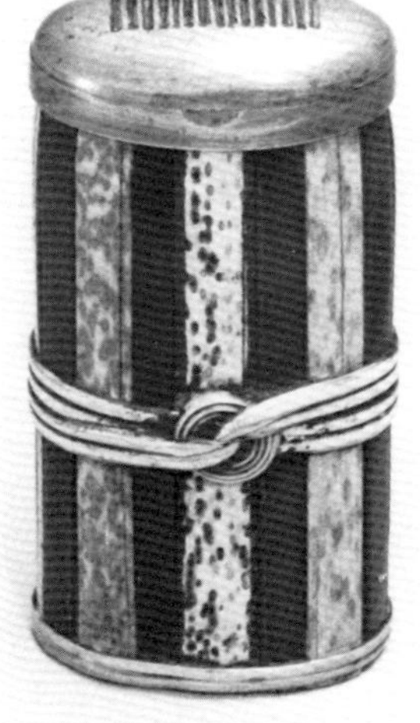

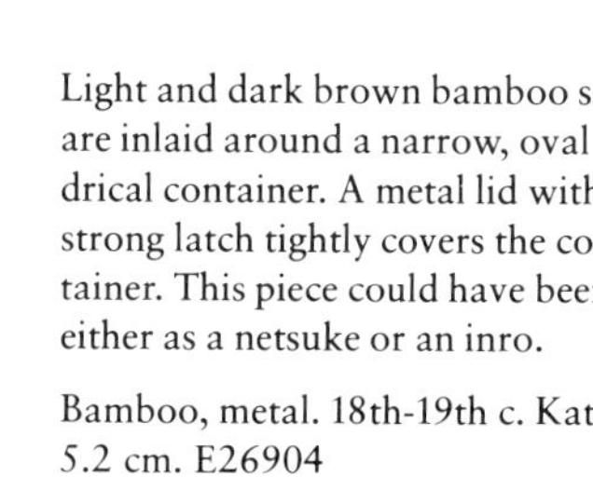

Light and dark brown bamboo strips are inlaid around a narrow, oval cylindrical container. A metal lid with a strong latch tightly covers the container. This piece could have been used either as a netsuke or an inro.

Bamboo, metal. 18th-19th c. Katabori. 5.2 cm. E26904

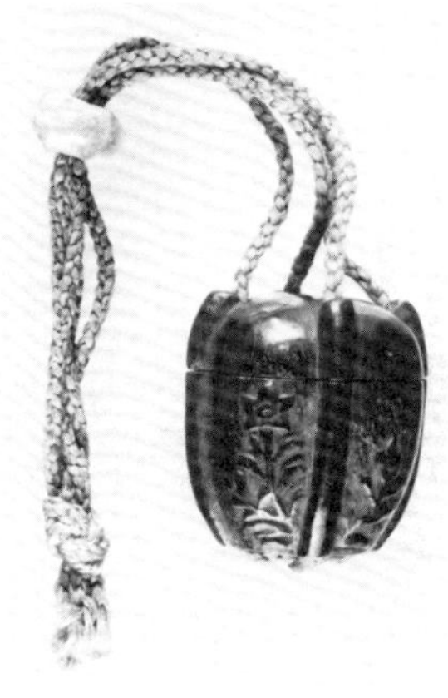

A wooden container is carved in an ideal shape for a netsuke, but could also have been used as an inro. The bottom of the box has a carved flower design, the top can be secured with a glass ojime.

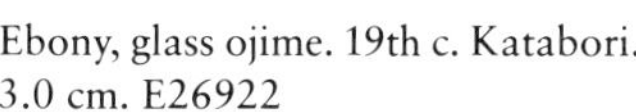

Ebony, glass ojime. 19th c. Katabori. 3.0 cm. E26922

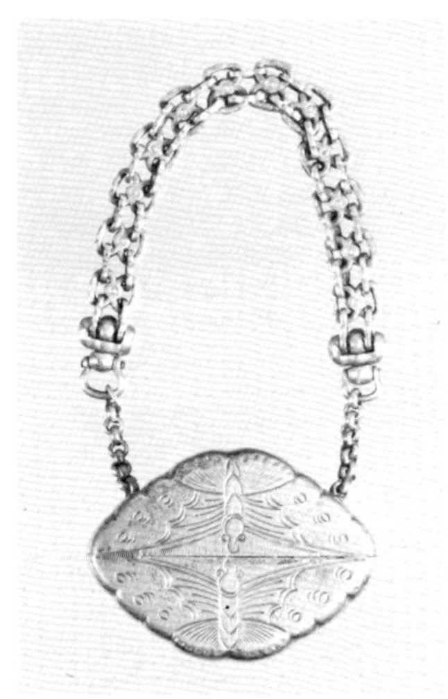

A white metal box with a brass chain is engraved with a design of stylized butterflies.

Metal, brass. 19th c. Katabori.
3.3 cm. E32640

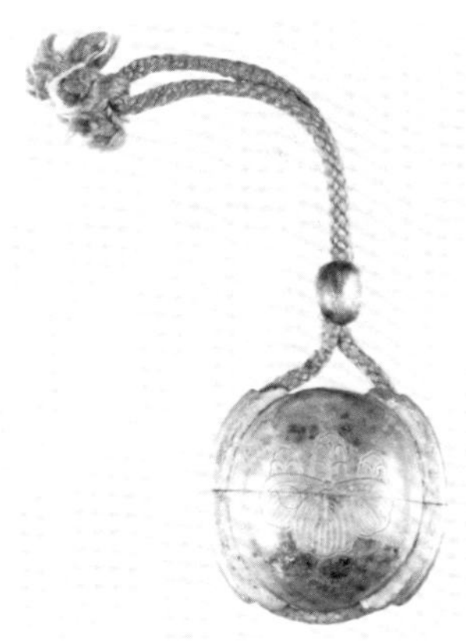

A silver netsuke engraved with a mon divides in half, creating a small container, probably for medicine.

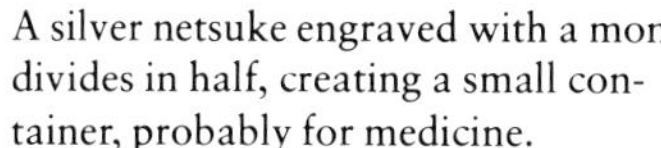

Silver. 19th c. Katabori.
3.5 cm. E32641

Flint and Steel Flint and steel netsuke were designed to be used as lighters and were used with tobacco pouches. Generally, both the cases and the lighter inside were made of metal and functioned by triggering a tiny hammer with a spring release on the side which struck a flint and ignited a small piece of inflammable material.

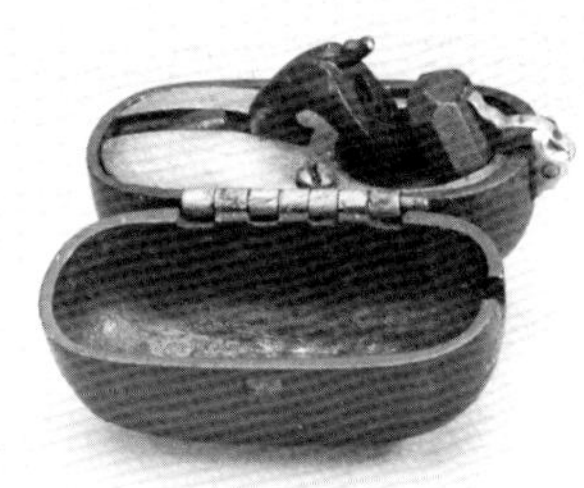

A hinged oval box has a hinged steel piece on one side of its interior, and a small hammer for the flint.

Iron, silver, copper. 19th c. Manju.
4.4 cm. E4444

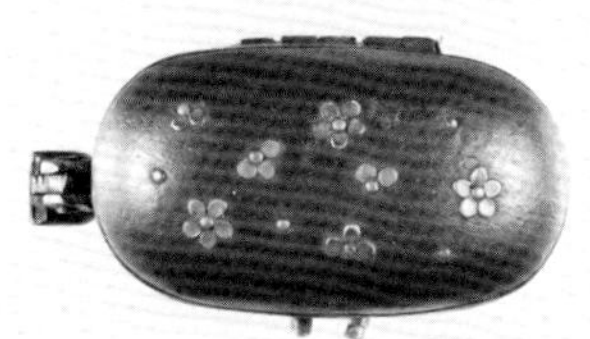

An oval flint and steel case, with flowers inlaid on the bottom, has a ring for a cord.

Iron, silver, copper. 19th c. Manju.
4.0 cm. E9423

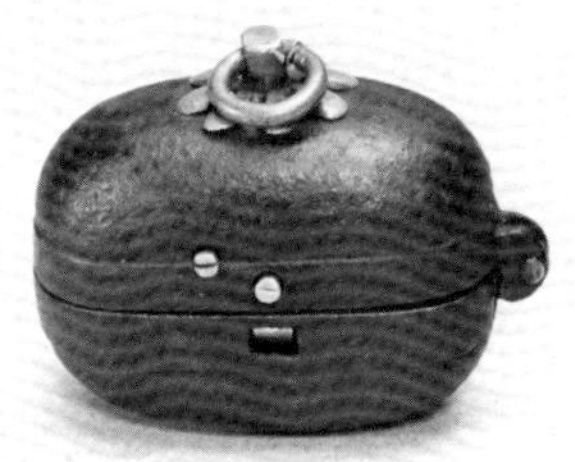

An oblong case, with a ring cord fastener, contains a flint and steel lighter.

Copper and iron. late 18th c. Manju.
4.3 cm. E26883

Gourd Bottles Natural gourds were among the earliest netsuke and continued to be used, though in later years they were often decorated and lacquered. Netsuke-shi were particularly fond of the shape of the narrow-waisted gourd, and copied its shape in ivory, metal, ceramic, and wood gourd bottles that were used primarily for medicines and scents.

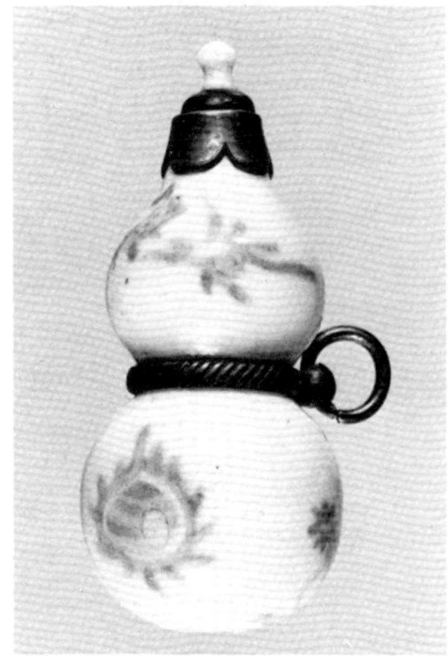

Blue dragons decorate a white gourd bottle.

Blue and white porcelain, metal ring, horn and ivory stopper. 19th c. Katabori. 5.2 cm. E5812

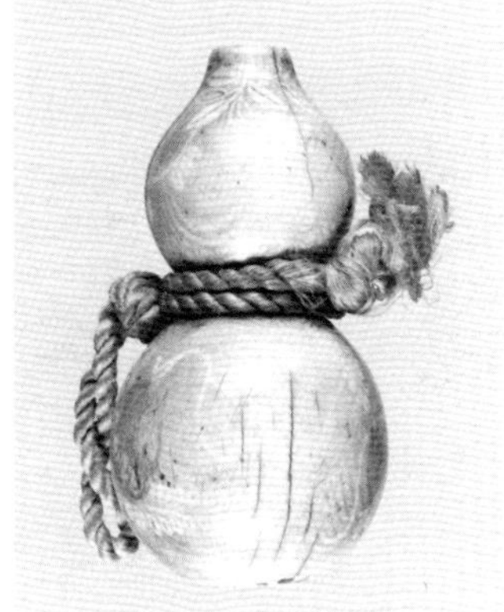

A simple gourd bottle with a silk cord tied around it has leaves and vines barely embossed on the surface of the bottle. The undecorated part of the bottle is stained brown, but the decorations have been left an unstained white.

Ivory. 18th c. Katabori.
4.4 cm. E26786

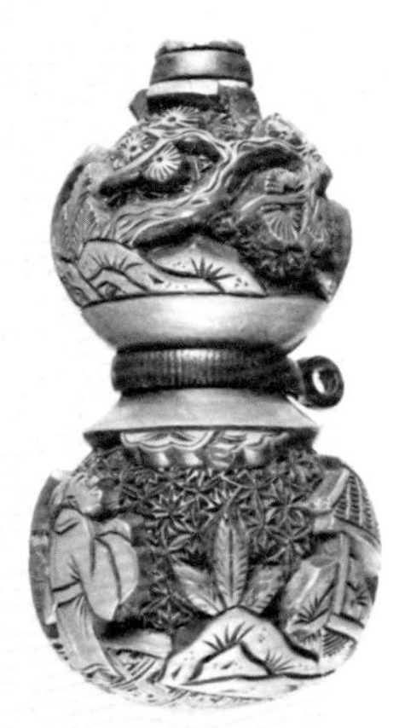

This piece depicts temple scenes carved in relief on the gourd bottle. A metal ring supplies the cord hole, and a stopper plugs the top.

Cinnabar lacquered wood, copper metal. 19th c. Katabori. 4.9 cm. E26798

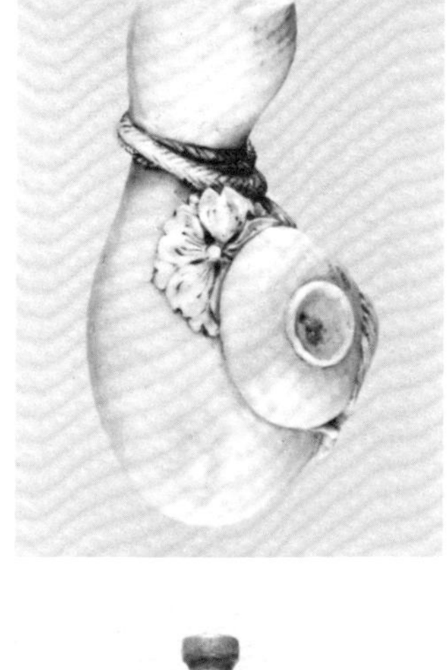

A saucer and a flower lie against a gourd bottle. An ivory rope tied around the bottle helps form a natural aperture for the cord.

Ivory. Senko, unrecorded artist. 19th c. Katabori. 5.0 cm. E26828

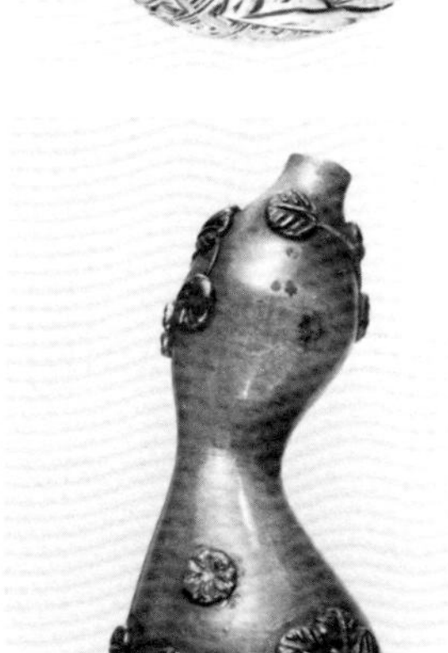

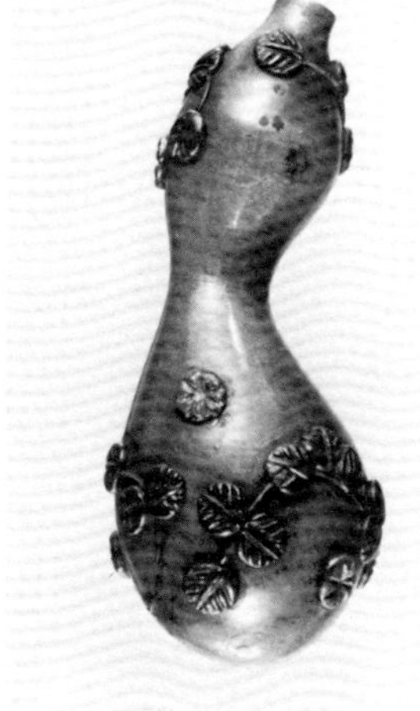

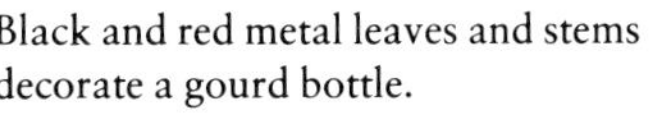

Black and red metal leaves and stems decorate a gourd bottle.

Copper alloy, metal. 19th c. Katabori. 5.2 cm. E26811

Inlaid mother-of-pearl circles decorate a black wood gourd bottle that has a metal ring for a cord fastener. The bottle is made of two round wood balls pegged together by a metal rod through their centers.

Wood, mother-of-pearl, metal. 19th-20th c. Katabori. 6.3 cm. E26859

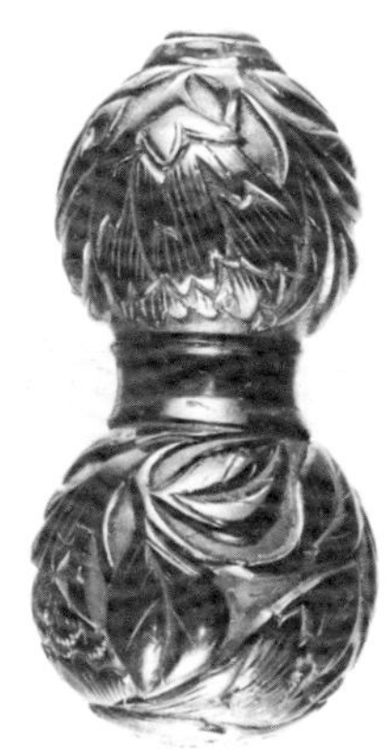

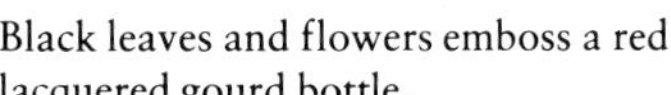

Black leaves and flowers emboss a red lacquered gourd bottle.

Lacquered wood. 19th c. Katabori. 4.8 cm. E26822

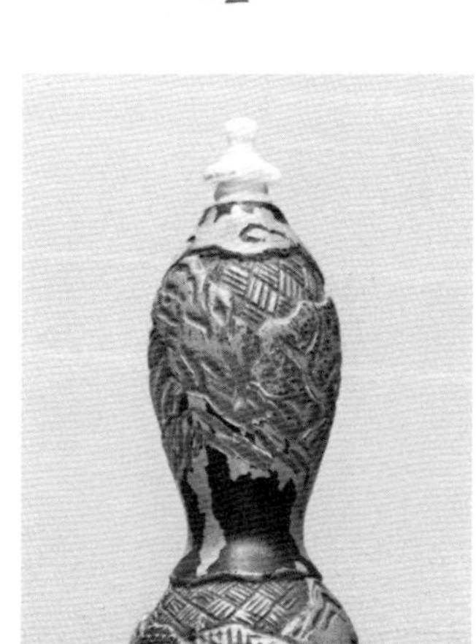

An ebony gourd bottle, with water scenes carved in relief, is coated with red paint and plugged with an ivory screw top.

Painted wood, ivory. 19th-20th c. Katabori. 6.0 cm. E26860

A brown ceramic gourd bottle has an ivory stopper.

Ceramic, ivory. 19th c. Katabori.
5.0 cm. E53699

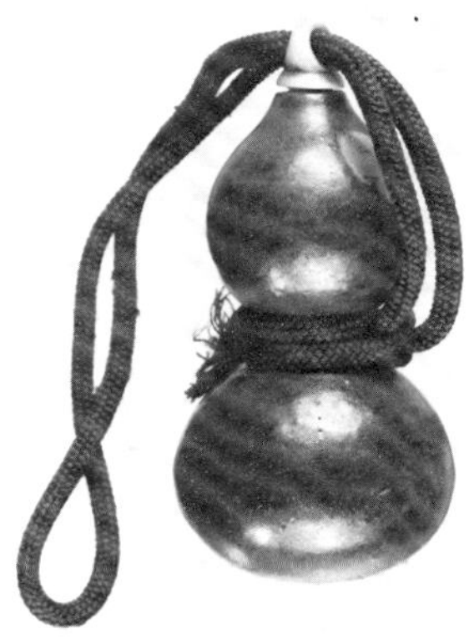

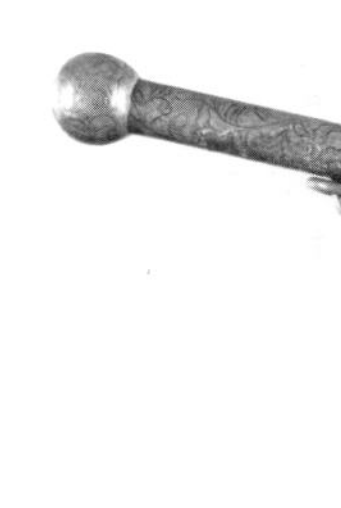

A short cylindrical case with a hinged lid is joined to a horizontally attached tube, forming a pen and ink case. The case holds ink, the tube holds the pen. Floral designs decorate the metal.

Copper alloy. 19th c. Katabori.
7.2 cm. E26926

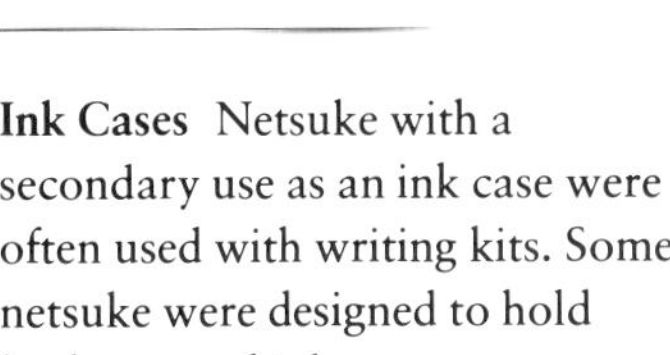

Ink Cases Netsuke with a secondary use as an ink case were often used with writing kits. Some netsuke were designed to hold both pen and ink.

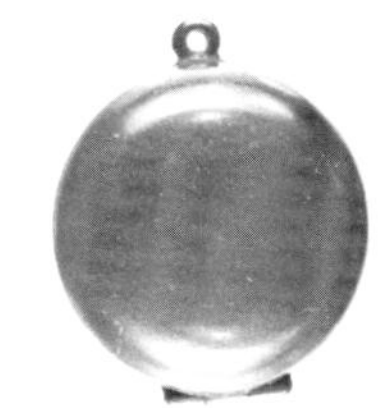

A small round metal case opens to store solid red ink.

Metal. 19th-20th c. Manju.
2.0 cm. E26556

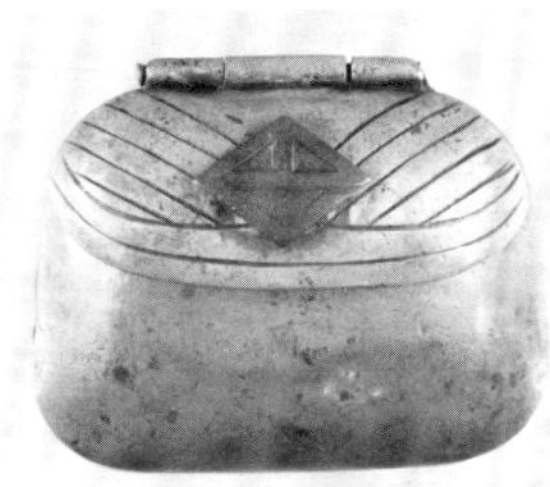

A copper case for ink has a lid that clasps shut. The metal piece simulates a tobacco pouch sagemono.

Copper alloy. 19th c. Manju.
4.4 cm. E26557

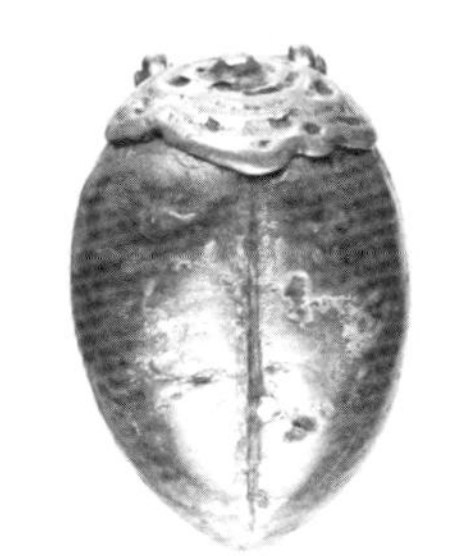

A silver inkwell in the shape of a fruit whose calyx forms the copper lid.

Silver, copper. 19th c. Katabori.
3.2 cm. E26801

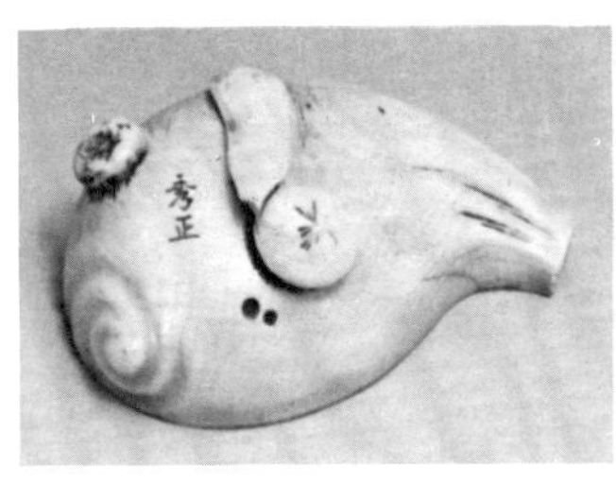

Half of an ivory gourd yields a shallow bowl for solid ink. A peapod forms the cord aperture on the back of the gourd.

Ivory. Hidemasa. early 1800's.
Katabori. 4.8 cm. E26844

Seals Seals for stamping signatures were introduced to Japan from China, becoming mandatory on government documents by the 8th c. The use of imported seals spread, and a craft of seal-making developed in Japan; artisans carved sculptural handles and engraved Chinese characters on the base, creating useful, decorative objects. When the Tokugawa dynasty decreed in 1603 that all legal papers were invalid unless stamped by the heads of families, seal-making flourished. Heads of families had to select seals to act as their signatures and register them legally. A convenient way to carry the seal and ink had to be devised, so compartmented boxes, inro, were used to hold the stamp pad or solid ink and the inro could be suspended from a seal that was attached to the cord and adapted as a netsuke. The majority of netsuke serving two purposes are seals.

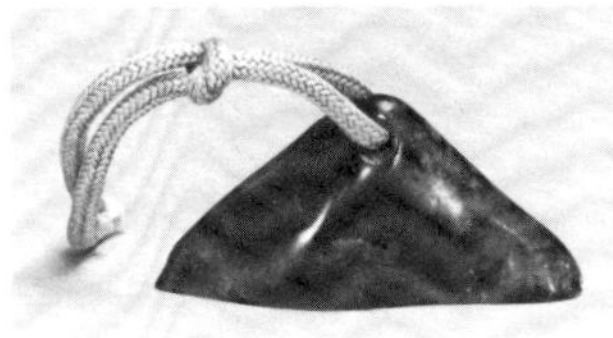

A piece of soapstone in the shape of Mt. Fuji

Soapstone. 19th c. Katabori.
4.3 cm. E11463

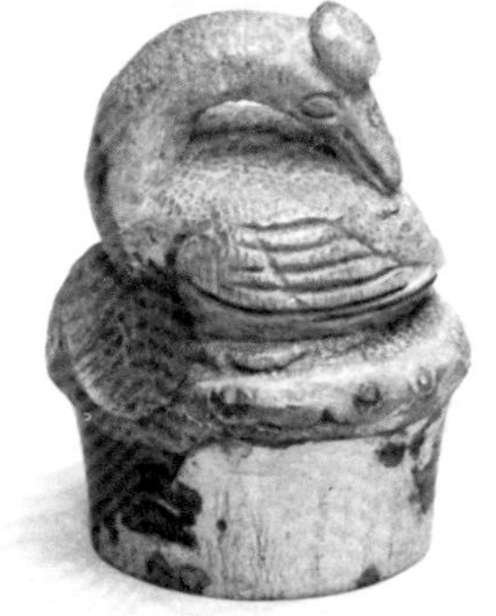

A sleeping goose is the handle for this seal.

Bamboo. 19th c. Katabori.
3.6 cm. E11464

A pile of nine monkeys serves as a handle for the seal which is carved on the base. The himotoshi obliterates part of the seal which suggests that the piece may have been converted to a netsuke after its original creation.

Ivory. 18th c. Katabori.
3.5 cm. E26717

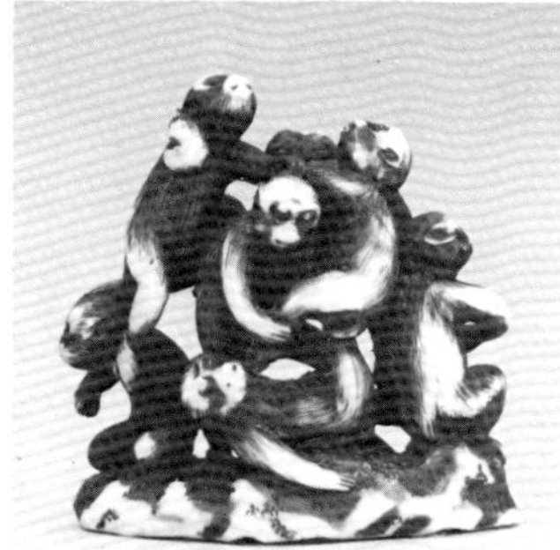

A water buffalo serves as a handle for the seal engraved on the bottom of the base.

Ivory. 19th c. Katabori.
3.7 cm. E26738

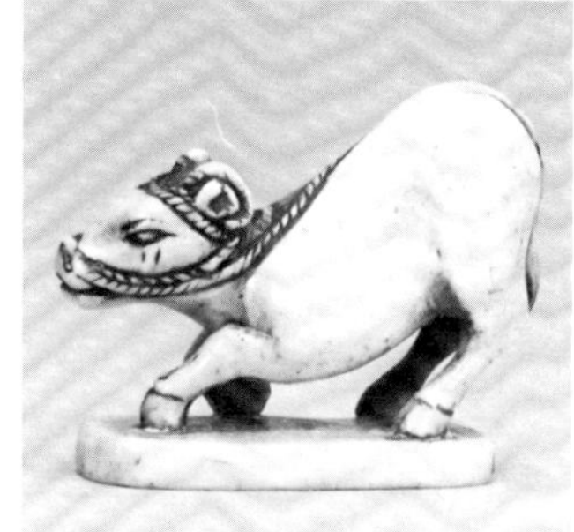

Sofu, leaning on his ox, provides a handle for the seal on the bottom of the base.

Ivory. 18th c. Katabori.
4.2 cm. E27148

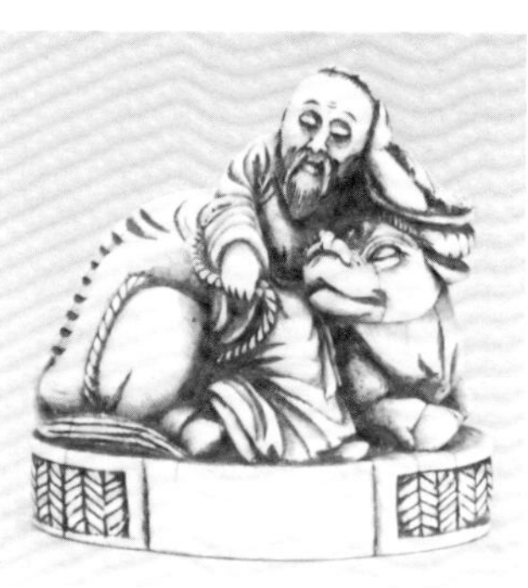

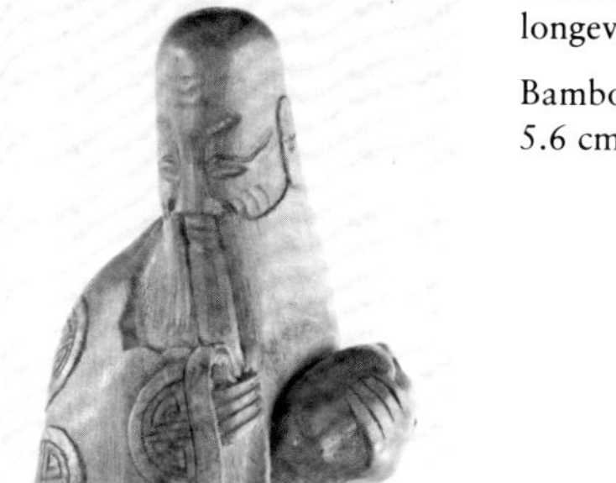

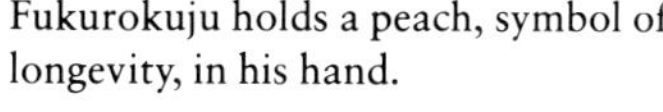

Fukurokuju holds a peach, symbol of longevity, in his hand.

Bamboo. 19th-20th c. Katabori.
5.6 cm. E31950

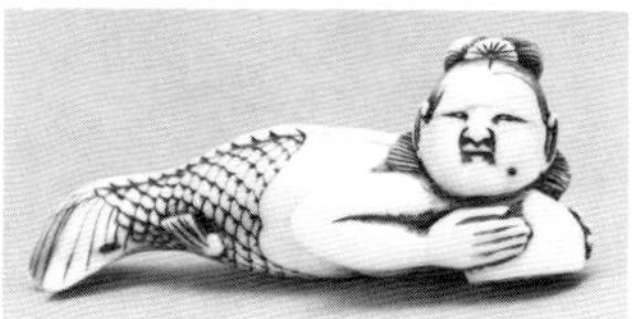

An ivory mermaid lies with her chin and hands resting upon a hemispherical seal.

Ivory. late 18th c. Katabori.
7.6 cm. E39022

Decorative Netsuke

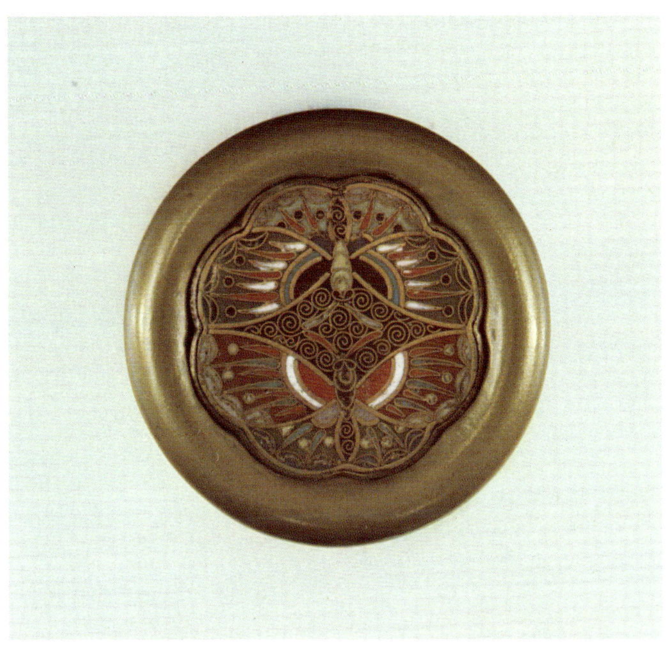

Artistic designs and shapes created in wood, ivory, lacquer metal, cloisonne and pottery, etc., were used to produce netsuke that did not represent animate or inanimate objects, but were highly decorative. Many non-representational netsuke were the work of netsuke-shi; often, artisans from other crafts such as potters, lacquer artists or metal-workers applied their techniques and patterns to create netsuke, using intricate diaper work, abstract designs, landscapes, family crests or geometric shapes for their ornamental effect.

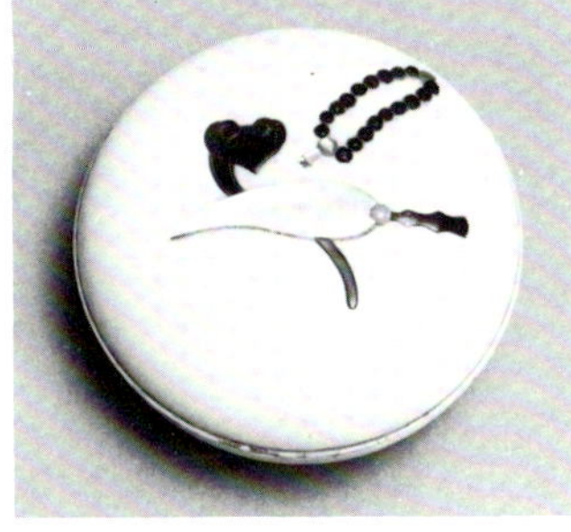

A temple whisk with shell and coral handle and mother-of-pearl brush, a shell lotus wand and a string of shell and mother-of-pearl beads decorate a round manju netsuke.

Ivory, coral, mother-of-pearl and shell inlay. 19th c. Manju. 4.5 cm. E12306

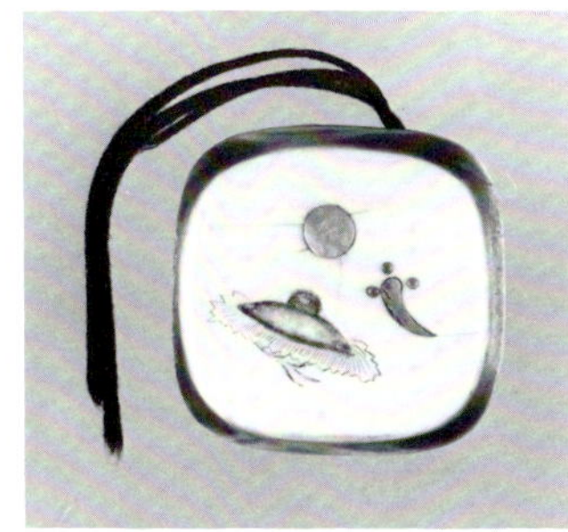

A squared white ivory piece is stained brown along the edges. Inlaid on the front are a round mother-of-pearl disk representing the sacred jewel, a green coral magatama and a shape, which had inlay, representing the hat of invisibility which renders its wearer invisible. These symbols are three of the many emblems of good fortune.

Ivory, coral, mother-of-pearl inlay. 19th c. Manju. 4.2 cm. E22506

The gold lacquer bowl lacks decoration; a stylized insect design in red, green, blue, white, gray, black and gold cloisonne decorates the lid.

Wood and cloisonne. 19th c. Kagamibuta. 3.7 cm. E26535

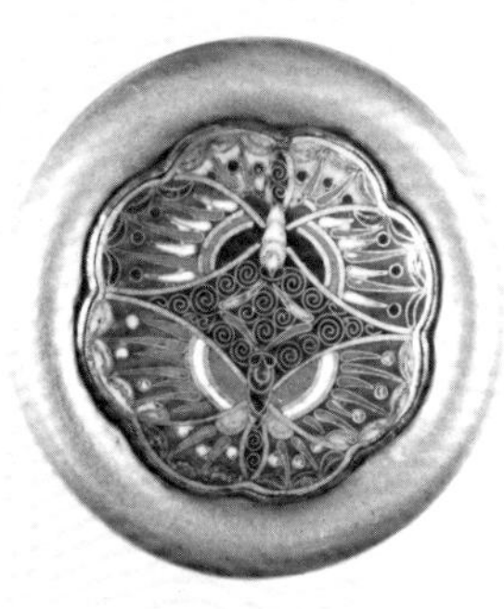

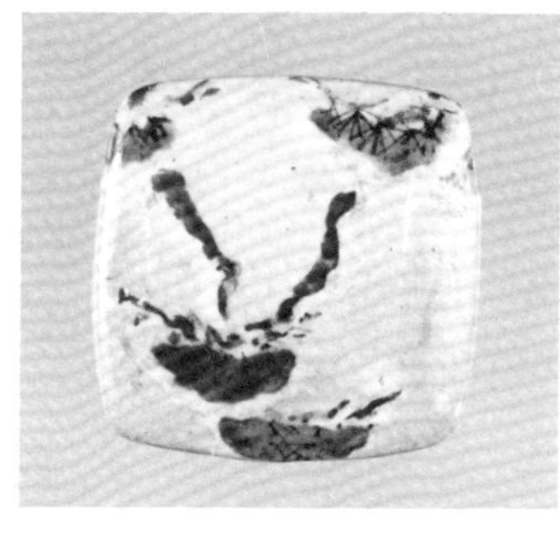

A square manju netsuke depicts green trees in brown pots on a gray background.

Ceramic. Kenzan. 18th c. Manju. 3.0 cm. E26563

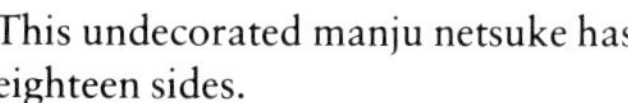

This undecorated manju netsuke has eighteen sides.

Wood. early 19th c. Manju. 4.2 cm. E26540

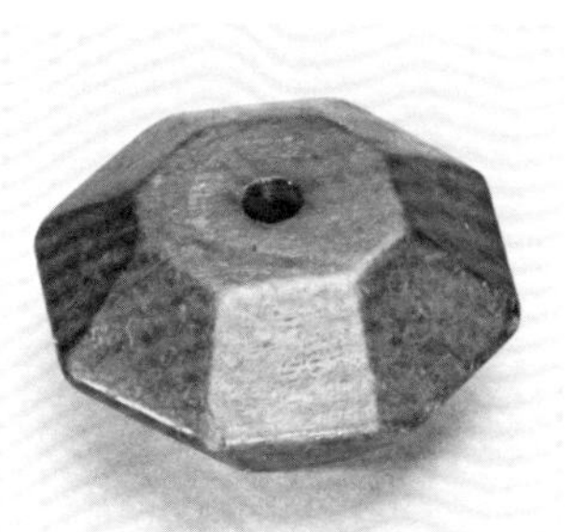

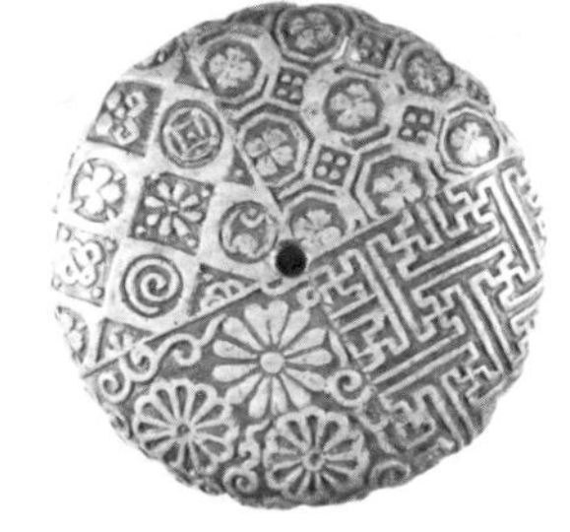

Both sides of this round button have been divided into quadrants, each of which displays a geometric or floral design. A metal ring serves as the cord fastener.

Brass. 19th c. Manju. 3.3 cm. E26575

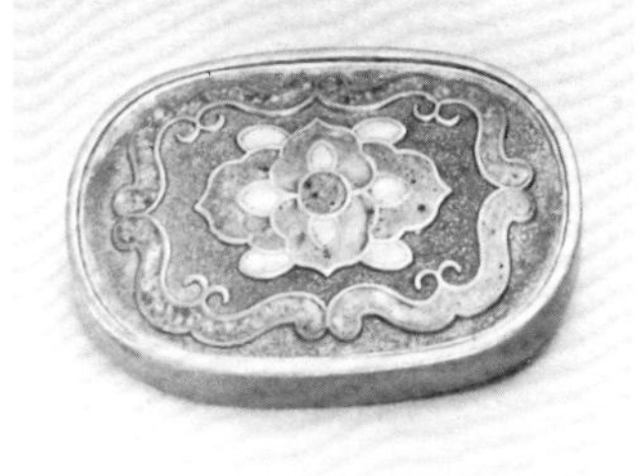

An oval-shaped pewter disk is decorated with green, yellow, and brown cloisonne designs on its front. A metal ring for the cord is attached to the back.

Pewter and cloisonne. 18th-19th c. Manju. 4.2 cm. E26576

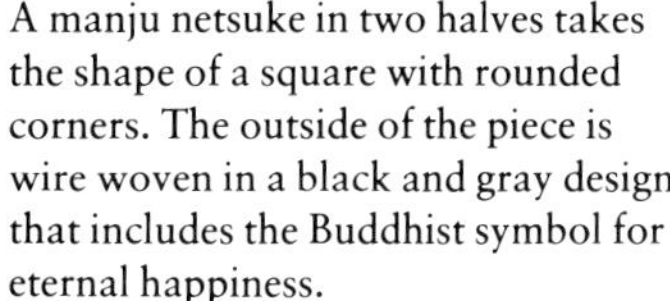

A manju netsuke in two halves takes the shape of a square with rounded corners. The outside of the piece is wire woven in a black and gray design that includes the Buddhist symbol for eternal happiness.

Metal. 19th c. Manju. 3.5 cm. E26551

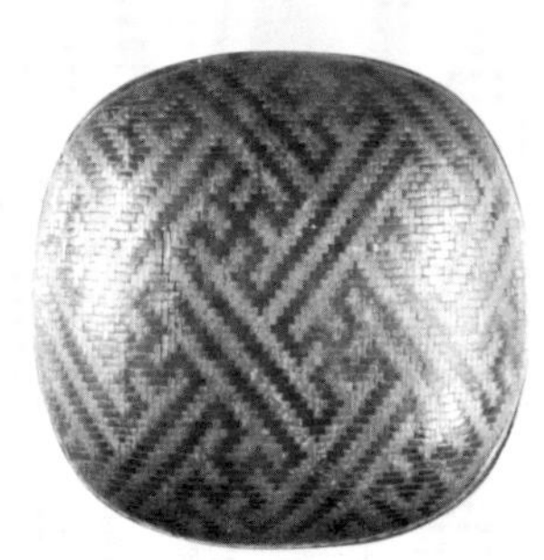

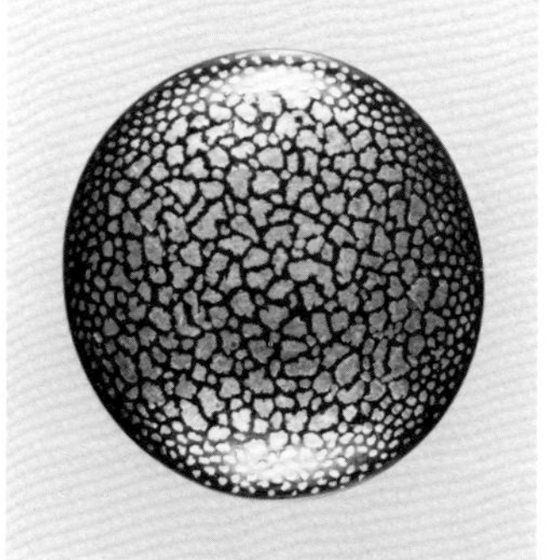

A round black lacquer piece has a metal ring for the cord on one side and a gold lacquer design on the other.

Lacquered wood, metal cord eyelet. Chikakazu, "83 years old". 19th c. Manju. 4.5 cm. E26577

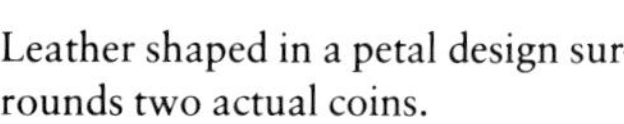

Leather shaped in a petal design surrounds two actual coins.

Metal coins, leather. 19th c. Manju. 4.2 cm. E26555

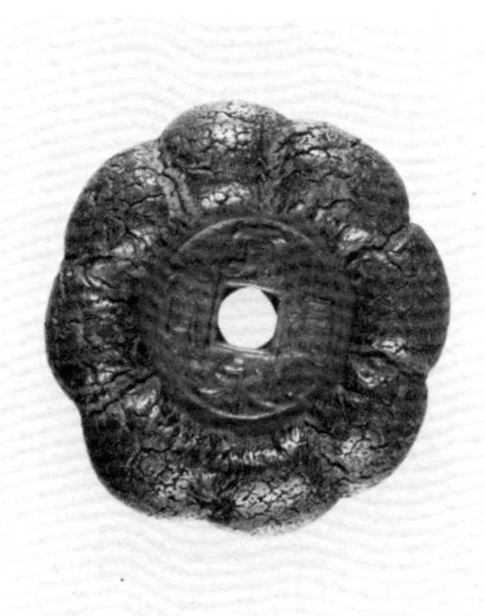

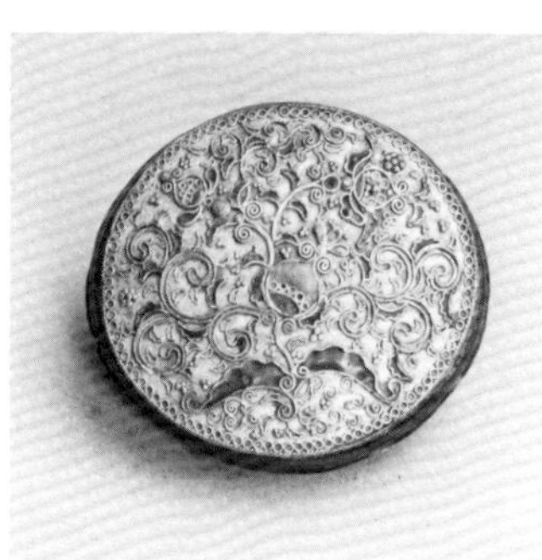

Two oval metal plates are joined by a wood rim. The black metal plate is decorated with a floral design and has a ring for the cord attached to it. Cloisonne flowers decorate the brass plate on the front side of the piece.

Wood, metal, brass and cloisonne. 19th c. Manju. 3.7 cm. E26583

This unusual piece depicts tall rocks with a waterfall running down them. Holes in the waterfall suggest there were inlays at one time in the design.

Ivory. 19th c. Katabori.
6.0 cm. E26825

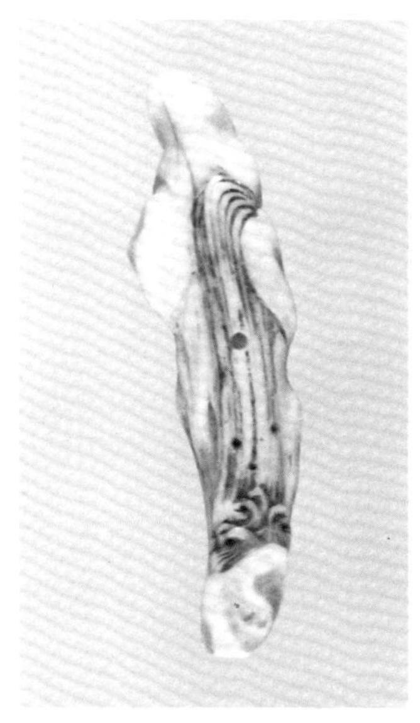

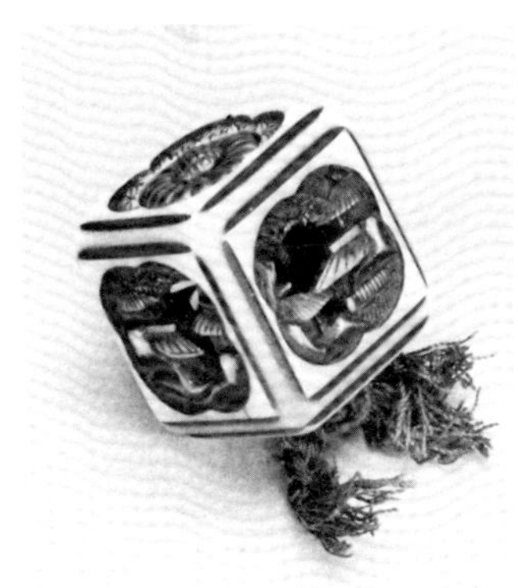

Individual scenes of buildings, trees, and mountains decorate four sides of a cube.

Ivory, metal cord fastener. 19th-20th c. Manju (ryusa). 2.3 cm. E26927

Mon Traditionally, mon were heraldic crests, family symbols, used exclusively by noble families and samurai during the feudal period. Each family chose a specific design, then used the crest to identify their carriages, horse trappings, clothing and other belongings. During the Tokugawa era wealthy merchants began to use mon to identify their businesses, for by the middle of the 18th c., anyone could adopt a mon for his personal use by selecting a design from a book.

Inlaid on Hotei's sack are four emblems of good fortune: a wood raincoat of invisibility, a red coral hat of invisibility, a gold sacred jewel and Daikoku's hammer in wood, as well as two of the seven precious things, coral and pearl.

Ebony, wood, red and green coral, gold, mother-of-pearl. mid 18th-19th c. Katabori. 4.5 cm. E26911

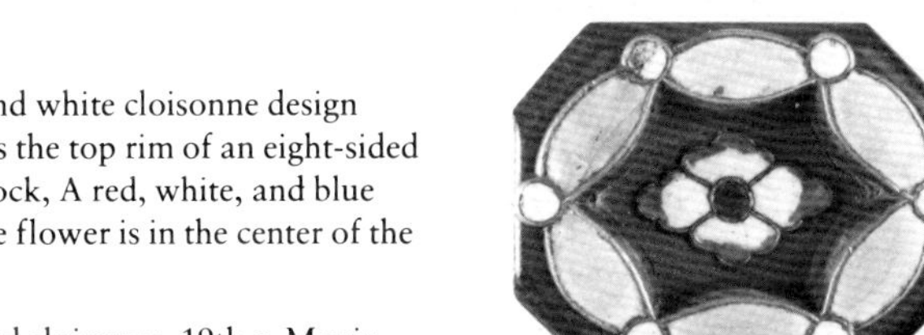

A blue and white cloisonne design decorates the top rim of an eight-sided wood block, A red, white, and blue cloisonne flower is in the center of the design.

Wood and cloisonne. 19th c. Manju.
4.6 cm. E26913

On each side, the crests of noble families are represented on small circles fitted into a large circle.

Metal. 19th c. Manju (ryusa).
4.6 cm. E9183

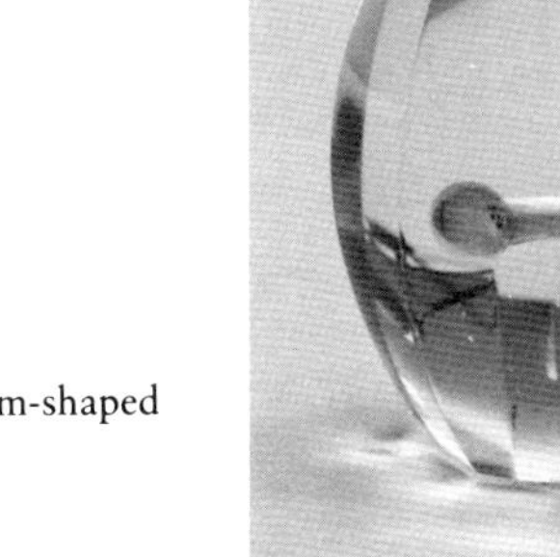

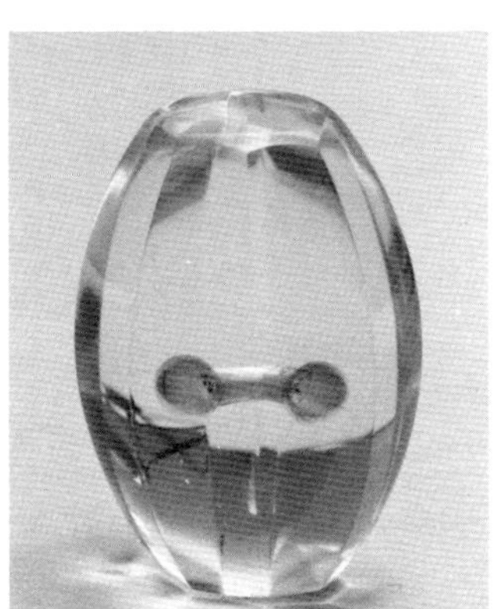

An eight-sided, crystal, drum-shaped piece

Crystal. 20th c. Katabori.
4.0 cm. E27081

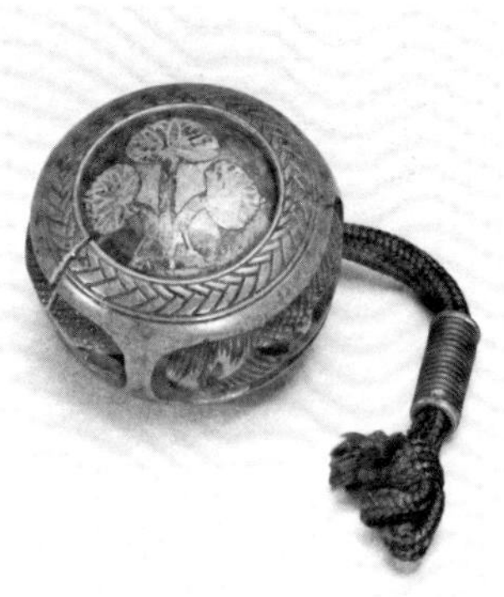

A gold metal lid is inlaid on the top of this piece painted with the hollyhock mon of the Tokugawa Iyeyasu family. An engraved butterfly and evergreen branch decorate the bottom. Three scenes, carved in openwork around the sides of the piece, depict an empty temple, a man walking to the temple, and the man in the temple.

Wood, metal. 19th c. Manju (ryusa).
3.8 cm. E29153

Sagemono

Netsuke would not have existed let alone evolved into an art form had not the style of traditional Japanese clothing necessitated the use of sagemono, the containers and objects suspended by cords or small chains from the obi of the kimono. Sagemono include, among other objects, inro, purses, writing kits, clocks, books, keys, small lanterns, flint pouches, powder flasks and tobacco accessories; in short, ways were contrived to suspend whatever needed to be carried. Some sagemono were of exquisite design, serving, like netsuke, aesthetic as well as utilitarian functions; others, however, were often objects suspended for convenience, not appearance. Included in this catalog are only the sagemono from the museum's collection that are attached to netsuke or to pipe holders, penholders, pipe cases, etc., which were used as netsuke to suspend the sagemono.

Inro are the type of sagemono most commonly associated with netsuke largely because inro, like netsuke, developed from a simple utilitarian object into an art form. Inro were originally intended to carry seals and/or ink (the word means "seal case") which were particularly needed by the upper classes for signing documents beginning with the Tokugawa period in 1603, so for a long period wearing inro was a privilege of the samurai and nobility. Eventually all classes had to affix a registered seal in place of a signature on legal papers; they generally used seal netsuke. Later, wealthy merchants began to wear inro, which were increasingly used as medicine boxes for medicinal herbs, pills and powders. Techniques of lacquer art developed to fulfill the requirements of tradesmen, artisans, actors and merchants who wanted lavishly ornamented as well as simple, refined inro. Beautiful and useful as inro may have been, however, they did not meet all the needs for sagemono and many other types of sagemono were commonly worn either with or instead of inro.

Once the ban on smoking was lifted early in the 18th c., smoking became a national habit, and tobacco pouches and pipe cases became the most prevalent types of sagemono. At the outset, merchants required matching sets of elegant pouches, pipe cases and netsuke, designed to equal the inro that were still the prerogative of the upper classes. As smoking became widespread, everyone needed pouches and pipe cases, and netsuke to suspend them from the obi. In this way, tobacco fostered the demand for netsuke, but the increased demand also hastened the demise of netsuke. For ultimately, the demand was met in part by using the pipe holder or pipe case itself to suspend the sagemono by thrusting it through the obi in the manner of a sashi netsuke. This use, combined with western dress and cigarettes shifted netsuke and sagemono to the realm of art.

Inro

Inro (in: seal, ro: case), compartmented boxes of varying shapes and sizes, are strung on cords and were used primarily for ink, seals or medicines. Working mainly in lacquer, inro makers demonstrated skill and imagination on a par with netsuke-shi. Inro that have netsuke attached are the only inro from the museum's collection that are included in the following list.

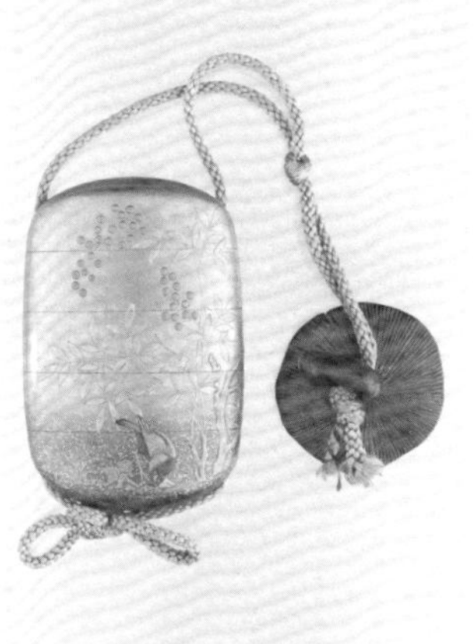

Netsuke: A wooden mushroom with two leaves engraved on the cup

Wood. 19th-20th c. Katabori. 4.5 cm. E5622

Sagemono: Lacquered inro with design of birds and cherry tree branches

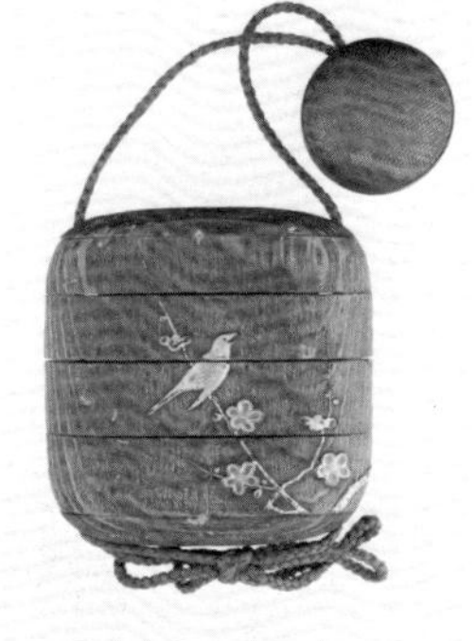

Netsuke: A metal manju netsuke woven in a herringbone pattern

Metal. 19th c. Manju. 3.3 cm. E1980

Sagemono: A wood inro with gold colored nightingale and plum blossoms

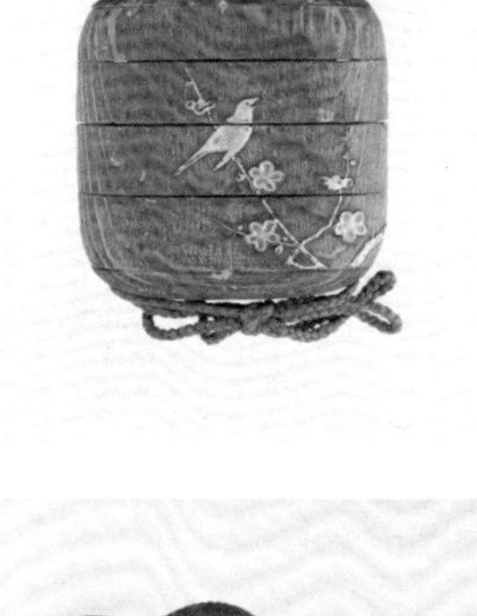

Netsuke: Polished, undecorated piece of amber

Amber. 19th-20th c. Manju. 4.9 cm. E9850

Sagemono and ojime: Various landscapes are depicted in pearl inlay on a wooden inro. The amber ojime has Daikoku and a rat etched on it.

Netsuke: The metal lid of the kagamibuta netsuke is made to resemble a lily pad and has a gold lily flower, a gold frog and a brown crab attached to it. The wood bowl is undecorated.

Wood and metal. 19th c. Kagamibuta. 4.2 cm. E4399

Sagemono and ojime: A lacquered inro with rats eating a katsuo (fish) and a wood ojime of a katsuo

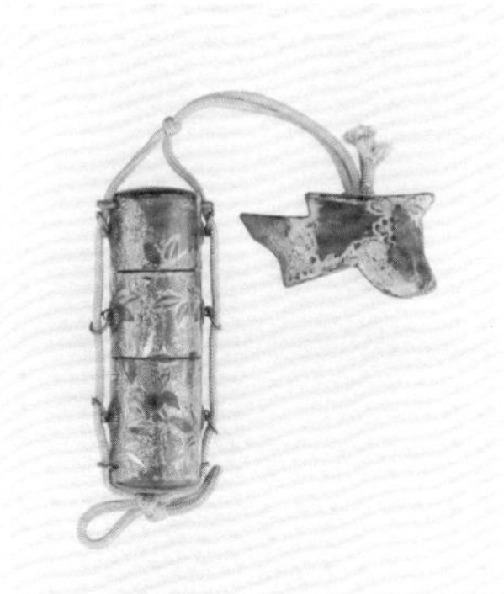

Netsuke: This oddly shaped flat piece is decorated with flowers and clouds in gold, black, red and silver lacquer.

Lacquered wood, metal cord ring. 19th c. Manju. 4.7 cm. E10290

Sagemono: A small, tubular inro with lacquered flower designs and metal himotoshi

Netsuke: A ryusa netsuke with swirling patterns

Brass. 19th c. Manju (ryusa). 4.0 cm. E14793

Sagemono and ojime: A metal sheath (saya) for a saya inro has openwork and chased designs. A compartmented case fits inside a saya inro.

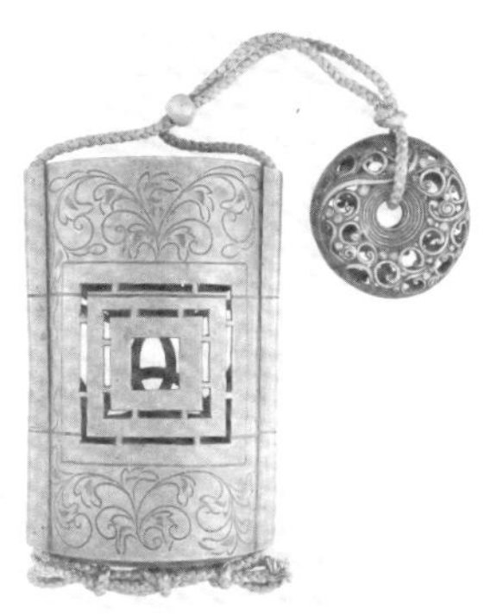

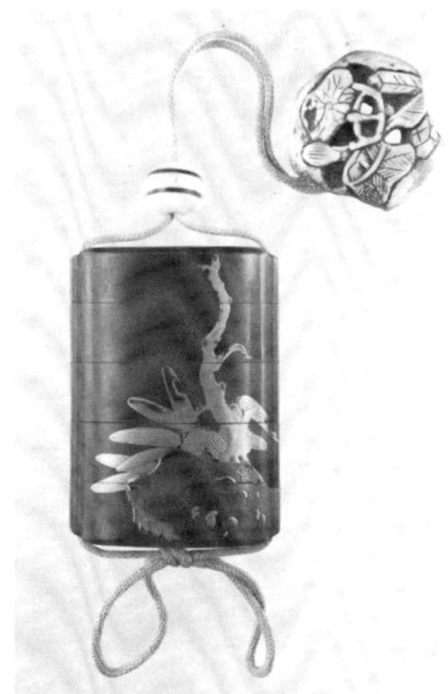

Netsuke: A ryusa netsuke with leaf design

Bone. 18th-19th c. Manju (ryusa). 4.3 cm. E22504

Sagemono and ojime: A bone and horn bead ojime fastens a lacquered inro with landscape.

Netsuke: On one side of a manju netsuke a smiling karako, carrying a basket of flowers on his back, reaches for a butterfly that has landed on his head. On the reverse is a fan and hat.

Wood. 19th-20th c. Manju. 3.7 cm. E16955

Sagemono and ojime: A cinnabar lacquer inro depicting the story of Kyoyu and Sofu.

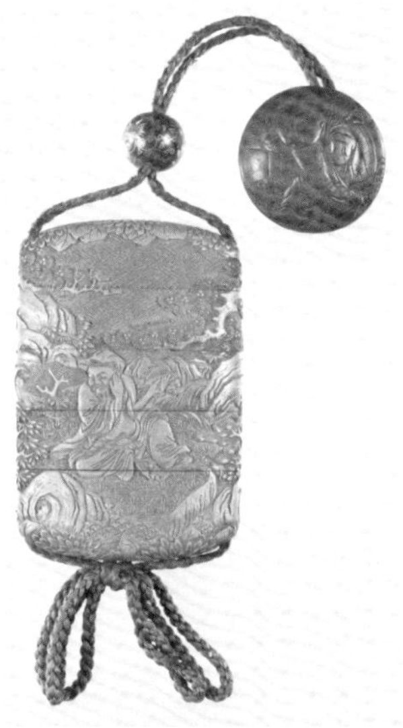

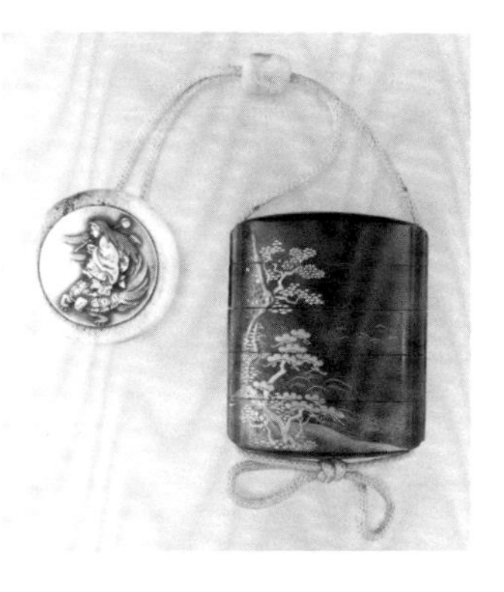

Netsuke: A red-haired shojo holding a long handled drinking cup dances on a distressed looking bushy-tailed turtle.

Bone and metal. 18th-19th c. Kagamibuta. 4.2 cm. E22505

Sagemono and ojime: A lacquer inro with landscape design

Netsuke: The head moves in and out of the bottom turtle in this stack of three turtles.

Wood. Masanao. 19th c. Katabori. 2.8 cm. E20860

Sagemono and ojime: A wooden inro carved in the shape of a turtle has three lacquered compartments.

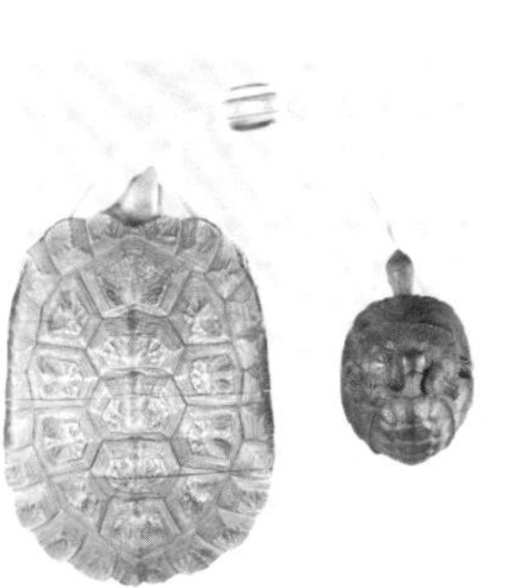

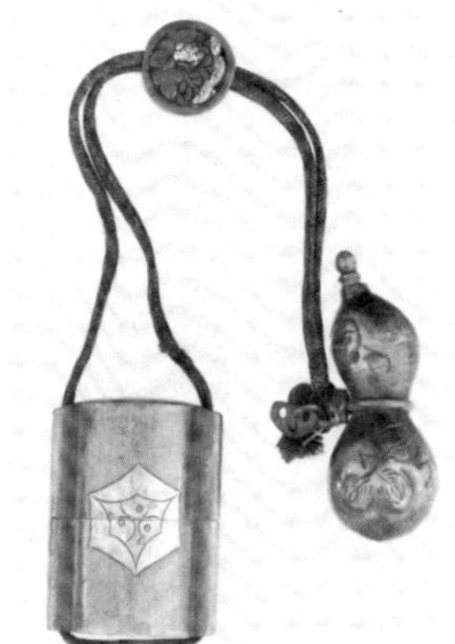

Netsuke: A tiny decorated metal gourd with removable stopper

Metal. 19th c. Katabori. 3.0 cm. E26900

Sagemono and ojime: A manju shaped ojime with flowers and butterfly secures a tiny one-compartment metal inro.

Netsuke: A black bird has geometric designs on its painted gold wings.

Wood. late 19th-20th c. Katabori. 2.7 cm. E29138

Sagemono and ojime: A lacquered inro has nacre and horn inlaid fish on lacquered water and reeds. The ojime is a lacquered bead.

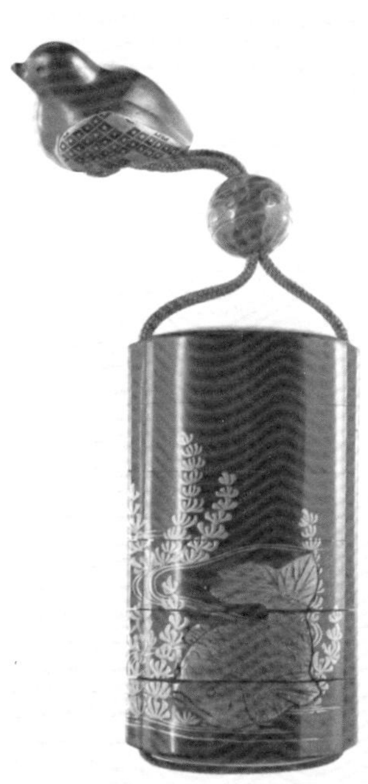

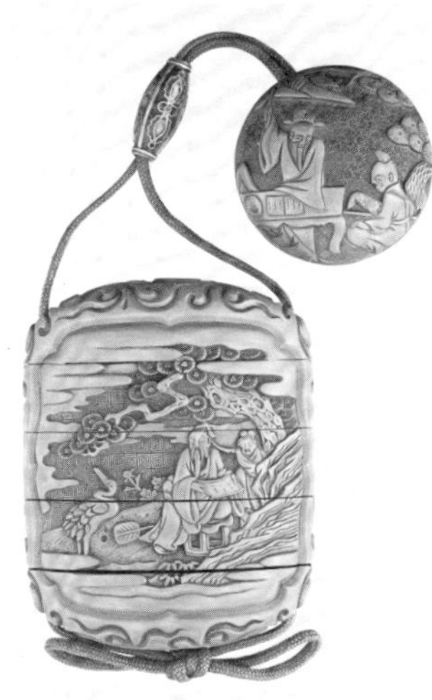

Netsuke: A cinnabar lacquer manju netsuke depicting a scholar writing and two servants or students attending him (one is on the reverse side of the piece)

Cinnabar lacquer. 19th c. Manju. 4.0 cm. E33335

Sagemono and ojime: A cloisonne ojime secures a cinnabar lacquer inro depicting Jurojin with scroll, fan, crane and attendant on one side, and a scholar and attendant on the other.

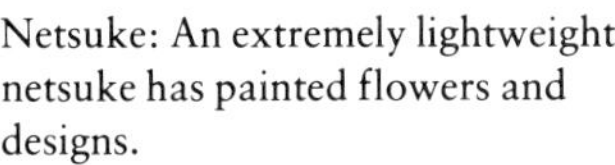

Netsuke: An extremely lightweight netsuke has painted flowers and designs.

Wood. 20th c. Katabori. 4.0 cm. E32702

Sagemono and ojime: A small balsa wood compartment is covered by green and white brocade. Kintaro, in cloth on the front of the inro, is wrestling a bear. The ensemble was probably made for a child.

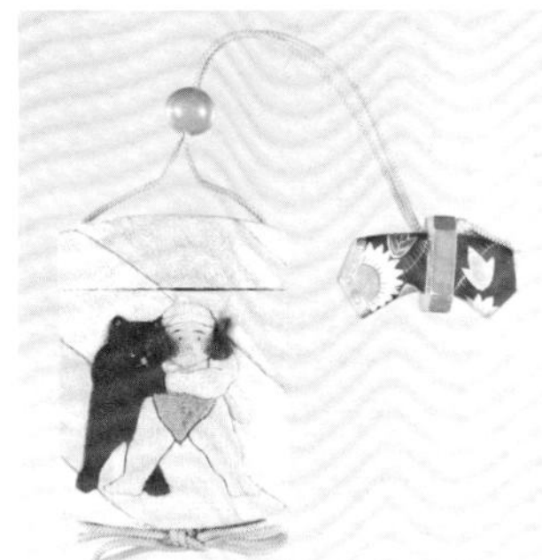

Netsuke: A wooden mushroom with writing on it

Wood. 19th c. Katabori. 4.0 cm. E34098

Sagemono: A lacquered inro with landscape design

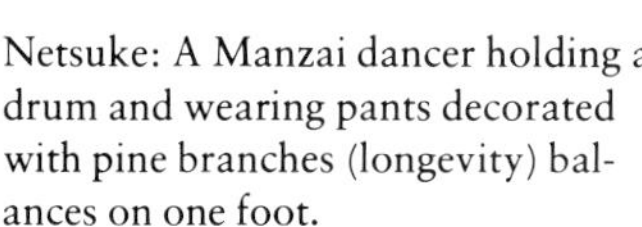

Netsuke: A Manzai dancer holding a drum and wearing pants decorated with pine branches (longevity) balances on one foot.

Ivory. late 19th-20th c. Katabori. 4.6 cm. E32878

Sagemono and ojime: The gold lacquered inro is filled with symbols for longevity.

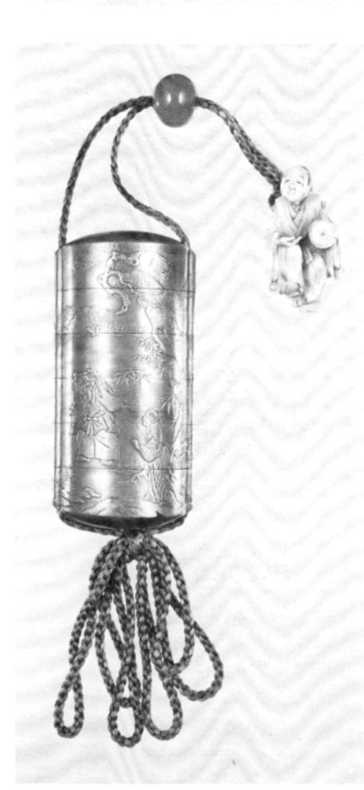

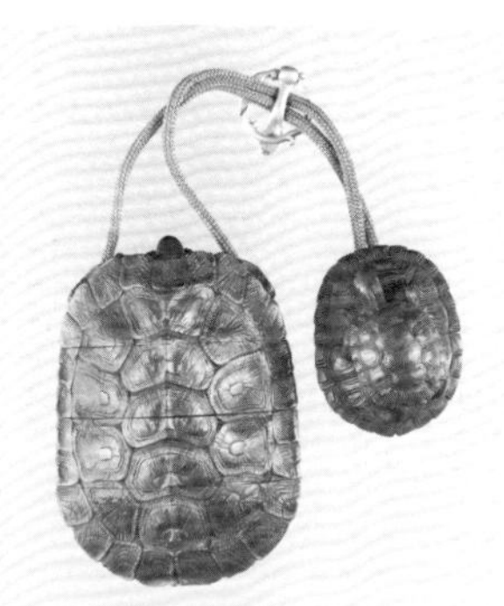

Netsuke: In an ensemble very similar to E20860, the netsuke depicts a stack of two turtles. Bushell in *Collector's Netsuke* (see Bibliography) discusses turtle netsuke signed by Masanao.

Wood with inlaid eyes. Masanao. 19th c. Katabori. 4.5 cm. E37151

Sagemono and ojime: An inro carved in the shape of a turtle is secured by a metal buckle ojime.

Netsuke: The lid of this kagamibuta netsuke pictures two mandarin ducks swimming. The bowl is undecorated.

Wood and metal. late 19th c. Kagamibuta. 3.1 cm. E38683

Sagemono and ojime: The hinged lid of the inro opens to reveal three egg-shaped metal containers. The metal ojime depicts a karako with a fan and a butterfly.

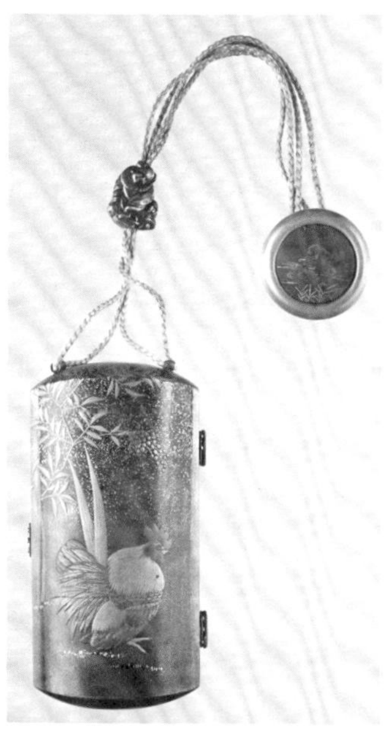

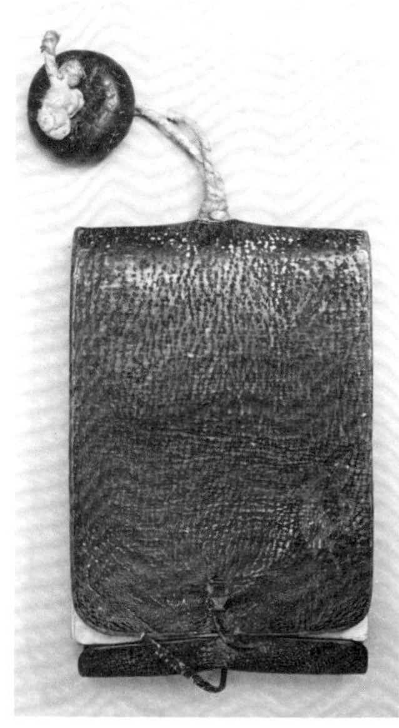

Miscellaneous Sagemono

Book

Netsuke: A nut with a hole drilled through it

Nut. 19th c. Manju. 4.0 cm. E65307

Sagemono: Tied to the netsuke by a piece of rope is a leather bound ledger from a rice store.

Netsuke: Gold lacquered netsuke with painted and inlaid flowers and leaves in nacre and enamel.

Lacquered wood, nacre, enamel, metal cord ring. 19th c. Manju. 4.7 cm. E44371

Sagemono and ojime: A gold lacquered and inlaid inro depicting the story of Choryo and the sandal. The ojime is metal with an openwork design.

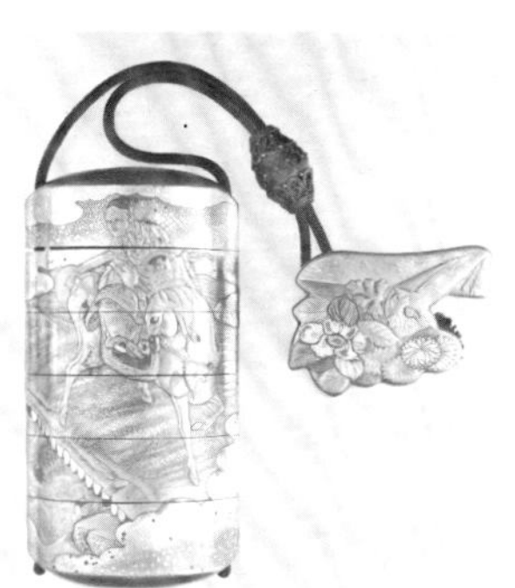

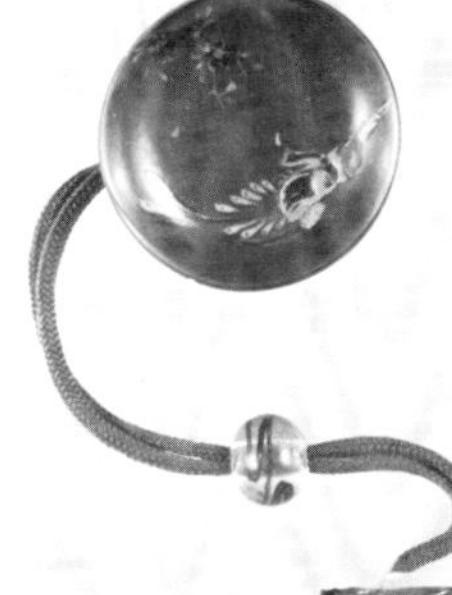

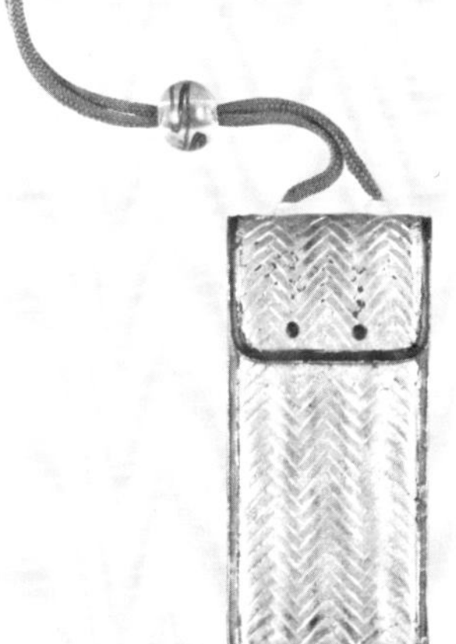

Box

Netsuke: A plain wood manju netsuke has a pheasant and flowers painted in lacquer on the top.

Wood. Torinsai, unrecorded artist. 19th c. Manju. 4.0 cm. E13730

Sagemono and ojime: The back slides off to open a small wood box painted gold and carved to look like a woven container.

Netsuke: On one side is a group of scholars and calligraphers writing, reading and talking. On the reverse, people engage in varied activities: two men play go, a woman plays a koto, a man kneels before a teapot on a heater.

Wood with pearl inlays. 19th c. Manju (ryusa). 5.0 cm. E54461

Sagemono and ojime: The lining of this inro is removable and consists of a small medicine box with a horned sennin painted on it. The ojime is a metal sack with two rats climbing in and out of it.

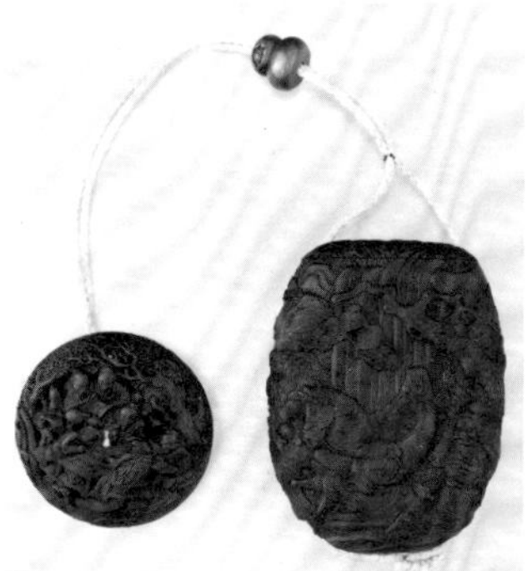

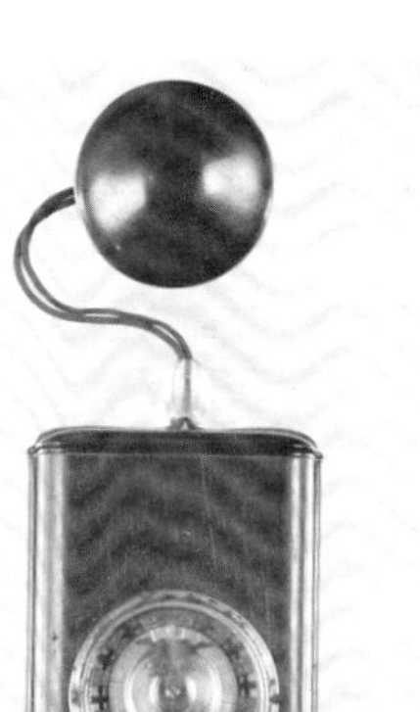

Clock

Netsuke: A plain wood Manju netsuke

Wood. illegible signature. 19th c. Manju. 4.0 cm. E16117

Sagemono and ojime: A portable Japanese clock

Flasks

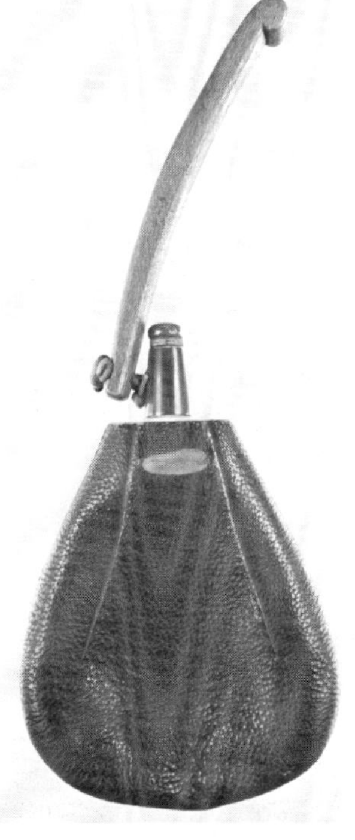

Netsuke: An undecorated sashi netsuke with a scrolled end

Wood. 18th-19th c. Sashi.
13.5 cm. E10333

Sagemono: A leather powder flask with horn stopper

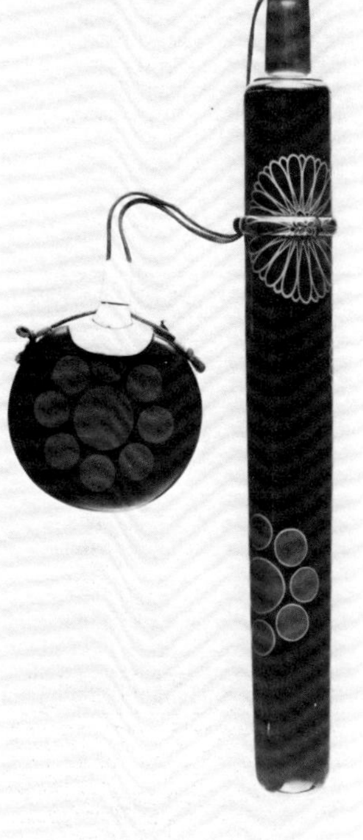

This large tubular flask could be thrust through the obi.

Lacquered wood, horn, bone.
Tube: 30.2 cm. Flask: 8.5 cm. E14584

Sagemono: A round flask is attached by cord to the tubular flask.

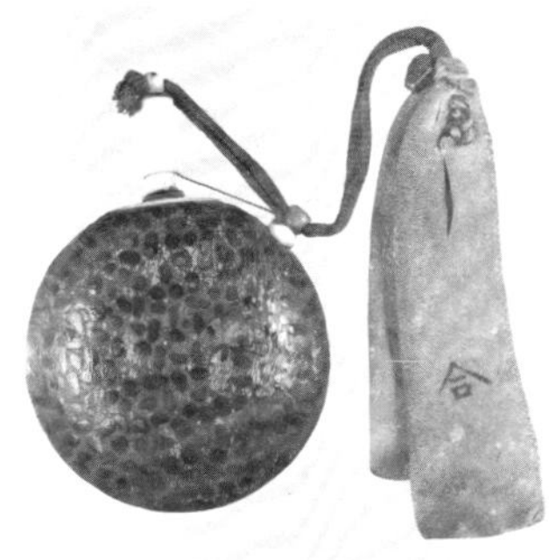

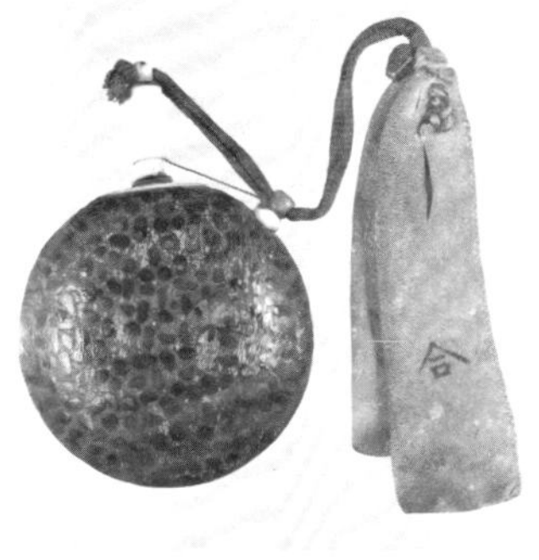

Two leather strips served as the netsuke.

Leather, bone, horn. 18th c.
Strips: 15.0 cm. Flask: 9.9 cm. E15615

Sagemono: Lacquered leather powder flask with bone spout, cloth plug and bone horn cap

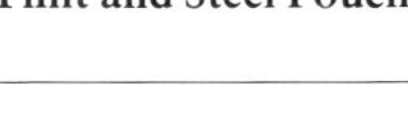

Flint and Steel Pouch

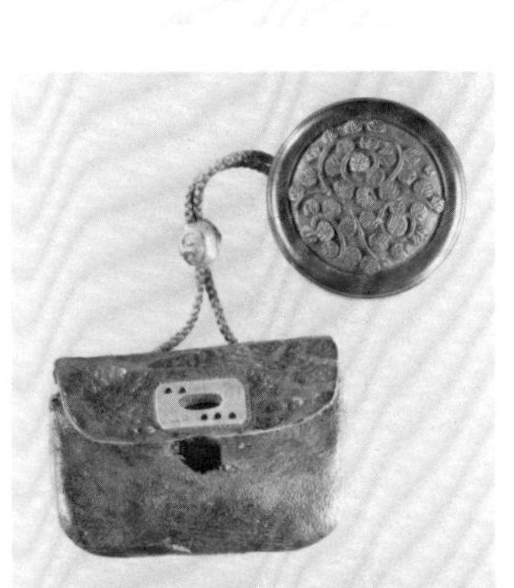

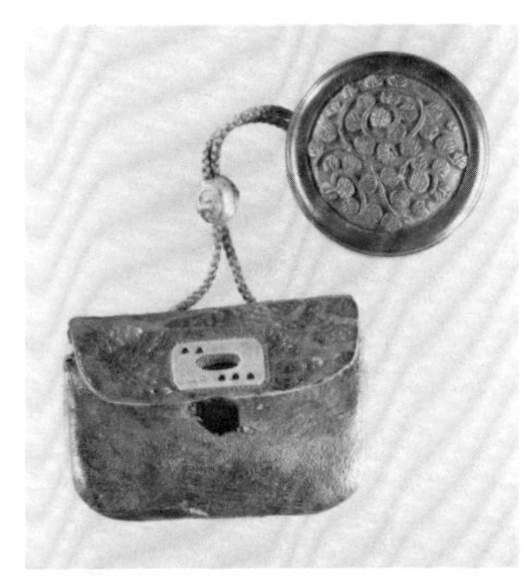

Netsuke: A manju netsuke has leaves and berries carved on the top.

Wood. 19th c. Manju. 4.0 cm. E26533

Sagemono and ojime: A small leather pouch with metal clasp contains a piece of flint and steel.

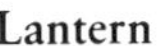

Lantern

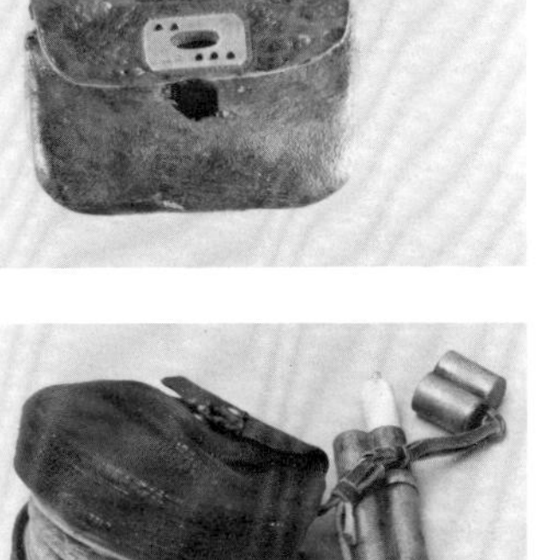

Candle holder: A candle holder for two candles was thrust through the obi like a sashi netsuke.

Brass. 19th c. 13.5 cm. E14707

Sagemono: A leather pouch with metal clasp contains a folding paper lantern, which has a narrow metal handle so that it can be carried or hung.

Pen and Ink Cases Sagemono to carry solid ink paste were often attached to pen holders which were thrust through the obi to suspend the container, as well as to netsuke.

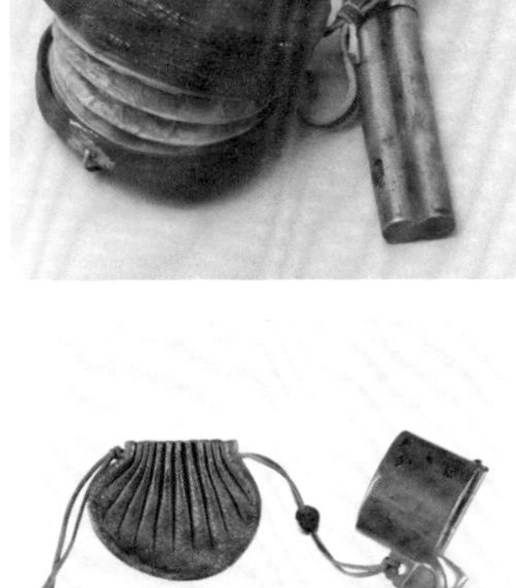

Pen Holder: A pen holder with ink well attached was thrust through the obi when carried.

Bronze. 18th-19th c. 25.1 cm. E6562

Sagemono and ojime: A small leather pouch for ink is tied to the kit with a slide cord with ojime.

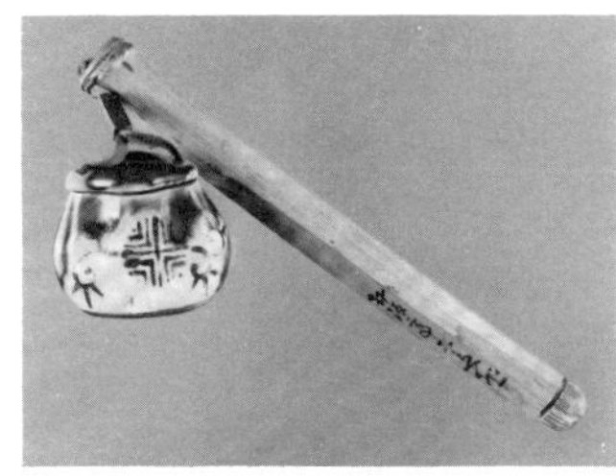

Pen holder: A bamboo tube for a pen is signed by Rokubei.

Bamboo. 19th c. 15.5 cm. E10061

Sagemono and ojime: A ceramic ink well with metal ojime was brought back by E.S. Morse as part of his pottery collection. It was made in 1840 at the Rokubei Pottery in Kyoto.

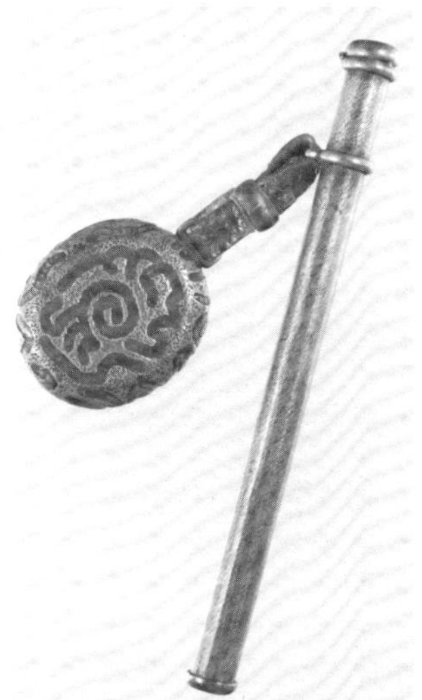

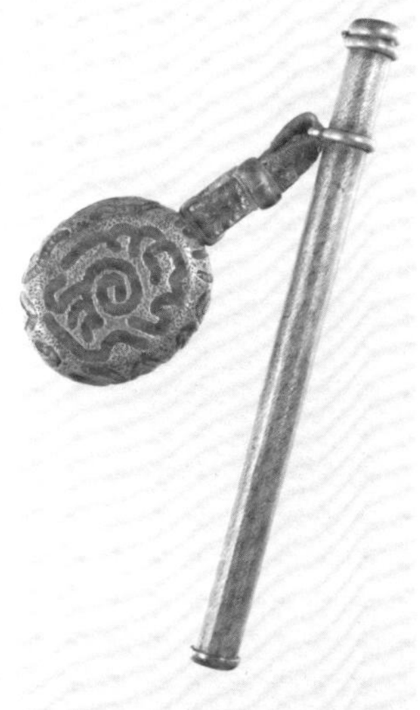

Pen Holder: A pen holder with a small knife inside was thrust through the obi like a sashi netsuke.

Brass. 18th-19th c. 15.6 cm. E24793

Sagemono: An oval ink well is attached to the pen holder with a leather strap.

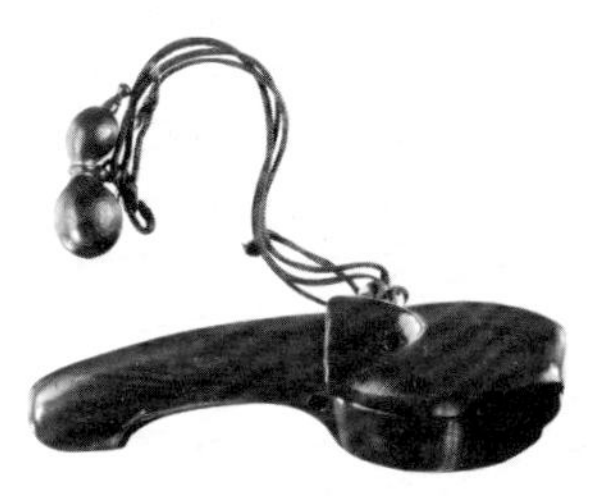

Netsuke: A silver gourd has a removable stopper that screws on.

Silver. 19th c. Katabori. 2.9 cm. E26923

Sagemono and ojime: A wood ink case has a metal liner for ink and a coral ojime.

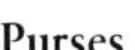

Purses

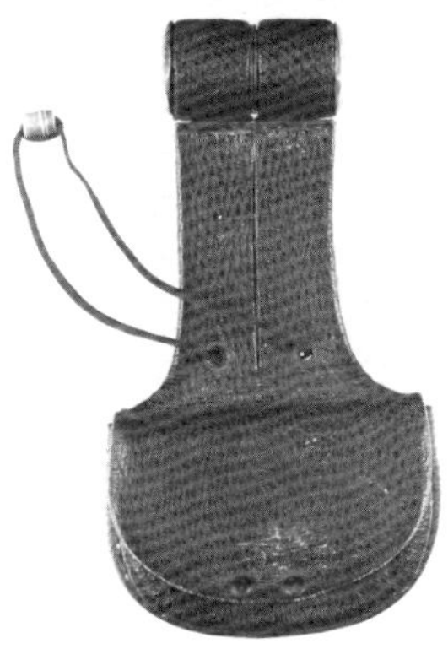

Netsuke: What served as a netsuke for this money pouch is a built-in change holder, made of metal covered with leather, which opens in the middle.

Metal and leather. 4.5 cm. E12625

Sagemono and ojime: A leather money pouch and leather strips (in place of a cord or chain) are made of the same piece of leather and sewn to the coin container. A cord with a bone ojime passes through two metal lined eyelets in the leather strips.

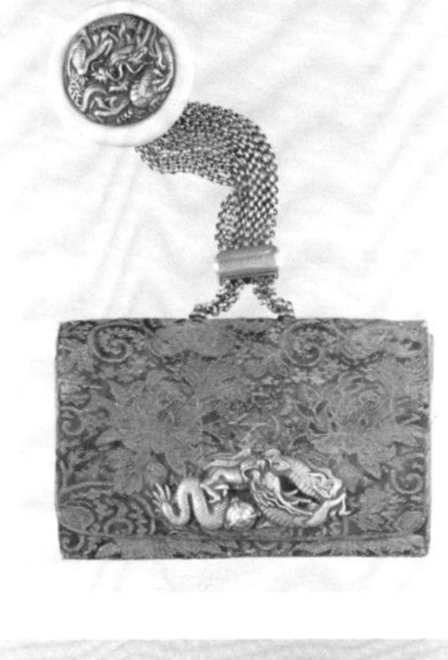

Netsuke: A fierce-looking dragon is curled up on the metal lid. The bowl is undecorated.

Wood and metal. 19th c. Kagamibuta. 5.2 cm. E17383

Sagemono and ojime: A brocade wallet with metal dragon clasp is secured by a rectangular metal ojime on a multiple chain.

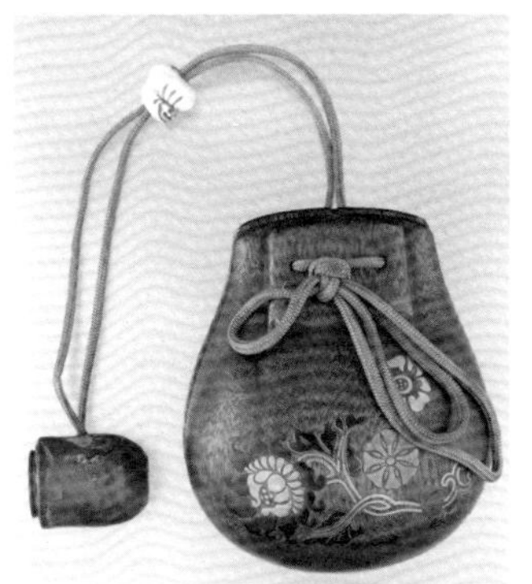

Netsuke: A lacquered wood carving made to look like a glazed ceramic jar.

Lacquered wood. 19th-20th c. Katabori. 3.0 cm. E23729

Sagemono and ojime: Wood carved in the shape of a money bag is open at the top, hinged at the bottom and lined inside with silk. Painted floral patterns decorate both sides. The ojime is an ivory Daruma toy.

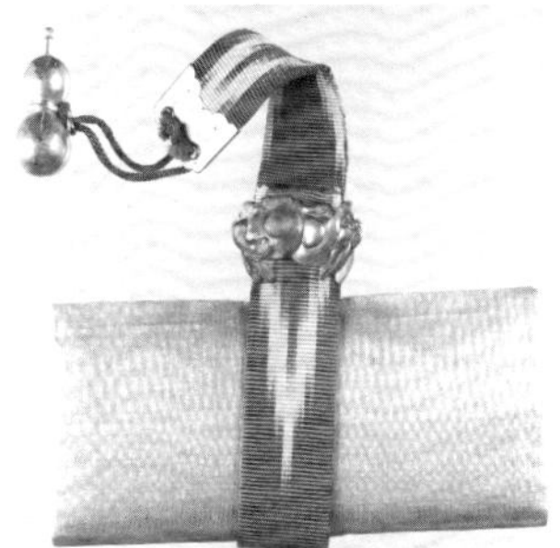

Netsuke: A silver metal gourd bottle with removable stopper

Metal. 19th c. Katabori. 5.1 cm. E32696

Sagemono and ojime: An open envelope made of woven gold thread and lined in white silk is held closed by a strip of purple and white woven silk with an ojime of metal rabbits. The metal tip of the silk strip has bamboo stalks etched on one side and flowers on the other.

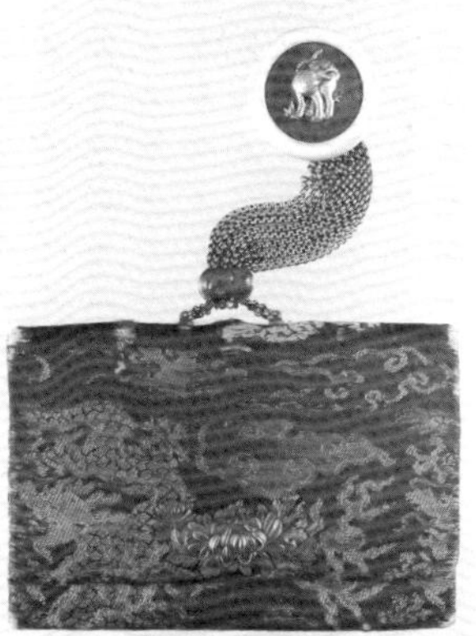

Netsuke: A gold metal tiger is attached to the metal lid of an undecorated ivory bowl.

Metal and ivory. 19th c. Kagamibuta. 4.0 cm. E36327

Sagemono and ojime: A blue silk damask purse with dragons and clouds and a chrysanthemum metal clasp is attached to a multiple chain. A rectangular metal ojime is decorated with a quail and flowers.

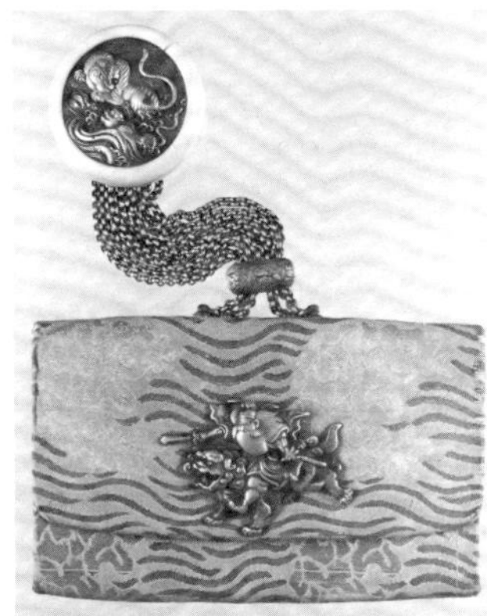

Netsuke: The metal lid depicts two tigers swimming. The bowl is undecorated.

Ivory and metal. 19th c. Kagamibuta. 5.0 cm. E36328

Sagemono and ojime: The brocade wallet has a carp design and a metal clasp of Shoki, sword drawn, riding a shishi in pursuit of an oni. The multiple chain is held by a rectangular ojime with floral designs.

Tobacco Accessories

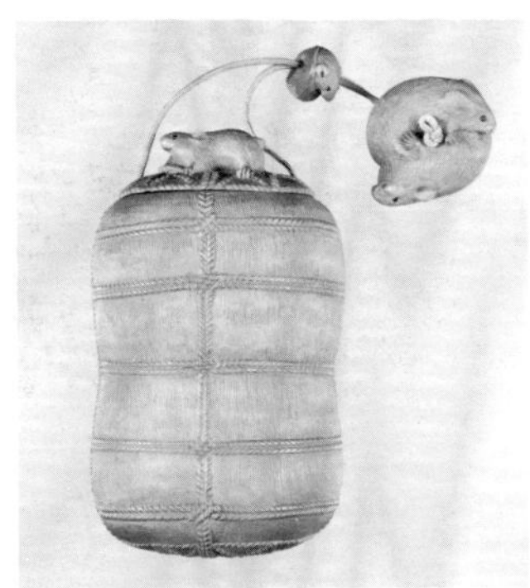

Tonkotsu and Netsuke In *The Inro Handbook* Bushell (see Bibliography) discusses Tonkotsu, containers for tobacco, which differ from inro in that they are larger, usually carved from wood, contain only one compartment, and were carried by the lower classes.

Netsuke: Two rats wrestling

Wood with inlaid eyes. 19th-20th c. Katabori. 3.8 cm. E9444

Sagemono and ojime: A wood tonkotsu in the shape of a rice bale has two rats carved on the lid. The ojime is also a rat.

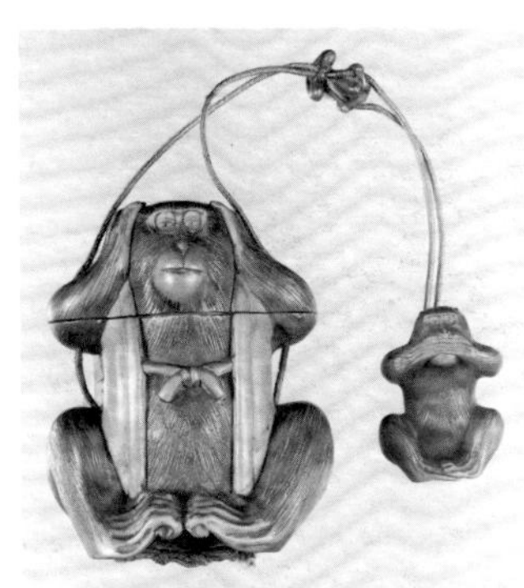

Netsuke: A "speak no evil" monkey

Wood. 19th-20th c. Katabori. 4.2 cm. E15374

Sagemono and ojime: A wooden ojime of the "see no evil" monkey serves a wooden tonkotsu of the "hear no evil" monkey.

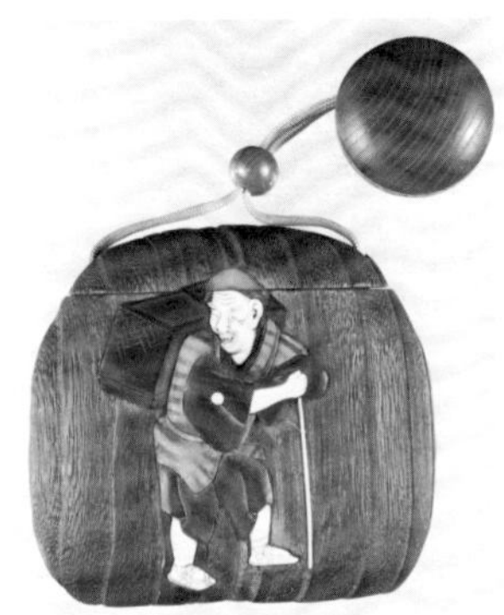

Netsuke: An undecorated manju netsuke

Wood. 19th c. Manju. 4.0 cm. E36925

Sagemono: A farmer carrying a basket is inlaid in ivory, wood and horn on one side of a plain wood tonkotsu. On the reverse two sparrows are inlaid in horn.

Tobacco Containers, Pipe Cases and Netsuke

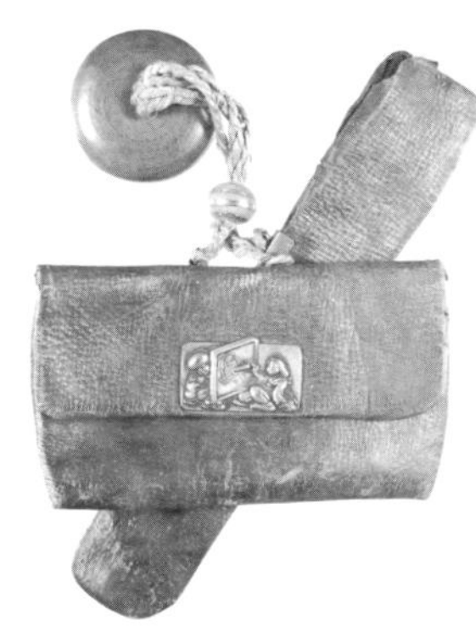

Netsuke: An undecorated wood ashtray netsuke

Wood. 19th c. Katabori. 5.0 cm. E70

Sagemono and ojime: The netsuke is attached by a rope to a leather tobacco pouch with metal clasp and a leather pipe case.

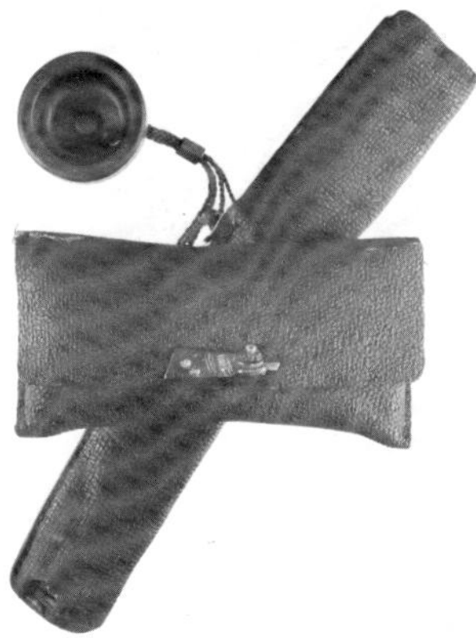

Netsuke: A plain wood ashtray

Wood. 19th c. Katabori. 4.2 cm. E1182

Sagemono and ojime: A leather tobacco pouch with metal clasp of fan and flowers and a leather pipe case with bamboo and metal pipe.

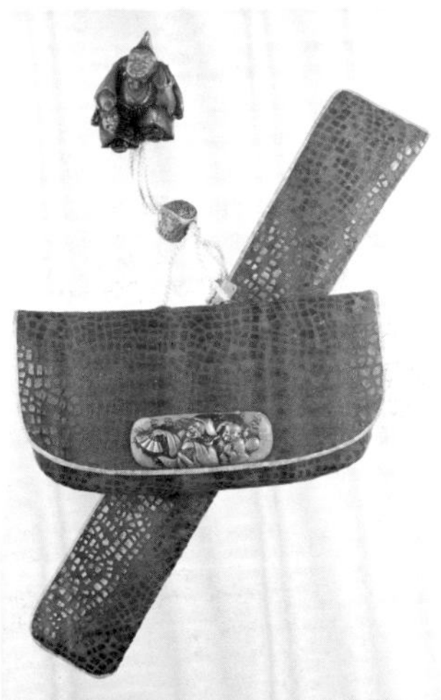

Netsuke: A sambaso dancer with rattle

Man-made material. 19th c. Katabori. 4.5 cm. E2636

Sagemono and ojime: A simulated leather tobacco case and pouch with metal clasp depicting festival dancers

Tobacco Containers and Netsuke

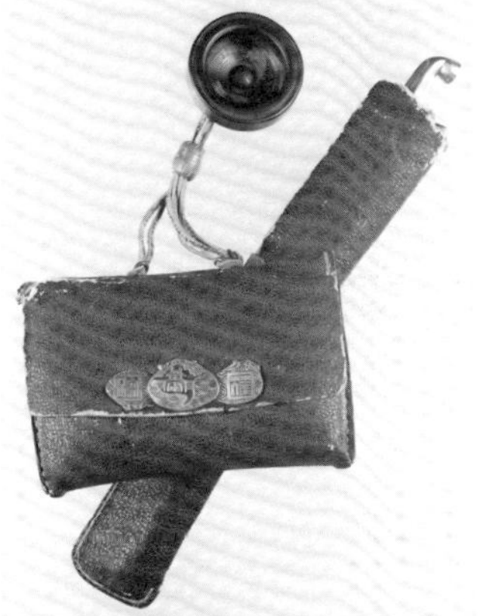

Netsuke: A plain wood ashtray

Wood. 19th c. Katabori.
5.0 cm. E16774

Sagemono and ojime: A simulated leather pipe case containing a bamboo and metal pipe is attached by leather strips to the netsuke and to a simulated leather tobacco pouch with metal clasp.

Netsuke: An ashtray netsuke

Wood. 19th c. Katabori.
3.9 cm. E6461

Sagemono and ojime: A leather tobacco pouch with metal clasp, wood bead

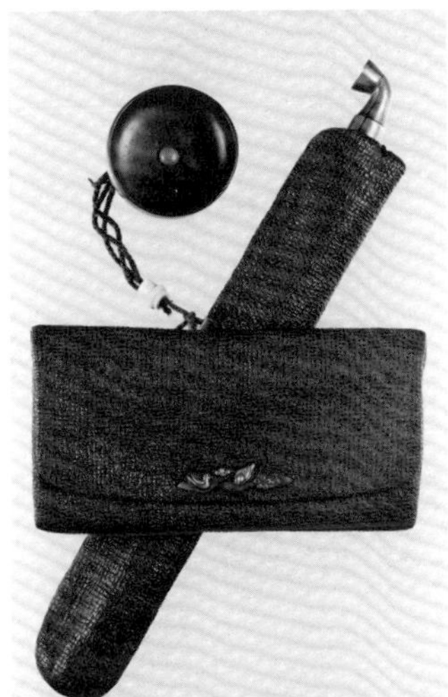

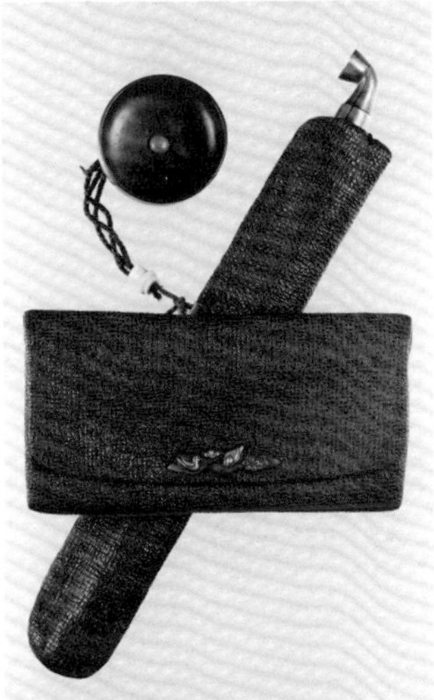

Netsuke: An undecorated ashtray

Wood. 19th c. Katabori.
4.5 cm. E21523

Sagemono and ojime: A leather tobacco pouch with metal clasp of two mandarin ducks, a leather pipe case with a bamboo and metal pipe and a bone ojime are fastened by silk cord to the netsuke.

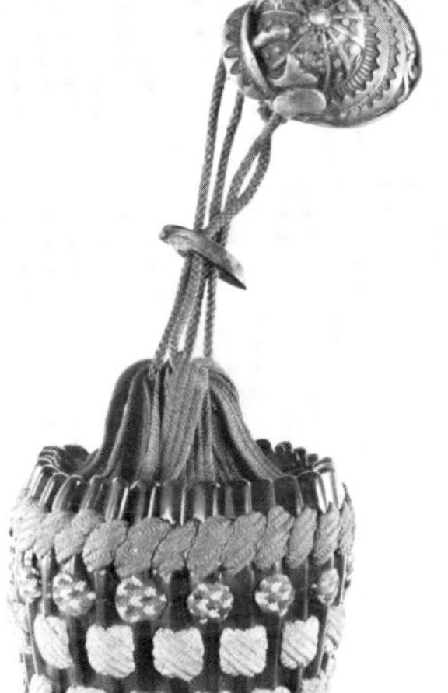

Netsuke: A helmet ashtray

Metal. 19th c. Katabori.
5.5 cm. E15618

Sagemono: A tobacco container made of armor

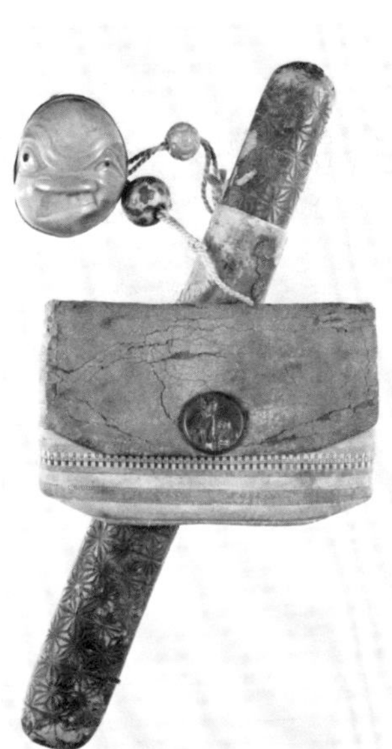

Netsuke: A Hyottoko face

Vegetable ivory. Gyokko. mid 19th c. Katabori. 4.2 cm. E24359

Sagemono and ojime: This small cloth and leather tobacco pouch with metal clasp depicting a woman and child may have been made for a woman. The pipe case is leather covered paper, and the pipe is bamboo and metal.

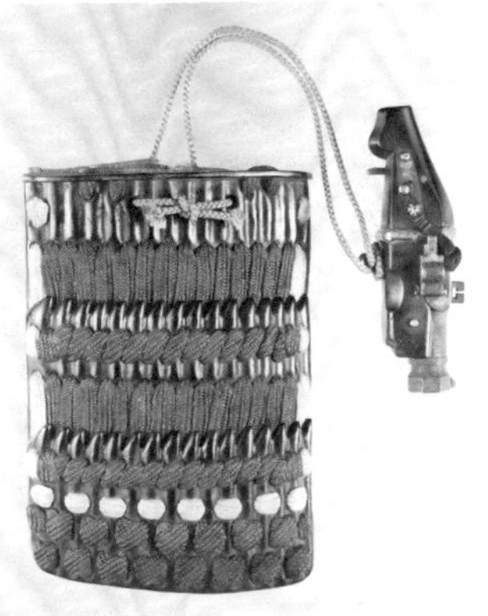

Netsuke: A matchlock gun

Wood and metal. 19th c. Katabori.
7.8 cm. E20383

Sagemono: A piece of armor is backed with silk to form a tobacco pouch.

Netsuke: A wood ashtray

Wood. 19th c. Katabori. 4.2 cm. E41580

Sagemono: The expression "Beware of fire" is painted on this large tobacco sack. *The Netsuke Handbook of Ueda Reikichi* (see Bibliography) says that pouches of an unknown material similar to leather were called kappa skin and were marked with this expression.

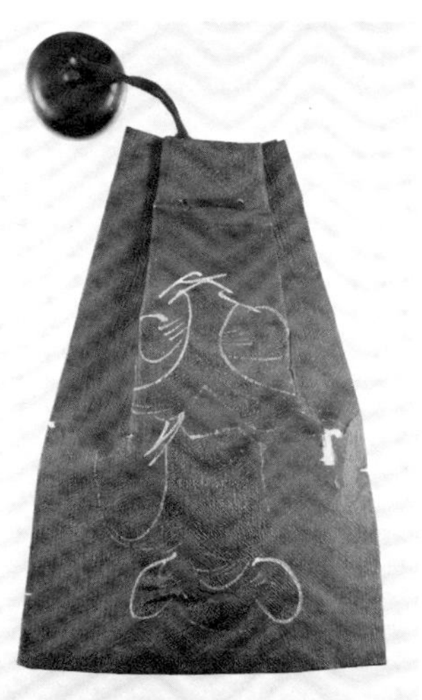

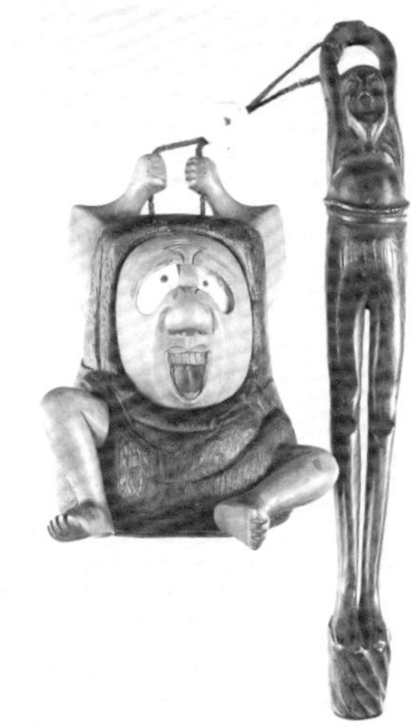

Pipe holder: The wooden pipe holder is a stretching Ashinaga.

Wood. 19th c. 20.0 cm. E44995

Sagemono and ojime: A yawning and stretching Daruma's face comes off to reveal the compartment inside this wood tonkotsu. The ojime is an ivory rabbit.

Tobacco Containers and Pipe Holders

Pipe holders were often used as sashi netsuke.

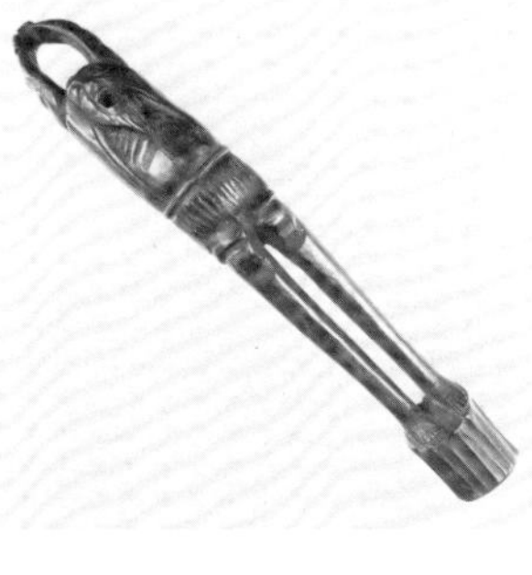

The Peabody Museum collection has two Ashinaga pipe holders which have no pipes or containers attached.

Wood. 19th c. 20.0 cm. E26966

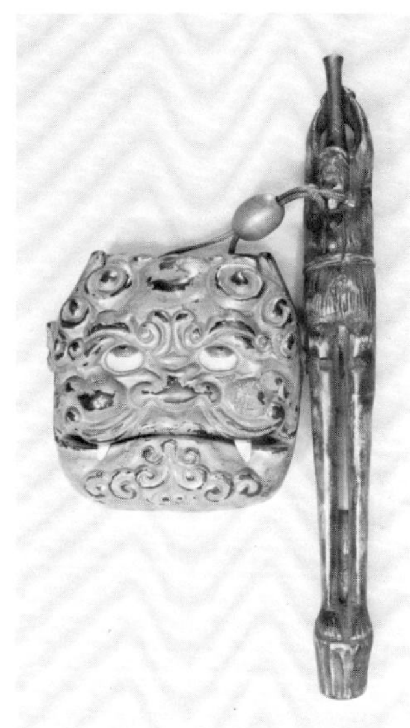

Pipe holder: A popular design for pipe holders was a stretching Ashinaga (Longlegs).

Wood. 19th c. 19.5 cm. E4425

Sagemono: A red lacquer tonkotsu carved in the shape of an oni's head opens at the mouth to reveal the compartment for tobacco inside. A figure of Daikoku is on the metal tip of the bamboo and metal pipe.

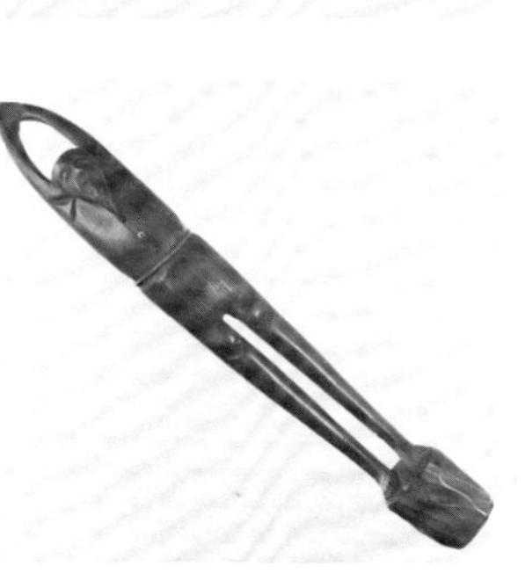

Wood, inlaid buttons. 19th c. 19.5 cm. E36656

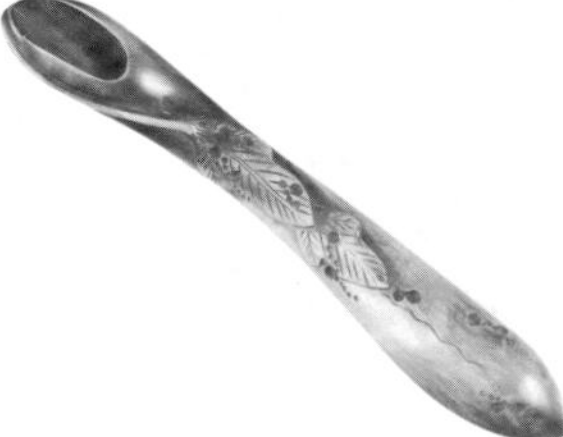

Pipe holder: A pipe holder is carved in the shape of an insect eaten squash with leaves.

Wood. 19th c. 20.5 cm. E14825

Tobacco Containers and Pipe Cases Pipe cases, like pipeholders, could be thrust through the obi to secure the pipe and tobacco container.

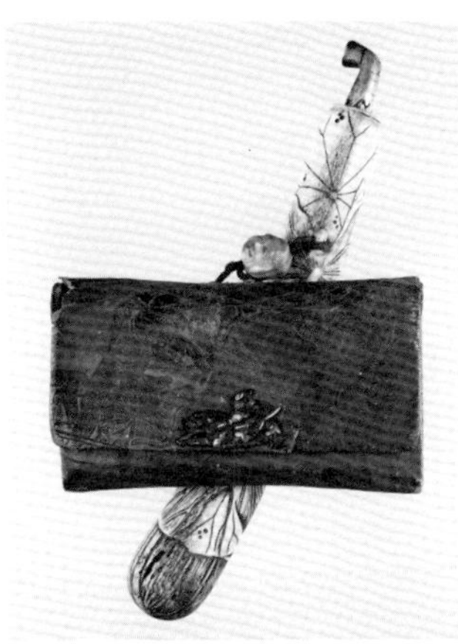

Pipe case: A bone pipe case with lotus leaf design holds a bamboo and metal pipe.

19th c. Case: 19.5 cm. E22917

Sagemono: The leather tobacco pouch is decorated with a battle scene, the metal clasp depicts a samurai slaying a tiger.

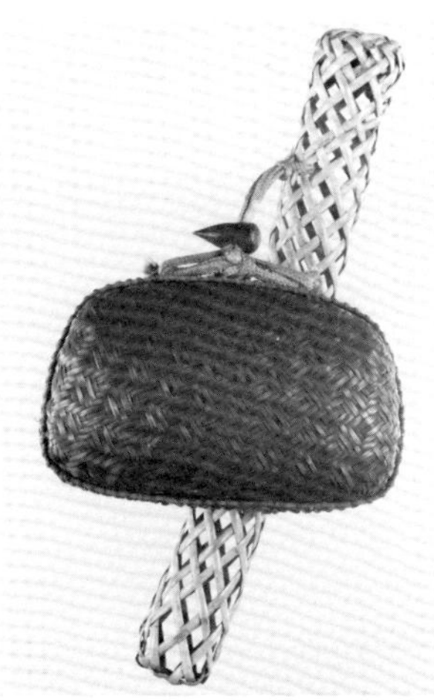

Pipe case: A woven straw pipe case.

19th c. Case: 22.0 cm. E23728

Sagemono and ojime: A silk-lined woven tobacco case is secured by a wood ojime.

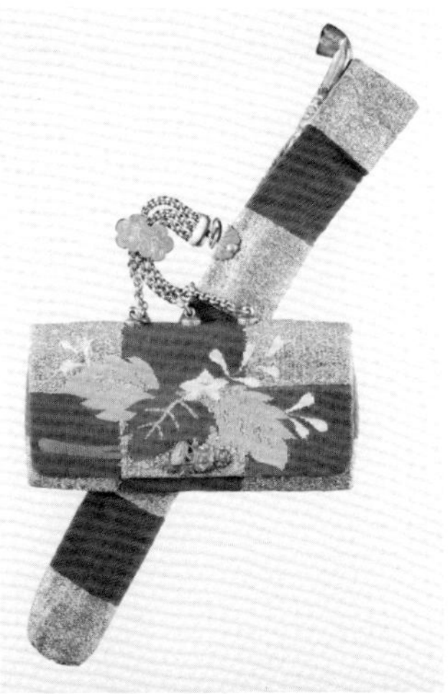

Pipe case: A purple and gold cloth pipe case with leaf designs holds a bamboo and metal pipe engraved with flowers.

19th c. Case: 24.7 cm. E32813

Sagemono and ojime: The matching tobacco pouch has a metal clasp depicting a drum and is fastened to the pipe case by a multiple chain with a metal ojime.

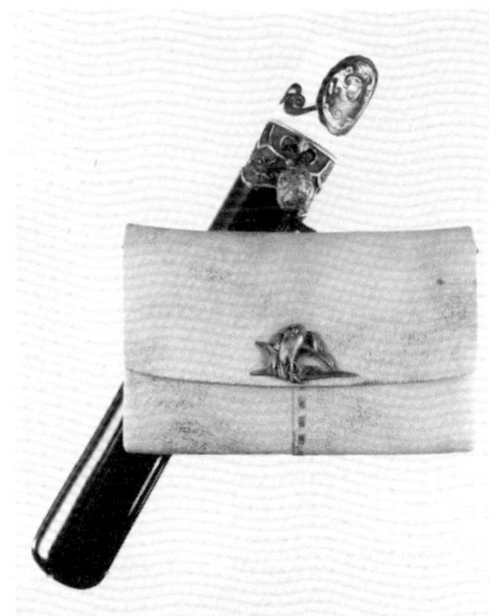

Pipe case: A lacquered horn pipe case with decorated bone and ivory top.

19th c. Case: 21.3 cm. E33340

Sagemono and ojime: A leather tobacco pouch with a metal clasp of a crane and an ojime with floral patterns engraved on it.

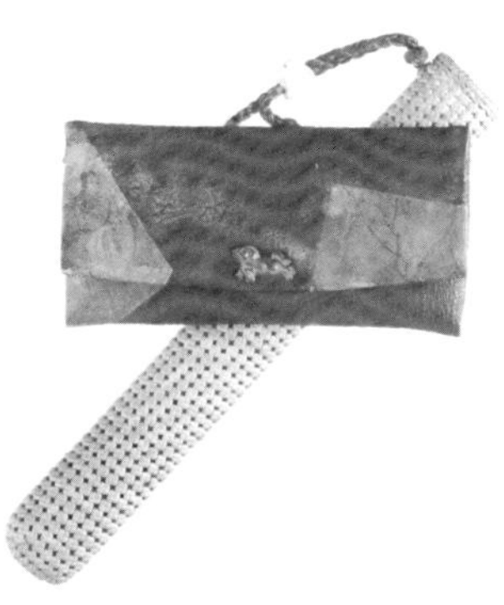

Pipe case: A woven pipe case.

19th c. Case: 17.4 cm. E54444

Sagemono and ojime: This ensemble of a leather tobacco pouch with scenes painted on it and an ivory ojime of a rabbit may have been intended for use by a woman.

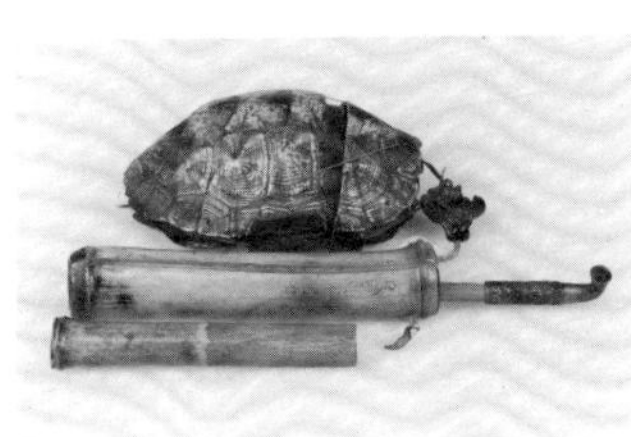

Pipe case: A bamboo pipe case

Bamboo. 19th c. 19.8 cm. E20357

Sagemono and ojime: A wood tonkotsu carved in the shape of a turtle with a wood ojime

Shop Signs

Shop signs (kamban) have had a long tradition in Japan, but during the Tokugawa era (1603-1868) they became more elaborate and impressive in size and design despite government sumptuary regulations ordering simplicity. Often decorated with gold and silver leaf, lacquer, mother-of-pearl inlay and rich metal fittings, they reflected the increasing affluence of the merchant class. Wealthy merchants, occupying the lowest rung of the social ladder, began to vie socially with samurai by lavishing their newly-acquired riches on luxury items previously enjoyed only by the upper classes. Shops sold various types of sagemono and netsuke that were not only useful, but were objects through which the lower classes could express their tastes and growing refinement. As the shops multiplied, so did the need for shop signs. The introduction of tobacco further stimulated the demand for shop signs which called attention to shops dealing in tobacco, pipes and accessories.

A painted leather and metal shop sign is in the form of a tobacco pouch and pipe holder suspended from a wooden manju netsuke. Calligraphy identifies the bridge depicted as that of Yodoya in Osaka.

56.0 cm. 18th-19th c. E16499

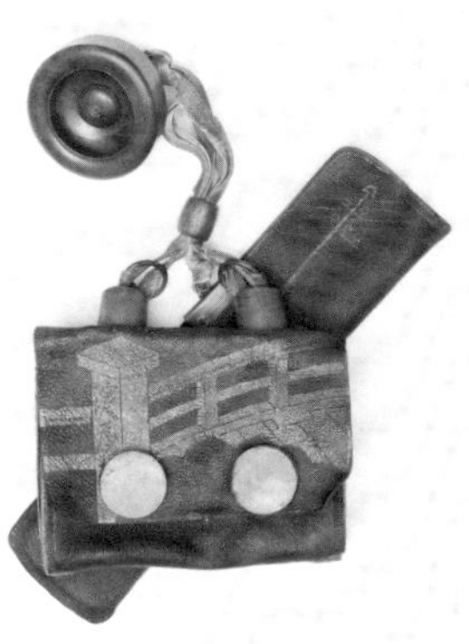

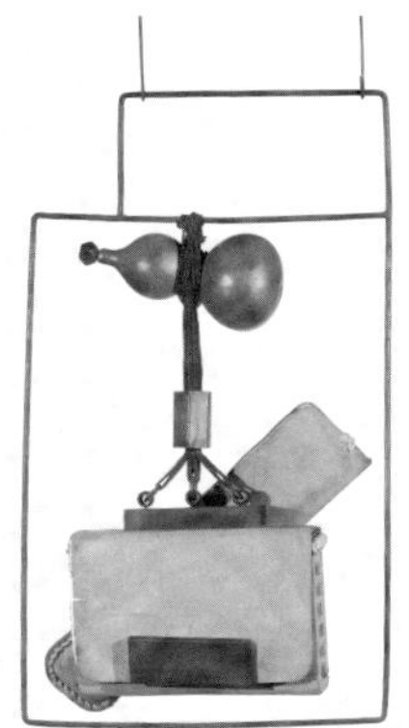

A fabric, metal and wood shop sign is in the form of a tobacco pouch and pipe holder suspended from a gourd netsuke that hangs from a metal frame.

95.0 cm. 19th c. E16536

This leather, metal, glass and lacquered shop sign is in the form of a tobacco pouch and pipe holder. These are attached to a comma-shaped netsuke in the form of a tomoe. Inside the pouch flap there is calligraphy indicating the sign is from Osaka and was made by Toda Kinhodo Juraku.

56.0 cm. 19th c. E19203

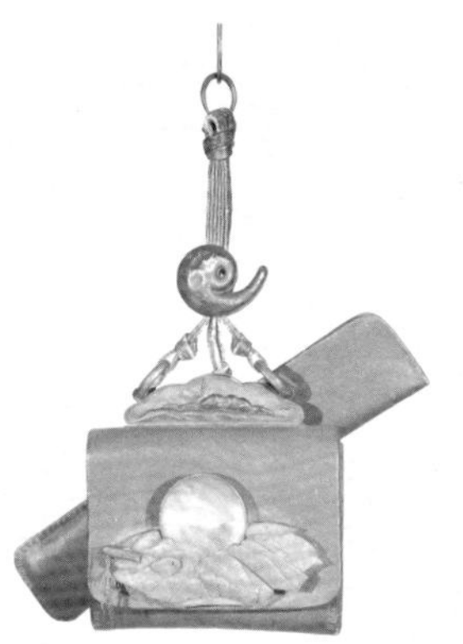

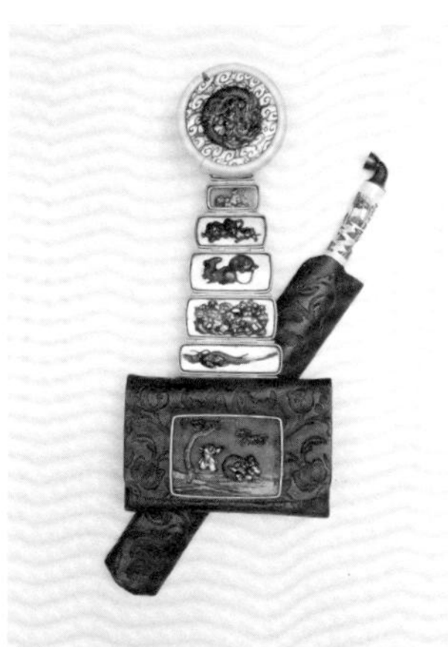

A metal, ivory and embossed leather shop sign for interior use is in the form of a tobacco pouch and pipe holder. These are attached by hinged metal pieces to a kagamibuta netsuke that depicts a gold metal dragon prowling on a background of gold waves.

50.0 cm. 18th-19th c. E23055

A lacquered wood shop sign is in the form of a tobacco pouch and pipe holder, which was attached to a netsuke. Calligraphy identifies the depicted bridge as that of Yodoya in Osaka.

102.0 cm. 19th c. E20996

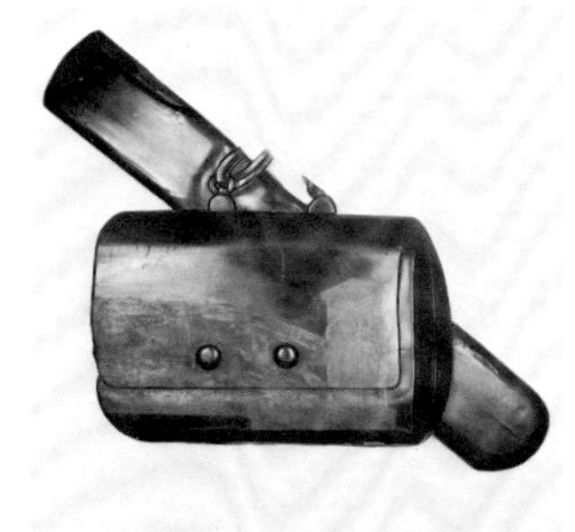

This lacquered and painted shop sign is in the form of a three-case inro with attached ojime and a comma-shaped netsuke in the form of a magatama (ancient jewel symbol).

65.0 cm. 18th-19th c. E20998

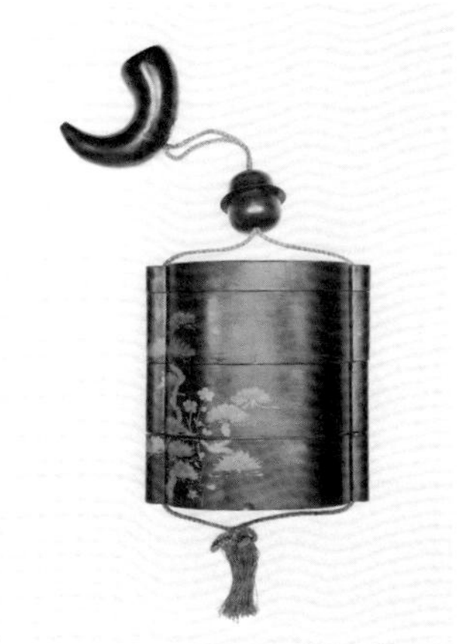

Bibliography

Allen, Maude Rex. *Japanese Art Motives.* Chicago: McClurg, 1917.

Anesaki, Masaharu. *History of Japanese Religions.* Rutland: Tuttle, 1963.

Bancroft, Ann. *Religions of the East.* New York: St. Martins, 1974.

Barbanson, Adrienne. *Fables in Ivory: Japanese Netsuke and their Legends.* Rutland: Tuttle, 1961.

Brockhaus, Albert. *Netsukes.* edited by E.G. Stillman. New York: Duffield, 1924.

Bush, Lewis. *Japan Dictionary.* New York: Philosophical Library, 1957.

Bushell, Raymond. *Collectors' Netsuke.* New York: Weatherhill, 1971.

———. *The Inro Handbook.* Tokyo: Weatherhill, 1979.

———. *An Introduction to Netsuke.* Rutland: Tuttle, 1971.

———. *Netsuke Familiar and Unfamiliar.* New York: Weatherhill, 1975.

———. *The Netsuke Handbook of Ueda Reikichi.* Rutland: Tuttle, 1961.

———. *The Wonderful World of Netsuke.* Rutland: Tuttle, 1964.

———. *Netsuke An Exhibition of Netsuke from the Raymond Bushell Collection.* Mikimoto, 1979.

Campbell, Joseph. *The Masks of God: Oriental Mythology.* New York: Viking, 1962.

Davey, Neil K. *Netsuke.* London: Bernet, 1974.

Davis, F. Hadland. *Myths & Legends of Japan.* New York: Crowell, 1932.

Department of Asiatic Art Gallery Book. *Japanese Netsuke.* Boston: Museum of Fine Arts, 1937.

Dorson, Richard M. *Folk Legends of Japan.* Rutland: Tuttle, 1962.

Earhart, H. Byron. *Japanese Religion: Unity and Diversity.* Encino: Dickenson, 1974.

Forman, Werner. *Japanese Netsuke.* Spring Books: 1960.

Fujiya Hotel, Ltd. *We Japanese.* Yamagata Press.

Hawley, W. and Chappelear, K. *Mon, The Japanese Family Crest.* Hollywood: Hawley, 1976.

Jahss, Melvin and Betty. *Inro and Other Miniature Forms of Japanese Lacquer Art.* Rutland: Tuttle, 1971.

Joly, Henri. *Legends in Japanese Art.* New York: Lane, 1908.

Jonas, F.M. *Netsuke.* Rutland: Tuttle, 1960.

Kato, G., Litt, D. *What is Shinto.* Japan Tourist Library No. 8. Tokyo: 1935.

Kitagawa, Joseph M. *Religion in Japanese History.* New York: Columbia University Press, 1966.

Koop, Albert J. and Inada, Hogitaro. *Japanese Names and How to Read Them.* London: Routledge and Kegan, 1960.

Meinertzhagen, Frederick. *The Art of the Netsuke Carver.* London: Routledge and Kegan, 1956.

Miyake, Syutaro. *Kabuki Drama.* Japan Tourist Library No. 23. Tokyo, 1938.

Morse, Edward S. *Catalogue of the Morse Collection of Japanese Pottery* vol. I. Cambridge: Riverside Press, 1900.

Nogama, Toyoichiro. *Noh Masks, Classification and Explanation.* Tokyo, 1938.

Nogami, T. *Japanese Noh Plays.* Japan Tourist Library No. 2. Tokyo, 1935.

O'Brien, Mary Louise. *Netsuke: A Guide for Collectors.* Rutland: Tuttle, 1965.

Okada, Barbra. *Japanese Netsuke and Ojime: From the Herman and Paul Jaehne Collection of the Newark Museum.* Newark: 1976.

Okada, Barbra T. and Neill, Mary G. *Real and Imaginary Beings.* New Haven: Yale University Printing Service, 1980.

Okada, Yuzuru. *Netsuke — A Miniature Art of Japan.* Japan Tourist Library No. 14. Tokyo, 1951.

Ono, Sokyo. *Shinto: The Kami Way.* Rutland: Tuttle, 1962.

Reischauer, E.O. and Fairbank, J.K. *East Asia the Great Tradition.* Boston: Houghton Mifflin, 1958, 1960.

Reischauer, E.O. *The Japanese.* Cambridge: Harvard College, 1977.

Religious Affairs Section, Ministry of Education, Government of Japan. *Religion in Japan.* Japan, 1959.

Ryerson, Egerton. *The Netsuke of Japan Legends, History, Folklore and Customs.* New York: Barnes, 1958.

Sheldon, Walt. *Enjoy Japan.* Tokyo: Tuttle, 1961.

Sunaga, Katumi. *Japanese Music.* Japan Tourist Library No. 15. Tokyo, 1936.

Tollner, Madeline R. *Netsuke The Life and Legend of Japan in Miniature.* San Francisco: Abbey, 1960.

Volker, Tys. *The Animal in Far Eastern Art.* Leiden, 1975.

Waley, Arthur. *The Nō Plays of Japan.* London: Allen & Unwin Ltd., 1921.

Wolfers, Nicholas. "Netsuke and Inro." *Discovering Antiques.* no. 45, 1971.

Appendix 1.

Artists represented by signatures in the collection

Index-Glossary